D1404701

NELSON

Science & Technology 7

Authors

Unit 1
Ted Gibb

Unit 2
Alan J. Hirsch

Unit 3
Deborah White
Steven White
Jim Wiese

Unit 4
Ted Gibb

Unit 5
Bob Ritter

Program Consultant
Marietta (Mars) Bloch

Contributing Authors

Skills Handbook
Nancy Dalgarno Alldred
Stephen Haberer

Australia • Canada • Denmark • Japan • Mexico • New Zealand • Philippines
Puerto Rico • Singapore • South Africa • Spain • United Kingdom • United States

Program Assessment Consultants
Damian Cooper
Halton District School Board

Nanci Wakeman-Jones
Halton District School Board

Safety Review
Patrick Hogan
Catholic District Board of Eastern Ontario.

Margaret Redway
Fraser Scientific and Business Services

Expert Review
Ron Garnham
Engineering Technologist, Stelco Inc. (retired)

David Logan
York University, Faculty of Pure and Applied Science

Steve Rogers
Technology Teaching Systems

Peter I. Russell
Earth Sciences Curator, University of Waterloo

Materials Review
Paul Hannan

Web Consultant
Peter Sovran

***Nelson Science & Technology* 7 Project Team**

Artplus Design & Communication
Marnie Benedict
Colin Bisset
Beverley Buxton
Angela Cluer
Ruta Demery
Peggy Ferguson
Fizz Design Inc.
Kyle Gell
Carol Glegg
Susan Green
Julie Greener
Geraldine Kikuta
Karen Kligman
Margo Davies Leclair
Kevin Linder
Kevin Martindale
Allan Moon
Renate McCloy
Ken Phipps
Peggy Rhodes
Todd Ryoji
Valentino Sanna
Silver Birch Graphics
David Steele
Rosalyn Steiner
Karen Taylor
Theresa Thomas
Janice Wormworth

1120 Birchmount Road
Scarborough, Ontario M1K 5G4
www.nelson.com
www.thomson.com

Printed and bound in Canada
1 2 3 4 5 6 7 8 9 0 /ML/ 8 7 6 5 4 3 2 1 0 9

Canadian Cataloguing in Publication Data

Main entry under title:
Nelson science & technology 7
Includes index.
ISBN 0-17-607495-3

1. Science – Juvenile literature. I. Ritter, Bob, 1950- . II. Title: Science 7.

Q161.2.N43 1999 500 C99-930747-9

Reviewers

Roni Abrahamsohn
The Leo Baeck Day School

Diane Aitken
Hamilton Wentworth District School Board

Karen Barnes
Toronto District School Board

Barbara Behan
Dufferin-Peel Catholic District School Board

Al Bernacki
Steve Bibla
Toronto District School Board

Ray Bowers
North York Board of Education

Bob Cooper
The Leo Baeck Day School

Jim Dawson
Faculty of Education, University of Windsor

Chris Eaton
Waterloo District Catholic School Board

Gord Felix
Dufferin-Peel Catholic District School Board

Maureen Innes
Waterloo Catholic District School Board

Claudia Jones
Dufferin-Peel Catholic District School Board

Paul Podesta
Dufferin-Peel Catholic District School Board

Franca Porcelli
York Catholic District School Board

Margaret E. Ramsay
Dufferin-Peel Catholic District School Board

Steve Rogers
Technology Teaching Systems

Melissa Stout
Toronto District School Board

Pamela Schwartzberg
Learning for a Sustainable Future

Linda Strey
Lakehead District School Board

Mary Jane Vowles
Dufferin-Peel Catholic District School Board

Allison Weagle
York Region District School Board

Janice Weir
York Region District School Board

Otto Wevers
Toronto District School Board

Table of Contents

UNIT 2: HEAT 70

UNIT 3: STRUCTURAL STRENGTH AND STABILITY 130

UNIT 4: THE EARTH'S CRUST **190**

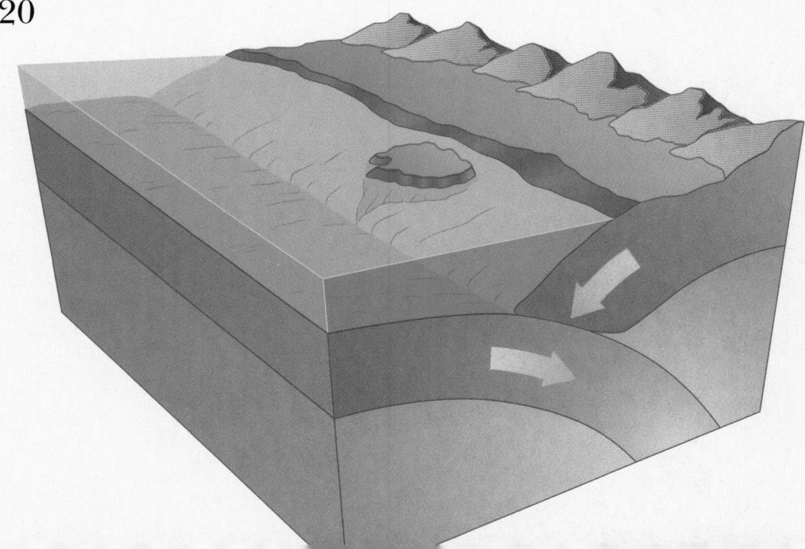

UNIT 5: INTERACTIONS WITHIN ECOSYSTEMS 250

UNIT 6: SKILLS HANDBOOK 310

Unit 1

Pure Substances and Mixtures

Unit 1 Overview

Matter is all around us: the air we breathe, the lakes and oceans, and Earth itself are all made of matter. To manufacture things or make them useful to us, we work with matter in all sorts of ways: we purify matter to obtain metals, mix up other types of matter to make foods or drinks, and we separate manufactured items to recycle the parts. But how do we know which substances will mix well for a particular purpose? Can we classify matter in a way that will help us make predictions?

Classifying Matter

Matter can be classified into many different categories. This helps us make sense of the thousands of different substances around us.

You will be able to:

- distinguish between pure substances and mixtures
- investigate different methods of separating the components of mixtures
- use the particle theory to explain how substances dissolve
- conduct experiments to determine the factors that affect the rate at which substances dissolve
- describe the difference between saturated and unsaturated solutions

Using Matter to Make Products

The products that we use in our everyday lives make use of the physical properties of the substances they are made from.

You will be able to:

- distinguish between raw materials and processed materials
- describe how raw materials are collected and processed to produce products
- identify a variety of manufactured products made from mixtures and explain their functions
- recognize that solutions in manufactured products can exist as solids, liquids, and gases

Sustainability Concerns

The use of large amounts of raw materials from the Earth to manufacture a wide range of products has an impact on the environment, the economy, and our health. Our environment is affected by manufacturing and agricultural processes. It needs to be protected by regulations and public awareness programs.

You will be able to:

- identify the sources and characteristics of pollutants that result from manufacturing and chemical fertilizers
- describe the effect of some toxic solvents on the environment, and regulations that ensure their safe use and disposal
- identify different types of waste present in the community and methods of disposal
- evaluate the quality of water from different sources by performing simple tests

Design Challenge

You will be able to ...
demonstrate your learning by completing a Design Challenge.

A System That Separates or Purifies Materials

Recycling substances and products, both liquid and solid, is an important way of preserving Earth's resources and reducing garbage. However, recycling and separating substances also requires many types of technology.

In this unit you will be able to design and build:

1 A Water Purification System
Design and build a model of a filtering system that removes solid particles from water.

2 A Recycling System for Plastic, Glass, Metal, and Paper
Design and build a model in which plastic, glass, metal, and paper items are separated from each other.

3 A Soil and Gravel Mechanical Separator
Design and build a model that efficiently separates soil and rocks into three different sizes.

To start your Design Challenge, see page 62.

Record your thoughts and design ideas for the Challenge when you see

Design Challenge

Getting Started

What Are Things Made Of?

1 We can see and feel most types of matter. We can also describe them in many different ways — for example, soft, hard, shiny, colourful, brittle, liquid, solid. Some things, like air, we cannot see or taste. Why is it important to have a way to classify things? Which classification system is best? Does one classification work for everything?

2 To make products, we mix raw materials together in combinations that may require heating, freezing, stirring, melting, hardening, or dissolving. Through a series of processes, we end up with the items that we buy and use every day. How do we know which materials mix best to give us the product we want? How do we decide which is the best process to use when manufacturing a product?

3 The raw materials we use to make products all come from the Earth. Some, like our food, we grow. Others, like metals and other minerals, we mine. And when we don't want something anymore, or it breaks, we throw it away. Both retrieving substances from the Earth and throwing things into landfills have an effect on the environment. How can we lessen this effect and create a balance between environmental concerns, health concerns, and economic concerns?

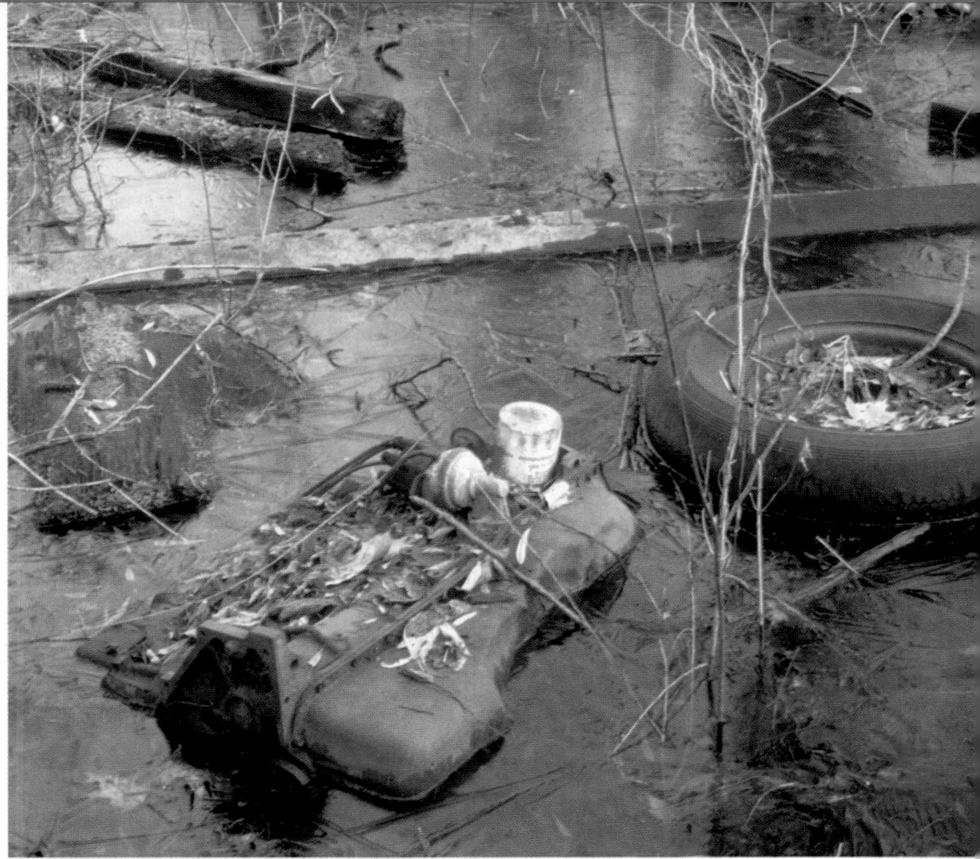

Reflecting

Think about the questions in 1, 2, 3. What other questions do you have about mixtures? As you progress through this unit, reflect on your answers and revise them based on what you have learned.

Try This Classifying Candy

Examine some chocolate candy bars and organize them into categories.

- Using a dinner knife, cut each candy bar into pieces.

1. Does each candy bar look the same throughout, or can you see other substances mixed in?

2. What makes a bar that contains only chocolate different from other chocolate bars?

3. Do you think chocolate is pure? Why or why not?

- Organize the candy bars into categories.

4. Did your group choose the same categories as other groups? Could you improve your system of categories?

5. What considerations do you need to make when designing a classification system?

1.1 Inquiry Investigation

SKILLS MENU
○ Questioning ● Conducting ● Analyzing
○ Hypothesizing ● Recording ● Communicating
○ Planning

Classifying Substances

Take a look around you. Everything is made of matter—including your own body, the products you use, Earth, and the universe (**Figure 1**). **Matter** is anything that has mass and takes up space. Matter is made up of many different kinds of substances. Some of these substances are similar to each other, and some have obvious differences. It is these similarities and differences that allow us to classify them.

Materials

- apron
- rubber gloves
- safety goggles
- substance samples, e.g., chalk, tennis ball, iron nails, salt, powdered drink mix, stainless steel nuts and bolts, air, water, celery, carrot sticks, mixed nuts, flour, alcohol, sand, charcoal
- magnifier
- test tube
- 50-mL beaker
- paper

Question

Which similarities and differences among substances can be used to organize, or classify, matter into different types?

Hypothesis

If we choose certain properties, then we can classify all forms of matter.

Procedure

Part 1: Observing Properties of Matter

1 Make an observation table like the one below.

6D • Examine the samples that are solid, hard objects.

(a) List all the properties you observe in your table.

2 Place a spoonful of each of the powdered solids onto a separate piece of paper.

- Use a magnifier to carefully examine each sample.

(a) Record all the properties you observe in your table.

3 Observe the liquid and gas samples (do not remove these samples from their containers).

(a) Record your observations in your table.

(b) Based on all your observations, classify the different types of matter into groups.

Observations

Sample	Observations	Observations after mixing with water	Observations after mixing with other solids
?	?	?	?
?	?	?	?

Figure 1
Matter includes all things that have mass and take up space. There are many useful ways to categorize matter.

Part 2: Observing Properties of Mixed Samples

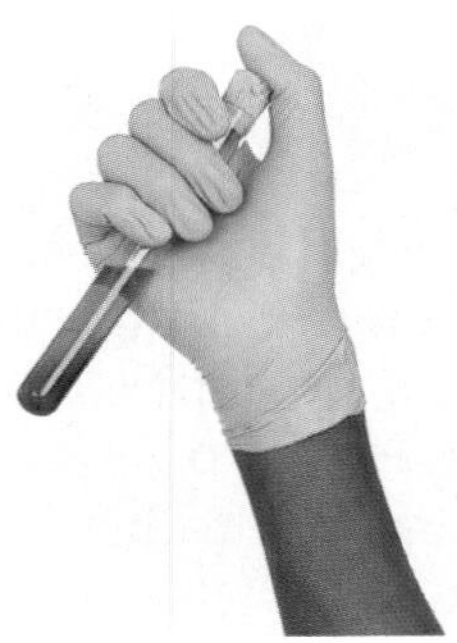

4 Place a spoonful of one of the powdered solids into a test tube. Add water to fill half the test tube.

- Put your thumb over the end of the test tube and invert it. Hold it away from your body and shake.

(a) Record your observations in the third column of your table.

- Wash out the test tube and repeat step 4 with each of the powdered solids.

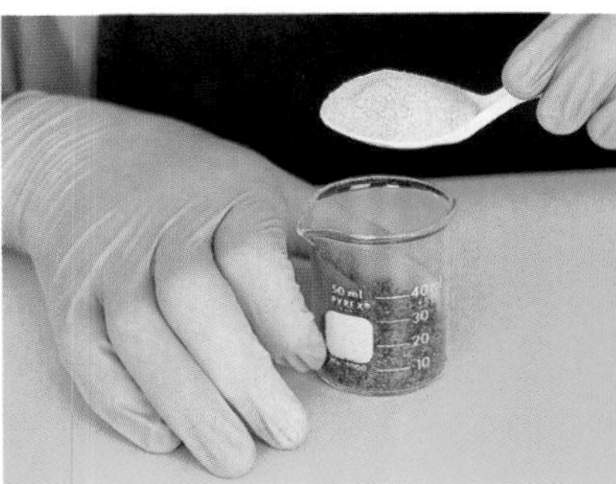

5 Select two of the powdered substances and mix together a spoonful of each in a beaker.

(a) Record your observations in your table.

(b) Do all of the mixtures you've made fit in your original classification system? If not, change your system so all of the forms of matter you've observed can be classified.

Making Connections

1. Using your classification system, describe how you would categorize the following:

(a) cheese and pepperoni pizza

(b) orange juice

(c) smoke

(d) wood

Exploring

2. In separate containers, mix water with cocoa, gelatin powder, and ground coffee. Record your observations, and classify each mixture according to your system.

Reflecting

3. Speculate why it is helpful to classify matter.

Analysis

6 Analyze your results by answering these questions.

(a) Compare your classification system with those of your classmates.

(b) What are the similarities and differences among the different classification systems?

(c) Create a flowchart of your classification system.

Design Challenge

Think about how you could separate each mixture you made in Part 2 of this investigation so that you could have the original substances you started with. Rate each mixture as "easy to separate," "difficult to separate," or "probably cannot be separated." Explain why you rated each mixture as you did.

SKILLS HANDBOOK: 6D Creating Data Tables

Pure Substances and Mixtures

In the previous investigation you looked at different substances. But why is each substance different from other substances? Why does each substance have its own properties?

The Particle Theory

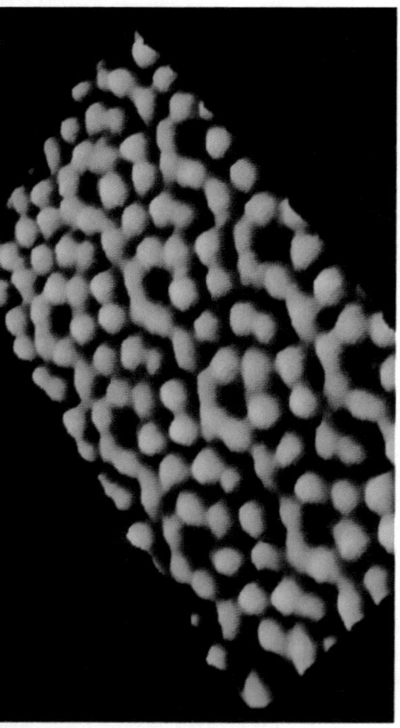

To answer these questions we need to look at the **particle theory**. The particle theory, developed over many centuries, explains that matter is made up of tiny particles with spaces between them (**Figure 1**). Particles are always moving. The more energy they have, the faster they move. The particle theory also explains that the tiny particles in matter are attracted to each other (**Figure 2**). This theory has been useful in explaining some observations about the behaviour of matter.

Figure 1
A magnified view of a thin metal foil supports the particle theory explanation that matter consists of tiny particles with spaces between them.

Figure 2

Solid
In a solid, the particles are close together and locked into a pattern. They can move, but only back and forth a little. Attractive forces hold the particles together.

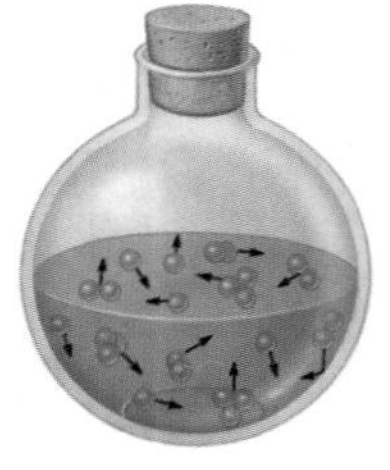

Liquid
In a liquid, the particles are slightly farther apart. Because the particles are farther apart, the attractive forces are weaker. They are able to slide past one another.

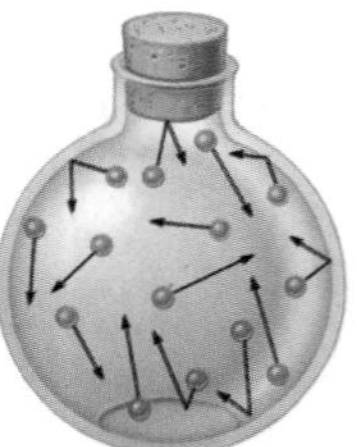

Gas
In a gas, the particles are far apart. The particles can move in any direction because the attractive forces are weakest.

Different Particles, Different Substances

According to the particle theory, there are many different kinds of particles. The differences between the particles cause the substances that contain them to have different properties.

Pure Substances

A **pure substance** contains only one kind of particle throughout. There are many pure substances, but only a few can actually be found in nature. We often think of our drinking water as being pure, but this water has chemicals in it to remove bacteria, so it is actually made up of several pure substances. In nature, pure substances tend to mix together. There are exceptions; for example, diamonds are pure. They are formed deep in the mantle of Earth's crust, but they are rarely found.

Almost all of the pure substances we encounter in our lives have been made pure by human beings. Aluminum foil is pure, and so is table sugar. To obtain these substances in a pure form, we take the **raw material** that contains them, and separate out the substance we want, as shown in **Figure 3**. All samples of pure substances have the same properties whether the sample is large or small.

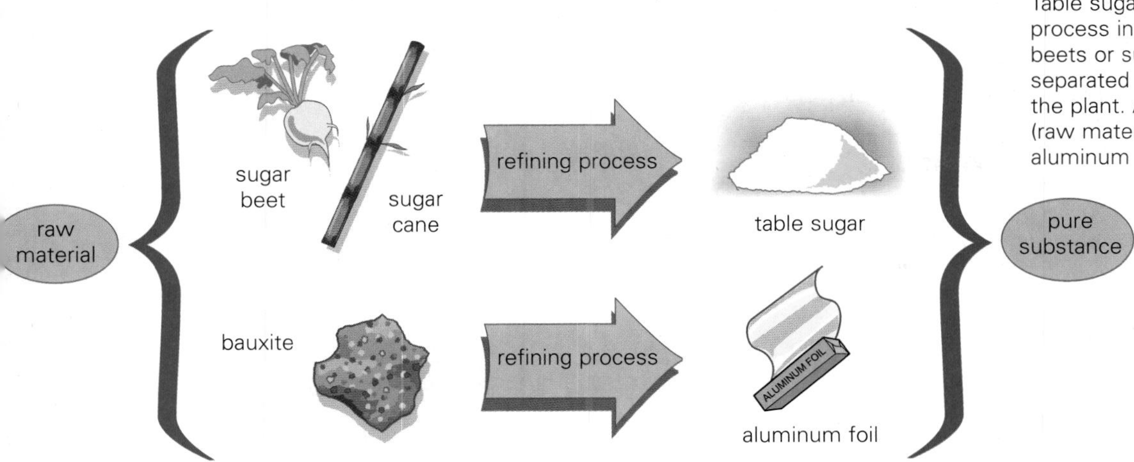

Figure 3
Table sugar is obtained by a refining process in which the sugar from sugar beets or sugar cane (raw material) is separated from the fibre and other parts of the plant. Aluminum comes from bauxite (raw material), a type of rock that contains aluminum mixed up with other minerals.

Mixtures

Almost all of the natural substances, as well as human-made and manufactured products, in the world are mixtures of pure substances. A **mixture** contains two or more pure substances, as shown in **Figure 4**. Mixtures can be any combination of solids, liquids, and gases. For example, soft drinks are a mixture that includes liquid water, solid sugar, and carbon dioxide gas. Bread is a mixture of yeast, flour, sugar, water, air, and other chemicals.

Figure 4
Most substances you will come in contact with are mixtures. Mixtures contain at least two pure substances.

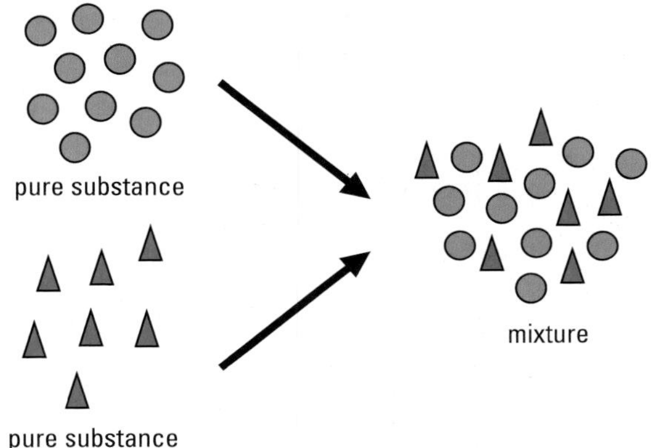

Try This Is Tap Water a Solution?

- Clean two glass containers or watch glasses, ensuring that there are no spots on them.
- Mark one container T (for tap water) and the other D (for distilled water).
- With a clean medicine dropper, add 5 drops of tap water to the container marked T, and 5 drops of distilled water to the container marked D.
- Place the containers near a sunny window or a heater, and let them stand until the water evaporates.
- Hold the containers up to the light.

1. What do you notice about each container?
2. Based on your observations, is tap water a solution? Explain.
3. How would you classify the distilled water? Explain.
4. Do you think evaporation is a reliable method for separating a dissolved solid from all liquid solutions? Why or why not?

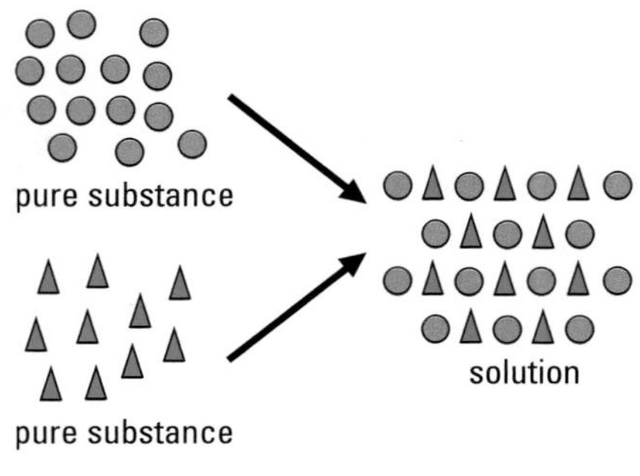

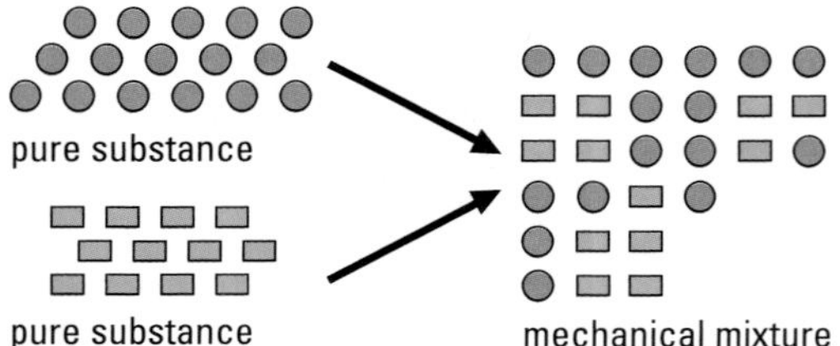

Figure 5
Pure substances mix to form mechanical mixtures or solutions. In a solution, the particles of the pure substances are mixed evenly so that neither original substance is visible. In a mechanical mixture, the substances do not mix evenly. Both substances are clearly visible.

Heterogeneous and Homogeneous Mixtures

In many mixtures, like concrete or granola, you can clearly see separate pieces in the mixture. Each spoonful of granola is different. If you take up a spoonful of wet concrete, it may or may not contain a pebble. This type of mixture is called a **heterogeneous mixture** (heterogeneous means "different kinds"), because two or more substances can be seen and felt. If you take a small sample from such a mixture, it may have different properties from another sample. Another name for a heterogeneous mixture is a **mechanical mixture** (see **Figure 5**).

In a **homogeneous mixture** (homogenous means "same kind"), the particles of the pure substances mix together so completely that the mixture looks and feels as though it is made of only one substance. No matter where you sample it, or how small the sample is, the properties of this mixture are always the same. Steel, composed of iron, oxygen, and carbon, is a homogeneous mixture. No matter where you cut a steel bar, it always looks the same. When you mix a small amount of salt with water you create a homogeneous mixture. Another name for a homogeneous mixture is a **solution**. We can classify matter based on its observable properties (see **Table 1**).

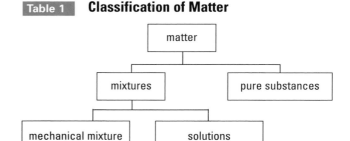

Table 1 **Classification of Matter**

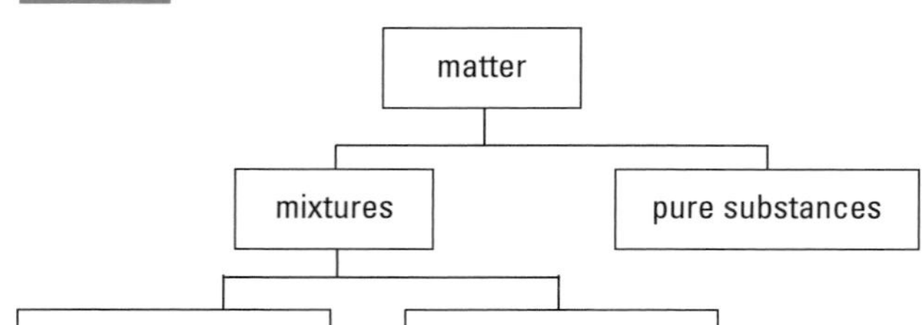

Try This: Mechanical Mixtures and Solutions from the Refrigerator

- Make a jelly dessert in a clear glass bowl following the package directions. When the jelly has set, observe it closely.

1. Is the jelly transparent?
2. Can you see more than one type of particle?
3. How would you classify it?
4. Is the jelly a solution?

- Try shining a flashlight through the bowl, so any fine particles will become visible.

5. What do you think now? Would you change your classification? State reasons.

- Add a tablespoon of chocolate syrup to a glass of water and stir until the syrup and water are thoroughly mixed.

6. Is the mixture homogeneous (a solution) or heterogeneous (a mechanical mixture)?

- Let the mixture stand for a while, then observe it again.

7. What do you notice?
8. Make a list of other mixtures that have similar properties to chocolate syrup and water.

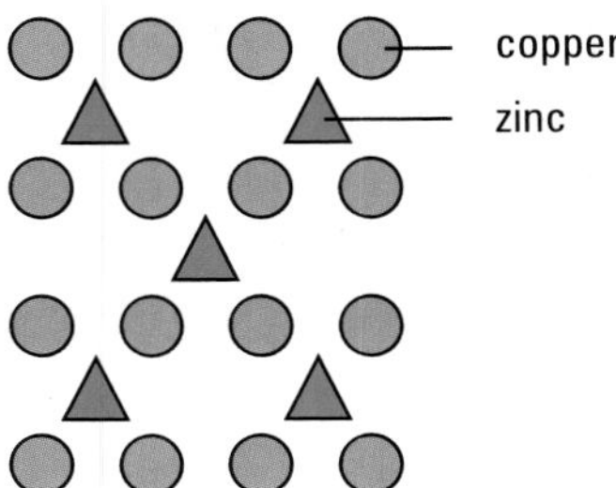

Figure 6

Brass, a decorative metal, is a solid solution in which a small amount of zinc (the solute) is dissolved in copper (the solvent) while it is molten hot. The zinc makes the brass harder than pure copper.

More About Solutions

In a solution, one substance has mixed completely, or **dissolved**, into another. Solutions can be solid, liquid, or gas. Steel, a solid solution, is made when oxygen (a gas) and carbon (a solid) dissolve into the main substance, iron. The substances that dissolve (in the case of steel, oxygen and carbon) are called the **solutes**. The substance into which they dissolve (iron) is called the **solvent**. Brass is another solid solution. The solvent in brass is copper, and the solute is zinc, as you can see in **Figure 6**.

Air, a solution of gases, consists mostly of nitrogen gas (the solvent). The gases dissolved in it include oxygen, argon, and carbon dioxide (the solutes).

Liquid solutions are formed when a solid, a liquid, or a gas dissolves in a liquid. For example, apple juice is a solution of sugar and minerals (the solutes) dissolved in water (the solvent). The oceans are a solution of many different salts dissolved in water. Another liquid solution is vinegar. Vinegar, used on French fries and salads, and for cleaning stains, is a solution that consists mostly of water (the solvent) and a small amount of liquid acetic acid (the solute).

Liquid solutions may also include dissolved gases. Pop is a sweet solution that is mostly water (the solvent), with both solid sugar and carbon dioxide gas (the solutes) dissolved in it. All solutions are homogeneous, so they look the same throughout, but liquid and gas solutions are also transparent (you can see through them). They may have a colour, however, as the solutions apple juice and tea do.

Understanding Concepts

1. **(a)** What is a pure substance? Give an example.
   (b) What is a mixture? Give an example.
2. Identify the solute and the solvent in the picture below.

3. Describe in your own words the difference between a mechanical mixture and a solution. Include the terms homogeneous and heterogeneous in your answer.
4. Which of the following is a solution, and which is a mechanical mixture? Explain the reason for your choice.
   (a) wood
   (b) orange juice
   (c) tap water
   (d) loonie coin

Making Connections

5. Give an example of each of the following types of solutions (not including those already mentioned in this section):
   (a) a liquid in a liquid
   (b) a solid in a solid
   (c) a solid in a liquid
6. Make a chart and list 10 liquids found at home. Examine the contents by reading the labels on the containers.
   (a) On your chart identify the liquids that meet the definition of a solution.
   (b) For each solution, list the solvent and the solute(s) on your chart.

Design Challenge

Are the mixtures you must separate for your Challenge mechanical mixtures or solutions?

SKILLS MENU
○ Questioning
● Hypothesizing
○ Planning
● Conducting
● Recording
● Analyzing
● Communicating

Filtering Mechanical Mixtures

Since most substances are mixtures, there are many situations when we want to separate the parts of a mixture. For example, you don't want to drink water that contains a mixture of soil, tiny plants and animals, and dissolved chemicals. Several techniques are available to separate mixtures. The water we drink is made safe by treating it at a water treatment plant to take out the impurities. Filtration is a technique that is frequently used in water treatment to separate particles from a mechanical mixture. Depending on the size of the particles that are being separated, the size of the mesh in the filter can be large, as in a screen, or very small, as in filter paper.

Materials

- apron
- safety goggles
- filter paper
- milk
- water
- ground pepper
- flour
- support stand
- ring clamp
- funnel
- 350-mL beakers
- water bottle with squirt top
- stirring rod

Question

Will filter paper separate all solid particles from a liquid mechanical mixture?

Hypothesis

(2C) **1** Write a hypothesis for this investigation.

Experimental Design

You will test whether filter paper can be used with three different mechanical mixtures.

Procedure

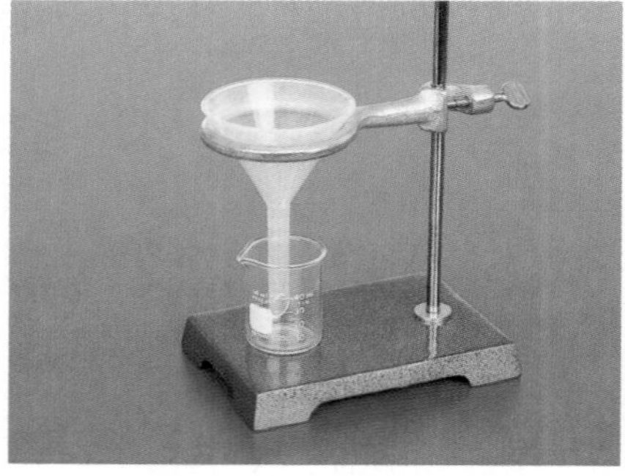

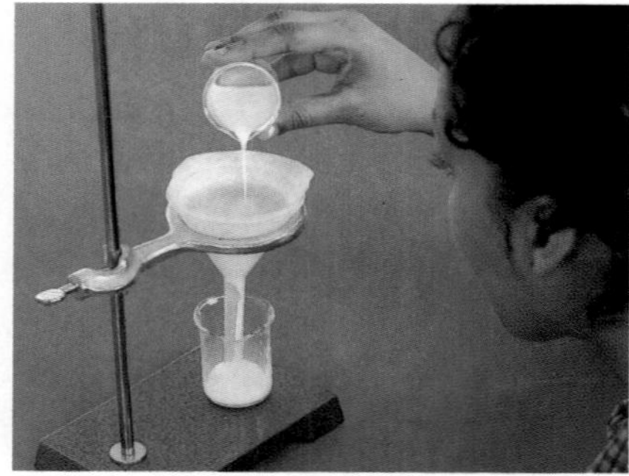

2 Set up a support stand, ring clamp, funnel, and beaker as shown above.

Wash your hands with soap and water after you complete this investigation.

3 Fold a piece of filter paper in half twice and shape it into a cone.
- Place the filter paper in the funnel.
- Squirt the paper cone with water so that it stays in place in the funnel.

4 Measure 25 mL of milk into a graduated cylinder.
- Pour the milk into the funnel.
- Wait a few moments for the liquid to pass through.

(a) Observe the filtered liquid in the beaker. How does it compare with the milk?

(b) Is there any residue left on the filter paper?

Figure 1
Water taken from a fast-moving stream will contain small particles of soil and microscopic living things. Filters can help to remove many of these particles from water. But even if water looks clear, does that mean it is safe to drink?

Design Challenge

Could you use a filter for separating materials in your Challenge? If so, what size must the mesh be? What forces will the filter have to resist? What materials should the filter be made of?

5 Remove the used filter paper and rinse the funnel with water.
- Measure out 25 mL of water in a graduated cylinder and pour it into a beaker.
- Mix 2.5 mL of flour into the beaker and stir.
- Repeat steps 2 to 4 using this mixture instead of milk.

6 Measure out 25 mL of water in a graduated cylinder and pour it into a beaker.
- Mix 2.5 mL of pepper into the beaker and stir.
- Repeat steps 2 to 4 using this mixture.

Making Connections

1. Describe how you could use kitchen utensils to separate each of the following mechanical mixtures:
   (a) sugar, toothpicks, and uncooked rice
   (b) chocolate chips, chocolate-covered peanuts, and small marshmallows

Exploring

2. Birdseed contains several types of seeds. With 250 mL (2E) of birdseed, design a procedure with your group to find out the amount of each type of seed, in units of mass or volume. With your teacher's approval, try it.

3. The screens on your windows and doors are filters that separate insects such as flies and mosquitoes from the air. Make a chart and list the different types of filters that might be found at home, at school, or in a car, as well as their purpose.

Analysis

7 Analyze your results by answering these questions.

(a) What evidence do you have that each of the liquids in this investigation is a mechanical mixture?

(b) What feature of the filter would you change to completely separate the substances in each of the mechanical mixtures?

(c) Based on your observations, was your hypothesis correct?

SKILLS MENU
- ○ Questioning
- ● Hypothesizing
- ○ Planning
- ● Conducting
- ● Recording
- ● Analyzing
- ● Communicating

Are All Solvents Alike?

As you learned earlier, a solvent is a substance in which other substances, or solutes, are dissolved. Centuries ago, scientists spent much time in their laboratories experimenting with solvents. They were hoping to find one solvent that dissolved everything. Instead, they found that solvents have different abilities to dissolve different substances (**Figure 1**).

Materials

- apron
- gloves
- safety goggles
- water
- ethanol
- test tubes
- rubber stopper
- flashlight
- salt, sugar, flour, rice, bath salts, butter, candle wax, drink crystals

Question

Are the solvents water and ethanol alike?

Hypothesis

2C **1** Read the Experimental Design and write a hypothesis that this investigation will attempt to prove.

Experimental Design

You will mix a variety of substances into both water and ethanol, and observe which ones form solutions, and which form mechanical mixtures.

Ethanol is toxic and flammable. Do not allow it to come in contact with your skin; do not allow an open flame in the room.

Procedure

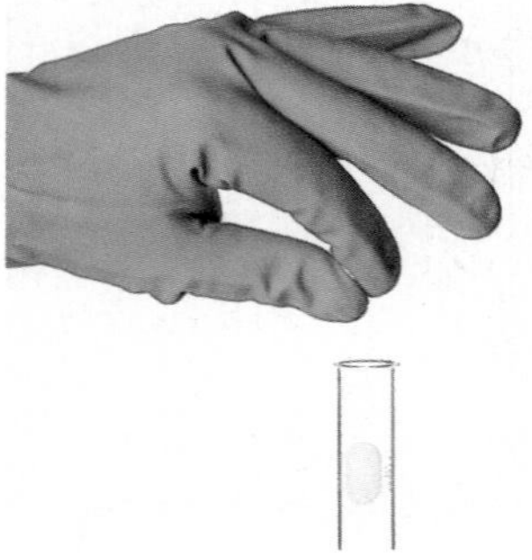

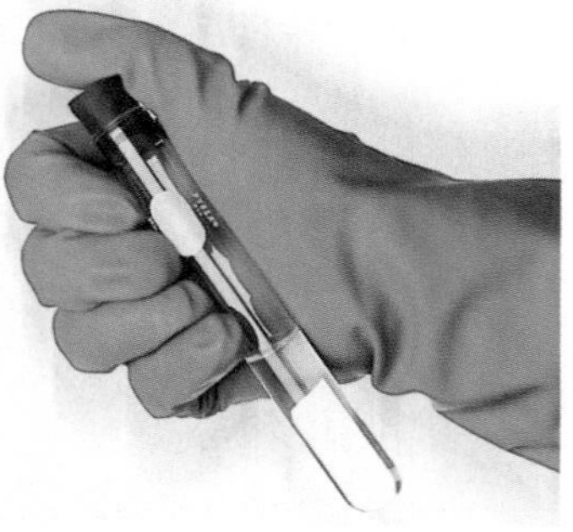

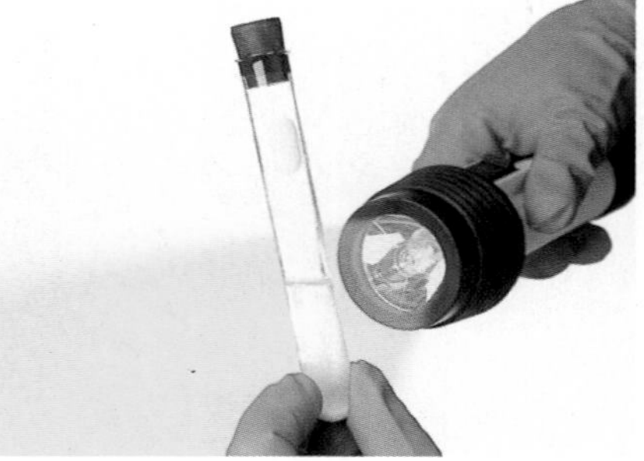

2 Pour 15 mL of water into a clean, dry test tube.
- Add a pinch of salt.

(a) What happens in the test tube? Record your observations.

3 Place the rubber stopper in the test tube and shake it away from your body while you count to 5.
- Let the test tube stand for a minute or so.

(a) Has any change occurred in the test tube? Record your observations.

(b) Record whether the test tube contains a mechanical mixture or a solution.

4 Repeat steps 2 and 3 with each of the substances you are given, using water as the solvent. If you are not sure if a mixture is clear or cloudy, try shining a flashlight through it, so any fine particles will become visible.

(a) Which mixtures have fine particles suspended in the water? Are they solutions or mechanical mixtures?

Figure 1
Different solvents have different properties. How will this affect their ability to dissolve various solutes?

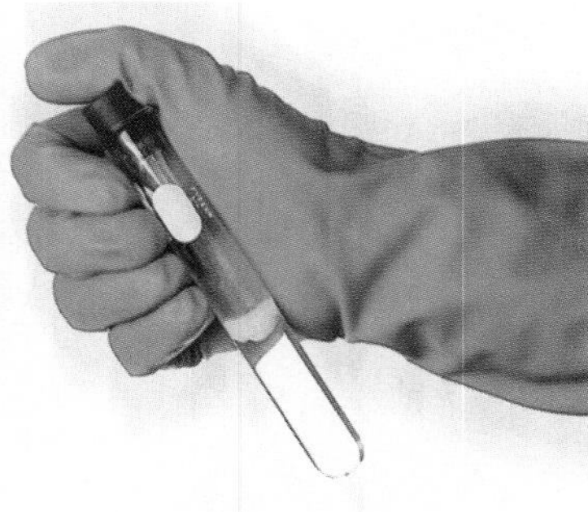

5 Dispose of the contents of the first set of test tubes, as directed by your teacher. Rinse the tubes and shake out any water.

6 Repeat steps 2, 3, and 4 using ethanol instead of water to test each of the solids you are given.

(a) Record your observations.

Making Connections

1. Dry-cleaning machines use a liquid to dissolve and remove grease, but the liquid is expensive. What are some possible ways of reducing this expense?

2. Imagine that you have accidentally spilled perfume into a bath. The perfume contains a rare, expensive oil, which you can see floating on the bath water. What steps could you take to recover as much of the oil as possible?

Exploring

3. Oil spills that occur near shorelines are often cleaned up with the help of powerful detergents. How do you think this works?

Reflecting

4. How would you classify the mixtures in this investigation? Which mixtures are possible to separate using the filtration technique from Investigation 1.3 or the evaporation technique from the Try This in 1.2?

Analysis

7 Analyze your results by answering these questions.

(a) Which substances formed a solution when mixed with:
- water?
- ethanol?

(b) Which substances formed a mechanical mixture when mixed with:
- water?
- ethanol?

(c) Write a summary paragraph to support or disagree with your hypothesis.

SKILLS HANDBOOK: 2C Predicting and Hypothesizing

How Do Solutions Form?

Why do some substances mix easily to form solutions, while others do not mix at all? For instance, in the previous investigation you observed that salt mixes readily with water to form a solution, yet does not form a solution with ethanol.

The Particle Theory and Drink Crystals

To answer this question we need to revisit the particle theory. When you make a drink, you may mix together drink crystals and water. Each solid drink crystal contains billions of small particles that are tightly attracted to each other. As long as they are in their package, they will stay in their crystal form. However, when the drink crystals are mixed into water, the particles at the surface of the crystal are attracted to water particles, as shown in **Figure 1**. If the attraction to the water particles is at least as strong as to other drink crystal particles, some of the particles on the surface of the crystal will break their connections to the rest of the crystal and float off into the water. This process continues until the drink crystals break apart and mix completely, or dissolve, in the water.

If the particles of the solute are not attracted to the particles of the solvent, the two substances generally cannot form a solution.

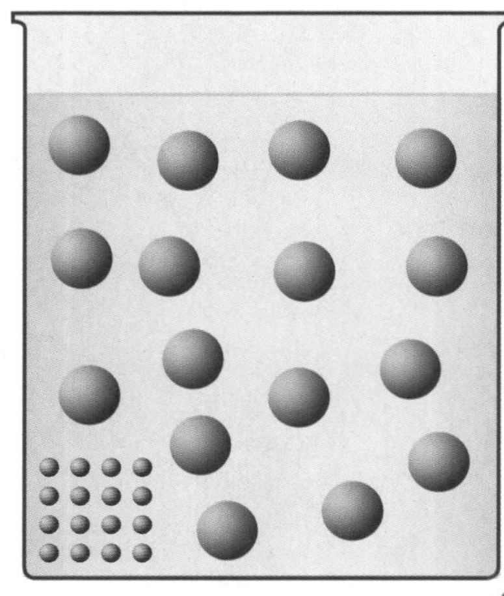

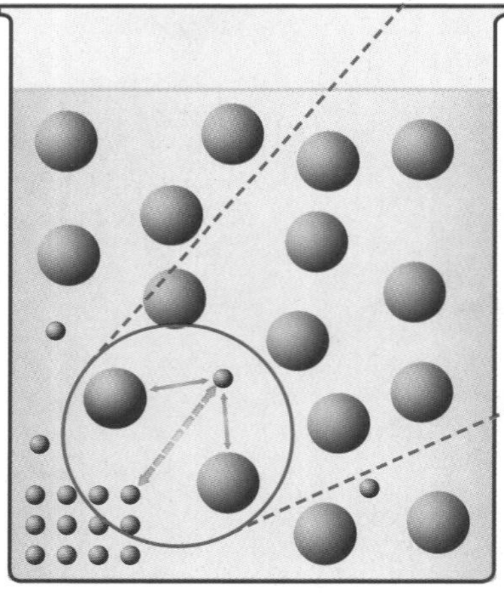

How Do Solute and Solvent Particles Fit Together?

When the tiny particles of a solute are dissolved, or mixed completely, with the particles of a solvent such as water, the solute particles fit in the spaces between the solvent particles.

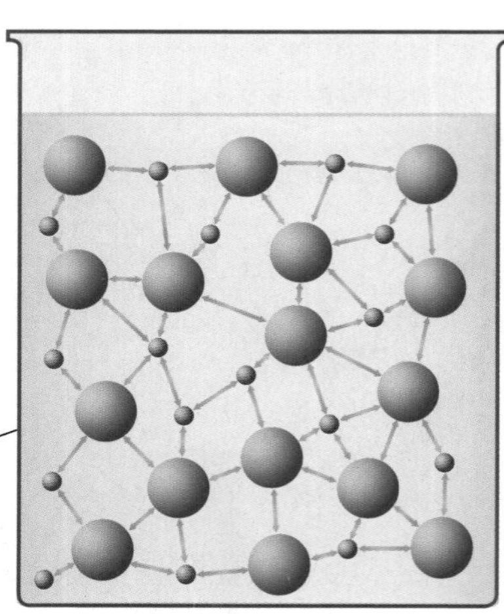

A solution occurs when all the drink particles break apart from the crystal, and mix completely with the water particles.

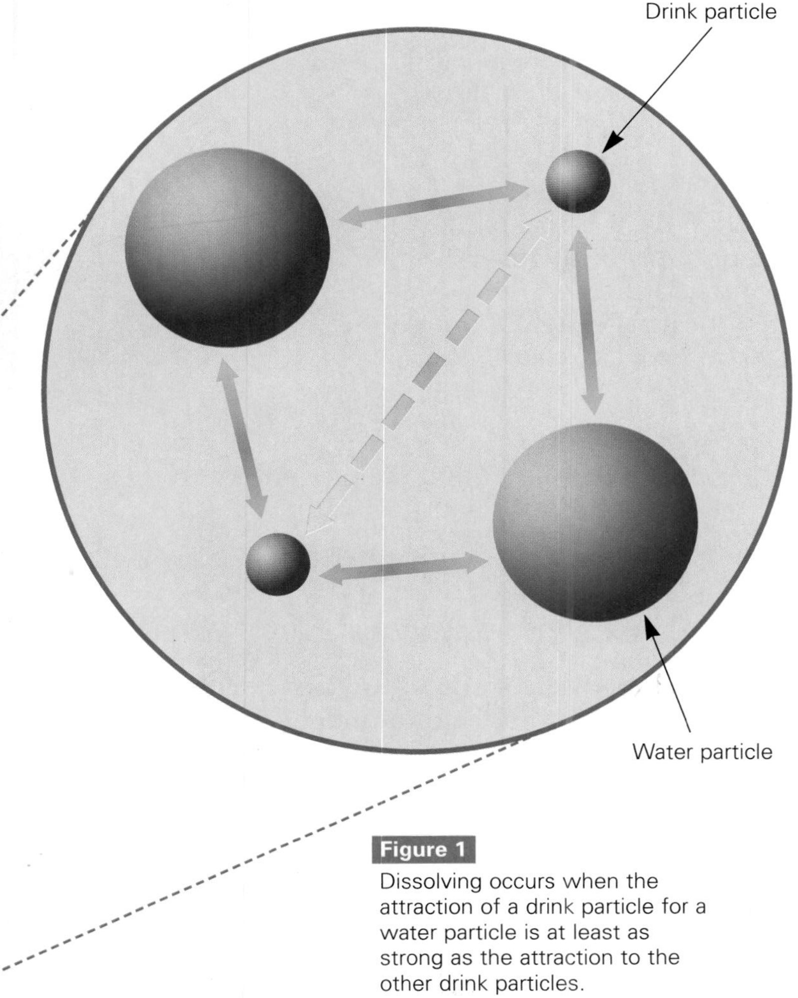

Figure 1
Dissolving occurs when the attraction of a drink particle for a water particle is at least as strong as the attraction to the other drink particles.

Understanding Concepts

1. Draw and label a series of diagrams to show the sequence of events that occurs when a sugar cube is dropped into water. (6C)
   (a) How does the particle theory explain how a solute dissolves in a solvent?
   (b) Based on the particle theory, why would a substance dissolve in one solvent, but not in another?

Making Connections

2. Imagine that you could take all the students in your class to the gym to help you illustrate the process of dissolving. What instructions might you give them?
3. Using what you know about particles, predict two ways you could shorten the time it takes to dissolve sugar in a drink. Explain your predictions.

Reflecting

4. Make a general statement relating the sizes of particles of substances and their combined volume when they are mixed.

Try This: A Model for a Solution

You can make a model of the solute and solvent particles in a solution. The advantage of a model is that you can observe a process that you ordinarily wouldn't be able to see.

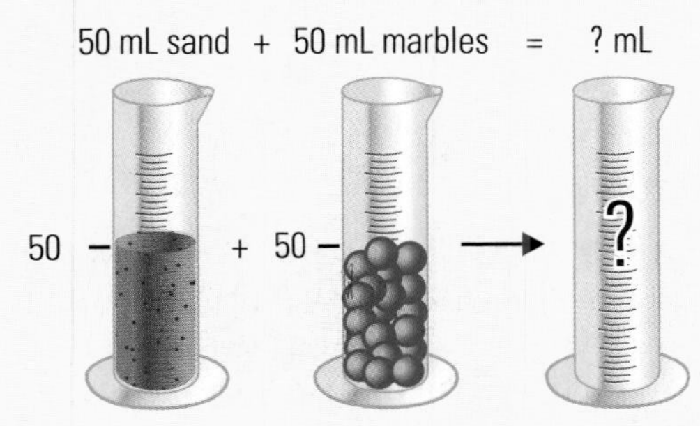

- Half-fill a clear container with marbles and mark the level with a grease pencil or marker. Then half-fill a second, identical container with sand.

1. Predict the total volume that will result when the marbles and sand are combined.

- Carefully pour the sand into the container of marbles and shake gently.

2. How accurate was your prediction of the volume of the mixture? Explain.
3. How is the container of sand and marbles like a solution?

1.6 Case Study

Flaky Baking

In baking, flour, fat, and water are mixed together. So why is making good pastry so difficult? The behaviour of matter is affected not only by the properties of the substance, but also by external factors such as temperature and humidity.

The main ingredients don't seem very mysterious (**Figure 1**), but getting the right mixture of these common substances remains a mystery that takes apprentice bakers years to master.

Flour and Water

The secret to flaky pastry lies in knowing how the three main ingredients work together. Flour contains many substances, including minerals and other nutrients, but the protein in the flour is pastry's "backbone." When flour mixes with water, the protein forms a substance called gluten, which gives dough strength and elasticity. But "sturdy" and "elastic" are not words you want to hear after critics have taken a bite of your pastry. What is needed is just enough strength to hold the crust together. That is why most of the steps and ingredients in a pastry recipe are designed to minimize gluten development. For example, pie crust is less likely to be tough if cake and pastry flour is used, instead of bread flour. Cake and pastry flour is 7% protein; bread flour is 12% protein.

(a) Explain how bread flour would make tougher pastry.

Fat and Flour

Liquid fat and oils do not form a water solution. Instead they will form a layer floating on water. If you force them to mix they will form a mechanical mixture, with fat forming globules in the water. It is this property that enables fat to play a major role in pastry by "waterproofing" flour particles. Small globules of vegetable shortening, lard, or butter can surround flour particles. Whenever water cannot reach the flour, gluten cannot form. When there is enough fat in the mixture, gluten forms only short strands.

(b) Why is the term "shortening" often used instead of "fat"?

(c) Why is it a good idea to add fat to the flour before adding water?

(d) What kind of mixture is dough? Explain.

Cold and Flaky

If you experiment with making pastry, you will find that cold, firm fat makes the flakiest pastry. The reason can be found in the oven.

Flaky pastry is made of many fine layers. In the oven, it is fat that separates the layers of dough. As the water in the dough turns to steam and expands, it pushes these layers of dough apart, forming the characteristic blisters or flakes of good flaky pastry. The greater the number of layers, the flakier the final pastry will be.

(e) Speculate as to why cold fat would create more layers in the dough than warm fat.

.... It's the Humidity

The dough mixture is sensitive. Even the weather has an effect!

Water holds the flour and fat together. When making pastry it is important to add only enough water until lumps of dough start to stick together. Any more water will develop extra gluten, which toughens the pastry. However, if bakers add precisely the amount of water their recipes call for, they'll find that on humid days their pastry will be tougher. Water vapour from the air becomes part of the mixture.

(f) On rainy and humid days, you should add less water than the recipe calls for. On dry days, you should add more. Speculate on what might happen to pastry dough that doesn't include enough water.

Figure 1
A flaky crust is all in the mix.

Hands Off

Too much stirring or handling of the dough toughens the pastry and also makes it less flaky. Chefs recommend you use a fork or pastry blender to mix the dough lightly, then push it into a ball with your hands.

(g) Speculate on why handling the dough too much is bad for the pastry.

Chill

Freshly mixed dough should be placed in a refrigerator for 20 min before rolling. Chilling allows the exposed flour particles to evenly absorb moisture, making the dough more uniform and easier to roll.

(h) If dough were set aside at room temperature the flour would still absorb water, but what else might happen in the dough?

Table 1 Other Pastry Ingredients

Ingredient	Function
sugars	Provides sweetness or aids yeast in producing the gas for raising dough. Sugar can tenderize dough and may help a baked product to brown.
salt	Brings out the flavours of other ingredients. Reducing or omitting salt can cause dough to rise too quickly, affecting shape and flavour.
baking soda, baking powder	Baking soda, combined with an acidic ingredient such as vinegar, lemon juice, or molasses, produces gas to raise dough. Baking powder is premixed. It contains baking soda and the right amount of acid to react with it.
eggs	Egg yolks provide uniform flavour and texture to cakes. Egg whites add air. When they are beaten, they form a froth that includes lots of air.

Understanding Concepts

1. Describe in your own words the role of each of the following dough ingredients:
   (a) flour
   (b) fat
   (c) water
   (d) salt
   (e) baking powder
2. (a) What is gluten?
   (b) What factors determine how much gluten is formed when mixing pastry ingredients?
3. Should you store shortening in a cupboard or in the refrigerator? Explain.

Exploring

4. Does noise affect rising dough or a baking cake? Could sound waves cause rising dough to collapse? Design an investigation to test the effect of sound on rising dough. Your procedure should include safety precautions. With your teacher's permission, carry out your investigation. (2E)

Other Ingredients

Recipes often call for other ingredients than the main three. Some of these are listed in **Table 1**.

Troubleshooting

An applesauce cake turned out flat, instead of airy. The recipe called for baking soda, brown sugar, and apple sauce. Both sugar and apple sauce add acid to the mix.

(i) Did the baker make an error? What could have gone wrong?

A couple from Edmonton who moved to Toronto are disappointed with their pastry, which is tougher now, at least in the summer.

(j) What would you recommend?

SKILLS HANDBOOK: (2E) Designing an Inquiry Investigation

SKILLS MENU
- ○ Questioning
- ● Hypothesizing
- ● Planning
- ● Conducting
- ● Recording
- ● Ana...
- ● Communicating

The Rate of Dissolving

Understanding factors that affect how quickly a substance dissolves is important to the manufacturing of medicines, dyes, and processed foods. For example, some kinds of cold relief remedies are powders that must be mixed with hot water. Scientists who work for drug companies do tests to ensure the powder dissolves quickly in hot water. Understanding how substances dissolve in other substances is an important part of their job. When you add sugar to a drink, several factors affect how quickly the sugar dissolves. Based on your experience, you probably have some idea of what these are. But have you ever tested your ideas?

Materials

- apron
- safety goggles
- beakers or clear plastic cups
- marker pen
- hot and cold water
- thermometers
- powdered sugar
- sugar cubes

Question

What factors affect how quickly a solute dissolves in a solvent?

Hypothesis

2C **1** Write a hypothesis for each variable you test in this investigation.

Experimental Design

This is a controlled experiment investigating the factors that affect the rate of dissolving. A test for one of the variables (temperature) is described in steps 6 and 7 below.

2E **2** Read steps 6 and 7. You will design and carry out tests for another two variables (particle size, stirring).

2D **3** Using sugar cubes and powdered sugar, plan a controlled procedure to test whether particle size has an effect on the rate of dissolving.

4 Plan a controlled procedure to test whether stirring has an effect on the rate of dissolving.

5 Write down the steps for your procedures and submit them to your teacher for approval.

Procedure

Part 1: Temperature

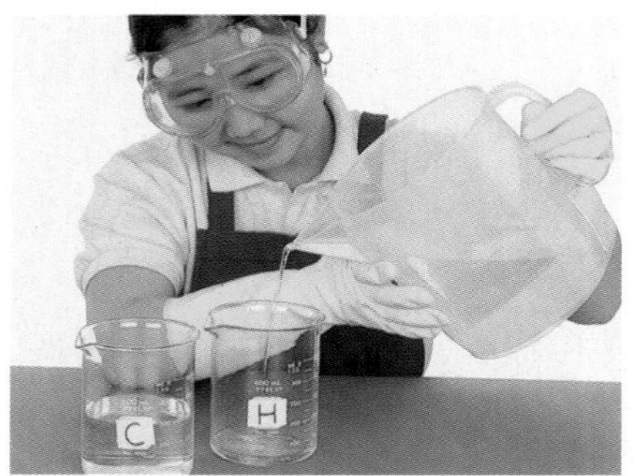

6 Mark two containers as follows: C (cold), H (hot).

- Pour cold tap water in the container marked C until it is three-quarters full.
- Pour the same amount of hot tap water into the container marked H.

(a) Record the temperature of the water in each cup.

7 Add 5 mL of sugar to each cup.

(a) In which cup does the solute dissolve faster?

SKILLS HANDBOOK: 2C Predicting and Hypothesiz

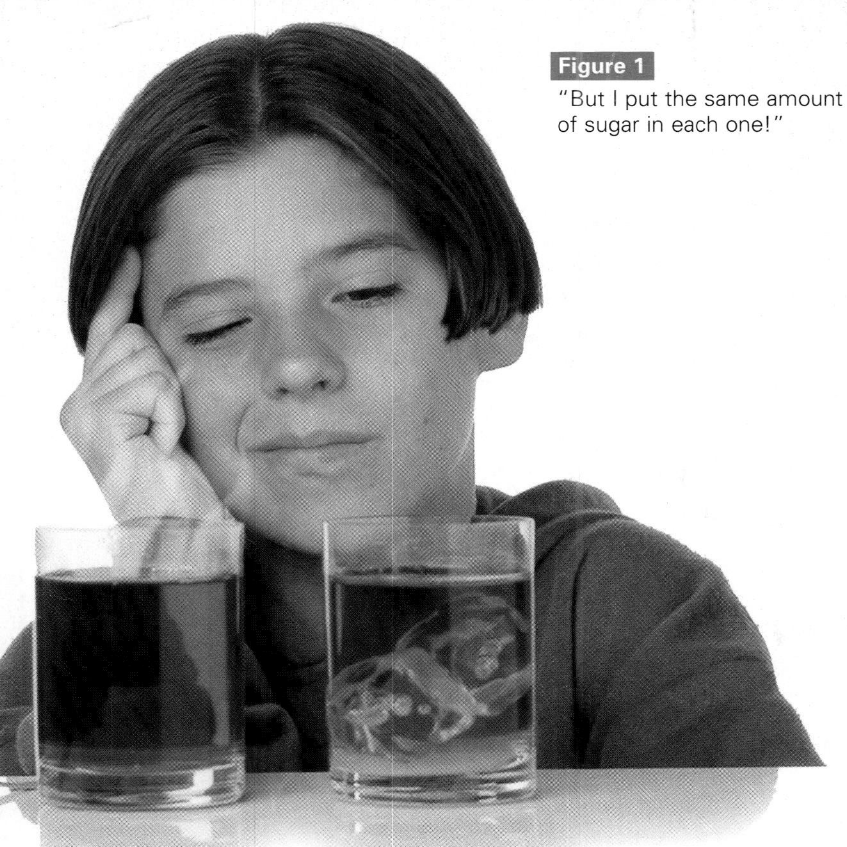

Figure 1
"But I put the same amount of sugar in each one!"

Parts 2 and 3: Other Factors

8 Carry out the procedures you have designed to test other factors.

Analysis

9 Analyze your results by answering these questions.

(a) List three factors that affect how quickly a solute dissolves in a solvent.

(b) What effect does each of these factors have?

(c) When testing the effect of stirring on dissolving, what was your independent variable?

(d) Explain how you controlled other variables.

(e) Use the particle theory to explain how each of the factors affects dissolving. Include a sketch in your answer.

Making Connections

1. Most brands of soda pop are solutions that contain water, dissolved sugar, and dissolved carbon dioxide gas. When you remove the cap from a cold bottle of soda pop, you will hear a faint whoosh as the gas escapes. But when the cap is removed from a warm bottle, the whoosh is much louder (**Figure 2**). What effect does changing temperature and pressure have on the rate that carbon dioxide gas comes out of a soda pop bottle?

Reflecting

2. Suggest at least two procedures that you hypothesize would have no effect on the rate of dissolving. Explain why you think they would have no effect.

Figure 2
Soft drinks are solutions that contain dissolved gases among other substances.

2E Designing an Inquiry Investigation   2D Identifying Variables and Controls

Saturated or Unsaturated?

Have you ever made a drink by dissolving flavour crystals in water and found that it tasted "watery" because you didn't add enough crystals? This happens when you don't have the right concentration of solute in the solvent. *Concentration* is the amount of solute dissolved in a given quantity of solvent or solution.

Solutions with a low concentration of solute are called **dilute solutions**. To make the flavour of your drink stronger, you must increase the concentration of the solute by adding more flavour crystals to the same amount of water. Solutions with a high amount of solute are referred to as **concentrated solutions**.

Since both dilute and concentrated solutions still contain unfilled spaces between the solvent particles (**Figure 1**), they are both **unsaturated solutions**.

The maximum amount of solute in a solution is the amount that fills all the available spaces between the solvent particles. A solution in which all the spaces are filled is a **saturated solution**. If you try to strengthen the flavour of your drink by adding still more flavour crystals to a saturated solution, the crystals will simply sink to the bottom of the glass without dissolving.

Exactly How Much Solute Can You Add?

The **solubility** of a solute is the exact amount of solute required to form a saturated solution in a particular solvent at a certain temperature.

The solubility is different for each combination of solute and solvent. The amount of solute needed to saturate a certain volume of solvent varies enormously. A solution of one substance in water, for example, may be saturated when only a little of it has been dissolved. On the other hand, a saturated solution of another substance in water may contain a lot of solute. In **Table 1** you can see that, at any temperature, the amount of sugar that will dissolve in 100 mL of water is greater than the amount of table salt, which in turn, is greater than the amount of baking soda.

Figure 1
Dilute, concentrated, and saturated solutions

(a) In a dilute solution, the solute particles fill only some of the available spaces between the solvent particles.

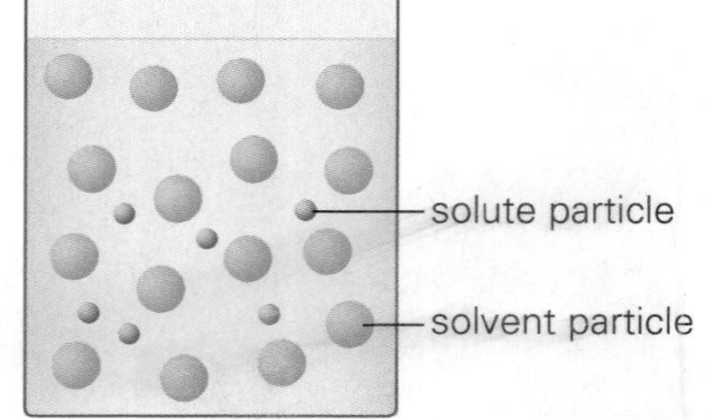

(b) In a concentrated solution, the solute particles fill most of the available spaces between the solvent particles.

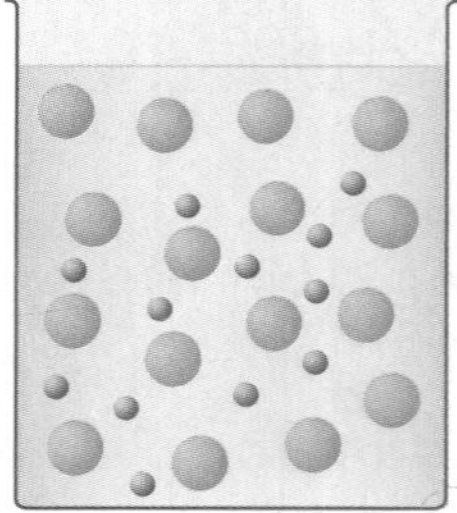

(c) In a saturated solution, the solute particles fill all of the available spaces between the solvent particles.

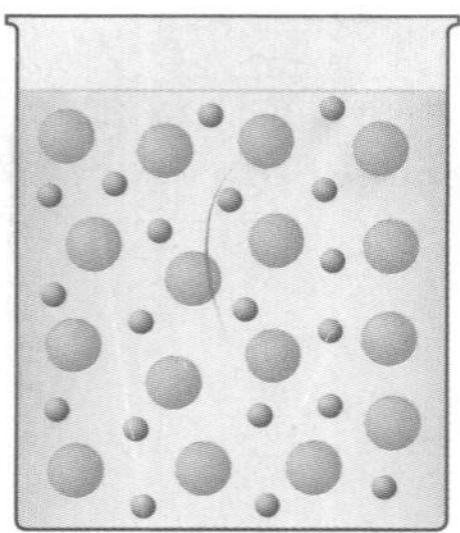

Table 1 Some Solubilities in Water

Solute	Temperature		
	0°C	20°C	50°C
baking soda	6.9 g/100 mL	9.6 g/100 mL	14.5 g/100 mL
table salt	35.7 g/100 mL	36.0 g/100 mL	36.7 g/100 mL
sugar	179 g/100 mL	204 g/100 mL	260 g/100 mL

Supersaturation

With very few solid solutes, it is possible to create a solution that is more than saturated. A solution that contains more of the solute than would be found in a saturated solution is called **supersaturated**.

A supersaturated solution can be made with certain solutes by starting with a hot saturated solution at high temperature, and then allowing the solution to cool slowly. If the solution is not disturbed, all the solute may remain dissolved. Normally, as a solution cools the solute particles lose energy. This allows the attraction between a few of the solute particles to draw them together into the crystal pattern of the solid. A crystalline solid forms in the solution. In a supersaturated solution, the solute particles are not able to get into the crystal pattern.

If the container holding a supersaturated solution is struck lightly with a solid object (a spoon or a stirring rod, for example), the resulting vibrations may cause some of the solute particles to move into the crystal pattern. Immediately, the rest of the extra solute will join the crystal and fall out of solution. You can produce a similar effect by adding a seed crystal of the solute for the excess solute particles to build on (**Figure 2**).

Understanding Concepts

1. Describe how you can tell the difference between a saturated solution and an unsaturated solution.
2. Is the solubility of all solutes the same?

Making Connections

3. Use the particle theory to explain why some substances do not dissolve in a particular solvent, while others do.
4. Rock candy is made by dissolving sugar in warm water to form a saturated solution, then allowing it to cool. Based on what you know about solutions, explain how the candy forms.

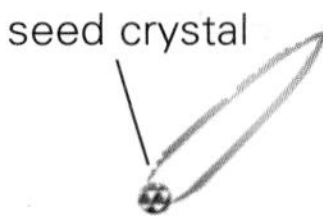

Figure 2

(a) Supersaturated solutions are rare because they are very unstable. They contain more dissolved solute than would normally occur at that temperature. Adding a seed crystal changes the nature of the solution.

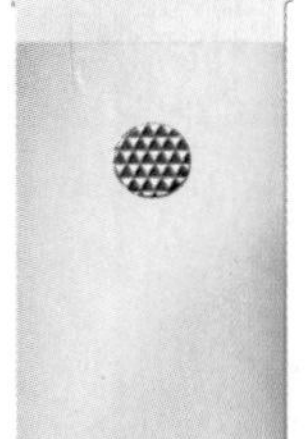

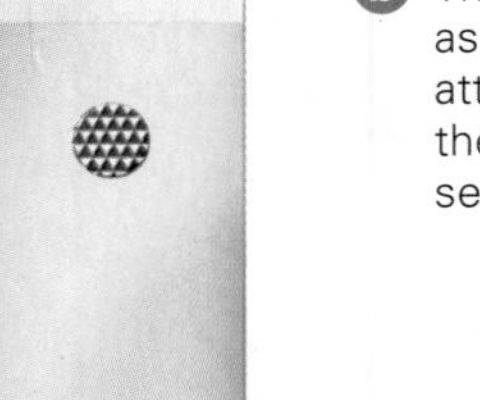

(b) The seed crystal begins to grow as excess solute particles are attracted to and become part of the pattern of particles in the seed crystal.

(c) All excess solute has now solidified around the seed crystal. The solution is now saturated at that temperature.

Design Challenge

What would you have to take into consideration designing your water purification system for Challenge 1?

Try This: Comparing Solubility

- Pour 100 mL of water into each of two 400-mL beakers.
- Add 50 g of salt to one beaker and 50 g of sugar to the other.
- Stir both at the same rate.

1. Does the same amount of both solutes dissolve in the water?
2. What does this tell you about the solubility of salt and sugar in water?

1.9 Inquiry Investigation

SKILLS MENU
○ Questioning ● Conducting ● Analyzing
● Hypothesizing ● Recording ● Communicating
○ Planning

Solubility and Saturation

You have already learned that the solubility of solutes in solvents is affected by temperature. But how much does solubility go up or down as the temperature rises?

Question

Are changes in the solubility of drink crystals in water predictable?

Hypothesis

2C **1** Write a hypothesis for this investigation.

Experimental Design

The solubility of drink crystals in water will be measured at different temperatures. You will be able to graph how solubility changes according to temperature.

Materials

- apron
- safety goggles
- drink crystals
- clear container
- 100-mL beaker
- 250-mL beaker
- 100-mL graduated cylinder
- water
- balance
- stirring rod
- thermometer

Procedure

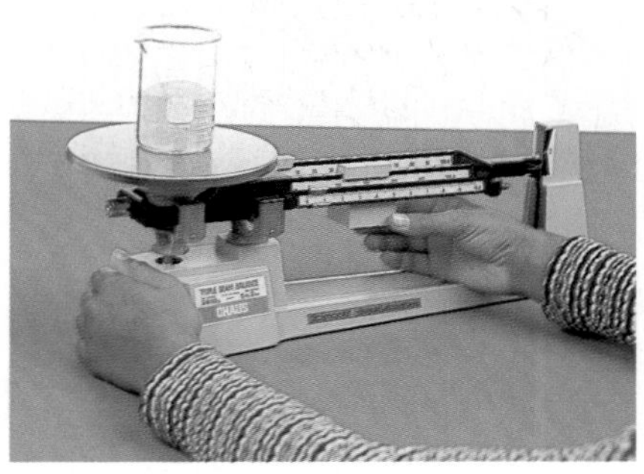

2 Measure the mass of a 100-mL beaker.

(a) Record the mass of the beaker.

- Half-fill the beaker with drink crystals.
- Measure the total mass of the beaker and the crystals.

(b) Record the mass of the beaker and crystals.

(c) Calculate the mass of the crystals.

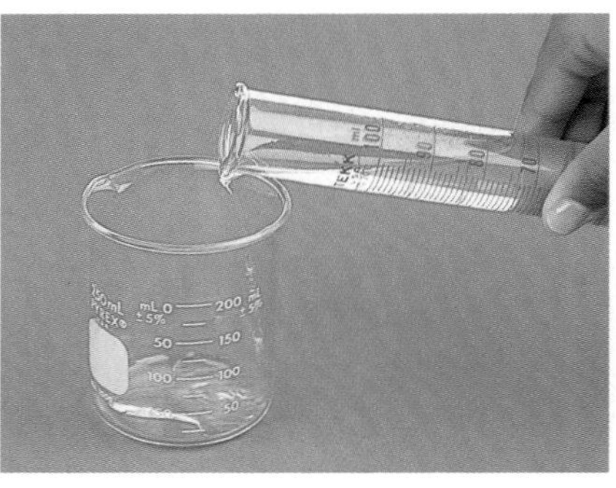

3 Fill a graduated cylinder with 100 mL of tap water.

- Pour the water into a clean 250-mL beaker.

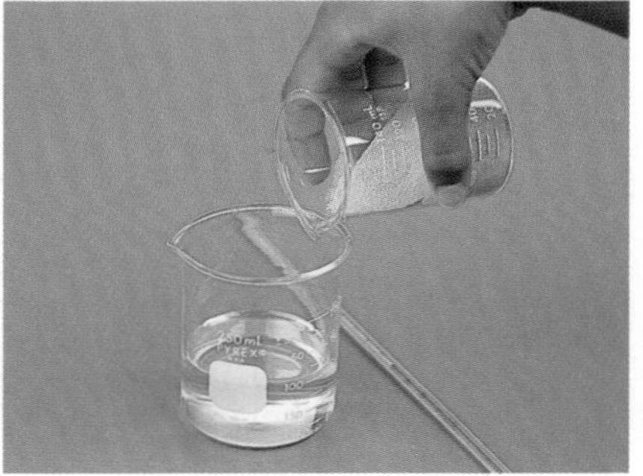

4 Slowly add crystals from the beaker to the water, stirring constantly, until no more crystals dissolve, and you see crystals starting to collect on the bottom.

- Measure the water temperature with a thermometer.

(a) Record the temperature of the water.

Figure 1
The solubility of all solutes changes according to temperature.

Understanding Concepts

1. If a solution is saturated at 20°C, will it also be saturated at 40°C? Explain your answer.

Making Connections

2. Suppose you mix lemon juice, sugar, and cold water to make lemonade. After stirring, there is still some undissolved sugar at the bottom of the glass.
   - **(a)** Why didn't all the sugar dissolve?
   - **(b)** Which type of sugar solution was formed?
   - **(c)** What type of sugar solution would form if you heated the lemonade?

Exploring

3. Predict what will happen to a hot, saturated solution of drink crystals in water as it cools. Explain your prediction. With your teacher's permission, try it. Was your prediction correct?

5 Measure the mass of the beaker and unused crystals and record it.

(a) Calculate the mass of the crystals you added to the water.

(b) Record the solubility of the drink crystals in water at the measured temperature, in g/100 mL.

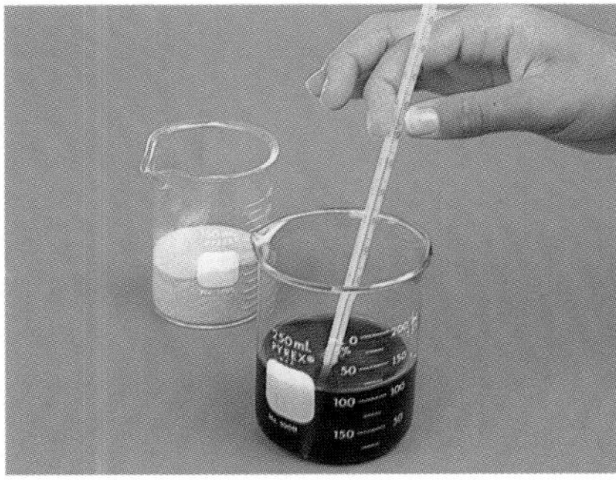

6 Repeat steps 2 to 5 using water at 3 other temperatures, using a mixture of hot and cold tap water.

(a) Record the solubility of the crystals at each temperature.

Analysis

7 Analyze your results by answering these questions.

(a) How did you know when you had created a saturated solution?

(b) From your data and the data of other groups in your class, draw a graph of solubility versus temperature for drink crystals in water. (7C)

(c) Based on your graph, what happens to the solubility of drink crystals in water as the temperature of the water increases?

(d) Using your graph, predict the solubility of drink crystals in water at 80°C.

SKILLS HANDBOOK: (2C) Predicting and Hypothesizing (7C) Constructing Graphs

SKILLS MENU
- ○ Questioning
- ○ Hypothesizing
- ● Planning
- ● Conducting
- ● Recording
- ● Analyzing
- ● Communicating

Separating Mixtures

You have learned that a mixture consists of two or more pure substances. Because each of these substances has different properties, they can be separated from each other, as shown in **Figure 1**. One of these properties may include the ability to form a solution in a particular solvent.

Materials

- safety goggles
- apron
- table salt
- pepper
- sand
- sawdust
- mechanical mixture (salt, sand, and sawdust)
- iron fillings
- magnet
- 3 plastic bags
- other materials and equipment as needed

Question

What methods can be used to separate a heterogeneous mixture consisting of three substances?

Hypothesis

Examining the properties of the substances in a mixture will enable you to choose a technique that allows you to separate each substance from the mixture.

Experimental Design

By analyzing a mechanical mixture and studying the separation techniques illustrated in **Figure 1**, you will come up with a procedure for separating the substances.

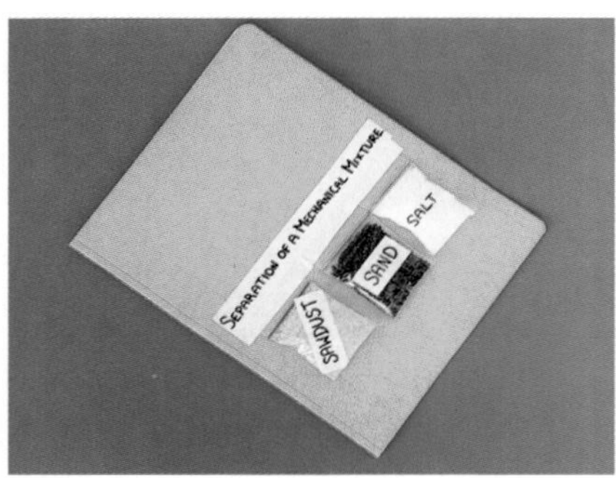

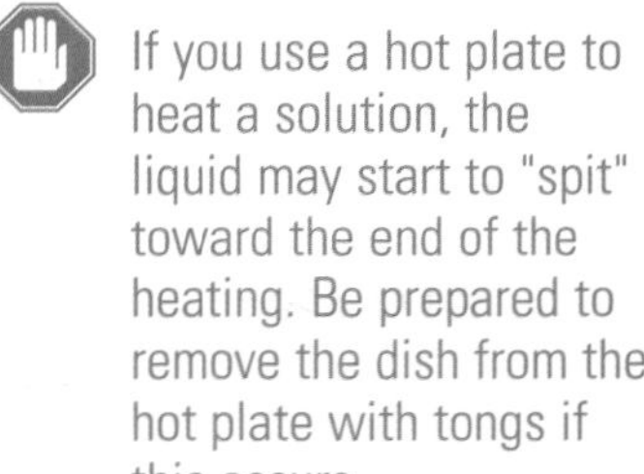

If you use a hot plate to heat a solution, the liquid may start to "spit" toward the end of the heating. Be prepared to remove the dish from the hot plate with tongs if this occurs.

1. Put on your apron and safety goggles.
2. Examine a small amount of each of the three substances in the mixture.
3. Using whatever equipment is available and your senses of sight and touch, observe and record in a table the physical properties of each substance.
4. (2E) Using what you have observed about the properties of the substances in the mixture and the information in **Figure 1**, develop a detailed procedure for separating the substances. At the end of your procedure, you must have three dry solids, each in a plastic bag. Your procedure must include labelled diagrams to illustrate how equipment will be used.
5. Submit the procedure to your teacher for approval.

Procedure

6 Once your procedure is approved, carry it out.

(a) Record the appearance of your substances and mixture after each step is complete.

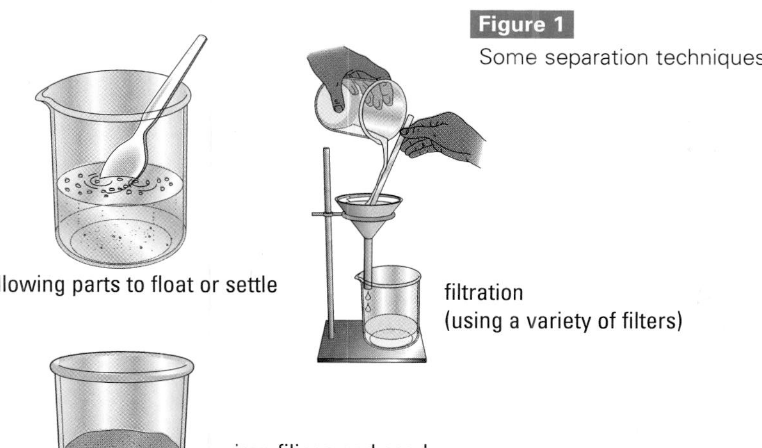

Figure 1
Some separation techniques

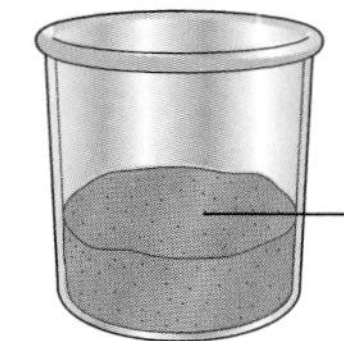

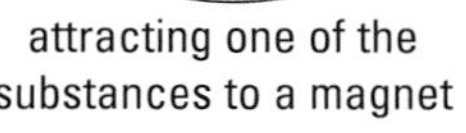

Design Challenge

Your Challenge requires that you separate substances in a mechanical mixture. Which of the techniques you have learned here will help you solve the Challenge?

Making Connections

1. Explain which separation techniques you might use to separate the substances in each of the mixtures below:
   - **(a)** water, sugar, and sand
   - **(b)** water, flour, and marbles
   - **(c)** vegetable soup, salt, and water
   - **(d)** water, iron filings, and soil
2. **(a)** Is there any commercial advantage to using settling instead of filtering to remove particles from a liquid? Explain.
   (b) Why isn't settling always used to separate particles suspended in a liquid?
3. Draw a flowchart to show how you would separate a mixture of iron filings, sand, salt, stones, and sawdust.

Analysis

7 Analyze your results by answering these questions.

(a) Which physical property did you use to separate the first substance from the mixture?

(b) Which physical property did you use to separate the remaining two substances in the mixture?

(c) Do you think you recovered all of each substance in the mixture? How might you improve your procedure to ensure that as much as possible of each substance is recovered?

(d) Submit a report on the investigation that includes your observations, the procedure you used, and a description of how you would improve your procedure if you had to do the separation again. (8A)

SKILLS HANDBOOK: (2E) Designing an Inquiry Investigation (8A) Writing a Report

1.11

Using Solutions of Gases

Figure 4
A good, warm fire needs dry wood that will burn easily and oxgyen from the air.

Because we can't see gases or feel them unless they move, we often forget that they exist! But we actually use many different gases in everyday life.

Air

You learned earlier that air is a solution of gases that includes nitrogen, oxygen, argon, and carbon dioxide. There are also varying amounts of water vapour and tiny amounts of several other gases. All of these gases are pure substances.

We breathe air every moment. Our lungs separate oxygen from the solution, and add carbon dioxide and water vapour. As a result, the solution of gases we breathe in is different from the solution we breathe out.

We also use air that has been compressed under high pressure for transportation and recreation (**Figure 1**).

Figure 1

a Compressed air is used to fill bicycle and car tires for a smooth ride.

b Compressed air is also used to fill air mattresses for floating on water.

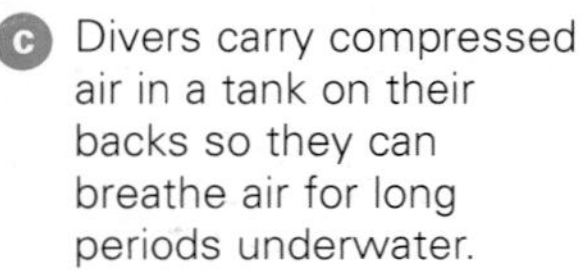

c Divers carry compressed air in a tank on their backs so they can breathe air for long periods underwater.

Neon for Light

Neon is a gas that has transformed our city streets. Brightly coloured neon lights are made of glass tubes that contain neon or other gases that glow when an electric current is passed through them (**Figure 2**). Neon glows an orange colour, but by changing the colour of the glass, it is possible to make neon-filled tubes that glow red, green, or even blue. Neon and the other gases are pure substances, but neon tubes usually contain a gas solution rather than pure neon.

Gases for Surgery

Gases are an important part of surgical operations (**Figure 3**). During an operation, the patient must stay unconscious, yet still breathe. This is arranged by giving the patient a gas solution that includes oxygen and another gas, such as nitrous oxide, that causes the patient to stay unconscious. The person responsible for controlling the flow of these gases during the operation is a specialized doctor called an anesthesiologist.

Figure 2
Neon light is made by passing an electric current through a glass tube that contains a gas solution that includes neon.

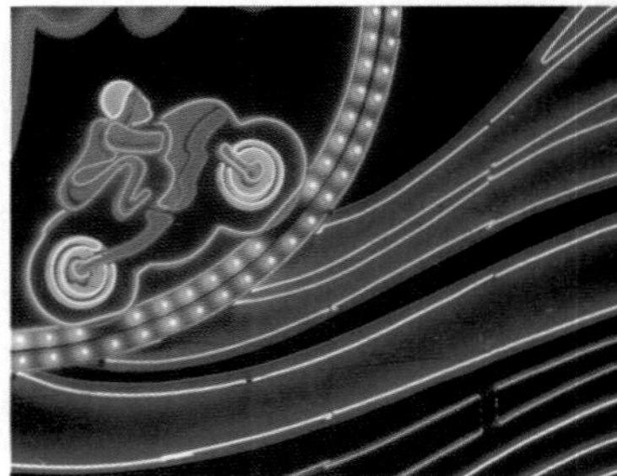

Figure 3
During surgery, the anesthesiologist controls the amounts of each gas in the solution the patient breathes. The patient must stay unconscious but also breathe normally during the operation.

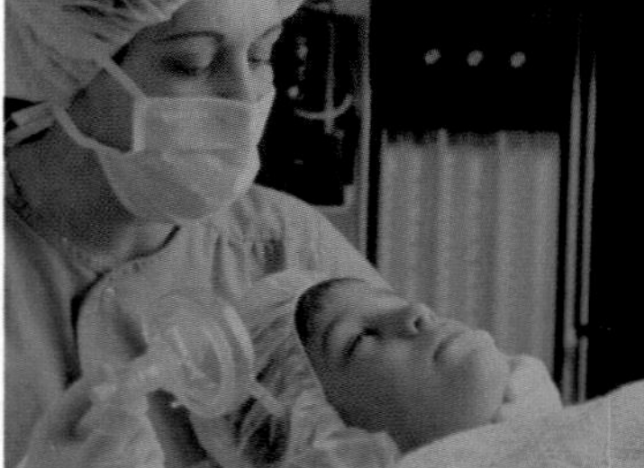

Exploring

1. Scuba divers who work at considerable depths underwater are careful not to surface too quickly to avoid a condition called the "bends" or decompression sickness.
   - **(a)** Use a variety of print and electronic sources to research this condition.
   - **(b)** Prepare an information pamphlet to inform scuba divers about this condition.
2. Methane gas has other surprising locations and uses. Use a variety of print and electronic sources to find out more about methane in the ocean, as an alternative fuel, and its effect on the atmosphere. Present your results as a poster that informs others about the importance of methane in our lives.

Gases for Burning

It is the oxygen in the air that allows fuels to burn. When we burn wood in fireplaces or gasoline in cars, the carbon in these fuels reacts chemically with oxygen in the air, forming carbon dioxide and water and giving off a lot of heat. This heat is used to provide warmth, cook food, or to supply energy for moving vehicles (**Figure 4**).

Sometimes the fuel itself is also a gas. For example, natural gas is piped into many homes to provide heat when it is burned in a furnace, a water heater, or a stove (**Figure 5**).

Natural gas is actually a solution of several similar gases, with methane as the solvent. Like wood, oil, and coal, methane contains carbon. Natural gas is found deep underground in pockets, usually near underground oil deposits. It is believed that oil and natural gas both formed from organisms that lived millions of years ago and were buried under many layers of rock and soil. Once a gas well is drilled down through the rock to a gas pocket, the gas flows up to the surface on its own. From the surface, thousands of kilometres of pipelines bring the gas into our homes. **Figure 6** shows a pipeline.

Figure 5
Natural gas is used as a fuel to heat food, water, or air.

Figure 6
Extensive networks of gas pipelines extend from gas wells in western Canada to the large cities of central Canada.

1.12

Products from Raw Materials

In the beginning of this unit you learned that pure substances can be mixed together to form solutions that are liquid, gas, or solid. What are solid solutions and are they an important part of our lives (**Figure 1**)?

Most metals we use are combinations of two or more metals mixed together in a solid solution called an **alloy**. An alloy is a homogeneous mixture of a metal with other substances. Alloys allow scientists and engineers to design metals that have specific properties depending on what they are used for. Steel is formed in a process that takes iron from iron ore and carbon from coal. Usually small amounts of other metals are mixed in to give the steel different qualities. Chromium and nickel, for instance, are often added to make the steel resistant to rust, giving it the name stainless steel. Adding zinc to copper makes brass, an alloy that is stronger than copper alone and is resistant to corrosion. It is used for ornamental objects on the exterior of houses, such as house numbers and mailboxes.

The idea of making alloys is actually thousands of years old. Early civilizations discovered that if you pour a small amount of melted tin into melted copper, the tin will dissolve in the copper to form a new substance, bronze, that is much harder than either metal. Bronze was made into furniture, jewellery, tools, armour, and weapons.

Modern Alloys

We still find uses for bronze, such as in statues. However, in the past few decades metallurgists (who study metals) have experimented and come up with thousands of different alloys, each having its own special properties. Some alloys are designed to resist heat, as in **Figure 2**, others to be strong, or light, or flexible.

One important modern addition to the list of useful metals is aluminum. Aluminum is very light and is used extensively in alloys used to make automotive engines, airplanes, and bicycle frames. Aluminum helps reduce weight.

Magnesium is a metal that is even lighter than aluminum, but it is more expensive. When light weight is crucial, as in the bicycle in **Figure 3**, magnesium alloys may be used.

Figure 2

Rockets and jet engines are made from alloys that include tungsten, which has the highest melting point of all metals (3410°C).

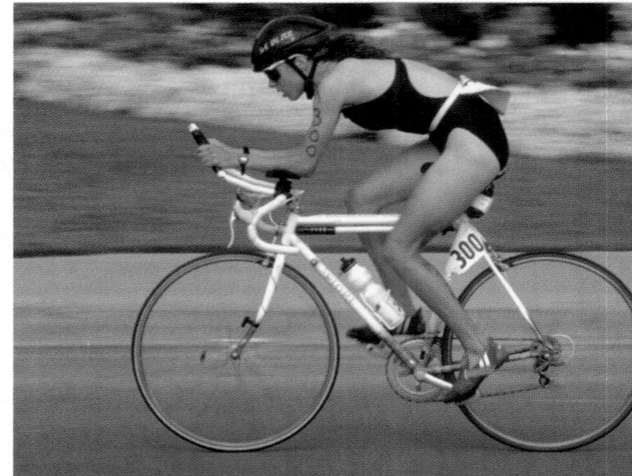

Figure 3

Bicycle frames used by racers are very light because of the magnesium dissolved in the other metals.

Ceramics

Ceramics, including pottery, bricks, cement, and glass, are made mostly from silica, and are another type of mixture. The mineral quartz is the crystalline form of silica and the source of raw materials for ceramic products. Silica particles are also often found in beach sand.

Figure 1
Many musical instruments, such as the saxophone, trumpet, and tuba, are made of copper and zinc mixed together to form brass.

Glass: One of the Ceramics

Glass is another type of solution—actually a supercooled liquid. The main raw material used to make glass is quartz.

Glass is a ceramic product we use daily. In the process of making glass, small amounts of limestone and potash are mixed with the silica at high temperatures, and then allowed to cool. While it is still liquid, glass can be poured onto a flat surface to form a sheet, from which we can make windows. Hot glass can also be moulded into shapes, such as vases, glasses, and bottles.

Glass Fibres

Glass can also be drawn out into fibres so thin that they are flexible but still allow light to pass through them, as shown in **Figure 4**. Thin glass fibres have revolutionized our worldwide communications systems. These optical fibres can carry thousands more signals than electrical cable made of copper wires. Optical fibres have provided the technology for the huge increase in electronic communication that has occurred in recent years.

Figure 4
Optical fibres, made of glass, can carry many signals at once in the form of pulses of light. They are also used in surgical viewing instruments. Light can pass along a curved fibre, allowing the surgeon to "see around a bend."

Other Types of Ceramics

Some new types of ceramics, with different combinations of ingredients mixed in with melted silica, are able to withstand extremely high temperatures. These materials are used in the heat shields of spacecraft so that they can withstand the fiery temperatures encountered when re-entering Earth's atmosphere.

Try This: Materials with a Purpose

Purified metals, such as aluminum, nickel, or copper, and alloys, glass, ceramics, and plastic are all processed or manufactured from raw materials. Many of the products we buy have been shaped from those raw materials. In every case, the raw materials used for each item have been chosen because of their special properties.

- Look around the classroom and make a list of the objects that you see.

1. Beside each object in your list, write the materials you think it is made from.
2. Indicate if the materials are natural, such as wood, or if they have been processed, such as plastic.
3. Record some of the properties of the object and explain why the particular materials were chosen for each object.
4. Are the materials used always the best choice in each case? List any alternative materials and explain why they would be better.

Glass for Insulation

Hot, molten glass can also be spun into small glass fibres, which are sprayed with a type of glue to form thick mats. These light, fluffy mats are used as insulation in houses and other buildings to keep in their heat. As an energy-conserving measure, as shown in **Figure 5**, the use of insulation in buildings has become an important feature.

Figure 5
Glass-fibre insulation matting is another important use of glass.

Plastics

Plastic is a modern material that we use in a huge number of products, from ice skates and toys to lawn chairs and tables (**Figure 6**). Plastic does not occur naturally. It is manufactured in a process that takes several steps, beginning with oil and gas.

Oil and Gas—the Source of Plastic

Crude oil pumped up from the Earth (**Figure 7**) is a raw material that is processed into many products, including plastic. Other products made from crude oil include gasoline, waxes, and asphalt for paving roads.

Crude oil is a mixture of many different pure substances that can be separated from each other in a refinery, as shown in **Figure 8**. The lighter substances in the crude oil are combined chemically with a pure substance from natural gas to form the many different types of synthetic materials that we call plastic.

Figure 7
Oil is the main raw material for making plastic products.

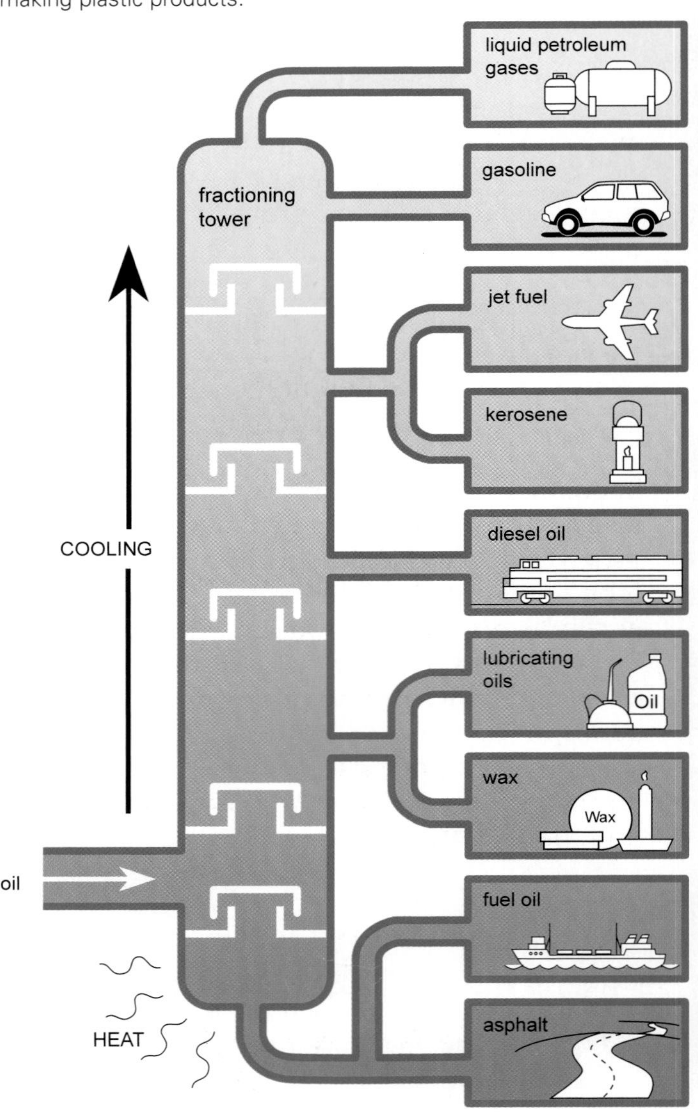

Figure 6
We use plastic everywhere, for almost any activity.

Figure 8

Crude oil is refined into many pure substances and solutions, which are then used in different manufacturing processes, for example, to make plastic and gasoline.

Materials Have Different Uses

Designers, engineers, scientists, and artists all work with materials, and must decide which material best suits the purpose that they have in mind. For example, when designing a spacecraft, engineers may have to select a different alloy or ceramic material for each part. Some parts must be extremely strong, while others must be resistant to heat, to cold, or to bending.

A glass blower may choose to add lead to glass to make a fine crystal. Glass with lead in it sparkles like a diamond when it is cut into patterns. And, of course, plastic varies widely, from the flexible form used to wrap food to the harder form used in casings, for example, around telephones and computers. We are surrounded by different materials. As consumers, we must not only make decisions about which items and which materials best suit our needs, but also about what will happen to the materials when the product is no longer useful.

Design Challenge

(a) You have learned about some finished products—plastics, glass, ceramics, metal alloys. Are any of these the best choice of material for the structures you must make for your Challenge? What other materials could you use?

(b) Different substances are used to make the various types of plastic. In the recycling Challenge, is it important to know which plastic objects can be recycled together? Are there plastics you cannot accept?

Understanding Concepts

1. Explain in your own words what an alloy is and describe its significance in the manufacturing of metallic products.
2. **(a)** What are the main raw materials used to make glass?
   (b) Which raw material is common to all ceramics?

Making Connections

3. If you had a choice of flying in a glider made of steel, or one made of a steel and manganese alloy, which would you choose? Why?
4. Many human body parts can now be replaced by artificial parts. What properties would designers and engineers need to consider when choosing the materials or substances to create an artificial limb?

Exploring

5. Soft packing beads, polar fleece jackets, and the wheels of inline skates are each made of a different type of plastic. Using electronic and print sources, research the differences between these plastics. Make a chart of the different types of plastics and what properties they have that make them suitable for the use specified.

Reflecting

6. There are many kinds of steel with many different properties. These different (4A) properties are the result of different materials added to the steel. Using electronic and print media, research how steel is made. Choose one kind of steel and create a poster illustrating how it is made, what it is made of, and how it is used.
7. "Modern products have better designs and are made of better materials than products in the past. Modern products may also have fewer environmental problems than products in the past". Do you agree with these statements? Give examples along with reasons for your answers.

SKILLS HANDBOOK: (4A) Research Skills

SKILLS MENU
○ Identify a Problem
● Planning
● Building
● Testing
● Recording
● Evaluating
● Communicating

Concrete for Construction

Designers and engineers must make decisions about using the best materials for a given purpose. Concrete is a material used in a variety of construction applications—buildings, dams, and sidewalks. It consists of two materials: crushed gravel and cement (**Figure 1**). The cement, when wet, is the "glue" that holds the crushed gravel together. Cement is made from clay and limestone. The gravel adds strength to the cement. But does a sidewalk need to be as strong as a dam? Is concrete as strong as cement?

Problem

How strong is cement alone compared to concrete? A construction company is preparing to build a bridge out of concrete. In order to safely ensure that the weight of people and equipment crossing the bridge will be supported, it needs to choose the stronger material of concrete or cement.

Design Brief

You will compare the strength of cement and concrete by building a cement beam and a concrete beam and comparing them.

Materials

- apron
- safety gloves
- mask
- empty 1-L milk carton
- scissors
- masking tape
- plastic sheet
- concrete mix
- cement mix
- 2 containers for mixing
- mortar trowel
- water
- wire
- hook
- pail
- bathroom scales

Note that time is an important element in this investigation.

Build

1 Seal the top of a milk carton with masking tape and lay the carton on its side.
- With scissors, cut away one side of the carton.
- With masking tape, tape the cutaway piece into the middle of the carton to form a barrier.

2 In a container, add water to 2 kg of concrete mix, stirring the concrete and water together until all the dry powder is wet.
- Use the trowel to fill one side of the milk carton with the concrete mix.

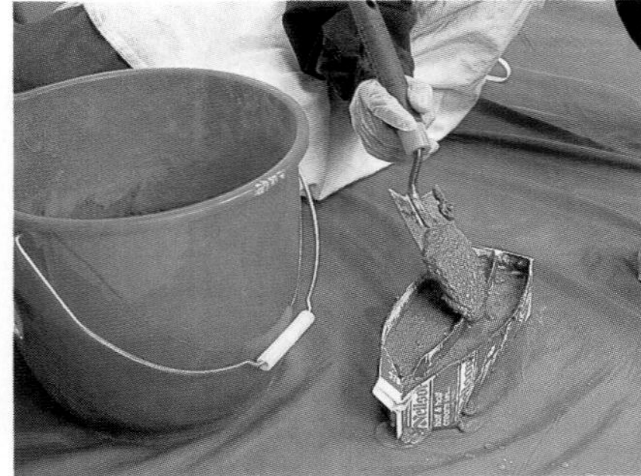

3 Repeat step 2 using cement mix instead of concrete mix, and pour this mix into the other half of the carton.
- Allow the cement and concrete to harden for two weeks, then peel away the carton.

Figure 1
Concrete is a very strong material that can withstand a lot of weight without breaking. The main raw materials of concrete are gravel and cement.

Concrete and cement mixes are corrosive. Do not handle with bare hands. Wash hands with soap and water after you complete this investigation.

Test

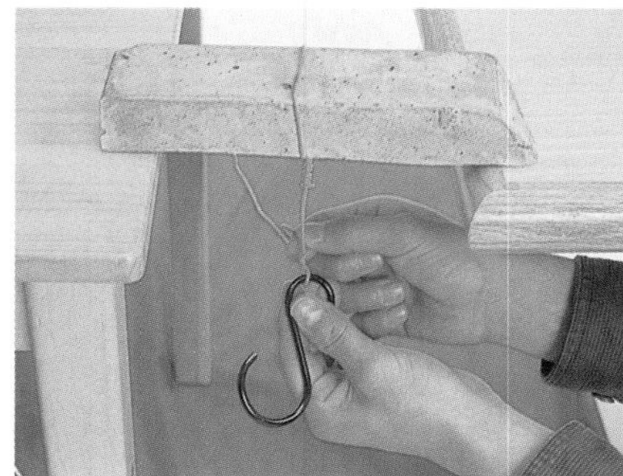

4 Place the cement beam over a gap between two tables.
- Loop a piece of wire around the middle of the beam and attach a hook.
- Suspend the pail from the hook.

5 Gradually add sand or water to the pail until the beam breaks.
- Measure the mass of the pail and its contents.

(a) Record the mass needed to break the cement beam.

6 Repeat steps 4 and 5 with the concrete beam.

Evaluate

1. Did you record any difference in the mass required to break the two beams?
2. What differences did you notice between the dry cement mix and the dry concrete mix? What differences did you notice in the beams? How do you explain the difference in strength of the two materials?
3. Which material would the construction company choose for its purpose?

Making Connections

4. Concrete varies according to how it will be used. What do you think might be the difference between the type of concrete used for dams and the type used for sidewalks?
5. (4A) The massive, 13 km Confederation Bridge links Prince Edward Island with New Brunswick. What special properties do you think would be required for the concrete in this bridge? (Hint: Consider year-round possibilities.) Research on the Internet what ingredients the engineers added to the concrete for the bridge and their purpose.

Exploring

6. (3F) Try making your own concrete mix by combining a different amount of gravel with the cement. Predict what will happen if you construct a beam with each different mixture and test its strength. With your teacher's permission, try it.

Design Challenge

Would concrete be a good choice of material for any part of your Challenge?

SKILLS HANDBOOK: (4A) Research Skills (3F) Testing and Evaluating a Prototype

1.14 Inquiry Investigation

SKILLS MENU
- ○ Questioning
- ● Hypothesizing
- ● Planning
- ● Conducting
- ● Recording
- ● Analyzing
- ● Communicating

Solvents in the Laundry

Most commercial cleaning agents are simply solvents. As you learned earlier, a substance may dissolve in one solvent but not in another. Stains are examples of substances that behave in this way. Water can dissolve some stains in clothes, but detergents are often added to dissolve many types of stains more effectively (**Figure 1**). The resulting mechanical mixture is then rinsed away.

Commercial dry cleaners also remove stains from clothes, but they use specific solvents, such as dichloromethane, that won't damage certain fabrics. From paint removers (**Figure 2**) to metal surface cleaners, industries are always on the search for better cleaning solvents.

Question

Will each of three common solvents (water, mineral spirits, and ethanol) be able to remove all of the different stains (lipstick, ballpoint ink, and felt-tip ink) from fabric?

Hypothesis

2C **1** Write a hypothesis for this experiment.

Experimental Design

2 Design a controlled experiment to test your hypothesis.
- 2E Your experimental design must include a method for placing the stained fabrics in the solvents and removing them without having your hands touch the solvents.
- Your experimental design must include a description of the variable you are testing and how you are controlling other variables.
- Your experimental design must include a description of how to dispose of the solvents safely.

3 Explain in detail how you will investigate the ability of each solvent to remove each stain.

4 Create a table for recording your data.

5 Submit your design, your procedure, and your table to your teacher for approval.

Procedure

6 Carry out your experiment in a well-ventilated room.

Materials

- safety goggles
- apron
- gloves
- labelling materials
- water
- ethanol
- mineral spirits
- graduated cylinder
- lipstick
- ballpoint pen
- felt-tip pen
- pieces of cloth
- other materials and equipment as required

Do not touch the solvents with your hands.
- Ethanol and mineral spirits can cause damage to the skin and eyes.
- Mineral spirits are poisonous if swallowed.
- Ethanol is flammable.

Figure 1
Detergents are excellent solvents for dissolving most common stains on clothes.

Figure 2

Turpentine is an effective solvent for cleaning (dissolving) oil-based paints from brushes. Water is effective for cleaning (dissolving) latex paints, which are made with water.

Table 1

Properties	Solvent				
	dichloromethane	**turpentine**	**methanol**	**isopropanol**	**ethylene chloride**
dissolves grease?	excellent	very good	very good	excellent	excellent
flammable?	no	yes	yes	yes	yes
toxic vapour?	yes	no	yes	no	yes

Making Connections

1. Make a list of cleaning solvents that you can find in your home. Carefully read the labels on each. Separate them into two groups: those that can be used without special precautions, and those that require special handling. What conclusion can you make about the safety of commercial solvents?
2. Imagine that you run a dry-cleaning business. You have a choice of five solvents to use. **Table 1** gives some important properties of each of them. Which solvent would you use? Explain your reasons.

Reflecting

3. Look at the properties of the given solvents in **Table 1**. What environmental concerns exist if they are disposed of by pouring them directly into the sewage system? Suggest some alternative methods of disposal.

Analysis

7 Analyze your results by answering these questions.

(a) Did any single solvent dissolve all three of the stains?

(b) If your answer to question (a) is no, which solvent removed the most stains?

(c) A good cleaning solvent must be nontoxic (not poisonous), should not be flammable, and must dissolve the stains it is being used on. Does your most effective solvent meet these criteria? Explain.

The Importance of Water

Did you know that water covers about 80% of Earth's surface? So why all the fuss about conserving water? The reason is that the oceans contain salt water that is undrinkable, and most of the rest is locked in polar ice and glaciers. That leaves less than 1% that is drinkable. But Canada, with less than 1% of the world's population, has 22% of the world's fresh water. And Ontario has 228 000 inland lakes, plus a large share of the Great Lakes. We must have more than enough.

Not quite! Water is used in more ways than you might think.

Everyday you use solutions that have water as their solvent. The tap water you drink, for instance, contains dissolved minerals that are absorbed by your body to help carry out your life functions and to strengthen your bones. You use water solutions to wash your clothes and your body. Water is also the solvent for solutions used in different industrial processes.

The problem is that people need *clean water*—water that has been filtered, processed, and purified; water they can safely drink. Tests show that our lakes and rivers contain more substances than ever that make the water less desirable for drinking. How do these substances find their way into our water supply?

Our lakes, once a source of clean water, now contain hundreds of dissolved substances. Some of the substances come from soil, rocks, and air, some from animals and plants, and some from the activities of people. Manufacturing, refining, sewage, waste disposal, farming, incinerating—these all produce substances that end up dissolved or mixed into the water that we depend on to live (**Figure 1**).

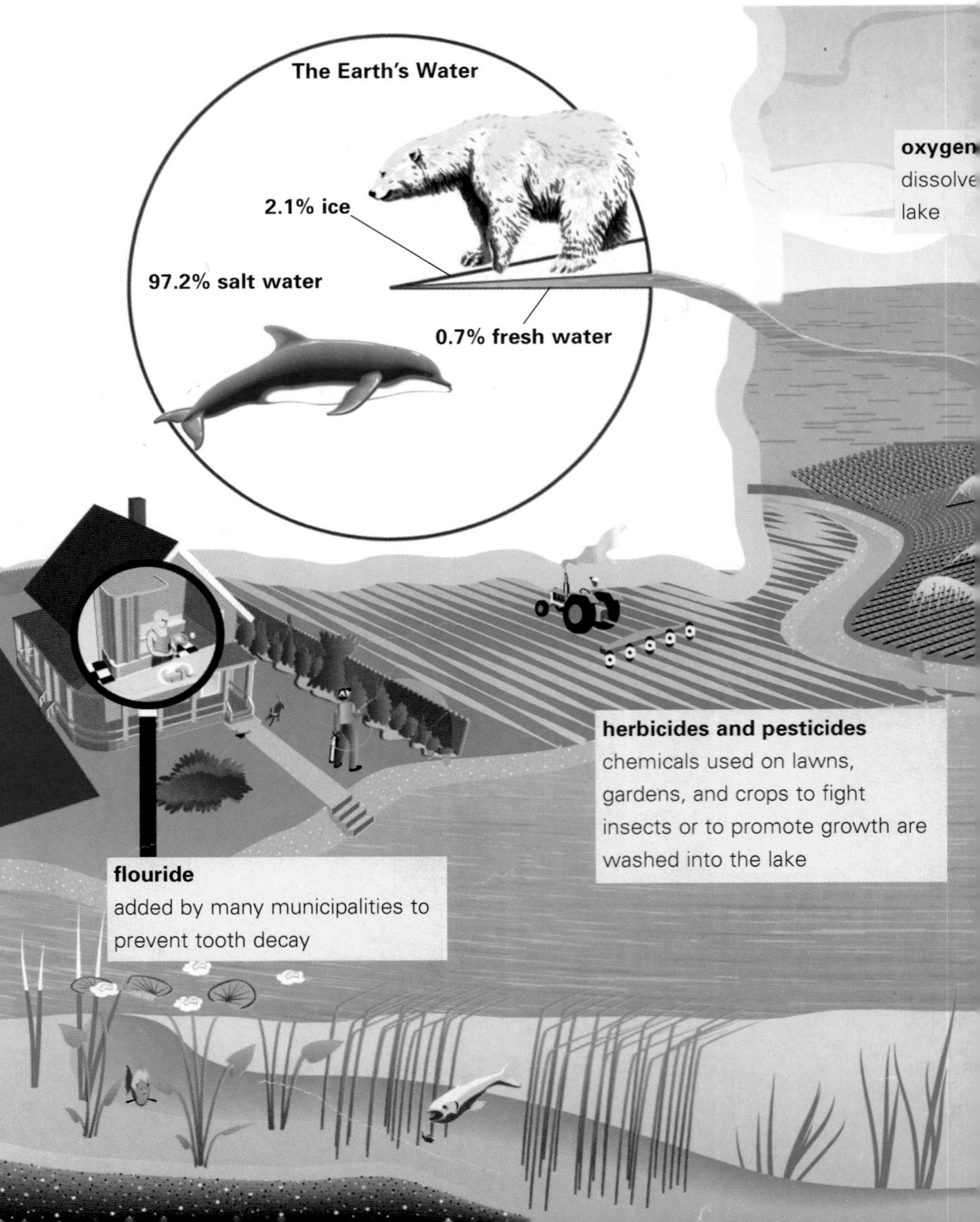
The Earth's Water
2.1% ice
97.2% salt water
0.7% fresh water
oxygen
dissolve
lake
herbicides and pesticides
chemicals used on lawns, gardens, and crops to fight insects or to promote growth are washed into the lake
flouride
added by many municipalities to prevent tooth decay

Design Challenge

A recent heavy rainfall overloaded a sewage treatment facility, causing sewage to flow into the river from which drinking water is taken. Nature can deal with such flows, if they are small. Bacteria will break down some solids, and particles of other solids will gradually fall to the bottom of the river. What can you learn from "nature's way" that will help you solve your Challenge of purifying water?

Figure 1

The fresh water in our lakes contains hundreds of dissolved and mixed substances. Some come from the soil, rocks, and air, some from animals and plants, and some from the activities of people. Manufacturing, refining, sewage, waste disposal, farming, incinerating— they all produce substances that either dissolve or settle in water.

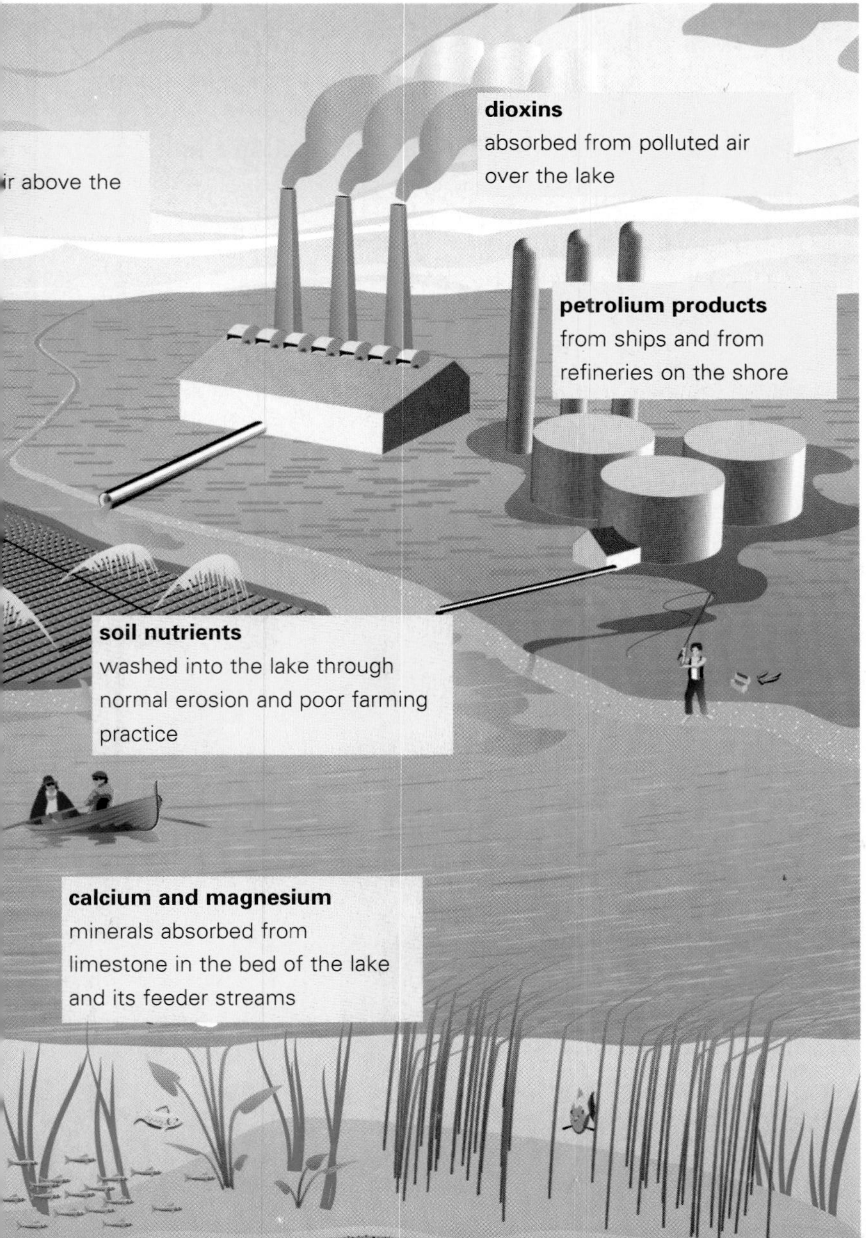
ir above the
dioxins
absorbed from polluted air over the lake
petrolium products
from ships and from refineries on the shore
soil nutrients
washed into the lake through normal erosion and poor farming practice
calcium and magnesium
minerals absorbed from limestone in the bed of the lake and its feeder streams

Understanding Concepts

1. With all the fresh water in Canada, why would Canadians worry about the supply of drinking water?
2. Describe two ways in which water can be polluted from distant sources. Draw a concept map to illustrate your findings.

Making Connections

3. **(a)** How is water being used by people or animals in the picture on these pages? Make a list of the uses. Add any other uses of water that you can think of.

   (b) Put a star (*) beside each use of water that you think involves the addition of substances to the water. If you know the names of the substances, write them down beside the use.
4. Suggest some strategies for conserving water in the following places:

   (a) bathroom

   (b) kitchen

   (c) outdoors

Exploring

5. Water is easy to waste. Place a plastic measuring cup under a slowly dripping tap, either at school or in your home. Measure the time it takes to fill the cup. How much water is lost in one hour by a leaky tap? in one day? in one month?

Reflecting

6. Often liquid wastes are disposed of by pouring them down the drain. What problems can be caused by this practice? What problems are caused by industries and municipalities that dump pollutants directly into lakes and rivers?

Testing Water Quality

Clean drinking water is essential for human survival. It must be clear and free of dangerous living things and chemical poisons. For aquatic animals such as fish, water must include enough dissolved oxygen for breathing. Mostly, though, clean water is defined by what it doesn't contain. There are tests we can do to show what is in the water we drink or swim in.

Dissolved Oxygen

The amount of oxygen dissolved in water is one of the most important indicators of water quality, since oxygen is necessary for aquatic organisms to live.

Oxygen in air is able to pass from the air and dissolve into surface water. Oxygen is also produced in the water by aquatic plants. In the process of converting the energy of the sun, water, and carbon dioxide into food, plants release oxygen as waste. At night, though, aquatic plants consume dissolved oxygen and release carbon dioxide. But oxygen is also consumed by animals and bacteria in the water, as you can see in **Figure 1**.

Most aquatic organisms require a dissolved oxygen concentration of 5 to 6 parts per million (ppm) for normal growth and activity. Levels below 3 ppm are stressful for most aquatic organisms, and levels below 2 ppm are too low for fish populations to survive.

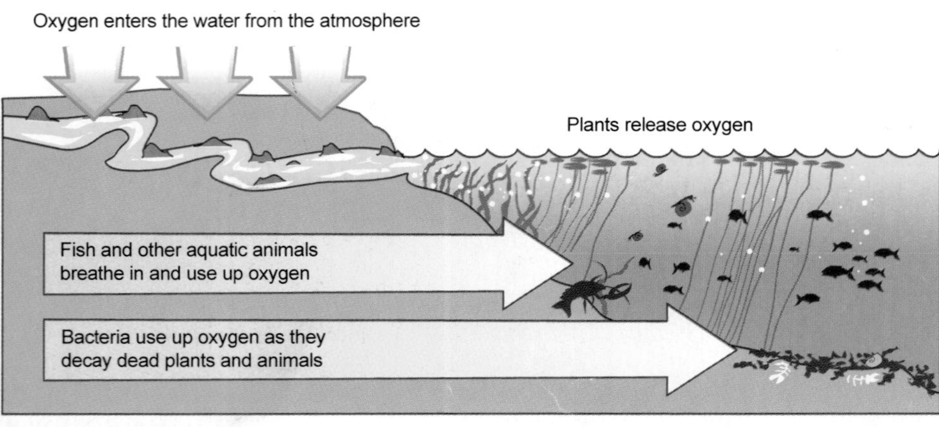

Figure 1
Oxygen is vital to living things. In a lake, there must be a balance between oxygen added and oxygen used.

Acidity

Most water in nature contains dissolved substances that make it slightly acidic or, the opposite, slightly alkaline. Strong acids and strong bases are dangerous to living things, as both are corrosive. **Figure 2** shows the **pH scale**, which is used to classify how acidic or alkaline a solution is.

A healthy lake typically has a pH of about 8, which is slightly alkaline. Lakes that receive a lot of acid from rain or snow may end up with a pH of 4 or 5, which is acidic. In water that is acidic it is difficult for certain species of fish to survive. However, many lakes are surrounded by rocks that naturally neutralize the acid, as you can see in **Figure 3**.

You can test how acidic or alkaline a water sample is with specially coated "pH paper" that changes colour. Each colour corresponds to a pH number.

Figure 2
The pH scale ranges from 0 (strongly acidic) to 14 (strongly alkaline). Solutions at both ends of the scale are highly corrosive. The middle of the scale, a pH of 7, is neither acidic nor alkaline, so it is described as neutral. Pure water is neutral—it has a pH of 7.

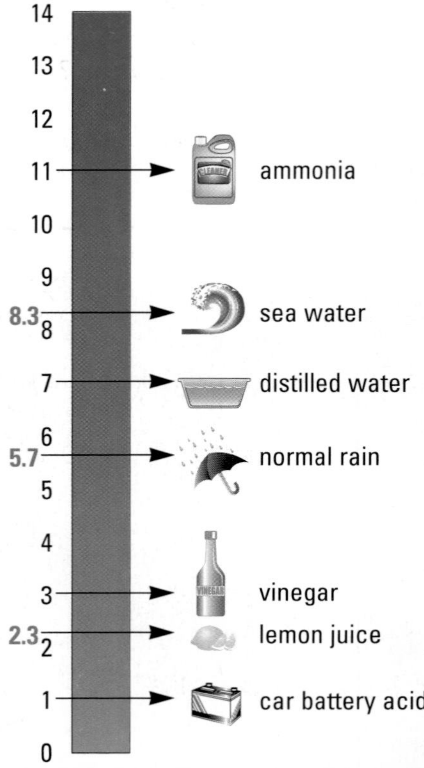

Turbidity

Small solid particles are often suspended (floating) in water. These particles make the water cloudy. **Turbidity** is a measure of how cloudy water is. If water contains large amounts of suspended solids, the water will be so cloudy that it blocks sunlight from reaching aquatic plants. Without sunlight, the plants will die. Suspended solids can be caused by soil erosion, wastes from animals and plants, human waste, and waste from industry.

Special meters, using light and a light detector, can be used to measure turbidity.

Hardness

Water that contains small amounts of dissolved minerals is called **soft water**. Rain water is the best example of natural soft water.

Most water in nature contains a variety of dissolved substances. Water that contains relatively high amounts of dissolved calcium, magnesium, or sulfur is called **hard water**. Hard water is difficult to clean with, as soap does not form a lather in it. Hard water containing dissolved sulfur may have an unpleasant taste.

The dissolved substances come from the soil and rock that water passes over or through. For example, rain water that ends up in a stream that flows over limestone will dissolve calcium from the rock.

Design Challenge

In the water purification Challenge, you must propose some tests to measure the safety of the water. Which of the tests of water quality mentioned here should you include? Would you need others?

Understanding Concepts

1. Make a chart that lists four important measures of the quality of water. Note how each is important to our survival and quality of life.

2. (a) Describe the cycle of oxygen in a lake.

(b) Predict what can occur if any part of the cycle is disrupted.

Making Connections

3. Imagine that people start pumping sewage into the stream that flows into the lake in **Figure 1**. Sewage water contains many small suspended solid particles. Explain what effects you would expect to see on:

(a) the turbidity of the lake

(b) the oxygen content of the lake

(c) plant and animal life in the lake

Exploring

4. Using electronic and print sources, research how hardness is eliminated from water, either during the water purification process or by consumers before they use it. Prepare a chart listing the different techniques.

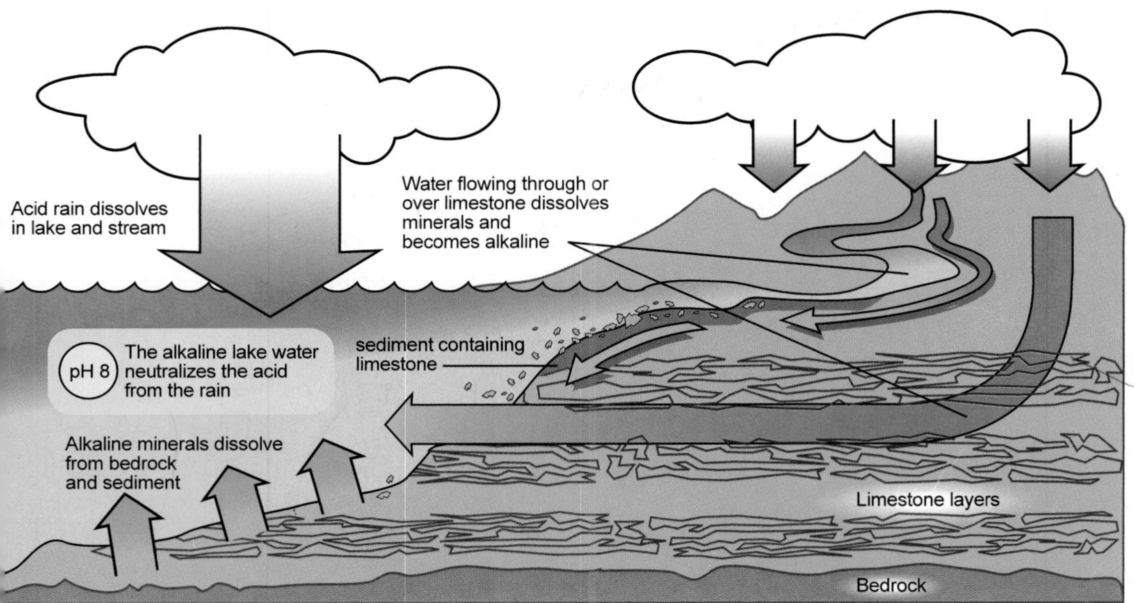
Acid rain dissolves in lake and stream
Water flowing through or over limestone dissolves minerals and becomes alkaline
pH 8
The alkaline lake water neutralizes the acid from the rain
sediment containing limestone
Alkaline minerals dissolve from bedrock and sediment
Limestone layers
Bedrock

Figure 3
In some lakes, naturally occurring alkaline substances, such as limestone, help to neutralize the acid in rain and maintain the pH at about 8.

1.17 Inquiry Investigation

SKILLS MENU
- ● Questioning
- ● Hypothesizing
- ○ Planning
- ● Conducting
- ● Recording
- ● Analyzing
- ● Communicating

How Hard Is the Water?

Hard water forms when certain substances, such as calcium and magnesium, dissolve in it, as shown in **Figure 1**. One of the properties of hard water is that soap does not lather very well in it. However, hard water tastes better, unless it contains dissolved sulfur, and is better for you because of its mineral content.

Materials

- apron
- safety goggles
- distilled water
- 1-L container
- liquid soap
- 5-mL spoon
- ruler
- tap water
- Epsom salts

Question

(2B) **1** Read this investigation. What question is it attempting to answer?

Hypothesis

(2C) **2** Create a hypothesis for this investigation.

Experimental Design

After adding known amounts of magnesium sulfate (also called Epsom salts) to water, you will measure changes in the amount of lather produced.

Procedure

3 Place 250 mL of distilled water in a 1-L container.
- Add 2 drops of liquid soap and stir thoroughly.
- Quickly measure the maximum height of the layer of suds on the surface.

(a) Record the height of the layer of suds.

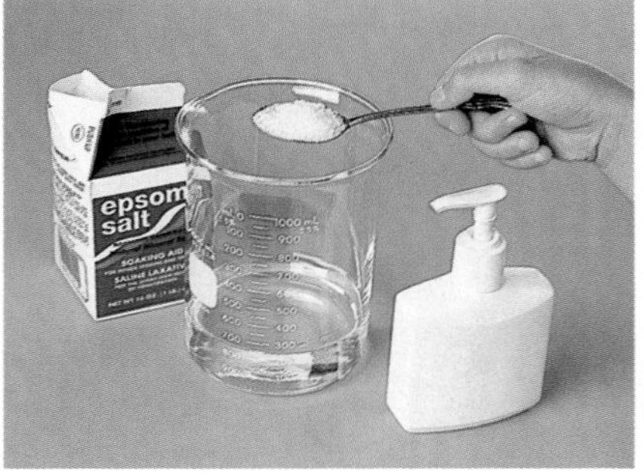

4 Thoroughly rinse and dry the container before refilling it with another 250 mL of distilled water.
- Stir in 5 mL of Epsom salt crystals until they have all dissolved.
- Add 2 drops of liquid soap, stir thoroughly, and measure the height of the suds.

(a) Record the maximum height of the layer of suds. Are the suds higher or lower than in step 1?

5 Repeat step 3 with fresh distilled water and 10 mL of Epsom salts.

(a) Record the maximum height of the layer of suds.

SKILLS HANDBOOK: (2B) Asking a Question (2C) Predicting and Hypothesizing

limestone
Calcium and magnesium from the rock dissolve in the rain water, making it hard.

Figure 1

Rain water, which is naturally soft, becomes hard as it runs over and through rocks and soil.

epsom salt
SOAKING AID
SALINE LAXATIVE

6 Continue this process, adding an additional 5 mL of Epsom salts each time, until no suds appear on the surface of the water, even after thorough stirring. Clean up any spills immediately.

(a) Record the maximum height of the suds each time.

(b) Describe the final contents of the beaker.

Analysis

7 Analyze your results by answering these questions.

(7C) (a) Use your data to draw a graph comparing the height of the layer of suds with the amount of Epsom salts added.

(b) Based on your graph, explain the relationship between the height of the lather and the amount of Epsom salts you added to your solution.

(c) What effect does Epsom salts have on water?

(d) Describe two observable characteristics of hard water.

Making Connections

1. Most manufacturers of hair shampoo say that their product is not affected by the hardness of water. How could you prove or disprove this claim? Design a procedure and, with your teacher's permission, carry it out.

(a) Based on your observations, what do you suspect is different in the ingredients of liquid soap and shampoo? Explain. Check the labels on some containers to verify your answer.

Exploring

2. (3F) Design a procedure to compare the hardness of local water samples from the school fountain, your home, a local stream or river, rain water, etc. You can use the graph you created in this investigation to compare the samples. Have your procedure approved by your teacher before you do any testing.

(7C) Constructing Graphs (3F) Testing and Evaluating a Prototype

Household Hazardous Waste

Do you contribute to water pollution like the people shown in **Figure 1**? You may not think so, but we all use many solvents and solutions at home because they help with cleaning, polishing, painting, and other activities. These **hazardous products** often require special handling and storage because they are dangerous to human health or to the environment. Labels on these products indicate how they are dangerous, as shown in **Figure 2**.

A second type of labelling, shown in **Figure 3**, gives detailed information on the safe handling of a much wider variety of chemical products. These are often found in the workplace, as well as in schools.

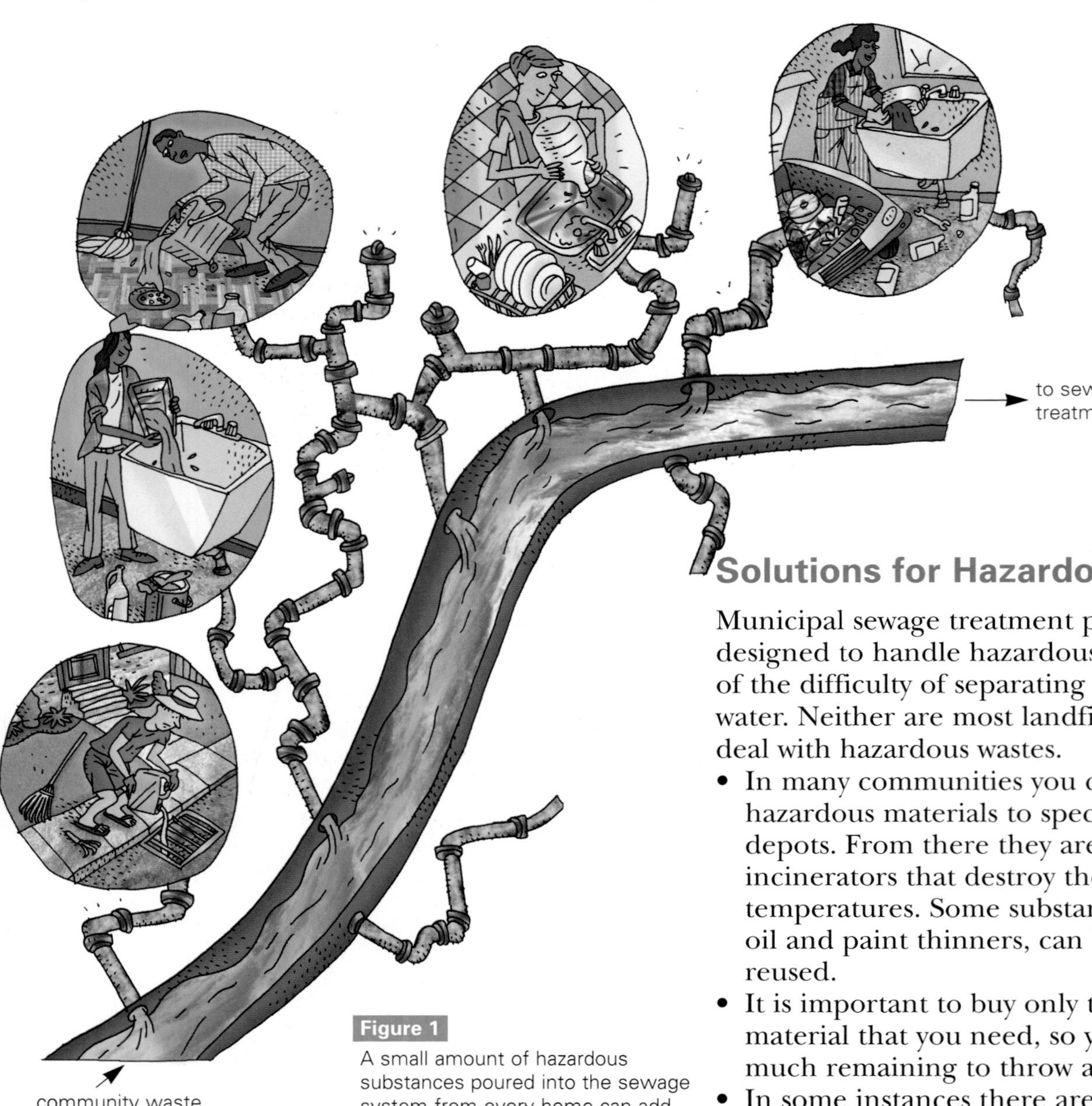

Figure 1
A small amount of hazardous substances poured into the sewage system from every home can add up to a lot of pollution.

Solutions for Hazardous Products

Municipal sewage treatment plants are not designed to handle hazardous products, because of the difficulty of separating them from waste water. Neither are most landfill sites equipped to deal with hazardous wastes.

- In many communities you can take your hazardous materials to special collection depots. From there they are taken to incinerators that destroy them at high temperatures. Some substances, such as motor oil and paint thinners, can be cleaned and reused.
- It is important to buy only the amount of material that you need, so you don't have much remaining to throw away.
- In some instances there are safer products that can do the same job.

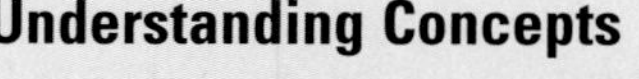

Figure 2
Government regulations require that hazardous household products must be marked with warning symbols that indicate why, and to what degree, a product is dangerous.

Understanding Concepts

1. What does the term "hazardous product" mean?

Making Connections

2. If methods of hazardous waste disposal are inadequate in your community, as a class, prepare recommendations on how disposal methods could be improved and forward them to local officials.

Reflecting

3. Some people believe that one way to solve pollution is to flush poisonous chemicals down the drain. What would you tell them?

Figure 3
Labels from the Workplace Hazardous Materials Information System **(WHMIS)**. Before using any products, always read the label to check how to handle the product safely.

Design Challenge

A recycling program may gather containers that hold hazardous products. How can you make the process safe for environment workers?

Try This How Is Waste Disposed of in Your Community?

Everyone has different types of hazardous wastes in their homes. Are they being disposed of correctly?

- Create a list of hazardous products in your home. Do not open containers. Check each room, including the garage and bathroom. Beside each item, indicate whether it belongs in one of the four categories of household hazards listed in **Figure 2**.

1. What have you and your family been doing with your "almost empty" containers of hazardous waste?

- Find out how hazardous wastes are collected and disposed of in your community.

2. How do you dispose of the products listed?

(4A) 3. Prepare an action plan for your family to dispose of hazardous waste.

Cleaning Up Our Water

You've learned that many substances dissolve in water. Unfortunately, this has resulted in pollution of many of our water systems, as people dump waste into lakes and streams.

The major source of water in Ontario, the Great Lakes, is the dumping ground for many pollutants from both sides of the border. This has been a problem for decades, as many Canadian and American cities and their industries are located on the shores of the Great Lakes. Thunder Bay, Sault Ste. Marie, Chicago, Windsor, Detroit, Buffalo, Hamilton... the list is long.

About 5800 tonnes of pollutants are added each year. Most of the industrial waste is added to Lake Erie (40%) and Lake Michigan (28%). Less of the total is dumped into Lake Ontario (19%), and the least is added to Lake Superior (7%) and Lake Huron (6%).

Measuring the Problem

Scientists on both sides of the border are trying to learn more about each of the vast amount of chemicals that has been dumped or washed into the huge chemical solution that fills the Great Lakes. Of course, that chemical solution is also the source of drinking water for millions of people. There are many questions that these scientists must answer. For example, many chemicals are dangerous only when they reach a certain concentration. But what is the dangerous concentration for each chemical? What are the sources of the chemicals? How can we reduce the amount of these chemicals that enter the lakes?

This research, along with increasing public awareness, is gradually resulting in a reduction in the amount of waste being dumped into the Great Lakes (**Figure 1**). Although there have been significant reductions in the amounts of municipal and industrial waste being dumped into the Great Lakes, many polluters still remain.

Figure 1
Pollution created by industry and our activities flows into the Great Lakes. How far should we go in reducing that flow?

Cleaning Up the Great Lakes (8D)

Statement

The Great Lakes have been a dumping ground for both industrial and municipal (human) pollutants for hundreds of years. With adequate treatment, water from the Great Lakes still remains safe for human consumption. Appeals to reduce or eliminate pollutants at their source are often countered with arguments about the economic consequences of such initiatives. Can we continue to move at the present pace of reduction and still be assured of a safe source of drinking water in the next millennium and beyond?

Point

- Companies and cities should be permitted to dump some waste into the Great Lakes. Since the volume of water in the lakes is so large, the waste will be diluted to safe concentrations.
- The cost of waste treatment is high. If companies based around the Great Lakes are forced to spend more money on pollution control than other companies located elsewhere, products from the Great Lakes area will cost more. This could mean lost sales and lost jobs.

Counterpoint

- Even a small amount of some pollutants can cause serious effects. As the pollutants accumulate through the food chain, the concentration for humans, at the end of the chain, can become high enough to be poisonous.
- Living things depend on clean water. If the water in the Great Lakes is polluted, all living things suffer, including people. People can find other jobs, but damage to health and the environment is difficult to fix.

What Do You Think?

- Consider the statement and the points and counterpoints. Discuss. What other points and counterpoints can you think of?
- Research the issue for both sides, using newspapers, a library periodical index, a CD-ROM directory, or the Internet for information on Great Lakes water pollution.
- Form a group to represent one side of the issue. Others in your class will form a group to represent the other side.
- Conduct a debate defending each group's position.

1.20 Career Profile

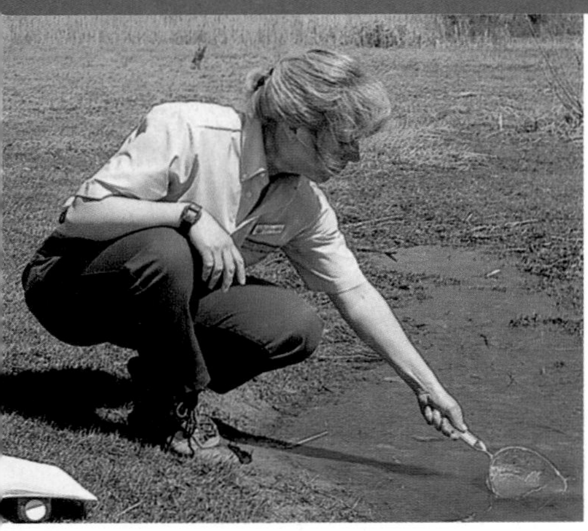

Wetlands Preservation

"Hip waders, binoculars, compass, and bug spray are some of the tools of my trade. My name is Joanna John and I am a wetlands specialist with the Upper Thames River Conservation Authority.

"Wetlands are more than just a haven for wildlife. Other benefits, such as improving water quality, decreasing downstream flooding, increasing flow in a drought, and controlling soil erosion, are also important.

"I spend a lot of time in the Thames River watershed carrying out evaluations of the wetlands. In the field, I take water samples and study the direction of water movement, make lists of plants and animals that live there, look for rare and endangered species, and note any disturbances by people.

"I work with the staff of the conservation authority and a variety of community groups and individuals to develop management plans for the wetlands. I also conduct hikes and prepare educational materials about the importance of wetlands."

Figure 1
Mornington Pond is an artificial wetland, created by the City of London. Wetlands are rich environments, formed in areas where water drains slowly.

An Artificial Wetland

Sewage treatment plants generally do not have the capability of removing household hazardous waste from sewage. Some cities are beginning to look to nature, specifically wetlands, to see how nature cleans water.

Based on what Joanna and her colleagues have learned about the wetlands in the Thames River watershed, engineers working for the City of London in Ontario have created Mornington Pond. Although it looks like a natural wetland, as you can see in **Figure 1**, it is a carefully designed system for controlling and purifying the huge amounts of water that collect during a storm, when the city's sewage system would normally become overloaded.

Mornington Pond is actually a series of ponds. The ponds hold and clean storm water until water flow to the sewage treatment plant returns to normal, and water levels in the river go down. The water is then gradually released into the Thames River in the same way that treated water from the sewage plant is released.

As water collects in the ponds, heavier sediment particles, often carrying contaminants, sink to the bottom, where they are periodically removed. More than 1000 native plant species planted in the ponds help purify the water by absorbing dissolved substances and controlling erosion in the same way that a natural wetland functions.

Mornington Pond is an environmentally friendly, cost-effective way of purifying water. So far, it has cost $3 million less than a traditional water treatment facility.

Try This Round Table—Wetlands or a Mall? (8D)

In your community, a developer, a local realtor, and the chamber of commerce are proposing to develop a new shopping mall. The mall promises to create 350 temporary construction jobs the first year, followed by 500 permanent jobs in various mall stores.

The proposed site for the new mall includes part of a wetlands area where many plants and animals live. The wetlands have also reduced flooding in the area over the years. The land is privately owned.

- List five arguments that might be used to justify moving ahead with the project as outlined.
- List five arguments that might be put forward to oppose the development.
- Decide which of the 10 arguments is the strongest and prepare to support the argument in a round table discussion. You may wish to contact local resource people while doing your research.
- Present your information and position at the round table, individually or as part of a "pro" or "con" group.

1. Did your views change during research and discussion of this issue? Explain.
2. Based on your research and the round table discussion, list the factors that are critical for deciding whether a wetland or other habitat should be destroyed when creating a new development.
3. Consider "sustainability." What implications would there be on the environment, the economy, society?

Water Additives

You have discovered that there are many substances dissolved in fresh water. After learning about water pollution, you may be wondering if all substances in the water are unsafe. In fact, some substances are beneficial. Iron, for example, is found naturally in water that flows over limestone, and is a key substance in hemoglobin, which carries oxygen in your blood.

Chlorine and Our Water

Water treatment plants, like the one in **Figure 1**, deliberately add substances to drinking water, taking advantage of its dissolving properties. Chlorine is dissolved in both drinking water and swimming pools for the same reason—to destroy bacteria. In the past, bacteria-containing water killed millions of people by causing diseases such as cholera. Chlorine is added to water supplies to eliminate such bacteria.

Most people never give chlorinated water a thought. However, scientific studies are showing a link between chlorinated drinking water and a variety of health effects. For example, chlorinated water may destroy some of the bacteria in our intestines that help us digest our food. Also, excessive amounts of chlorine in swimming pools can aggravate asthma in children.

Fluoride and Our Water

Another chemical added to drinking water to protect teeth is a compound that contains fluoride. Several studies have indicated that water fluoridation is a safe and cost-effective means of reducing tooth decay, as shown in **Figure 2**. For residents of communities that don't have water fluoridation, the alternative is regular visits to a dentist for fluoride rinses.

Since there is an alternative to fluoridating all of our drinking water, some groups feel that if there is a slight chance that fluoride might be harmful, then it should not be added to community water supplies. For example, some research suggests that long-term use of flouride may be slowly destroying our bones, teeth, and general health. Too much flouride can actually weaken teeth, making them porous and easily stained. It turns out that fish and other aquatic life don't react well to the addition of fluoride at higher-than-recommended levels.

Should we continue to add fluoride and chlorine to drinking water? Are there safer alternatives? If we continue, what is the minimum amount of these substances that we can add? Scientifically aware citizens must ask such questions to encourage study and ensure that responsible decisions will be made.

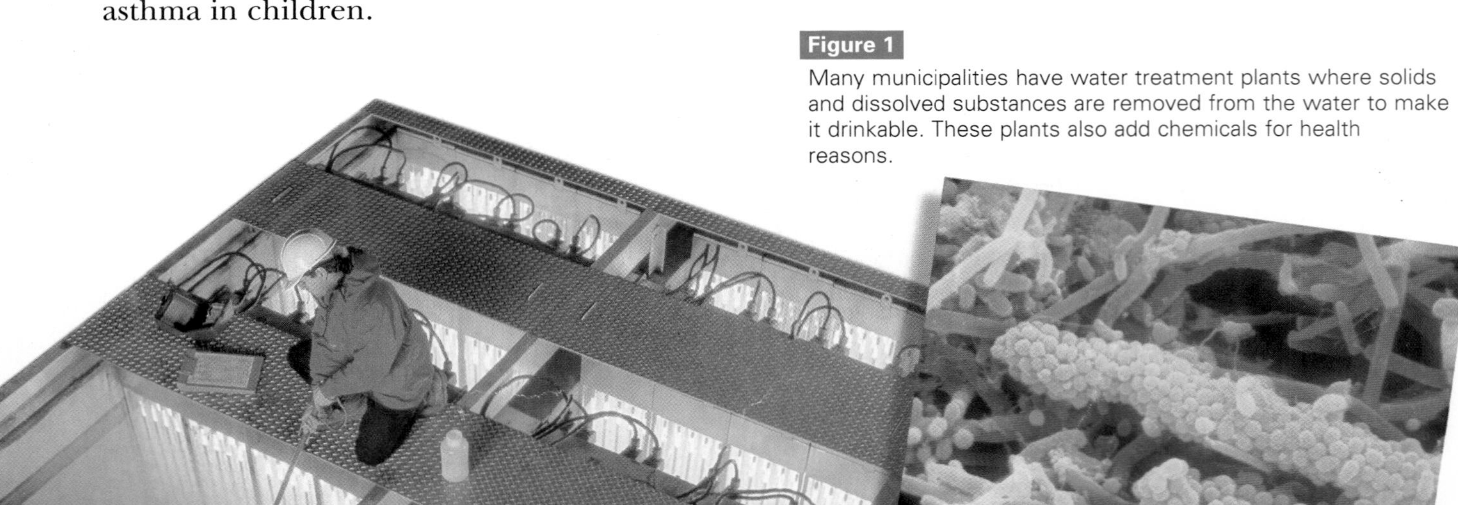

Figure 1

Many municipalities have water treatment plants where solids and dissolved substances are removed from the water to make it drinkable. These plants also add chemicals for health reasons.

Figure 2
The bacteria that live in our mouths can be a threat to teeth.

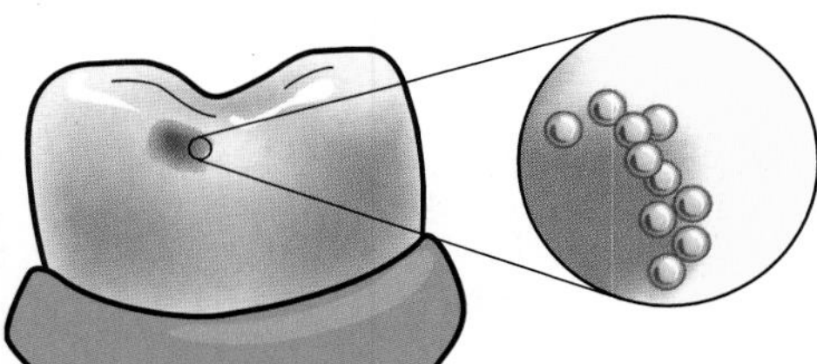

ⓐ Bacteria that feed on sugar in the mouth produce acids.

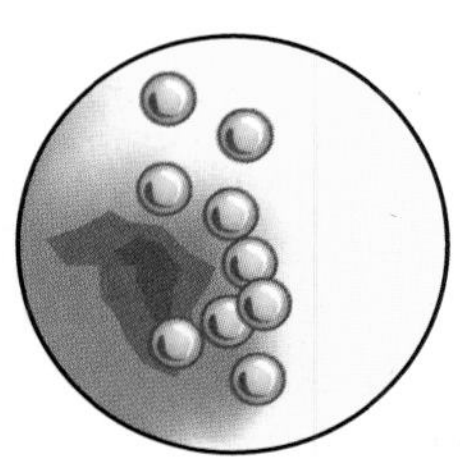

ⓑ The acid produced by the bacteria eats through tooth enamel.

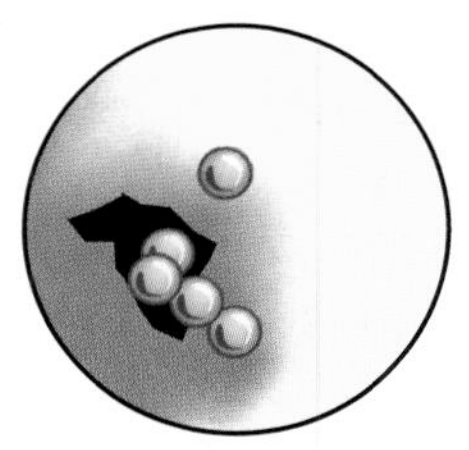

ⓒ Bacteria enter the tooth through the hole in the enamel and infect the tooth.

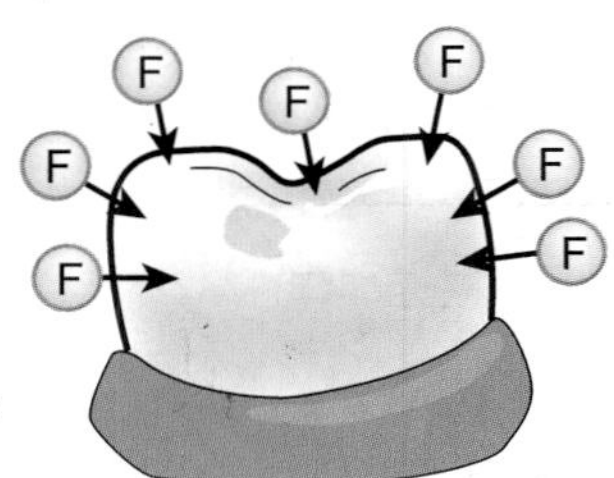

ⓓ Fluoride compounds dissolved in water enter the tooth enamel and make it stronger.

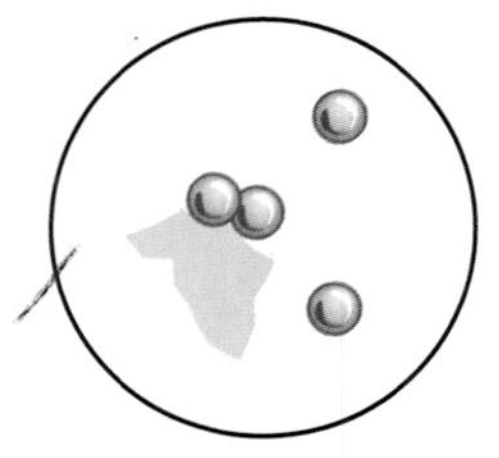

ⓔ The tougher enamel resists bacterial acid.

Understanding Concepts

1. What is one benefit and one drawback of dissolved chlorine in water?
2. Describe in your own words what is meant by fluoridation and chlorination.
3. Draw a comic strip describing the life of a bacteria on your tooth.
4. State one risk in using unchlorinated drinking water.

Making Connections

5. A thirsty hiker finds a stream in the wilderness. She has special water purification tablets in her pack but decides not to use them, since there are no houses or industries in the area. Is she right to drink the water untreated? Give your reasons.

Exploring

6. Travellers to remote parts of the world often carry small kits with them that purify water. Find out how one of these works. Where else do you think similar types of water purifiers might be useful?
7. Using electronic and print sources, research the advantages and disadvantages of adding flouride to our drinking water. Present your report to the class.

Design Challenge

How large are bacteria? Will your design for purifying water remove them?

Design Challenge

Design and Build a System That Separates or Purifies Materials

Reusing and recycling all sorts of substances and products, both liquid and solid, has become ever more important as our growing population uses more of Earth's resources and creates more garbage. Our mineral resources are limited, and so is our supply of fresh, clean drinking water. Purifying our water and separating different materials for reuse requires many types of technology.

Figure 3
Carrots are sorted mechanically by size and then by visual inspection.

1 A Water Purification System

Problem Situation

Although people in cities have access to purified water, those who live in rural and more remote areas may take their water from lakes and rivers, where the water is often murky due to particles mixed in it.

Design Brief

- Design and build a filtering system that removes solid particles from water.

Design Criteria

- The device must be able to remove microscopic particles from the water (verified with a microscope).
- The water must move through the filtering system under pressure.
- Additional tests must be outlined for establishing the safety of the water for drinking.

Figure 1
Water is purified for drinking. The first step in this process is to improve the clarity of the water.

2 A Recycling System for Plastic, Glass, Metal, and Paper

Problem Situation

Although many people separate the different types of recyclable materials before putting them out on the curb, recycling companies must separate the substances more accurately before they can be processed into new materials.

Design Brief

- Design a system in which a mixture of plastic, glass, metal, and paper items are separated from each other.

Design Criteria

- Each component (plastic, glass, metal, paper) must be removed from the mixture in a set sequence.
- The separation processes must be safe and efficient.
- A flow chart outlining the system must accompany the model.

Figure 2
All the materials in this yard can be recycled, but they must first be separated from one another.

3 A Mechanical Soil and Gravel Separator

Problem Situation

Earth that is dug up often contains a mixture of many different particle sizes, from tiny clay particles to large pieces of gravel. However, gardeners and landscapers need these substances separated so that they are usable. For example, the gravel is useful for driveways or walkways; gardeners need clay to improve sandy soil; and so on.

Design Brief

- Design and build a separating device that efficiently separates the particles in stony soil into three different sizes.

Design Criteria

- The separating device must be capable of separating at least 1 kg of soil.
- The separator must collect each of the three different-sized particles in separate compartments.
- The separator must work without being touched directly by a human operator.

Assessment

Your model will be assessed according to how well you:

Process
- Understand the problem
- Develop a safe plan
- Choose and safely use appropriate materials, tools, and equipment
- Test and record results
- Evaluate your model, including suggestions for improvement

Communicate
- Prepare a presentation
- Use correct terms
- Write clear descriptions of the steps you took in building and testing your model
- Explain clearly how your model solves the problem
- Make an accurate technical drawing for your model

Produce
- Meet the design criteria with your model
- Use your chosen materials effectively and carefully
- Construct your model
- Solve the identified problem

When preparing to build or test a design, have your plan approved by your teacher before you begin.

Unit 1 Summary

Reflecting

- Reflect on the ideas and questions presented in the Unit Overview and in the Getting Started. How can you connect what you have done and learned in this unit with those ideas and questions? (To review, check the sections indicated in this Summary.)
- Revise your answers to the Reflecting questions in ❶, ❷, ❸ and the questions you created in the Getting Started. How has your thinking changed?
- What new questions do you have? How will you answer them?

Understanding Concepts

- distinguish between pure substances, mechanical mixtures, and solutions using the particle theory 1.1, 1.2
- use the particle theory to explain how substances dissolve, based on attractions between the particles of solute and solvent 1.2, 1.5
- describe the difference between saturated and unsaturated solutions, between dilute and concentrated solutions 1.8, 1.9
- identify factors that affect the rate at which a substance dissolves 1.4, 1.7, 1.14

- identify solutes and solvents in various kinds of solutions 1.1, 1.11, 1.12

Applying Skills

- classify a sample of matter as a pure substance or a mixture; as a solution or a mechanical mixture 1.1, 1.2

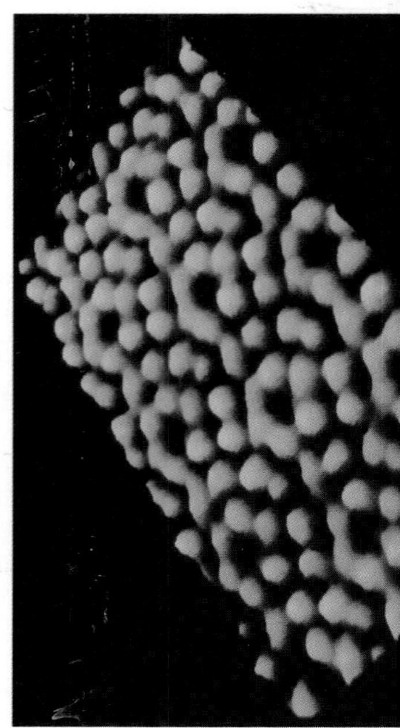

- conduct experiments to determine various factors that affect the rate at which substances dissolve 1.4, 1.7, 1.14
- determine the amount of solute required to form a saturated solution with a fixed amount of solvent at various temperatures 1.9
- investigate different methods of separating the components of mixtures 1.3, 1.10, 1.20

- evaluate the quality of water from different sources by performing simple tests 1.16, 1.17, 1.21
- identify different types of waste present in the community and the environmentally acceptable methods for their disposal 1.14, 1.15, 1.18

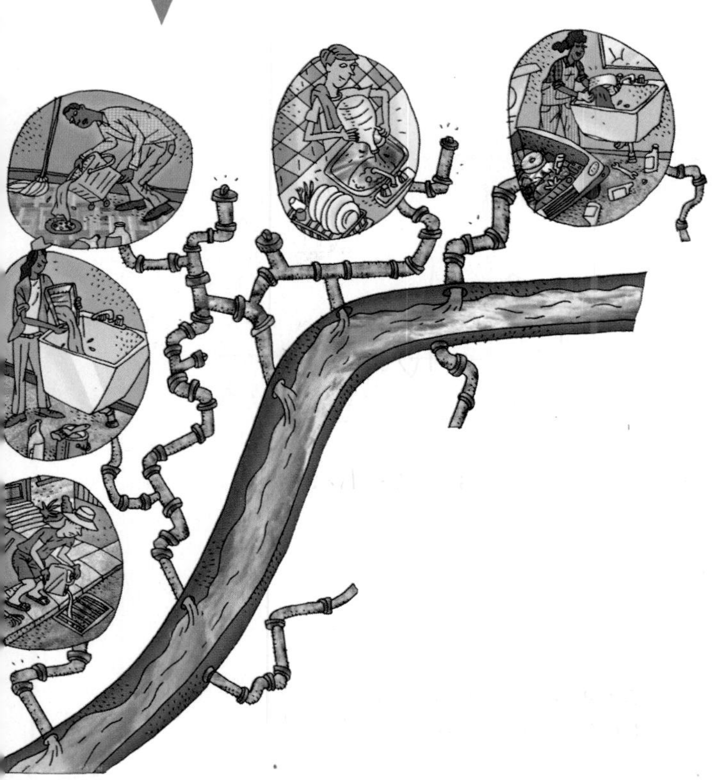

- understand and use the following terms:

alloy	plastic
ceramic	pure substance
concentrated solutions	raw material
dilute solutions	saturated solutions
glass	soft water
hard water	solubility
hazordous product	solute
heterogeneous mixture	solution
homogeneous mixture	solvent
matter	supersaturated
mechanical mixture	turbidity
mixture	unsaturated solutions
particle theory	WHMIS
pH scale	

Making Connections

- recognize that solutions in manufactured products can exist as solids, liquids, and gases 1.1, 1.11, 1.12
- distinguish between raw materials and manufactured products 1.12, 1.13
- identify a variety of manufactured products made from mixtures and explain their functions 1.6, 1.12, 1.13
- describe how raw materials are collected and processed to produce a variety of products 1.12, 1.13
- identify the sources and characteristics of pollutants that result from manufacturing and agricultural processes 1.15, 1.19
- describe the effects of some toxic solvents on the environment and regulations that ensure their safe use and disposal 1.18
- demonstrate the use of water as a solvent and as a chemical reactant 1,1, 1.4, 1.6, 1.10, 1.13, 1.14, 1.15, 1.17, 1.21
- evaluate how human use of natural resources has affected water systems 1.4, 1.17

Unit 1 Review

Understanding Concepts

1. Copy the terms in Column A into your notebook. Match each term with the most correct description from Column B.

Column A	Column B
mechanical mixture	a solute that "disappears" in a solvent
solvent	mix together very well
solute	a tiny bit of solute in a large amount of solvent
concentration	contains more dissolved material than is required for saturation, at that temperature
dissolve	something in which a substance dissolves
insoluble	the mass of dissolved material in a specified amount of solvent
dilute	all spaces between solvent particles filled with solute
saturated	two or more pure substances in the same container
unsaturated	the substance that gets dissolved
soluble	mix together very well

2. State, with a reason, whether each of the following is a solution or a mechanical mixture:
   (a) hotdog relish
   (b) freshly squeezed grapefruit juice
   (c) soda water
   (d) apple juice
   (e) granola
   (f) vegetable soup

3. Decide whether each of the following is a solution or not. Give reasons for your choice.
   (a) a mixture of clay and water
   (b) a mixture of salt and water
   (c) tomato juice

4. Give examples of the following:
   (a) two pure substances
   (b) two solid solutions
   (c) two liquid solutions that do not contain water
   (d) a solution that is a gas

5. Is an alloy a pure substance or a mixture? Use the particle theory to explain your answer.

6. How do each of the following affect the solubility of a solid solute in water?
   (a) temperature
   (b) stirring

7. The Moon was once believed to have no water anywhere on its surface. If this were true, could there be solutions on the Moon? Explain.

8. Read the following statements. Rewrite those that are incorrect so that they become correct.
   (a) If a solution is saturated at 20°C, it will also be saturated at 25°C.
   (b) When some solvent evaporates, a solution becomes more saturated.
   (c) When a saturated solution is cooled, some crystals begin to appear in the solution. The solution is now unsaturated.
   (d) A solvent is a liquid that dissolves sugar.
   (e) A solute is always a solid.
   (f) Dissolving means mixing two things together.
   (g) Oil is insoluble.

9. Describe the information that you would obtain from each of the labels below
   (a) 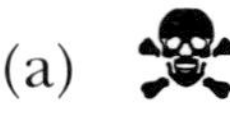
   (b) 
   (c) 

10. Use the particle theory to explain
    (a) the difference between a pure substance and a mixture
    (b) the difference between a solution and a mechanical mixture
    (c) how a small amount of sugar dissolves in a container of water.

11. Identify a solute and the solvent in each of the following solutions:

(a) salt water

(b) air

(c) brass

(d) steel

12. What is the ideal pH for fresh water? Why? What is the effect on fresh water organisms if the water becomes too acidic? How are some bodies of water able to offset acidic precipitation? Explain your answers.

13. Why are each of the following added to drinking water?

(a) chlorine

(b) fluoride

14. What does the term "hazardous" mean when it is used to describe a substance? You dump a small amount of paint thinner down the drain before putting the can at the curb for recycling. Are you being environmentally responsible? State your reasons.

15. You add one teaspoon of lemon juice to a 400-mL cup of water. A friend adds four teaspoons of lemon juice to her 400-mL cup of water. Into whose cup would more sugar need to be added to make the drink sweet? Explain.

16. A perfume chemist determines that 5 g of Brand X perfume can dissolve in 50 g of water at room temperature. She also finds that 10 g of Brand Y perfume can dissolve in 100 g of water. She concludes that Brand Y perfume is more soluble in water than Brand X. Do you agree with her findings? Explain.

Applying Skills

17. Using a flashlight, how can you distinguish between a solution and a mechanical mixture ?

18. Prakesh makes the following entry in her notebook: "On Friday we were given a clear blue liquid in a shallow container. We placed it on the windowsill over the weekend. On Monday morning, there was no liquid left, but the dish had some solid blue stuff in it."

(a) Was the blue liquid in the dish a heterogeneous mixture, a solution, or a pure substance? Design a procedure to verify your choice.

(b) Write a hypothesis to account for what happened in the dish.

19. Use the solubility data for solid potassium nitrate in water at various temperatures from **Table 1**. Graph the data and answer the following questions.

Table 1

Temperature (°C)	0	10	20	30	40	50	60
Solubility of potassium nitrate (g solute/100g water)	14	21	31	45	60	85	110

(a) How many grams of potassium nitrate will dissolve in 100 g of water at 30°C? At 35°C?

(b) At what temperature will 40 g of potassium nitrate dissolve in 100 g of water to form a saturated solution?

(c) At what temperature will 85 g of potassium nitrate dissolve in 100 g of water to form a saturated solution?

(d) If 30 g of potassium nitrate are dissolved in 100 g of water at 18°C, is the solution saturated? Explain.

20. Use the data provided in **Table 1** in **1.8** to draw the solubility graphs for both sugar and salt. Use the graphs to answer the following questions.

(b) How much sugar will dissolve to form a saturated solution in 100 g of water at 60°C? Salt?

(b) If 20 g of salt is completely dissolved in 100 g of water at 50°C, what kind of solution will result?

21. Genna decides that, while she brushes her teeth, the tap should only be running while the toothbrush is being rinsed. She decides to investigate how much water is used if the tap is left running all the time she brushes. To her surprise, the extra water fills one 1.75-L bottle, along with half of another. If she brushes three times daily, how much water will Genna save in a year by turning off the tap?

22. A laboratory receives a bottle of red liquid for analysis. After it sits overnight, bits of red powder are found on the bottom of the container. When lab technicians shine a light into the container, the top of the beam appears pink, while the bottom appears red. Tiny particles are also observed in the beam of light. Does this bottle contain a solution? Explain.

23. Suggest a method to separate each of the following mixtures:

(a) sand, salt, and bird seed

(b) sugar, flour, and pennies

(c) water and salad oil

(d) iron powder, salt, and iron nails

24. Michael's results in a dissolving investigation are not consistent with the results of other students in the class. For solute 1, Michael half-filled a test tube with tap water, put in some solute, and then shook the test tube until his arm got tired. For solute 2, he put 5 mL of water into a beaker, added two crystals of solute 2, and stirred the contents once or twice with a stir stick.

(a) What would you suggest to Michael to improve his experimental technique?

(b) Effram and Michael argued over solute 3. Effram described it as "not very soluble." Michael insisted that it is "insoluble." How might you determine who is right?

25. Water is used to deliver fluoride to the citizens of a community because it is an excellent "carrier." What makes water such a good carrier?

Making Connections

26. Why does air, a solution, feel much more humid on a hot day than on a cool one, even if the relative humidity on both days is the same?

27. A good angel food cake does not appear to have any icing. Your grandmother tells you that she sprinkled some powdered sugar on the moist cake when it came out of the oven. What happened to it?

28. A student carefully removes the cap from a chilled bottle of pop. The open top is covered with a balloon that is secured with tape. When she shakes the bottle, the balloon fills with gas. This sequence is repeated with an identical bottle of pop at room temperature.

(a) Which balloon will fill with the greatest amount of gas? Explain.

(b) How is the solubility of carbon dioxide gas related to the temperature of the beverage?

29. Galvanized nails are now used for most outdoor applications. Investigate how a metal is galvanized and determine whether galvanized nails are, in fact, an alloy.

30. Gases that dissolve in water can make it look cloudy. Will hot water or cold water likely produce a cloudy ice cube? Explain.

31. Laura observes her friend Ingrid preparing to make a glass of lemon iced tea from a drink mix. Ingrid first fills a tall glass with ice cubes. She then adds a spoonful of drink mix and two sugar cube to the glass before adding cold tap water. A considerable amount of undissolved solid remains at the bottom of the glass.

(a) Describe four suggestions that Laura could make to reduce the amount of undissolved solid.

(b) Is Ingrid's first drink saturated, unsaturated, or supersaturated? Explain.

(c) If Laura's suggestions are taken and there is no evidence of undissolved solid in the glass, how would you now describe the drink?

32. If pure gold is described as 24 karat, then 18-karat gold must consist of 18 parts gold and 6 parts other metals, such as copper.

(a) Name the solute in 18-karat gold.

(b) Name the solvent.

(c) Bill's girlfriend gives him a pure gold chain for his birthday. After a few weeks of wearing it, his skin becomes discoloured under the chain. What advice would you give Bill?

33. Rock candy is made by dissolving sugar in warm water to form a saturated solution and then is allowed to cool.

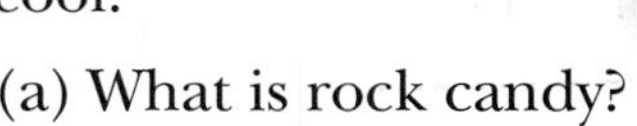

(a) What is rock candy?

(b) Explain how it is formed based on what you know about saturated solutions.

34. Imagine that you are an industrial chemist. Part of your job is to think of new and useful mixtures that your company can make. Using the following list of substances and their properties, name three mixtures that you would make, inventing a use for each one.

Substance	Useful Property
A	sticks to plastic
B	is bright blue
C	boils at 20°C
D	smells like bananas
E	is elastic
F	glows in the dark
G	conducts electricity
H	bends without breaking
I	repels insects

35. The instructions on an aerosol can of oven cleaner advises the user to wear rubber gloves while using the product. The can also contains two WHMIS warning labels. Which two?

36. You decide to enter a competition to build a mountain bike that has no metal parts.

(a) What materials that you have learned about here would you use to replace the metal parts of your mountain bike? Explain the reasons for your choices.

(a) If you wanted to build a racing bike, would your choice of materials change? Explain.

37. Lake trout prefer oxygen-rich water. Where would you expect to find trout in mid-summer—at the bottom of the lake or near the surface?

38. A soup recipe calls for the addition of bouillon. A cook finds both bouillon powder and bouillon cubes in the spice cabinet. Which form of the substance will speed up the process of making the soup?

39. A large bottle of liquid laundry detergent states that it contains enough detergent to wash 100 loads of laundry. A different brand in a smaller bottle also states that it contains enough detergent to wash 100 loads of laundry. Both are true. Explain how this could be.

40. It is discovered that a newly developed chemical reduces the desire to eat. Politicians in a small municipality decide that it would be a good idea to add small amounts of this chemical to drinking water. They argue that dissolving the chemical in everyone's drinking water would result in a lowered demand on countries to produce food and would help overweight people lose weight. State your position on this issue. Give some reasons to support your position.

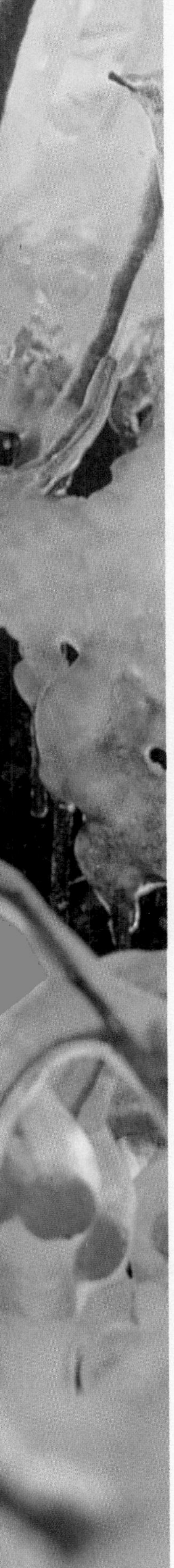

Heat

Unit 2 Overview

You use and control heat every time you cook food, or change the temperature of the room you are in. Your body works hard to prevent or encourage heat transfer so your internal temperature is constant. The weather outside depends on heat transfer from the Sun to the atmosphere and water. The steel in the spoon you used for your last meal was made using huge quantities of heat. The electricity you use to dry your hair or drive your games may have been generated using heat from fossil fuels. In this unit, you will learn about the many ways we depend on and control heat.

Temperature and Heat

Temperature and heat are not exactly the same.

You will be able to:

- explain the difference between heat and temperature
- estimate and compare the temperatures of different objects
- investigate examples in nature of sensitivity to temperature
- record the temperature of a substance as it changes state and analyze the results
- identify factors that can affect the rate of temperature change

Heat Transfer

Heat transfers between objects of different temperatures.

You will be able to:

- observe and describe what happens to solids, liquids, and gases when they are heated
- describe how convection currents in Earth's atmosphere and oceans can affect weather everywhere
- choose appropriate materials when designing a device that conducts or insulates
- experiment with absorption of radiant energy
- compare the heat capacities of various substances

Producing and Using Heat

The sources and effects of heat are important when designing and building.

You will be able to:

- explain and demonstrate how insulating materials control heat transfer
- classify different sources of heat as renewable or nonrenewable
- describe how solar heating can be applied to reduce our need for other sources of heat
- recognize the causes and effects of heat pollution and describe ways to control it
- identify and explain how feedback devices are used to control heating systems

Design Challenge

You will be able to ...

demonstrate your learning by completing a Design Challenge.

Devices That Control or Use Heat

Through science and technology, people have learned to build various structures and devices to control or transfer heat to their advantage.

In this unit, you will be able to design and build

1 A Device That Delays Heat Transfer

Design a container that will keep a cold pop can as cool as possible from breakfast until lunch time.

2 A Swimming Pool Heated by the Sun

Design a device that uses only energy from the Sun to heat the water for a model swimming pool to 25°C.

3 A Greenhouse to Protect Plants

Design a greenhouse that will allow plants to grow even when outdoor temperatures are low.

To start your Design Challenge, see page 122.

Record your thoughts and design ideas for the Challenge when you see

Design Challenge

Getting Started

Thinking About Heat and Temperature

1 You know from experience that these onion rings are hot. After all, they were just deep-fried in very hot oil. But how will you know when they are cool enough to eat? Can you tell by touching them with your finger? Just how reliable is your sense of touch?

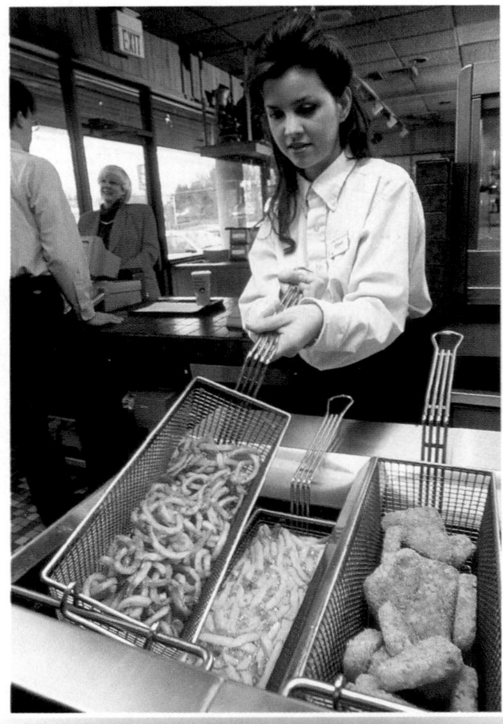

2 Hang gliders and many birds rely on a form of heat transfer. Rising warm air keeps them aloft. But why does the air rise? What is the source of the heat?

3 Electricity is produced at this generating station by burning natural gas. The heat released by the burning fuel is used to make steam, and the steam drives a turbine that creates electricity. The electricity is then transmitted through wires to our homes, where it may become a source of heat in appliances or even a furnace. At every step, heat escapes. Is this the best way to get energy from one place to another? What are the advantages and disadvantages of burning fuel? What other ways can you think of to heat your house that would be more sustainable?

Reflecting

Think about questions ❶, ❷, ❸. What other questions do you have about heat? As you progress through this unit, reflect on your answers and revise them based on what you have learned.

Try This Judging Temperatures (6A)

It is not always easy to judge temperatures by looking at a photograph. Is it any easier if you can feel a substance? In this activity you'll find out how well your hands can judge temperature.

(9D) Work with a partner to record your reactions. Then switch roles and let your partner try this.

- Fill three plastic bowls and place them in a line: one with hot water (but not too hot!), one with lukewarm water, and one with cold water.
- Place your left hand in the bowl of hot water and your right hand in the bowl of cold water for at least one minute.

1. Record what each hand senses.

- Place both hands in the bowl of lukewarm water.

2. Record what each hand senses.

- When your hands have returned to their normal temperature, touch several objects in your classroom. Do they feel warm or cold?

3. Record whether each object feels warm or cold.
4. What makes objects feel hot or cold?

2.1 Inquiry Investigation

SKILLS MENU
- ○ Questioning
- ○ Hypothesizing
- ○ Planning
- ● Conducting
- ● Recording
- ● Analyzing
- ● Communicating

Identifying Temperatures

As you have seen, it's difficult to judge exactly how hot or cold something is just by touching it. A better way is to find out the temperature of the object. For now, you can think of temperature as a measurement of how hot or how cold an object is. We usually measure temperature in degrees Celsius (°C). For example, the temperature of the palm of your hand is probably about 35°C.

In this investigation you will use your experience and cues from photographs to estimate temperatures in degrees Celsius. After you have arranged the temperatures in order from lowest to highest, you can evaluate your own arrangement.

Materials

- 28 index cards
- pencil

1. The oven when a pizza is cooking

Question

Can we estimate temperatures?

Hypothesis

From our own experience, we can create a scale of temperatures, using familiar objects and events as markers.

2. Hottest day ever recorded on Earth's surface

3. Comfortable room temperature

Experimental Design

Using your experience and deduction, you will assign a temperature to 14 objects or events.

Procedure

1 In a group, record items 1 to 14 on separate index cards.

9D **2** After discussion in your group, sort the cards into three piles: "low temperatures," "everyday temperatures," and "high temperatures."

3 Discuss which of the items in each pile of cards is the coldest and which is the hottest.

- Arrange the cards in each pile in order from coldest to hottest.

4 Make a set of temperature cards, one card for each of the temperatures (a to n) listed in **Table 1**.

- Match the temperature cards with item cards 1 to 14, making your best estimate of the temperature in each situation.

(a) Record the temperature that your group decided for each of items 1 to 14, listing them from the lowest to the highest.

Analysis

5 Your teacher will supply the actual temperatures for items 1 to 14. Record these temperatures on your item cards. Compare your group's estimate with the actual temperature for each item.

(a) Which temperatures were the easiest to predict? Why?

(b) Which temperatures were the hardest to predict? Why?

(c) Describe ways you could improve your skill at estimating temperatures.

SKILLS HANDBOOK: 9D Working Together 4A Research Skills

4. Boiling water

Table 1

a) –273°C	**h)** 15 000 000°C
b) –89°C	**i)** 37°C
c) 80°C	**j)** 160°C
d) –10°C	**k)** 0°C
e) 100°C	**l)** 40°C
f) 20°C	**m)** 6000°C
g) 58°C	**n)** 7°C

Making Connections

1. How does knowing the predicted outdoor temperature help you plan an outdoor activity? Give examples for both summer and winter.

Exploring

2. (4A) Using a variety of electronic and other sources, research the Fahrenheit (°F) and Kelvin (K) scales. How are they the same as the Celsius temperature scale? How are they different? Where is each used? Summarize your information in a chart.

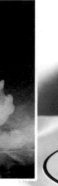

5. Lowest temperature possible

6. Air in a refrigerator

10. Hot tea

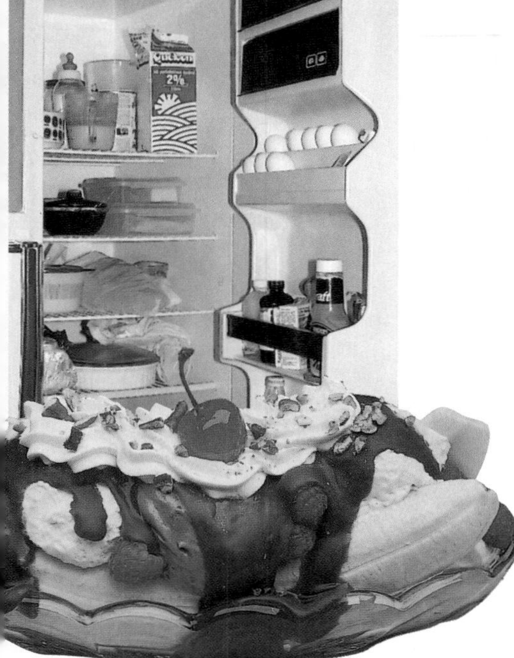

11. Healthy human being

12. Coldest weather ever recorded on Earth's surface

7. Ice cream

8. Interior of the Sun

9. Surface of the Sun

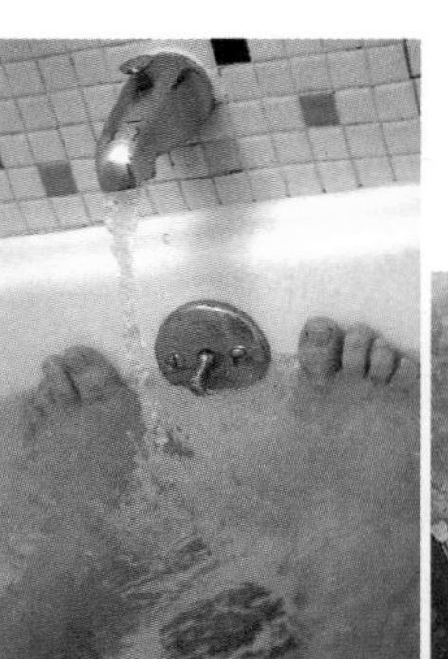

13. Comfortable bath water

14. Freezing water

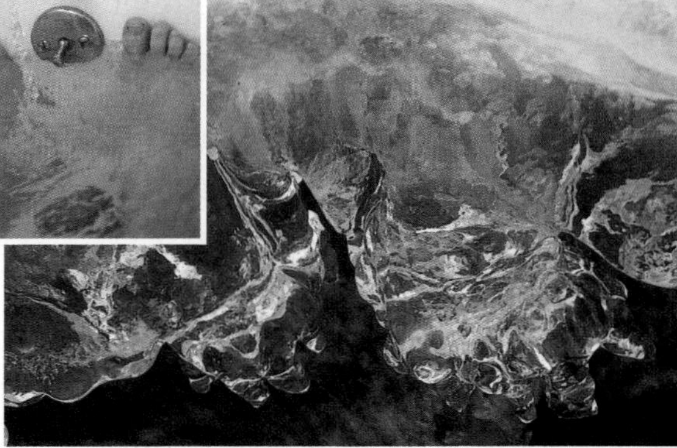

Design Challenge

Temperature is important in each of the Challenges.

(a) Estimate the temperature of cold pop from the refrigerator. Explain your answer.

(b) In the swimming pool challenge, you are asked to heat water to 25°C. Based on what you have learned, is this a good temperature for water in a swimming pool? Explain.

(c) People have a standard body temperature, but what about plants? Do pine trees or roses have a "body temperature"? Explain.

2.2 Inquiry Investigation

SKILLS MENU
○ Questioning ● Hypothesizing ○ Planning ● Conducting ● Recording ● Analyzing ● Communicating

Heating and Cooling

It is not wise to put a cold glass plate onto a hot stove. The plate could crack and break easily. All forms of matter change when they are heated or cooled. What happens to a plate as it is heated also happens to other materials, such as water and air. Learning about the effects of heating and cooling will help you understand how many things work, such as hot-air balloons and thermometers.

Materials

- apron
- safety goggles
- water
- food colouring
- Pyrex flask
- rubber stopper with inserted glass tubing
- hot plate
- retort stand
- clamp
- glass-marking pen
- ball and ring apparatus
- pulse glass

Question

What happens to a liquid, a solid, and a gas when each is heated or cooled?

Hypothesis

(2C) **1** Make a prediction for what you would observe for each type of substance, and write a hypothesis for your prediction.

Experimental Design

Water at room temperature, a ball and ring apparatus, and a pulse glass will be used to observe what happens to each substance when it is heated or cooled.

Do not attempt to remove glass tubing from the stopper. The glass may break.

Once you have turned on the hot plate, do not touch the surface of the plate.

Procedure **Part 1: A Liquid**

2 Fill the flask completely with room temperature water and add a few drops of food colouring.
- Insert the stopper with the glass tubing into the flask so that there is no air in the flask.
- Mark the water level in the glass tubing with a glass-marking pen.

(a) Why do you think you were asked to put food colouring in the water?

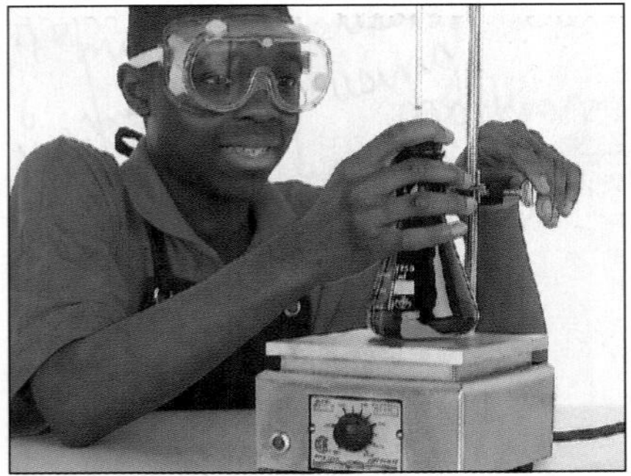

3 Put the flask on the hot plate and clamp it.
- (5C) Turn on the hot plate and slowly heat the water. Do not allow it to boil.
- Mark the water level in the glass tubing again when you have finished heating the water.

(a) What happened to the water level after the water was heated?

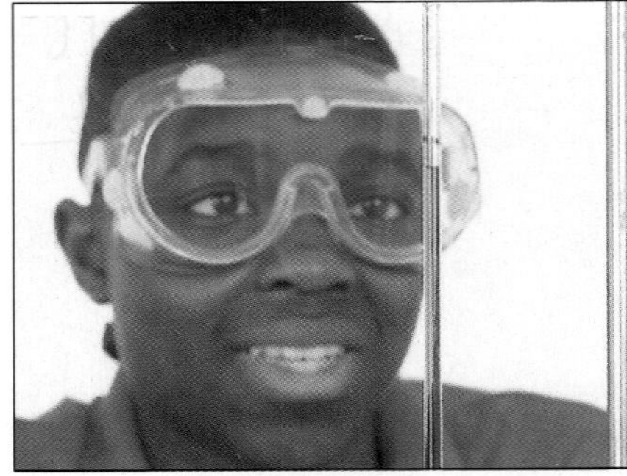

4 Turn off the hot plate. Allow the flask to cool and observe any change in the water level.

(a) Does the water level rise or fall during cooling?

SKILLS HANDBOOK: (2C) Predicting and Hypothesizing (5C) Using Other Scientific Equipment (9D) Working Together

Design Challenge

How might knowing that materials change size when they are heated or cooled affect your choice of materials for your Challenge design? How could you test materials to discover if they are appropriate?

Exploring

1. Do other liquids expand by the same amount when heated? Repeat the investigation using vegetable oil. Compare the results.

   Do not heat vegetable oil directly on the hot plate. When you are heating the liquid, place the flask in a hot-water bath.

2. How could you prepare your flask thermometer so it gives readings in degrees Celsius? (This process is called calibration.) For example, many thermometers use the temperature of ice water to calibrate 0°C and boiling water to calibrate 100°C. Explain how your calibrated thermometer could be used to measure the temperature of other liquids.

Part 2: A Solid

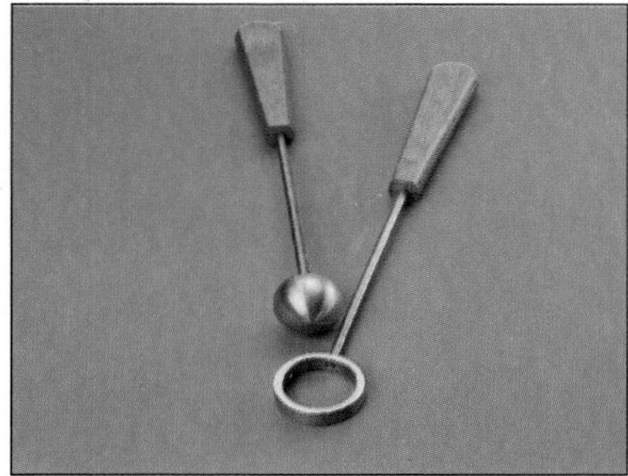

5 Look at the design of the ball and ring apparatus. How will the ball and ring behave when heated or cooled with hot or cold running water? Discuss with your partner(s) what tests you could perform on the apparatus. Perform the tests.

9D

(a) Describe how you tested the apparatus.

(b) Record what you observed.

Part 3: A Gas

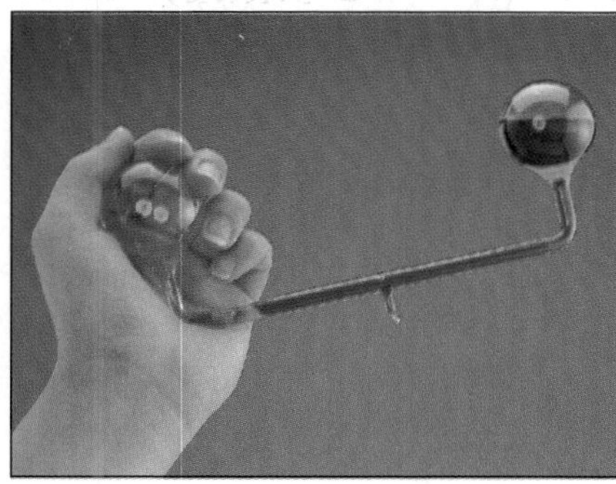

6 Hold one bulb of the pulse glass in your hand and observe what happens. Then hold the same bulb under cold running water and observe again.

(a) Describe what you observed.

Do not heat the pulse glass with the hot plate. Body temperature is enough.

Analysis

7 Analyze your results by answering the following questions.

(a) Did the water expand or contract when it was heated? How do you know?

(b) Predict what would happen to the water level in the tubing if you placed the flask in the refrigerator.

(c) What happened to the solid and gas when they were heated? when they were cooled?

(d) Summarize in a paragraph how the observations you made are significant when designing products.

Measuring Temperatures

Why do you need to measure temperature? Think of all the ways temperature measurement is important in your life. If you know the temperature outside, you know how to dress to go out. If you know the temperature inside your oven, you know if it is hot enough to cook a pizza. No doubt you can think of many more examples.

Many thermometers operate because of expansion and contraction. **Expansion** is an increase in the volume of an object or substance. For most substances, adding heat causes expansion. **Contraction**, which is a decrease in volume, usually occurs when heat is removed from an object or substance. Since solids, liquids, and gases usually expand when heated and contract when cooled, almost any substance can be used in a thermometer.

Not all thermometers rely on expansion and contraction; some rely on electricity or battery power to operate. The choice usually depends on the way the thermometer will be used.

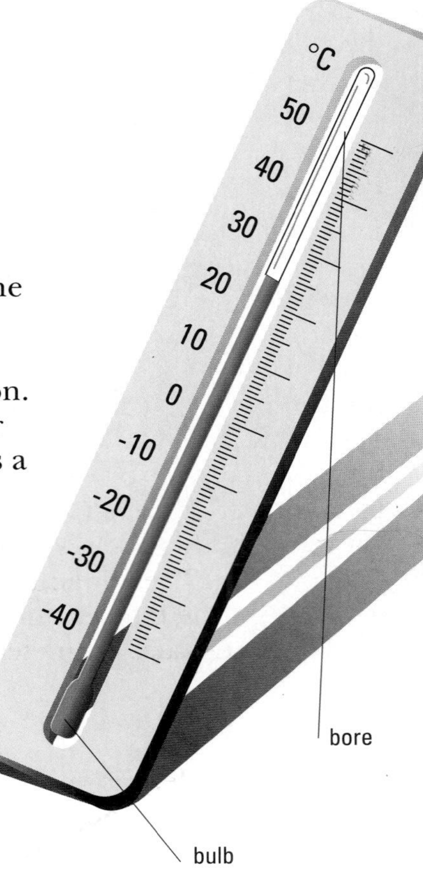

Figure 1
An outdoor thermometer

Liquid Thermometers

You are probably familiar with outdoor thermometers, like the one in **Figure 1**. **Thermometers** use the expansion and contraction of a liquid to measure temperature. The liquid in the bulb (usually coloured ethyl alcohol) expands when it is warmed and is forced up the narrow bore of the thermometer. The more the liquid is warmed, the higher it rises in the bore. When the liquid cools, it contracts, dropping lower in the bore.

The clinical thermometer, **Figure 2**, is a modification of this design. As the liquid is warmed by the patient's body heat, it expands past the constriction to show the patient's temperature. The liquid cools and contracts when the thermometer is removed from the patient, but the liquid cannot move back past the constriction. This allows the patient's temperature to be read long after it is taken. To use the thermometer again, the liquid must first be forced back by shaking the thermometer downward.

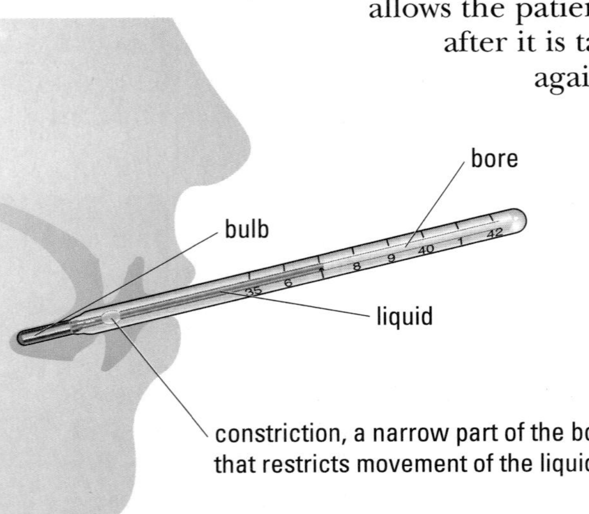

Figure 2
A clinical thermometer. This type of thermometer is sensitive to very small changes in temperature but is able to measure temperatures only within a few degrees of normal body temperature (37°C).

The Thermostat

A thermostat, such as the one in **Figure 3**, can be used to measure temperature in a room or in an appliance, such as a furnace. It can also switch appliances on or off at a preset temperature. In other words, it can act as a feedback system.

Thermostats use the expansion and contraction of solids to measure temperature. They contain a strip made of two metals (called a bimetallic strip). Because the metals are different substances, when they are heated or cooled, the two metals will expand or contract by different amounts, causing the strip to bend. The amount of bending depends on the temperature. This provides a measure of the temperature.

Figure 3

A thermostat can be set to control a furnace to keep the room temperature at 17°C.

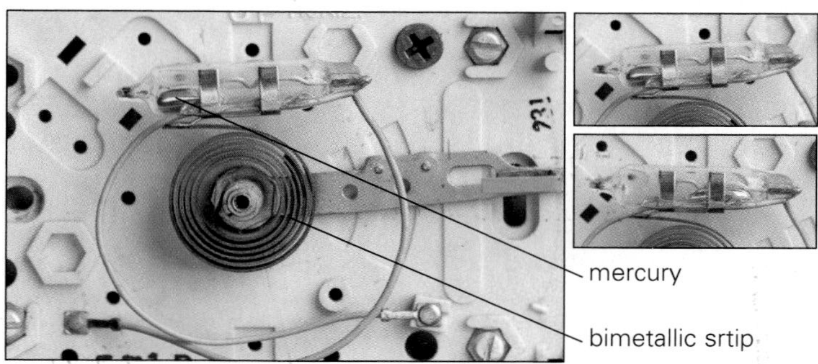

(a) As the temperature in the room rises above 17°C, the bimetallic strip expands. This tilts the glass casing slightly, causing the mercury to flow away from the contact. This breaks the circuit, and the furnace turns off.

(b) When the temperature drops back below 17°C, the strip contracts, causing the mercury to flow to the contact. This completes the circuit, turning the furnace back on.

The Thermocouple

A thermocouple, shown in **Figure 4**, uses electricity to operate. A **thermocouple** contains two wires, each of a different metal, that are joined (coupled) at one end. When two different metals touch each other, a tiny electrical current is generated. The amount of electricity depends on the temperature. The other ends of the wires are connected to a meter that measures electricity. By measuring the amount of electricity that flows through the meter, you can measure the temperature of the metal wires.

Figure 4

The thermocouple is useful for measuring very high temperatures in places where people cannot go, such as inside a kiln or a blast furnace. Also, since the thermocouple creates electricity, it can be connected to a computer to record the temperature.

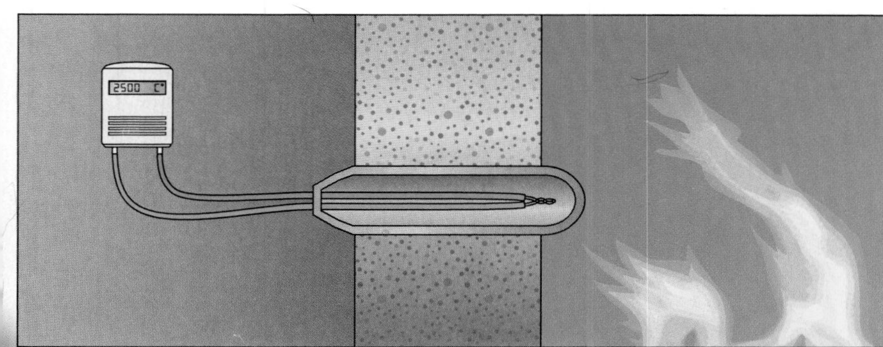

Figure 5

A bimetallic strip

Understanding Concepts

1. Describe in your own words the main features of each device that measures temperature and where it is used.
2. Describe how a thermostat keeps your home at a constant temperature. How does it work as a feedback system?
3. Explain how a thermocouple works. Why can it be connected to a computer?

Exploring

4. The first thermometer was invented by the astronomer Galileo in 1593. Research, using electronic and print sources, and write an explanation describing how it worked.

Design Challenge

Hold a bimetallic strip (**Figure 5**) under hot running water, then under cold running water. Describe what you discover. How can such a strip be used as a switch in a feedback system? Could a bimetallic switch be useful with your Challenge design? Explain.

Temperature and the Tomato

Have you ever wondered why apples grow in the Okanagan Valley and southern Ontario, but not on the Prairies? Or why tomatoes like those in **Figure 1** are often grown in greenhouses rather than in fields? Temperature is an important factor in determining where plants and animals can survive.

The tomato is a native of South America. In the tomato's native land there is no frost, and tomato plants can live for years. In North America, however, tomato plants live and die in less than a year, because they cannot survive if the air temperature drops below 0°C.

Figure 1
Commercial growers of tomatoes often rely on greenhouses to protect their crop from frost.

The Growing Season

Plants begin to grow at temperatures over 5°C. The growing season is the number of days in the year with an average temperature above 5°C. Of course, daily temperatures much higher than 5°C are needed to produce a good crop. **Figure 2** shows the growing season across Canada.

(a) How long is the growing season where you live?

(b) How long is the growing season in Timmins? in St. Thomas?

(c) Which parts of Canada have the longest growing seasons?

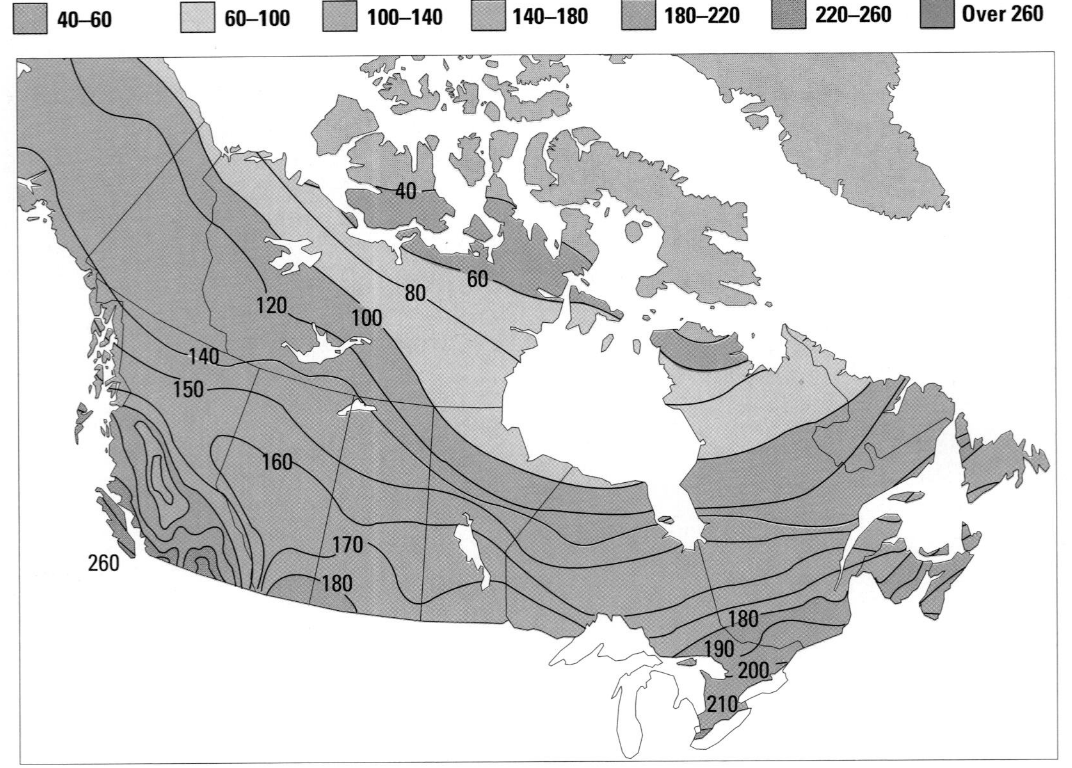

Figure 2
This map shows the number of days in the average growing season. The growing season in any year may be longer or shorter, depending on the weather. Refer to an atlas to locate places.

Variety and the Tomato

The tomato life cycle creates problems for growers in Canada. If you plant a tomato seed outdoors, it will not germinate until the soil is at least 10°C, which may happen 20 or more days into the growing season. After germination the plant will not grow unless night temperatures are higher than 7°C, and it will grow only slowly on cool days.

Tomato breeders have responded by creating varieties that will grow quickly and in cool weather, so they bear fruit in areas with short growing seasons. However, even these varieties, if grown entirely outdoors, will take 60 to 80 d before they grow enough to flower.

After the tomato flowers and is fertilized, the fruit begins to mature. The length of time from flowering until fruit can be picked is called the time to maturity. The amount of fruit that can be picked is called the yield, and is measured in kilograms. The **Tomato Varieties Table** shows the time to maturity for several varieties, and the yield you might expect from each plant.

(d) Using information from **Figure 2** and **Table 1**, which varieties could you grow in your area from seed and expect to get fruit? (Assume 100 d before flowering.) Which varieties of tomatoes could produce fruit in Timmins? in St. Thomas?

(e) Which variety would produce the greatest yield of fruit in your area? in Timmins? in St. Thomas?

Helping Mother Nature

Most of Canada has a short period for growing crops. What if you could extend this period? Well, you can! One way is to plant seeds indoors or in a greenhouse. In a warm location, tomato seeds will start to germinate in three to four days. When the plant is about 40 d old, it can be planted in the garden, where it will continue to grow, as long as the soil is warmer than 10°C.

(f) How would starting the seeds indoors change your answers in (e)?

Table 1

Variety	Time to maturity (days)	Yield for determinate* varieties (kg per plant)	Yield for indeterminate* varieties (kg per plant every 10 d)
A	80	?	6.8
B	40	?	2.6
C	70	?	5.2
D	60	10	?
E	70	?	4.2
F	65	10	?
G	55	15	?
H	50	10	?
I	75	?	5.6

* NOTE: Some varieties of tomatoes are called determinate—they produce all of their fruit in a short period at the end of the maturity time. Other varieties are called indeterminate—they produce fruit continuously until the first frost. For indeterminate varieties the yield is listed in kilograms per plant every 10 d after maturity. Where in Canada would it be difficult to grow tomato plants, even in a greenhouse? Why?

Understanding Concepts

1. Suppose you want to grow as many tomatoes as possible. Plan a growing calendar for a variety listed in **Table 1**. Show planting, germination, flowering, and harvesting dates.

Making Connections

2. In 1998, weather around the world was influenced by El Niño. In much of Canada, temperatures were higher than normal. What effect, if any, might this have on plant growth?

Exploring

3. (4A) You are a reporter for a nature magazine. Choose an animal and research how changes in temperature affect its habitat, its food sources, and its ability to reproduce. Write your information as a magazine article.

Temperature, Heat, and the Particle Theory

What exactly is the difference between water at 10°C and water at 80°C? What is the difference between heat and temperature? Over the years, scientists have tried to answer these questions with theories about heat and temperature. A theory is an explanation based on all the available information. As new evidence emerges, a theory may change. This is an important part of science.

Many times scientists' theories about big things are changed by observations of very tiny things. For example, in 1827 Robert Brown was looking at pollen. Pollen grains are small—too small to be seen with the eye. Under the microscope they can be seen clearly, if you can get them to sit still. Brown watched pollen grains bounce back and forth, even though the water they were in looked totally motionless. The motion of the pollen grains, now called Brownian motion, provided evidence that helped scientists propose a theory about matter. **Figure 1** shows Brownian motion.

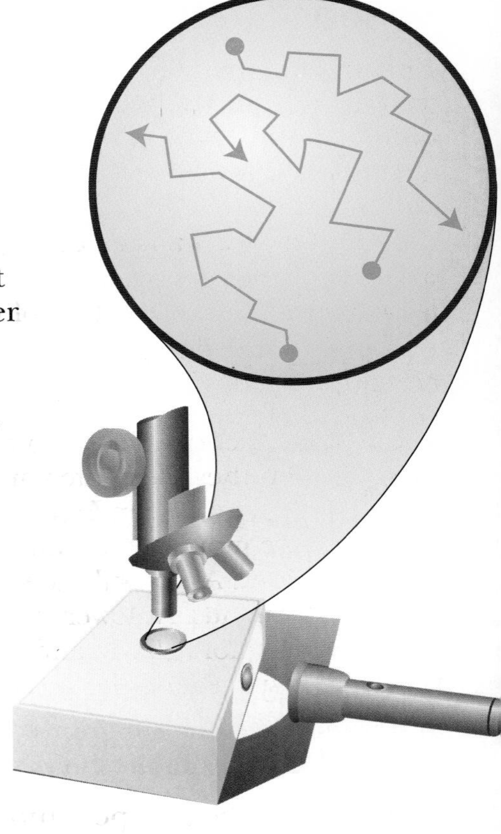

Figure 1

Brownian motion was discovered when pollen grains were observed in water. The same kind of motion can be seen if you look through a microscope at smoke particles.

The Particle Theory

By about 150 years ago, scientists had gathered enough evidence to be able to explain heat and temperature by combining ideas about energy and particles of matter. The kinetic molecular theory, or **particle theory**, says that all matter is made up of tiny particles too small to be seen. According to this theory, these particles are always moving—they have energy. The more energy the particles have, the faster they move.

So far, all the evidence that scientists have about matter supports the idea that all substances are made up of moving particles. That is why we call the particle model for matter a theory. According to this theory, Brown's pollen grains moved because they were being pushed around by invisible particles of water.

(a) cold water

(b) hot water

Figure 2

Both hot and cold water are made up of moving particles, some moving quickly, and some moving slowly. Overall, there are more particles moving quickly in hot water than in cold water, so the average energy of the particles is higher.

Heat and Temperature

Heat and temperature are different things. According to the particle theory, **heat** is energy, which transfers from hotter substances to colder ones. **Temperature** is a measure of the average energy of motion of the particles of a substance.

When heat is transferred to particles of cold water, the particles of water move faster, so they have more energy of motion and the temperature of the water rises (**Figure 2**).

Expansion and Contraction

The particle theory is useful to explain why substances expand when they are heated and contract when they are cooled, as you can see in **Figure 3**. At high temperatures, particles have more energy, move more quickly, and have more collisions. As a result, they take up more space, and the substance expands. At lower temperatures, particles have less energy, move more slowly, and have fewer collisions. They take up less space, and the substance contracts.

Figure 3

As a substance is heated, the particles move faster and take up more space.

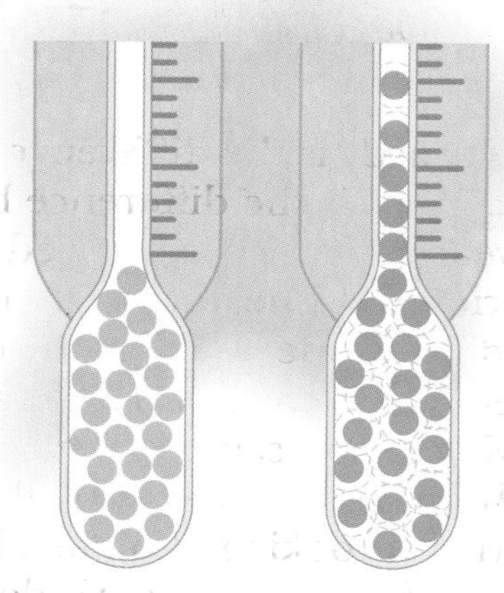

States of Matter

All matter can be grouped into one of three states: solid, liquid, or gas. Each state has certain characteristics, or properties. As shown in **Figure 4**, the particle theory is useful to explain the differences among the properties of solids, liquids, and gases.

Figure 4

The particle theory can be used to explain the properties of the three states of matter.

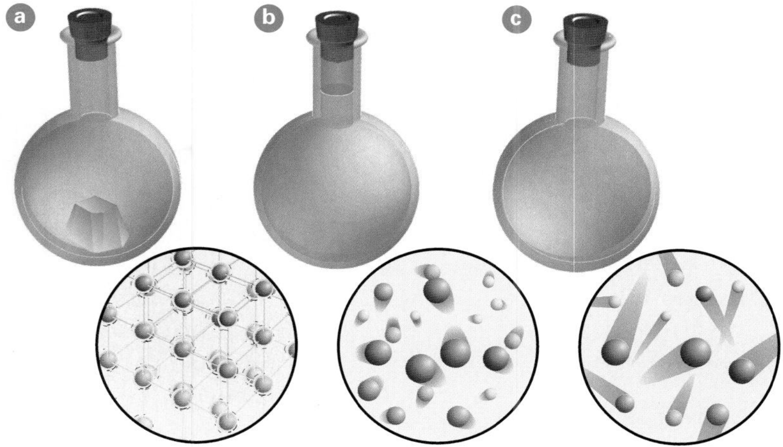

(a) A **solid** has a set volume and a rigid shape; it cannot flow like a gas or a liquid. Particles in a solid move, but only by vibrating in the same spot.

(b) A **liquid** has a set volume, but it will take the same shape as the container it is in; a liquid can flow. Particles in a liquid are free to move around.

(c) A **gas** fills any container it is in and takes on the shape of the container; a gas can flow. Particles in a gas are free to move around and are separated by relatively large spaces.

Understanding Concepts

1. **(a)** What is Brownian motion?
   (b) How did observing this motion help develop a theory about heat and temperature?
2. In your own words, describe the difference between heat and temperature.
3. Explain how a thermometer helps you compare the energies of particles.
4. Use the particle theory to explain how water differs in its three states.
5. Use the particle theory to explain how a clinical thermometer works.

Reflecting

6. How could you use a bottle of perfume in a room to show that the molecules in a gas are in constant motion?

Design Challenge

Is the average energy of particles important in your Challenge? Explain.

2.6 Inquiry Investigation

SKILLS MENU
- ○ Questioning
- ● Hypothesizing
- ○ Planning
- ● Conducting
- ● Recording
- ● Analyzing
- ○ Communicating

Ice to Water to Steam

Water can exist in the three states shown in **Figure 1**. If you leave an ice cube at room temperature, heat from the surrounding air will transfer to the ice, and the ice will become water. Then if you heat the water enough, it will boil and change into water vapour. In this investigation, you will explore what happens to the temperature of water as it changes state.

Question

What happens to the temperature of a substance as it changes state?

Hypothesis

(7C) (2C) **1** Draw a line graph of temperature vs. time, predicting what you think will happen to the temperature of a beaker full of ice as it is heated. Make sure your graph includes temperature values. Write a hypothesis to support your prediction.

Experimental Design

In Part 1 of this investigation you will heat water from ice to a liquid while measuring its temperature. In Part 2 the liquid will be heated until it boils. (For safety reasons, your teacher will demonstrate Part 2.)

(6D) **2** Create a table to record your data.

Materials

- apron
- safety goggles
- 250 mL crushed ice
- 250-mL Pyrex beaker
- stirring rod
- thermometer
- timing device
- hot plate
- clamp
- stand and ring apparatus
- insulating mitt
- cold metal pie plate

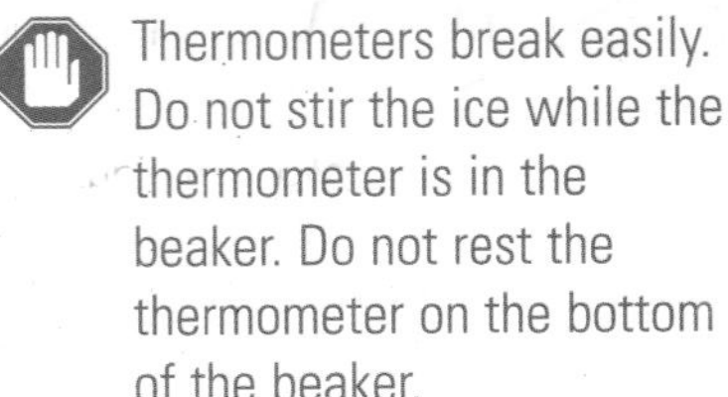

Thermometers break easily. Do not stir the ice while the thermometer is in the beaker. Do not rest the thermometer on the bottom of the beaker.

Procedure

Part 1: Ice to Water

3 Place the crushed ice in a beaker and stir it.
- Place the thermometer in the beaker and record the temperature at 0 min.

(a) Why should you stir the ice/water mixture?

(b) Where should the bulb of the thermometer be to get the most accurate reading? Why?

4 Remove the thermometer and stir the ice again.
- At 1 min, measure the temperature.

(a) Record the temperature each minute until 5 min after all the ice has melted.

(b) Record your observations of any changes.

Part 2: Water to Steam

5 To find out what happens to the temperature of water as it boils, a demonstration will be set up as shown above.

(a) Record temperature observations every minute before the water boils, and for at least 5 min after it begins to boil.

SKILLS HANDBOOK: (7C) Constructing Graphs (2C) Predicting and Hypothesizing (6D) Creating Data Tables

Figure 1
Water can be solid (ice), liquid, or gas (water vapour).

Making Connections

1. While camping in the fall, you leave some water in a bucket overnight. The next morning, you notice a layer of ice on the top of the water. What is the temperature of the water just beneath the ice?

Exploring

2. Design an experiment to find out if the melting temperature (2E) of water changes for different amounts of water. Check your design with your teacher before starting.

Reflecting

3. Compare the graph you drew for your hypothesis with the graphs you drew from your data. Was your hypothesis correct? Explain.

Part 3: Steam to Water

6 Use an insulating mitt to hold a cold metal pie plate above the boiling water for 10 s.

(a) Describe what you observe.

Analysis

7 To analyze your results, answer the following questions.

(a) Create line graphs of temperature vs. time (7C) for your data from Parts 1 and 2.

(b) Describe the shape of (7B) the graphs.

(c) Predict what your graph would look like if you had continued to heat the melted ice.

(d) Predict what your graph would look like if you had continued to heat the steam.

Design Challenge

Describe how you might use tables, charts, or graphs to present the data from your Challenge.

(e) What happens to the temperature of water during a change of state?

(f) On the basis of your observations, do you agree with the following statement? "When heat is added to a solid, the heat can cause a change of state or an increase in temperature." Explain your answer.

(7B) Reading a Graph (2E) Designing an Inquiry Investigation

The Particle Theory and Changes of State

You found that adding heat to ice at 0°C did not cause much change in temperature—it simply changed the ice to water. The temperature at which a substance melts is called its **melting point**. For ice, that point is 0°C.

Adding heat to water at 100°C does not cause a change of temperature—it simply changes the water to steam or vapour. The temperature at which a substance boils is called its **boiling point**. What is the boiling point of water?

In **Figure 1**, the particle theory of matter is used to explain why the temperature of a substance remains constant during a change of state.

Figure 1

In (a) water is changing from ice to water. In (b) water is changing from a liquid to water vapour.

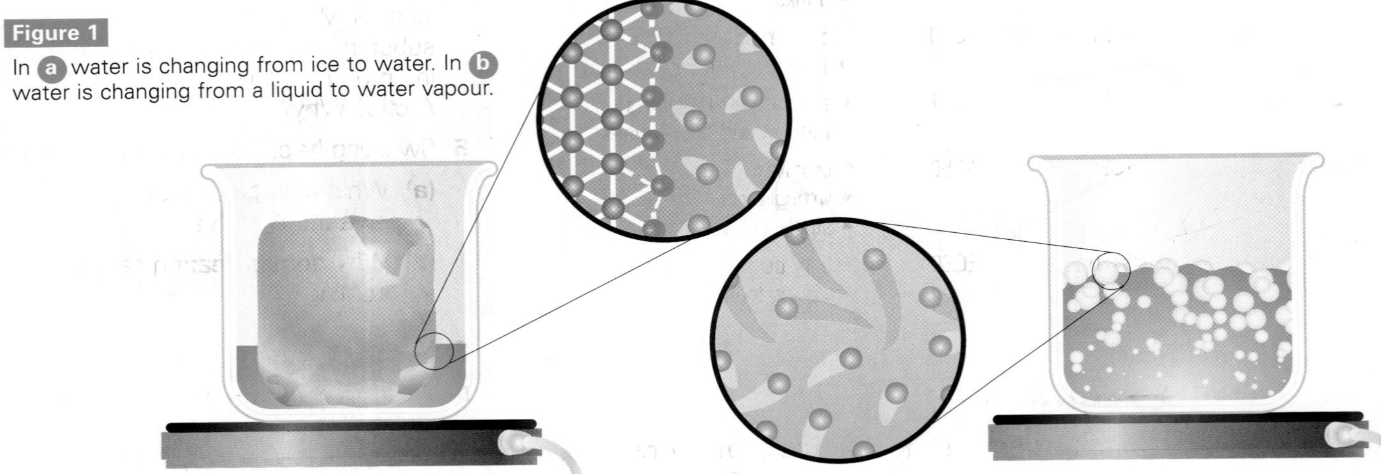

(a) When you add heat to ice at 0°C, the temperature does not rise. Instead, the heat is used to free the water particles from their set places in the solid. Since the heat has not increased the motion of the water particles, their temperature is the same. Particles that have been set free are in the liquid state.

(b) As water is heated, its particles gain energy and now move faster and faster. The temperature rises until the liquid reaches its boiling point. At this point the temperature does not continue to rise. Instead, the heat is used to help the particles move more freely and escape from the surface of the liquid. Particles that have been set free are now in the gas state.

Heating Curves

A **heating curve** is a graph showing how a substance's temperature changes while being heated. An example is shown in **Figure 2**. The flat part of the curve, where the substance is melting or boiling, is called a plateau. What do you think a cooling curve is?

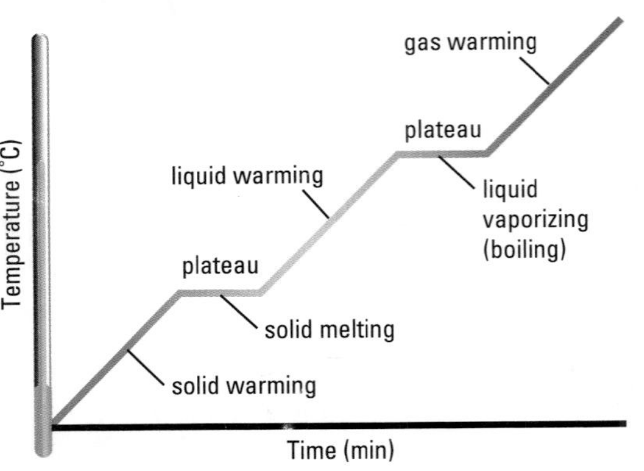

Figure 2

A heating curve

Differences in Substances

Different substances are made of different particles, so they have different melting and boiling temperatures.

Substance	Melting point/ freezing point (°C)	Boiling point/ condensation point (°C)	Some uses for substance
oxygen	–218	–183	• welding • breathing apparatus
carbon dioxide	–78	–78	• as "dry ice" in refrigeration
ammonia	–78	–33	• fertilizer • explosives
mercury	–39	357	• barometers • switches
ethyl alcohol	–114	78	• solvent
water	0	100	• ice cubes • drinks
paraffin wax	71	360	• candles • sealing jars of jam and jelly
aluminum	660	2467	• auto and aircraft parts • window and door frames
iron	1535	2750	• cast iron • wrought iron • steel
tungsten	3410	5660	• light bulbs • cutting tools

Changes of State

Figure 3 sums up changes in state. Notice that there are two changes of state called sublimation. The liquid state is skipped when frost forms from water vapour on windows in winter, or when a solid air freshener slowly disappears.

Understanding Concepts

1. Use the particle theory and a series of diagrams to explain what happens to ice as it is gradually heated and turns to water and then steam.
2. Draw a heating curve for paraffin wax as it goes from 0°C to 400°C. Label its melting point, boiling point, and its state in each section of the curve.
3. Draw a cooling curve for steam to (7C) water to ice. Label your graph.

Making Connections

4. Look at the melting and boiling points of mercury and ethyl alcohol. Which of these two substances would be better to use in an outdoor thermometer in the Arctic? Why?
5. Sweating helps cool a person's body.
   - **(a)** What change of state does sweating involve?
   - **(b)** Why does sweating cause cooling?

Exploring

6. The Celsius temperature scale relies on fixed points, the melting and boiling points of water, and divides the interval between them into 100 degrees. The reason water was chosen is that it is a common and very useful substance. Make up a temperature scale for a planet where the oceans and lakes are filled with ammonia instead of water.

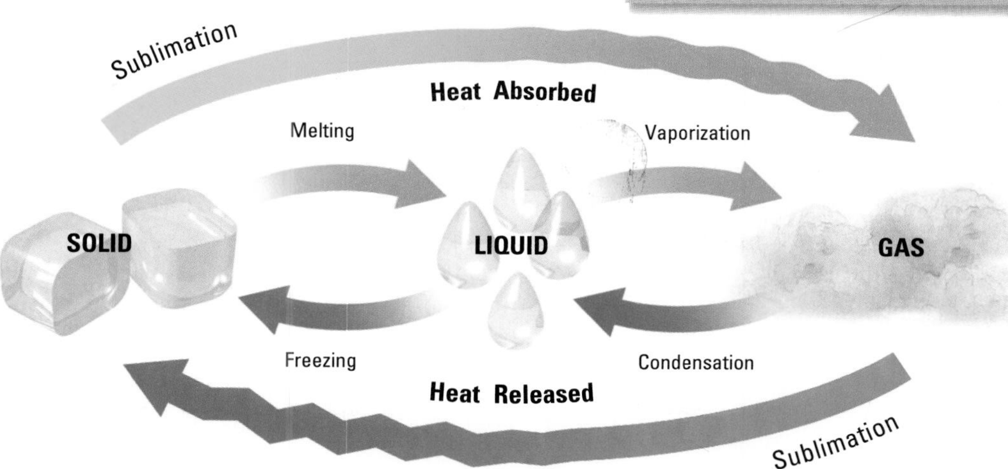

Figure 3
When heat is absorbed or released by a substance, a change of state can occur. Heat that is absorbed causes the changes shown by red arrows. Heat that is released causes the changes shown by blue arrows.

2.8 Inquiry Investigation

SKILLS MENU
- ○ Questioning
- ● Hypothesizing
- ○ Planning
- ● Conducting
- ● Recording
- ● Analyzing
- ● Communicating

Heat and Convection

Do all parts of your classroom feel as if they have the same temperature? Does the air near the floor or window feel the same as the air near the middle of the room? Heat can cause the air in a room to move. In this investigation, you will learn how heat transfers (or moves) in air and other fluids (**Figure 1**).

A fluid is a substance that is free to flow. Liquids and gases are fluids. To transfer heat, fluids use a method called convection. **Convection** is the transfer of heat by the movement of particles from one part of a fluid to another. The motion of many fluid particles is called a **convection current**.

Question

What are the properties of a convection current?

Hypothesis

1 Read the procedure for this experiment. Then draw diagrams predicting how you think the pieces of nutmeg and the smoke will move. Write a hypothesis for your prediction. 2C

Experimental Design

In this experiment you will use markers (the nutmeg in Part 1 and the smoke in Part 2) to reveal the movement of two fluids.

Materials

- apron
- safety goggles
- grated nutmeg
- large Pyrex beaker
- cold water
- retort stand and clamp
- hot plate
- ring stand
- gas convection apparatus
- candle
- wire gauze
- smoke paper

Follow the safety rules in the *Skills Handbook* when using an open flame.

Procedure Part 1: Convection in a Liquid

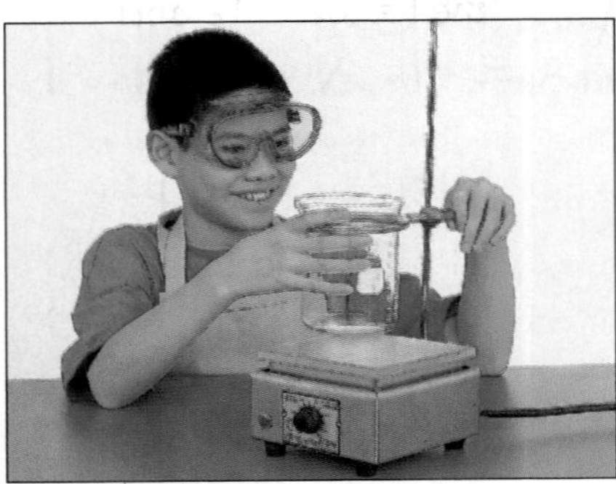

2 Set up the beaker so that one side will be heated more than the other.

3 Fill the beaker with cold water. Sprinkle about 15 to 20 pieces of nutmeg into the water.

(a) What do you think will happen to the pieces of nutmeg? Why?

4 When the water and pieces of nutmeg have become still, turn on the hot plate.

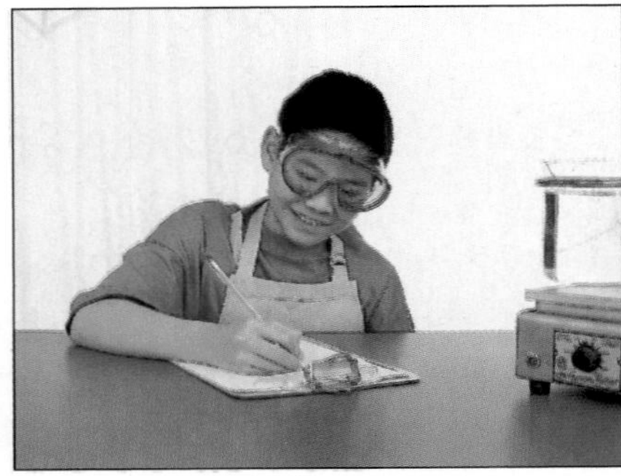

5 Heat the water until you can see a pattern in the motion of the nutmeg pieces.

(a) Record your observations.

(b) Draw a diagram showing the pattern you observed.

(c) Beside your diagram, describe any evidence that there is a convection current.

Figure 1
"Heat waves" are caused by rising air.

Making Connections

1. (a) Predict how convection currents will form in the air in your bedroom when the furnace or heater is turned on. Sketch your prediction.
   (b) How could you investigate your prediction?
2. (a) Your town council decides to heat the town's swimming pool. If you had to put a heater directly in the pool, where could you install it to take advantage of convection currents? Explain.
   (b) The town council decides to put the heater and a pump in a shed away from the pool. Design a circulating system for the heater that takes advantage of convection currents. (8B)
   (c) Explain why the town council decided not to put the heater in the pool.

Part 2: Convection in a Gas

6 Your teacher will set up the gas convection apparatus with a candle on the right side.

(a) Predict what will happen when smoke paper is held first above the right chimney, then above the left chimney. Record your prediction.

(b) Record your observations.

(c) Draw a diagram showing the pattern you observed.

Analysis

7 Analyze your results by answering the following questions.

(a) You set up your experiment in Part 1 to cause uneven heating. In your drawing from step 5, show where you think the water would be warmer, and where it would be cooler.

(b) You have learned that substances expand when they are heated, because they are made of particles. Using the particle theory, explain how a convection current could start in a fluid.

Design Challenge

How can you adapt your design for the town pool in question 2(b) to help you with your design for a solar-heated pool?

SKILLS HANDBOOK: (2C) Predicting and Hypothesizing (8B) Creating a Design Folder

Heat and Weather Patterns

Heat transfers in fluids using convection currents. Convection currents in Earth's atmosphere and oceans are important because they affect weather everywhere.

Thermals, Winds, and Sea Breezes

On a clear day, energy from the Sun warms the land and the air near it. The warm air expands and becomes less dense. (Can you use the particle theory to explain why this happens?) As the warm air expands it rises and is replaced by cooler, denser air. This kind of convection current is called a thermal. **Figure 1** shows the formation of a thermal.

As the thermals grow in size, drawing more and more cool air in at the bottom, people on the ground can begin to detect the movement of air. We call the flow of air a wind. This kind of wind is most likely to develop near a large body of water, such as a large lake or an ocean. Water warms up more slowly than soil, so the air over the water tends to be cooler. The cooler air over the water moves toward the base of the thermals on land. If the convection current is near a sea or an ocean, the wind that forms is often called a sea breeze.

Thermals help large birds, such as turkey vultures and eagles, glide in the air for hours, searching for prey. As the warm air rises, the birds can ride it higher by gliding in circles within the thermal. When the thermal isn't strong enough to keep them aloft without effort, or they want to move to a new area, they glide down to the next thermal and start the cycle again.

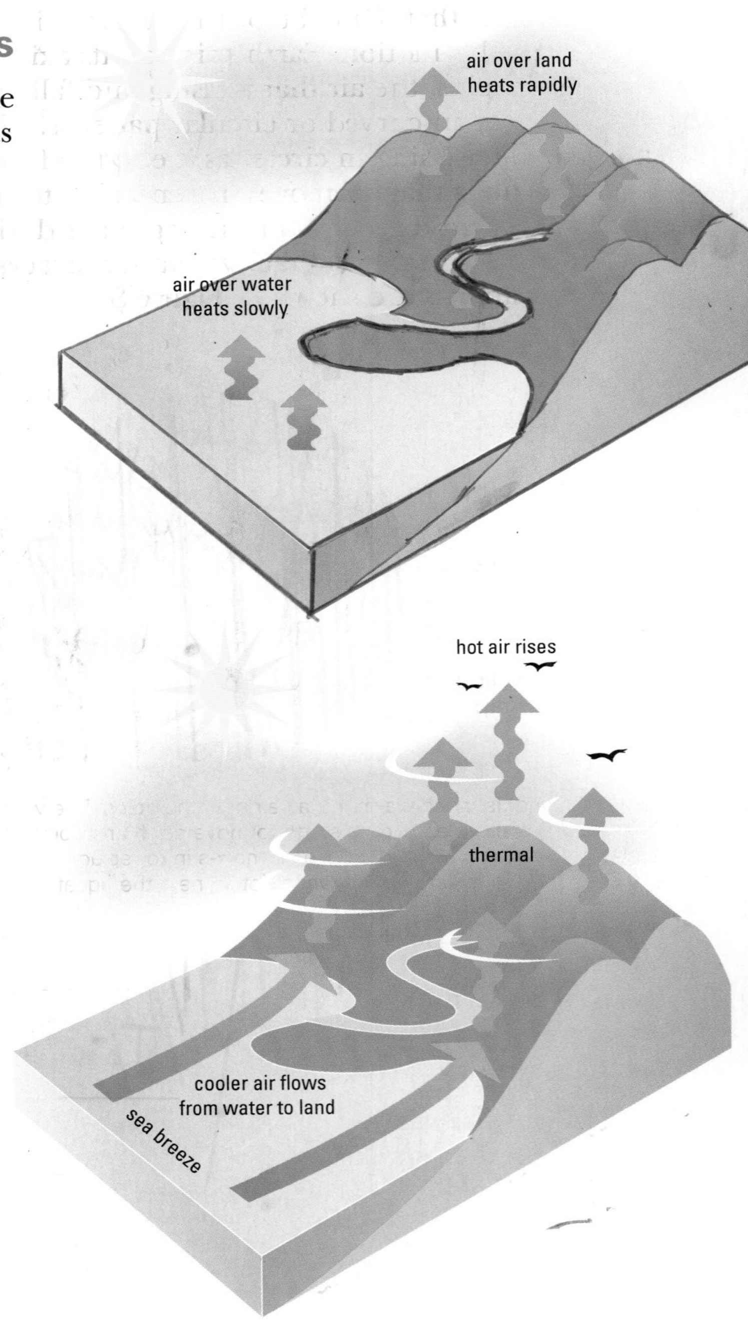

Figure 1
Heating of the air by the Sun causes thermals and sea breezes to form.

SKILLS HANDBOOK: 4A Research Skills 8C Multimedia Presentations

Large Wind Patterns

What we see in thermals is also happening on a much larger scale. As you can see in **Figure 2**, huge convection currents are created by the Sun in Earth's atmosphere, causing global wind patterns to develop.

Based on the simple convection model, you might expect winds at Earth's surface to blow only from the poles to the equator. But the circulation of air is much more complicated than that. One factor that affects wind direction is Earth's motion. Earth spins on its axis once each day. As it spins, the air that is rising and falling can also start to move in curved or circular patterns. (This effect is like water going in circles as it empties from a sink.) The result is that air moves in general patterns, but at a local level wind direction and strength are difficult to predict—as you can tell from faulty weather forecasts! Global wind patterns are shown in **Figure 3**.

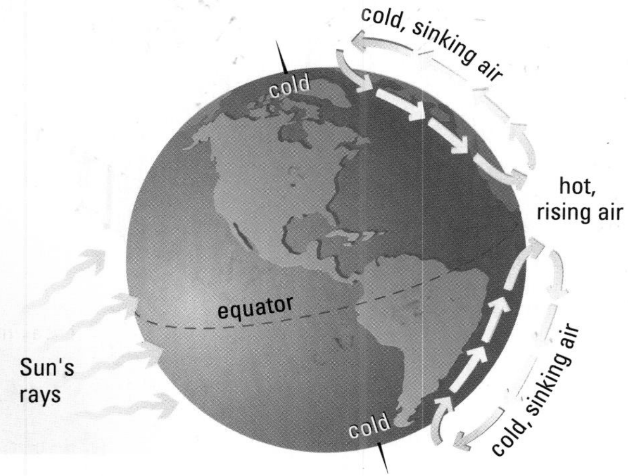

Figure 2

Air near the equator is much warmer than air near the poles. The warm, less dense air rises above the equator. It starts to move north and south, away from the equator, as cooler, more dense air moves in to replace it. Large convection currents of air are set up when hot air near the equator rises.

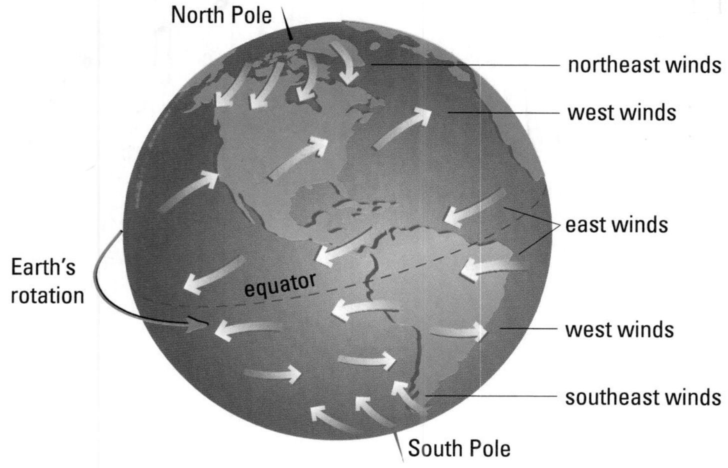

Figure 3

Earth's motion causes patterns in the large movements of air in the atmosphere. Notice that the winds near the equator tend to travel westward. The winds in southern Canada tend to travel from west to east. What direction would you expect the wind to blow on most days in Dawson City?

Understanding Concepts

1. Explain the expression "hot air rises."
2. (a) Are thermals more likely to be set up in winter or in summer? Why?
   (b) Are thermals more likely to be set up on a cloudy day or a sunny day? Why?
3. Draw and label a sequence of three diagrams to show how a thermal is set up over land.
4. What conditions help a sea breeze begin?
5. A land breeze, blowing from the land out over the water, can begin when the sun sets. When this happens, lakes often become calm near the shore. Use a diagram to help you explain how a land breeze is set up.
6. Describe the main factors that cause the air in Earth's atmosphere to move.

Exploring

7. (4A) (8C) Using electronic and print sources, research the sport of hang-gliding. Relate what you discover to thermals and the way birds soar on thermals. Make a visual presentation about what you discover.
8. (4A) Hurricanes are large storms that occur on and near the Atlantic Ocean. Research how these storms are set up by heat transfers.

Design Challenge

You have learned that heat transfer in water and air sets up convection currents. How can knowledge of convection currents help you with your challenge design?

2.10 Design Investigation

SKILLS MENU
- ○ Identify a Problem
- ○ Planning
- ○ Building
- ● Testing
- ● Recording
- ● Evaluating
- ● Communicating

Heat and Conduction

Imagine that your first few steps in bare feet in the morning are on a rug. Then you walk on to a wooden floor. Which do you think would feel cooler? Can you suggest a reason?

The wooden floor feels cooler than the rug even though they are at the same temperature. Wood has a better ability than a rug to transfer heat away from your body. You can notice a similar effect when you touch objects around you in the room: a metal chair leg transfers heat away from your fingers more quickly than a piece of paper.

The transfer of heat by the collisions of particles in a solid is called **conduction**. **Figure 1** shows conduction. A substance that conducts heat well is called a **heat conductor**. Wood is a better heat conductor than a rug, and metal is a better heat conductor than paper. In this investigation you will test substances to rank them according to which are the best heat conductors.

Materials

- apron
- safety goggles
- glass and metal rods of approximately equal size
- 2 support stands
- 2 clamps
- candle
- hot plate
- equal-sized rods made of various metals
- timing device

Use care with an open flame.
Do not touch wax while it is liquid. Hot wax can burn.

Do not allow the glass or metal rod to touch the hot plate.

Problem

You are going on a camping trip and will be cooking over an open fire.

Design Brief

Test a variety of materials to determine which would be the most suitable cookware to design and make for a camping trip.

Design Criteria

- A utensil is necessary for cooking hot dogs and making hot chocolate.
- The material should conduct heat quickly and be safe to hold.

Test

Part 1: Comparing a Metal and a Nonmetal

1 Clamp a glass rod and an equal-sized metal rod to separate support stands.
- Use a lit candle to make small beads of wax equally spaced along the rods.

2 After the wax beads are solid, arrange the rods horizontally so that each rod has one end above the hot plate.
- Turn on the hot plate and time how long it takes each wax bead to melt.

(a) Record your observations.
- Turn off the hot plate after the last bead has melted.

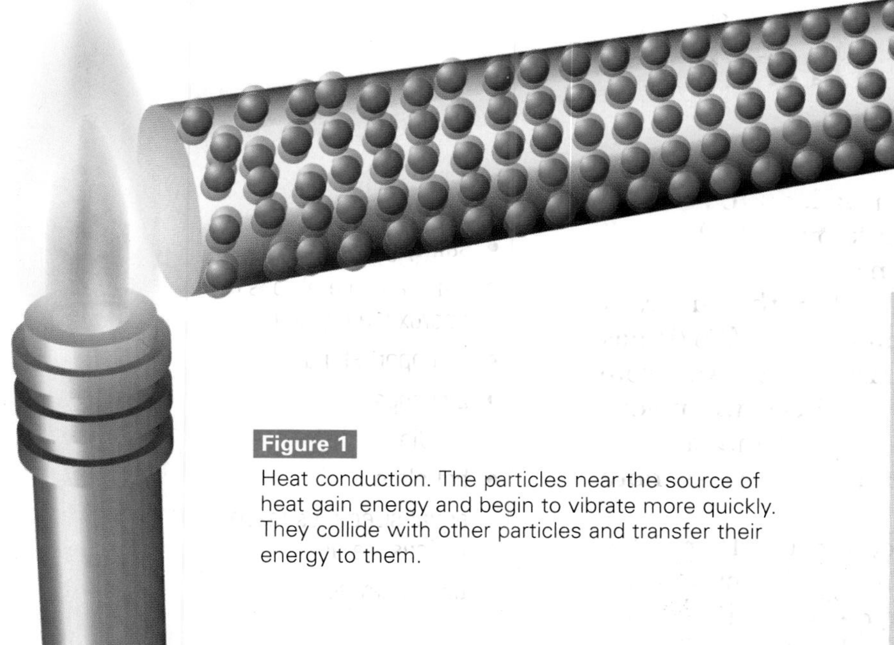

Figure 1

Heat conduction. The particles near the source of heat gain energy and begin to vibrate more quickly. They collide with other particles and transfer their energy to them.

Part 2: Comparing Metals

3 Design a way to test various other metal rods so you can rank the metals from best conductor to worst.

- Design a table for your data.
- Have your teacher approve your design.
- Carry out your test.

Evaluate

4 Evaluate your results by answering the following questions.

(a) In step 2, did the wax melt more quickly on one rod than the other? Explain why.

(b) When conducting this test, what were the independent and dependent variables? List the controls that you used.

(c) Which materials would be best suited for camping cookware?

Making Connections

1. Design a set of camp (3D) cookware using technical drawings.
2. The ability to transfer heat quickly is important in products we use in our homes. Describe three products that transfer heat through a solid by conduction.
3. A baker can choose between using a glass pan or a metal pan. In which pan would bread develop a firm brown crust on the bottom and sides? Explain how.
4. Explain why cooks stick metal objects in potatoes when they bake them.

Exploring

5. Describe how you could use a set of temperature probes connected to a computer to test how quickly various solids transfer heat.

Reflecting

6. Use the particle theory to explain how heat is transferred along a metal rod.

Design Challenge

Substances can be good or poor conductors of heat. How will this affect your choice of materials for your Challenge? How could you test your materials?

SKILLS HANDBOOK: (3D) Planning a Prototype

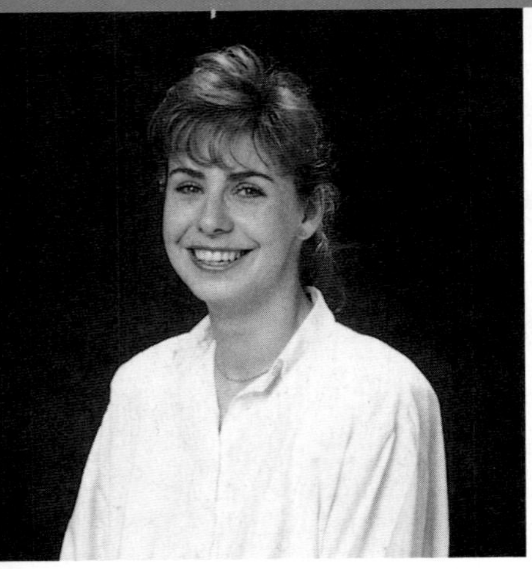

At the Scene of the Crime

Susan Kern is a forensic biologist at Ontario's Centre of Forensic Sciences. That means Susan spends a lot of time looking at blood and other body fluids. "We determine if a particular body fluid is present on an item," she says. "If it is, we try to determine who the fluid may have come from, using DNA typing."

Susan sometimes goes to the crime scene to help figure out what happened. "The size, shape, and pattern of blood stains can tell us a lot about what occurred," she says. A quick chemical test tells Susan whether a stain is probably blood, and she uses a small hand-held magnifier to measure very small stains.

After she has analyzed all the evidence and made her conclusions, she goes to court as an expert witness. "Being in the witness stand can be stressful, but it's the culmination of all we do," she says.

Susan enjoys her work and finds it challenging, but what about the gory crime scenes, do they upset her? "Not really—it takes a certain type of person to look at it as just work. It's an interesting job."

Heat and Crime

Often, the temperature of an object plays an important role in solving a crime. Heat from the engine of a vehicle may indicate that it has just been driven. A warm cup of coffee on a kitchen table may mean that a suspect has just left. The temperature of a body can indicate when death occurred.

A forensics lab. Here evidence collected by police officers is analyzed and tested.

When an object is removed from a source of heat, its temperature begins to drop. It cools until it reaches the temperature of the surrounding air, at which point its temperature stabilizes. For same-sized objects at the same initial temperature, surrounded by material with the same insulating properties, heat loss occurs at the same rate. This allows forensic scientists to determine, with some degree of accuracy, the time that the object was removed from the heat source.

At death, a body stops generating heat and its temperature drops gradually. At first the cooling is relatively rapid—approximately 0.8°C per h—but this rate slows after a few hours. In addition to the initial temperature, the temperature of the surroundings, and the effectiveness of any insulation, the size of the body will also affect the cooling time. A small body will cool more rapidly than a large one. By taking a body's temperature, a forensic scientist can estimate the time of death.

The Alibi—A Forensic Investigation (2A)

A suspect in a jewel robbery tells police that he was at home pouring a cup of coffee when the theft occurred. The theft took place at 10:00 p.m. When police arrived at 10:15 p.m., the temperature of the suspect's coffee was 45°C. Was he telling the truth?

- Make a data table like the one below.

Time (min)	Temperature (°C)
0	?
1	?
2	?
3	?

- Pour 250 mL of hot coffee into a coffee cup.
- Put a thermometer into the coffee and measure the temperature of the coffee.
- Record the temperature at 0 min.
- Measure and record the temperature each minute for 20 min.
- Make a graph of your data.

1. Does your data support the suspect's alibi?
2. How could your graph help in other investigations?
3. How would your data be affected by changing the insulating properties of the cup?

2.12 Inquiry Investigation

SKILLS MENU
- ○ Questioning
- ● Hypothesizing
- ● Planning
- ● Conducting
- ● Recording
- ● Analyzing
- ● Communicating

Radiation

You have learned that heat transfer occurs by convection in fluids and conduction in solids. Both convection and conduction depend on the motion of particles. Between Earth and the Sun there is much empty space—there are almost no particles. Yet we receive heat from the Sun; if we didn't, there would be no life on Earth. There must be a third way of transferring energy, one that does not need particles. This method is called radiation. **Radiation** is the transfer of energy by means of waves. Energy transferred by radiation is called **radiant energy**. Light is an example of radiant energy.

Some objects absorb radiant energy better than others; some objects emit (give off) radiant energy better than others. In this investigation you will test a variable to see what effect it has on absorbing or emitting radiant energy.

Questions

(a) How can the absorption of radiant energy be increased?

(b) How can the emission of radiant energy be increased?

Hypothesis

1 (2C) Your experiment will study one of the two questions, and one independent variable. For your experiment, create a hypothesis in the form "If we…, then…."

Experimental Design

2 You will create a controlled experiment that studies the effect of changing either the colour or the surface area of an object. **Figure 1** may help you with your design.

- You should use water as the substance to be heated or cooled. Any other materials (3D) you choose should be inexpensive and safe to use.
- The experiment must be controlled. While you are carrying out your tests, you must change only one variable at a time.
- Since different groups will be testing (2D) different variables, you must be prepared to share your results.

3 Discuss with your partner(s):
- the experimental design
- the materials you will need to test your hypothesis
- how you are going to record and present the data you collect

4 Prepare a procedure, including safety precautions.

Materials

5 List the materials you will need.

6 Ask your teacher to approve your procedure and materials list.

Procedure

7 Carry out your experiment.

8 Share your results with the other groups in your class.

SKILLS HANDBOOK: 2C Predicting and Hypothesizing 3D Planning a Prototype 2D Identifying Variables and Controls

Figure 1

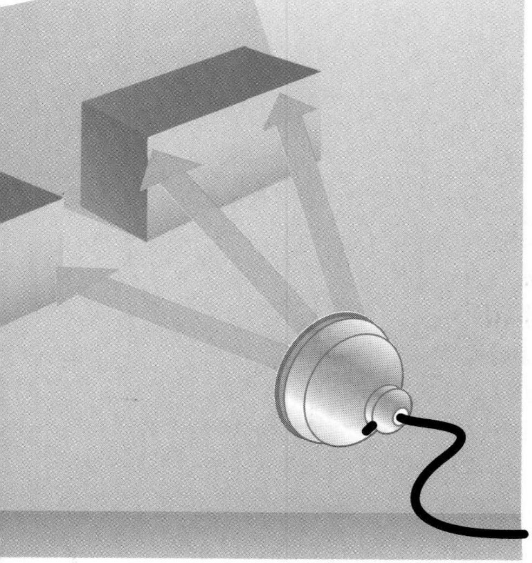

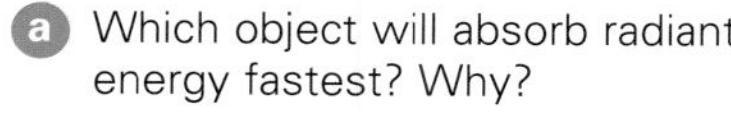

(a) Which object will absorb radiant energy fastest? Why?

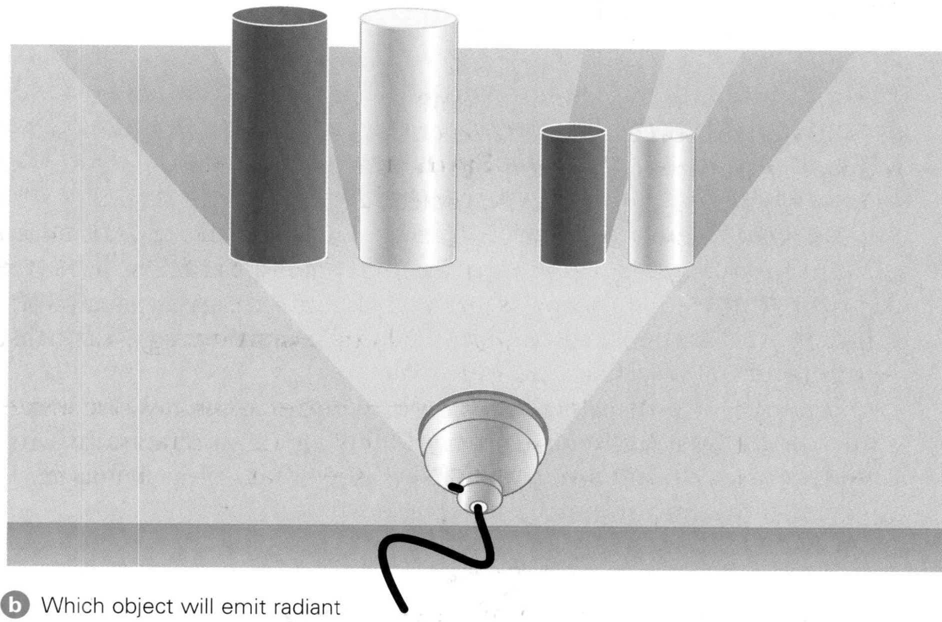

(b) Which object will emit radiant energy fastest? Why?

Analysis

9 Analyze your results by answering the following questions.

(a) Which colour or colours tend to absorb radiant energy best?

(b) How does the surface area of an object affect its ability to absorb radiant energy?

(c) Which colour or colours tended to emit radiant energy best?

(d) How does the surface area of an object affect its ability to emit radiant energy?

(e) Does an object that absorbs radiant energy well also emit radiant energy well? Explain your answer.

(f) In your experiment, what was the independent variable? What was the dependent variable? What variables did you control?

(g) If you were to try this experiment again, what would you do to improve your choice of materials and procedure? Explain.

Exploring

1. (2C) (2E) Are good conductors or poor conductors better emitters of energy? Describe how you would test your hypothesis. If possible, carry out the experiment and share the results with your class.

Reflecting

2. What are some properties of materials that get hot when solar energy hits them? Explain.

Design Challenge

Should the materials you choose for your challenge design be good absorbers of radiant energy or good emitters? What changes should you make in your design based on your knowledge of radiant energy?

(2E) Designing an Inquiry Investigation

Heat and the Water Cycle

Without water, life as we know it would not be possible. The water cycle, **Figure 1**, is the repeated movement of water from oceans and lakes, to atmosphere, to land, and back to oceans and lakes. The cycle begins when radiant energy from the Sun is absorbed by the oceans and other bodies of water.

1. Raindrops

High above Earth's surface, the temperature is lower, so the water vapour cools. Tiny water droplets form around some of the dust particles in the air. The droplets or crystals keep growing until they are large enough to be pulled down by gravity. As they fall, they meet other droplets and form drops of rain.

2. Freezing Rain

Freezing rain forms and falls like ordinary rain, but freezes when it hits cold surfaces. **Figure 1** shows the conditions needed to cause freezing rain. Usually these conditions do not last very long, but in one case, the 1998 ice storm in Quebec and eastern Ontario, they lasted several days.

Figure 1

Earth's water cycle starts with water vapour from the surface of Earth, including oceans, lakes, and living things, rising with air currents.

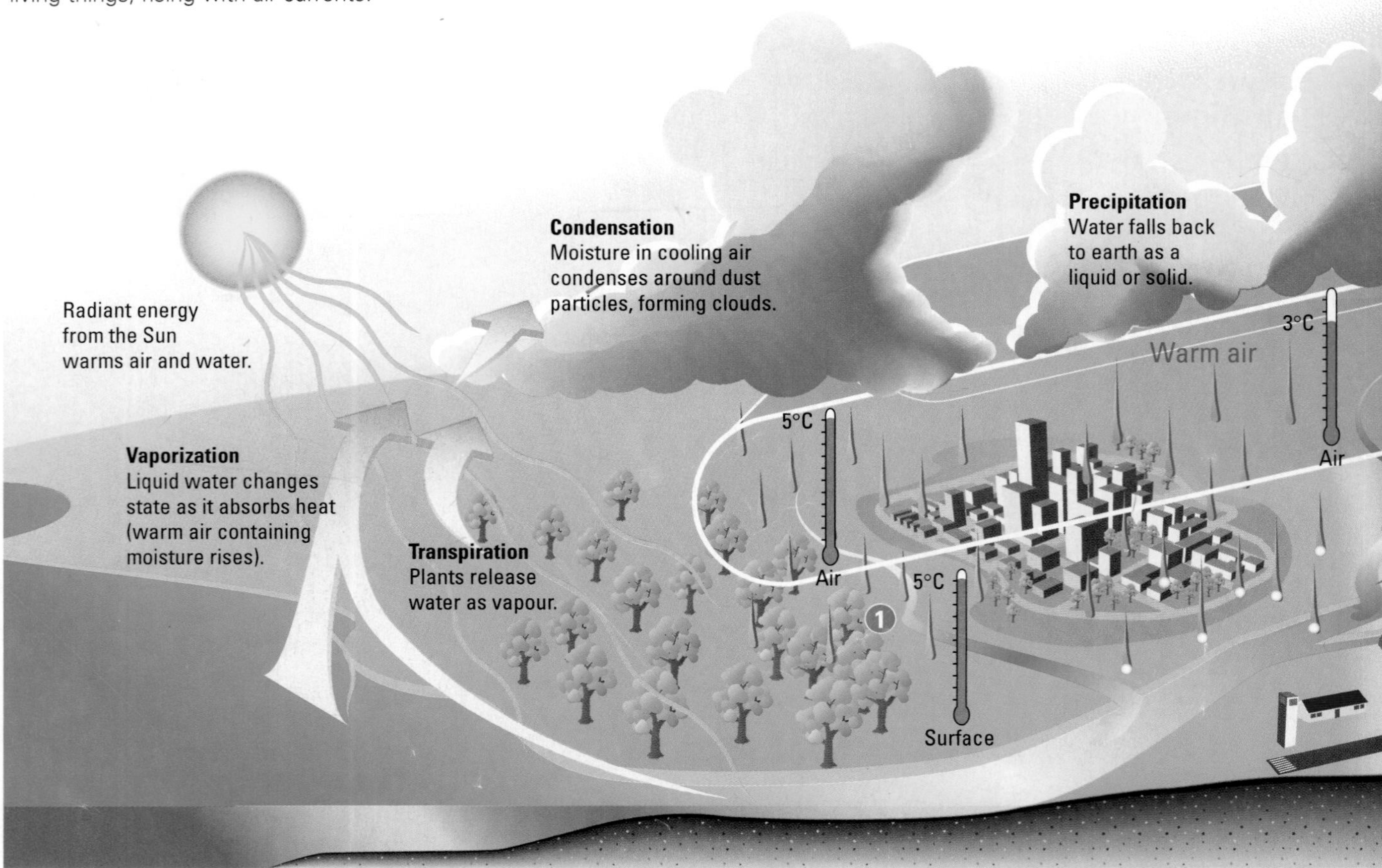

Radiant energy from the Sun warms air and water.
Condensation
Moisture in cooling air condenses around dust particles, forming clouds.
Precipitation
Water falls back to earth as a liquid or solid.
3°C
Warm air
5°C
Air
Vaporization
Liquid water changes state as it absorbs heat (warm air containing moisture rises).
Transpiration
Plants release water as vapour.
Air
5°C
1
Surface

Try This Weather Response

Freezing rain can build upon power lines and pull them down, cutting off electricity. It can make roads and sidewalks slippery and dangerous to use. A weather advisory predicts freezing rain for your area.

(3D) 1. Design a device to reduce the effects of freezing rain.

3. Snow

At colder temperatures, snowflakes form instead of raindrops.

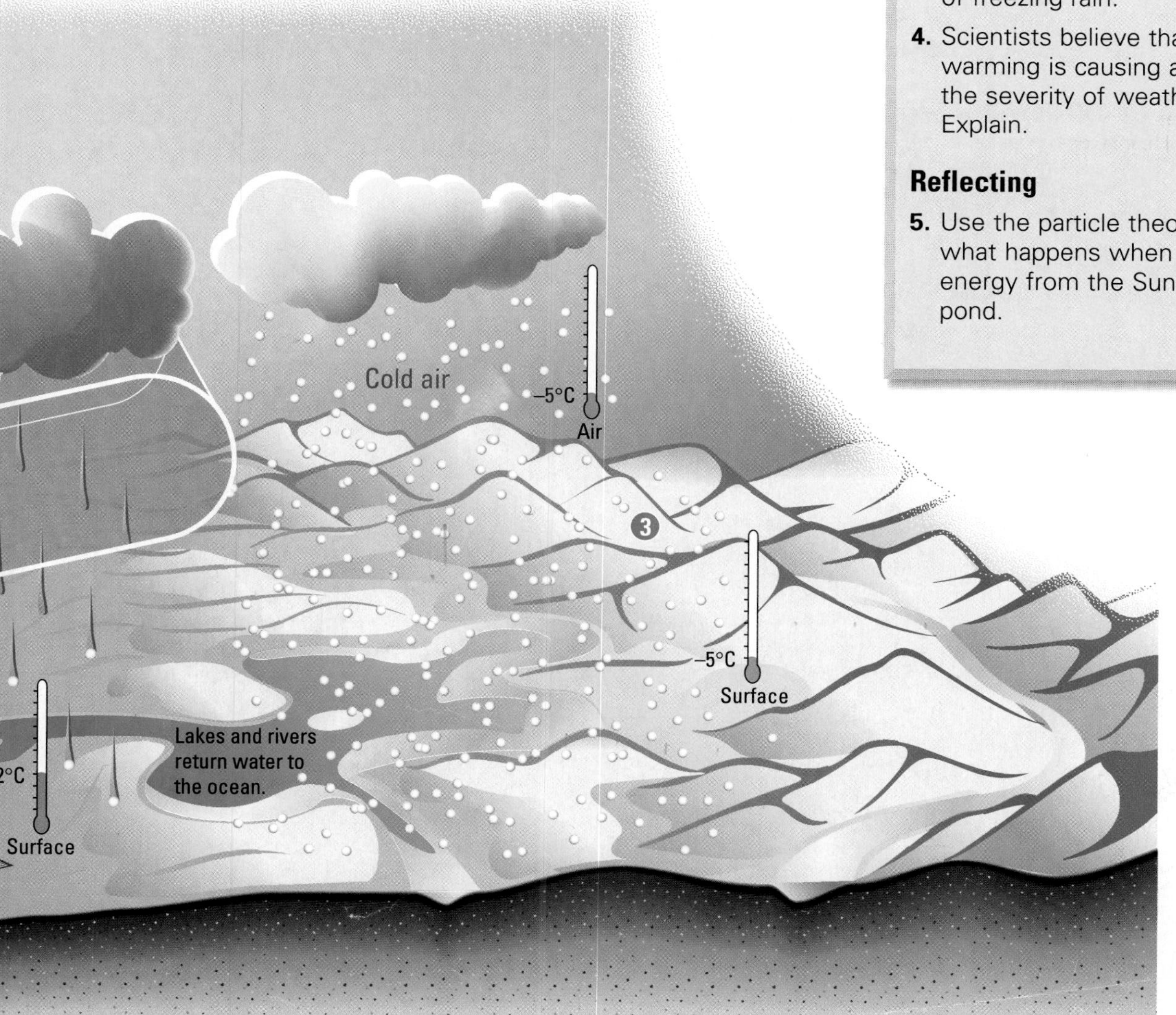

Understanding Concepts

1. What is the main source of energy for the water cycle on Earth?
2. (a) Starting with water on the Earth's surface, list all the changes of state that occur in the completion of one water cycle when rain falls.
   (b) How does the list of changes of state differ for a snowfall?
   (c) How does the list differ for freezing rain?

Exploring

3. Hail, like rain and snow, is a type (4A) of precipitation. It can damage property and destroy farmers' crops. Research how hail is formed. Draw a diagram showing how its formation differs from that of freezing rain.
4. Scientists believe that global warming is causing an increase in the severity of weather storms. Explain.

Reflecting

5. Use the particle theory to explain what happens when radiant energy from the Sun heats a pond.

SKILLS HANDBOOK: (3D) Planning a Prototype (4A) Research Skills

Heating Homes

Think about heating the place where you live: Where does the energy come from to heat your house or apartment? How does the heat get sent to each room? Which of the three methods of heat transfer (convection, conduction, and radiation) occur? Does the heating system use energy efficiently? Is there a feedback device to control the system? Try to relate these questions to the ideas about home heating described here.

Heating a Single Room

Air is a good heat insulator, which, of course, means it is a poor heat conductor. So in order to efficiently heat air in a room, a convection current must be set up. **Figure 1** shows how a convection current is created by an electric heater.

Figure 1
An electric heater creates a convection current.

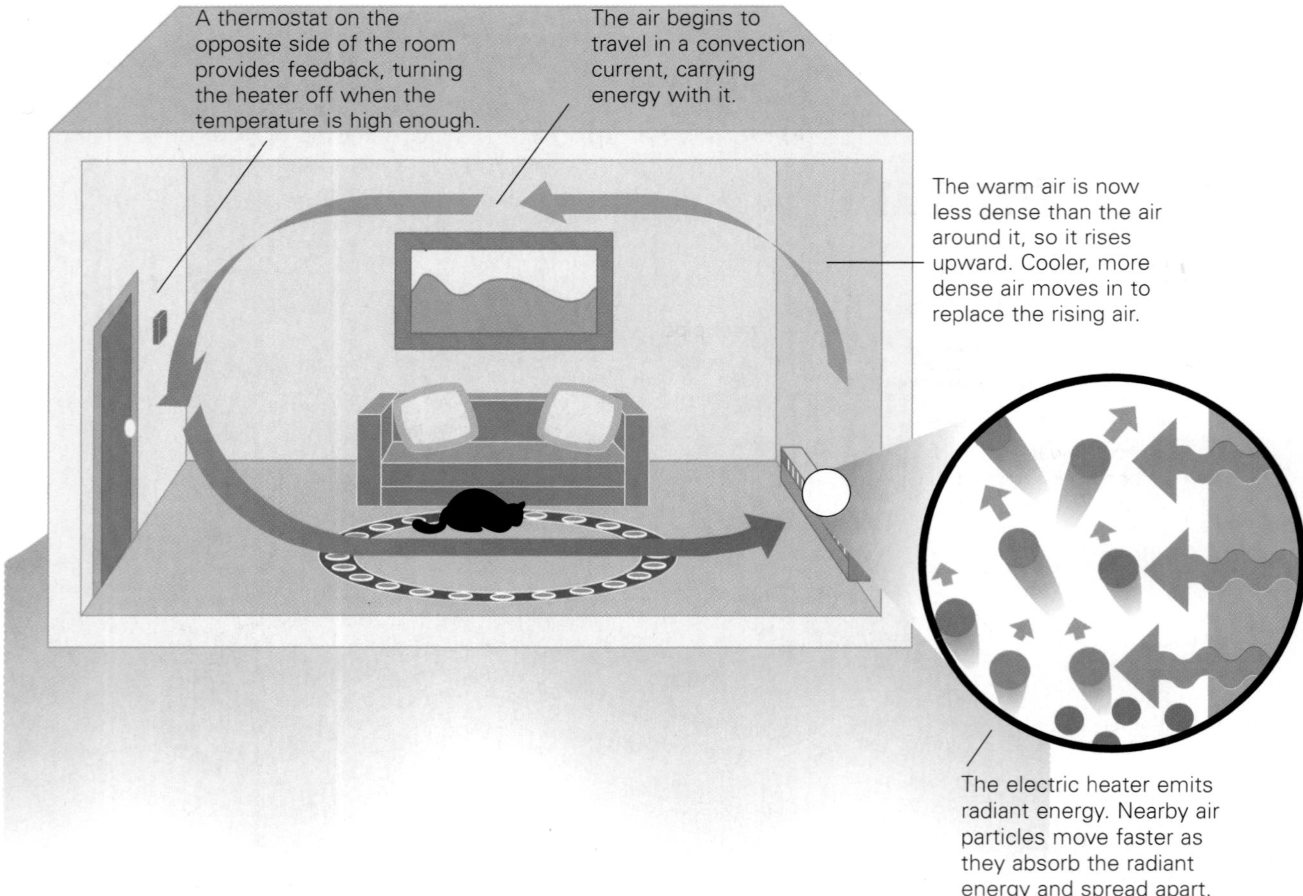

A thermostat on the opposite side of the room provides feedback, turning the heater off when the temperature is high enough.
The air begins to travel in a convection current, carrying energy with it.
The warm air is now less dense than the air around it, so it rises upward. Cooler, more dense air moves in to replace the rising air.
The electric heater emits radiant energy. Nearby air particles move faster as they absorb the radiant energy and spread apart.

Hot-Water Heating Systems

Some homes and other buildings use hot water to provide heat. The water is under pressure, just like the water that goes to the taps in a home. **Figure 2** shows how hot water can be used to heat a home.

Figure 2

Some heating systems use hot water as a source of heat.

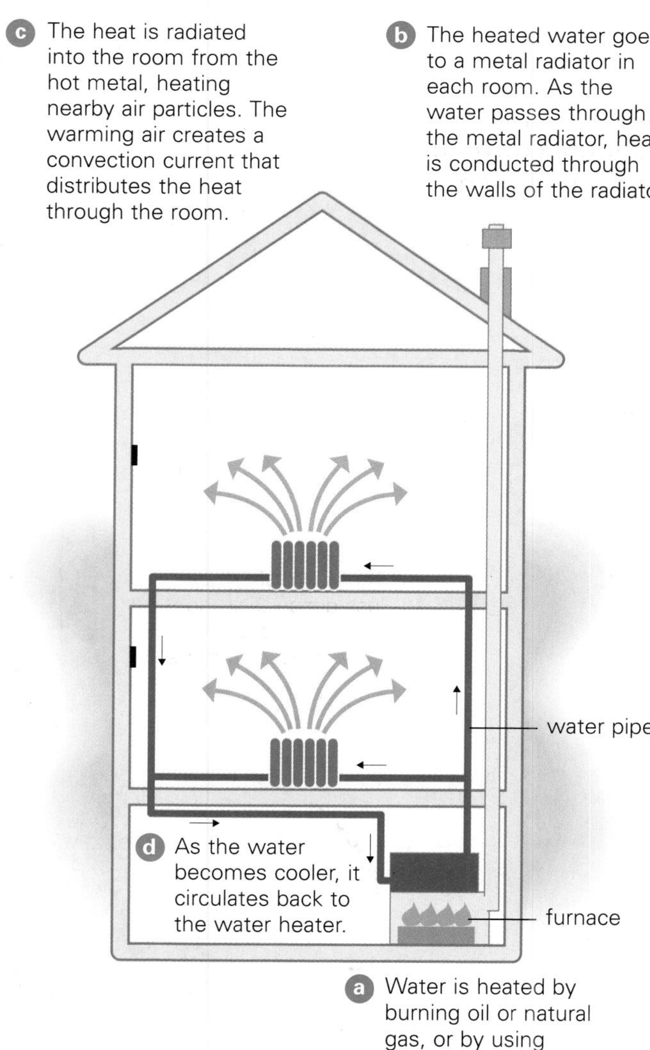

c The heat is radiated into the room from the hot metal, heating nearby air particles. The warming air creates a convection current that distributes the heat through the room.
b The heated water goes to a metal radiator in each room. As the water passes through the metal radiator, heat is conducted through the walls of the radiator.
water pipe
d As the water becomes cooler, it circulates back to the water heater.
furnace
a Water is heated by burning oil or natural gas, or by using electricity.

Forced-Air Heating Systems

In a forced-air heating system, air is heated in a furnace and then driven by a fan through ducts to the rooms. **Figure 3** shows a forced-air system.

Understanding Concepts

1. Where does the energy come from to heat the air in a single room in a hot-water heating system? in a forced-air heating system?
2. (6C) Using diagrams, compare the heating of air in a room to the development of a sea breeze.
3. How many methods of heat transfer are involved in a hot-water heating system? Give an example of each method.
4. Describe how a forced-air heating system works.

Making Connections

5. Two families, one with a hot-water heating system and the other with a forced-air system, leave for a one-week winter vacation. They turn down their thermostats to the same temperature to conserve energy. When they return, they increase their thermostats to the same temperature. Will the two homes heat up at the same rate? Explain your answer.
6. (6C) Describe the heating system used where you live. Use diagrams to show how the air is warmed, the method of heat transfer, and the feedback device that controls the system. Do you think the system uses energy efficiently? Explain.

Figure 3

A forced-air heating system

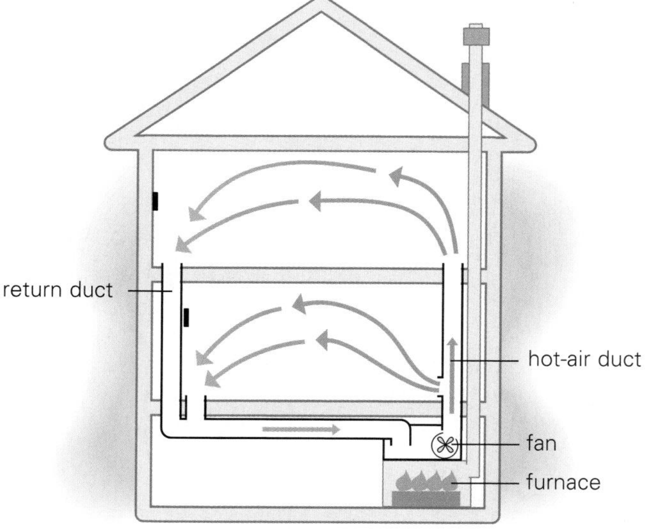

Design Challenge

Suggest a way to set up a feedback system to control the heat in the greenhouse challenge or the model pool challenge.

SKILLS HANDBOOK: (6C) Scientific & Technical Drawing

2.15 Explore an Issue

Wasting Heat

Heating bills are high for your school. This means that money that might be spent on books, computers, and sports equipment is being used to pay for heat. One way to reduce heating bills is to find out where warm air is escaping from the building.

To do this you could use an instrument called a thermal scanner. It measures invisible radiant energy. Then, with the help of a computer, the scanner changes the measurements into a "picture of heat" that you can see on a video screen. This process is called thermography. It helps show where heat is being lost from a building. **Figure 1** shows an example of a thermograph.

Figure 1
A thermograph. This house is losing lots of heat through its windows (white and orange areas), and a little through the front wall (green). The snow on the roof and the ground is cold (red).

Saving Heat

There are many ways to decrease loss of heat and other energy (**Figure 2**).

Figure 2
Some features that reduce heat loss from homes.

Source of heat loss

Remedies

walls and roofs

- Increase the amount of insulation in the basement walls, the roof, and the exterior walls.

air leakage

- Use a sealed air/vapour barrier to reduce air leakage and the buildup of moisture. The barrier is made of plastic and is placed on the inside of the insulated walls.

windows and doors
basement walls

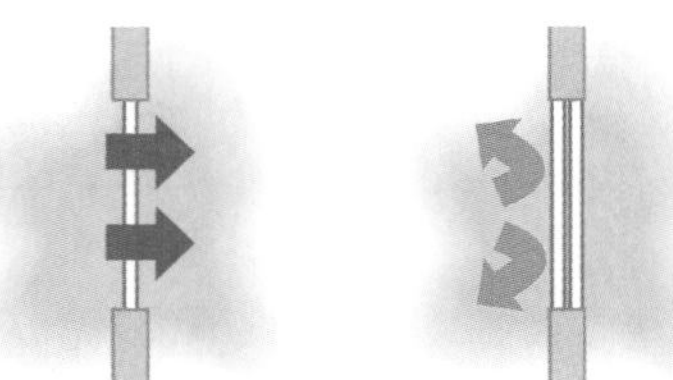

- Install windows that are either double- or triple-glazed, or use storm windows.
- Use doors that are made from good insulating materials or use a double-door system.
- Ensure that all windows and doors have tight weather seals.

lack of exposure to sunlight

- Whenever possible, face the home toward the Sun (east-west, with southern exposure) and use special designs to take advantage of solar energy.
- Use a screen of evergreen trees to protect the north side of the home from cold winds.
- Use a screen of deciduous trees to shade south-facing windows in the summer.

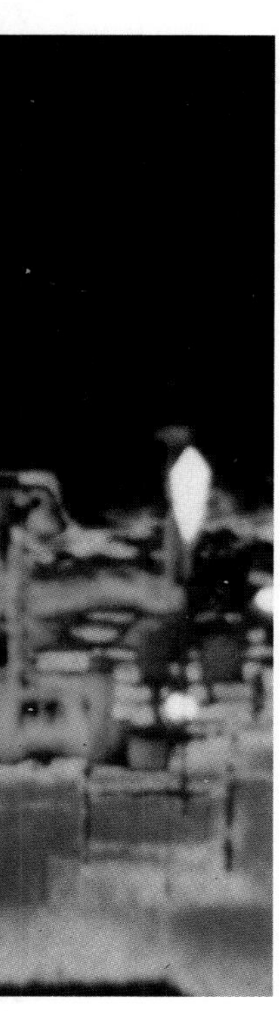

The Cost of Saving

Each energy-saving feature that is added to a building makes it more expensive. Many people cannot afford these features. And some people think that not all the features are necessary, or that they cost more than they save.

The Cost of Not Saving

We know that we must have heat for our buildings. But we also know that when we burn fuels, we add carbon dioxide to the atmosphere, increasing global warming, and we are using up a nonrenewable resource.

Understanding Concepts

1. **(a)** What are the advantages of adding heat-conservation features to a building?
   (b) How does each feature help save energy?
2. Why do we need to conserve energy?

Making Connections

3. Suggest another use for thermography and explain the benefits.

Design Challenge

Can you use any of the remedies for heat loss in your Challenge? Explain.

Debate — Heat Conservation

Statement

All new buildings constructed in our community must include the latest energy-saving features.

Point

- We waste too much energy. We are also using up precious fossil fuels. Better insulation would reduce heat loss and the amount of fuel we use.
- Although adding features will cost more initially, it will save money in the long run through lower energy expenses.

Counterpoint

- We already have good building standards. By adding more standards, all we do is increase costs, making buildings too expensive.
- Energy-conserving features may not be cost effective. There are other, less expensive ways to conserve energy, such as turning off lights when they are not needed, or turning down the thermostat at night.

What do you think?

- (4A) (8D) Are you in favour of allowing only energy-conserving building standards in your community? Would you favour some energy-conserving features, but not others? Why or why not? Research the topic thoroughly and prepare to defend your opinions in a class discussion.

2.16 Inquiry Investigation

SKILLS MENU
- Questioning
- Hypothesizing
- Planning
- Conducting
- Recording
- Analyzing
- Communicating

Controlling Heat Transfer

In our homes, schools, and other buildings, we like to keep the air temperature at a comfortable level. This requires energy—energy that costs money and that should not be wasted. To reduce the amount of energy needed to heat our buildings in the winter, we must learn how to control heat transfer. One way to do this is to make sure that our buildings have good insulation, as in **Figure 1**. Good insulators reduce heat transfer out of a building in winter and into a building in summer.

In this investigation, you will be testing the insulating abilities of various materials. Because convection and conduction transfer heat by the movement of particles, the best way to prevent heat transfer is to eliminate all particles—create a vacuum. A vacuum is difficult to create and maintain. The next best insulator is a substance that has particles that are well separated, like air. A region where air does not form a convection current is called a dead air space. Materials that include dead air spaces make good insulators. Think about where such spaces may exist when you write your hypothesis.

Question

Create a question for this investigation.

Hypothesis

1 Explain why the material you are testing should be a good or a poor insulator.

Experimental Design

2 You will design and carry out a controlled test of an insulator by measuring the rate of cooling of water in a container. The container should be surrounded by a single layer of the insulator you are testing.

- You will need a control container.
- Think about what variables you must keep constant and what variables you must change and measure.

3 Design your experiment, including a procedure, safety precautions, and a method for recording your data. (2E)

Materials

4 Create a list of materials you will use.

5 Have your teacher approve your design and materials list.

Procedure

6 Carry out your experiment and record your observations.

Figure 2
Which materials do you think are the best insulators?

SKILLS HANDBOOK: (2E) Designing an Inquiry Investigation

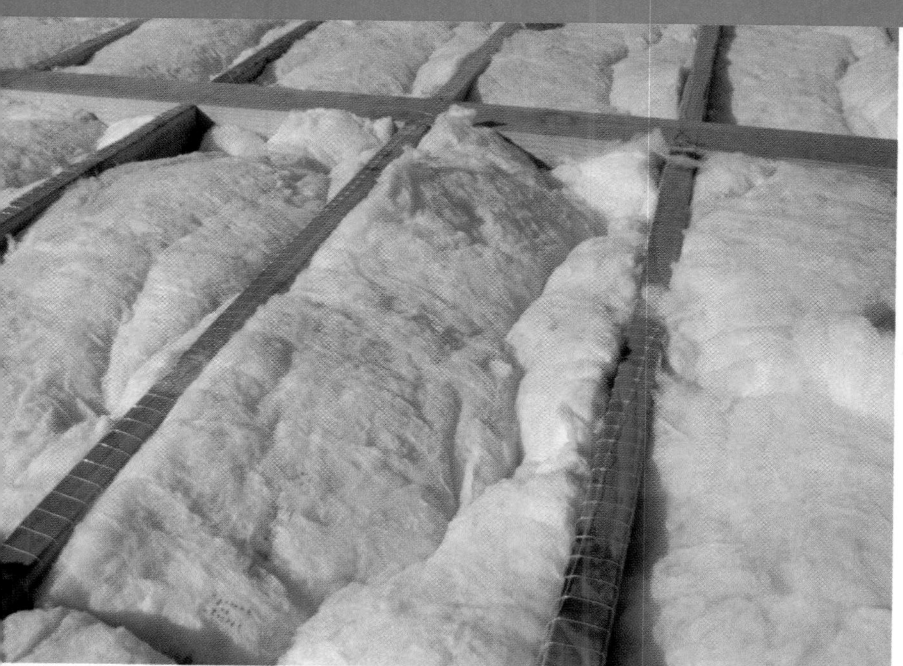

Figure 1

Insulation prevents heat flowing, and so saves energy.

Analysis

7 To analyze your results, answer the following questions.

(a) Why was a control necessary in this investigation?

(b) Identify the dependent and the independent variables in your experiment.

(c) Create a graph of temperature vs. time for the insulator you tested. (7C)

(d) Compare your graph with the graphs of other groups who tested different materials.

(e) List the materials your class tested in order of best insulator to poorest.

(f) Use the particle theory to describe the feature(s) of the best insulators.

(g) How good was your prediction in your hypothesis? Explain any variation.

Making Connections

1. Which of the materials tested by the groups in your class would be best to wear to:

(a) a Grey Cup game played in –5°C weather? Explain.

(b) a baseball game in 30°C weather? Why?

2. A thermos bottle keeps cold liquids cold and hot liquids hot. Explain **Figure 3** and use a diagram to describe how a thermos bottle prevents conduction, convection, and radiation.

Figure 3

A thermos

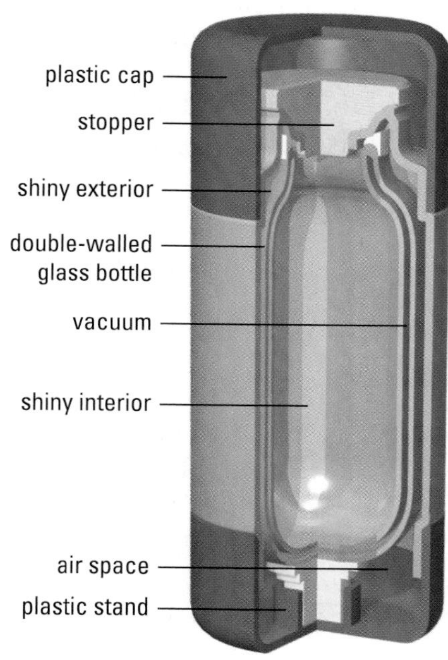

Design Challenge

Will your choice of material for the container in the swimming pool challenge affect how quickly the water can be heated?

Knowing some of the characteristics of a good insulator, should you change your choice of materials in the design of your pop can cooler?

(7C) Constructing Graphs

SKILLS MENU
- ○ Questioning
- ● Hypothesizing
- ○ Planning
- ● Conducting
- ● Recording
- ● Analyzing
- ● Communicating

Heating Various Liquids

From experience, you probably know that it is not smart to bite into an egg roll or a Jamaican patty that is fresh out of the oven, as shown in **Figure 1**. The outside may cool down fairly quickly, but the filling does not. Different substances cool down at different rates. They also heat up at different rates—but substances that heat up slowly also cool down slowly. Knowing that, which part of a Jamaican patty do you think should take longer to heat up—the pastry or the filling?

In this investigation, you will determine the heating rate of a liquid and then compare its heating rate with those of other liquids. What you learn can also be applied to solids and gases.

Materials

- apron
- safety goggles
- water
- vegetable oil
- glycerin
- hot plate (or other source of constant heat)
- Pyrex beakers
- support stand
- clamp
- thermometer
- stirring rod
- timing device
- balance
- tongs or insulating mitts

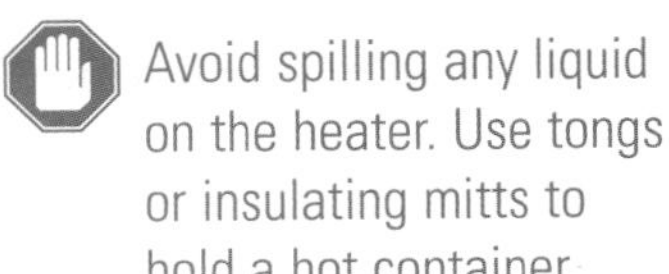

Avoid spilling any liquid on the heater. Use tongs or insulating mitts to hold a hot container.

Do not allow warm glycerin or vegatable oil to contact your skin. Do not breathe in over the warm liquids.

Question

Do all liquids change temperature at the same rate?

Hypothesis

1 (2C) Will 100 g of water need more time or less time than 100 g samples of vegetable oil or glycerin to go from 30°C to 60°C? Write a hypothesis for your prediction.

Experimental Design

This is a controlled experiment in which the mass and starting temperature of each liquid must be the same. You will measure the temperature of the liquid samples every 30 s as heat is added.

2 In your notebook, create a table to record data.

Procedure

3 (2A) Turn on the hot plate to medium so that it can heat up and reach a constant temperature while you are carrying out the next step.

4 Use a balance to measure 100 g of the liquid to be tested.

5 Place the beaker and liquid on the heater.
- As you stir with the stirring rod, observe the temperature of the liquid.
- When the temperature reaches 30°C, start taking readings of the temperature every 30 s until the temperature reaches 60°C.

(a) Record your observations.
- Carefully remove the beaker from the hot plate, using tongs or mitts. Your teacher will collect your liquid for proper disposal or storage.

SKILLS HANDBOOK: (2C) Predicting and Hypothesizing (2A) Process of Scientific Inquiry

Figure 1
Why is the filling so much hotter than the pastry, since they both came out of the oven at the same time?

Making Connections

1. Which type of substance would likely make a better heat insulator, one that heats up rapidly, or one that heats up slowly? Explain.
2. **Figure 2** shows the results of an investigation comparing the heating rates of 1.0 kg samples.
   - **(a)** What can you conclude from this investigation?
   - **(b)** Which solid would be best for storing heat received from the Sun?
   - **(c)** Some cooking pots are made with copper bottoms and aluminum sides. Does this make sense? Explain.

Exploring

3. (7F) Describe how you would perform a controlled experiment to test your answer to question 1.

Analysis

6 Analyze your results by answering the following questions.

(a) (7C) Gather data for the other liquids from your classmates. In a line graph, plot the temperature–time points for your liquid, and then, in the same graph, for the other liquids. Use a different colour for each liquid.

(b) List the liquids in order from the longest to the shortest time it took each to heat from 30°C to 60°C.

(c) What variables were controlled in this experiment? Explain.

Figure 2
Data from an investigation

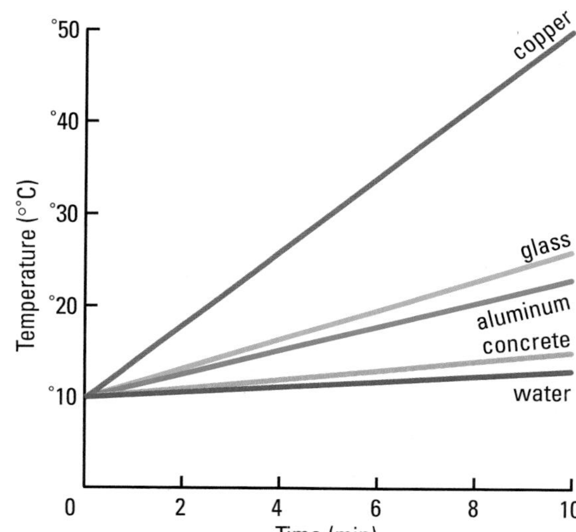

Design Challenge

When designing a control device that reacts quickly to temperature changes, should you choose materials that heat up rapidly or slowly? Could you use such a device in your Challenge?

(7C) Constructing Graphs (7F) Reflecting on Your Work

Comparing Heat Capacities

Imagine you are at a beach by a lake on a clear summer morning. The water and sand temperatures are both at 20°C. As the Sun rises higher in the sky, you notice that the temperature of the water stays about the same, but the temperature of the sand rises fairly quickly. The water and the sand have different capacities to hold heat.

As you have learned, different substances heat up (and cool down) at different rates. The **heat capacity** of a substance is a measure of the amount of heat needed to raise the temperature of the substance; it is also a measure of how much heat the substance releases as it cools. The bar graph in **Figure 1** compares the heat capacities of several substances. Notice that water has a very high heat capacity.

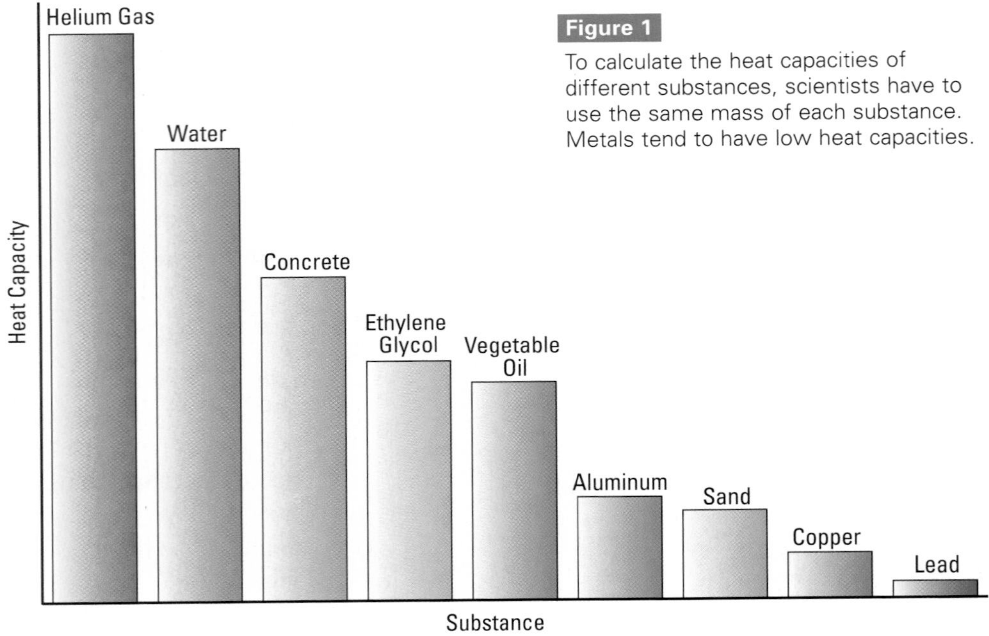

Figure 1
To calculate the heat capacities of different substances, scientists have to use the same mass of each substance. Metals tend to have low heat capacities.

How Does Water's High Heat Capacity Affect Climate?

Look at the map of Canada in **Figure 2**. The graph on the map shows the average January temperature in several cities. You might think Edmonton is so cold because it is farthest north. But why are Regina, Winnipeg, and Quebec City so cold? What makes Victoria, Toronto, and Halifax warmer in winter?

One thing the warmer cities have in common is that they are close to large bodies of water. As the weather gets colder in the fall and winter, the water takes a longer time to cool down than the land and the air do. Places such as Toronto are kept warmer by the water (Lake Ontario) than inland areas like London.

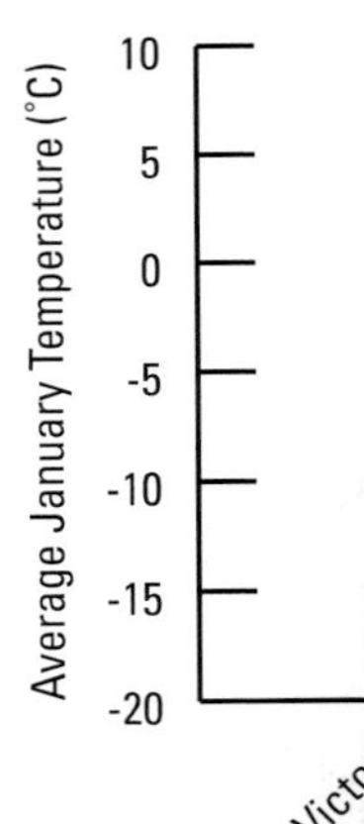

Heat Capacity and Solar Heating

How would your knowledge of radiant energy from the Sun and heat capacities of various substances help you design a solar-heated home? Look at the bar graph of heat capacities. Water and concrete have high heat capacities, so they would be good to store energy in a solar-heated home. Water could absorb radiant heat and become warm during sunny days. The water could be pumped to a storage tank, then energy in the water could be released during the night or when it is needed.

Concrete can be used in a similar way. As radiant heat from the Sun hits the concrete, the concrete slowly warms up. Then when night arrives, the energy stored in the concrete can keep the room warm as the concrete slowly releases heat.

Understanding Concepts

1. Assume you use a hot plate to heat equal masses of vegetable oil, copper, and aluminum from 20°C to 50°C. List the materials in order of fastest to slowest in reaching 50°C. Which has the highest heat capacity?
2. After a sunny day at the beach, which cools down more rapidly at night, the sand or the water? Explain.

Making Connections

3. You take a baked potato covered with aluminum foil out of a hot oven. You remove the foil, and very soon you can hold the foil in your hand, but not the potato. It remains hot for a long time. Explain why there is such a difference between the foil and the potato.

Exploring

4. (2E) Design an experiment to show that a substance that takes a long time to heat up also takes a long time to cool down.

Reflecting

5. What are some of the problems of harnessing solar energy in Canada?

Design Challenge

Based on what you have learned about the heat capacities of various substances, how could you modify your greenhouse and pool designs to prevent the internal temperature from dropping quickly at night? How could this information help you choose material for the design of your pop can cooler?

Figure 2

Average January temperature across Canada

SKILLS MENU
- ○ Questioning
- ○ Hypothesizing
- ○ Planning
- ● Conducting
- ● Recording
- ● Analyzing
- ● Communicating

Using Mechanical Ways to Produce Heat

Have you ever received a skid burn on your knees or elbows after falling on a gym floor? During the skid, heat was produced by the friction between the floor and your skin, as shown in **Figure 1**. Friction is a force that occurs between objects in motion that are touching. Friction can occur between solid objects. It can also occur between a fluid and a solid, such as a boat in water or the space shuttle in air as the shuttle lands.

Friction is just one example of a mechanical force, a force caused by objects in contact with each other. In this investigation you will study four mechanical ways of producing heat, including friction.

Question

What are some ways of producing heat using mechanical means?

Hypothesis

Mechanical forces can produce heat.

Experimental Design

In this investigation you will explore four ways of producing heat by mechanical means: friction, distortion (bending), percussion (pounding), and compression (squeezing).

Materials

- apron
- safety goggles
- protective gloves
- metal coat hanger
- wooden block
- clamp
- hammer
- bicycle pump (or fire syringe)

Be careful when working with sharp objects. Use bare hands only to test an object's temperature.

Make sure the wood is secure before pounding. Do not use your hand to secure the wood.

Procedure

Part 1: Friction

1 Open your hands and hold your palms together. Rub your hands together about 20 to 25 times. Observe what happens when you press your hands closer together as you rub.

(a) Record your observations.

Part 2: Distortion

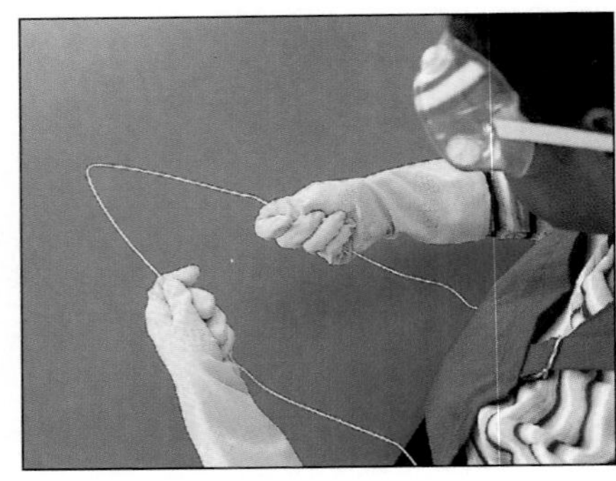

2 Use the palm of your hand to test the temperature of a metal coat hanger.

- Put on your gloves and bend the hanger back and forth quickly about 10 to 12 times.
- Test the temperature of the region that was bent.

(a) Record your observations.

SKILLS HANDBOOK: 2E Designing an Inquiry Investigation 2D Identifying Variables and Controls

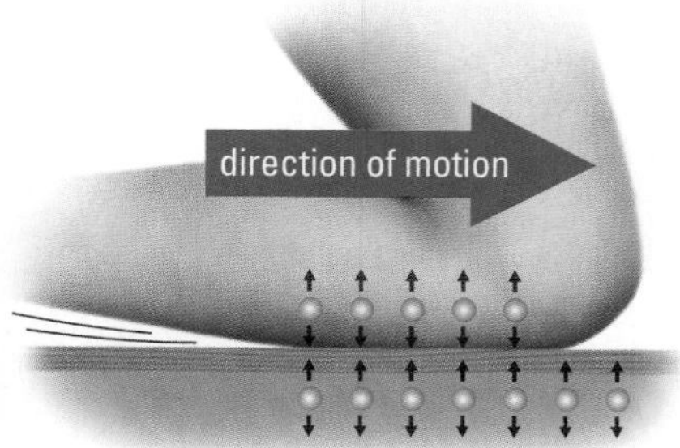

Figure 1
As two substances move past each other, the particles of one substance pull on the particles of the other substance. This causes resistance to motion and increases the motion of the particles in each substance, which increases the temperature.

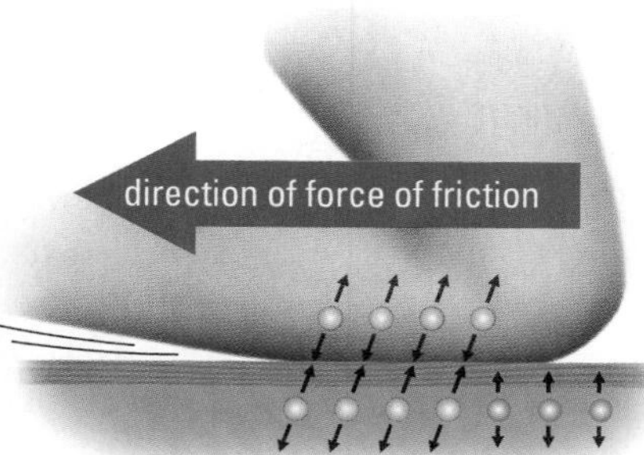

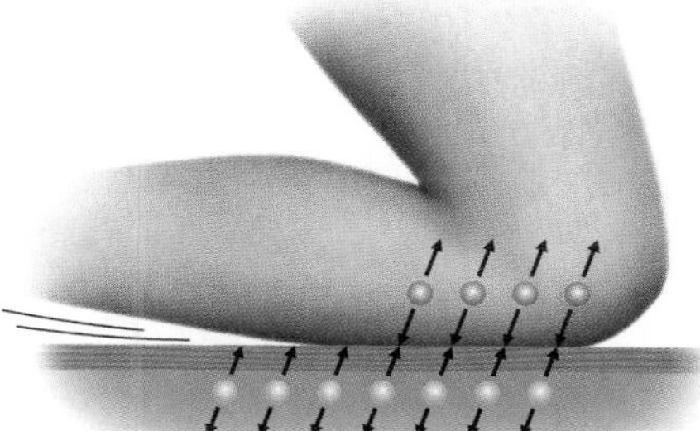

Making Connections

1. Give two examples from outside your school of where you might find each of the four mechanical means of producing heat.
2. Motorcyclists often wear shiny, smooth leather, especially when riding at highway speeds. Explain why.
3. A dentist's drill requires water to be sprayed on to it when it is being used. Why is the water needed?

Exploring

4. Choose one of the mechanical (2E) ways of producing heat and design a controlled experiment to investigate it. What would be the independent variable? (2D) What variables would you have to control?

Part 3: Percussion

3 Use the palm of your hand to test the temperature of a wooden block.
- Put on your gloves and use the hammer to pound the same place on the block about 15 to 20 times.
- Test the temperature of the wood where you pounded it.

(a) Record your observations.

(b) Was heat the only type of energy you observed?

Part 4: Compression

4 Feel the valve of the bicycle pump and test its temperature.
- Compress the air in the pump by pumping hard.
- Test the temperature of the valve again.

(a) Record your observations.

Analysis

5 Analyze your results by answering the following questions.

(a) Use the particle theory to explain why the temperature of the surface of an object can increase because of friction.

2.20

Producing Heat

The Sun is our most important source of energy. However, energy from the Sun can be used to provide heat directly only in the daytime in clear weather. Even then the Sun's energy is not as convenient to use for heat as some other sources. An energy source is a material or method that provides energy we can use.

Energy sources can be grouped as renewable or nonrenewable. Renewable energy sources are those that are not destroyed in the process of being used; examples are solar energy and electricity produced from the moving water of rivers. Nonrenewable energy sources are gradually being used up and one day may run out entirely; examples are coal and oil. In the last few hundred years, people have used nonrenewable resources at an increasing rate.

We are now using wood more quickly than it can be replaced. Would you consider wood renewable or nonrenewable? As you read about examples of energy sources, think about whether they are renewable or nonrenewable.

Figure 1

The friction of spinning tires on the road surface produces lots of heat and some sound. The heat causes the air inside the tires to expand and inflate the tires. The energy transformation is: mechanical energy → heat and sound.

Heat from Mechanical Energy

In friction, distortion, percussion, and compression, mechanical energy changes into heat and perhaps some sound energy. In ancient times, people used friction between solid objects, such as two pieces of wood, to light fires. In modern times, we have created many more uses for friction (**Figure 1**).

Heat from Chemical Energy

Fuels such as oil, wood, coal, and natural gas have energy stored in them. This kind of energy is called chemical energy. Through the chemical process of burning, the energy is released as heat (**Figure 2**).

Figure 2

As the wood burns, chemical energy stored in the wood provides the heat needed to roast these hot dogs. The energy transformation is: chemical energy → light and heat.

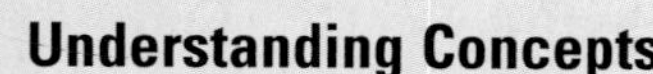

Figure 3

Electricity flowing through this burner produces heat. The energy transformation is:
electrical energy → light and heat.

Heat from Electrical Energy

Electrical energy can change into heat, but first we must produce the electricity. There is more than one way to produce electricity. The energy in moving water can be used to produce electricity. It is also produced at generating stations by burning fuels such as coal and natural gas.

Once produced, electricity is sent through wires to our homes, where it is changed to heat in stoves, dryers, and many other appliances. For example, in a stove (**Figure 3**), an electric current passes through an element made of a material that resists the flow of electricity. The resistance causes the element to heat up. The greater the current, the hotter the element becomes until it is red hot (in a stove) or white hot (in a light bulb). Like other forms of energy, electrical energy ends up as heat.

Heat from Nuclear Energy

Tiny particles of materials are called atoms, and at the centre of each atom is the nucleus. Energy stored inside the nucleus is called nuclear energy. This energy can be changed into other forms of energy, such as heat, through processes called fusion and fission. In nuclear fusion, some small nuclei (plural of nucleus) join to form larger nuclei. In this process, some mass changes into energy. This is the way the Sun produces so much energy.

In nuclear fission, nuclei of a substance such as uranium split into smaller nuclei. Again, some mass changes into energy. Technologists use this process to produce heat at nuclear generating stations (**Figure 4**). The heat is used to create steam under pressure, and the steam causes large turbines to spin. As the turbines spin, both electrical energy and waste heat are produced. In both fusion and fission, the final form of energy produced is heat.

Understanding Concepts

1. List three ways that heat can be produced. Indicate whether the method is renewable or nonrenewable. Give an example of how each is used in your daily life.
2. State two examples, other than those given here, in which heat is produced from:
   (a) mechanical energy
   (b) chemical energy
   (c) electrical energy
3. Where does the electrical energy come from for use in your home? in your school?

Making Connections

4. Tungsten is an important substance often used in light bulbs. Look at the table of melting and boiling points on page 21. Use the information there to explain why tungsten is a good substance to use in light bulbs.

Exploring

5. Write a science fiction story about a technological breakthrough in which a totally new and cheap source of heat is discovered. How would it affect our environment, business, and industry?

Reflecting

6. Someone once called heat the "graveyard" of forms of energy. Why is that a good description of heat?

Figure 4

A nuclear generating station produces electrical energy from nuclear energy. The energy transformations are:
nuclear energy → heat (to heat water) → mechanical energy (of the spinning turbine) → electrical energy and heat.

Design Challenge

Describe how your Challenge design can be applied to help reduce our need for nonrenewable resources.

Heat Pollution

When you use an electric light bulb, only about 5% of the electrical energy becomes light energy. The rest becomes wasted heat. This is just one example of waste heat. All of our appliances, vehicles, factories, and buildings generate waste heat.

Because we use so much energy, there is more waste heat being produced than ever before. This waste heat is called **heat pollution**, because, like chemical pollution, it affects our environment.

Heat Pollution in and near Cities

The average air temperature in and near a big city is almost always a few degrees warmer than in the countryside several kilometres away. Buildings, roads, sidewalks, and cars absorb solar energy. Also, a lot of waste heat is produced by everything that uses energy, such as cars, trucks, heating, and lighting. Even the waste water from a city includes waste heat. The waste heat from all these factors combines to cause the air temperature in a city to rise.

In the summer, as the air gets hotter, air conditioning systems also produce waste heat. This creates a feedback loop: people react to the increase in temperature by turning up their air conditioning, which generates even more waste heat.

(a) Identify three sources of waste heat in the city in **Figure 1**.

(b) Explain how these sources produce waste heat.

Heat Pollution in Industries

Imagine how much water it would take to fill your science classroom. Now imagine a way to heat that much water so that in just five seconds its temperature goes up by 10°C! That is what happens at an electric generating station where fossil fuel (coal, oil, or natural gas) is burned to produce electricity.

At an electric generating station, like the one in **Figure 2**, about 60% of the chemical energy in the fossil fuel becomes waste heat.

Similar waste heat occurs at big industries, such as steel mills or pulp and paper mills, located along rivers and lakes. In a steel mill, for example, raw materials are heated in a blast furnace with temperatures as high as 1650°C. Large quantities of water are used to cool the finished metal.

(c) Why would an industry use water to cool heated materials rather than another substance?

(d) Which industries in your community would use a lot of water in their production process?

Figure 1
Waste heat from cities and industry raises the temperature of the air and of water in lakes and rivers.

Waste Heat and Wildlife

When hot water used in industry and electricity generation is discharged directly into a lake, it raises the temperature of the surrounding water, as shown in **Figure 1**. The temperature increase also reduces the water's oxygen content. This can disrupt the habitat of marine plants and animals. Living things are adapted to certain conditions in their habitat. Changes in habitat can be fatal. Some species, such as lake trout, need cold water and cannot survive increases in water temperature. If the water temperature rises, they must move out of the area or die. If other species that prefer warm water and require less oxygen can reach the warmer water, they may replace the cold-water species. Large-mouthed bass and pike are fish species that prefer warmer water.

(e) Suppose an electric generating station that has been running for years has to shut down for one week for repairs. What would happen to the water in a week?

(f) Describe what might happen to the surrounding marine life.

Waste Heat and Agriculture

Temperature increases can affect field crops and orchards. For example, the change could create a longer growing season. Changes in temperature might also affect precipitation patterns, for example by reducing the amount of snow that falls. Without snow cover the soil heats up more quickly when the sun shines. During a warm spell in winter, as the soil warms, plants and other organisms in the soil might be fooled into thinking it is spring. Snow is also a source of ground water in the spring, which plants can draw on with their roots.

(g) How would a longer growing season and changes in precipitation patterns affect a farmer's choices of what to grow?

(h) What might happen if plants and organisms are fooled into thinking it's spring?

Figure 2

a Steel Mill
Steel mills pump their hot coolant water into ponds, where the waste heat escapes into the air. The pond water is cleaned and reused.

b Electric Generating Station
Every second, more than 30 000 L of water from the lake pass through this electric generating station. The water takes away the waste heat and comes back to the lake almost 10°C hotter.

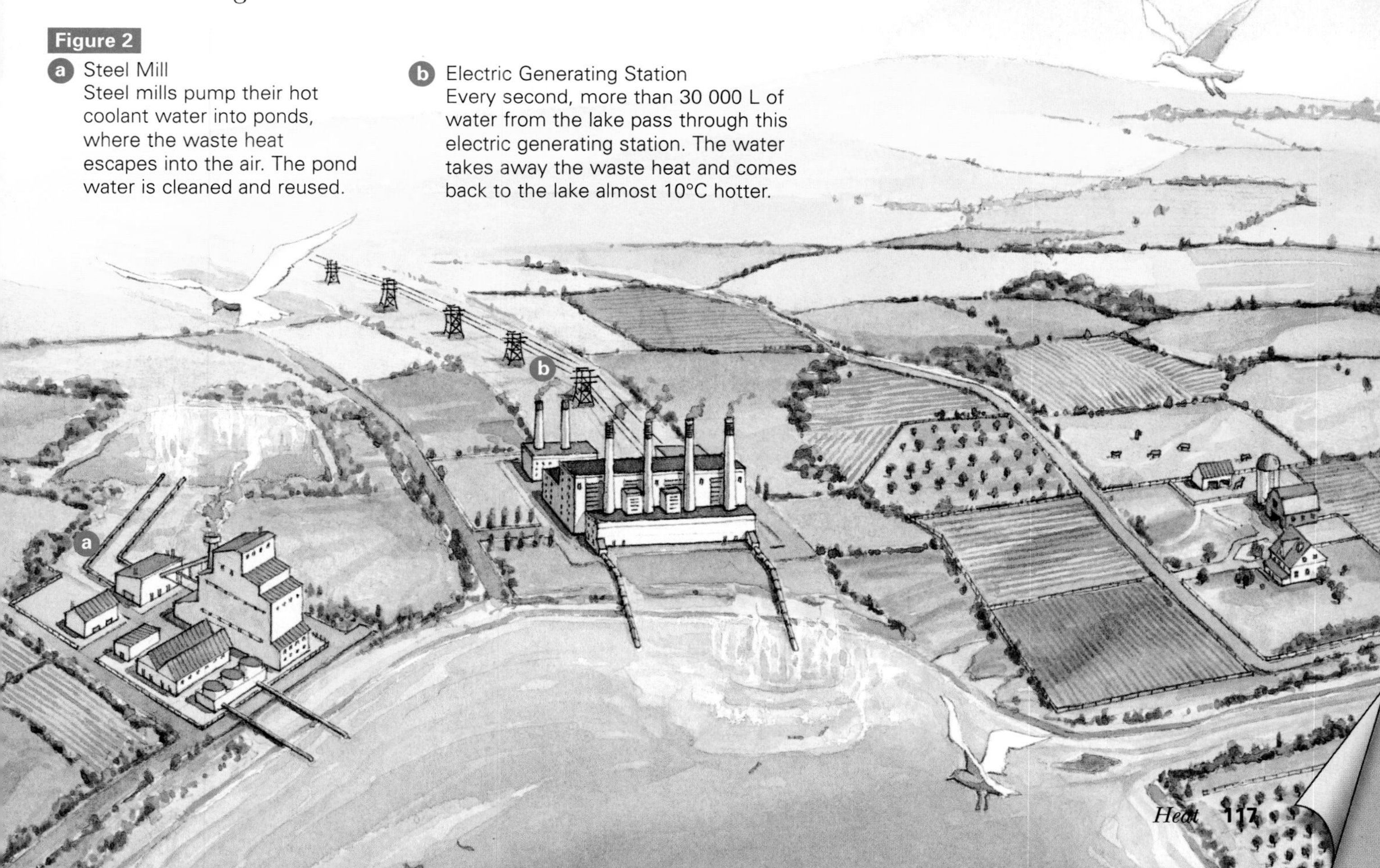

How Much Energy Is Wasted?

An incandescent light bulb has an efficiency of only 5%, as shown in **Table 1**. This means only 5% of the energy input (electricity) becomes useful output (light). The other 95% becomes waste heat. Knowing the efficiencies of various devices may help you decide which device to use.

(i) Look at the efficiencies of the devices in **Table 1**. In each case, what percentage of the energy used is wasted heat?

(j) Why is an electric heater rated at 100% efficiency?

Table 1: Efficiencies of Some Devices

Device	Efficiency
incandescent light	5%
fluorescent light	20%
automobile	25%
fossil-fuel electric generating station	40%
wind generator	55%
gas furnace	85%
falling-water generating station	95%
large electric motor	95%
electric generator	98%
electric heater	100%

Reducing Waste in Mechanical Systems

The moving parts of any mechanical system add to heat pollution, mainly because of friction. This happens in machinery, in motors of all sizes, and in all vehicles. The friction of moving parts, such as the wheels and motor parts, is reduced by making the parts smooth and using a substance that reduces friction, called a **lubricant**. Oil is a lubricant.

Another form of friction, called air resistance, pushes against moving vehicles. Cars, trucks, and other vehicles can be designed to reduce air resistance, for example, by using a curved shape that goes through the air smoothly.

Reducing friction and air resistance helps to reduce heat pollution, as the less friction in the moving parts of a vehicle, the less fuel the vehicle must burn to operate.

(k) Look at the vehicles in **Figure 3**. What features of each model would make it more efficient in using the chemical energy from gasoline?

(l) What other methods could be used to reduce the amount of gasoline used by vehicles?

Figure 3
Two possible vehicles

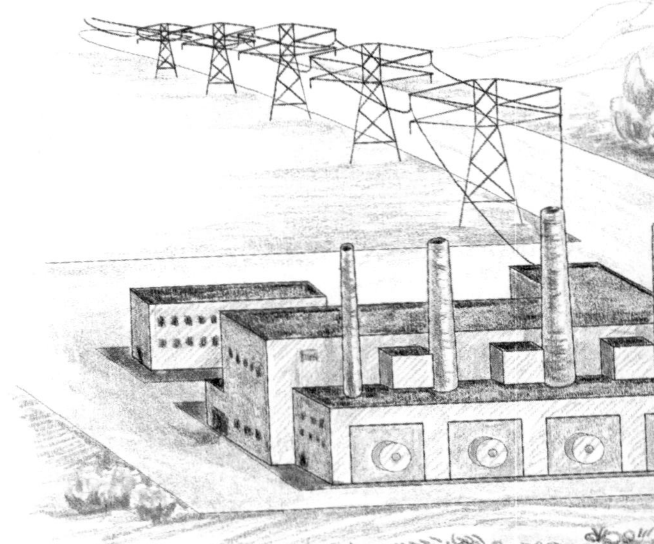

Figure 4
Commercial greenhouses could use hot water from a generating plant to help maintain a constant temperature.

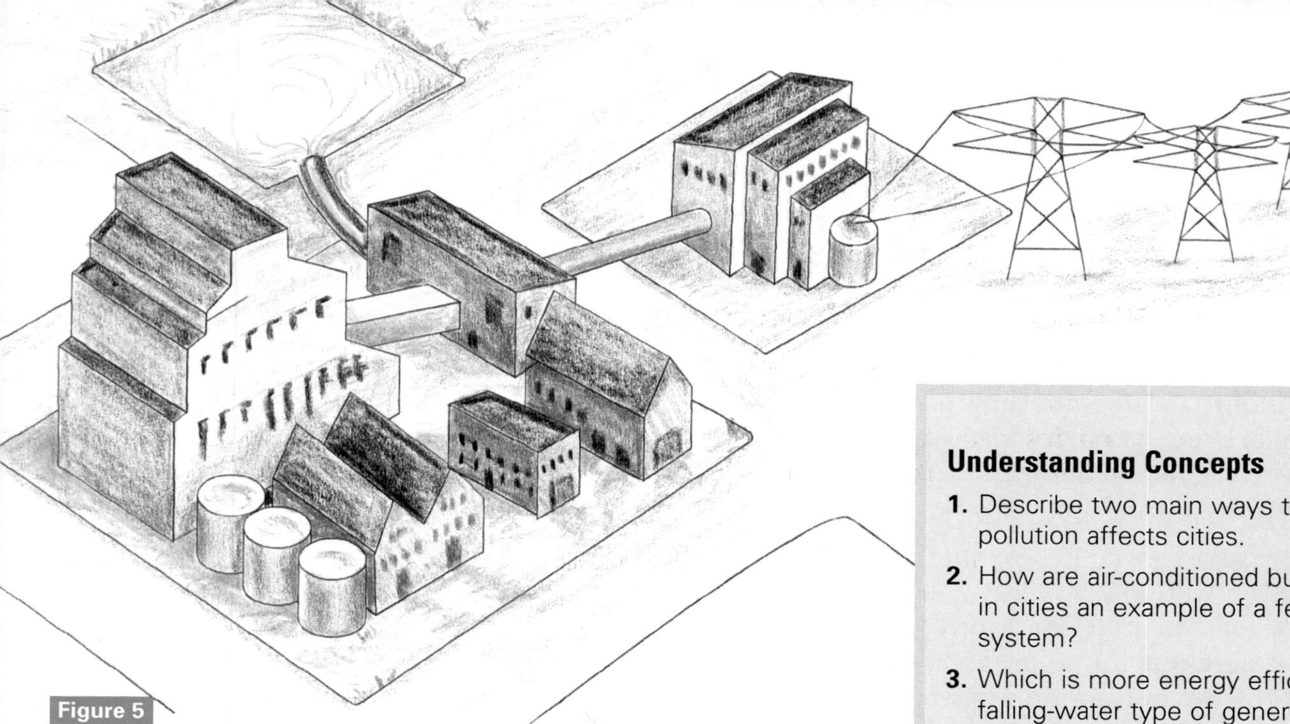

Figure 5
A steel plant could use waste heat to generate electricity.

Recycling Waste Heat

Waste heat doesn't need to be wasted. Heat from generating stations could be used in industrial processes and to heat nearby buildings. The process of providing electricity and heat at the same time is called **cogeneration**. **Figure 4** shows how waste heat from an electric generating station can be used by a nearby industry. **Figure 5** shows how an industry can burn fuel to provide the heat it normally needs and use any extra heat to produce electricity that can be sold to the local power company.

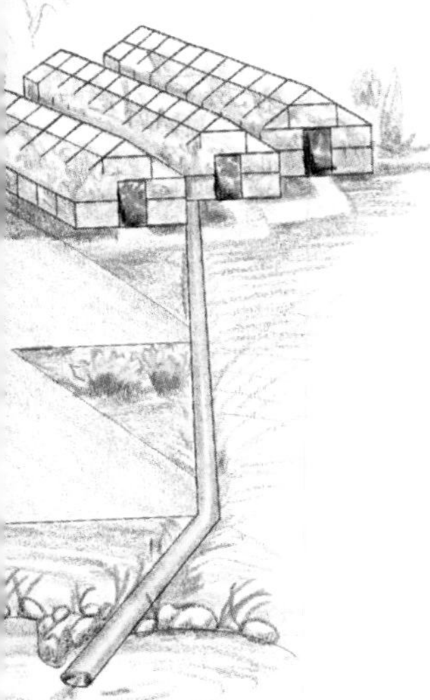

(m) Suggest another way waste heat from an electric generating station could be used.

(n) It is possible to heat homes using waste heat from generating stations or industry, but the homes would have to be close to the source of heat. List some economic, social, and environmental advantages and disadvantages of using waste heat in this way.

Understanding Concepts

1. Describe two main ways that heat pollution affects cities.
2. How are air-conditioned buildings in cities an example of a feedback system?
3. Which is more energy efficient, a falling-water type of generating station or a fossil-fuel one? Explain.

Making Connections

4. If you were designing a car, what (3D) could you do to ensure that friction and air resistance were kept to a minimum?
5. **(a)** Waterfowl (birds that spend much of their time in or on the water) need open, unfrozen water to survive. How could waste heat from cities affect the habitat and behaviour of waterfowl?
   (b) Most waterfowl eat fish or small animals that feed on water plants. How might the change in waterfowl behaviour affect other living things near the city? Explain.

Design Challenge

Will your greenhouse or swimming pool model generate excess heat? What could you add to your design to recycle some of that extra energy for other purposes? What could you do with your pop can cooler to keep it from being exposed to waste heat?

Solar Heating

Solar energy is important for life on Earth. It may become even more important to us as our need for energy increases. Solar energy can be used to heat places where we need to warm water or air, such as homes, larger buildings, and swimming pools.

There are two basic ways of using solar energy to provide heat. One way is passive; the other is active. As you read about these ways, think about why the passive way is much cheaper to set up than the active way.

Passive Solar Heating

In passive solar heating, the word "passive" means that the system lets the solar energy in and prevents much heat from getting out. Passive solar heating is not expensive and is easy to maintain. Most homes use passive solar heating simply by allowing sunlight to shine in the windows. **Figure 1** shows a house where passive solar heating has been planned.

The Greenhouse Effect

Windows are important in solar-heated homes as well as in other structures, such as greenhouses. The **greenhouse effect** is the process of trapping radiant heat inside a structure. The name came from the greenhouse, where glass is used to trap heat. The greenhouse effect is shown in **Figure 2**.

Figure 1
Window treatment and building materials are very important in a home designed to make best use of passive solar heating.

Sun's rays in summer
i wide overhangs: prevent the Sun's rays from enterin in the summer, when the Sun is higher in the sky, bu not in the winter
a small windows facing north: reduce heat loss in winter
b window shutters: prevent heat transfer. In summer can be closed during the day and opened at night; in winter opened during the day and closed at night.
c good insulation: prevents heat transfer through the walls
d walls with a high heat capacity: absorb radiant energy during the day and emit it later
e evergreen trees and shrubs on the north: provide shelter from the cold north wind in winter
f flooring that absorbs radiant energy: darker colours absorb more sunlight in winter; substances with high heat capacity store the energy and release it at night
g deciduous trees on the south: provide shade in the summer but lose their leaves in winter, allowing the Sun's rays to enter the windows

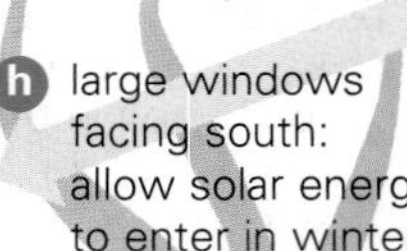
h large windows facing south: allow solar energy to enter in winter

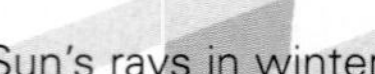
Sun's rays in winter

Figure 2

The greenhouse effect

(a) Radiant energy from the Sun is made up mainly of waves that can travel through glass.

(c) At the higher temperature, the objects emit their own radiant energy, but it is composed of waves that cannot get through the glass. This trapped radiant energy helps keep the greenhouse warm, even in winter.

(b) Plants and other objects in the greenhouse absorb the radiant energy. This causes their temperature to increase.

Active Solar Heating

Another way to heat buildings is active solar heating. The word “active” means that the system absorbs as much solar energy as possible and distributes it throughout the building. **Figure 3** shows an active system. An active solar-heating system usually requires another source of energy besides the Sun, at least as a backup during times when there is little sunshine.

Figure 3

One type of active solar-heating system. In the solar collector for this system, radiant energy passes through a clear plastic or glass covering and is absorbed by a dark-coloured collector plate.

(a) Heat from the water is transferred to the air, which is pumped through the house using a forced-air system. The water is pumped back to the solar collector.

(d) Radiant energy from the Sun is absorbed by a solar collector on the roof. A steep roof allows the Sun's rays to hit more directly in winter months.

water pipes

insulation: dark material absorbs light

(b) The hot water is pumped through pipes to a storage tank.

(c) The absorbed energy is used to heat up a liquid, usually water.

Understanding Concepts

1. List several advantages of passive solar heating in homes.
2. How is the greenhouse effect used in passive solar heating?
3. Figure 3 shows the water storage tank in the basement. Would the attic be a better location for this tank? Why or why not?
4. What is the function of the insulation in the solar collector?

Making Connections

5. What special considerations would be important in a solar-heated home in your own region? Assume no other sources of heat are allowed.
6. (6C) Draw diagrams showing how solar heating could be used in two of the following places: apartment buildings, schools, hospitals, barns, industrial buildings.

Exploring

7. Describe and evaluate solar heating in your area.
   - **(a)** (4A) Research how many hours of sunshine there are on an average day in midsummer and midwinter.
   - **(b)** Describe how climate affects the type of solar heating suitable for buildings in your area.

Reflecting

8. How does knowing about the heat capacity of various substances assist an architect in designing a solar house?

Design Challenge

Would an active or a passive solar system work best in the Challenge design for the swimming pool? for the greenhouse?

SKILLS HANDBOOK: (6C) Scientific & Technical Drawing (4A) Research Skills

Design Challenge

SKILLS MENU
- Identify a Problem
- Planning
- Building
- Testing
- Recording
- Evaluating
- Communicating

Design and Build a Device That Controls or Uses Heat

All life on Earth depends on heat. If plants and animals get too hot or too cold, they cannot survive. In nature, we can find many examples of animals that keep a healthy temperature by controlling heat transfer. Humans use what they learn from nature to develop technologies to control heat.

Figure 1
Warm pop isn't as pleasant as cold pop—but sometimes a fridge isn't handy.

1 A Device That Delays Heat Transfer

Problem situation

We use appliances to cook food and to keep it cool. Ovens, refrigerators, and similar devices will not waste nearly as much energy if they are designed to prevent heat transfer to or from the outside.

Design brief

- Design a container that will keep a cold pop can as cool as possible from breakfast until lunchtime.

Design criteria

- The container must fit inside a standard lunch box.
- The pop can should be 355 mL. It should start at refrigerator temperature.

2 A Swimming Pool Heated by the Sun

Problem situation

As the world's population increases and our standard of living rises, we use more energy. But many of our sources of energy are not renewable, for example oil and gas. Using oil or gas heaters to warm a swimming pool is wasteful.

Design brief

- Design a controllable device that uses only energy from the Sun to heat the water for a model swimming pool to 25°C.

Design criteria

- The device should work either in sunlight or light from a bright lamp.
- The model pool must hold at least 250 mL of water, all of it usable for swimming.
- The water must be cold water from the tap.
- The device must be safe for swimmers.

Figure 2
A lot of energy is needed to heat water in a swimming pool.

3 An Environment to Protect Plants

Problem situation

Every year, more people in Canada discover the advantages of growing their own plants for food or simply for beauty. But the growing season in Canada is short, because many plants die when struck by frost.

Design brief

- Design a greenhouse or other environment that would allow a plant to grow even when outdoor temperatures are low. The environment must also resist overheating, to prevent plants from dying from too much heat.

Design criteria

- The environment must support at least one plant.
- To avoid energy waste, only energy from the Sun, either direct or stored, can be used.
- The temperature in the environment should remain fairly constant. It should not drop below 10°C, even if outside temperatures are lower than 10°C for five hours. It should not rise above 30°C, even in bright sunshine on a warm day (25°C).

Figure 3 This greenhouse protects tropical plants from the outside cold.

Assessment

Your model will be assessed according to how well you:

Process
- Understand the problem
- Develop a safe plan
- Choose and safely use appropriate materials, tools, and equipment
- Test and record results
- Evaluate the sustainability of your model, including cost, health, and social implications, as well as suggestions for improvement

Communicate
- Prepare a presentation
- Use correct terms
- Write clear descriptions of the steps you took in building and testing your model
- Explain clearly how your model solves the problem
- Make an accurate technical drawing for your model

Produce
- Meet the design criteria with your model
- Use your chosen materials effectively
- Construct your model
- Solve the identified problem

When preparing to build or test a design, have your plan approved by your teacher befr you begin.

Unit 2 Summary

Reflecting

- Reflect on the ideas and questions presented in the Unit Overview and in the Getting Started. How can you connect what you have done and learned in this unit with those ideas and questions? (To review, check the sections indicated in this Summary.)
- Revise your answers to the Reflecting questions in ❶, ❷, ❸ and the questions you created in the Getting Started. How has your thinking changed?
- What new questions do you have? How will you answer them?

Understanding Concepts

- describe how thermometers operate using expansion and contraction 2.3
- explain matter and moving particles 2.5, 2.7, 2.8, 2.10
- distinguish between temperature and heat 2.5
- observe energy transfers from hotter objects to cooler ones by convection, conduction, or radiation 2.5, 2.8, 2.9, 2.10, 2.12
- describe how adding or removing heat from a substance may change its state 2.6, 2.7
- observe how substances heat up and cool down at different rates, depending on their capacity to store heat 2.17, 2.18

Applying Skills

- create a scale of temperatures, using experience and deduction 2.1
- plan and conduct an investigation to identify the property of matter that explains how a thermometer works 2.2
- describe and investigate the characteristics and changes of the states of matter 2.5, 2.6, 2.7
- observe and experiment with the properties of a convection current 2.8
- design, plan, and carry out an investigation to determine which solids are the best heat conductors 2.10
- communicate ideas, procedures, and results of investigations of heat transfer by convection, conduction, and radiation 2.8, 2.10, 2.12
- investigate and explain the use of insulating materials to control heat transfer 2.15, 2.16

- investigate and compare the heat capacities of various substances 2.17, 2.18
- classify mechanical, chemical, electrical, and nuclear ways of producing heat and indicate whether they are renewable or nonrenewable 2.19, 2.20

Making Connections

- observe how plants and animals are sensitive to changes in temperature and depend on heat for survival 2.4
- describe how convection currents affect weather 2.9
- identify some careers that require knowledge of heat and temperature 2.11
- explain how Earth's water cycle is a series of heat transfers 2.13

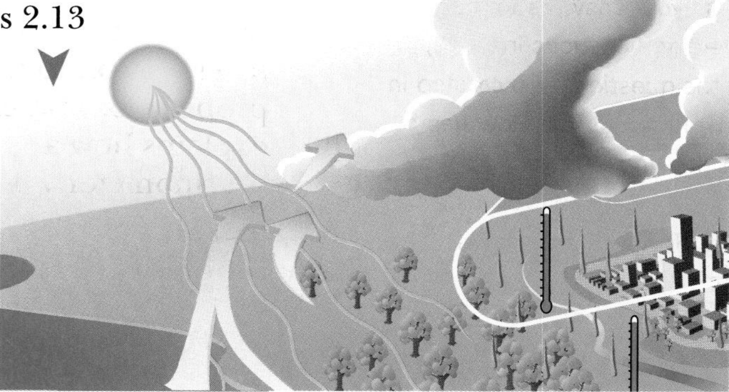

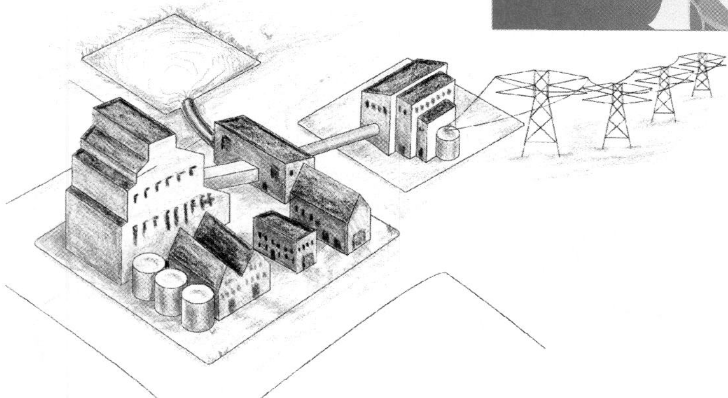

- explain how homes can be heated with hot-water systems or forced-air systems 2.14
- identify ways that waste heat can be reduced through energy-saving measures and recycled to reduce the amount of heat pollution 2.15, 2.21
- describe the use of solar energy to heat buildings, using either passive or active systems 2.22

- understand and use the following terms:

boiling point	heating curve
cogeneration	liquid
conduction	lubricant
contraction	melting point
convection	particle theory
convection current	radiant energy
expansion	radiation
gas	solid
greenhouse effect	temperature
heat	thermocouple
heat capacity	thermometer
heat conductor	thermostat
heat pollution	

Unit 2 Review

Understanding Concepts

1. When Marco first enters a swimming pool, he thinks the water is cold. After a couple of minutes in the pool, he thinks the temperature is just fine. Why does he change his mind?
2. Describe how a liquid thermometer and a thermocouple are the same and how they are different.
3. Vegetables are being cooked in a pot on the stove. Use the particle theory to explain why the lid starts to jump up and down.
4. A boy who feels ill touches his forehead with his hand to see if he has a fever. Will he be able to tell? Explain.
5. Explain why a liquid clinical thermometer has
   (a) a small range of Celsius degrees;
   (b) a narrow bore just above the bulb.
6. Describe situations where a solid thermometer would be more useful than a liquid one.
7. Describe how you and your class could act out Brownian motion.
8. Use the particle theory to explain expansion and contraction of a solid when its temperature is changed.
9. Is it possible to add heat to a material without changing its temperature? Explain.
10. Identify the three states of matter and give two examples of substances in each state.
11. Use the particle theory to explain why water expands when it changes from the liquid state to the gas state.
12. In which of the three states of matter does convection occur? Why can convection not occur in the other state(s) of matter?
13. A magician at the fall fair had five copper pennies like those in **Figure 1**, each from a different year. She put the pennies into a hat and asked someone in the audience to pick out one coin. Then she said, "Pass the coin around so everyone can see the year on it. Then put the coin back into the hat, and I'll try to pick out the same coin." When she reached into the hat, there was a brief pause and then she pulled out the correct penny. How did she do it?

Figure 1

14. What happens to the average energy of the particles in milk when the milk is taken from the refrigerator and begins to warm up? Use the concept of heat transfer and the particle theory to explain your answer.
15. What colour of clothing should be worn to keep cool on a hot, sunny day in summer? Explain your answer.
16. Give some examples of materials that slow heat transfer. In each case, state an example of where the material is used.
17. Describe how mechanical energy can be changed into heat.
18. State the type of energy that is the source of heat in each situation described below.
    (a) A dentist's high-speed drill becomes hot when drilling teeth.
    (b) Ancient people used flint, a very brittle type of stone, to start fires.
    (c) Water from Earth's oceans and lakes evaporates, forming clouds.

19. Explain why wearing loose clothing on a cold day might provide good insulation. What else might be needed?

20. A down jacket temporarily loses some of its insulating ability when it becomes wet.
    (a) Explain why this occurs.
    (b) What would you do, and why, to restore much of the jacket's insulating ability?

21. Which is better for keeping food and drinks cool in a picnic cooler: water at 0°C or ice at 0°C? Explain your answer.

22. Look at the experimental setup in **Figure 2**. The water in both beakers starts at the same temperature and the hot plates produce the same amount of energy. Will the water boil first in the beaker on the left or on the right? Use the words "particles," "average energy," and "heat" in your explanation.

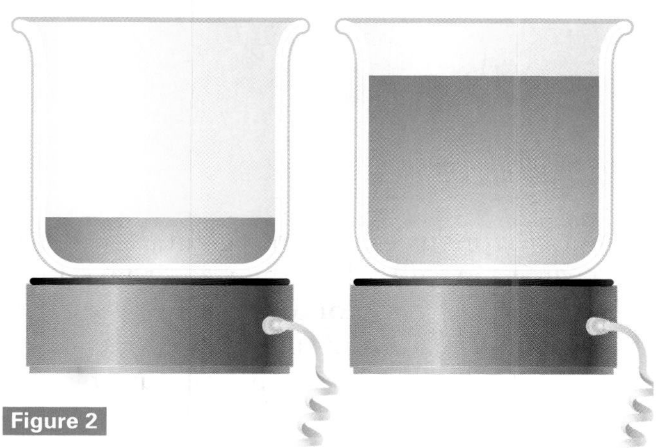

Figure 2

Applying Skills

23. Explain the significance of these temperatures:
    (a) 100°C (b) 37°C (c) 0°C

24. Make up a poem or short story about heat and temperature using words in the vocabulary list on page 125.

25. Describe how a bimetallic strip could be used to make a thermometer. How would you calibrate it? Would it be very accurate? Explain.

26. Suppose you are helping someone find a house to buy.
    (a) What questions related to heat could you ask to be sure the buyer is getting an energy-efficient home?
    (b) Identify the steps that you could take to find answers to the questions in (a).

27. Describe a controlled experiment to determine which method of cooking corn or potatoes would require the least amount of energy.

28. A consumer magazine hires you to test kettles used to heat water to see which should be recommended.
    (a) What would you test?
    (b) How would you perform a controlled investigation to test those factors?
    (c) Design data tables for the tests.

29. In an investigation equal masses of two liquids were allowed to cool from the same starting temperature. The results are shown in **Figure 3**. From the graphs, describe what you can about:
    (a) the change of state of each liquid
    (b) the heat capacity of each liquid

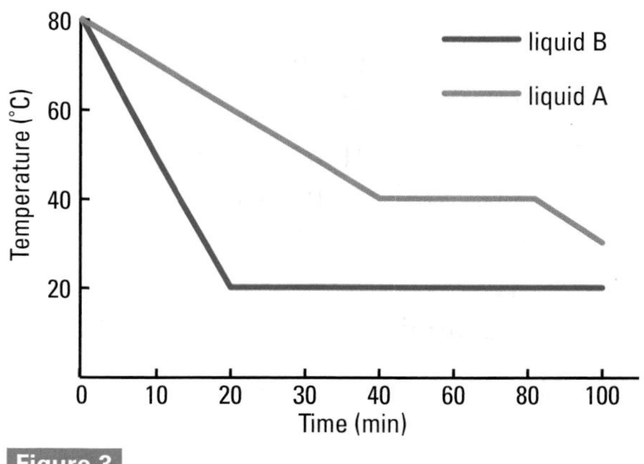

Figure 3

30. Design a home for a tropical climate. Include reasons for the design features.

31. Plan an investigation to determine how good snow is as an insulator.

32. Using terms you've learned in this unit, design a concept map that illustrates heat transfers.

Making Connections

33. State one useful application for each of the observations listed below:
    (a) Liquid mercury expands when heated and contracts when cooled.
    (b) Metals conduct heat better than glass does.
    (c) Some metals expand more than others when heated.
34. How does thermal underwear help prevent the loss of body heat?
35. Use the particle theory to explain why steam causes a more serious burn than hot water.
36. If you are planning a winter hiking trip, how will you keep warm and dry on the hike?
37. In winter, many people turn down the heat in their homes before going to bed. Then they may hear the floors start to creak. Why does this creaking occur?
38. Although snow is cold, it can act as a very good heat insulator.
    (a) Explain why snow is a good insulator.
    (b) Describe how the insulating properties of snow are useful for plants, animals, and people in Canada's north.
39. Look at the paved surface of a highway bridge in **Figure 4**. Which diagram represents the paved surface in the summer? Explain your answer.

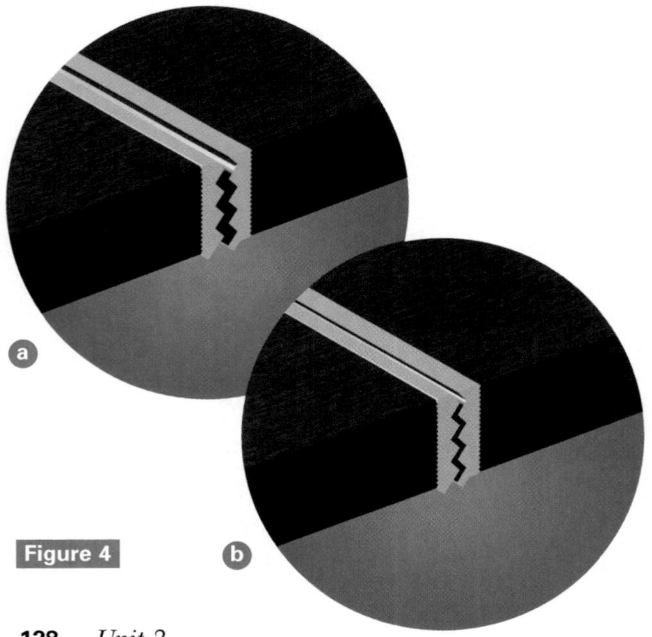

Figure 4

40. How would you restore a dented table tennis ball it to its original shape?
41. **Figure 5** shows that steel rods are used in concrete to strengthen the concrete. Fortunately, steel and concrete expand the same amount when heated. Describe what might happen if they didn't.

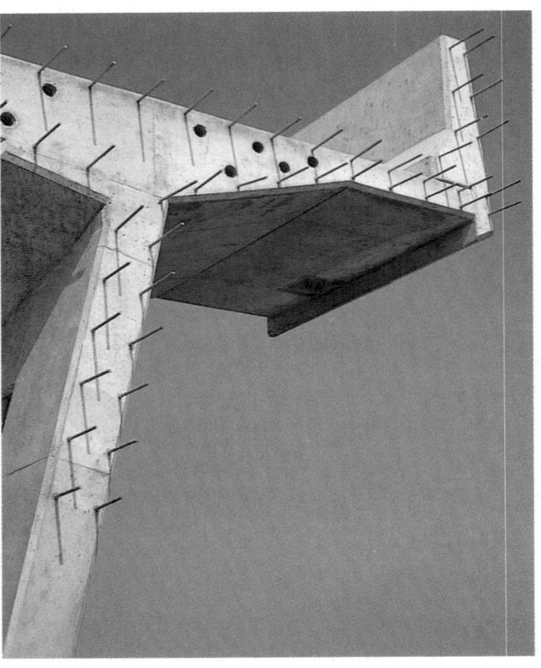

Figure 5

42. Explain why each of the following are concerned about heat transfer:
    (a) an architect
    (b) a hot-air balloonist
    (c) a chef in a restaurant
    (d) a manufacturer of winter boots
    (e) a long-distance runner
43. Newspapers sometimes refer to solar energy as "free." Is it really "free"? Explain what expenses you would have in converting your home to active solar heating.
44. Using what you know about the properties of metals, speculate on how Canadian pioneers made metal rims fit tightly on the wooden wheels of wagons like the one in **Figure 6**.

45. Draw your own home. Redesign it to be as energy-efficient as possible. Make it use little energy in the winter and stay cool in the summer. Label the new features that you would include. Explain how each feature would control heat transfer. What are the costs you would incur?

46. Design an electric kettle so it wastes as little electrical energy as possible.

47. Heating and cooling systems become inefficient when they are not properly maintained. One problem is dust that gathers on heating and cooling coils.

(a) Why is dust a problem?

(b) What other maintenance problems can you suggest should be addressed?

48. Design a system that uses garbage to produce electricity for a small community. (If you research "biomass," you will find out more about this method of conserving energy.)

49. The diver in **Figure 7** is wearing a wet suit for protection in cold water. Research and report on the properties of the materials used in wet suits.

Figure 6

Figure 7

50. **Figure 8** shows an astronaut in space, where temperatures in the shade are extremely low and there is no air. Describe ways that the astronaut is protected from the cold, and explain why the suit is light in colour.

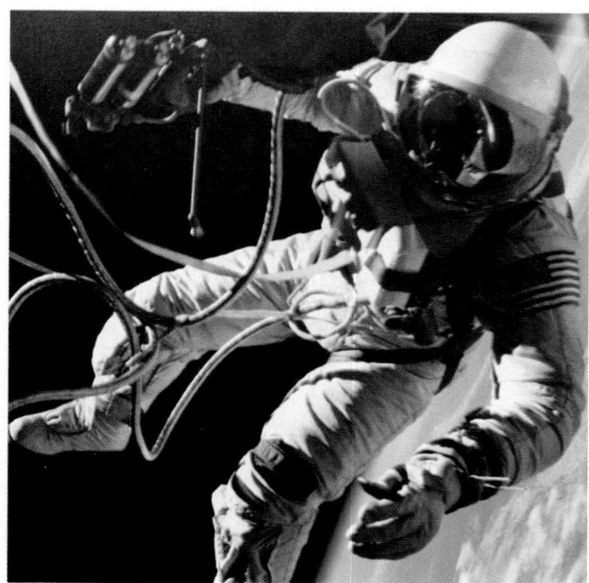

Figure 8

51. Outdoor swimming pools lose a lot of heat to the air, especially at night in spring and fall. This heat is often replaced using a heater. Design a cover for a pool to reduce the amount of heat needed.

Structural Strength and Stability

Unit 3 Overview

Mouses, chairs, bridges, cars, umbrellas, towers, shoes, televisions. All of these are structures, and all of them meet needs, whether it is to to protect us from the weather, help us move, store our goods, allow us to work faster or more effectively, help us communicate with each other, or just make our lives easier or more pleasant. All of these structures have been carefully designed to resist the forces that are expected to act on them. A chair that collapses when we sit on it is not useful; a school that blows down in a strong wind is dangerous. But what are the forces that can be expected? How do they affect structures? And how do we build structures so they resist those forces?

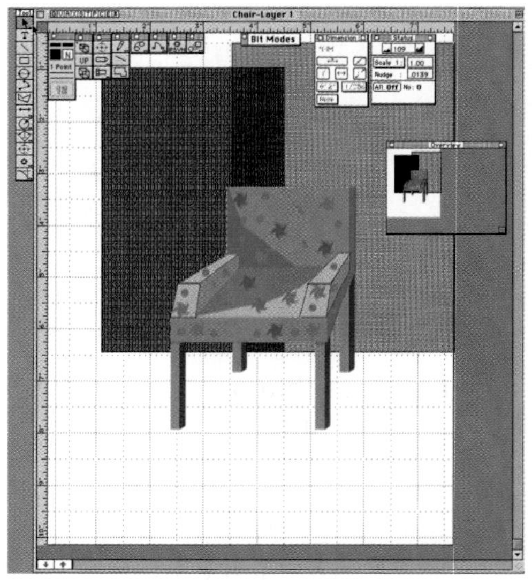

Designing Structures

Structures are designed to perform a specific function.

You will be able to:

- identify the needs that a product fulfills and describe its production, use, and disposal
- recognize that, in meeting needs, designers face limitations, including the types and amounts of materials that can be used
- design and build structures to meet specific needs and test that they meet those needs
- evaluate structures you have designed and built and make suggestions for their improvement
- create a work plan and database to organize the building of a product
- classify structures as solid, frame, or shell, and identify the advantages and disadvantages of each type

Forces and Structures

In performing its function, a structure is exposed to forces. These forces can make the structure fail.

You will be able to:

- investigate ways to increase the stability of structures
- demonstrate that the magnitude, direction, and points of application of a force affect the stability of a structure
- test and evaluate a structure you have designed and built, and determine the structure's factor of safety
- identify forces that act within structures and can cause structural failure
- investigate and use techniques to strengthen structures and materials
- explain how symmetry improves the strength and stability of a structure
- identify structural weaknesses in a structure
- measure the performance of a structure you have designed and built

Design Challenge

You will be able to ...

demonstrate your learning by completing a Design Challenge.

Design and Build a Structure for Everyday Life

Structures are designed based on needs. Those needs influence the choice of materials, the form, and the size of the structure. To build successful structures, designers must always keep these needs in mind.

In this unit, you will be able to design and build:

1 A Recyled Chair

Design and build a dining room chair using cardboard.

2 A Baseball Catcher

Design and build a structure that catches a pitch and returns the ball to the pitcher.

3 A Lightweight Pack for Hiking or Biking

Design and build a lightweight, collapsible pack.

To start your Design Challenge, see page 182.

Record your thoughts and design ideas for the Challenge when you see

Design Challenge

Getting Started

Designing Products

1 You expect that your new backpack will hold all the books, paper, pencils, and so on you want to carry. You expect that the straps will be comfortable and that the pack will not dig into your back when it's full. And you expect that the pack will last longer than a week. You are right to expect all of those things. But how did the designer of your new backpack know what to do to meet all of those expectations? How do designers create products that meet the needs of the user? ➤

Reflecting

Think about the questions in 1,2,3. What other questions do you have about structures' strength and stability? When you have finished this unit, reflect on your answers and revise them based on what you have learned.

2 Think of a concrete block, how heavy it is. Now picture thousands of slabs of concrete, all piled on top of each other. Add to your picture thousands of tonnes of steel and glass, cable, and ducts. How could all of this stand hundreds of metres tall? Why doesn't it collapse? Without actually building the structure, how can a designer predict whether it will stand or collapse into a broken pile? ➤

3 An airplane carries passengers quickly and safely from one place to another. Each piece of the plane has been carefully designed to be strong so the structure is safe and fulfills its function. The wings don't flap about. The fuselage (where the passengers sit) doesn't bend in two. The landing gear doesn't collapse when the plane lands. The structure of each piece of the plane is carefully chosen and designed so the plane can carry out its function. What makes certain kinds of structure best for certain uses? How do we make those structures stable and strong?

Try This Building with Newspaper ③

CDs always seem to present a storage problem. In this activity, you will design and build a prototype of a CD rack.

- You may use only newspaper and sticky tape to build the rack.
- The rack must hold five CDs, and it must be stackable. (A second rack can be put on top of or underneath your rack.)
- The rack should store the CDs safely, so they will not fall out. The user should be able to take out one CD at a time.
- Once you have your basic design, try to make the rack pleasing to the eye.

1. How many of your racks do you think you could stack? How could you test the structure without damaging any CDs?
2. How much tape and newspaper did you use? If you had to build another rack, how could you reduce the amount of materials you used?
3. Would your structure be different if you were limited to using 50 cm of tape? Explain.
4. Examine the racks made by your classmates. Do any of them give you ideas for improving the design of your own rack?
5. How successful were you at improving the appearance of your rack? Could you make a CD rack made of newspaper that someone would be willing to buy? Explain.

3.1

The Life Cycle of a Product

From idea to disposal, every product has a history—one that consumers may not know very much about. The can opener (**Figure 1**) is an example. The structure of the hand-operated can opener has gone through many small changes since 1858, when it was invented. However, its purpose has not changed. Not surprisingly, the can opener was invented soon after cans were first used to store food. Products are created to meet a need.

Figure 1
The can opener was invented and designed to enable users to remove the lid of a can safely and with as little effort as possible.

Meeting a Need: The Production Process

1. The Idea: All products start with ideas. The inventor either identifies a need that isn't met by other products and then invents a new product to meet that need, or thinks of ways to improve an existing product so it meets its need better.
2. A Model: The inventor may create several designs for the product in rough form, but chooses the one that appears best. The first detailed plans can then be constructed on paper or using a computer design program (**Figure 2**). A working model may be produced.
3. Choosing Materials: The materials chosen will affect the strength of the product's structure, how easy it is to manufacture, and whether the product is recyclable. Materials also affect the cost of manufacturing. For example, materials that must be heated will use more energy. Materials that are rare or that must be shipped from a great distance will be more expensive.
4. Research: Not all ideas are good. Inventors research how people would use the product, looking for ways to make the product better.
5. Improving the Design: The design of the product is refined (**Figure 3**) based on the research. This may involve changing the structure of the product and the materials used. A new model is created and more user research is done, followed by more changes in the design, a new model, more research.... The cycle continues until the product seems ready.

Figure 2
Increasingly, product design is done using computer-assisted design (CAD) software.

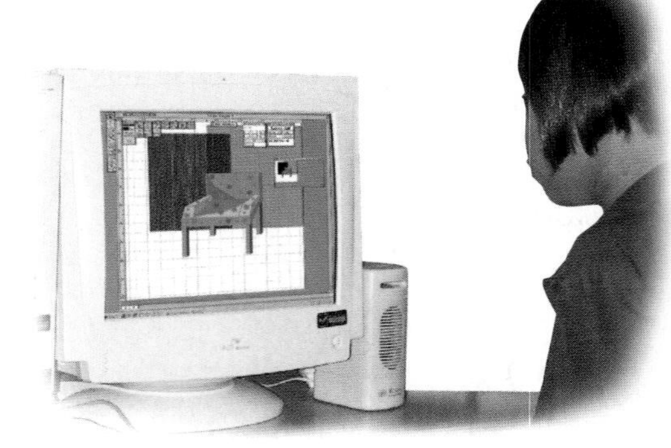

Figure 3
Even something as simple as an umbrella has many different designs, depending on need: compact umbrellas are easy to carry; large umbrellas protect a larger area.

6. The Prototype: A full-scale version of the final design, using final materials, is built and tested to check that the product works as imagined. The prototype is also used to design a manufacturing process. The product may be completely redesigned if it does not work well, is not easy enough or safe to use, or if it is too expensive or difficult to manufacture.
7. Market Research: Research is done to discover how many units of the product are likely to be sold, and at what price. This is important information. If the manufacturer produces too many units, it will have wasted resources. If the manufacturer produces too few units, customers may decide not to wait and buy a competing product instead. If the price is more than consumers are willing to pay, the product may be redesigned to make it cheaper.
8. Preparing for Production: The manufacturer prepares to mass-produce the product. This may involve creating a whole new factory or just modifying an existing one.
9. Production: The manufacturer begins making the product.
10. Advertising: No one can decide to buy a product if they don't know it exists. Advertising informs possible customers about the product and the need it meets. If the ads are effective, buyers will want the product.
11. Distribution: The product is distributed to stores for sale.
12. The Buying Decision: Before buying a product, the consumer evaluates it in some of the same ways as the inventor and manufacturer. Is it useful? How much will it cost to use (**Figure 4**)? Can it be recycled? Consumers who are satisfied with the answers to these and other questions will buy the product.
13. The End: When the consumer is finished with the product, it must be disposed of safely. Some products can be recycled and some can be used for other purposes, but many end up in landfill sites. Inventors, manufacturers, and consumers are all responsible for the effects the product has on the environment.

Figure 4
When buying a product, a consumer must consider how expensive the product will be to use. Would you buy a game if you had to change the batteries every hour?

Understanding Concepts

1. Why is the choice of materials important when designing a new product?

2. Why is the amount of energy needed in manufacturing important to consider when creating a product?

3. For each stage in the production process, explain why a product might not go on to the next stage.

Making Connections

4. (4A) (8C) Choose a product to investigate and tell its "story." Who thought of the product? What need does it meet? Which company manufactures it? How is it advertised? How is it used? What happens to the product when it wears out? Present your findings using posters, video, or a computer.

Reflecting

5. Make a list of things to consider before buying a product. Rank your criteria in order of importance. Do you always follow your criteria? Explain.

Design Challenge

For your Challenge you must design a product. Using the production process as a model, create a plan for your design process.

SKILLS HANDBOOK: (4A) Research Skills (8C) Multimedia Presentation

Product Testing

You've probably noticed that some products look different than they used to. The running shoes you wore as a little kid would probably look funny next to the ones you wear today. The new sneakers may also help you jump higher or run faster. Cars also look much different from those of 10 years ago. They're also safer in a crash. Why and how do the structures of products like these change?

Designers are always trying to improve the products they are creating. To do this, designers do a lot of testing. Testing not only ensures that a product will act as intended, but it also sparks ideas for improvement.

Figure 1

Crash testing shows investigators how a car will act in a crash. By analyzing the results, they find ways to improve the structure and safety of the vehicle.

Crash Tests

When a car is being designed, prototypes are put through rigorous tests to see how well the car protects its human passengers in an accident. Of course, real humans can't be used during the test because of the danger involved. Instead, crash-test dummies are put behind the wheel. The car is then crashed into a concrete barrier to simulate a real collision (**Figure 1**). Cameras record the test so the results can be analyzed and changes made where necessary. Unfortunately, the process is very expensive: each test can cost over $150 000 to run!

Virtual crash tests save money. A model of the real car, a virtual prototype, is generated on the computer. Then the model is put through a simulated test, where it is crashed into a virtual barrier. It's a lot cheaper than a real test, since computers can carry out the same test over and over again without wrecking a single car. Designers can also get close-ups of particular parts, even those hidden inside the car, to see what's going wrong during the crash. They can then change the design and try again.

When all the necessary improvements have been made, a real prototype still must be built and tested to make sure the results are accurate. However, using simulations lets the designers try different things out without wasting money on the real thing.

Trial and Error

At one car company, car designers who used computer simulations discovered an unexpected way to make their cars safer. When hit from the side, the frame of their car tended to buckle dangerously near the head and body of the driver. The car designers first tried the obvious solution: reinforcing the frame with steel to make it stronger. Unfortunately, when they ran the computer tests on the new model, they found that this change actually made the buckling worse!

The designers experimented with different combinations on their computers until they found the answer. They discovered that making the lower part of the frame weaker, not stronger, made the buckling less severe higher up, near the driver's head and body. Like the crumple zone in the front of the car, this little weakness in the structure made the rest of the structure stronger. It's not likely they would have discovered this innovation except through trial and error and the power of simulation.

Try This: Testing the Rack

In the Try This in the Getting Started, you designed and built a CD rack. Imagine how that rack might be used and where it might be stored.

- Create three tests you could carry out on your (3F) CD rack.

1. What results do you expect from the tests?

- Carry out the tests.

2. Based on the test results, how could you improve the design of your CD rack?

Understanding Concepts

1. Why are prototypes tested before they are mass-produced?
2. How does testing help to improve the products we use?

Making Connections

3. Cars are expensive to build and test, which is why car manufacturers use computer simulations instead of real crash tests. Shoes are much cheaper to make. What benefits could a shoe manufacturer gain from using simulations in testing?
4. (3F) Do you ever have trouble with a door handle? Do your clothes seem to wear out before you want to buy new ones? Can you think of a way to improve a product that you use every day? How would you test your innovation?

Reflecting

5. Testing a prototype can yield unexpected results. Car designers discovered they should weaken, rather than strengthen, part of the car body to improve safety. Why would an unexpected result be important? What things should you consider if the results of your tests are unexpected?

Design Challenge

(3F) Testing a structure often reveals areas for improvement, and different tests will reveal different things. How will you test your designs for your Challenge?

3.3 Case Study

Planning to Fly

How do you build something as large and complicated as an airplane? Where do you start?

A class of aerospace manufacturing students figured out how: not only do you need a good design, but you also need a work plan and the right tools to track your progress. Using a work plan and databases to stay organized, the students were able to construct and sell a two-seater airplane (**Figure 1**).

Figure 1
A team of high school students was able to construct and sell a plane much like this one.

The Kit

The teacher and students chose to build an ultralight airplane from a kit. The raw materials (sheet metal, screws for use in airplanes, rubber, materials to build seats, cables for the controls, and so on) came from a factory in British Columbia. A manual suggested which parts to build first, how to design and manufacture some components, and how to join pieces together. Some pieces were shipped as raw materials that had to be cut and formed. Some decisions were left to the builders, such as whether the seats should be upholstered. The design of some pieces, such as the instrument panel, were left completely to the builders.

(a) What are the advantages of using a kit instead of designing your own airplane?

(b) Speculate on why the factory leaves some elements of the design to the builders.

Table 1 The Work Plan

Headings	Descriptions
1. Materials	(i) The arrangement of all the tools, materials, and completed parts to keep them accessible and free from harm and dirt
2. Personnel	(ii) The division of tasks among the teams of people involved in building the airplane
3. Physical Plant	(iii) The order of work to be done, with the small, easy parts built first, and then assembled into larger components
4. Storage	(iv) A map of the construction site, separated into work stations, with adequate tools and energy available for each team
5. Schedule of Construction	(v) The pieces needed to make the plane

The Work Plan

Assembling an airplane is complicated and time-consuming. To make the process more efficient, the teacher and the students started by planning how to organize their tools and materials, as well as deciding in what order the work would be done, just as a factory would do. They created a document called a work plan. The plan described who was going to work on which parts, in what order the parts were to be made and assembled, and where they would be assembled. They drew up a detailed list with the following headings: Materials, Personnel, Physical Plant, Storage, and Schedule of Construction. A team leader was assigned to each part of the work plan to ensure that it was carried out.

(c) Match each of the headings in **Table 1** with the appropriate description.

Materials

When the parts arrived, it was clear there was a management problem. What to do with an assortment of boxes and crates of all different weights and sizes? The students had to make sure that the parts they needed were really all there. They had to find a way to store the parts so they could find a part when they needed it. They knew that as they worked they would have to record how much of each material was used, so they would know how much was left. They also knew they would need to store parts as they were created, together with scraps of waste material, in case a repair of some part was needed further down the road.

They decided to put each type of part in a separate bin, then count or measure the pieces in each bin, and record the results in a computer database (**Figure 2**).

Figure 2

As materials were used, entries were added to the various fields in the database.

Bin Number	1
Description of Material	5-cm stainless steel screws
Date Received/Created	1998-09-30
Quantity Received/Created	1250
Quantity Used	100
Date Used	1998-10-15
Balance on Hand	1150

AIRPLANE PARTS

(d) What other fields of information could the students have added to their database?

(e) Why is it important for a database to be updated regularly?

Finishing the Product

The students built smaller, easier parts first, such as the flight controls, to learn the skills they needed before progressing to more difficult parts. The wings and the fuselage were built simultaneously. The landing gear parts were assembled into larger components and then installed on the fuselage. The wings were then put on. Next came the tail assembly and the flight controls, and after that, the fuel system wiring and the engine. Finally, the students worked on the interior, and painted and polished the exterior.

The systems were ground-tested (to make sure everything was performing well) and then flight-tested before the airplane was delivered to the new owner.

(f) If you were thinking of buying the finished plane, what concerns would you have?

Understanding Concepts

1. Using the headings Materials, Personnel, Physical Plant, Storage, and Schedule of Production, create a work plan to organize a project that interests you. For example, you might consider a complicated meal or the building of a go-kart as your project.

2. (9C) Design a database to store information about a CD collection. How would such a database be useful?

Making Connections

3. (9C) In order to find out how much material was left in each bin, the students could subtract the quantity used from the quantity received for each bin. They could also design a spreadsheet to do the work for them. Design a spreadsheet that could use information from the database to keep track of materials.

4. The airplane in this case study took approximately 1000 person-hours to build.

(a) For a class of 20, how many calendar days would this be?

(b) Do you think it would it take that long to build the airplane in a factory? Why or why not?

Design Challenge

It makes sense to use a database if you have a project with many pieces of information that you wish to record and need quick access to. What kinds of information might you wish to record while working on your Challenge? Would a database help you?

SKILLS HANDBOOK: (9C) Using Your Computer Effectively

Stability

Figure 1
The tall, slender tower is about to fall. The short, broader tower is not. Why are some structures more stable than others?

When you were designing and testing a product earlier—your CD rack—you probably noticed that it is difficult to stack objects to any height before they fall over. Children learn the same lesson when stacking building blocks—a stack of single blocks is more likely to fall than a stack built on a wider foundation (**Figure 1**).

A structure is **stable** if it remains on its base, undamaged, when acted on by the forces it is designed to withstand. The stability of a structure depends on the materials the structure is made from, and how its mass is distributed.

All structures have mass, which is acted on by gravity. In every object, there is a point at which you can picture the mass of the object being concentrated. This point is called the **centre of gravity**. When you support an object at its centre of gravity, the object will stay perfectly balanced. You can demonstrate this principle with a book and one finger (**Figure 2**). If you place your finger under the book's centre of gravity, the book will balance on your finger.

Figure 2
The centre of gravity of the book is directly over the tip of the finger.

The centre of gravity of a book is fairly easy to find (try it!). For other objects, the centre of gravity can be hard to visualize, but understanding where it is in a given structure can be very important. Designers use this principle to construct towers, tables, and other structures. A structure will remain stable only if its centre of gravity is between the points where it is supported. If the centre of gravity is located outside the structure's support base, the structure may topple over. As you can see in **Figure 3**, the support base for a structure does not have to be solid.

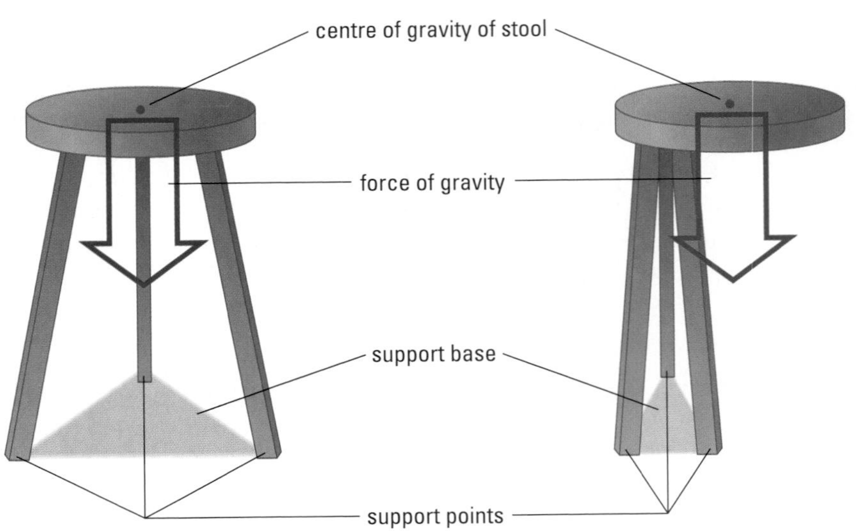

Figure 3
The legs of a stool form an imaginary triangle that is the support base for the stool.

a The centre of gravity of this stool, located near the middle of the seat, lies over the support base, so the stool is stable.

b The centre of gravity of this stool is not over its support base, so it is unstable. It will fall over.

Try This Finding the Centre

The centre of gravity of an object is revealed when you pick it up—if you do not resist the motion, the object will move so that its centre of gravity is directly below your hand. You can use this property to pinpoint the centre of gravity of any flat object, if you have cardboard, a long pin, some thin string, a weight, a ruler, and a bulletin board.

- Cut 1 m of string and tie the weight to one end. Tie the other end of the string to the pin. You will use this structure as a plumb line.
- Cut a square from a sheet of cardboard.
- Pin the square of cardboard to the bulletin board with your plumb line. You can pin the square through any part, but make sure the cardboard can move freely. Once the square is settled, carefully draw a pencil line on the cardboard along the length of the string of the plumb line (**Figure 4**).
- Remove the plumb line and pin the square to the board again through any other point in the square. Once again, draw a line on the cardboard along the length of the string.
- The centre of gravity of the square is where the two lines intersect. You can demonstrate this is true by unpinning the square and putting one finger under the point of intersection. Does the square balance?

1. Describe the location of the centre of gravity of the square.

- Find the centre of gravity of more shapes. Cut a rectangle, a circle, and some more irregular shapes.
- Before measuring the centre of gravity of each object, make a dot where you predict the centre of gravity will be.

2. How accurate were your predictions?

- Add a small piece of Plasticine anywhere in a few of your shapes.

3. How does the extra mass change the location of the centre of gravity?

Figure 4

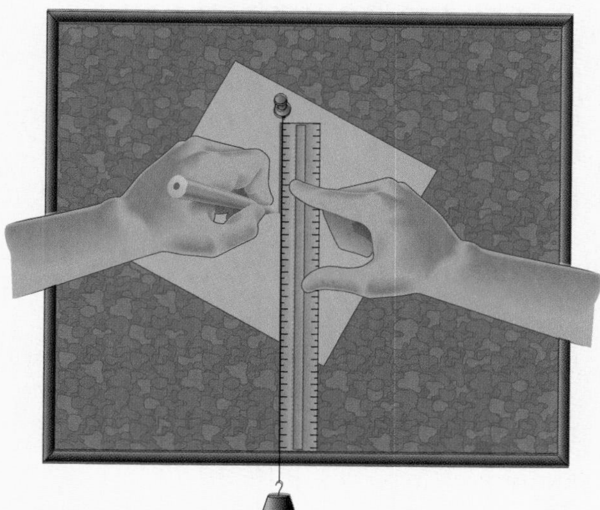

Centre of Gravity and Stability

Generally, widening the base of a structure will make it more stable (**Figure 5**). A structure can also be made more stable if its centre of gravity is low, rather than high. Buildings, lamps, and even staplers use this principle: they are built with broad, heavy bases and lighter tops to keep them from toppling over.

Tapering a structure is one of the best ways to ensure the structure stays standing. Tapered structures, such as pyramids (**Figure 6**), have a wide base for stability. The wide base and narrow top also mean that the centre of gravity is close to the ground.

Figure 5
A wide base and a low centre of gravity make a structure stable. Triangle 1 will topple onto the line BC when tilted 45°, but triangle 2 will not. Can you explain why?

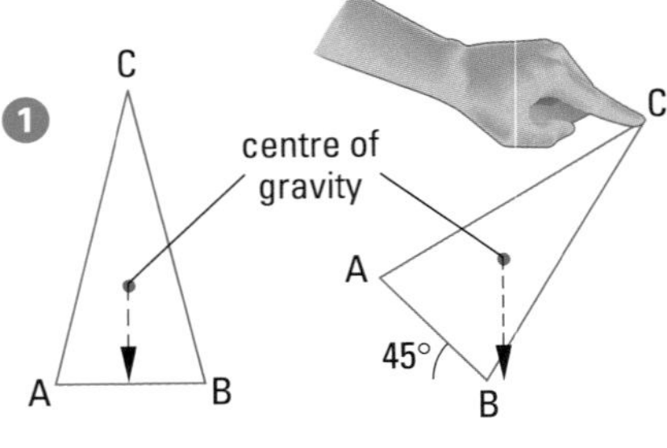

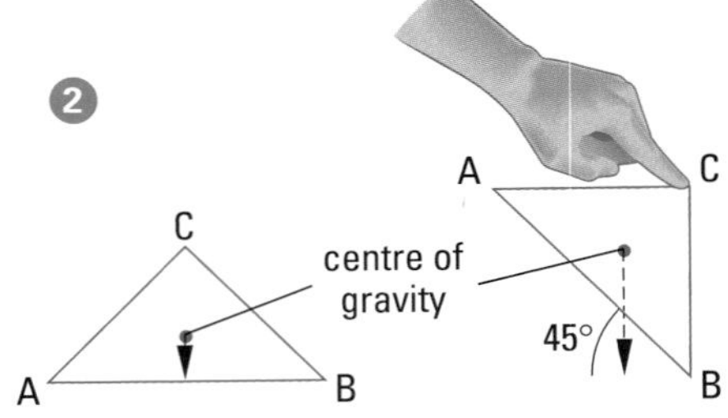

Try This — Moving the Mass (3F)

Using a building you have designed, you can measure how changing the centre of gravity of a structure affects its stability.

- After reading this activity, as a class create a test that will measure how stable your buildings are. The test must be repeatable, and the effect of the test must be measurable.
- In your group, design and build a model of a building using only 30 straws, 50 cm of tape, and one sheet of cardboard.
- Your building must be at least three floors tall, and should be able to support a 100-g mass on each floor. The building must be as stable as you can make it.

1. Estimate the location of the centre of gravity of your building. Explain your estimate.

- Put the mass in the middle of the bottom floor of your building.

2. Estimate the location of the centre of gravity of the building after the 100-g mass is added. Explain your estimate.

- Test the building's stability with the extra mass.
- Repeat your test for each floor of the building.

3. Is your building more or less stable when the mass is placed on higher floors?

4. Describe how the centre of gravity moves as the 100-g mass moves up each floor.

- Try putting the 100-g mass close to the edge of each floor, rather than in the middle.

5. What differences do you notice in the stability of the building?

- Share the results of your tests with the other groups in your class.

6. Which building was the most stable at each floor?

- Examine the design features of the other buildings in your class.

7. What changes could you make to your design that would make the building more stable when the centre of mass is high or near the edge of a floor?

SKILLS HANDBOOK: (3F) Testing and Evaulating a Prototype

Figure 6

This pyramid has been standing for a very long time. Tapered structures are stable because they have a low centre of gravity and a broad base.

Football players illustrate how lowering the centre of gravity and widening the base can make a structure more stable (**Figure 7**). Spreading your feet apart gives you a wider base, while crouching down brings the bulk of your mass closer to the ground. That is why it is so much harder to knock players over when they are crouching than when they are standing up straight.

Figure 7

Football players know they are harder to knock down when they are in a crouch.

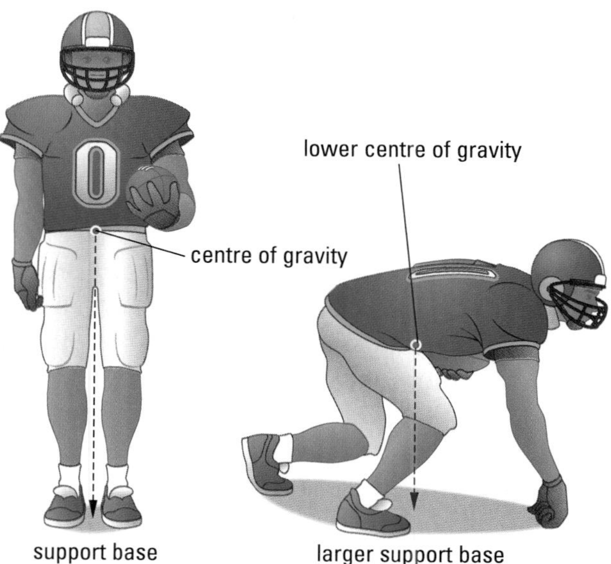

Design Challenge

Stability is important for the chair and the baseball catcher challenges. If they topple, the chair could cause an injury and the catcher will probably not work. How can you use your knowledge of centre of gravity to build a stable structure?

Understanding Concepts

1. In your own words, explain centre of gravity and how it affects the stability of a structure.
2. (a) What are the support points and support base of the structures in **Figure 8**?
   (b) Which of the structures in **Figure 8** are stable? Explain your evaluation.

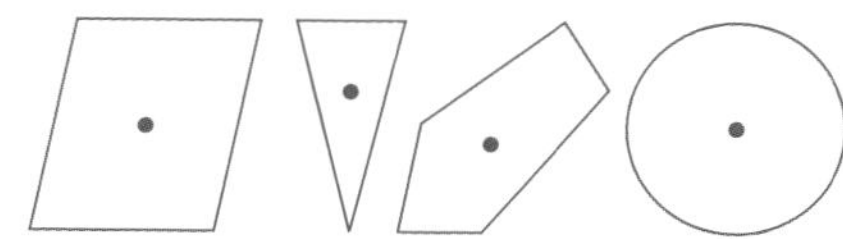

Figure 8

Making Connections

3. The towers used by radio broadcasters are tall and slender. Using the term centre of gravity, describe three ways you could make a radio tower more stable without decreasing its height.
4. Giraffes have long, heavy necks, but they do not tip over, even when they run or drink. Giraffes do not bend their knees when they drink from ponds, and they keep their necks straight (**Figure 9**).

Figure 9

   (a) Draw diagrams showing where you think a giraffe's centre of gravity is when it is eating leaves from a tree and when it is drinking.
   (b) Speculate on how the giraffe's structure prevents it from tipping over.

Stabilizing the Tower of Pisa

Figure 1
The Leaning Tower of Pisa. Engineers are working to reduce the tower's lean so it will not fall.

The Leaning Tower of Pisa in Italy (**Figure 1**) is one of the wonders of the Middle Ages. The structure is known as a *campanile*, a kind of bell tower. Eight storeys high, the tower reaches 55.9 m into the air. The structure is made of stone—white marble—and the foundation walls are 4.0 m thick. The tower is strong and it has stood for centuries, but it is not stable.

Building the Tower

Construction of the tower started in 1173. In 1178, when the base and three more storeys had been built, construction was interrupted by a war. Even then, it was obvious that the tower was leaning to the south. After the war, the people of Pisa decided to continue construction, but with a slightly changed plan—they built the next two levels on a slight curve, opposite the direction of the lean. They hoped this would allow them to make the bell chamber at the top flat.

(a) The lean of the tower was a problem. The people of Pisa decided to solve it by curving the tower. Was this the best solution? What other solutions can you think of?

Completing the Tower

The curve didn't work. As the tower grew taller, it began to lean even more. Construction was interrupted several times, but the tower was finally completed in 1350, almost 200 years after the start of the project. At that point, the lean, measured from the seventh storey to the ground (**Figure 2**), was about 1.5 m. It was visible, but not dangerous. However, the lean has increased since then, as you can see from **Table 1**.

Figure 2

(b) Speculate on the position of the tower's centre of gravity. What happens to the stability of the tower as its lean increases?

(c) In 1990, the tower was closed to the public. Why do you think this was done?

Why the Tower Leans

The reason for the tower's instability is the sandy soil under the foundation. This soil is gradually shifting from under the great weight of the tower. There is a layer of more solid clay 10 m below the surface. If the original architects had considered the soil, they could have compensated by building the foundation deep into the ground. However, the foundation is only 3.0 m deep—not nearly enough to stabilize the tower against shifting soil!

(d) If there were a way to straighten the tower, is there any reason to believe it would stay straight? Explain.

Table 1 A Growing Lean

Year	Lean (m)
1298	1.43
1550	3.79
1787	3.79
1817	3.84
1911	4.04
1935	4.80
1997	5.20

Reducing the Lean

The first commission to deal with the problem of the leaning tower was established in 1298. There have been 17 more commissions since then. Most have done nothing that helps, and a few have done harm. The attempts to inject concrete under the tower in 1934 and to freeze the soil around the foundation in 1995 both made the lean significantly worse.

A new plan, scheduled for 1999 and 2000, involves bracing the tower with cables and removing some of the soil from under the north side of the foundation (**Figure 3**). The plan is to reduce the lean by only a small amount, about 0.4 m, enough to make the structure safe for visitors.

(e) Why would removing some of the soil from under the north side of the tower reduce the lean?

(f) No one wants to completely straighten the tower, especially the people of Pisa. Suggest some reasons why.

Understanding Concepts

1. The stones used in the foundation of the Leaning Tower are thicker than the stones used higher up. How does this affect the stability of the tower?
2. The original architects wanted to create a tower that would stand for centuries, so they chose marble as their building material. If durability was less important, what materials could they have chosen that would have made the tower more stable? Explain your choices.

Exploring

3. (a) Research, using the Internet or a library, the measurements of the Leaning Tower. Make a scale model of the Leaning Tower and use it to predict how much the tower must lean before it falls. (4A) (3D)

   (b) In 1990, it was estimated that the tilt of the tower was increasing 1.2 mm every year. Based on your model, if engineers did not intervene, when would the tower fall?

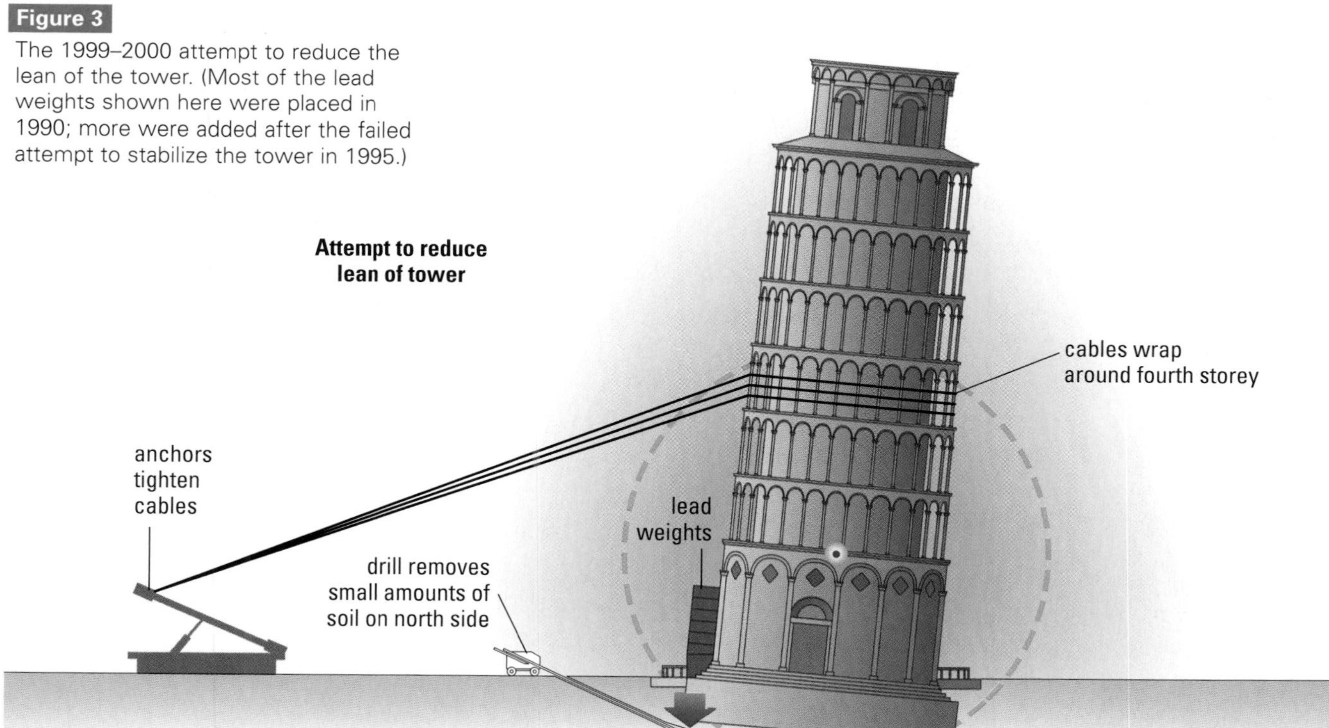

Figure 3
The 1999–2000 attempt to reduce the lean of the tower. (Most of the lead weights shown here were placed in 1990; more were added after the failed attempt to stabilize the tower in 1995.)

3.6 Career Profile

Building Sets for Television

We all know that much of what we see on television isn't real. This is just as true for many of the buildings on television: these special structures are often built and torn down again in a matter of weeks or even days. Although these sets are not real, they still must be carefully constructed by set carpenters, who use lightweight materials while creating structures that are stable. The structures must also accommodate cameras and lights.

Mitsu Yano is a set carpenter for various television productions. He has always been interested in building things. Mitsu began his career in architectural drafting and house construction, but turned to set construction because the projects were more challenging. He has built everything from a Greek temple for a skating show, to a submarine tower for *Due South*, to futuristic sets for the television series *Nikita* (**Figure 1**) and *Total Recall.*

Figure 1
The underground fortress from the *Nikita* television series was constructed as a frame structure from lauan. The concrete blocks tied to the top of the frame gave the structure stability during construction.

Moving Pieces

Constructing a set involves a lot of problem-solving, especially when the set must be movable. First the art director or set designer creates plans or a concept. The carpenters usually choose the materials, the framework, and decide how the set will be built.

For *Due South,* an actual-size conning tower of a submarine was constructed. It then had to be transported from the studio in Toronto to a lake in northern Alberta where the episode was filmed. "We make sure that there are always small pieces in any set to make it easy to move," Mitsu says. "We call this 'making it wild' because it's not fixed or permanent." Even permanent sets, such as a police headquarters in a cop show, have a couple of "wild" sections that can be pulled out and replaced by lighting and cameras. The wild sections are held at the back by a triangle support called a jack. The jack is weighted down by a sandbag for stability.

Because sets don't have heavy bases, set materials must be as light as possible. "We usually use lauan, which is a lightweight plywood," Mitsu says. "We also use a lot of Styrofoam, especially for rocks and ice." Sheet acrylics and plastics are also used, because they're easy to bend and shape. Plexiglas replaces glass to ensure the safety of the actors.

Reusing Sets

Building sets can be expensive, especially when a set that takes two weeks to build is used for a shot that will last for only 30 seconds. But there are ways to save on costs. "One set can be used over and over again with little changes made to doorways and windows," Mitsu explains. "Once, we used one set for nine different locations: a factory, a hospital, an office… If you change a couple of windows and doorways it looks like a whole new set, but you save on materials and time."

Reusing sets is also important because many of the materials used for sets are not recyclable. Some companies store and then resell sets or parts of sets to other production companies. It may take a lot of creativity to turn an existing set into a new set, but Mitsu enjoys solving the problems that arise during his job. "Meeting famous movie stars is also an added bonus," he says.

Setting the Scene 

You are building a set for a single scene in a TV production. During the scene, two actors enter an alley from one building, go around a corner, and enter another building. Cameras must catch the actors' faces as they enter the alley and must follow them to the corner. The actors' faces must be shot again as they move to the second building.

- Design a set for this scene in a drawing, making sure the cameras can be set up in appropriate places. You may need "wild" sections in your set. (Remember that a scene does not have to be shot all at once—it can be broken up into sections that are shot separately.)
- Use your drawing to create a rough model of the set.

1. What materials would you use if you had to build the set full-scale?
2. How would you modify your design if you knew one of the actors had to lean against a wall at one point in the scene?

Planned Obsolescence

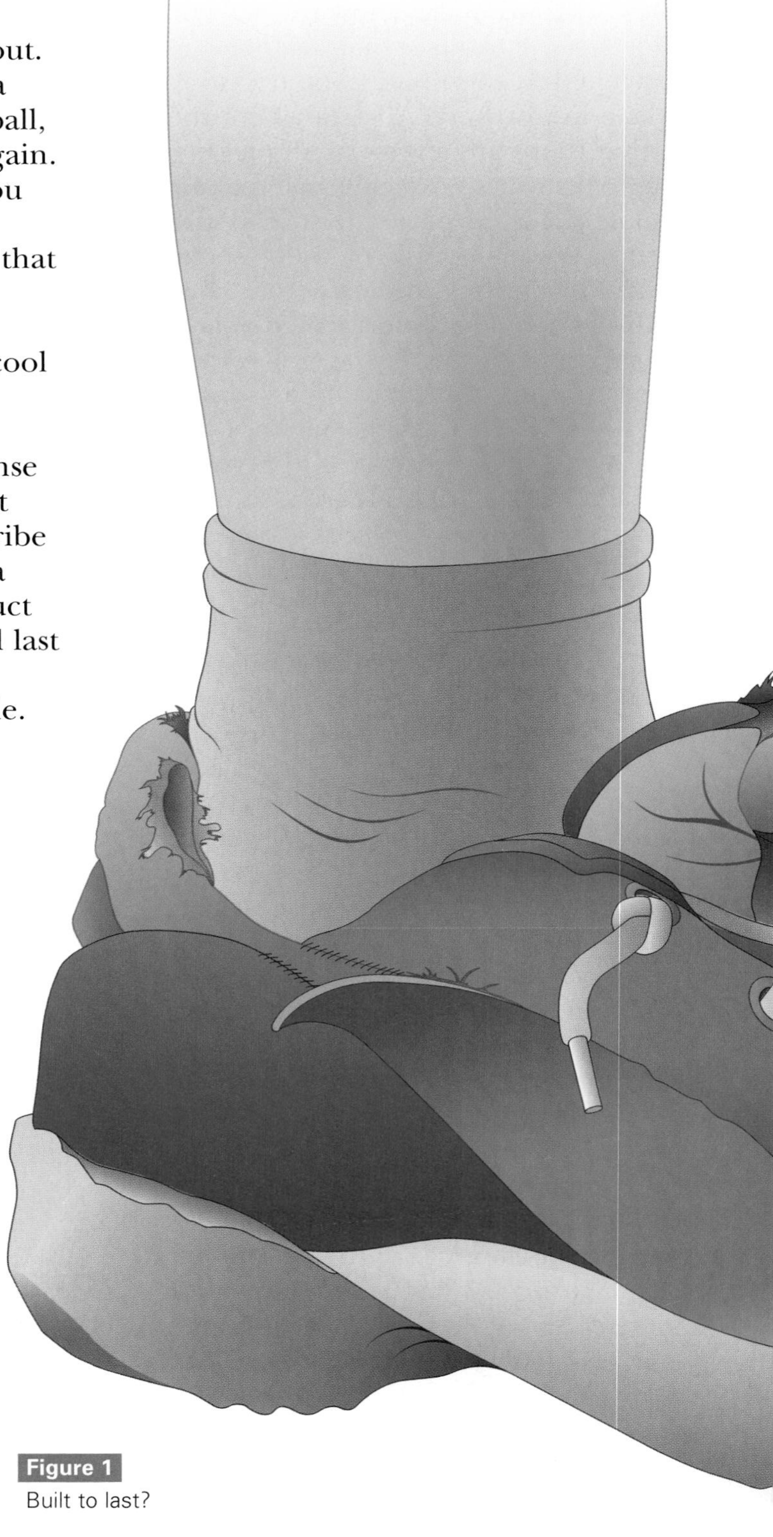

Imagine a world in which things never wore out. Once you bought something, whether it was a bicycle, a sweater, a pair of socks, or a basketball, you would never have to replace that thing again. Does this sound like the kind of world that you would like to live in?

The problem with permanent products is that people and their needs are not permanent. Children become adults and outgrow their bicycles and socks. The sweater that seemed cool last year is the wrong colour this year.

It doesn't always make sense to design a product to be used forever. It makes more sense to design a product so that it lasts as long as it needs to. The term that is often used to describe this concept is **planned obsolescence**. When a manufacturer produces a product, that product has an expected life, or amount of time it will last under conditions of reasonable use.

Children's shoes **(Figure 1)** are an example. They are designed to last for as little as one season, because children's feet are growing. Shoes that fit this summer will not fit next summer—so why build them to last? Consumers are expected to use a product for a reasonable amount of time, dispose of it, and buy a replacement product.

But what about the waste? Those worn-out shoes go to the dump.

Figure 1
Built to last?

Understanding Concepts

1. Why aren't products designed to last forever?
2. In your own words, describe planned obsolescence.
3. Give three new examples each of products that are designed to last a long time and products that have a short planned life. Explain why these products have different product lives.

Planned Waste (8D)

Statement

We should reduce the amount of waste our society creates. Designing products to be thrown away after a short time just creates waste. New products should be designed to last as long as possible; people should not be allowed to buy new products until the old ones are worn out or they find someone else to use the product.

Point

- We are producing too much waste and pollution. Landfill sites full of thrown-away products occupy land that could be productive, or left to nature. Industries churning out temporary products fill the air and water with pollutants.
- There is no need to design short-lived products. People who don't want a product any more can always find someone else to use the product rather than throwing it away.

Counterpoint

- Workers depend on planned obsolescence. Once everyone has a pair of shoes that won't wear out, how are the workers in the shoe factory going to make a living?
- Without planned obsolescence, products would never get better. Why would companies design new, better products if they knew no one would be allowed to buy them?

What Do You Think?

- Consider the statement and the points and counterpoints above. (4C) What other points and counterpoints can you think of?
- Discuss the statement, and then decide whether you agree or disagree.
- Search newspapers, a library periodical index, a CD-ROM directory, (4A) or the Internet for information on planned obsolescence.
- Prepare to defend your position in a class discussion.

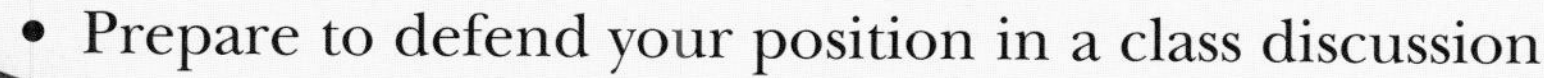

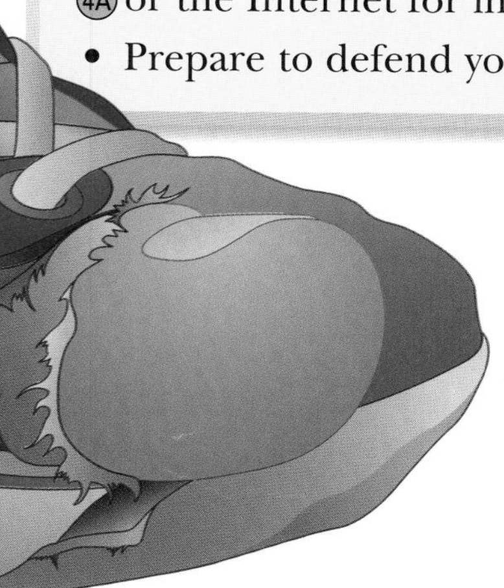

SKILLS HANDBOOK: (8D) Exploring an Issue (4C) Critical Thinking (4A) Research Skills

3.8

Forces and Structures

Why don't bumper cars cause serious injuries in amusement parks, while cars hitting each other on the road do? How can one force, such as the impact of one car hitting another in a crash, have a variety of effects? The answer is that forces are not created equal. The effect of a force on a structure depends on its magnitude, direction, and the point of application of the force.

Magnitude of Force

Every force has a magnitude. **Magnitude** is a measure of how strong the force is. If you were to gently tap a nail on its head with a hammer, the nail would not be driven into the wood. The tap is a low magnitude force. If you struck the nail hard, you would have more success. A hard strike is a higher magnitude force. The structure in **Figure 1** will react differently to two forces of different magnitude.

Figure 1

Magnitude of force. In diagrams, the magnitude of a force is indicated by the length of the arrow.

(a) A weak force (low magnitude) is not enough to make the block move.

(b) A strong force (high magnitude) moves the block to the right.

Direction of Force

The effect of a force on a structure depends on the direction of the force. If a door says "push," it won't open if you use a pulling force. The structure in **Figure 2** will not react in the same way to two forces that have the same magnitude but different directions.

Figure 2

The direction of a force affects how a structure will react to it. These two forces have the same magnitude but different directions. Both forces will cause the structure to collapse.

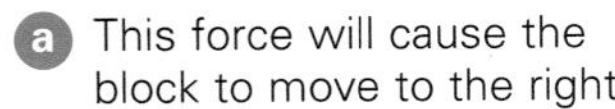

(a) This force will cause the block to move to the right.

(b) This force will cause the block to move to the left.

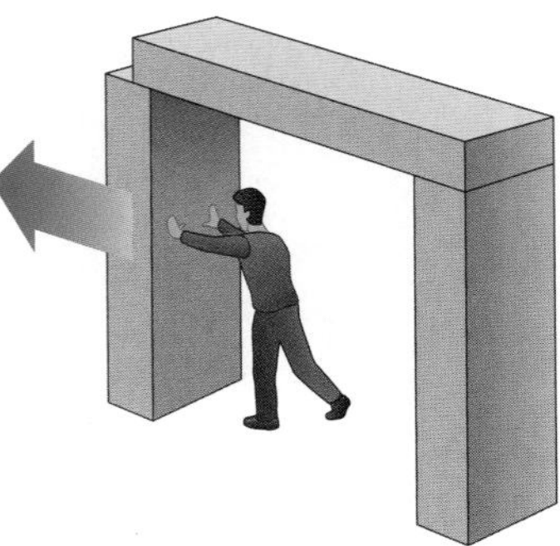

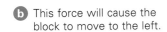

Point and Plane of Application of Force

You may have tried to push a chest of drawers from the centre of a room toward a wall. If you push low on the chest, it will slide toward the wall. However, if you push with the same magnitude of force higher up, the chest may topple over. As you can see in **Figure 3**, the point and plane of application of a force make a difference.

Figure 3
Where and how a force is applied to a structure affects the results.

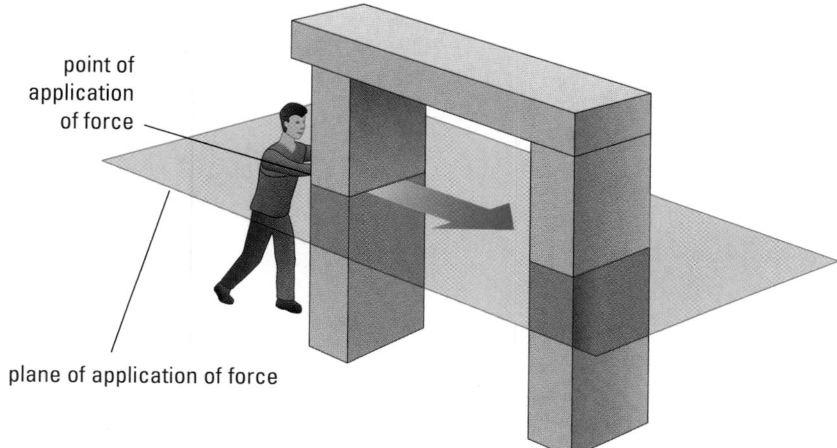

ⓐ As before, the force pushing on the block will cause the structure to collapse by moving the block to the right. Any force of this magnitude in the same plane (applied to the right or left of the point of application) will have the same effect.

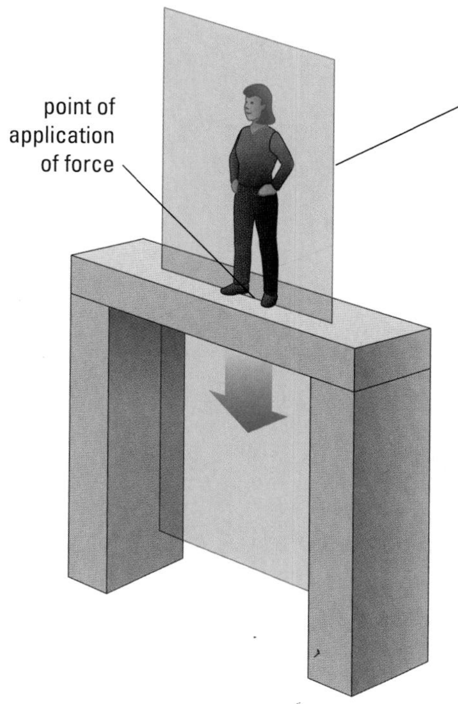

ⓑ Here the force is pushing on the top of the structure. The structure is designed to handle a force applied from above, so the force has no effect. Any force in this plane of application will have the same effect.

Understanding Concepts

1. The wind exerts a force on structures. Using the terms force, magnitude, and direction, describe how changes in the wind might affect the structure of the tree.
2. Describe the forces acting on a nail as it is
   (a) driven into a piece of wood with a hammer.
   (b) pulled from the wood with a crowbar.
3. Using diagrams of a bicycle wheel, (6C) show how forces of different magnitude, direction, and point of application can have different effects on the wheel.

3.9 Inquiry Investigation

SKILLS MENU
- ○ Questioning
- ● Hypothesizing
- ● Planning
- ● Conducting
- ● Recording
- ● Analyzing
- ● Communicating

Applying Force

While demolishing a building, the crew may use a wrecking ball (**Figure 1**). But how can operators make the ball most effective? In practice, the wreckers examine the structure of a building very carefully and decide where it is weakest. Then, they hit the weak point.

Materials

- 9 building blocks
- paper
- pencil
- string
- one-hole rubber stopper
- ring stand

Question

How are structures affected by forces of different magnitude and point and plane of application?

Hypothesis

2C **1** Write a hypothesis for this experiment after reading through the procedure.

Experimental Design

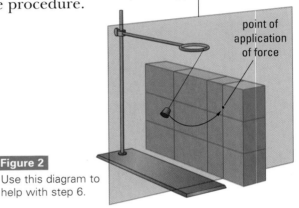

You will investigate the effects of changing the point and plane of application of force on a structure by using a pendulum to simulate a wrecking ball.

2 Read steps 6 and 7 carefully and design a measuring system that will allow you to apply the same levels of force to each block.

6D **3** Create a chart to record your data.

plane of application of force

point of application of force

Figure 2
Use this diagram to help with step 6.

Procedure

4 Using 9 blocks, build a wall with 3 rows and 3 columns on a piece of paper.
- On the paper, carefully mark the position of the blocks on the bottom row.

5 Create your wrecking ball.
- Make a pendulum by tying the rubber stopper to the string.
- Tie the pendulum to the ring stand, making sure it is 20 cm long.
- Attach the measuring system you have designed to measure level of force.

6 By moving the ring support up or down, adjust the height of the rubber stopper so it will hit the centre of a block in the top row.
- Hold the pendulum so it will swing as in **Figure 2**.
- Using the smallest level of force, allow the pendulum to strike the block.
- Gradually increase the level of force you apply to the block until the block falls.

(a) Record the level of force that was needed to make the block fall.

(b) Record the number of other blocks that fall with the moved block.

SKILLS HANDBOOK: 2C Predicting and Hypothesizing 6D Creating Data Tables

Figure 1
A wrecking ball works like a pendulum: the ball generates the most force at the bottom of its arc, where it is travelling fastest.

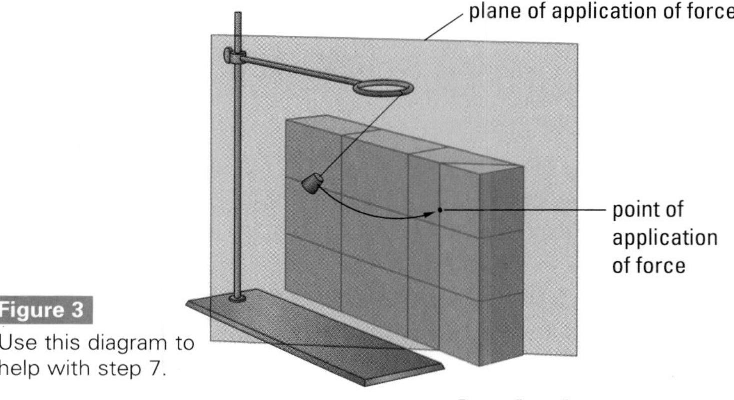

Figure 3
Use this diagram to help with step 7.

7 Hold the pendulum so it will swing as in **Figure 3**. As in step 6, gradually increase the level of force applied to the block.

(a) Record the level of force that was needed to make the block fall.

(b) Record the number of other blocks that fall with the moved block.

8 Repeat the tests in steps 6 and 7 for each block.

- Carefully restore the wall after each test, using the reference marks on the paper.

Analysis

9 Analyze your results by doing the following.

(a) Did changing the plane of swing of the pendulum affect the results? Explain the results of steps 6, 7, and 8.

(b) Which blocks were easiest to move?

(c) Removing which blocks had the most effect on the stability of the wall?

(d) Create and test a plan to demolish the wall using the fewest number of swings of the pendulum.

(e) Create and test a plan to demolish the wall using the smallest level of force.

Making Connections

1. Predict which would cause more damage to two cars, a head-on collision or a collision at an angle. Explain your prediction.

2. In the middle ages, invaders would attack castles with battering rams. To withstand the battering ram, the main door was reinforced by placing a plank of wood across the centre of the door and securing the plank to either side of the frame. Why would this change to the structure of the door make it better able to withstand the force being applied?

Exploring

3. (3C) (3D) Design a way to modify the wall, using 12 wooden dowels, glue, and wood fasteners, so it will not collapse when struck at any point by the wrecking ball. Draw a diagram of your design. Test your design. Based on what you learn in the test, improve your design and test it again. Draw the final version of your design and explain how it prevents the wall from collapsing.

4. (4A) What techniques, other than wrecking balls, are being used to bring down tall buildings? Research the techniques and create a poster showing the process of demolition.

Reflecting

5. What were the dependent and independent variables in this investigation? How did you control other variables?

(3C) Selecting the Best Alternative (3D) Planning a Prototype (4A) Research Skills

3.10

Loads

What happens when you put too many groceries in a shopping bag? The handle of the bag breaks (**Figure 1**). The **load**, the effect of the forces acting on the bag, is too great for the structure.

Loads are usually grouped into two categories: **static loads**, which are caused by the force of gravity, and **dynamic loads**, which are caused by other forces.

Figure 1
This shopping bag was overloaded.

Static Loads

Consider a bicycle (**Figure 2**). When you are riding a bicycle, the static load caused by the force of gravity has two components. The first component, the weight of the bicycle's wheels, frame, gears, cables, seat, and handlebars, is called the dead load. The **dead load** on any structure is caused by the force of gravity acting on the structure itself. It does not change.

The second component of the static load on the bicycle is the weight of the rider, called the **live load**. The live load is also caused by gravity, but it can vary. Some riders are heavy, some are light. Sometimes the bicycle has no rider at all, so there is no live load.

Figure 2
The static loads on a bicycle

Dynamic Loads

When you are riding the bicycle, you turn the handlebars to go around corners. To turn, you must exert a force on the handlebars. To go faster, you push down on the pedals with your feet. That force is transmitted from the pedals through the front gear to the chain, to the gear on the rear wheel, to the axle, which turns more quickly. Potholes in the road can cause forces that act on the wheels. The wind is a force pushing on the structure of the bicycle. These forces acting on the structure or parts of the structure of the bicycle create the dynamic loads, which may change rapidly.

Structural Design and Loads

The designer of a structure must try to anticipate the loads that the structure will bear. Obviously, a structure that cannot even bear the dead load of its own weight is a failure, but anticipating the other loads is more difficult. For example, the designer of the grocery bag expected the live load on the bag would be fairly small, perhaps a loaf of bread and some apples. The designer did not expect that the user would create a live load made up of a bag of milk and a kilogram of potatoes.

Dynamic loads can also test the foresight of a designer. The Tacoma Narrows Bridge **(Figure 3)** is a classic example. The bridge could handle the dead load caused by its own weight and the live load caused by the vehicle traffic crossing the bridge. However, the dynamic load created by a strong, steady wind caused the bridge to start swaying and twisting. Eventually, the bridge collapsed.

Figure 3

The Tacoma Narrows Bridge was not well designed to handle the dynamic load caused by the wind.

Try This Reducing the Load

You can use an empty cereal box and an electric fan to demonstrate the effects of a dynamic load.

- Place the empty box face-on about 1 m from the fan, and turn on the fan.

1. The box should be blown over. What were the dead load and the dynamic load on the cereal box?
2. Suggest as many ways as you can to change the dead and dynamic loads so the structure will not be blown over.

- Test your ideas.

3. What would a live load be in this situation? If the structure had to support a live load, would it alter your solutions to the problem? Explain.

Understanding Concepts

1. Hydro towers form a structure that is used to carry electricity from generating stations to homes and businesses. In **Figure 4**, identify the dead load, the live load, and the dynamic loads caused by forces acting on this structure.

Figure 4

2. (6C) Draw diagrams of structures that are supporting a dead load, a live load, and a dynamic load. Identify the forces that create the loads.
   (a) a chair
   (b) an apartment building
   (c) a running shoe as it hits the ground
3. Describe the loads that might affect the structure of a sailboat.

Making Connections

4. Shopping bags have a low dead load. Would a shopping bag with a high dead load still serve its purpose? Explain.
5. Using diagrams, explain how the magnitude, direction, and point of application of the force caused by the wind affects the dynamic load on a building.

Design Challenge

A chair, a pack, and a baseball catcher must bear much different loads. What static and dynamic loads must your structure bear? What about the dead load on your structure—should it be large or small?

SKILLS MENU
- ○ Identify a Problem
- ● Planning
- ● Building
- ● Testing
- ● Recording
- ● Evaluating
- ● Communicating

Determining Factor of Safety

Grocery bags break fairly easily if you add even a small amount more than the recommended weight limit. What if elevators, bridges, and bicycles were designed the same way? If you look on the wall of an elevator (**Figure 1**), you will see a licence. On this licence is the recommended rider capacity and maximum weight for the elevator—the maximum live load. But there is no need to get nervous if too many people squeeze on—the elevator cables won't snap. Why? Because to be safe, elevators are designed to support a live load 20 times greater than the licence number. This means that if the rider capacity is 500 kg, the elevator can safely support 10 000 kg (500 × 20)—more than the heaviest African elephant!

The **factor of safety** for elevators is 20. Other structures may use larger or smaller multiples of the maximum expected live load as their factor of safety.

Materials

Elevator

- 2 pulleys
- 2 m string
- 1 m^2 cardboard
- 12 paper fasteners
- hole punch

Test

- toy action figures
- mass balance
- standard masses

Figure 1
How many people can this elevator really support?

Problem

Elevators must be designed to safely lift the heaviest group of people who can fit in the elevator. How does a designer determine the maximum live load for an elevator?

Design Brief

Design and construct a model elevator and determine its factor of safety.

Design Criteria

- At least 5 passengers (action figures) must fit in the passenger compartment of the elevator.
- The elevator must be able to raise the compartment at least 20 cm.
- The elevator is safe if it can be raised and lowered at least 5 times without failing.

Build

(3D) **1** Design and draw a diagram of an elevator using the materials available.

(3E) **2** Based on your design, build your model elevator.

Test

3 Carefully fit as many action figures as you can into the passenger compartment of your elevator.

- Test the elevator by raising it and lowering it to make sure it meets the design criteria with the action figures on board.

4 (5B) Measure the total mass of the action figures that were in the elevator. This is your maximum live load.

(a) Record the mass of the action figures.

(b) What kind of load is represented by the mass of the action figures?

SKILLS HANDBOOK: (3D) Planning a Prototype (3E) Building a Prototype

Making Connections

1. It is always possible to increase the factor of safety of any design. Elevators could be built with safety factors of 30, 60, 100, or even more—but they are not. Based on your experience with this investigation and outside the classroom, suggest some reasons why not.
2. How would you test the factor of safety of a hockey helmet? What kinds of loads would you simulate during the test?

Reflecting

3. (3D) There is more to designing an elevator than getting the factor of safety to 20. What other features should a good elevator have? Create a set of design criteria for an elevator that will carry people from the ground floor to the 50th floor of a skyscraper.

5 Using standard masses equal to twice the mass of the passengers, test your model elevator.

(a) What factor of safety does this test represent?

6 Test your elevator for increasing factors of safety, until it fails. Remember, the factor of safety is the multiple of the maximum live load that the elevator can raise without failing.

(a) What is the factor of safety for your elevator?

Evaluate

7 Evaluate your design by doing the following.

(a) What part of the structure of your model elevator failed? What could you do with that part to make it stronger?

(b) Which of the elevator designs in your class had the highest factor of safety? What design features made that elevator different?

(c) Modify the design of your elevator to improve the factor of safety as much as possible.

(d) Build and test the new design.

Tension, Compression, Torsion, and Shear

Loads put stress on structures. The structures respond by stretching, compressing, twisting, and bending. If the stress is severe enough, the structure will collapse.

Tension and Compression

If you try to walk across a stream on a board, you put stress on the board. You are the load. One effect of a load on a beam is to make the beam bend (**Figure 1**). When a beam bends under a load, the bottom surface becomes longer—it is stretched. This pulling or stretching force is called **tension**. Meanwhile, the upper surface of the beam is being squeezed. The pushing force that squeezes the upper surface is called **compression**.

Tension and compression are often at work in the same part of a structure. For example, hydro wires are pulled tight as they are hung on the towers (tension), but there is also tension and compression caused as the wires sag. (The sag or bend is caused by the dead load created by the force of gravity pulling on the mass of the wires.) However, tension and compression can also act separately. When you pull on an elastic band (**Figure 2**), the band is under tension. When you squeeze a rubber ball (**Figure 3**), the ball is under compression.

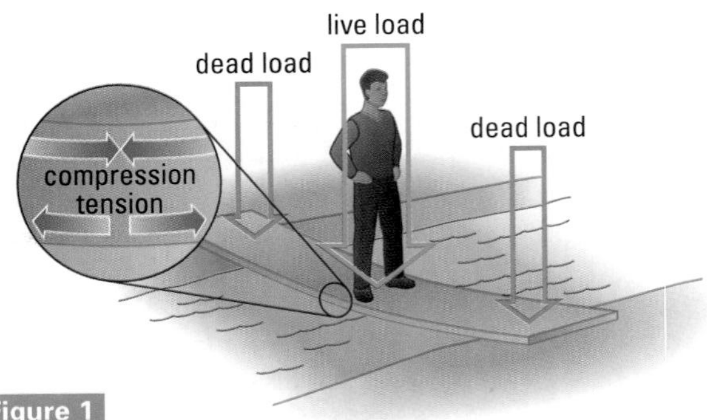

Figure 1
When you cross a stream on a board, you add to the load on the board. The board bends under the stress, creating forces of tension and compression within the structure.

Torsion

When you wring out a wet dishcloth by twisting the ends of the fabric, you are creating a force within the cloth. This force, created by applying opposite rotational forces on different parts of a structure, is called **torsion**. Objects that are under torsion twist (**Figure 4**).

A rotational force applied to any part of a structure, if the part is anchored, will result in torsional forces within the part. This is because the opposite rotational force is created by the structure itself, which resists the rotation of the part (**Figure 5**).

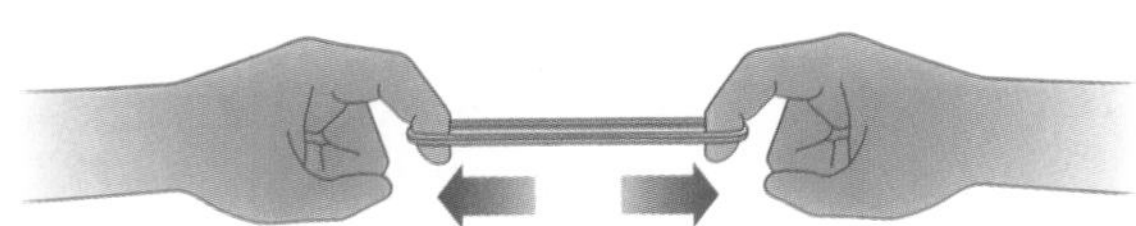

Figure 2
When forces pull in opposite directions, the force of tension is created in a structure. The object responds by stretching.

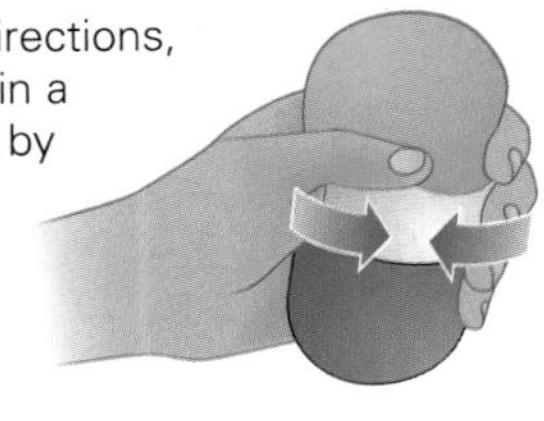

Figure 3
When forces push in opposite directions, the force of compression is created in a structure. The object responds by becoming smaller.

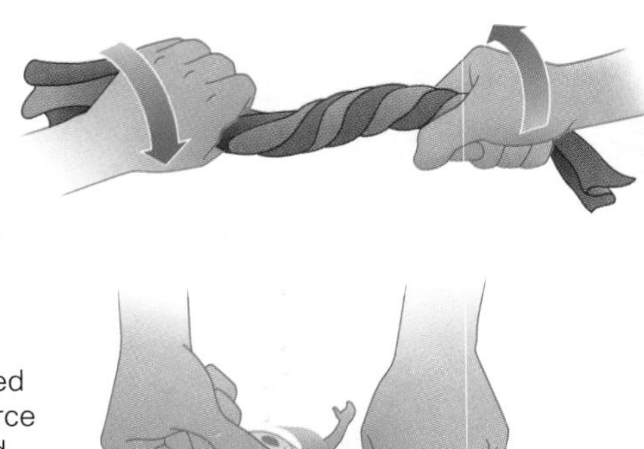

Figure 4
Torsion is created when opposite rotational forces are applied to an object. The object responds by twisting.

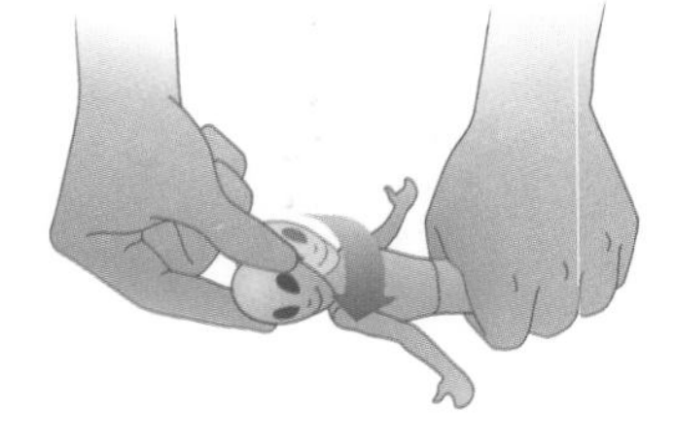

Figure 5
Torsion is also created when a rotational force is applied to one end of an anchored object.

Shear

When parallel forces acting in opposite directions are at work on a part in a structure, the part is said to be under **shear**. When you pull apart two pieces of licorice that are stuck together, you are creating a shear force (**Figure 6**).

When scissors are cutting paper, the two blades are moving in opposite directions at the surface of the paper. Scissors use forces of shear to cut through paper (**Figure 7**).

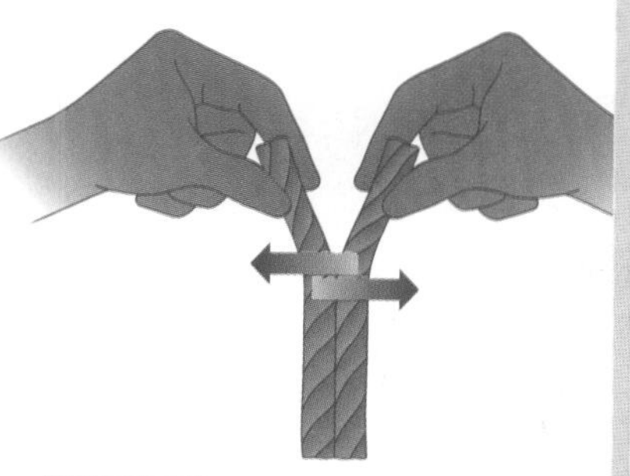

Figure 6
Shear forces are created when two parallel but opposite forces are at work at the same place within an object. When the opposing forces are pulls, the part responds by tearing, usually along a flat plane.

Figure 7
When the shear forces are opposite pushes, the structure may also tear.

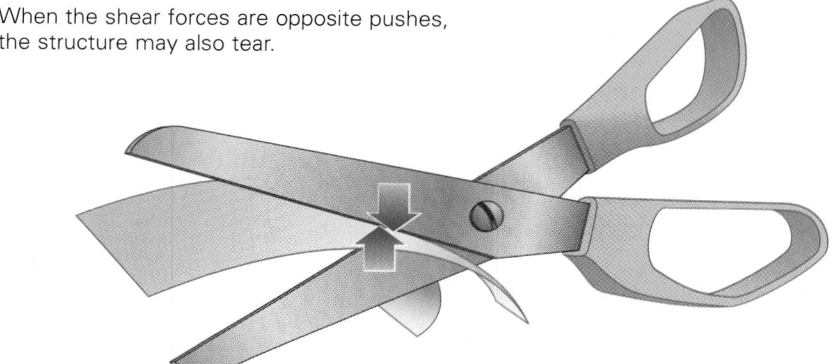

Understanding Concepts

1. In your own words, describe tension, compression, torsion, and shear.

2. (6C) Draw diagrams of each of the following situations and identify which forces are at work within the structure when they are being used:

(a) a gymnastic balance beam

(b) a diving board

(c) a model airplane powered by an elastic band

(d) a chain on a child's swing

Making Connections

3. (6C) Draw and label a diagram sharing the forces acting on and within a flagpole and its flag in a strong wind.

Try This Straw Drawing

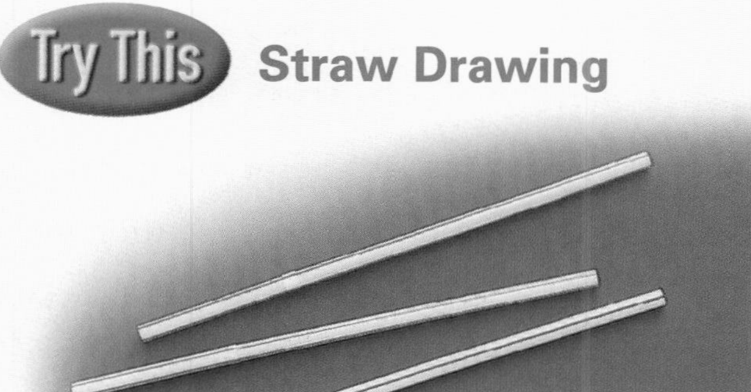

Buildings are designed to resist forces that cause compression and tension. But not all structures are designed this way. Some are designed to yield to these forces, such as straws with corrugated (ridged) sections. The corrugated section allows the straw to bend when it is bearing a dynamic load (when you are drinking!). You can use a flexible straw to observe the forces of tension and compression.

- Sketch the ridges in the corrugated section of the straw when the straw is straight.
- Bend the straw. Sketch the ridges in the corrugated section.

1. On which side are the ridges closer together? Is this evidence of tension or compression?

2. What force is at work where the ridges are farther apart?

3. Explain how the ridges make this structure more flexible than an ordinary straw.

Choosing Structures

When designers are creating a product, whether it is a building, a rack for CDs, or a jungle gym for a playground, they must start by assessing the forces that will work on the structure of the product. Then, they must decide which type of structure works best to handle the loads.

Shell Structures

Have you ever wondered why a clam shell is shaped the way it is? Its curved, hollow structure protects the delicate creature living inside. A **shell structure** has a solid surface and a hollow interior. Eggs and the cartons they are stored in, domed roofs, helmets, shoeboxes, and aircraft wings are all shell structures. Shell structures are used in many situations, but in all cases it is the shape of the shell that gives the structure its strength. In general, shell structures with curved surfaces are stronger than shell structures with flat surfaces (**Figure 1**). Strong shells can be made out of weak materials. Eggshell material is easily broken using small forces, but eggs resist being slowly crushed (compression), even when a high-magnitude force is applied. Because of their hollow interior, shell structures can be of low mass. They are useful for protection and as containers.

Figure 1
A domed roof is an example of a shell structure. Forces applied to a shell are transmitted through the whole structure.

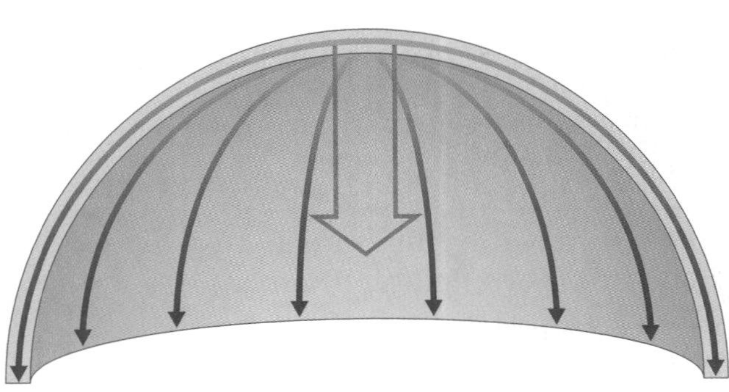

Solid Structures

Walls, dams, concrete pillars, and telephone poles are all solid structures. A **solid structure** has only one part and contains no hollow spaces. The strength of solid structures depends on their bulk—they resist forces either because they are too massive to move (**Figure 2**) or because the materials they are made of resist compression. Generally, the thicker a solid structure is, the stronger it is.

Since their strength comes, in part, from their mass, solid structures are also called **mass structures**. Solids tend to be stronger than shells, but they are also more massive. They add significantly to the dead load on any structure that includes them. The main use of solid structures is as supports.

Figure 2
This solid structure, a concrete gravity dam, resists the force generated by the water because it is too massive to move.

Testing a Shell

Paper cups are shell structures. You may be surprised to discover how strong they are.

- Turn a cup upside down on a flat surface.
- Predict how much mass the cup will support.
- Add masses to the base of the cup a little at a time until the cup collapses.

1. Describe how the cup gave way. What could you do to strengthen the cup?
2. Based on this test, predict how many cups you would need to support your weight. Describe how you would arrange the cups.

- Test your prediction.

SKILLS HANDBOOK: 2C Predicting and Hypothesizing

Figure 3
Properly supported, a frame structure can be strong.

(a) The structure of the picture frame has no internal support, so it is easy to make it lose its shape.

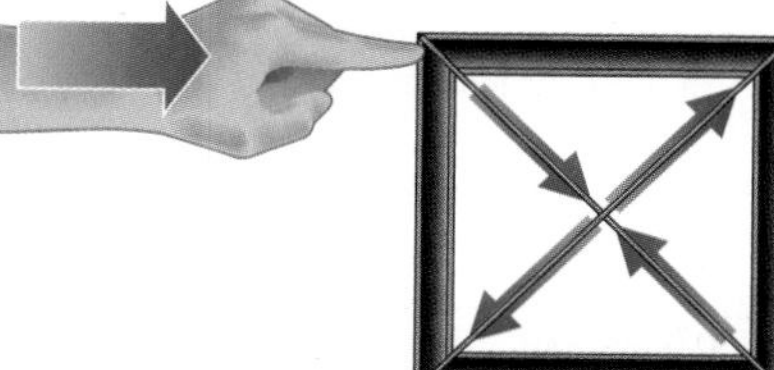

(b) Supports help the structure resist the force. Forces of tension and compression are set up inside the supports.

Frame Structures

Goal posts, your skeleton, hydro towers, and the girders that make up a bridge have something in common: they are all frame structures. **Frame structures** are formed from a combination of parts. None of the components of a frame structure is capable of supporting the load by itself. However, once the components are fastened together, they support and strengthen each other (**Figure 3**).

Because of their flexibility, frame structures are generally better at handling torsion and tension forces than solid structures, although they do not resist compression as well.

An important advantage of frame structures is that they use less material than solid structures and are therefore lighter. However, they may require more work to construct, because each component of the structure must be attached to the others.

Understanding Concepts

1. Make a chart with these headings: Solid (Mass), Frame, Shell. Under each heading, give three new examples of each kind of structure. Under each heading, one example must be smaller than a person, and one must be larger than a person.
2. Why are some structures a combination of more than one structural type?
3. The ancient Greeks and Romans used stone columns to support the roofs of their buildings. What type of structure is a column? What type of structure is a building made of columns and beams?
4. List the advantages and disadvantages of using a frame structure as a helmet.

Making Connections

5. Most animals have structures to support and protect inner organs and to help them move.
   (a) Classify and compare the structures of a beetle, a turtle, and a bird.
   (b) The wing bones of birds are hollow rather than solid. What advantage does this give birds?

Structures in Combination

Because shell, solid, and frame structures each have their advantages, they are often used in combination. For example, most tents are frame-shell structures. Can you explain why the structure shown in **Figure 4** was designed in a similar way?

Most buildings are solid-frame-shell structures. The foundation and other supports are solid; a frame of steel or wood supports the outer shell of brick or cement.

Figure 4
An umbrella is an example of a frame-shell structure.

Design Challenge

For your chair challenge, try creating designs using each of the three types of structure. Which do you think will work best? Would a combination of structural types be better?

Finding Stability in Symmetry

Next time you look at yourself in a mirror, study your face. If you draw an imaginary line down the centre of your face you will find the two halves look very much alike (**Figure 1**). The structure of human beings, like that of most animals, is symmetrical. An object or structure is **symmetrical** if it can be divided in two by a line or plane in a way that creates two pieces that are mirror images of each other (**Figure 2**).

Symmetry is common in living things, and it is also common in human-made structures. Structures are designed to be symmetrical to make them more stable and to distribute loads evenly.

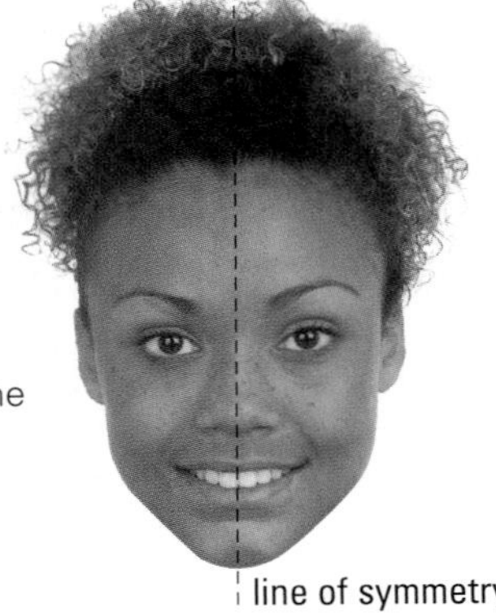

Figure 1
Human faces are symmetrical. The eyes are the same shape and the same distance from the nose; the mouth is balanced and the same shape on each side of the central line. What other features are the same in each half of the face?

Figure 2
Two symmetrical structures

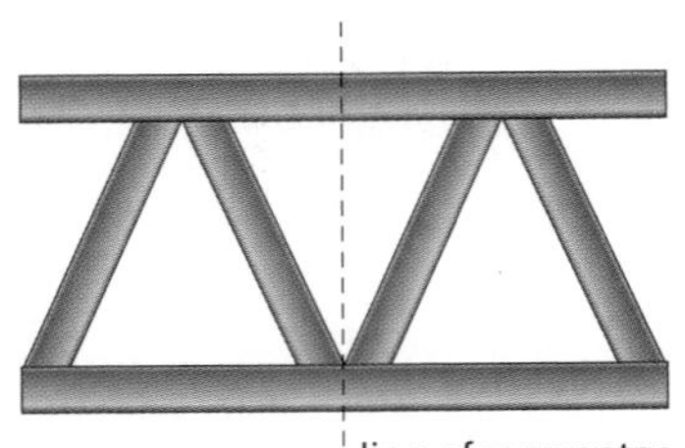

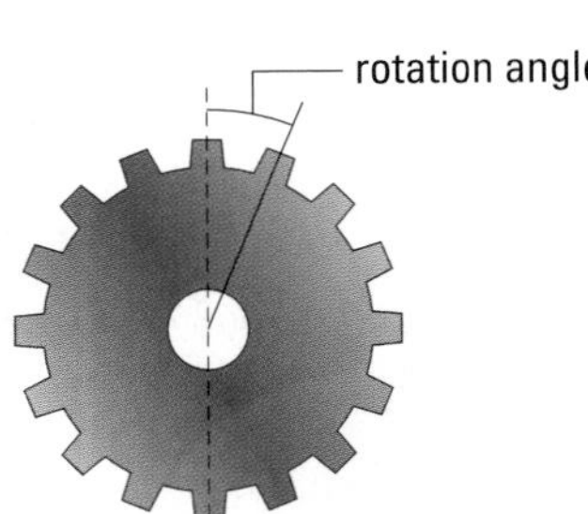

a This structure has **reflectional** symmetry. Each side of the line of symmetry is a reflection of the other side.

b This structure has **rotational** symmetry. If you rotate the structure repeatedly through the angle of symmetry, its appearance will remain the same. The gear also has reflectional symmetry. How many lines of symmetry could you draw through the gear?

Symmetry and Stability

Imagine that your left arm is much bigger and stronger than your right arm. Imagine that it is so long that the knuckles of your left hand brush the ground when you walk. There might be advantages to having such a long, powerful arm. It would certainly make playing basketball easier! However, there would be many more disadvantages. Consider that to support that big arm you would need much bigger muscles in your left shoulder and side, and bigger bones to support those muscles. The arm, the muscles, and the bone would make your left side weigh much more than your right. Now think about where your centre of gravity would be if you were standing with that big arm straight out from your shoulder. If someone were to give you a small push on your right side, you would fall over.

Symmetry improves the stability of structures. A structure that has its centre of gravity over the centre of its support base can resist external forces better than a structure that does not (**Figure 3**).

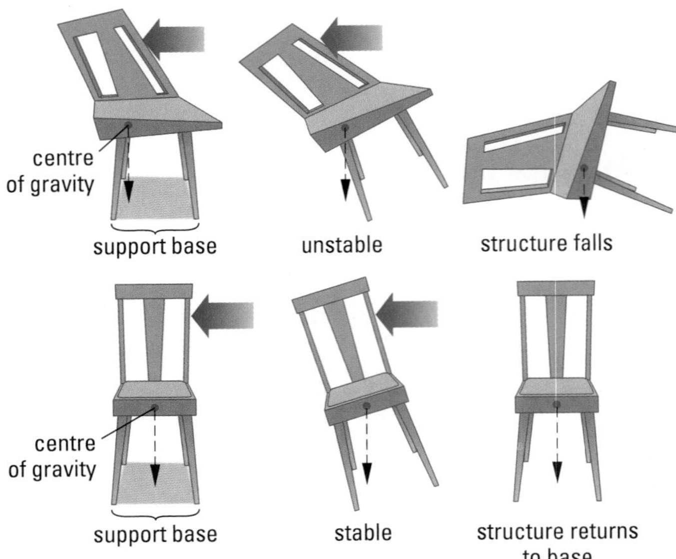

Figure 3
Symmetrical structures are more stable when the same force is applied.

Symmetry and Loads

Study **Figure 4**. Concrete is very good at resisting compression, but its tensile strength is poor. If the support were made of concrete and the load were large, the support would break because of the large tension force inside. In **Figure 5**, the load is even, and the support must deal only with a compression force. This support will not break.

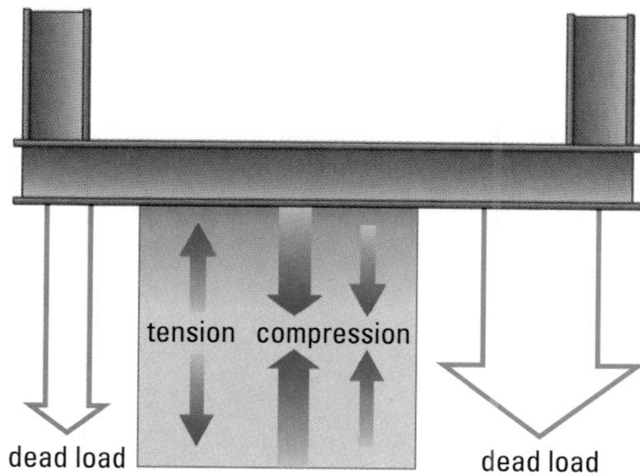

Figure 4

The dead load on this structure is not applied evenly, creating extra tension and compression forces in the support.

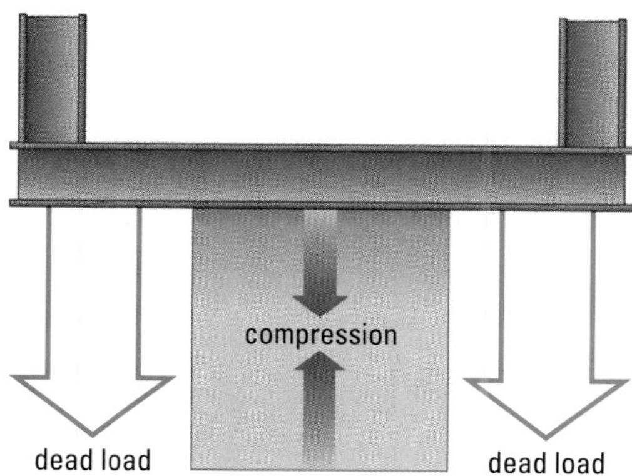

Figure 5

The dead load on this structure is applied evenly. The only force created inside the support is compression.

Symmetry and Expense

Symmetry has another important benefit—it makes structures easier to build, especially if the structure has many repeated sub-structures. For example, an office tower may have thousands of windows. If the structure is symmetrical, the windows will be the same shape—they can be designed once, and repeated. The manufacturer can mass-produce the windows, instead of having to custom-build each one. Finally, creating the frame and installing the windows is quicker and easier if they are all the same size.

Understanding Concepts

1. Draw diagrams of each of the following showing their symmetries:
   - **(a)** a human body
   - **(b)** a maple leaf
   - **(c)** the CN Tower

Making Connections

3. Find three examples each of symmetry in structures in your classroom, your schoolyard, your home, and the street where you live. In each case, make a diagram of the structure showing how it is symmetrical. Speculate on how symmetry makes the structure more stable and better able to support the loads it must bear.
4. In 1999, the Petronas Towers in Malaysia (**Figure 6**) was the tallest building in the world. The structure has two separate towers, connected by a walkway high above the ground.
   - **(a)** How might the symmetry of the Petronas Towers make it more stable?
   - **(b)** How might the structure's symmetry have made it less expensive to build?

Figure 6

Exploring

5. A stepladder must be stable to be safe.
   - **(a)** Draw a sketch of a stepladder. What parts of this structure are symmetrical? Why do they need to be symmetrical?
   - **(b)** Try designing a stepladder that has no symmetry. What are the disadvantages of your stepladder?

3.15 Design Investigation

SKILLS MENU
- ○ Identify a Problem
- ○ Planning
- ● Building
- ● Testing
- ● Recording
- ● Evaluating
- ● Communicating

A Stronger Beam

When the forces of tension, compression, torsion, and shear in a structure are strong enough, they can permanently change the structure. Permanent changes that result in a structure being unable to function are called **structural failures**. When you crush a pop can, you are causing a structural failure in the can. **Figure 1** shows the ways a part of a structure can change under a load.

There are techniques that can be used to reinforce parts of structures so the structure will not fail. In this investigation you will explore some techniques that modify the material.

Problem

To maintain stability in a structure, the parts of the structure must be prevented from bending, buckling, twisting, or shearing.

Design Brief

Build and test parts of structures under loads. Use techniques to strengthen these parts, and then test them again.

Use the following test for each beam:

- Place the beam across two pencils.
- Place the beaker on the centre of the beam.
- Add marbles, one at a time, to the beaker until the beam fails.
- The beam has failed if any part of it touches the table surface. If you fill the beaker with marbles and the beam has still not failed, record the test result as "pass."

Design Criteria

Using reinforcing techniques, build beams that pass the marble test.

Figure 1

Depending on the nature of the force, a structural member can fail in four different ways.

(a) **bend:** tension and compression forces cause the part to curve or to curve in a different way if it is already curved

(b) **buckle:** a compression force can causes the part to wrinkle, to lose its shape in one area

(c) **twist:** torsion forces cause the part to form a spiral

(d) **shear:** opposing forces (shear forces) cause the part to split and slide

Materials

Build

- apron
- goggles
- 3 polystyrene beams (2 cm × 4 cm × 20 cm)
- bamboo skewer
- 9 popsicle sticks
- low-temperature glue gun
- glue
- card stock
- sheets of paper
- scissors

Test

- 2 pencils
- 100-mL plastic beaker
- marbles

Build

Part 1: A Single Beam

1. Make a reinforced beam by carefully pushing a wooden skewer the length of the beam.

Test

2. Test an unreinforced polystyrene beam with its broad side up and with its narrow side up.
   - Test your reinforced beam.

(a) Record the number of marbles in the beaker when each beam fails.

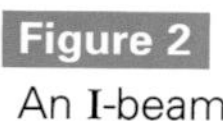

Figure 2
An I-beam

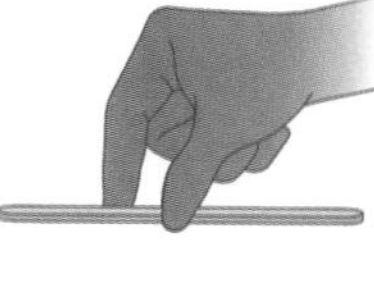

Figure 3
A laminated beam

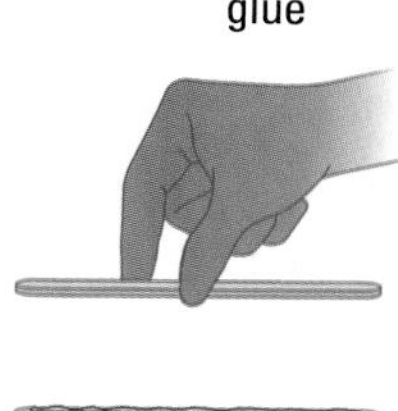

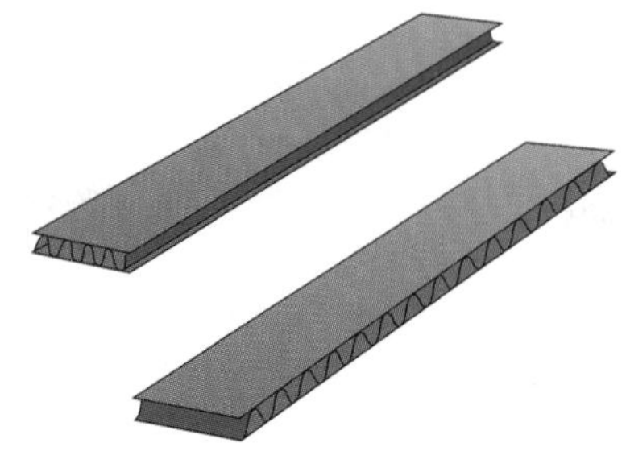

Figure 4
Two ways to corrugate

Build

Part 2: Beam Combinations

3 Using popsicle sticks and glue, make an I-beam as shown in **Figure 2**.
- Make a laminated beam, as shown in **Figure 3**.

Test

4 Test three popsicle stick beams by laying them side-by-side across the pencils.

(a) Why would you test three beams at once instead of one?
- Test your I-beam.
- Test your laminated beam.

(a) Record the number of marbles in the beaker when each beam fails.

Wear goggles and an apron when using the glue gun. Hot glue and the tip of the gun can burn exposed skin.

Build

Part 3: A Corrugated Beam

5 Using scissors, cut 6 sections of cover stock that are 5 cm × 20 cm.
- Cut a 5 cm × 20 cm section from a sheet of paper. Glue the paper between two sections of cover stock to make a flat beam.
- Fold two pieces of paper into pleats, as in **Figure 4**, and glue each one between two sheets of cover stock to make two corrugated beams.

Test

6 Test your paper beams.

(a) For each beam, record the number of marbles in the beaker when the beam fails.

Use care when cutting with scissors. Always cut away from your body.

Design Challenge

Which of the techniques you applied in this investigation would help you reinforce the structure in your Challenge?

Evaluate

7 Evaluate your results by doing the following.

(a) What kind of structural change happened in each beam?

(b) Which technique produced the strongest beam?

(c) It isn't fair to compare the three types of beam you tested in this investigation. Explain why not.

(d) How could you change the tests to better compare the techniques?

(e) In the test of the I-beam and the laminated beam, you made the test with the flat side up. Based on the results of your tests, predict which of these beams would be stronger with the other side facing up. Test your prediction.

Making Connections

1. You may have had trouble with your I-beam collapsing. In construction, I-beams are usually made of steel, and they are formed in one continuous piece (no glue!). An I-beam is not as strong as a beam made of solid steel, but it is lighter. What advantages are there in using I-beams instead of solid beams in construction?
2. Look around the school, your home, and your community and note where you see each of the techniques you have learned in this activity. Make a chart that includes the following headings: structure where technique is used; reinforcing technique; materials used; function of reinforced structural part. Which technique seems to be most common? Do you see a pattern in the use of each technique? (6A) (7E)

SKILLS HANDBOOK: (6A) Obtaining Qualitative Data (7E) Reaching a Conclusion

3.16 Design Investigation

SKILLS MENU
○ Identify a Problem
○ Planning
● Building
● Testing
● Recording
● Evaluating
● Communicating

A Stronger Structure

In the last investigation you learned how to make materials stronger using corrugation, lamination, I-beams, and internal reinforcement. In this investigation you will investigate techniques used to strengthen structures.

Problem

In some structures, modifying the materials isn't enough to make the structure strong and stable.

Design Brief

You will test a beam under a load, then build reinforcements for the beam using some standard techniques and test the beam again. Use the same test you used in the previous investigation. In this case the beam will have failed when it collapses or the beaker falls off the beam.

Design Criteria

Use three techniques to maximize the load a beam can carry.

Build

1 Cut 5 equal strips of cardboard, each about 30 cm long. Three of these will act as a main beam; the other two will be used to form supports.

Use care when cutting with scissors. Always cut away from your body.

Materials

Build

- cardboard
- scissors
- 4 index cards, 7.5 × 12.5 cm
- paper fasteners
- single-hole punch

Test

- books (to make two piles of equal height)
- 50-mL plastic beaker
- marbles

Test

2 Place two equal piles of books of equal height about 20 cm apart. Use the books to support the beam. (You may have to adjust the height of the piles for each test.)

- Place one of the thin strips of cardboard so it rests on each pile of books.
- Test the beam using the beaker and marbles.

(a) Record the number of marbles in the beaker when the beam failed.

3 Lay a second strip of cardboard across the books.

- Use another strip of cardboard to make an arch. Being careful not to "break" the cardboard, wedge the arch between the books and below the top piece of cardboard. You may need to adjust the height or position of the books.
- Test the beam supported by the arch.

(a) Record the number of marbles in the beaker when the beam failed.

Figure 1
The arm of this crane is a truss. Triangular supports can make a structure very strong.

4 Lay a third strip of cardboard across the books.
- Use another strip of cardboard to make two supports. Fold the strip in half. Wedge the support beams in an upside-down V between the books and the other piece of cardboard. You may need to adjust the heights and position of the books.
- Test the beam supported by the support beams.

(a) Record the number of marbles in the beaker when the beam failed.

Build

5 Cut 3 index cards into 12 long, equal strips.
- Punch a hole in each end of the strips.
- Attach strips with paper fasteners to make a triangle, a square, and a pentagon.

6 Lay the shapes on the table. Push and pull on each shape.

(a) Which shape is most stable?

7 Add a diagonal strip to the square so it doesn't change shape when pushed. You have created a truss.

(a) Draw a diagram of the truss.

8 Design and build a truss made out of cardboard that will support a beam. (3C)

Test

9 Test a beam while it is being supported by your truss.

(a) Record the number of marbles in the beaker when the beam failed.

(b) Record your observations of how the truss failed.

Evaluate

10 Evaluate the results of your tests by doing the following.

(a) Describe how an arch and support columns each increase the strength of a beam. According to your tests, which is stronger?

(b) Why is a triangle a stronger shape for a structural support than a square?

(c) Compare your truss to the arch and the support columns. Which is strongest?

(d) Draw a diagram of your truss under load. Show where you think forces of tension and compression are acting in the truss.

(e) Using your own ideas and the design ideas and observations of other groups, design, build, and test a new truss.

Making Connections

1. **Figure 1** shows an example of a structure that includes a truss. Look for more examples of arches, trusses, and support beams in structures in your home, at school, and in the community. For each example, speculate on why that support technique was used.

Design Challenge

Could you use any of the techniques you used in this investigation in the design of your chair challenge? If so, explain how the technique will strengthen the structure of the chair.

SKILLS HANDBOOK: 3C Selecting the Best Alternative

Strengthening Structures

If a structure is likely to fail, it might seem easiest for the designer to simply use a stronger material. However, that stronger material may be too heavy, too expensive, or just not available. To stay within budget and to keep dead loads low, designers must often choose weaker and cheaper construction materials and support them to overcome their weaknesses.

Using Triangles

As you have learned, triangles are strong shapes for structural forms. A **truss** is a frame that takes advantage of the strength of triangles by linking many of them together (**Figure 1**). Each triangle in a truss is made up of three members or parts. Trusses can be used to support other parts of a structure or on their own as an alternative to solid structures such as beams.

Gussets are used to reinforce the triangle. A **gusset** is a piece of solid material used to reinforce a seam or a joint (**Figure 2**). Gussets can be used to resist tension, compression, or torsion forces.

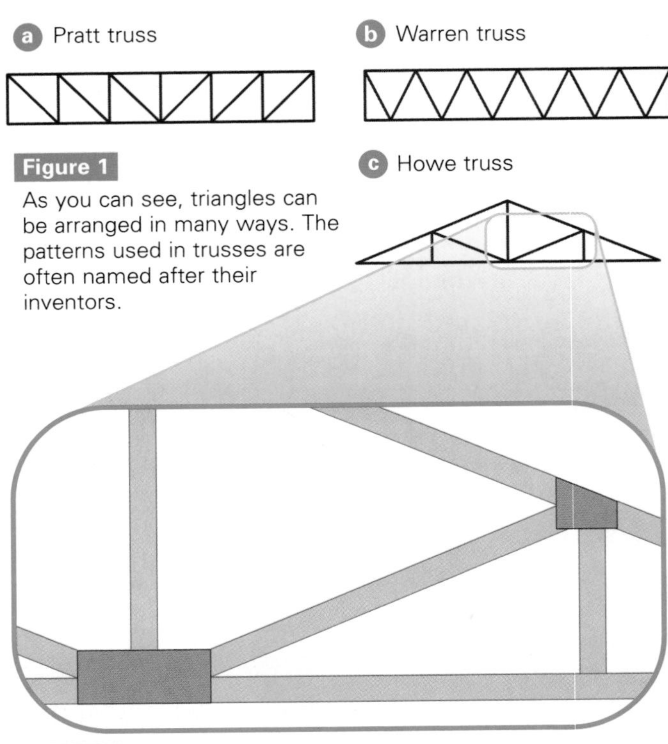

Figure 1 As you can see, triangles can be arranged in many ways. The patterns used in trusses are often named after their inventors.

Figure 2 A gusset prevents the separation, twisting, or collapse of parts meeting at a joint. They are attached to both of the parts making up the joint. Here gussets are being used to reinforce a Howe truss.

Using Curves

As you have learned, the curve of an **arch** can form a very strong support. The arch "channels" the force caused by the load to the supports of the arch.

Figure 3 shows an arch made of separate stones. However, one-piece arches, made of wood, plastic, steel, or concrete, work the same way. It may help you to imagine how if you think of the one-piece arch as being made up of tiny bricks that are too small to see.

Arches are just as strong as or stronger than walls, but they use less material, and they leave openings in a structure. Those openings can be used, for example, as entrances, or to reduce the area of the structure exposed to wind.

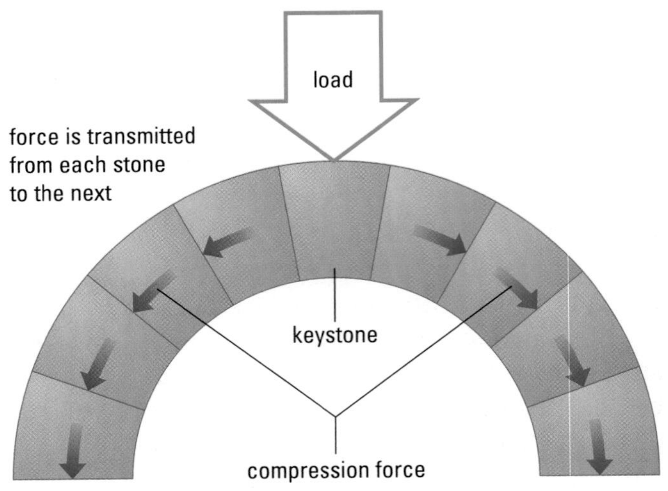

Figure 3 A stone arch. Compression forces are transmitted through the arch and are converted to a pure vertical compression force at the base.

Ties and Struts

Sometimes a structure needs only a little help to become strong. A **tie** is a support that does its work by resisting tension forces. A **strut** is a support that resists compression forces. Unlike columns, struts do not have to be vertical.

Figure 4
In these examples the tie and the strut are two ways of doing the same job—supporting the sign.

Corrugation

If you look at the edge of a piece of cardboard, you will see that the interior is corrugated. The waves in the edge of corrugated cardboard look and act like a series of arches. This pleated material is much better at resisting compression than would be expected from paper. This makes cardboard a good packaging material, as it is light, protects the contents, and is strong enough to allow stacking. Corrugation may also be formed as a V-shaped pleat.

Lamination

Making a material thicker will increase its strength. When it is not possible to make one thick piece, lamination (bonding of two or more layers of the material) is used (**Figure 5**).

It is possible to laminate different materials, taking advantage of the special properties of each material. For example, to make a kitchen counter that is strong and light but won't be destroyed by accidental spills, a layer of waterproof material is laminated to a wooden base.

Figure 5
When wood is laminated, each layer is turned at a 90° angle to the layer below. This takes advantage of a property of wood: it is stronger in one direction (the grain) than in others. Wood that is laminated in this manner is stronger than a single piece of wood of the same thickness.

Understanding Concepts

1. Create a chart that includes the name of each of the strengthening methods, a description in your own words of how it is effective, and a diagram showing an application that hasn't been mentioned in this section.

Making Connections

2. Examine a running shoe, a computer, or a bicycle. Have any of the strengthening techniques you've read about here been used in these products? Describe where, and how they strengthen the product.

Exploring

3. The single sheet of steel that forms the hood of a car is structurally weak. Create diagrams showing the hoods of at least five different cars, identifying how they are strengthened. Label each diagram with the maker's name and the model.

Design Challenge

Which of the ways of strengthening materials might be useful in your Challenge?

SKILLS MENU
- Identify a Problem
- Planning
- Building
- Testing
- Recording
- Evaluating
- Communicating

Getting Under Foot

When we think of floors, we usually think of being on solid ground. This is rarely true, of course—floors are structures, or parts of structures. A floor must be strong enough to support people and furniture and to help support walls, but there are good reasons why most floors are not simply solid structures (**Figure 1**).

Materials

- 40 toothpicks
- 4 bamboo skewers, with the pointed tips cut off
- 4 letter-size sheets of paper
- 4 drinking straws
- white glue
- paintbrush
- scissors
- ruler
- pencil
- string

Test

- books
- 5-g masses, 10
- 50-g mass

Problem

3B **1** Identify a problem that is solved in this investigation.

Design Brief

You will construct a floor system using lamination, corrugation, and other reinforcement techniques to make the floor strong and stable.

Design Criteria

- The floor must be stable and able to support a load of at least 50 g.
- The floor surface must measure at least 20 cm × 20 cm.
- The floor must be thick enough to allow simulated wiring and plumbing (string).

Build

2 Draw a rough sketch of
3C your floor design.
- Identify the weak points in your design, then design reinforcements.
- Draw diagrams explaining how you will construct each type of reinforcement.
- Draw a final diagram of
3D your design. Submit this
6C diagram and your reinforcement diagrams to your teacher for approval.

3 Build your model floor based on your design and using the materials provided.
- Make sure you include string to represent plumbing and wiring.

Test

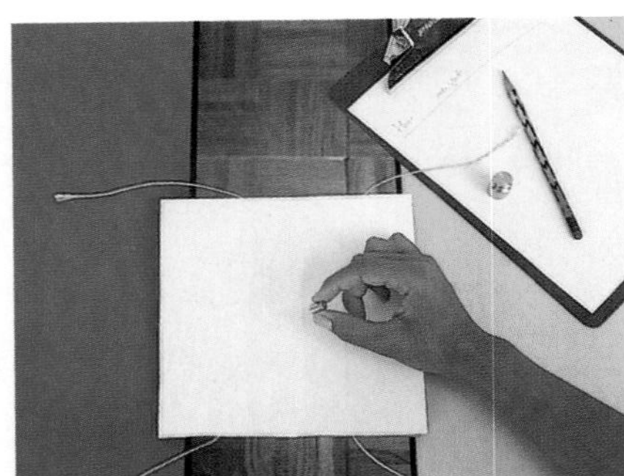

4 Place your floor across two equal piles of books with 1 cm of the floor supported at each edge.
- Slowly add 5-g masses, to a total of 50 g, to different parts of the floor. As you add the masses, observe how the floor reacts.

(a) Record your observations.

- If the floor collapses, redesign the floor so it will support the load.

SKILLS HANDBOOK: 3B Identifying a Problem 3C Selecting the Best Alternative

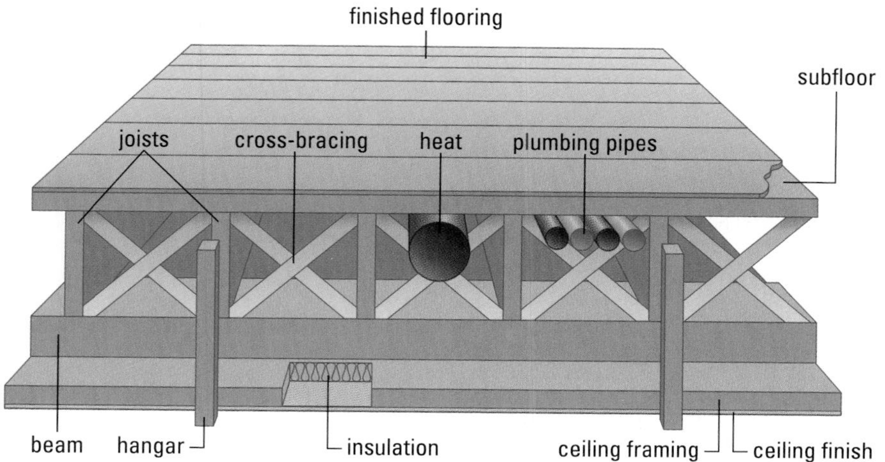

Figure 1

Floors must allow plumbing, heating, and electrical systems to be routed through a building.

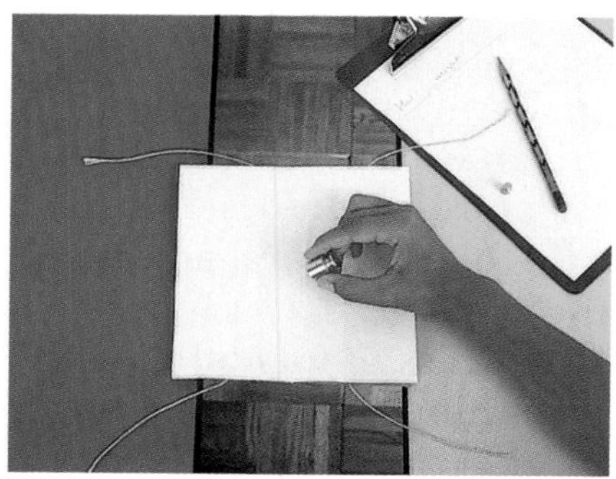

5 Remove the masses and place a 50-g mass on different parts of the floor, one area at a time, to test if the structure can withstand a concentrated mass.

- Observe how the floor reacts to the 50-g mass.

(a) Record your observations using drawings.

Evaluate

6 Evaluate your floor by answering the following questions.

(a) Did your floor structure fail during step 5? If so, draw a diagram showing how the structure failed. How would you make it stronger?

(b) Study the other floors designed by your class. Would any of their design features improve the strength of your floor? Explain.

(c) A bumpy floor is a safety hazard. Did the surface of your floor stay flat during testing? How could you improve the structure of the floor so that the surface would remain flat under a load?

Making Connections

1. What type of structure (solid, frame, shell) is the floor you designed?
2. **(a)** Draw a diagram showing (6C) how external forces act on the structure of your floor.
   (b) Draw diagrams showing how and where the external forces create internal forces within your floor.
3. You used string to represent wiring and plumbing in the floor. But plumbing is made of straight pipes, not flexible string. What adjustments would you make in your design if you had to include real plumbing?
4. Study the webbed floor in **Figure 2**. Does this resemble the structure you built? What design features of the webbed floor could you use to improve your design?

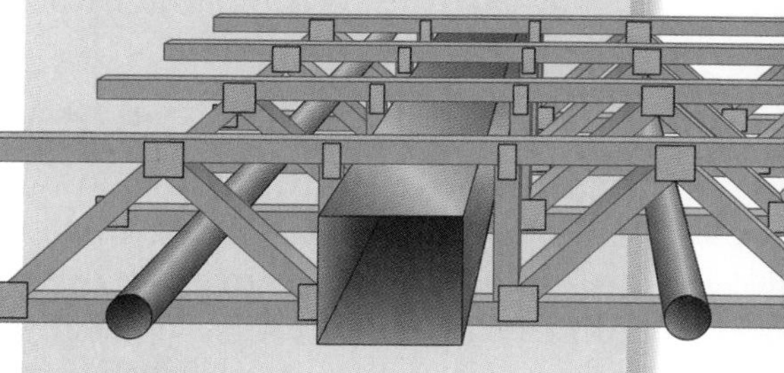

Figure 2

Reflecting

5. If you had to build a roof, rather than a floor, what would stay the same in your design? What would you change?

Design Challenge

Can any of the techniques you've tested in this investigation help with the design of your chair?

(3D) Planning a Prototype (6C) Scientific & Technical Drawing

Fasteners and Function

A structure's strength depends not only on the design of the structure and the materials it is made of, but also how it is held together. A device or material that holds two or more pieces of a structure together is a **fastener**. Nails, screws, rivets, and glue are all fasteners.

Forces and Clothing

Every piece of clothing—whether a shirt, a skirt, a jacket, or a pair of shoes—is a structure. Most clothing is made of several pieces, carefully shaped and fastened together. Clothing must not suffer structural failure when being worn, put on, or taken off.

(a) What forces act on clothing? Brainstorm a list of forces that could be expected to act on an item of clothing during a normal day. Classify them as tension, compression, torsion, or shear forces. Rank the forces according to their magnitude.

Withstanding Forces: Zippers

Fasteners for clothing are designed to open easily when we want to remove the item, and to remain closed otherwise. While the type of fastener selected for a piece of clothing depends on the type and magnitude of the main force the garment must withstand, there are other reasons for choosing a particular kind of fastener. Ski jackets, for example, almost always use a zipper (**Figure 1**) as their main fastening device.

(b) Brainstorm as many kinds of fasteners as you can that would hold a ski jacket closed during normal use. What advantages do zippers have over the other fasteners for this use?

(c) Zippers have disadvantages. You've probably experienced a zipper that has broken. What kind of force causes zippers to have a structural failure? In what ways are zippers most likely to fail?

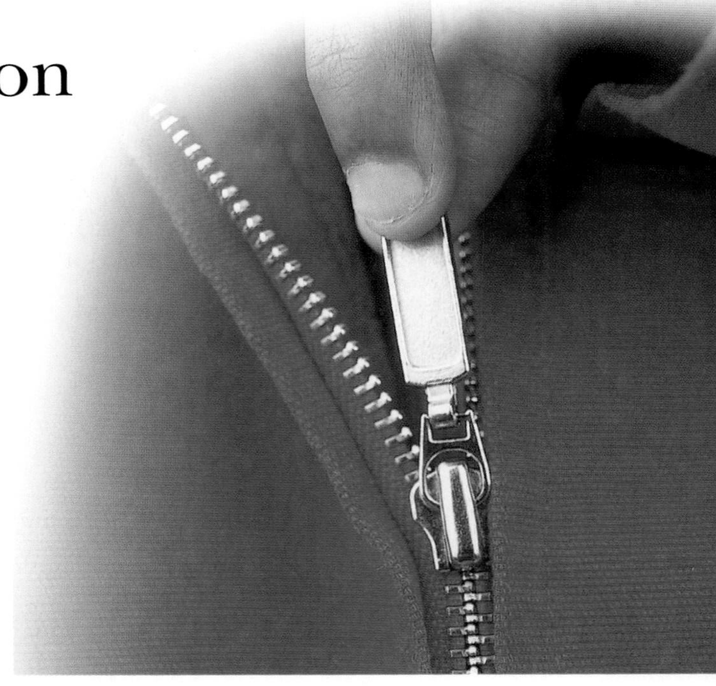

Figure 1
The teeth of a zipper interlock when closed, making them very difficult to separate.

Fasteners That Don't Fail: Dome Snaps

Zippers are relatively easy to break—and once broken, hard to fix. For most uses, dome snaps (**Figure 2**) are an excellent alternative. When locked, the snap resists forces of tension. However, the big structural advantage of the snap over the zipper is that it helps clothing to deal with forces of torsion. Under torsion forces, the clothing can rotate around the snap.

If the force acting on the snap becomes too great, the two pieces of the snap will simply separate rather than failing permanently, as a zipper does.

(d) Where are dome snaps often used in clothing?

(e) Draw a diagram showing how the two locking parts of a snap help clothing adjust to torsion.

(f) Some forms of clothing combine a zipper with a separate layer above that is fastened using dome snaps. Speculate on the advantages of this combination.

Traditional Fasteners: Buttons

Buttons have a lower resistance to forces than snaps, but are the preferred fasteners if cost is a consideration. Buttons are inexpensive and easy to replace if broken. Snaps must be hard, so are often made of metal. A button can be made from a much wider variety of materials, so buttons are often chosen when visual appeal is more important than strength.

(f) When a strong force is applied, a button is more likely to break than a snap. Explain why.

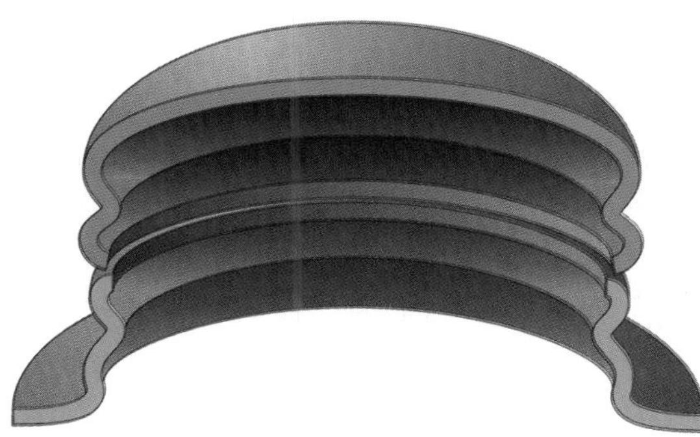

(a) Force is applied by the thumb

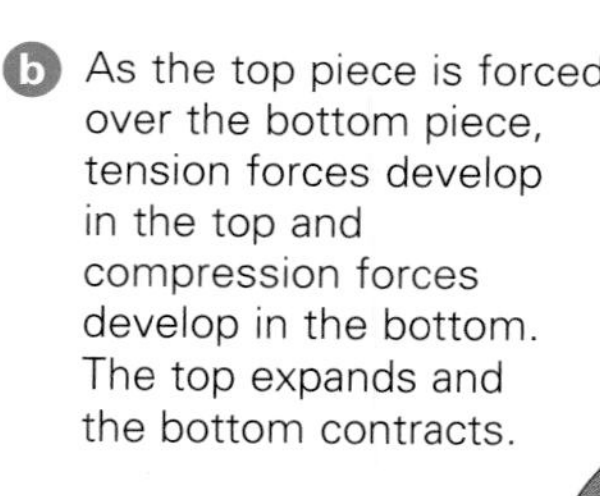

(b) As the top piece is forced over the bottom piece, tension forces develop in the top and compression forces develop in the bottom. The top expands and the bottom contracts.

(c) The two pieces fit snugly, but because they are round and smooth, they can rotate around each other.

Figure 2

Snaps do just that: the top of the device slips over the bottom with a snap. Snaps work because the narrowest part of the top piece is slightly smaller in diameter than the mouth of the bottom piece. Snaps are effective against torsion forces, but they open fairly easily using a shear force.

Understanding Concepts

1. Would strength always be the most important reason for choosing a fastener? Think of three examples where the strongest available fastener would not be the best choice.
2. Hook-and-eye fasteners (**Figure 3**) are also used in clothing. What are the advantages of the hook-and-eye over the button or the snap? What are the disadvantages of this kind of fastener?

Figure 3

3. Velcro is a fastener with many miniature hooks on one side of the tape and loops on the other. When they are pushed together, the hooks slip into the loops. Velcro is used for many purposes, from running shoes to medical splints and braces. What advantages does Velcro have over other fasteners?

Exploring

4. All of the fasteners in this section (4A) are temporary and reusable. However, other fasteners are permanent and can be used only once. Research to find as many fasteners as possible, and make a chart with the following headings: Permanent or Temporary; Reusable or One-Time Use; Materials Used to Make the Fastener; Examples of Use. Make a poster showing some interesting uses of fasteners that you have discovered.

Design Challenge

You will need fasteners to complete your Challenge. How will you decide which ones to use? What tests will you carry out before you make your choices?

SKILLS HANDBOOK: (4A) Research Skills

SKILLS MENU
- Identify a Problem
- Planning
- Building
- Testing
- Recording
- Evaluating
- Communicating

Designing a Childproof Container

When a product is being designed for safety, the choice of fasteners can be especially important. The childproof cap (**Figure 1**) has saved many lives. Small children are very curious and often investigate objects by putting them in their mouths. This is dangerous if the object is poisonous or small enough to swallow. In this investigation, you will design a childproof container that is used to hold small objects that might be dangerous, such as pills or matches.

Materials
- cardboard
- scissors
- tape
- hole punch
- other materials as required

Problem

(3B) 1 Write a problem statement for this investigation.

Design Brief

Design and construct a container that infants cannot open, but that can be opened by an adult.

Design Criteria

- The container must be able to hold several small objects, such as sewing needles or pills.
- An infant should not be able to open the container, but an adult should be able to open it with moderate force.
- The fastener must allow the container to be opened and shut more than once.

Figure 1
Opening a childproof cap usually requires two movements (a push and a precise turn) at the same time. Infants find this very difficult.

Build

(3C) 1 Three different styles of container are shown in **Figure 2**. Examine each closely and discuss which design is best for the use you have in mind.

2 Make a list of the design features you want to include in your container.

(6C) 3 Draw a diagram of the container and its fastening.

4 List any additional materials you will need to build the structure.

(3D) 5 Write a description of how your container works and why a child would have difficulty opening it.

6 Submit your description, drawing, and materials list to your teacher for approval.

(3E) 7 Build the container according to your design.

Figure 2
Three styles of container

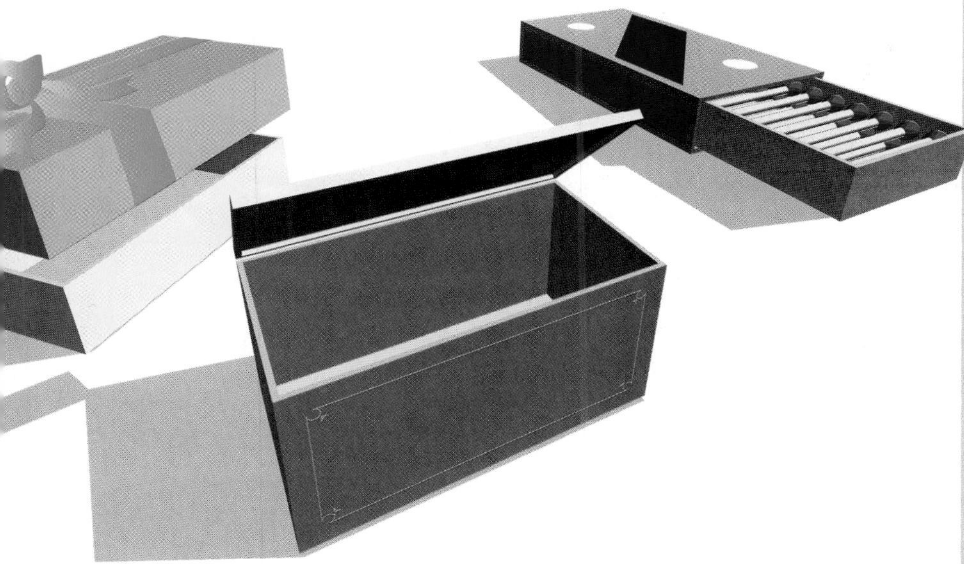

Test

8 Test how difficult your container is to open and close.
3F Would a child have enough force or ingenuity to open the container?

(a) Record your observations of the tests and your conclusions.

Evaluate

9 Evaluate your design by answering the following questions.

(a) Would it be a problem if a child could open your structure even partially? Did your container pass this test? If not, how could you improve your design?

(b) Study the other designs your class has created. Based on the design features of other containers and the results of your tests, how could you improve on your design?

(c) Is cardboard a good choice of material for a final product? What would be the best material to use in building your container?

Making Connections

1. Some food products, such as pop bottles, have a special fastener called a seal. The seal is broken when the product is opened—it is designed to fail. An intact seal tells consumers that the product has not been opened and is safe to use.

(a) Draw a diagram showing 6C the forces that act on the seal of a pop bottle as it is opened.

(b) Investigate the seals on food products at a local grocery store or in your home. How many different kinds can you find? Draw diagrams showing how each works.

2. You are working for a company that must store and use a liquid that is toxic if it is swallowed or if the fumes are inhaled. The liquid is also flammable. Small amounts of the liquid are used while making a special plastic. Write a design brief and design criteria for a container for this liquid.

Exploring

3. People with arthritis in their fingers sometimes find pill bottles with childproof caps difficult to open. Arthritis makes it difficult to grip the small cap, and it can be painful to apply force while twisting the cap. Design a childproof container for medicine that can be opened easily by people who have arthritis.

Reflecting

4. Did your design change after you drew your initial diagram? What problems did you run into as you moved from your diagram to the product you tested?

6C Scientific & Technical Drawing

Making Bridges

Bridges all have the basic function of enabling people and products to move over an obstacle, so why aren't they all alike? As with other structures, a bridge's design depends on the needs it meets. Some bridges are designed to cross over great distances; some carry only pedestrians, others cars and trucks, and still others trains. Local weather conditions and what support can be expected from the local rock are also important design considerations.

While engineers have developed several types of bridge to respond to the range of needs, all bridges are made of one or more spans. A **span** is a section of bridge that lies between two supports.

Figure 1
Larger beam bridges rely on a frame to improve stability.

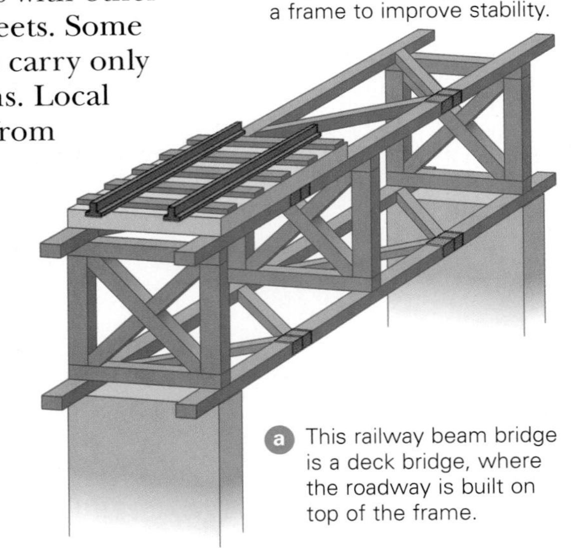

(a) This railway beam bridge is a deck bridge, where the roadway is built on top of the frame.

(b) In a through bridge, the roadway is inside the frame.

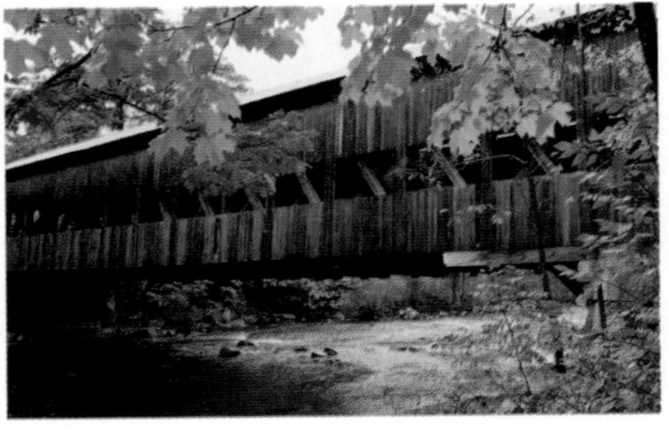

The Beam Bridge

As you have already seen, **beam bridges** consist of one or more beams supported at both ends and sometimes by columns underneath. Modern beam bridges use steel or concrete reinforced with steel for the beams. Concrete resists compression well, and steel resists tension.

Bridges with several beams usually add a frame structure using steel stiffeners and triangles to improve the stability of the bridge (**Figure 1**).

The Truss (Framed) Bridge

The **truss bridge**, usually made of steel, relies on a system of triangular supports (trusses) to support its load (**Figure 2**).

Figure 2
Truss bridges use a variety of different forms of truss.

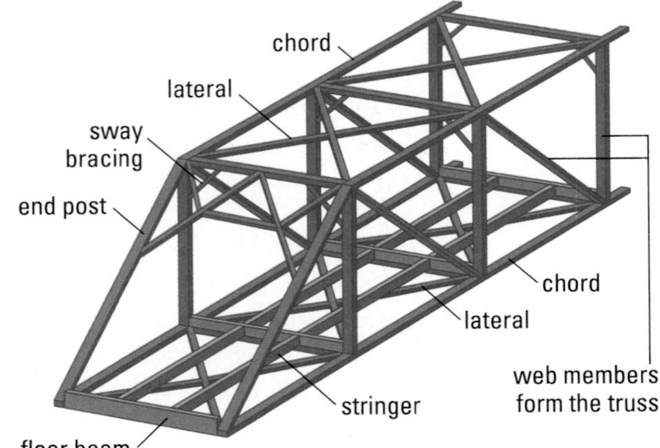

(a) A Pratt truss through bridge. Forces of compression and tension in the web members change as traffic crosses the bridge.

(b) The Champlain Bridge in Montreal, also a through truss bridge. In this case the truss is a Warren. Its longest span is 215 m.

The Arch Bridge

As you can see in **Figure 3**, depending on the material chosen, an **arch bridge** supports its load from below (concrete or stone) or above (steel). The static load creates a compression force in the arch.

Figure 3

Arch bridges are often used in locations where a support column would be difficult to place.

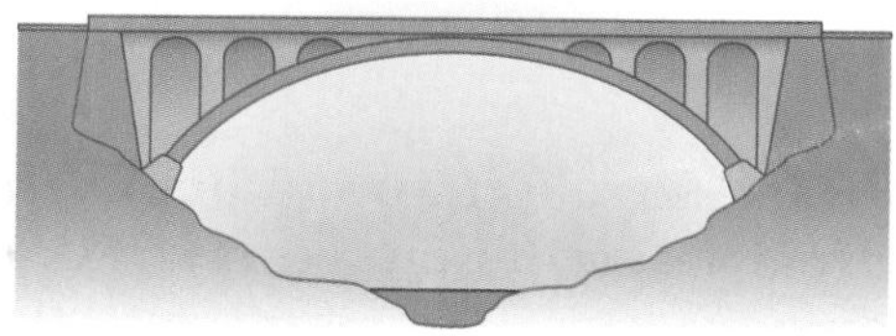

(a) The load creates forces of compression that are directed down the arches to the supports.

(b) The Rainbow Bridge in Niagara Falls is a steel arch bridge. It has a span of 300 m.

The Suspension Bridge

A **suspension bridge** uses cables strung from towers to support the bridge from above (**Figure 4**). Steel cables and concrete towers are used because of the enormous load created by the weight of the bridge.

Figure 4

Suspension bridges are designed to cross wide bodies of water.

(a) Tension forces in the tightly strung cables are of very high magnitude. Compression forces are created in the towers.

(b) The longest span of the Ambassador Bridge in Windsor is 564 m, but a few suspension bridges have spans of more than 1200 m.

The Cantilever Bridge

A **cantilever bridge** works like two seesaws connected by a span (**Figure 5**). Mass on either end supports the mass of the span in the middle. Cantilever bridges are made of massive steel girders supported by concrete piers.

Figure 5

Like suspension bridges, cantilever bridges are usually used to cross water, however, cantilever bridges are much more massive.

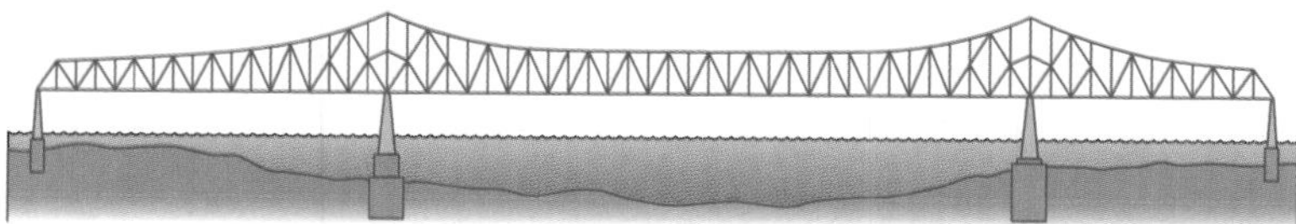

(a) Cantilever bridges have a high dead load because they depend on their mass to support the middle of the bridge.

(b) The middle span of the Quebec Railway Bridge over the St. Lawrence is 549 m long.

Understanding Concepts

1. Describe the differences between:
   - (a) a beam bridge and a suspension bridge;
   - (b) an arch bridge and a cantilever bridge;
   - (c) a truss bridge and a cantilever bridge.
2. Beam bridges are often used for short distances because they're more economical than other types. Explain why a beam structure might not be the best choice for a bridge that needs a long span.

Making Connections

3. (a) Identify some local bridges and make a chart with the following headings: Function of the Bridge; Type of the Bridge; and Materials Used.
   (b) (4A) (8A) Choose one of the bridges and research when and why it was built, and why the engineer chose the type. Write up your findings in a report.

SKILLS HANDBOOK: (4A) Research Skills (8A) Writing a Report

3.22 Design Investigation

SKILLS MENU
- Identify a Problem
- Planning
- Building
- Testing
- Recording
- Evaluating
- Communicating

Bridging the Gap

In this investigation, you will build a model of bridge that will cross water. Building over water is more complicated than building over land. In addition to the normal forces acting on a bridge, other factors must be taken into account. Ships must be able to go underneath the bridge—should the main span be high, or is a mechanism that raises or moves part of the bridge the best choice (**Figure 1**)? If piers or towers are part of the design, how can they be built safely and economically in the water? There are also tides, currents, the possibility of ice damage, and even strong impacts if a ship were to collide with the bridge.

You will also measure the performance of your bridge by comparing the bridge's mass with the load it can carry.

Materials

- materials as available

Test

- mass balance
- other materials as needed

Problem

Your team has been hired to design a bridge that meets the needs of the town of Bridgeton. Bridgeton is growing rapidly and has decided to replace an old stone bridge over the canal that runs through the town. The town also plans to expand its harbour so it can handle freighters. These ships must get past the bridge to reach the harbour. Storms with high winds occur every summer in Bridgeton.

Design Brief

Design and build a model of a bridge over Bridgeton's canal (**Figure 2**) that carries two lanes of traffic and a pedestrian walkway, will withstand the dynamic loads caused by high winds and moving traffic, support the static loads created by its own weight and the weight of traffic, and allow ships to pass.

Design Criteria

- The bridge must span a 50-cm gap.
- Freighters must be able to pass safely through or under the bridge. (Use the same scale.)
- The bridge must safely withstand the loads created by high winds and by a traffic jam. You must provide an estimate of the factor of safety of the bridge.
- The bridge must be strong, but should also be as light as possible to conserve materials.

Build

1 (3A) Begin by thinking about how your design will provide a solution for Bridgeton, and how you can use the materials available.

2 (6C) Before starting to build, create a detailed diagram of your design and submit it for approval to your teacher. On your diagram, identify the loads that your bridge must support.

3 (5E) Build your bridge according to your design.

Test

4 (3F) As a class, create tests that will measure the safety of the bridges your class designs under high winds and under a traffic jam.

- Use those tests to determine if your bridge is safe. If the bridge has a structural failure, it is unsafe and must be redesigned and rebuilt.

(a) Record your observations during the tests.

(b) How could you make your bridge stronger?

SKILLS HANDBOOK: (3) Process of Design (6C) Scientific & Technical Drawing

Figure 1
This bridge moves to allow ships into and out of a port on Kaministiqua River near Thunder Bay, Ontario.

5 Create a test to study how your bridge performs when traffic is moving over it.

(a) Record your observations.

(b) How can you improve the stability of your bridge?

6 Create a test to measure the factor of safety of your bridge under a traffic jam. What is the load created by a traffic jam? What is the maximum live load the bridge can bear?

(a) Calculate and record the factor of safety of your bridge.

7 Measure the mass of your bridge. You will use the mass to calculate the performance of your bridge. (5B)

(a) Record the mass.

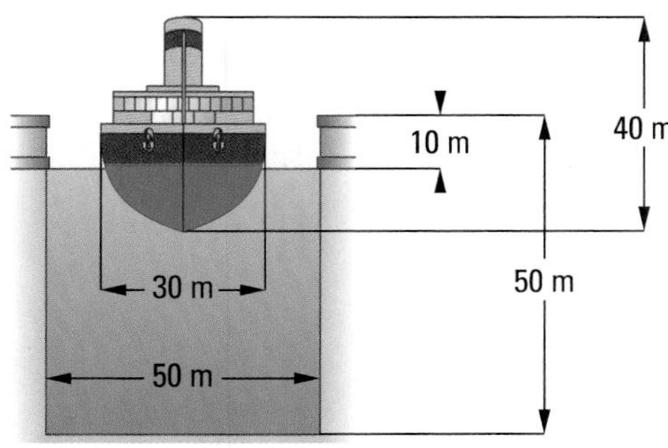

Figure 2
Your model should span 50 cm. On this scale, how large would the ship be?

(5E) Fabrication Techniques (5B) Working with Scales and Balances

Making Connections

1. You performed several tests on your bridge. What other tests would you recommend for models of a bridge before the actual bridge is constructed?

Design Challenge

What is the maximum load you expect for your chair? For your pack? Can you use the strength-to-mass ratio to improve the design of your product?

Evaluate

8 Evaluate your bridge by doing the following.

(a) One way to measure the performance of your bridge is to calculate how strong your bridge is compared to its mass. A strong structure that has a small dead load is ideal. Calculate your bridge's strength-to-mass ratio.

Example:
Maximum live load: 3500 g
Mass of bridge: 1000 g
Strength-to-mass ratio: = 3500 g:1000 g
= 3.5:1

The bridge will safely support 3.5 g for every gram of its mass.

(b) Compare your bridge with your classmates' bridges. Use a chart to display the following information: structural form; material selection and use; forces; mechanisms; fastenings; factor of safety; strength-to-mass ratio. Which of the bridges do you think is the best design for the needs of Bridgeton? Explain.

(c) Using ideas from other bridges in your class and your own ideas, how would you modify your bridge to improve its strength-to-mass ratio, its factor of safety, and its stability?

Design Challenge

SKILLS MENU
- Identify a Problem
- Planning
- Building
- Testing
- Recording
- Evaluating
- Communicating

Design and Build a Structure for Everyday Life

To design a good product, the designer must keep the user in mind. Who will use the product? How will the product be used? How can the product be made safe? What can be done to make its structure stable and strong enough to withstand normal use? To complete these challenges successfully, you must think like designers of a product.

1 A Recycled Chair

Problem situation

One way to encourage recycling is to show evidence that recyling works. Products made out of recycled materials give that evidence. You want to produce a product line made of recycled materials.

Design brief

Design and build a chair for a dining room using recycled materials of your choice.

Design criteria

- The chair must fit at a dining room table.
- The chair will be on display—it must be pleasing to the eye.
- The chair must safely hold your weight.
- The use of non-recyled materials, such as glue and tape, must be kept to a minimum.

Figure 1
Can some of these ideas be used to make a chair of cardboard?

2 An Automated Baseball Catcher

Problem situation

Baseball teams have long used pitching machines so that batters can practise hitting. The pitching machine throws baseballs through the strike zone over home plate sixty feet and six inches away. So how do pitchers practise pitching? A catcher stands behind the plate and returns the pitched balls to the pitcher.

Design brief

Design and build a machine that will catch a baseball pitched from 2 m away.

Design criteria

- The baseball catcher must catch the ball and return it safely to the pitcher.
- The baseball catcher should work just as well on calm and windy days.
- The baseball catcher should indicate to the pitcher whether the pitch would be a strike.

Figure 2
Why keep a catcher crouching?

Figure 3
What does the perfect pack look like?

3 A Lightweight Pack for Hiking or Biking

Problem situation

When you have to travel a long way, you don't want to carry any more than you have to. On the other hand, you don't want to leave behind something you need. How much you can carry depends on your pack.

Design brief

Design and build a lightweight, collapsible pack that can be carried while cross-country cycling, hiking, or on a school field trip.

Design criteria

- The pack must be able to carry or support a water bottle, a compass, a waterproof coat, a helmet, a notebook, and a small amount of food supplies.
- The pack must weigh at most 500 g when empty
- The pack must be collapsible, when empty, into a space of 5 cm × 10 cm × 10 cm.

When preparing to build or test a design, have your plan approved by your teacher before you begin.

Assessment

Your product or device will be assessed according to how well you:

Process

- Understand the problem
- Develop a plan
- Choose and safely use appropriate materials, tools, and equipment
- Test and record results
- Evaluate your product, including suggestions for improvement

Communication

- Prepare a work plan before beginning your design that includes a description of the development and building sequence you will follow, a shedule, and responsibility assignments
- Prepare a presentation
- Use correct terms
- Write clear descriptions of the steps you took in building and testing your product
- Explain clearly how your product solves the problem
- Make an accurate technical drawing for your product

Product

- Meet the design criteria with your product
- Use your chosen materials effectively
- Construct your product
- Solve the identified problem

Unit 3 Summary

In this unit, you have learned that structures can be designed to withstand the loads placed on them in normal use, and some techniques that can be used to make structures stronger and more stable.

Reflecting

- Reflect on the ideas and questions presented in the Unit Overview and in the Getting Started. How can you connect what you have done and learned in this unit with those ideas and questions? (To review, check the sections indicated in this Summary.)
- Revise your answers to the Reflecting questions in 1, 2, 3 and the questions you created in the Getting Started. How has your thinking changed?
- What new questions do you have? How will you answer them?

Understanding Concepts

- demonstrate that the position of the centre of gravity of a structure determines whether the structure is stable or unstable 3.4, 3.5, 3.14

- describe how the magnitude, direction, and point and plane of application of external forces affect the stability of a structure 3.8, 3.9
- describe how loads affect the stability of a structure by causing internal forces such as compression, tension, torsion, and shear 3.10, 3.12, 3.15, 3.16
- classify structures as solid, frame, or shell structures 3.13
- describe techniques and devices that can be used to strengthen structures 3.17, 3.19, 3.21
- measure the performance of a bridge by comparing its mass to the mass of the maximum load it can support 3.22

Applying Skills

- compile qualitative and quantitative data while testing structures 3.9, 3.11, 3.18, 3.20, 3.22
- plan and carry out an investigation into how structures can be strengthened 3.15, 3.16
- design and build, using appropriate materials, structures that meet specific needs 3.18, 3.20
- design, build, and test a bridge that includes a mechanism 3.22

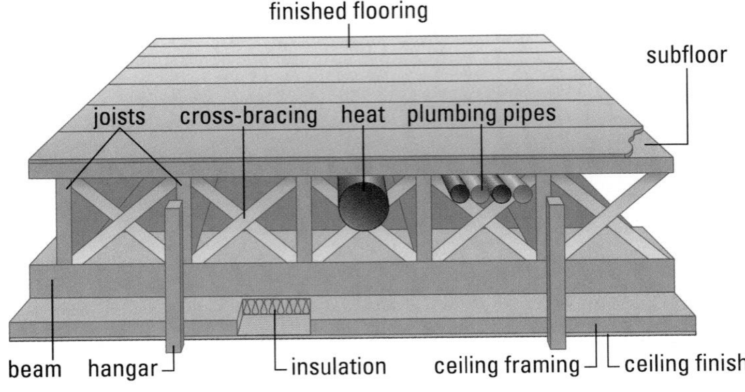

- understand and use the following terms:

bend	magnitude of force
buckle	mass structure
centre of gravity	plane of application of force
compression	planned obsolescence
corrugation	point of application of force
database	shear
dead load	shell structure
direction of force	solid structure
dynamic load	static load
factor of safety	symmetry
field	tension
frame structure	torsion
gusset	truss
lamination	twist
live load	work plan

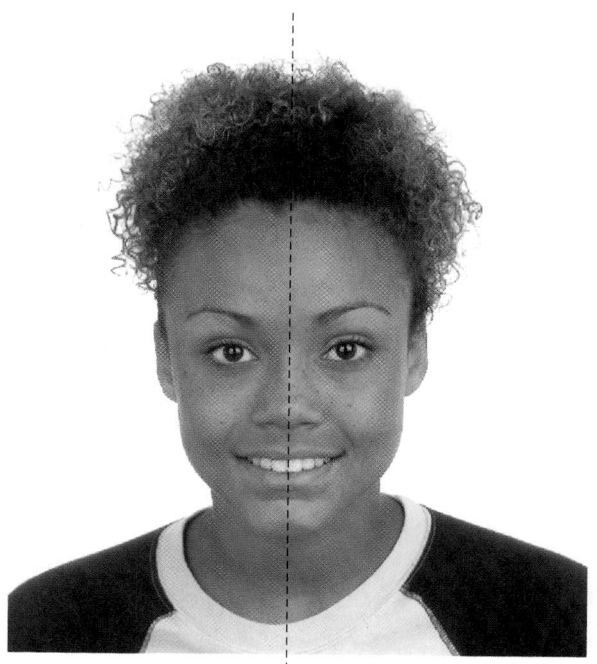

Making Connections

- describe the life of a product from design through production, use, and disposal 3.1
- explain the importance of researching needs before developing a product 3.1

- demonstrate how a plan for production can be organized using a database 3.3
- identify factors to consider when creating products that satisfy specific needs 3.6, 3.20

- describe how symmetry improves the stability and strength of structures 3.14
- use knowledge of materials and strengthening techniques to design and build structures that will stand up to stress 3.18, 3.22

Unit 3 Review

Understanding Concepts

1. Draw a copy of each of the structures in **Figure 1**.
   (a) Where is the centre of gravity in each structure?
   (b) Which structure is most stable?
   (c) Which structure is least stable? Why?
   (d) Give three examples of ways you could improve the stability of the least stable structure.

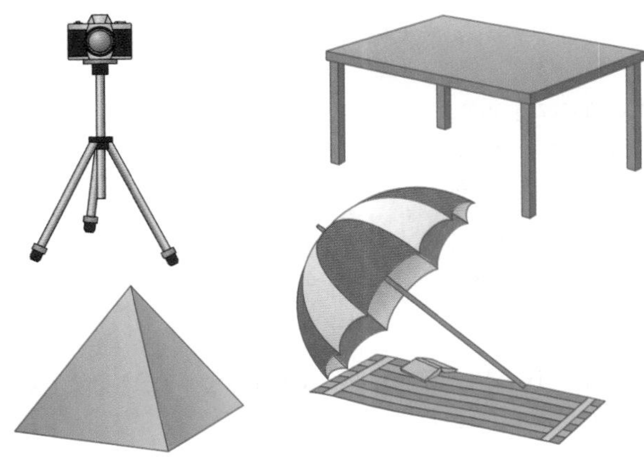

Figure 1

2. Using what you have learned about stability, explain why it is unsafe to stand in a canoe.
3. Some of the following statements are true and some are not. State whether each is true or false and write an explanation or correction for each.
   (a) A structure with a higher centre of gravity is more likely to stay standing.
   (b) Materials that stretch can withstand tension.
   (c) A nail clipper is an example of the use of shear forces.
   (d) Using computer simulations is the only way to test the safety of a prototype.
   (e) Dynamic loads are caused by the force of gravity acting on a structure.
   (f) Lamination strengthens a structure by improving a material's resistance to torsion forces.
4. Describe the force(s) at work in the structures in the following scenarios.
   (a) A portable CD player falls in a trash compactor and is crushed.
   (b) A large dog jumps into its owner's lap, breaking her frame chair.
   (c) An earthquake causes a block of the Earth's surface to rise 2 m. Half of a house is on the block that rises, the other half is not.
5. Provide three examples each of shell, frame, and solid structures. For each example, explain why the structure type is a good choice for that use.
6. What weight can an elevator support if its factor of safety is 18 and the maximum weight allowed is 300 kg?
7. For each of the structures in **Figure 2**,
   (a) classify the type of structure
   (b) explain, using diagrams that show the forces acting on and in the structure, how the structure is likely to fail
   (c) suggest ways to reinforce the structure

Figure 2

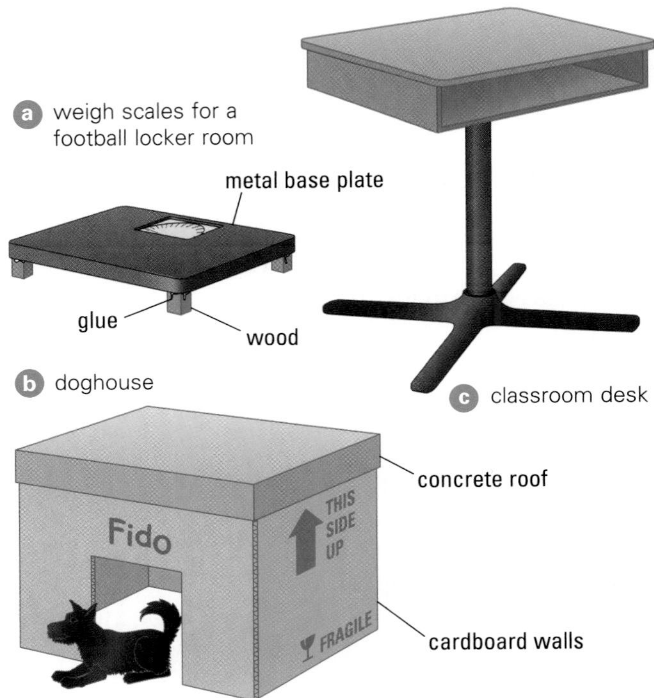

8. The seal on pop bottles breaks when you twist the top. It is designed to fail. Give three more examples of structures that are designed to fail when sufficient force is applied. What kinds of forces make the structure fail?

9. Calculate the strength-to-mass ratio of a ladder that has a mass of 25 kg and can support 200 kg.

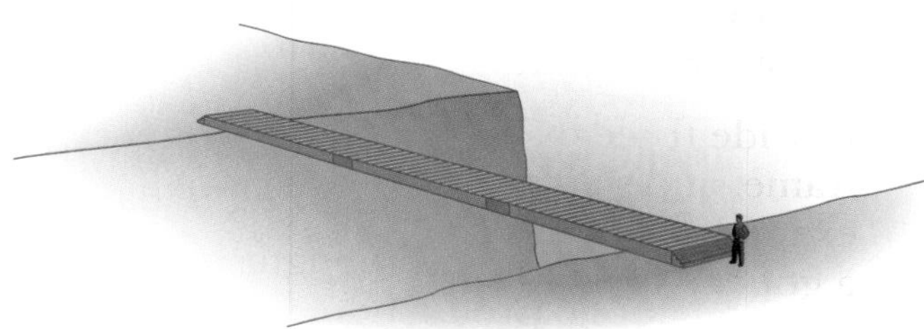

a A bridge to allow pedestrians to cross a gorge

b A bookcase to hold a set of encyclopedias

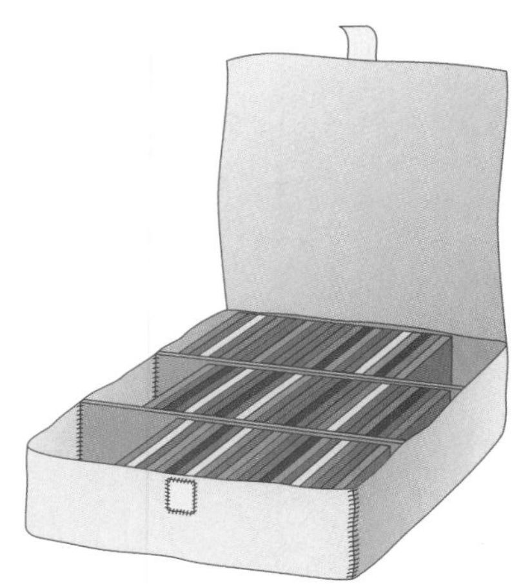

c A carrying case for CDs

Applying Skills

10. Match each of the terms on the right of **Table 2** with the correct statement on the left. You may use each statement once, more than once, or not at all.

Table 2

Description	Term
A structural damage resulting from strong torsion forces	1. buckling
B a term describing objects that are the same on both sides	2. torsion
C the weight a structure has to support	3. corrugation
D structural damage resulting from a strong compression force	4. twist
F a triangular-shaped part used to strengthen a structure	5. static load
H a squeezing force	6. gusset
I parallel forces acting in opposite directions	7. compression
J load caused by forces other than gravity	8. shear
K a twisting force	
L creases or pleats added to strengthen flat materials	

11. Which of the following design features strengthen a structure?
    (a) lamination
    (b) factor of safety
    (c) buckling
    (d) low centre of gravity
    (e) trusses
    (f) layering
    (g) planned obsolescence
    (h) flexibility

12. For each of the structures in **Figure 3**
    (a) identify any flaws in the design and describe how the structure might fail
    (b) redesign the structure to make it more stable and stronger

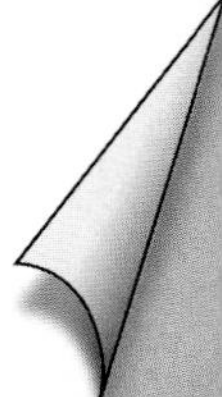

13. Draw a sketch of a 100-m bridge over water. Indicate all the forces acting on the bridge that have to be considered in the design. How might the design be different if the bridge were 5 km long?

14. Draw a sketch of a cable car that carries people up a mountain 1000 m tall. Indicate all the forces acting on the cable car system that have to be considered in the design.

15. Create a work plan to build a storage shed for bicycles at your school. Divide the plan into five parts that different people can oversee.

16. Design a structure to carry a wheelchair up a flight of stairs. What materials would you use? What mechanisms would be part of the design? What are the forces you would have to consider? Indicate the forces on your sketches.

17. Using at least 10 of the key terms listed in the unit Summary, write a short story in which an important structure fails.

18. Design an investigation to determine what materials would be best to use to make a playground swing.
    (a) Formulate design criteria for the swing, using concepts such as stability, tension, and factor of safety. What structural needs would the swing have to fulfill?
    (b) List the materials you would test.
    (c) Describe the testing procedure. What variables would you measure? Which variables would you control?
    (d) Create a chart that would present the results.

Making Connections

19. Select a product you use and describe its life cycle.

20. (a) Prepare a work plan for a project to build four matching bookcases for a school library.
    (b) Which materials would you use? Why?

21. List two benefits and two drawbacks of planned obsolescence.

22. Which of the following statements are true? Explain your assessment.
    (a) Structures are usually designed to withstand forces of magnitudes much greater than they're exposed to daily.
    (b) If product design is thought well enough, the product doesn't need testing.
    (c) Databases can help a researcher analyze information.
    (d) If you've done your research, you can predict the results of a product test.

23. There are many different types of vehicle, but consider three: a race car, a transport truck, and a bus. Explain how the structural differences of these three types of vehicles are related to the differences in their function.

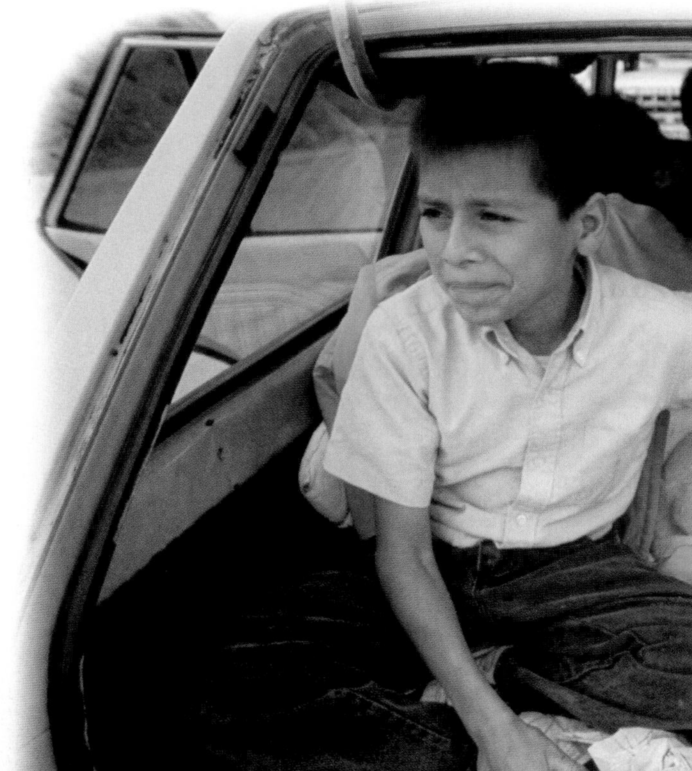

24. Some of the most impressive monuments in the world are so well built that they are still standing after hundreds of years. Choose one famous structure and describe features that make it stable despite the forces that act on it.

25. Discuss the advantages and disadvantages of three different types of fasteners that could be used to close shoes.

26. The sets made for television shows are broken into sections and stored in large warehouses. Create a storage system and a database that a set designer could use to retrieve the pieces to recreate a set or to use in constructing a new set.

27. Access to materials is not equal throughout the world. In many countries, people don't have access to materials that would make the sturdiest homes. As a result, damage can be especially severe when natural disasters hit. For example, many people have died in earthquakes when their homes, made of bricks of dried clay, collapsed on them. If there is no wood available locally, suggest ways of reinforcing a clay-brick home. How would you test your ideas?

28. Create an advertisement for an improvement of an everyday product. Your ad will tell viewers how the product's design meets their needs, and explain how the design makes the product energy-efficient.

29. In the 1970s, station wagons (**Figure 4**) were popular as family cars. Now families are more likely to own mini-vans.
   (a) Imagine you are the designer of the first mini-van: you suspect that station wagons can be improved, but you're not sure how. What questions might you ask users of station wagons to discover their needs?
   (b) Can mini-vans can be improved? Design a survey for users of mini-vans that will reveal problems in the design of the mini-van.

30. Fifty years ago, soda pop was sold in glass bottles. Today, pop is more likely to be sold in plastic bottles or aluminum cans.
   (a) Why do you think this change came about? In your answer, consider the stages that a pop container goes through, from production to disposal.
   (b) In your opinion, which is the best material for pop containers? Give reasons for your opinion.

31. Bridges often have one end fixed solidly, while the other end is allowed to slide. Explain why this is necessary.

32. In 1998, a major ice storm in Quebec and Eastern Ontario caused electrical transmission towers to collapse or topple like bowling pins. Many people said that the towers must have been poorly designed or made of inferior materials, or they wouldn't have failed. Research the storm of 1998 and respond to this criticism.

Figure 4

Unit 4

The Earth's Crust

Unit 4 Overview

Rocks hold clues to a mystery that is slowly being unravelled. The mystery is how the Earth came to be as it is, and the rocks in your neighbourhood had a role. Those rocks could be millions of years old, and may have travelled thousands of kilometres from where they were first formed. What events are part of their story? What can we learn from that story to help us survive and live in harmony with our ever-changing planet?

Minerals and Mining

Minerals are the natural substances that form the building blocks of rocks. Human beings extract minerals from the Earth to use as raw materials.

You will be able to:

- understand how minerals formed into rocks over millions of years
- classify minerals according to their characteristics
- describe the many uses of minerals in everyday life
- illustrate how minerals are mined from the Earth
- simulate the economic and environmental issues surrounding the mining of minerals

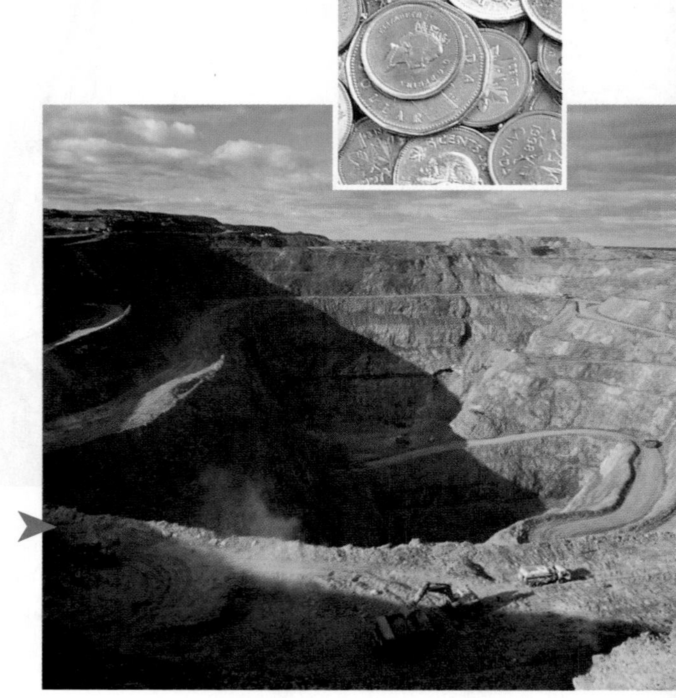

Weathering and Erosion

Soil consists of weathered rocks and decomposed organic materials. It is essential to the growth of plants and many other living things.

You will be able to:

- describe the different layers of soil
- build models of how soil gets washed away and test ways of reducing that movement
- understand how water moves through the different layers of rock and soil, and the importance of preventing unwanted chemicals from entering the water system
- test soil for qualities that allow a variety of plants to grow in it
- discuss environmental issues related to the reduction of available farmland in Canada

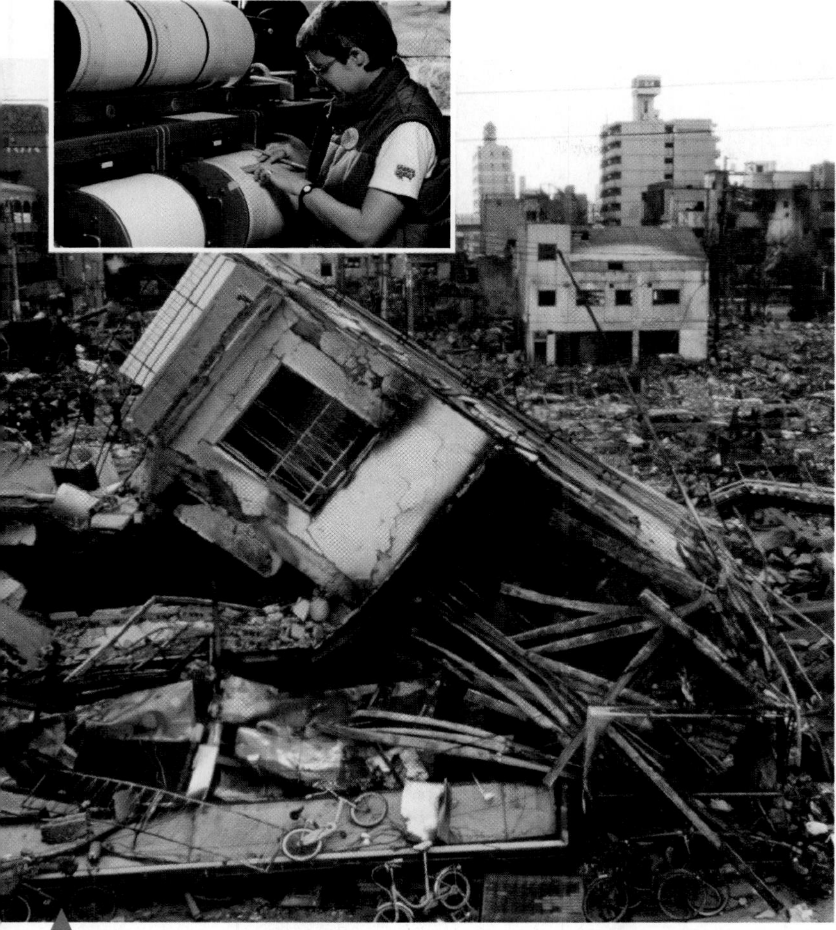

The Dynamic Earth

The Earth's surface is constantly changing as forces uplift, push down, bend, and break the Earth's crust.

You will be able to:

- understand how movements and forces within the Earth's crust gradually created many of Earth's features
- describe how fossils form and what evidence they provide about Earth's history
- identify the three main types of rocks and describe how they formed
- describe how and why volcanoes occur
- build structures that can withstand the vibrations of an earthquake
- predict how earthquakes, mountains, and volcanoes are related to one another
- evaluate evidence that Earth's continents used to be one large continent

Design Challenge

You will be able to ...

demonstrate your learning by completing a Design Challenge.

Model Showing Responsible Use of the Earth's Crust

We depend on mining and farming to provide us with the minerals and food we need to live. But it is essential to carry out these activities in a way that preserves the environment.

In this unit you will be able to design and build:

1 A Responsible Mine
Design and build a model of a working mine that causes minimal environmental damage.

2 A Mine-Tailings Pond
Design and build a model of a pond that safely contains the toxic waste products of a mine.

3 An Erosion-Proof Field
Design and build a model of a field in which the soil resists erosion and water runoff.

To start your Design Challenge, see page 242.

Record your thoughts and design ideas for the Challenge when you see

Design Challenge

Getting Started

Where Do Rocks Come From?

1 All of the metal objects that you see around you originally came from minerals that formed millions, even billions, of years ago in the Earth's crust. Many of these minerals are found deep in the crust, mixed with other minerals. How are they removed from the Earth and purified so that they can be made into things like copper wire?

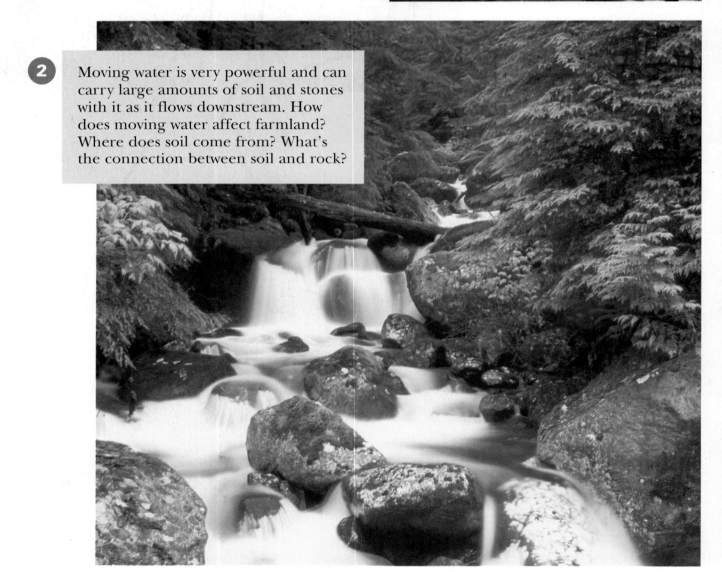

2 Moving water is very powerful and can carry large amounts of soil and stones with it as it flows downstream. How does moving water affect farmland? Where does soil come from? What's the connection between soil and rock?

3 From the time it formed, the Earth's crust has changed continuously. Volcanoes have erupted, pouring molten lava onto the Earth's surface, which has cooled and formed new rock. Why do volcanoes exist in some places and not in others? What are the forces in the Earth's crust that cause earthquakes?

Reflecting

Think about the questions in 1, 2, 3. What other questions do you have about the Earth's crust? As you progress through this unit, reflect on your answers and revise them based on what you have learned.

Try This: The Great Rock Investigation (6A)

Before beginning this activity, find two or three small, interesting-looking rocks in the schoolyard or on the way home. Each should have some features that make it different from the others. Examine and record the properties of your rocks. In doing so, you might ask the following questions:

1. What colour(s) are they?
2. (a) What do they feel like?
   (b) Are they round or sharp? How do you think they got their shape?
3. Do they look the same throughout, or do they have different types of rock mixed in?
4. Do they feel heavy or light in comparison to their size?
5. Do they have any unusual features (for example, colour, shape, markings)?
6. Do any of your rocks have pieces that sparkle or reflect light?
7. Do your rocks look like most other local rocks? If not, speculate on why they are different, and how they got where you found them.

SKILLS HANDBOOK: (6A) Obtaining Qualitative Data

Earth: A Layered Planet

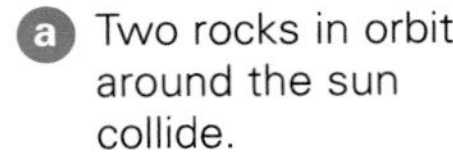

a Two rocks in orbit around the sun collide.

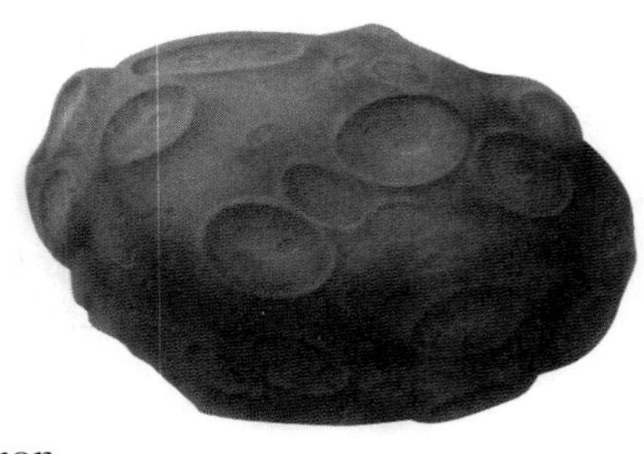

Just over 4.5 billion years ago, Earth was being formed, as shown in **Figure 1**. According to the most recent astronomers' model, at that time many rocks, large and small, were in orbit around the newly forming sun. As the rocks collided, they joined together to form even larger rocks, and planets like Earth began to form. Because the rocks in space were travelling at high speed, each collision generated huge amounts of heat. This caused the rock to become so hot that it melted. Heavy materials, such as liquid iron, sank to the core of the growing Earth.

As Earth grew larger, more rocks collided with it. Once most of the rocks near Earth were gone, Earth was left about the size it is now. It was also very, very hot.

b The collision generates heat, which melts the rock.

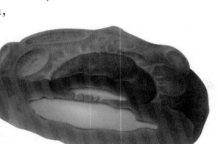

c Heavy liquids, such as iron, flow down to the centre of the new body.

Figure 1
Astronomers believe Earth formed from the collision of large and small rocks.

Try This An Eggsact Model?

Is there a good model that can help you visualize the idea of Earth as a layered planet? What about a hard-boiled egg?

- Peel away a piece of the shell of a hard-boiled egg. Compare the thickness of the shell with the rest of the egg.
- Remove the shell from one-half of the egg. Carefully use a knife to cut the egg in half. Use a permanent marker to place a dot at the centre of one-half.

Be careful with sharp objects.

1. Which layer of Earth would the shell represent?
2. Including the centre, how many layers are there in the peeled egg?
3. Does the egg model accurately represent the number of layers of the Earth?
4. Does the thickness of each layer in the egg compare well with the corresponding layer of the Earth?
5. Discuss whether the hard-boiled egg is a good model of the layered Earth.

The Hot Earth

Billions of years later, Earth is still hot. Only the thin crust on the outside has cooled enough to harden into solid rock. Depending on where it is measured, this thin crust varies in thickness from 6 to 64 km—not much compared to the 6400 km from the crust to the core. **Figure 2** shows a model of our layered planet.

1. The Crust

The **crust** is a thin layer of solid rock. The material that makes up the crust tends to be lighter than the materials below—the Earth's crust "floats" on the inner layers.

2. The Mantle

Just below the crust is a hot, partly molten layer called the **mantle**. The mantle is made up of a thick, heavy material. When it cools, it forms rock. The mantle moves sluggishly, like thick syrup.

3. The Outer Core

Toward the centre of the Earth is the core. The **outer core** is a molten mass of mostly iron with some nickel in the mix. Like the mantle, material within the outer core flows.

4. The Inner Core

At the very centre of the Earth is the **inner core**, a large ball of iron and nickel. Despite the heat (almost as hot as the surface of the sun), the inner core is solid, crushed under the enormous weight of the outer core and the mantle.

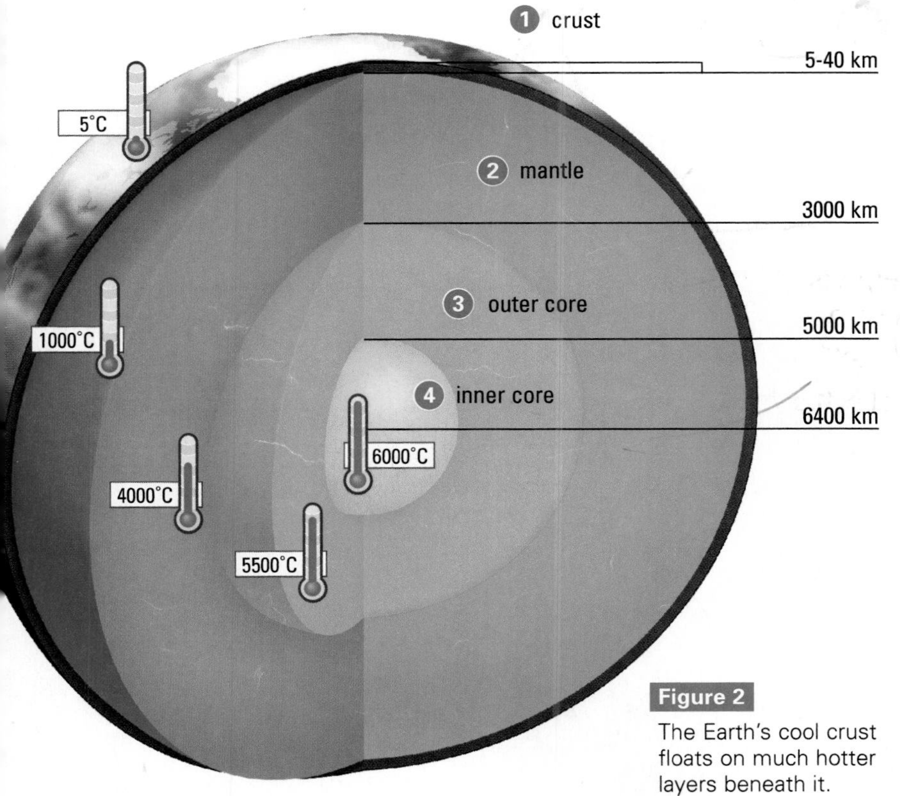

Figure 2

The Earth's cool crust floats on much hotter layers beneath it.

Understanding Concepts

1. (a) Name the layers of the Earth.
   (b) How are they different from one another?
2. Imagine that there was a highway from your school to the centre of the Earth—and that you had a vehicle that wouldn't melt before you got there! At 100 km/h, how long would it take to get from your school to
   (a) the mantle?
   (b) the outer core?
   (c) the inner core?
   (d) the centre of the Earth?
3. Why is the inner core of the Earth solid even though it is so hot?
4. (a) What two metals are found in large quantities at the centre of the Earth?
   (b) Why is there so much more of these metals at the core than in the Earth's crust?

Making Connections

5. Earth is gradually cooling. Draw what you think the Earth's layers might look like in several more billion years.

Reflecting

6. What feature on the Earth's crust gives us an occasional view of how the Earth looks inside?
7. Even on the very coldest days of winter, you can dig a hole through the ice on a lake and always find water. Why doesn't the lake freeze all the way to the bottom?

Minerals: Building Blocks of Rocks

Diamonds, iron, and gold—what are they? They are all minerals, and all come from rock. **Minerals** are the pure, naturally occurring building blocks of rocks. Rocks are made of combinations of minerals. The differences among rocks are due to the minerals they contain.

All minerals are non-living, but a few contain materials that were living things. For example, the mineral calcite, found in chalk, is composed of the shells of tiny organisms that lived in the sea and became fossilized. You will learn more about fossils later.

Because minerals are substances that occur naturally, synthetic substances like steel (iron mixed with carbon) are not minerals.

Minerals and Their Uses

Minerals play a big part in our everyday life (**Table 1**). Gold, iron, and diamonds are all minerals that are used to make a wide variety of objects, including tools, electronic parts, and beautiful jewellery. Gold is used in jewellery because it can be melted and formed into many shapes, and its scarcity gives it value. Like gold, diamonds are also rare. Diamond is prized because it is the hardest mineral known, which makes it useful in tools that cut or scrape, and, of course, it sparkles in light and can be split into smaller pieces, which makes it ideal for jewellery. Iron is rarely used by itself these days but is the main component of steel, used in everything from cars to cutlery.

Minerals Usually Contain Several Substances

Although a few minerals, like gold, may be found in a pure form, most minerals are made of several substances. For instance, iron is found in several different minerals. Two common minerals that contain iron are hematite (iron combined with oxygen) and pyrite (iron combined with sulphur).

Table 1 Some Minerals and the Substances They Contain

Mineral	Location	Valuable substance	Properties of substance	Uses of substance
gold	Northern Ontario	gold	soft, can be shaped, doesn't rust	money, jewellery
diamond	South Africa, Northwest Territories	diamond	extremely hard, reflects light	cutting tools, jewellery
hematite	Northern Ontario	iron	very strong	steel, stainless steel
chalcopyrite	Ontario	copper	conducts electricity, can be easily shaped	wiring, plumbing, coins
uraninite	Ontario	uranium	radioactive	nuclear generation of electricity
chrysotile	Quebec	asbestos	fibrous, doesn't burn	car brake linings, insulation around fireplaces

Minerals Are Crystals

All minerals are pure crystals. Crystals have regular geometric shapes because they are made up of tiny particles connected in a repeating pattern (**Figure 1**). Large crystals form if the mineral cools slowly. Small crystals indicate that the mineral cooled rapidly.

Figure 1
Sulphur crystals. Sulphur is used to make sulphuric acid, which in turn is used to make fertilizer, special steels, plastics, and other chemicals.

Other Ways of Identifying Minerals

- **Lustre** or shininess. Some minerals, like gold, have a metallic sheen. Others, like diamond, look glassy, while asbestos has a dull, fibrous appearance.
- **Cleavage**. Almost all minerals split into smaller pieces with flat surfaces due to their crystal structure. The way they split is called **cleavage**. For example, mica (see **Figure 2**) will always split to form thin sheets. Halite (also called table salt, in **Figure 3**) always splits into cubes. The type of cleavage depends on the shape of the mineral's crystals.
- **Hardness**. Every mineral can make a scratch on other minerals that are softer than itself but cannot scratch a mineral that is harder than itself. Using some standard minerals ranging from very hard to very soft, it is possible to discover quickly the hardness of an unknown mineral. For example talc (see **Figure 4**) is very soft, while quartz (see **Figure 5**) is very hard.
- **Colour**. Although colour isn't as reliable as hardness, it often gives a clue as to a mineral's identity. Gold, for instance, is always yellow. Jade (see **Figure 6**) is usually a shade of green. Quartz is frequently white but can be colourless, violet, grey, or black.

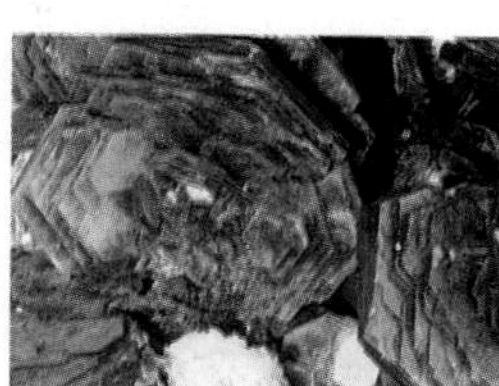

Figure 2
Mica

Figure 3
Halite

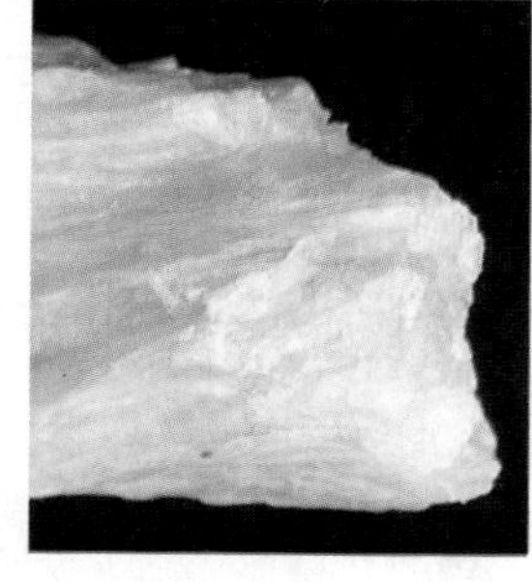

Figure 4
Talc is very soft and has a greasy feel. It is used in cosmetics.

Understanding Concepts

1. Describe the differences between a rock and a mineral.
2. What properties make diamond useful?
3. Describe three properties that all minerals have in common.
4. Why isn't it possible to identify all minerals by colour?

Making Connections

5. Gold, like copper, conducts electricity. Why do you think electrical wiring isn't made of gold?

Exploring

6. People often wear a ring containing their birthstone. Birthstones are minerals that are also called gemstones, or precious or semiprecious stones. A different mineral represents each month of the year. Investigate your birthstone and report on its properties, value, and where it is mined.

Design Challenge

Rocks contain minerals, and minerals may be composed of valuable substances. In your model mine, how could you represent rocks composed of a mineral that contains copper?

Figure 5
Quartz is hard. It comes in many colours depending on how it was formed. Amethyst, carnelian, agate, and onyx are all forms of quartz.

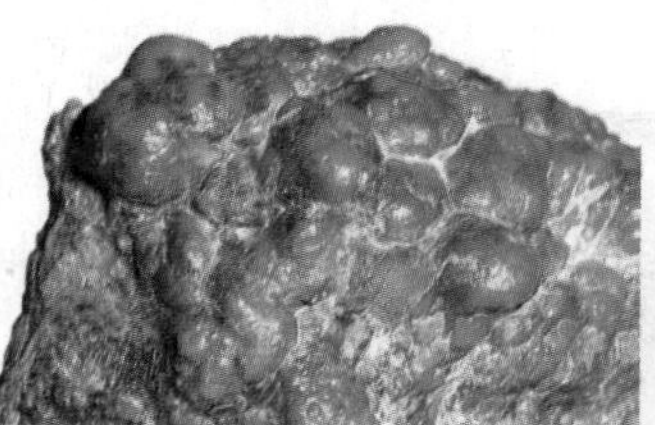

Figure 6
Jade is used to make jewellery and figurines.

4.3

How Minerals Are Mined and Processed

Small amounts of many different minerals can be found in most rocks. However, minerals can sometimes be found in high concentrations or **deposits**. For example, the rocks near Sudbury, Ontario, contain huge deposits of minerals that contain nickel and copper. It is these deposits that make mining possible and profitable.

Rock that contains a valuable mineral is called **ore**. High-grade ore contains rich concentrations of a mineral and is the most profitable type of ore to mine. Because it contains less of the valuable mineral, low-grade ore may not be worth mining.

Searching for Deposits

Many geologists spend much of their lives looking for deposits of useful minerals. Due to the increasing demand for certain minerals, and because known deposits of minerals are being used up, geologists must study the Earth's crust carefully to find new deposits. Once an important deposit is discovered, it is often a complicated process to extract the ore because it may be deep underground, trapped in hard rock. This means that the mine developer must choose the best method for removing the ore from the ground: strip mining (**Figure 1**) or underground mining (**Figure 2**).

Figure 1
Strip mining is often used when a mineral deposit is discovered near the surface. The top layer of soil and rock, called **overburden**, is removed until the ore is exposed. Then the ore is dug out with large loaders and loaded into trucks.

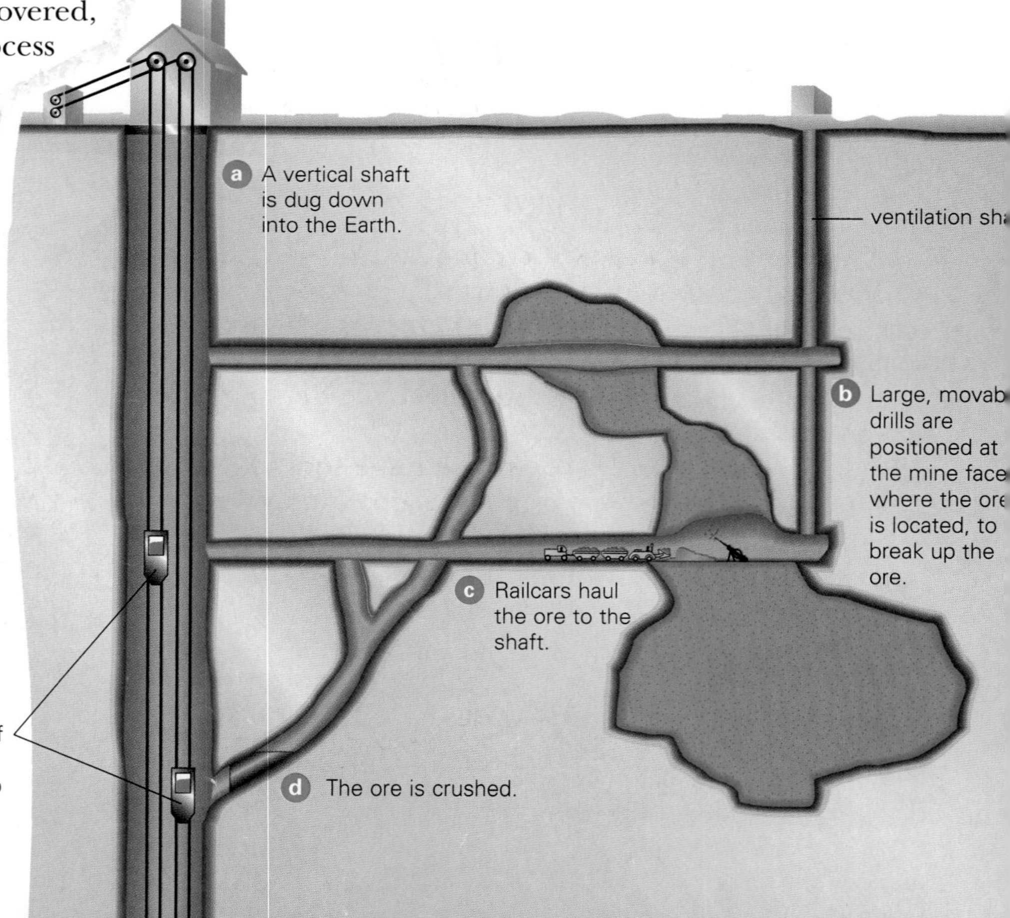

a A vertical shaft is dug down into the Earth.
ventilation sh
b Large, movab drills are positioned at the mine face where the or is located, to break up the ore.
c Railcars haul the ore to the shaft.
d The ore is crushed.
e Cages full of crushed ore are raised to the surface.

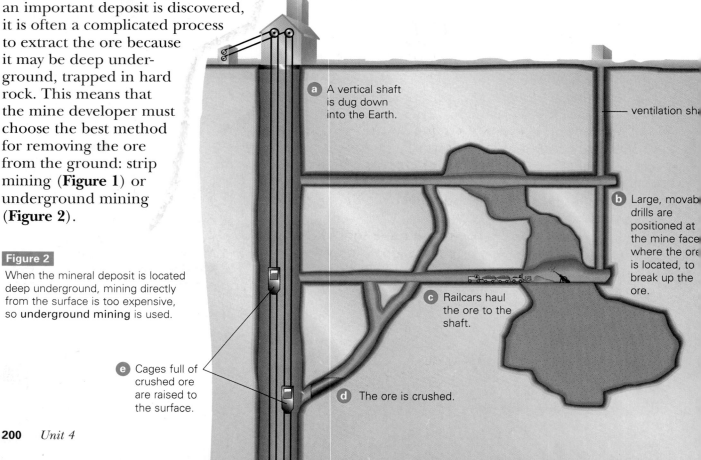

Figure 2
When the mineral deposit is located deep underground, mining directly from the surface is too expensive, so **underground mining** is used.

Ⓐ In a flotation tank filled with water and a variety of chemicals, the mineral floats in froth while the unwanted rock sinks.

minerals
sand or chemicals
high temperature smelter
copper

Ⓑ In a high-temperature furnace, a chemical reaction breaks down the mineral. The reaction requires mixing sand or chemicals with the mineral. This separates valuable substances such as pure copper or nickel.

Figure 3

Separating the valuable mineral from rock

Processing the Ore

All types of ore must be processed to separate unwanted rock from the mineral. The exact process for each type of ore is slightly different, but the key steps are often the same (see **Figure 3**).

These processes use a large amount of water and chemicals, which are recycled as much as possible. However, there are liquid wastes, which are placed in a **tailings pond**. Because these liquids are toxic to people and the environment, the tailings pond must be carefully built so that nothing leaks out (see **Figure 4**).

Figure 4

The tailings pond of this mine is next to the shore, so it is essential that it does not leak.

Deciding When to Close a Mine

For a mine to be profitable, the value of the mineral must be great enough to make it worth the expense of extracting the ore and processing it. Once the high-grade ore runs out, the low-grade ore is usually not worth the cost of processing, and owners will make the decision to close a mine.

Closing a mine also has costs. The mine should be returned as closely as possible to its original natural state, and the liquid waste in the tailings ponds must be removed and disposed of.

Design Challenge

For shallow deposits, miners will create a strip mine. Would a strip mine be suitable for your Design Challenge? Explain. What features would make a tailings pond safe for long-term storage of toxic waste?

Understanding Concepts

1. What is meant by the expressions:
   (a) copper deposit?
   (b) copper ore?
2. Which mining method is used when an ore deposit is far below the surface?
3. Why is the processing of ore an essential part of a mining operation?
4. The mineral deposits for a proposed mine are located as shown in **Figure 5**. Describe how you would extract the ore from each deposit.

Figure 5

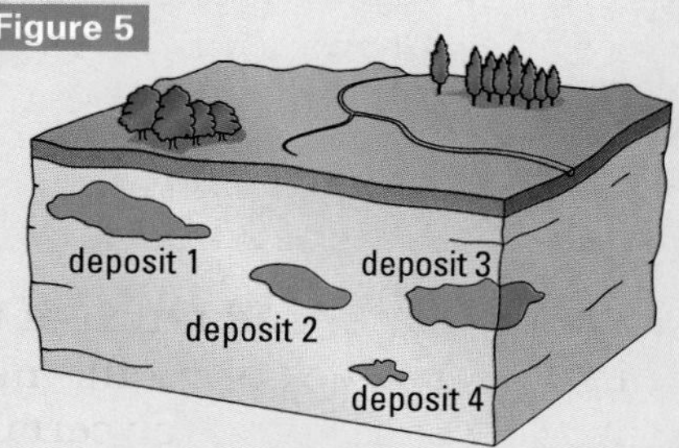

5. A mine operator creates a tailings pond around a natural depression in the land (**Figure 6**). A dam is created to hold in the tailings water by piling overburden at one end of the depression. Is this tailings pond environmentally safe? Give reasons to support your opinion.

Figure 6

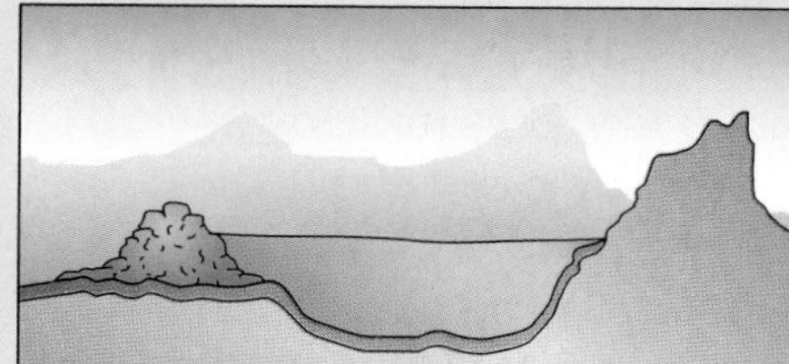

Making Connections

6. How might the varying prices of metals affect a mine operator's decision to close or reopen a mine?

Reflecting

7. Mining is expensive. It requires expensive heavy machinery and many skilled workers. Is there any other source of metals that people could use?

SKILLS MENU
- ○ Questioning
- ○ Hypothesizing
- ○ Planning
- ● Conducting
- ● Recording
- ● Analyzing
- ● Communicating

Mining Chocolate Chips

Ore is mined only if it is profitable to do so. After the ore is cut from the rock face, the desired metals or minerals must be separated from the ore (**Figure 1**). There are many ways to do this, but the value of the minerals being mined must always be greater than the cost of the separation process.

In this investigation, you will explore a method to separate chocolate chips from cookies to simulate separation of minerals from ore.

Question
Are some ores more valuable than others?

Hypothesis
Each kind of ore (cookie) will yield a different amount of valuable mineral (chocolate).

Experimental Design
Chocolate chip cookies will be used as a model of ore to explore the costs and benefits of mining.

1 After reading the Procedure, create a method for measuring the amount of chocolate in each cookie.

2 Create a data table to record your observations.

Materials
- 4 chocolate chip cookies (2 each of 2 different brands)
- toothpick
- spoon
- ruler
- several 5-cm lengths of plastic drinking straws

Procedure

3 Use the toothpick to pick the chocolate chips from both the top and bottom surfaces of one of the cookies.

(a) From which surface is it easier to remove the chocolate chips? Why?

4 Use your fingers to break the cookie into smaller pieces so that all the chocolate can be removed with the toothpick.
- Separate the chocolate and the remaining cookie pieces into two piles.

(a) Estimate how much of the cookie was made of chocolate chips. Express your estimate as a fraction.

5 Repeat steps 3 and 4 with a second cookie of the same brand.

(a) How does the amount of chocolate "mined" from the second cookie compare to the amount from the first one?

(b) Using the pieces of drinking straw, make a more accurate measurement of the amount of chocolate in each cookie.

Figure 1

A large part of the expense of mining is removing the valuable mineral from the surrounding rock.

6 Follow steps 3, 4, and 5 using 2 cookies of another brand.

(a) Does one brand of cookie contain more chocolate than the other?

Analysis

7 Analyze your results by answering the following.

(a) Do your results support the hypothesis? Explain.

(b) Why were two cookies of each brand "mined" for chocolate instead of just one?

(c) Was the investigation a fair test of the two brands of cookies? Explain.

Making Connections

1. (a) If geologists from a mining company are estimating the richness of an ore deposit, how many samples do you think they should take? Explain.

(b) Should the samples be taken close together or far apart? Why?

2. (a) If the chocolate "mineral" has a market value of $10 per gram, calculate how much the chocolate is worth for each brand of cookie.

(b) Which brand of cookie "ore" is more valuable?

3. (a) Did the chocolate chips separate more easily from one brand of cookie than the other?

(b) Suppose it costs $20 per hour to pay workers to separate chocolate from the cookie "ore." Explain how the amount of difficulty in removing the chips would affect the value of the ore.

Exploring

4. Invent a machine to separate (3D) chocolate chips from cookies. Draw a diagram of your machine, labelling the parts, and explain how it would work.

Design Challenge

There are many factors that affect how profitable a mine is. You've explored two: the richness (or grade) of the ore and how easy it is to separate the valuable mineral from the ore. How can you represent the ore in your model mine so that it makes sense to mine it?

SKILLS HANDBOOK: (3D) Planning a Prototype

Mining for Minerals

There are many different uses for the minerals that are extracted from the Earth, and the number of those uses is increasing. In Ontario, each person uses 16 tonnes of new material from the Earth every year. As the demand for minerals increases, the Earth's mineral resources are being depleted. Is the solution to open more mines, including inefficient ones with low-grade ore?

In addition to the costs of extracting minerals from low-grade ore, there are also environmental considerations. In the past, mines have damaged nearby land and polluted water systems. Strip mines have an additional problem: if not carefully refilled and landscaped afterward, they can leave an ugly scar on the land on which nothing grows (**Figure 1**).

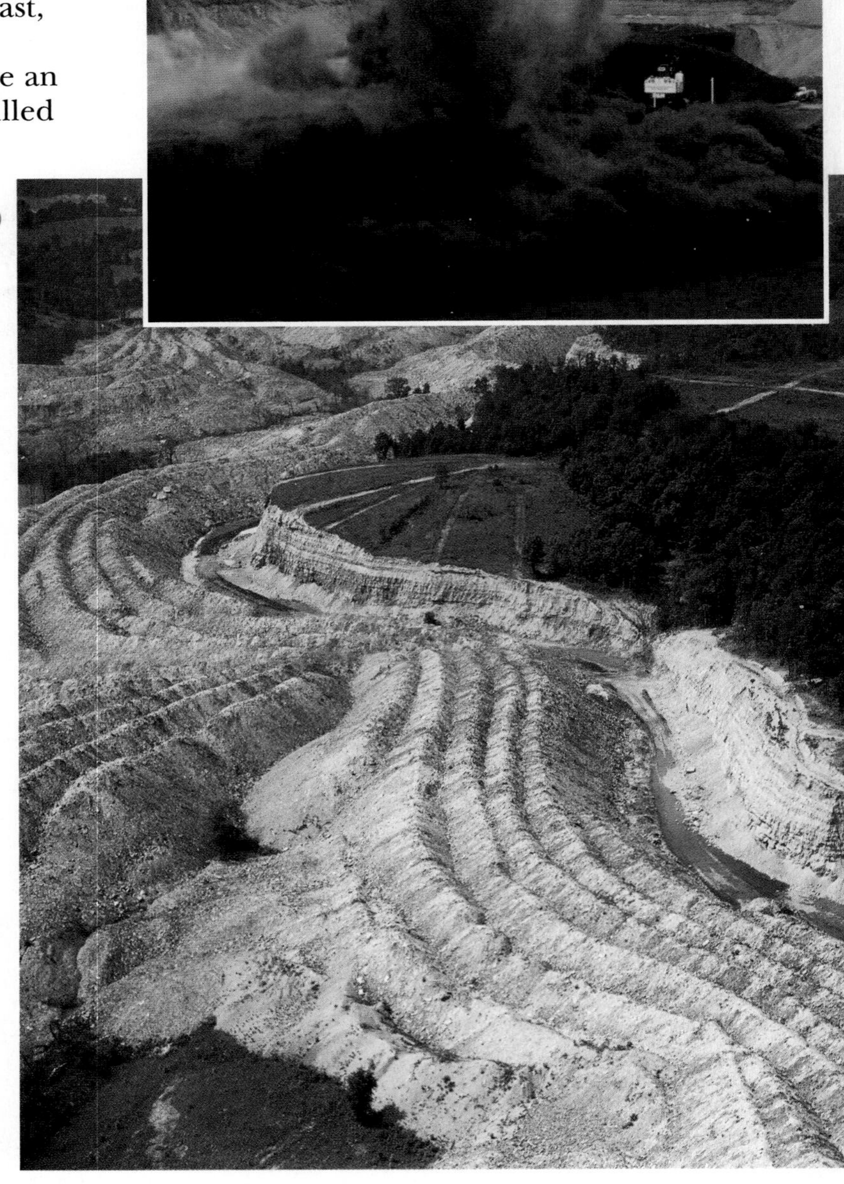

Figure 1
Before beginning a strip mine, extensive environmental planning must be done. (a) Expanding a strip mine. (b) An abandoned strip mine.

Restoring the Land

Recently, citizens in mining towns have been demanding that strip-mine operators restore the land when the mine is closed. This involves filling the hole by carefully replacing the rock and topsoil that was scraped off the deposit. The mine operators would also be responsible for replanting native grasses, trees, and shrubs in order to restore the land to its natural state.

Although this kind of restoration is an improvement over simply abandoning a closed strip mine, even with replanting, it does take several years for the natural diversity of plant and animal life to return to the area.

Understanding Concepts

1. What kinds of environmental issues need to be considered:

(a) before a mineral is extracted?

(b) after a mine closes?

Role Play Mining Economics

Near a town, a deposit of a mineral has been found. The deposit is near the surface, so the company that owns the deposit would prefer to build a strip mine.

The town has a high unemployment rate, and so the citizens welcome development of the mine. However, many of the citizens want a promise from the mining company that the land will be restored after the mine is closed.

The value of the mineral in the deposit is not high at the moment, although it may increase later. The company has said that if it must restore the land completely, this will make the mine unprofitable.

The citizens and their politicians have a difficult choice. They have two options:

1. Wait until the value of the mineral increases so that the mine will become profitable.
2. Offer to subsidize the mine, by paying for restoration of the land, so that the company will be guaranteed a profit.

Sample Opinions of Town Residents

- A subsidy will mean that taxes will increase. We should wait. Jobs will come once it is profitable to build the mine.
- Strip mines disrupt the environment when they are open, and even after a mine site is restored, it takes years for the plant and animal life to return. We should concentrate on finding alternative materials and recycling, and not open any more mines.
- An operating mine will create jobs. We should offer to subsidize the mine and guarantee jobs for local residents. If we wait, the jobs might never come.
- We should subsidize restoration of the land. If we are putting up the money, we can ensure the restoration will be done as we want it done.

What Do You Think? 

Should the town give money to the mining company to cover the extra costs of restoring the land so the mine can begin operating immediately? Or should the town wait for the value of the mineral to rise, with the risk that the mine will never open? Research the arguments further, at the library or on the Internet.

The Roles 

The people listed at right have been appointed to a special committee responsible for making recommendations to the town council about the mine. Choose one of the roles and then prepare your report for the council.

- an executive with the mining company
- an environmental activist
- a local businessperson
- a representative from the provincial environment ministry
- a citizen on a limited, fixed income
- a local politician
- a geologist
- an ecologist

4.6

Erosion and Weathering

On your way to school, you may see the same rocks, lawns, and streams every day, and they appear to remain unchanged. But they do change over a long period of time. The changes are caused by erosion. **Erosion** is the wearing away and transport of the Earth's materials. Water, wind, chemicals, and living things all cause erosion.

Erosion by Water

If you live near a lake, you may have noticed that the water appears to be much dirtier after a big storm. This is partly due to large waves hitting the shoreline and knocking soil from the banks into the water. In a river or stream, as shown in **Figure 1**, fast-moving water does the same thing, especially during the spring when melting snow causes the water level to rise and the flow to increase.

On a rocky shoreline, you'll find large boulders, small rocks, pebbles, and sand. Over many thousands of years, the force of the pounding waves breaks rocks into smaller and smaller pieces. Eventually the rocks are broken down into sand.

Erosion by water can occur slowly or suddenly. Over many thousands of years, a mountain stream can gradually wear away even the hardest rocks. But in just hours or days, a swollen river can cause huge clumps of riverbank to fall into the water.

Both the soil washed away by the river and the rocks pounded by waves are undergoing **mechanical weathering**, a form of erosion, shown in **Figure 2**.

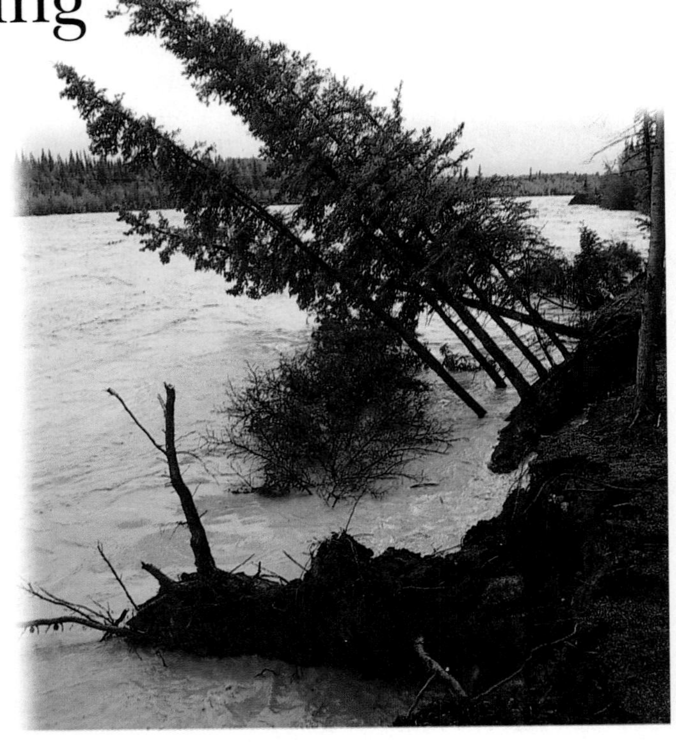

Figure 1
Water erodes riverbanks.

Erosion from Running Water

Make a cone-shaped pile of sand in a shallow pan. Flatten the top, as in **Figure 5**, and place an ice cube carefully on the cone. Allow the ice cube to melt.

Figure 5

1. What changes do you observe in the sand mountain as the ice cube melts?

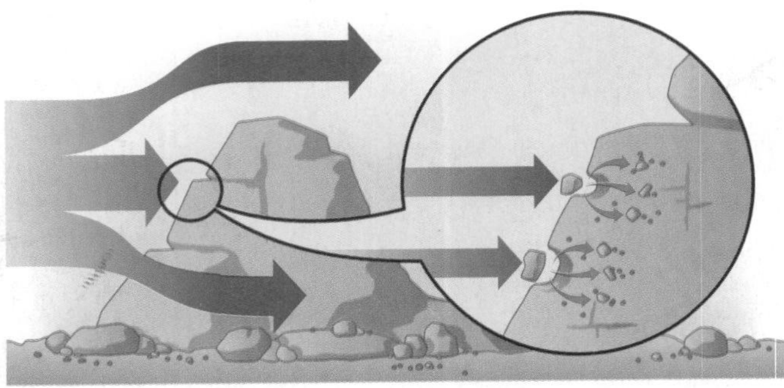

Figure 2
Mechanical weathering by water or wind. As sand particles carried by water or air hit a rock, they wear away the rock.

Erosion by Wind

Wind is another force that can cause mechanical weathering. The devastating dust storms in the Prairies during the severe droughts in the 1930s demonstrated the wind's power. Due to a lack of rain, the rich surface soil became very dry. This allowed the strong winds sweeping over the surface to pick up the light, dry soil particles and blow them many kilometres away. In many places, the rich soil was completely blown away, leaving behind layers that were unsuitable for growing crops. Many farmers were forced to abandon their farms.

Wind not only erodes soil, but it can also erode rock. Over time, windblown particles of soil or sand can wear away rock, much as sandpaper wears away wood. Some layers of rock are softer than others and wear away faster, producing interesting rock formations like the Hoodoos in Southern Alberta (**Figure 3**).

Figure 3

The Hoodoos in Alberta were formed by wind erosion. Wind has worn away the rock by driving soil and sand particles against it for thousands of years.

Erosion by Ice: Nature's Bulldozer

One of the more dramatic causes of mechanical weathering is glaciers. Although they seem to stay in one place, glaciers actually move very slowly downhill due to their immense weight.

As these huge masses of ice move down a mountainside, they slowly scrape the rock layer below, causing it to break up, as shown in **Figure 4**. The erosive force of a moving glacier is so great that it can even scrape a U-shaped valley from the rock beneath it.

Once a glacier starts to melt, it leaves the broken rocks it eroded in enormous piles, called **moraines**. Moraines are often as high as 100 m. Long, narrow moraines may be deposited along either side of a melting glacier or at the front of a glacier, where it is melting and receding. Moraines can be found in many places in Ontario, but they're especially noticeable on the northern shores of Lake Ontario and Lake Erie. Those hills, and the gravel they are mined for, were left by the last great glacier.

(a) One of the glaciers of the Columbia Icefield in the Rockies.

(b) During the last Ice Age, a huge glacier covered most of the continent. You may find a rock like this, with marks that have been cut into it by moving ice.

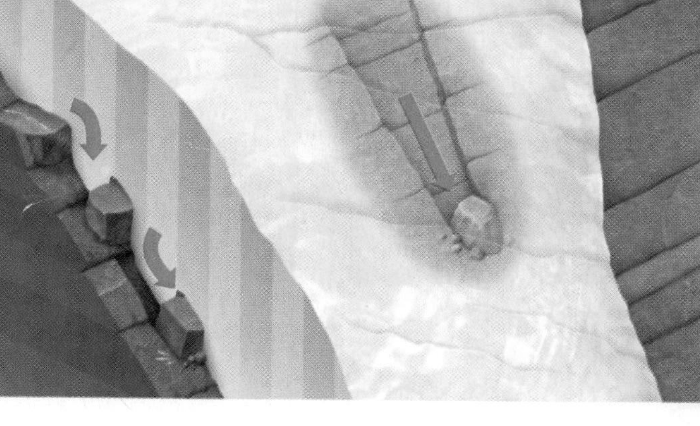

(c) Rocks are broken off as the glacier moves.

Figure 4

Slowly moving glaciers cause massive erosion of the Earth's surface as their immense weight scrapes along the ground.

Erosion by Ice: Nature's Chisel

Another type of mechanical weathering occurs when rainwater seeps into cracks and pores in rock surfaces. When the temperature dips below the freezing point, the water changes to ice. Water expands as it freezes. As the water expands, it puts pressure on the walls of the crack, forcing it to widen. Eventually the rock may split down the crack, or pieces may break off, as shown in **Figure 6**.

Figure 6

Water expands when it freezes, putting pressure on surrounding rock.

Erosion by Living Things

Lichen, a form of living thing that is part fungus and part plant, grows on rocks. Lichen uses the minerals in the rocks as a source of nutrients. It produces an acid that dissolves the rock on which it's growing. The acid wears the rock down. When the lichen dies, it leaves a thin layer of material—soil—in which other plants can grow.

Cracks formed by expanding ice can also be a home for plants. The wind may deposit soil particles in a crack, or soil may be formed there by lichen. Then, if windblown seeds also get carried into the crack, the small amount of soil may support the growth of plants. The roots of these plants will often penetrate deep into the cracks in their search for water and nutrients, causing the cracks to deepen and widen, as shown in **Figure 7**. Again the rock may split or pieces may break off.

Weathering due to the action of living things is called **biological weathering**.

a Trees grow very slowly where there is little soil. This tree may be hundreds of years old.

b As the tree's roots grow, they split the rock.

Figure 7

Trees and other plants cause biological weathering with their roots.

Try This: Ice versus Water

Use a permanent felt-tip marker to mark a horizontal line near the top of 4 to 6 compartments in an ice-cube tray As shown in **Figure 8**, carefully add water to each compartment up to the line you drew. Place the tray in the freezer and leave it until solid ice cubes have formed. Remove the tray and examine the cubes.

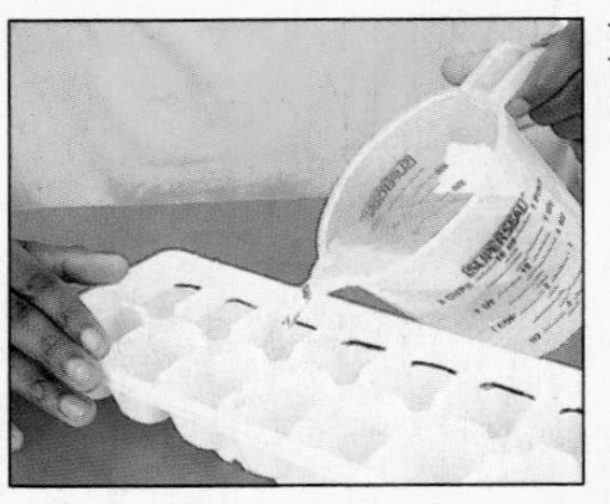

Figure 8

1. How does the size of the solid cube compare to the amount of liquid that was in each compartment?

Erosion by Chemicals

Rocks can also be broken down by chemical weathering. **Chemical weathering** occurs when water, air, and other materials react with the rocks, changing the substances that make up the rocks.

Water causes mechanical weathering, and it is also the main cause of chemical weathering. As shown in **Figure 9**, when water passes over or through rock, it dissolves certain minerals and carries them away, changing the makeup of the rocks.

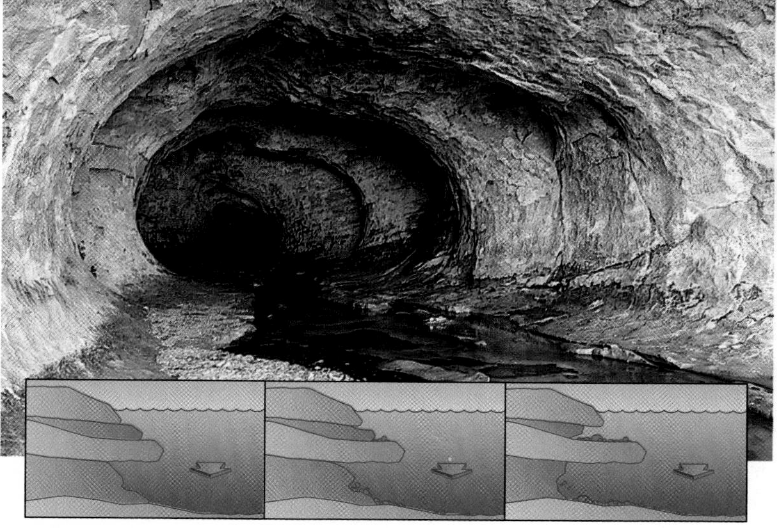

Figure 9
Water dissolves the mineral calcite in limestone, sometimes forming large underground tunnels.

Another example of chemical weathering is acid precipitation (either snow or rain) caused by pollutants and natural acids in the air. Acid rain dissolves more minerals than ordinary water. An example is the limestone rock used for statues and other monuments and buildings (**Figure 10**). Over many years, the mineral calcite in this rock dissolves as acid rain pours over it, causing the rock to crumble.

Figure 10
The chemical weathering of ancient statues has been speeded up by the modern pollutants in acid rain.

Chemical weathering and biological weathering are sometimes difficult to tell apart. Is the acid made by lichen an example of chemical weathering or biological weathering?

Weathering: Fast or Slow

Weathering can occur quickly or slowly depending on several factors. A small rock will often weather faster than a large rock because smaller rocks have proportionately more surface exposed to the forces of erosion.

The minerals in a rock will also affect the rate of weathering. Granite, for example, is much more resistant to chemical weathering than limestone or marble because the minerals in granite do not dissolve easily in water.

Climate is also important. For example, during our cold winters, mechanical weathering by ice occurs. On the other hand, areas near the equator, where there is no ice, are more likely to suffer from huge storms, which can do more mechanical weathering in a few hours than ice in the North could do in a century.

Understanding Concepts

1. Develop a concept map about erosion. (9E)
2. Make a chart explaining the differences between mechanical, biological, and chemical weathering.
3. Water is an agent of both mechanical and chemical weathering. Explain.

Making Connections

4. Some scientists list gravity as one of the causes of erosion because sloping land erodes more quickly than flat land. Explain why.
5. Name a natural or human-made feature near where you live that shows the effects of erosion. Make a diagram to show the kinds of weathering that are occurring. Has an attempt been made to prevent the weathering? If so, describe it. (6C)

Exploring

6. Use the Internet to take a virtual field trip to a glacier in the Rockies. Is the glacier advancing or receding? Use web site evidence to support your answer. (4A)

Design Challenge

What kinds of erosion would you expect to act on a farmer's field? List the possibilities.

Learning About Soil

Over time, rocks can be broken down into smaller pieces by weathering. These particles of rock are the beginning of a process that leads to the formation of soil in which plants can grow. As soil develops, it creates a series of layers called **horizons**, as you can see in **Figure 1**. In each deeper layer, the size of the rock particles tends to increase.

1. Litter

The surface of soil is usually covered with leaves, broken branches, and fallen trees. This layer, known as the **litter**, keeps the ground damp by preventing too much water from evaporating.

2. Topsoil

Beneath the litter is a layer of **topsoil**. Topsoil usually contains dark, decaying plant and animal matter called **humus**. Humus is important because it contains the rich supply of nutrients and minerals that new plants need for growth.

3. Subsoil

The **subsoil** contains larger pieces of rock and clay. It is usually a lighter colour because it contains little humus.

4. Bedrock

A layer of solid, unbroken rock called **bedrock** marks the dividing line between soil and rock. The bedrock may be under soil, but it is still subject to biological weathering from plant roots.

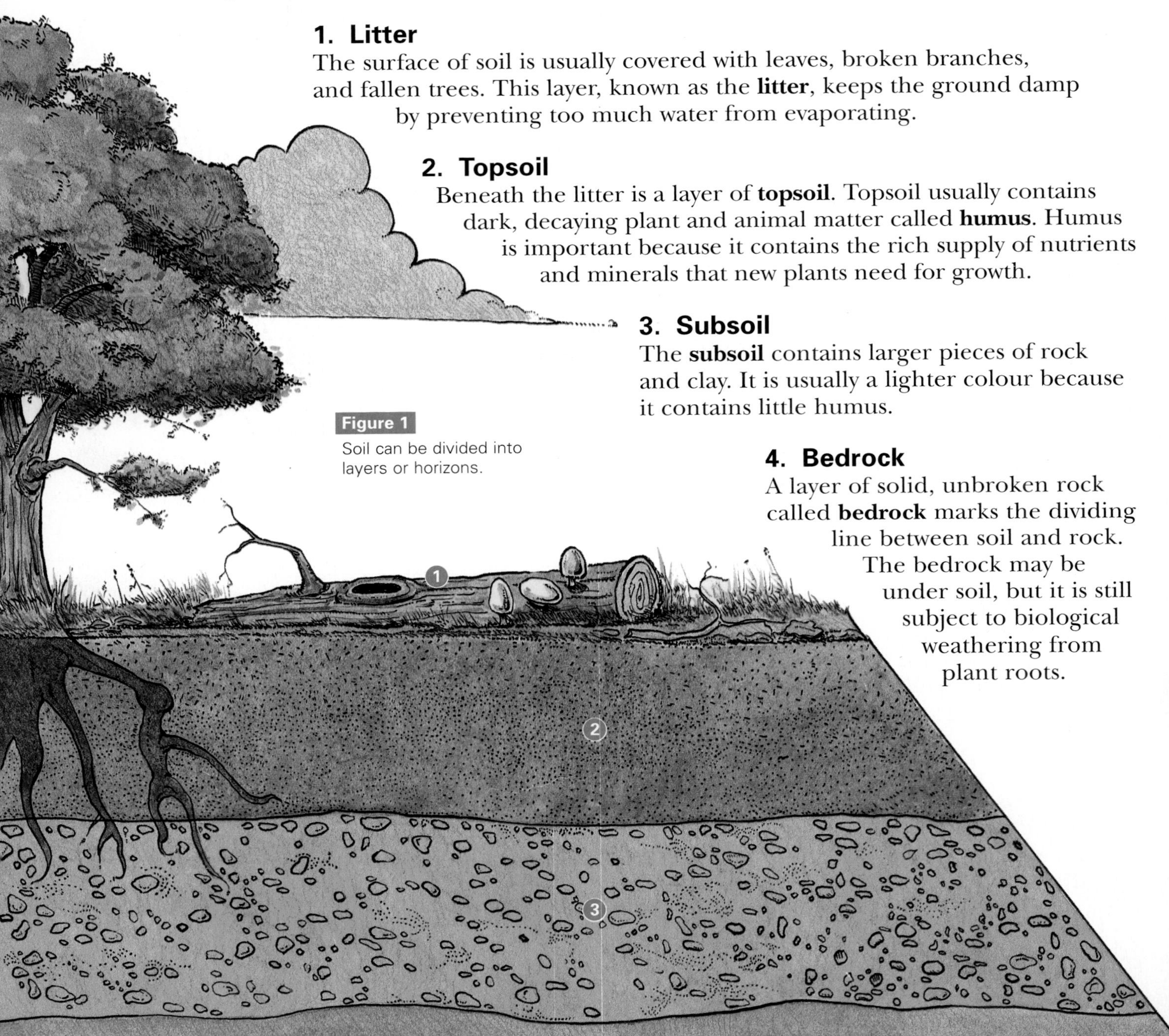

Figure 1
Soil can be divided into layers or horizons.

Is Soil the Same Thickness Everywhere?

As bedrock is weathered, small rocks break off, deepening the subsoil. The subsoil is also being weathered by plant roots and small burrowing animals, such as moles and worms, which bring humus down into the subsoil. As a result, the top of the subsoil slowly becomes topsoil. This process takes time—thousands of years.

Depending on how long the soil has had to form, how much material was left by the glaciers, and the amount of erosion that has occurred, the soil has different thicknesses in different parts of the country. In southern Ontario, where great trees and countless animals have lived, died, and contributed their bodies to soil humus for 10 000 years, soil layers tend to be deeper. In northern Ontario, where the glacier of the last Ice Age lasted much later, there has been less time for soil to form. It is also cooler in the north, so plants grow more slowly and there is less biological weathering. Near the glaciers of the Columbia Icefield in the Canadian Rockies, little pine trees can be seen growing in rocky soil that is just a few centimetres deep. There has been little time there for soil formation.

Design Challenge

In addition to forming humus, trees and other plants have another important function in soil: their roots help soil resist erosion by water and wind. How could you use trees in your model field?

Understanding Concepts

1. Why is soil important?
2. What features distinguish each soil layer from the others?
3. Describe how soil is formed.

Making Connections

4. (6C) Examine the picture of the northern forest shown in the Try This. Draw a diagram showing what you would expect to happen to soil formation if the trees were cut down and removed.

Exploring

5. (4A) If there is little or no oxygen in the soil, decayed plant matter will form a material called peat instead of humus. Research some of the important uses of peat.

Reflecting

6. The treeline is the northern boundary at which trees are able to grow. Using a map showing the treeline across Canada, explain why this boundary might move when considering changes in climate and soil layers.

Try This: Soil Horizons

Compare the soil horizons in **Figure 2**. Which soils do you think would be best for growing crops? Give your reasons.

Figure 2

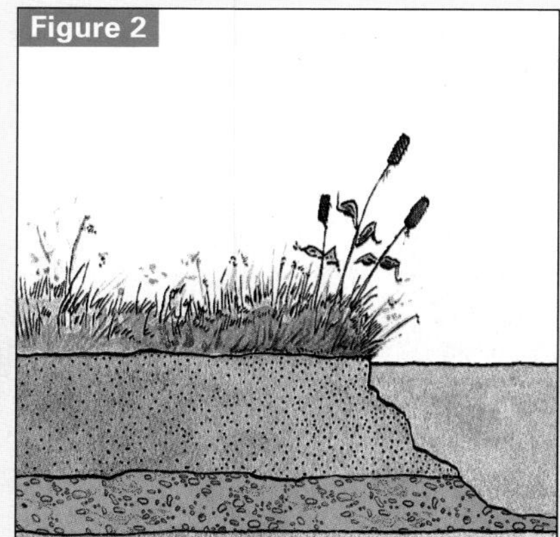

grassland

southern forest

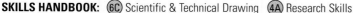

northern forest

SKILLS MENU
- ○ Questioning
- ● Hypothesizing
- ○ Planning
- ● Conducting
- ● Recording
- ● Analyzing
- ● Communicating

Components of Soil

You've probably noticed that soil seems to be different when you dig in different areas. Some soils are soft, dark, and rich; others are thick and grey. In some soil, many different kinds of plants grow easily; in others, only very hardy plants can grow. Topsoil also contains particles of various sizes. In this investigation, you will explore how these particles affect soil quality.

Question

What factors make topsoils differ?

Hypothesis

1 (2C) Based on what you know about soil, write a hypothesis that explains why topsoils differ.

Materials

- safety goggles
- apron
- trowel
- plastic bag
- 100-mL graduated cylinder
- clear plastic jar or bottle with lid
- 50-mL beaker
- plastic tablespoon

Do not handle the soil. Soil may contain sharp objects, such as glass or nails.

Experimental Design

In this investigation, each group will examine a sample of topsoil. You will compare your results to those of the other groups and analyze differences.

2 (6D) After reading the Procedure, design a chart to record all of your observations.

Procedure

Part 1: Viewing Particles in Topsoil

3 Find an area where you can remove some soil.

(a) Describe the soil. Is it easy to dig? What colour is it? Are there many small rocks in it or only a few? What kinds of plants grow in the soil?

4 Using a trowel, place 1 scoop of soil into a plastic bag.

(a) Record where the sample was taken.

5 Fill a clear plastic jar one-quarter full with soil from your sample.
- Add water until the jar is three-quarters full.
- Screw the lid on and shake the jar well.
- Leave the jar for 2 min or until the contents settle.

(a) Draw what you observe. Include any measurements you can make in your drawing.

(b) Are the larger particles found near the top or bottom of the jar?

SKILLS HANDBOOK: (2C) Predicting and Hypothesizing (6D) Creating Data Tables

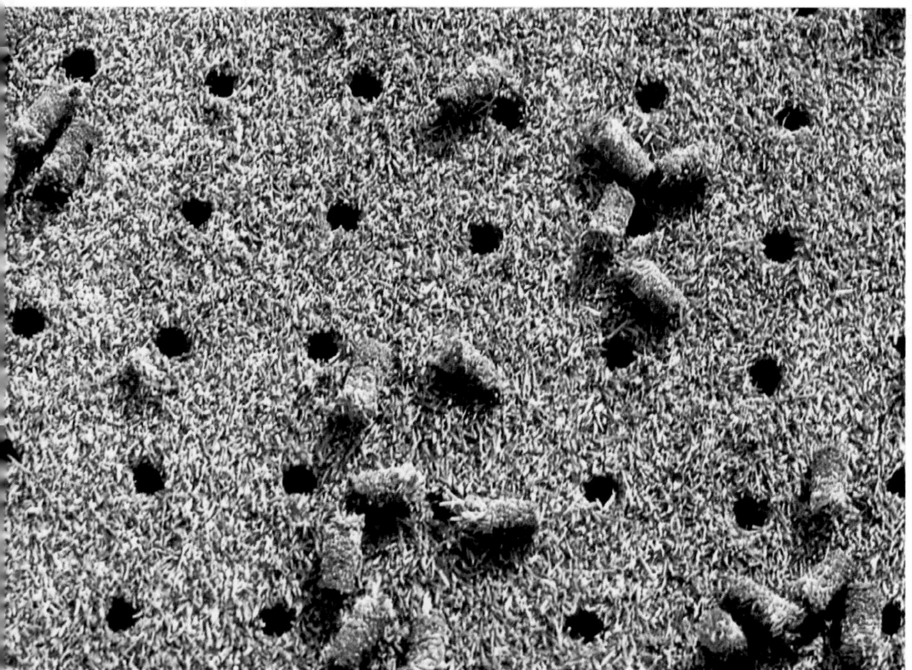

Figure 1

Gardeners and groundskeepers sometimes go over their lawns with a machine called an aerator. Can you explain why?

Part 2: Measuring the Air Content

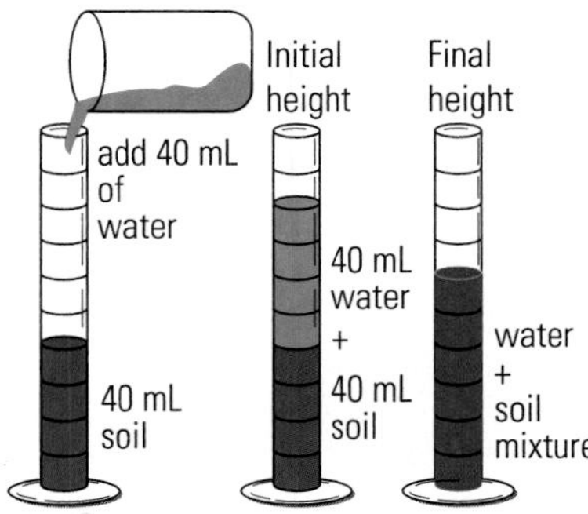

6 Put on your safety goggles.

- Using the graduated cylinder, measure 40 mL of water and pour it into a small beaker.
- Dry the graduated cylinder and, using a spoon, measure 40 mL of your soil sample in the graduated cylinder.
- Slowly pour the 40 mL of water onto the soil in the graduated cylinder.

(a) Record the final level of the soil and water.

(b) Did you observe any bubbles coming from the soil when the water was added? What does this tell you?

(c) Calculate the change in volume of the water and soil when they were combined:

Initial volume = 80 mL
Final volume =
Change in volume =

(d) Why is the final volume less than the initial volume?

Making Connections

1. **(a)** Why might plants grow best in soils that have air spaces?

   (b) Use your answer to explain why the plugs of earth have been removed from the grass in **Figure 1**.

Exploring

2. In this investigation, you tested soil for particle size and air content.

   (a) What other factors might make soil better or worse for growing plants?

   (b) (2E) Design an investigation to explore one of these factors. If your teacher approves your design, carry out the investigation.

Reflecting

3. How could you improve on the way you gathered and recorded observations in this investigation?

Analysis

7 Analyze your results by answering these questions.

(a) In step 5, did all the groups in your class get the same results? Describe any differences.

(b) In step 6, which of the soil samples in your class held the most air? Which held the least air?

(c) Compare all the groups' descriptions in step 3 and the results from steps 5 and 6. What do you notice?

(d) Do the results of this investigation support your hypothesis? Explain.

(2E) Designing an Inquiry Investigation

4.9

Soil and Plant Growth

Fertile soil is one of the world's most valuable resources. Soil that can support the growth of crops has always been in limited supply. In Canada, less than 1% of the total land area is prime agricultural land. For gardeners, good soil for both indoor and outdoor plants is essential. But what makes good soil?

Rich Soil Means Lots of Humus

Black or brown soil, rather than grey soil, has the most humus in it. It is the decaying plant and animal material in humus that gives soil its dark colour and supplies plants with most of the nutrients and minerals necessary for growth. Humus has a damp and sticky texture.

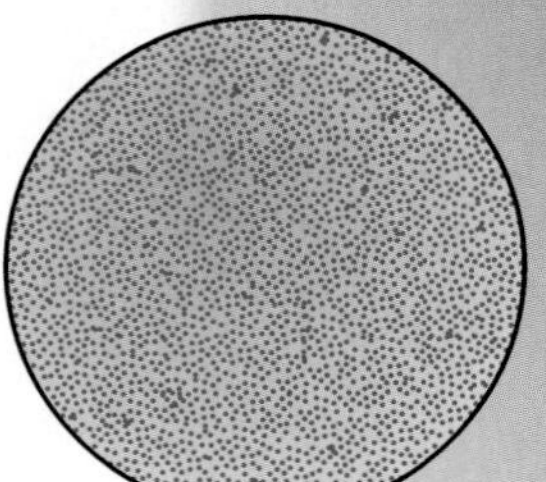

Fertile Soil Includes Sand, Silt, and Clay

Good soil includes roughly equal proportions of sand, silt, and clay. Each has a different texture because it is made up of particles of different sizes, as shown in **Figure 1**.

Between the soil particles are spaces. The spaces are important, because that is where the other ingredients of good soil can be found—water and air. Water and air are essential for plant growth. Plants absorb water with their roots. They use the water to make food. Bacteria and other organisms in the soil need air before they can break down humus into a form that plants can use. Minerals and other nutrients are also drawn into plants through their roots. Good farming soil contains roughly half particles and half spaces.

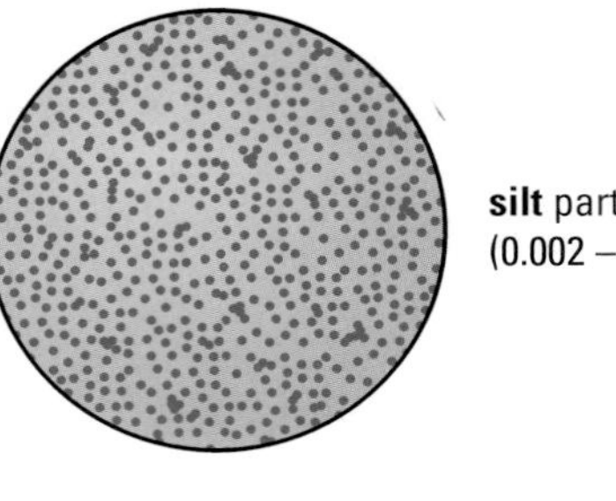

Because sand particles are large, the spaces between the particles are also large. These large spaces allow the tiny roots of plants to grow down through the soil more easily. However, the large spaces also allow water to drain away quickly, leaving plants with no water. Corn is just one plant that does not grow well in sandy soil because it requires a lot of water.

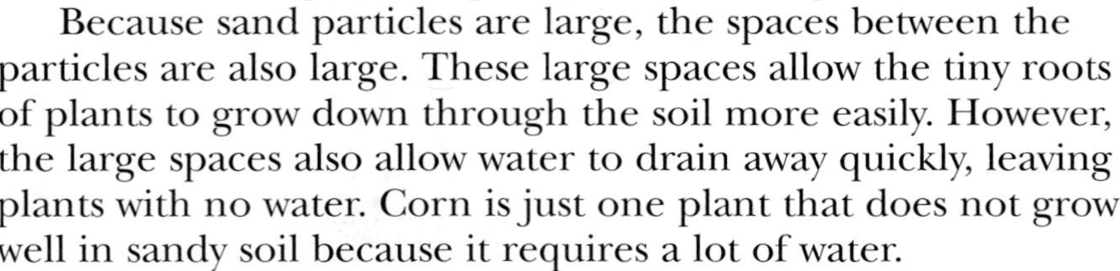

Because the spaces between clay particles are so small, clay holds water much better than sand. But clay particles also pack together tightly, preventing water from entering the soil easily. The small spaces between clay particles also make it difficult for plant roots to grow, and soil with lots of clay in it will have less air available to soil organisms.

Silt particles are in between sand and clay in size. They hold water better than sand, and they allow plant roots to grow better than clay. It's good to have some silt in soil, but soil made only of silt will not be as good as a mixture of all three types of particles.

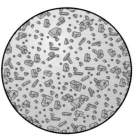

Figure 1
Soil is made up of humus and particles of rock. The rock particles have different names, depending on how large they are.

Understanding Concepts

1. Why is the humus content in soil important?
2. Why are the spaces between soil particles so important?
3. Why does clay alone make a poor soil for growing most plants?

Making Connections

4. (a) On a baseball field after a rainstorm, puddles have formed around home plate and the pitcher's mound, and along the paths between the bases but nowhere else on the field. How can you explain this observation?
   (b) How could you improve the condition of the field?
5. Some houseplants, such as cacti, thrive in environments where there is very little water. What kind of soil mixture would be good for these plants? Why?

Design Challenge

When designing a tailings pond, what type of soil in the pond bed would best prevent the tailings from leaking into the environment?

Water-Holding Capacity of Soil

Soil particles affect how much water the soil can hold.

- Examine 3 different 50 mL samples of soil with a hand lens.

1. What types of particles can you observe in each sample? Describe the differences between the samples.
2. Predict which soil sample will hold water best.

- Place each soil sample in identical folded pieces of cheesecloth, and fasten the corners together with a rubber band, as shown in **Figure 2**.
- Measure 50 mL of water in a graduated cylinder.
- Hold the first cheesecloth sack over a pail.

Figure 2

- Slowly pour the water over the sack. Stop pouring when water begins to drip into the pail.
- Record the amount of water left over in the graduated cylinder.
- Repeat with the second sack.

3. Which soil sample held the most water? Was your prediction correct?

4.10 Case Study

Farming and the Soil

All organisms, including humans, alter their environment simply by living in it. Farming is a dramatic example of a human effect on the environment. The way we grow food can change the soil, increase the chance that it will be eroded, and add chemicals to the environment.

Heavy Machinery

Heavy, mechanized farming equipment has greatly improved the efficiency of farmers in growing and harvesting crops, as shown in **Figure 1**. However, the frequent use of this heavy equipment presses down the soil, forcing soil particles closer together. The soil becomes compacted. Compacted soil has fewer and smaller spaces between the soil particles.

(a) How would soil compaction affect the soil's ability to grow crops?

Figure 1
Modern farms use heavy machinery to cultivate the soil and harvest crops.

Ploughing

Since the invention of the mechanized plough, farmers have been using it to till, or break up, the surface of the soil efficiently. During tilling, any hard crust on the soil is broken. This allows water and air to enter the upper layers of the soil. Planting seed becomes easier. Young plants grow more quickly in the loosened soil. But tilling also has a downside: it leaves the soil exposed to erosion.

Soil erosion results not only in the loss of valuable topsoil, but also in the removal of soil nutrients. **Zero tillage** (**Figure 2**) is one way of dealing with this problem. Using this method, stubble from the previous crop, including the roots, is left in the ground, and new seed is planted into the old stubble. No plough is used.

(b) Why would tilled land be more vulnerable to erosion than untilled land?

(c) How would stubble from the previous crop help to prevent erosion?

Figure 2
Planting in a zero-tillage field. This farmer has not ploughed the soil before planting.

Other Methods of Preventing Erosion

Some farmers plant rows of trees next to their farms and between fields. Others who have sloping land plant their crops in level rows that carefully follow the contours of the land, as shown in **Figure 3**, so that water does not run downhill along any row.

(d) Which type of erosion is prevented by trees?

(e) Which type of erosion is prevented by level rows of crops?

Figure 3

This field has been ploughed following the contours of the land to reduce erosion.

Changing the Crop

Although planting one crop in the same area every year is easier for the farmer, it does cause problems. Each crop removes different nutrients from the soil. For example, the nutrients used by the wheat plant to make its stalk and leaves may be returned to the soil when its stubble decays, but the nutrients in the wheat seeds (the grain) are taken by the farmer. If those nutrients are not replaced, the soil will become less and less productive. Farmers replace missing nutrients with fertilizer (see **Figure 4**).

There are other problems associated with repeatedly growing the same crop in the same field—pests and diseases. Insect pests, bacteria, and moulds that feed on that crop will stay in the field over winter and be ready to attack the next crop in the spring. Weeds that compete with the crop for the soil's nutrients will leave their seeds in the soil, ready for the next year. To deal with these problems farmers may resort to repeated use of insecticides, fungicides, and herbicides.

(f) Some farmers practise **crop rotation**, growing a different crop every year in the same field. How might crop rotation help farmers?

(g) Water runs off and through fields into neighbouring streams and rivers. What kinds of problems could the use of herbicides and insecticides cause downstream from the farm?

(h) Would growing two different crops in alternate rows reduce the farmer's need to add chemicals to a field? Explain.

Figure 4

Using the soil for the same crop every year forces farmers to add fertilizer to keep the soil fertile.

Understanding Concepts

1. Explain how the use of heavy machinery on farmland causes problems with the soil.
2. Name one problem related to modern farming methods and a possible solution.
3. What are the advantages of zero tillage?

Making Connections

4. Motorized machinery is a relatively new development for farmers. Its use has increased the production from most farmland, but there are problems involved in using it.
   (a) What disadvantages would there be to farmers who didn't use heavy machinery on their farms?
   (b) Is it likely that any new technology will bring only positive changes with it? Explain.

Design Challenge

Would any of the methods presented here help in the design of your field? How could you integrate them into your design?

4.11

Erosion: Carving the Landscape

Canada is a land of contrasts. In many places in the north, as in northern Ontario, the underlying rock of the Earth's crust, the bedrock, is exposed. Farther south, the bedrock is less visible, covered as it is in rich, thick soil. How can we explain this difference?

Ancient Ice Ages

Ancient glaciers are the surprising answer. Over the last 2 million years, five periods of glaciation have occurred in North America, creating huge changes in the features of the land. Each time, as the climate of Earth cooled, a thick ice sheet advanced slowly southward, covering much of North America. The most recent period of glaciation ended about 10 000 years ago. This last glacier, called the Wisconsin Glacier, covered North America from the Arctic to south of the Great Lakes, as shown in **Figure 1**.

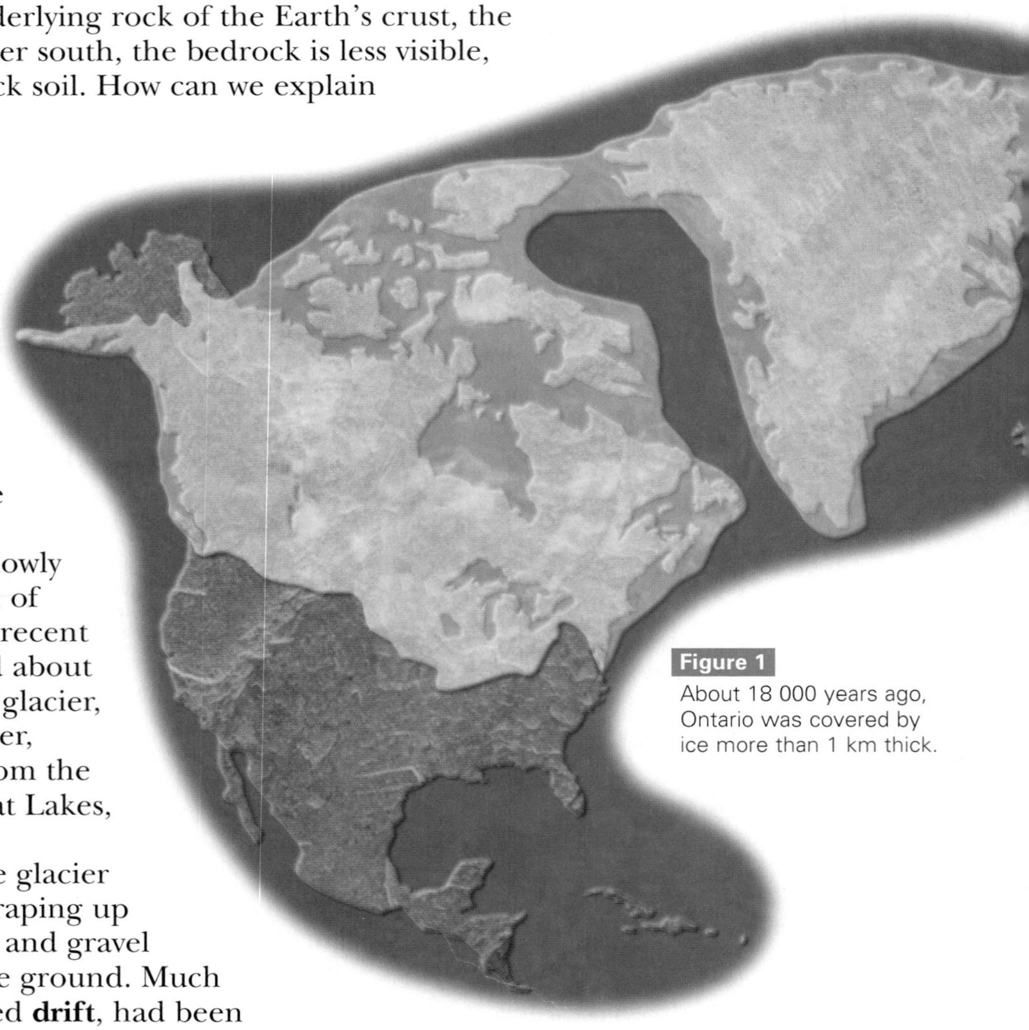

Figure 1
About 18 000 years ago, Ontario was covered by ice more than 1 km thick.

The great weight of the glacier caused it to spread out, scraping up bedrock, loose rock, sand, and gravel as it slowly pushed over the ground. Much of this loose material, called **drift**, had been left behind by previous glaciers. The glacial movement carried this material south and eventually deposited it in moraines, leaving the northern bedrock scraped clean. Many of the hilly areas north of Lake Ontario and Lake Erie are actually moraines, now covered with trees, fields, and towns.

Another feature of receded glaciers is called a **drumlin** (**Figure 2**). Drumlins look like narrow moraines, but are often in groups, all pointing in the same direction. Drumlins are caused by a glacier rearranging the moraine of a previous glacier, pushing the drift in the new direction.

Figure 2
Drumlins are narrow hills, usually in groups, formed from glacial drift. All point in the direction the glacier was moving.

How Ontario Looks Today

Many of the features that you see in Ontario's landscape can be traced to glacial action. Most of the small lakes, for example, were gouged from the bedrock by the glaciers. The Great Lakes' basins, too, were scraped larger and deeper with the passing of each glacier during the five ice ages. Ontario's many rivers drain the small lakes. They have eroded their channels through the layers of rock and gravel left behind by the glaciers.

Rivers and Flood Plains

Figure 3 shows how the erosive force of moving water has continued to shape the land since the last glacier receded. The first streams and rivers were fast flowing and fairly straight. Then, over thousands of years, they cut away at their banks, eroding material from the outside of curves, and depositing it at the inside of curves where the water moves more slowly. The curves eventually got larger and rounder, and the rivers became slower and winding. During the spring, when a river is full of meltwater from snow, it may overflow its banks and cover the shores with muddy water. The mud settles and helps build up and level out the **flood plain** on either side of the river.

Understanding Concepts

1. Why is there more soil in southern Ontario than in northern Ontario?
2. What erosive force created most of the lakes in Ontario?
3. Using a series of diagrams, explain how a river changes from being young and straight to old and winding.
4. Glaciers slow down the formation of soil on the one hand, yet speed it up on the other. Explain how this is true.

Exploring

5. A topographical map shows the change in height of the land, indicating the location of hills, lakes, and mountains. Obtain a topographical map of your area from the Geological Survey of Canada, and see if you can find evidence of old and young rivers, moraines, and drumlins left behind by glaciers.

Reflecting

6. There have been five ice ages in the last 2 million years. Do you think we have seen the last of the ice ages? Why or why not?

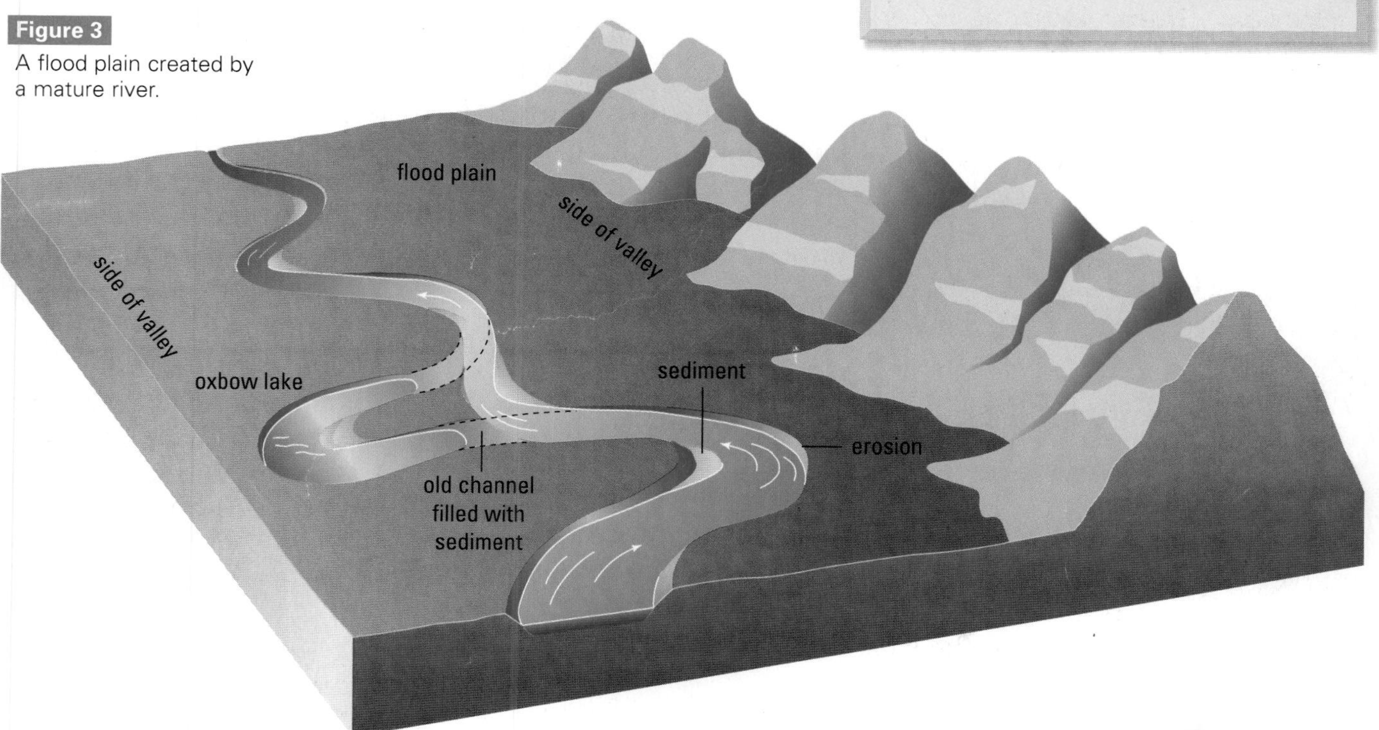

Figure 3
A flood plain created by a mature river.

SKILLS MENU
- Questioning
- Hypothesizing
- Planning
- Conducting
- Recording
- Analyzing
- Communicating

Mountains to Molehills

You have learned that many factors, including running water, cause rock to erode and that some rocks erode faster than others. Mountains are made of rock. What are the effects of rain, snow, ice, and streams on mountains over time? **Figure 1** shows the Rocky Mountains and the Laurentian Mountains. Water, wind, and ice continue to affect these mountains.

Materials

- apron
- paper
- potting soil
- clay
- sand
- popsicle sticks
- dishpan
- water
- watering can

Question

1 What question is being answered through this investigation?

Hypothesis

2C 2 Create a hypothesis for this investigation.

Experimental Design

In this investigation, you will design and build a mountain that will resist erosion. Erosion will be caused by a watering can full of water. Your design will influence how much your mountain erodes.

3 6C Design and draw a mountain shape that will use any of the materials available. Your mountain must be as resistant as possible to erosion. Include an explanation for the features of your mountain.

Procedure

4 In the dishpan, build your mountain according to your plan with the materials you have chosen.

5 Once you have finished building, examine the other mountains.

(a) Predict which mountain will best resist the erosion from the watering can. Explain your prediction.

6 One student will use the watering can to erode each mountain. Observe each mountain, including your own, as the water is poured onto it.

(a) How well did your mountain withstand the water? Draw a diagram showing your mountain after erosion.

SKILLS HANDBOOK: 2C Predicting and Hypothesizing 6C Scientific & Technical Drawing

Figure 1

Weathering and erosion work on (a) the Rocky Mountains, and (b) the Laurentian Mountains. What differences do you notice in the two ranges?

(a) The Rocky Mountains

Making Connections

1. As you have learned, erosion can also be a problem below ground since water seeps through soil and rocks. What features of the mountain you designed would help prevent this kind of erosion?
2. Look at **Figure 1**. The two photographs look very different.
   - **(a)** Make a T-chart and list some differences you notice between the two mountain ranges.
   - **(b)** How would you account for the differences?
   - **(c)** Predict what will happen to each mountain range over millions of years of erosion.

Design Challenge

Could you use any of the features you built into your mountain design in the design for a model field?

Analysis

7 Analyze your results by answering these questions.

(a) How good was your prediction? Which mountain stood up best to the watering-can test?

(b) From observations of your mountain and the others, which materials and features seem to work best at resisting erosion?

(c) Should you modify the hypothesis you wrote at the start of this investigation? Explain.

(d) If you had other materials available, what could you have done to prevent your mountain from eroding?

(b) The Laurentian Mountains

Mountains to Rock

You have learned how erosion breaks down mountains of rock. Streams and rivers carry all the soil and rock pieces, or **sediment**, downstream, as you can see in **Figure 1**. Where does all this sediment end up?

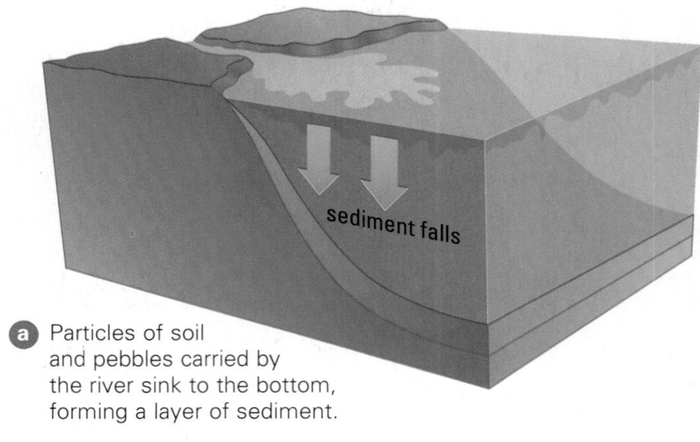

a Particles of soil and pebbles carried by the river sink to the bottom, forming a layer of sediment.

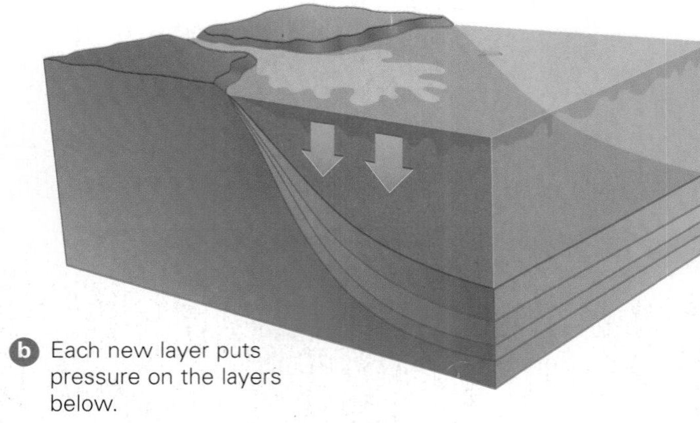

b Each new layer puts pressure on the layers below.

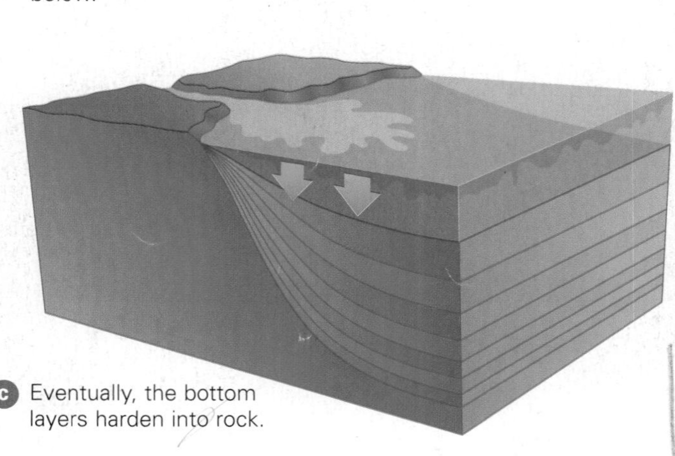

c Eventually, the bottom layers harden into rock.

Figure 2
Sedimentary rock is formed as layers of sediment are added by a river.

Figure 1
As this satellite photo shows, sediment carried by the Fraser River pours out into the sea.

Sediment Layers

The sediment is carried downhill by the strong current of small rivers and streams into larger rivers. Eventually, as the water approaches a lake or an ocean, the current slows, and the water can no longer carry the sediment along. The sediment gradually sinks to the bottom. There, on the lake or ocean floor, the sediment gradually piles up in layers. Over millions of years, the enormous weight of the many layers of sediment presses down on the lower layers. Under that pressure, water is squeezed out and the lower layers slowly harden into **sedimentary rock** (**Figure 2**).

Types of Sedimentary Rock

Different types of rock are formed from different types of sediment, as shown in **Figure 3**.

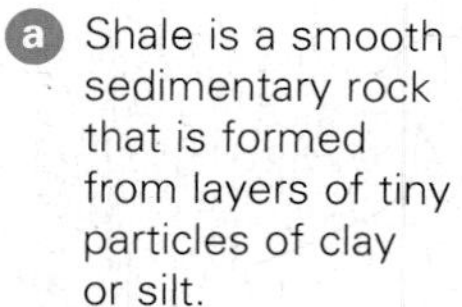

a Shale is a smooth sedimentary rock that is formed from layers of tiny particles of clay or silt.

b Sandstone, a rougher rock, is formed from layers of compressed sand.

c Conglomerate is made from sediment that contains pebbles and small stones.

Figure 3
As the layers of sediment are compressed into rock, they tend to form different kinds of rock, depending on the nature of the particles in the sediment.

Understanding Concepts

1. What part does erosion play in the formation of sedimentary rock?
2. Explain why there are different types of sedimentary rocks.
3. In a series of diagrams, show what (6C) eventually causes sedimentary layers to become hard.

Making Connections

4. The Niagara Gorge is being created by erosion caused by the Niagara River. What will happen to the rock eroded by the river?
5. In many parts of the world, including North America, there are areas of sedimentary rock that extend for hundreds of kilometres. What does this clue tell you about the ancient history of these areas?

Reflecting

6. The oldest rock in the world is about 4 billion years old, almost as old as Earth itself. However, this rock is not sedimentary. Speculate on how this rock might have formed.

Evidence of Sediment

There are many places we can see evidence of sedimentation and the formation of sedimentary rocks. The Niagara Escarpment, as shown in **Figure 4**, and the Grand Canyon, as shown in **Figure 5**, are just two examples.

Figure 4
The sedimentary layers that can be seen in the Niagara Escarpment were laid down millions of years ago in an ancient ocean bed that covered large parts of North America.

Figure 5
The Grand Canyon, which is over 1500 m deep, is being created as the Colorado River slowly erodes a path through layers of sedimentary rock laid down in an ancient ocean.

Fossils: Rock's Timekeepers

Figure 1
These fossil dinosaur bones, discovered in sedimentary rock in the Alberta Badlands, were reconstructed to form an entire skeleton. This animal lived about 75 million years ago.

You've probably heard of, if not seen, fossils of dinosaurs and other animals that lived on our planet millions of years ago. The dinosaur in **Figure 1** is an example. But what are fossils? How do they form?

How Fossils Form

Fossils are rocklike casts, impressions, or actual remains of organisms that were buried after they died, before they could decompose. Only a tiny fraction of organisms are preserved as fossils. This is because most dead organisms decay or are eaten by scavenging animals. Also soft tissue, such as muscle and other organs, does not fossilize well. Animals that have neither bones nor shells will not leave fossils.

An organism that is suddenly buried, for example if it falls into mud or quicksand, or is covered quickly by a landslide of sediment or blowing volcanic ash, may become a fossil. As the layer that contains the organism is covered by other layers of sediment, it gradually becomes sedimentary rock.

As wet sediment becomes rock, minerals that are dissolved in the water gradually replace minerals in the body of any buried organisms. Bone, shell, and the body parts of plants can all be replaced this way. Eventually, particle by particle, the fossilizing organism is replaced by minerals. The final result is a fossil that looks exactly like the original organism but is in a rocklike form (see **Figure 2**).

Figure 2
A fossilized log. Minerals have replaced the original wood, preserving the wood's structure. Entire forests, killed and preserved by volcanic eruptions or mudslides, have been fossilized in this way.

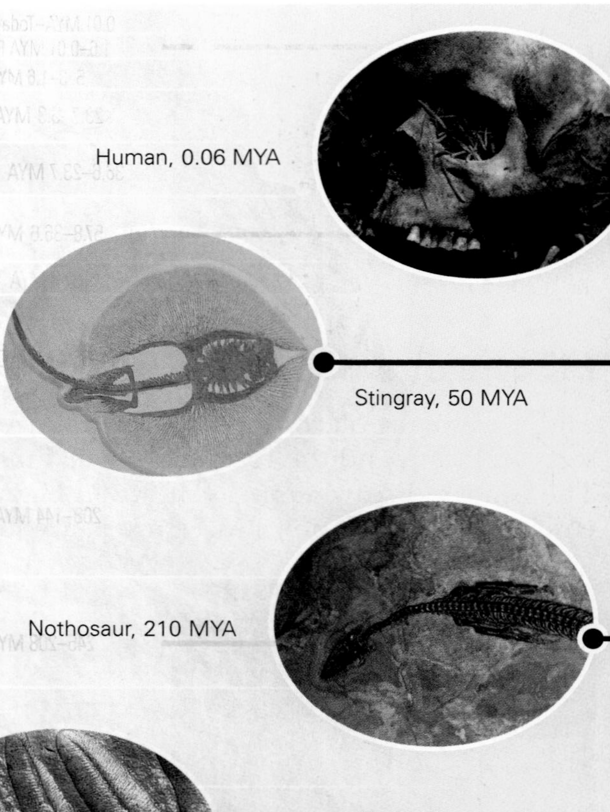

Figure 3
Geological time scale. MYA = millions of years ago

SKILLS HANDBOOK: 4A Research Skills

Fossils: Ancient Snapshots in Sedimentary Rock

Fossils are important because they show us what types of animals and plants lived on Earth hundreds of millions of years ago. If you look at exposed layers of sedimentary rock, from bottom to top, the fossils are like a series of snapshots of how life has changed on Earth, from the distant past near the bottom to more recent times near the top, as shown in **Figure 3**.

Fossils are also used to compare the age of rocks. For example, if a certain type of ancient fossil is found in two different places, then those two rock layers were probably formed at about the same time.

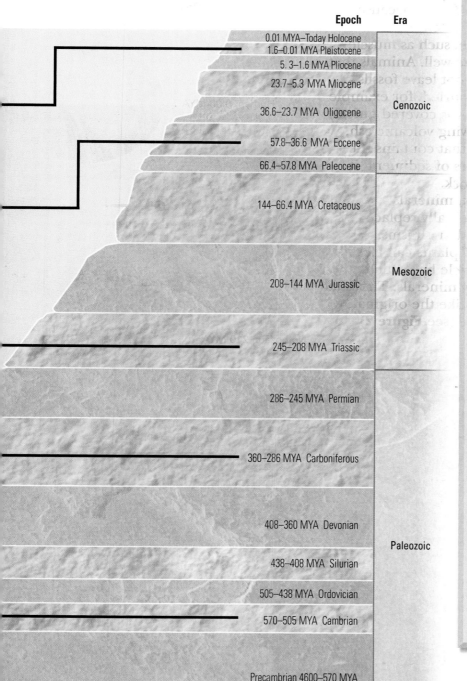

Epoch	Era
0.01 MYA–Today Holocene	Cenozoic
1.6–0.01 MYA Pleistocene	
5. 3–1.6 MYA Pliocene	
23.7–5.3 MYA Miocene	
36.6–23.7 MYA Oligocene	
57.8–36.6 MYA Eocene	
66.4–57.8 MYA Paleocene	
144–66.4 MYA Cretaceous	Mesozoic
208–144 MYA Jurassic	
245–208 MYA Triassic	
286–245 MYA Permian	Paleozoic
360–286 MYA Carboniferous	
408–360 MYA Devonian	
438–408 MYA Silurian	
505–438 MYA Ordovician	
570–505 MYA Cambrian	
Precambrian 4600–570 MYA	

Understanding Concepts

1. What are fossils and how are they made?
2. Why are fossils rare?
3. If you found a rock with a fossil that looked like **Figure 4**, how old would the rock be?

Figure 4

Making Connections

4. No fossils have been found in the lowest sedimentary layer in the Grand Canyon. Does this mean that life did not exist on Earth when that layer of sediment formed? Explain.

Exploring

5. From fossil evidence, it appears that dinosaurs and many other animals died out suddenly about 65 million years ago. Some scientists think the mass extinction was caused by an asteroid that hit the Earth. Others believe massive volcanic eruptions were the cause. In both cases, the air would have filled with dust or ash, blocking the sun and cooling the Earth rapidly. What might have happened to a dinosaur caught in this disaster? Create a diagram showing the life, death, and fossilization of a dinosaur.
6. (4A) The Burgess Shale, near the town of Field in British Columbia, is one of the most famous fossil finds in the world. Research what types of fossils can be found there and create a brochure explaining why they are so important.

Reflecting

7. Based on what you have learned, why would scientists who have only fossil evidence have to be careful about interpreting what life was like on Earth?

4.15 Case Study

Drifting Continents

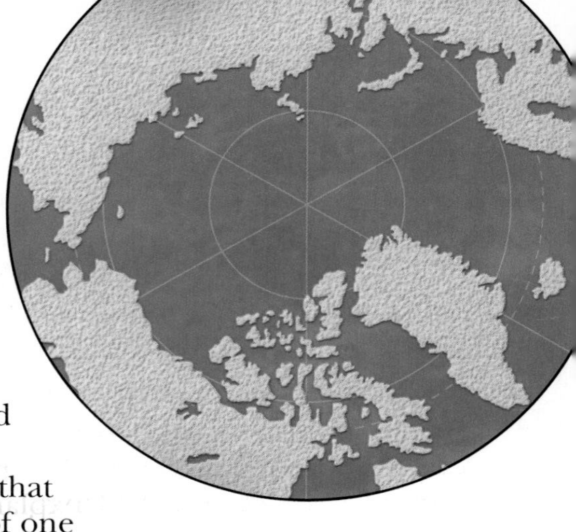

Many people have looked at the map of the world and noticed that some of the continents look like jigsaw pieces that have somehow become separated. Some came up with fanciful explanations, for example that missing continents had sunk into the sea. Among the explanations was the visionary hypothesis of Alfred Wegener, in the year 1912. He proposed that millions of years ago, all of the continents were actually part of one supercontinent he called Pangaea. The supercontinent had broken up and the continents had gradually moved apart to where they are now. He called his hypothesis **continental drift**.

At the time, most other scientists completely dismissed Wegener's idea because they could see no evidence to support it. Besides, they argued, how could huge continents move thousands of kilometres?

Figure 1
Were the continents once part of one giant supercontinent?

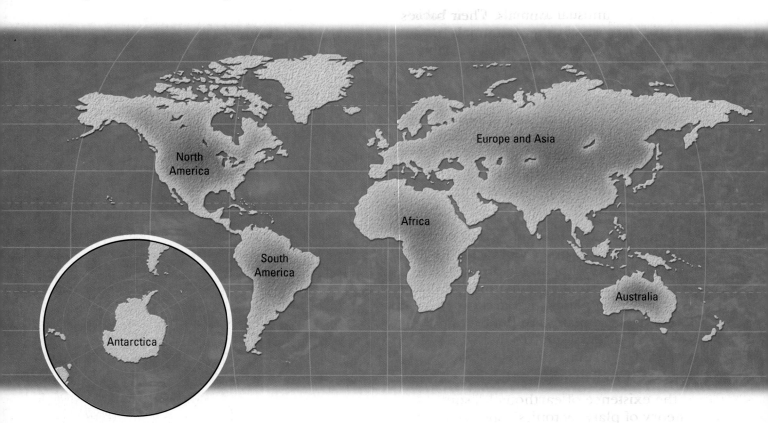

(a) Look at the continents in **Figure 1**. Do any of the continents look like they could fit together? Which ones?

(b) How might you explain why those continents seem to fit quite well but not perfectly?

(c) If you were a geologist, what features might you look for on the continents or in the rocks themselves that would help support or disprove continental drift?

The Search for Evidence

Once Wegener had put forward his hypothesis, geologists, biologists, and other scientists began to search the Earth for evidence that would support or disprove his idea. As the years passed, the supporting evidence became stronger and stronger.

(d) Ancient fossils of a small, extinct aquatic reptile have been found only in South America and Africa. Could this be evidence to support continental drift? Explain.

(e) Fossils of tropical trees and animals have been found in Antarctica. That continent is now almost completely covered in ice that is many kilometres thick. How can the presence of these fossils be explained? Is there more than one explanation?

(f) Marsupials are unusual animals. Their babies are born like those of other mammals but in an earlier stage of development. The babies crawl into a pouch in their mother's body, where they continue to develop. Most marsupials live in Australia, but not all. Opossums are marsupials, and opossums live in North and South America. Does the existence of opossums support continental drift? Explain.

Plate Tectonics

Wegener's hypothesis is now widely accepted and is part of an established theory called **plate tectonics**. The theory of plate tectonics is that the Earth's crust is actually made up of several large sections, called **plates**, that are always moving slowly. These plates are floating on the hot, thick mantle kilometres below. The continents move by riding piggyback on top of these vast, thick plates of rock.

(g) Does the existence of earthquakes support the theory of plate tectonics? Speculate on how moving plates might cause earthquakes.

Understanding Concepts

1. Describe the theory of plate tectonics.
2. What clues are there that continental drift has been occurring for millions of years?

Making Connections

3. A large deposit of gold is discovered on the west coast of Africa. According to the theory of plate tectonics, where else in the world might a similar deposit be found? Use a map to support your opinion.
4. You can create a model of the Earth's crust using a hard-boiled egg. Lightly crack the shell of a hard-boiled egg, and use a felt-tip pen to outline the cracks. Remove a few pieces of the shell.
   - **(a)** Try sliding the remaining pieces around the surface of the egg. How is the eggshell a model of the Earth's crust?
   - **(b)** What happens when you slide pieces of eggshell into one another? Does anything similar happen to the Earth's crust?
   - **(c)** What activity at the Earth's surface cannot be modelled using an eggshell?

Reflecting

5. Wegener was laughed at when he first told other scientists about his hypothesis. A huge amount of evidence from every area of science was required before continental drift and the plate tectonic model that explained it were finally accepted. All new scientific theories must have a lot of evidence to support them. Are there drawbacks to this approach?

4.16

Moving Plates

The Earth's crust is not one continuous piece but is actually composed of several huge, solid sections, called plates (see **Figure 1**), that move slowly as they float on the semi-liquid mantle below. The plates are moving relative to one another. For example, the plate that carries North America and the plate that carries Europe are moving away from each other at the rate of about 3 cm every year. Some plates are moving toward each other. Some are slipping by each other. Wherever plates meet, earthquakes signal their movement.

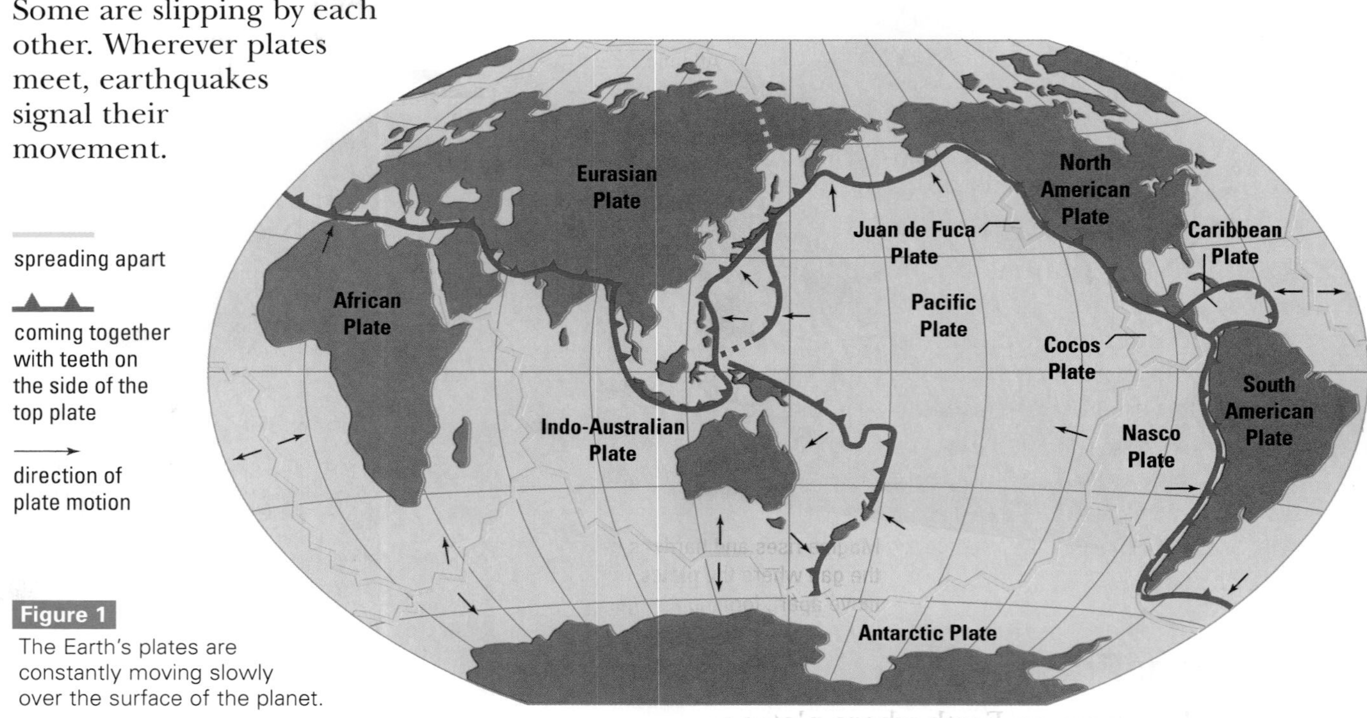

Figure 1
The Earth's plates are constantly moving slowly over the surface of the planet.

Slipping By: A Fault

The San Andreas Fault in California (see **Figure 2**) is an example of a place on the Earth's crust where plates are slipping by each other. Here the Pacific Plate, which carries part of Baja California and a small strip of the west coast of the United States, is moving north past the North American Plate. Places where plates meet in this way are called **faults**.

Figure 2
The famous San Andreas Fault in California. Here the Pacific and North American Plates meet. The Pacific Plate is moving north, and the North American Plate is moving south.

Collision: Subduction

Plates can collide as they move toward each other. When they do, something must give. Usually one plate slides below the other (see **Figure 3**). As the lower plate plunges underneath, it pushes into the hot mantle, where it heats up and melts. This process is called **subduction**. It is occurring in many places in the world, including along the coast of British Columbia.

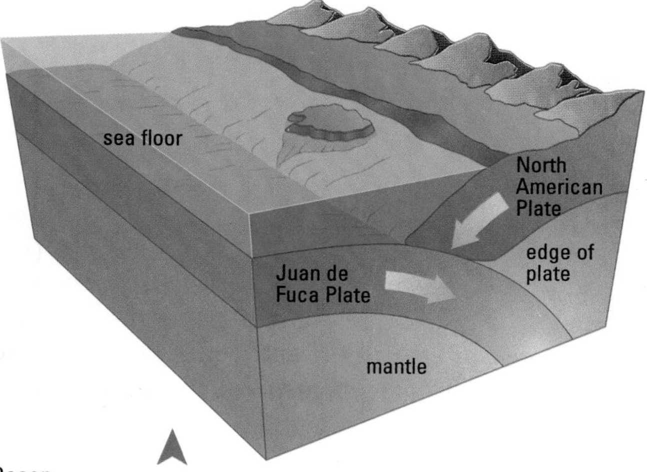

Figure 3
The Juan de Fuca Plate has been forced under the North American Plate, which is moving west.

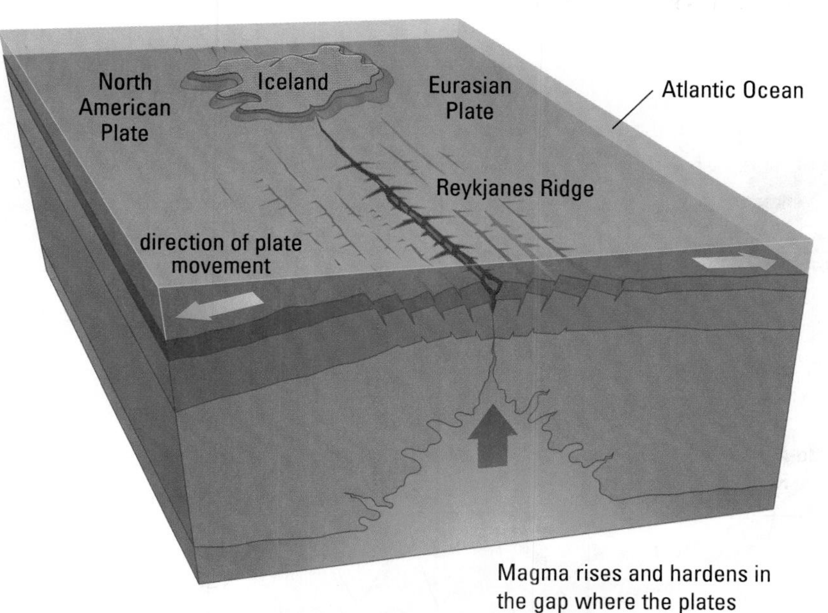

Figure 4
Iceland formed on the rift in the middle of the Atlantic Ocean where two large plates are moving apart. Magma from below continually rises up into the newly formed gap and flows out onto the Earth's surface as lava.

Separation: Ridges

There are also places on Earth where plates are moving apart from each other. At these spots, hot magma rises up into the crack between the plates and hardens, forming **ridges** of new rock (see **Figure 4**). Ridge formation usually occurs beneath the oceans, but one place on the Earth's surface where you can actually see this happening is in Iceland (see **Figure 5**).

Figure 5
In 1963, the new island of Surtsey formed off the coast of Iceland as large amounts of magma flowed out of the oceanic rift between the Eurasian and North American Plates.

Understanding Concepts

1. What are plates?
2. **(a)** Describe what happens when two plates meet and when two plates move apart.
   (b) (3) Design a simulation of plates meeting.

Making Connections

3. Look at **Figure 1**. Why might Vancouver have more earthquakes than Toronto or Halifax?

Exploring

4. Where on the Earth would you expect to find young, newly formed rock? Where would you expect to find old rock? Explain.
5. (4A) In Iceland, where hot magma is close to the surface, many people use its heat, called geothermal energy, to warm their homes. Research this form of energy. Is it renewable? Would it be practical to use geothermal energy in your area? Prepare a report.

SKILLS HANDBOOK: (3) Process of Design (4A) Research Skills

SKILLS MENU
- ○ Questioning
- ● Hypothesizing
- ○ Planning
- ● Conducting
- ● Recording
- ● Analyzing
- ● Communicating

Earthquakes, Volcanoes, and Mountain Ranges

The plates that make up the Earth's crust are constantly moving. They are also pushing against one another. Is there a direct connection between plate movement and earthquakes? Are mountain chains and volcanoes related to plate movement?

Question

Is there a pattern in the location of earthquakes, volcanoes, and mountain ranges (**Figure 1**)?

Hypothesis

1 (2C) Based on your knowledge of plate tectonics, create a hypothesis for each of the following questions.

(a) Where are earthquakes most likely to occur?

(b) Where are volcanoes most likely to occur?

(c) Where are mountain ranges most likely to occur?

Experimental Design

On a map of the world, you will plot the location of mountain ranges and recent earthquakes and volcanic eruptions to see if any patterns exist.

Materials

- map of the world
- atlas or globe
- coloured markers

Procedure

2 Practise finding latitude and longitude on a map.
- To find latitude, measure from 0° at the equator up to 90° north at the North Pole or 90° south at the South Pole.
- To find longitude, measure from 0° at Greenwich, England, either east or west up to 180°.
- As a trial example, find the city in Ontario that is located at 46° N latitude and 76° W longitude.

3 On your copy of the world map, place a small blue circle ● at the location of each earthquake listed in **Table 1**.

4 For each volcano listed in **Table 2**, place a small red triangle ▲ on your world map.

5 Use a third colour ✎ to mark the location of the following mountain ranges: Rockies, Andes, Himalayas, Alps, Urals, and Appalachians. (You can use an atlas or globe to help you find these features.)

Analysis

6 Analyze your results by answering these questions.

(a) Compare your map with Figure 1 in 4.16. What patterns do you see in the locations of:
- earthquakes?
- volcanoes?
- mountain ranges?

(b) Are volcanoes always located near mountain ranges?

(c) Were your predictions correct? If not, explain why.

SKILLS HANDBOOK: (2C) Predicting and Hypothesizing

a The 1989 earthquake in San Francisco, California was devastating.

Making Connections

1. Explain, using evidence from your map, why the edge of the Pacific Ocean is often called the Ring of Fire.

Design Challenge

Earthquakes are dangerous to miners. Could an underground mine be made safe during an earthquake? Would a tailings pond contain its waste during an earthquake?
How would you simulate an earthquake in your models? What extra precautions would you have to take if your mine were on the west coast of Canada?

b Kilauea Iki, in Hawaii erupted in 1959.

Figure 1
Some areas of our planet seem to be more dangerous than others.

Table 1 **Major Earthquakes**

Year	Location	Coordinates
1556	Shenchi, China	39° N, 112° E
1755	Lisbon, Portugal	39° N, 9° W
1811–12	New Madrid, Missouri	36° N, 89° W
1906	San Francisco, Calif.	38° N, 122° W
1920	Kansu, China	40° N, 75° E
1923	Tokyo, Japan	36° N, 140° E
1935	Quetta, Pakistan	30° N, 67° E
1939	Concepcion, Chile	37° S, 73° W
1964	Anchorage, Alaska	60° N, 150° W
1970	Yungay, Peru	9° S, 78° W
1972	Managua, Nicaragua	12° N, 86° W
1976	Guatemala City	14° N, 91° W
1976	Tangshan, China	40° N, 119° E
1985	Mexico City, Mexico	19° N, 99° W
1988	Shirokamud, Armenia	41° N, 44° E
1989	San Francisco Bay, Calif.	38° N, 122° W
1990	Rasht, Iran	37° N, 49° E
1991	Valla de la Estrella, Costa Rica	10° N, 84° W
1993	Maharashtra, India	23° N, 75° E
1994	Northridge, Calif.	34° N, 119° W
1995	Kobe, Japan	34° N, 135° E

Table 2 **Some Active Volcanoes**

Volcano and Location	Coordinates
Etna, Italy	37° N, 15° E
Tambora, Indonesia	8° S, 117° E
Krakatoa, Indonesia	6° S, 105° E
Pelée, Martinique	14° N, 61° W
Vesuvius, Italy	41° N, 14° E
Lassen, California	40° N, 121° W
Mauna Loa, Hawaii	21° N, 157° W
Paricutin, Mexico	19° N, 103° W
Surtsey, Iceland	63° N, 20° W
Kelud, Indonesia	8° S, 112° E
Arenal, Costa Rica	10° N, 84° W
Eldfell, Iceland	65° N, 23° W
Mount St. Helens, Wash.	46° N, 122° W
Laki-Fogrufjoll, Iceland	64° N, 18° W
Kilauea, Hawaii	22° N, 159° W
Mount Katmai, Alaska	58° N, 155° W
Avachinsky, Russia	53° N, 159° W
El Chichon, Mexico	17° N, 93° W
Ubinas, Peru	16° S, 71° W
Villarica, Chile	39° S, 72° W
Asama, Japan	36° N, 138° E
Shikotsu, Japan	41° N, 141° E

4.18 Career Profile

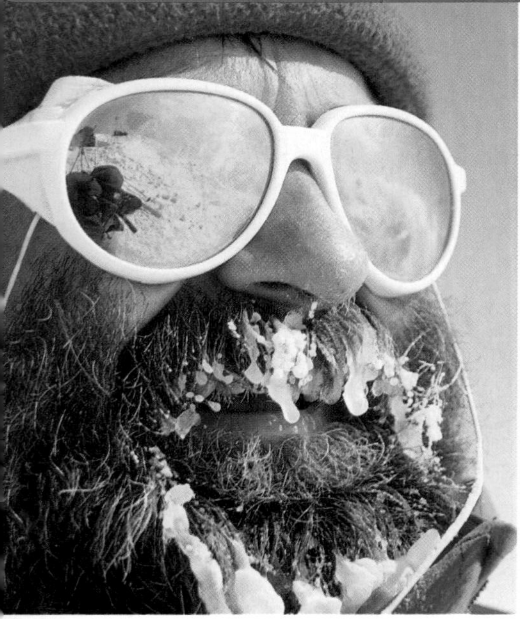

Cracking the Secrets of the Earth's Crust

Meet Michael Schmidt. He is on "earthquake watch." He keeps an eye on the shifting continental plates of Canada's biggest earthquake zone.

People have always used stars for navigation. Michael Schmidt uses artificial stars that are 20 000 km above us. They're satellites that make up the global positioning system, or GPS. With GPS, Michael can pinpoint the slow creep of huge continental plates.

"The concept of how it works is very simple," says Michael. The GPS satellites send radio signals to Earth. Each signal includes a message that says exactly when it was sent. It's accurate to a billionth of a second! On Earth, GPS receivers pick up the signal and record when the signal arrives. The difference between sending and receiving is the signal's travel time. The signal moves with the speed of light, a number we know. The GPS computers multiply the speed of light by the signal's travel time to give the distance between the satellite and receiver.

This same multiplication is done with signals from at least four separate satellites. This gives the exact location of the receiver on the Earth.

Michael uses receivers that are attached to concrete pillars driven into the crust. When a continental plate moves, the receivers move with it (**see Figure 1**).

Figure 1
Michael Schimdt placed this temporary GPS receiver near the top of Mount Logan in B.C.

A Sticky Situation on the West Coast

Michael is most concerned about the North American and Juan de Fuca Plates on Canada's west coast. Scientists believe the Juan de Fuca Plate started to slip under the North American Plate, but, at the moment, the plates are stuck, as shown in **Figure 2**. Michael measures the movement of the western edge of the huge North American Plate as it is being squeezed out of shape or deformed. Each year the underlying Juan de Fuca Plate is pushing the North American Plate up about 4 mm and backwards (east) about 1 cm.

Added up over hundreds of years, these tiny movements store a huge amount of energy, like a tennis ball being squeezed tightly. When the plates unlock some day, the bulging North American Plate will suddenly leap forward over the Juan de Fuca Plate. "That's an incredible force happening all at once," says Michael. A tremendous earthquake will rock the coast.

Predicting the "Big One"

"GPS helps tremendously," says Michael. "If an earthquake like this happens under Vancouver, it's going to have an incredible effect."

Scientists believe the earthquake will happen where the most deformation takes place. Michael's GPS research shows that that spot is under the ocean about 120 to 150 km off Vancouver Island. Knowing this, Michael and his fellow scientists will be able to predict how strong the shock will be in nearby cities and towns. Using that information, architects and engineers may be able to make sure schools and other buildings are earthquake-proof and that will save lives.

Try This Unsticking Plates

You can demonstrate the movements of the continental plates that Michael observes using a sheet of paper, a sheet of heavy cardboard, and a ruler.

- Label the paper "North American Plate" and the cardboard "Juan de Fuca Plate."
- Place the cardboard and paper side by side, with the paper on the right. Put your right hand on the right half of the paper to hold it still.
- With your left hand, push the cardboard to the right against the edge of the paper. The left portion of the paper sheet should bulge up as it is squeezed. Keep pushing until the paper slips over the cardboard.
- Repeat this exercise with a partner. Let your partner slowly push the cardboard, then measure the distance the cardboard moved underneath the paper before the paper regained its shape.
- Start again, but this time measure the maximum height of the paper bulge before it slips.

1. Explain what might happen with real continental plates if this sudden movement took place next to the ocean.
2. How might this sudden motion affect living things?
3. Do you think your model of plate movement accurately represents what is occurring (or will occur) with the real plates on the coast of British Columbia? What are the weaknesses of this model?

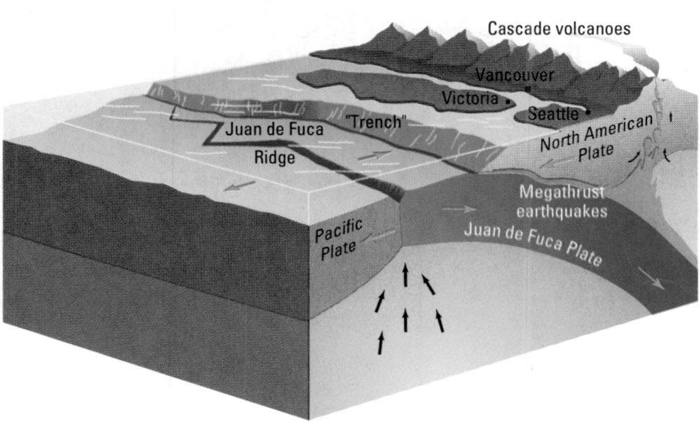

Figure 2
When the plates unlock, the "big one" will be let loose.

SKILLS MENU
- Identify a Problem
- Planning
- Building
- Testing
- Recording
- Evaluating
- Communicating

Preparing for Earthquakes

If an earthquake happens near a city, it can be devastating, as **Figure 1** shows. During an earthquake, people are most in danger from collapsing buildings and falling pieces of concrete, stone, or steel. So the most effective way to minimize damage from an earthquake is to construct better buildings. Even in eastern Canada, where earthquakes are uncommon and usually mild, engineers must design office buildings to withstand at least small earthquakes.

Materials

- 1 m of masking tape
- 3 balls of modelling clay
- 100 toothpicks
- 30 thin wood sticks, each 4 cm long
- 2 thin pieces of wood, each 10 cm × 10 cm

The shaker must be careful not to damage desks or injure nearby students.

Problem

3B **1** What problem can you identify in the paragraph above?

Design Brief

Design and make an earthquake-proof building using only the materials available.

Design Criteria

- The building must be at least 30 cm tall and not more than 20 cm wide.
- The building must be taped to the desk on which it is built. A building that comes loose will be judged to have collapsed.

Build

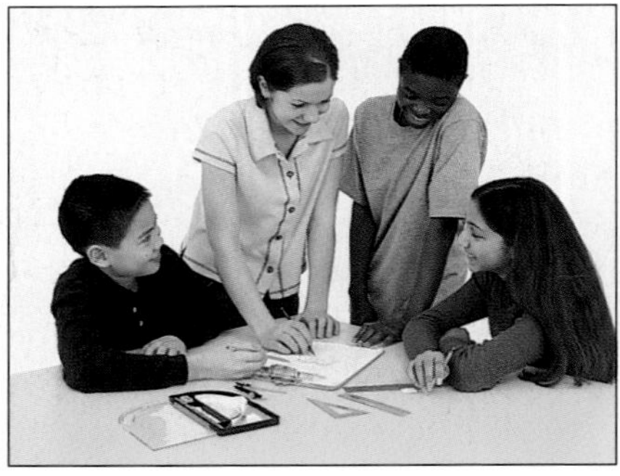

2 Design at least two earthquake-proof buildings. 3D

3 Pick the design you think is better, and build it. 3C

(a) How did you decide which design is the better? What are the important features of the design?

4 When your model has been built, present it to the rest of the class, pointing out the features of your design that you think make your model earthquake-proof. 3E

Test

5 Study each of the other models. 3F

(a) Predict what will happen to each structure when the desk it is sitting on is shaken. Record your prediction.

6 One person will be chosen to shake the desk under each model.

- Starting with a very gentle shake, increase the amount of shaking every 10 s until the model falls down or the shaker gives up.

(b) Record your observations for each model.

SKILLS HANDBOOK: 3 Process of Design

Figure 1

The powerful earthquake that struck Kobe, Japan, in 1995 lasted only 20 s, yet it left 5502 people dead and $99 billion in property damage.

Evaluate

7 Evaluate your results by answering these questions.

(a) Based on the results of the testing, create a new design for an earthquake-proof building. Label the features of your new building and explain their purpose.

(b) Are the models you designed good examples of what real buildings might be like? Why or why not?

Making Connections

1. Why don't all new buildings contain features that will help them withstand earthquakes?

2. Look around at the buildings, bridges, and other large structures in your town or city.

- **(a)** Can you see any evidence of reinforcements for earthquakes?
- **(b)** Are these reinforcements just for earthquakes? If not, list other possible functions they might have.

Exploring

3. (4A) The CN Tower in Toronto is the highest structure in Canada. Research what features it has to protect it from earthquake damage.

Reflecting

4. No one yet knows how to predict earthquakes, but there is some evidence that some animals can. For example, rats and mice have been observed running from buildings just before an earthquake.

- **(a)** What do you think these animals might be sensing?
- **(b)** How could scientists test the reliability of these observations?

Design Challenge

You have tested several designs for a structure that resists earthquakes. Can you use any of the design features you created in your mine model? In your tailings pond model?

(4A) Research Skills

Mountains from Rocks

You have learned that mountains seem to be associated with the edges of plates. They form where two of the Earth's plates meet.

Fold Mountains

Where plates meet head-on, as the lower plate plunges into the mantle, the crust on the upper plate may fold under the pressure, forming **fold mountains** like the Rocky Mountains of North America and the Himalayas of Asia.

The Coast Mountains

The west coast of North America is mountainous. This is because the North American plate is moving generally west, colliding with the plates under the Pacific Ocean. The Juan de Fuca Plate under the Pacific Ocean at British Columbia is being forced down under the plate carrying the continent. As you can see in **Figure 1**, the tremendous pressure created by the lower plate causes mountains to form on the upper plate. Over millions of years, this continuous folding into high ridges and deep valleys has formed the Coast Mountains and the Rockies in North America.

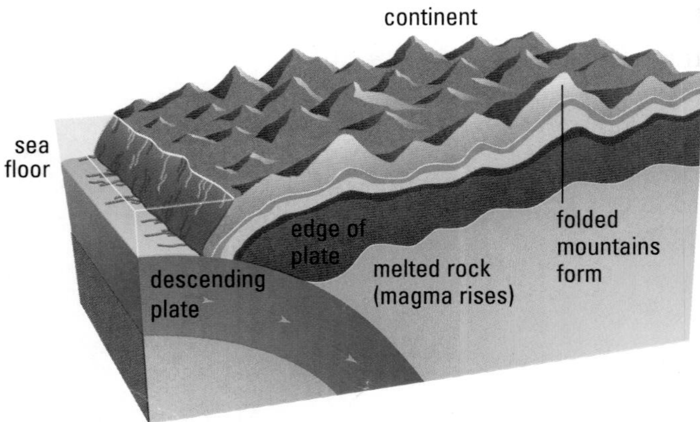

Figure 1

At the British Columbia coast, the North American Plate is sliding over the Juan de Fuca Plate. The huge force of the lower plate pressing against the upper plate as it thrusts downward causes the upper plate to rise, bend, and fold.

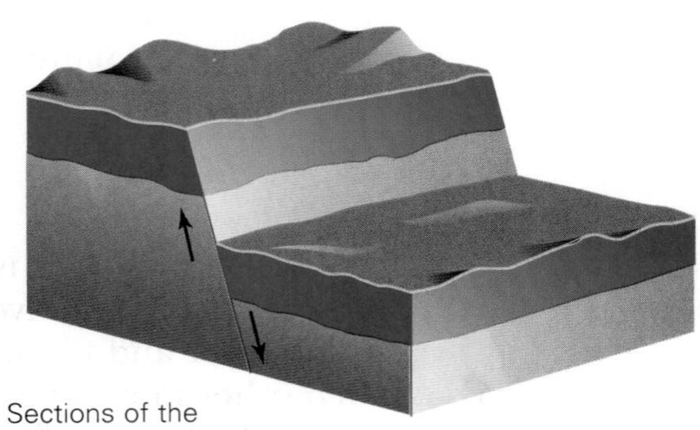

a Sections of the Earth's crust may float up or sink down past each other.

b A block of the Earth's crust may sink between two fault lines, forming a huge valley, or it may rise, forming a large mountain.

c Blocks of the Earth may move upward and tilt at the same time. The Sierra Nevada Mountains and the San Andreas Mountains in California are examples of block mountains that formed as blocks of the Earth's crust tilted and rose along two fault lines.

Figure 2

Block mountains or deep valleys may form along faults in the Earth's crust.

The Himalayas

The mountains in the highest range in the world, the Himalayas, are also fold mountains that have formed from two plates colliding. The plate carrying India is moving north, colliding with the large Eurasian Plate in front of it, and is plunging beneath it. Mount Everest, the highest mountain in the world, is getting still higher, by about 6 mm each year.

Mountains from Faults

Folding of plates during head-on collisions is not the only way mountains can be created. You have learned that plates move away from each other and toward each other, and they also slip past each other in areas called faults. However, plates are not smooth. As they slip by each other, they tend to have a grinding stop-and-start movement as the edges of the plates catch and push on each other. The pushing generates great pressure in the plates and can cause cracking as pieces of one plate or the other are forced up or down. The results of movement along a fault can be seen in **Figure 2**. **Block mountains** form as the crust tilts under pressure from a neighbouring plate.

Mountains from Below

A third type of mountain, not nearly as high as fold or block mountains, is called a **dome mountain**. Dome mountains form when magma moving up through the mantle encounters sedimentary rock in the Earth's crust that will not crack. The magma then simply pushes the layers above into a dome that rises higher than the surrounding land (see **Figure 3**).

Mount Royal, in the centre of Montreal, is a dome mountain. In the countryside surrounding Montreal, there are several other dome mountains. They rise only a few hundred metres, but they stand out prominently against the flat background.

Understanding Concepts

1. Use diagrams to explain the formation of:
   (a) fold mountains
   (b) block mountains
   (c) dome mountains

Making Connections

2. Can earthquakes be linked to the formation of all mountains? Explain.

Exploring

3. (a) Research how geologists (4A) estimate the age of mountains.
   (b) Which mountains are older, the Rocky Mountains in western Canada or the Laurentian Mountains in Quebec?

Reflecting

4. (8A) People have often considered burying toxic or radioactive waste far underground, where they hope it won't harm the environment. Based on your knowledge of plate tectonics, mountain formation, and earthquakes, is there a place where it would be safe to bury toxic waste? Prepare a report to support your opinion.

Figure 3
Formation of dome mountains

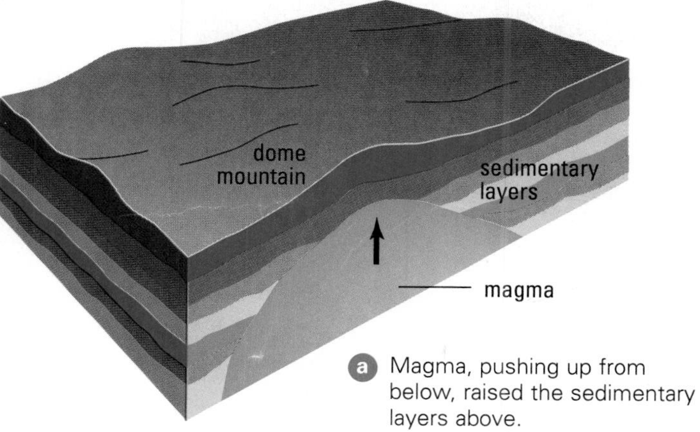

(a) Magma, pushing up from below, raised the sedimentary layers above.

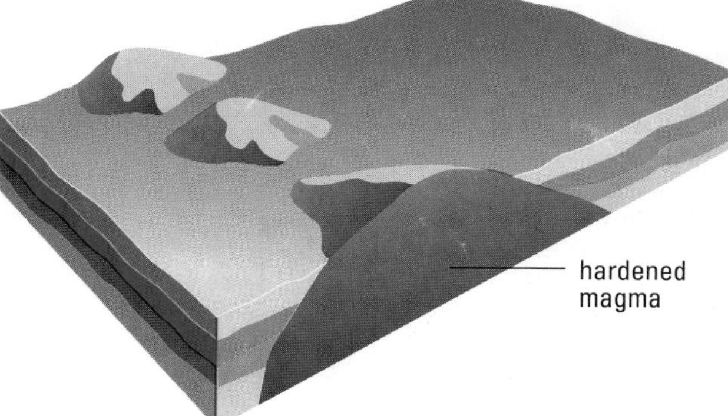

(b) As glaciers advanced and receded across the mountain, they eroded away much of the sedimentary rock, leaving the hardened magma exposed.

SKILLS HANDBOOK: (4A) Research Skills (8A) Writing a Report

Igneous and Metamorphic Rocks

About 4 billion years ago, the Earth's crust formed when the liquid magma on the surface cooled and hardened. Rock that forms from the hardening of liquid magma is called **igneous rock**. Four billion years ago, all of Earth's rock was igneous. Since then sedimentary rocks have formed, but there are also other types of rock formed by processes in the Earth's crust.

Igneous Rock

Most of the world's rock is still igneous, and igneous rock is still being formed.

Just below the Earth's surface, slowly cooling magma forms **intrusive igneous rock** that can be seen only after erosion removes the layers above it. Granite forms in this way.

Extrusive igneous rock is formed when magma (lava) pours out of volcanoes and hardens. Basalt is an extrusive igneous rock. It is the most common rock in the Earth's crust.

Metamorphic Rock

Below the Earth's surface, where rock is exposed to high heat and pressure, igneous rock and sedimentary rock form new types of rock called **metamorphic rock**. **Figure 1** shows how all of the rocks mentioned in this section are formed.

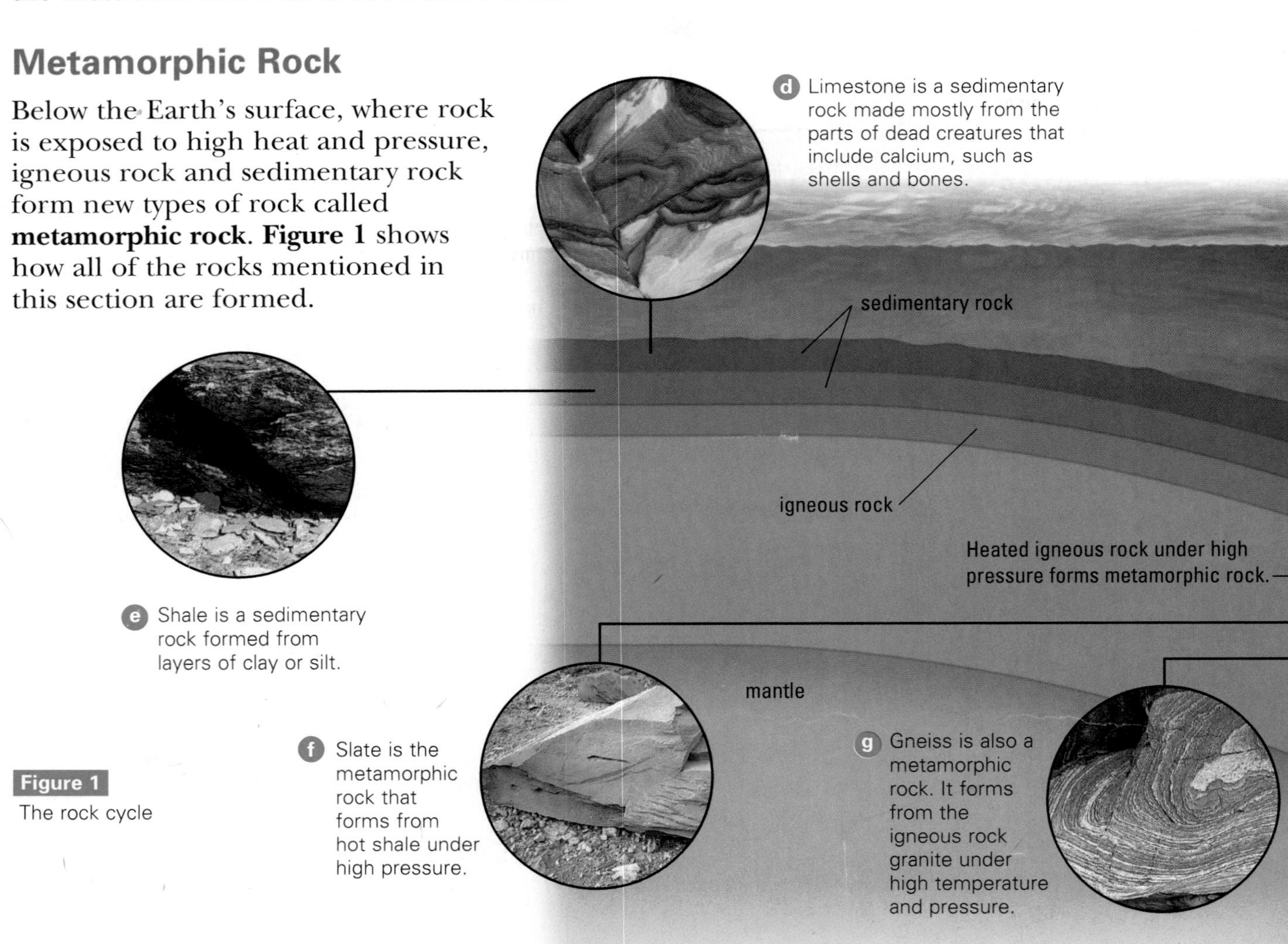

d Limestone is a sedimentary rock made mostly from the parts of dead creatures that include calcium, such as shells and bones.
sedimentary rock
igneous rock
Heated igneous rock under high pressure forms metamorphic rock.
e Shale is a sedimentary rock formed from layers of clay or silt.
mantle
f Slate is the metamorphic rock that forms from hot shale under high pressure.
g Gneiss is also a metamorphic rock. It forms from the igneous rock granite under high temperature and pressure.

Figure 1
The rock cycle

The Rock Cycle

Rocks, no matter what type, can gradually change into another type. All three forms of rock—sedimentary, igneous, and metamorphic—may eventually become exposed on the Earth's surface, where erosion will wear them down. The resulting sediment then gradually forms into layers that get compressed into sedimentary rock.

Any rock, if pushed far enough into the Earth, will become metamorphic due to the high temperatures and pressure. If the rock is part of a plate plunging far into the mantle underneath another plate, it will become extremely hot and melt, turning into magma. The magma can, in turn, rise and erupt out of a volcano or cool gradually near the surface, forming igneous rock.

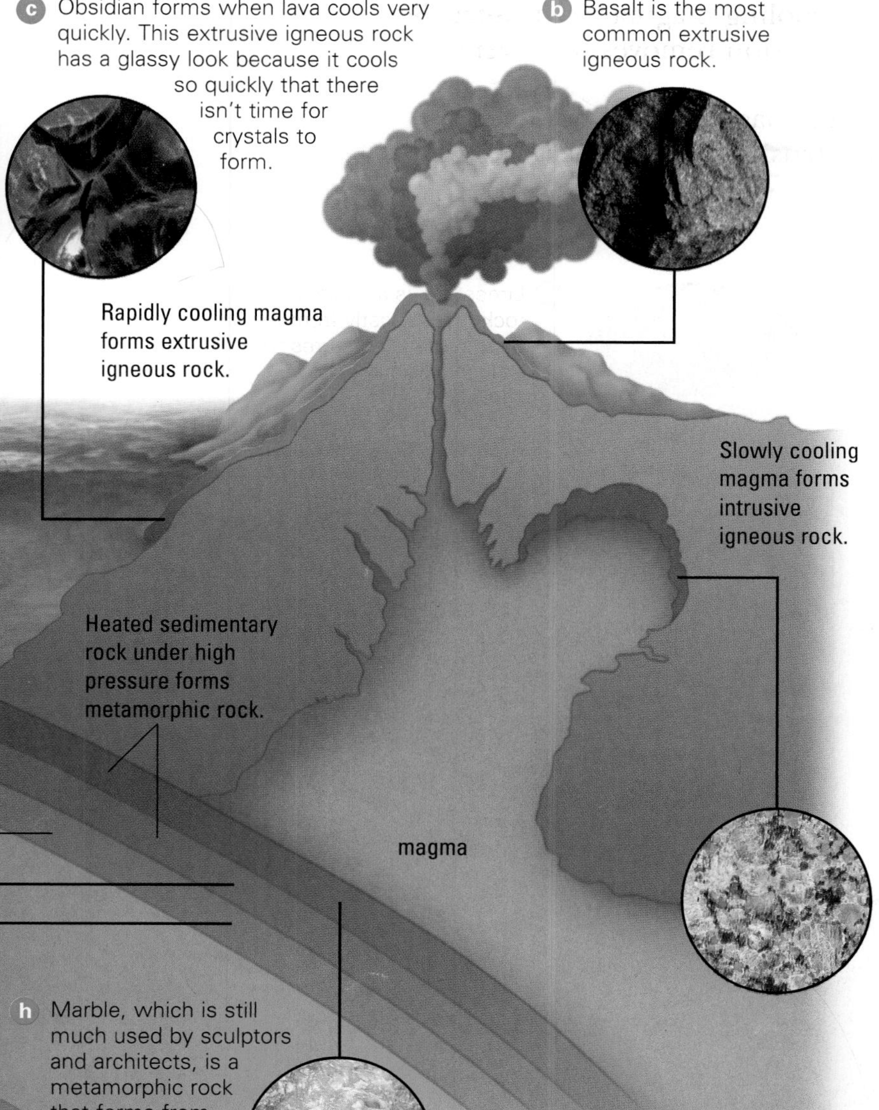

Rapidly cooling magma forms extrusive igneous rock.
Slowly cooling magma forms intrusive igneous rock.
Heated sedimentary rock under high pressure forms metamorphic rock.
magma
All rock, if pushed into the mantle, will be heated enough to melt and form magma.

c Obsidian forms when lava cools very quickly. This extrusive igneous rock has a glassy look because it cools so quickly that there isn't time for crystals to form.

b Basalt is the most common extrusive igneous rock.

a Granite is an intrusive igneous rock. Some of the oldest rocks on Earth are granite, such as the Canadian Shield rocks of central and northern Ontario and Quebec.

h Marble, which is still much used by sculptors and architects, is a metamorphic rock that forms from limestone that is heated under high pressure.

Understanding Concepts

1. Which type of rock is formed by:
   (a) weathering and erosion?
   (b) pressure and heat, but no melting?
   (c) melting and cooling?
2. What is the difference between intrusive and extrusive igneous rock?
3. Illustrate and describe how particles in a rock could go through the rock cycle from igneous to sedimentary to metamorphic and back to igneous rock.

Making Connections

4. **(a)** Which type of igneous rock was probably the first to form on the early Earth? Explain.
   (b) The most common type of rock on Earth is basalt. Speculate on why this is the case.
5. Coal and diamonds are formed from the same substance—carbon. Diamond is much harder than coal.
   (a) Which one do you think is formed farthest underground? Explain.
   (b) Speculate on how these differences might affect mining.

Exploring

6. Before the invention of modern materials, slate used to have many uses because it is a hard rock that cleaves into sheets. Research what some of these uses were and what materials have replaced slate. What advantages do modern materials have over slate?

Volcanoes: Mountains from Magma

The Earth's surface is pockmarked with volcanoes. Some of them erupt frequently and relatively quietly, and you can actually watch the lava flow out of them from a safe distance. Others erupt only once every few hundred years, but when they do, it is wise to be as far away as possible.

Shield Volcanoes: Rivers of Lava

Shield volcanoes do not occur at the edge of plates, unlike the major mountain ranges of the world. Instead, they can be found anywhere in a plate, even rising out of the ocean floor. Shield volcanoes are formed above hot spots in the mantle, as shown in **Figure 1**. In a hot spot, magma collects in enormous pools. The hot magma eventually melts the rock above it and pours out through the hole onto the Earth's surface as **lava**. The lava of shield volcanoes tends to be runny and hardens into basalt rock. Basalt lava is so fluid that shield volcanoes tend not to erupt explosively. The lava simply pours out of the volcano like a river and then hardens. Because of this, shield volcanoes build up gradually and have gently sloping sides.

When a shield volcano forms on the ocean floor, the lava pouring out hardens more quickly than it would on land. More lava pours on top, forming a volcanic **cone**. The cone may build up until it rises above sea level and forms an island. **Figure 2** shows Mauna Loa, a shield volcano that has formed the island of Hawaii.

volcano
lava flow
ocean
Earth's crust
magma
hot spot

Figure 1
Shield volcanoes form at hot spots where a huge pool of hot magma has risen through the mantle and melted a hole through the solid rock of the Earth's crust.

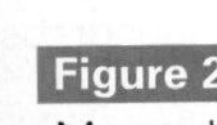

Mauna Loa, on the island of Hawaii, is a shield volcano. From its base at the bottom of the Pacific Ocean to its summit, it rises 9750 m, which makes it taller than Mount Everest.

SKILLS HANDBOOK: 8A Writing a Report 4A Research Skills

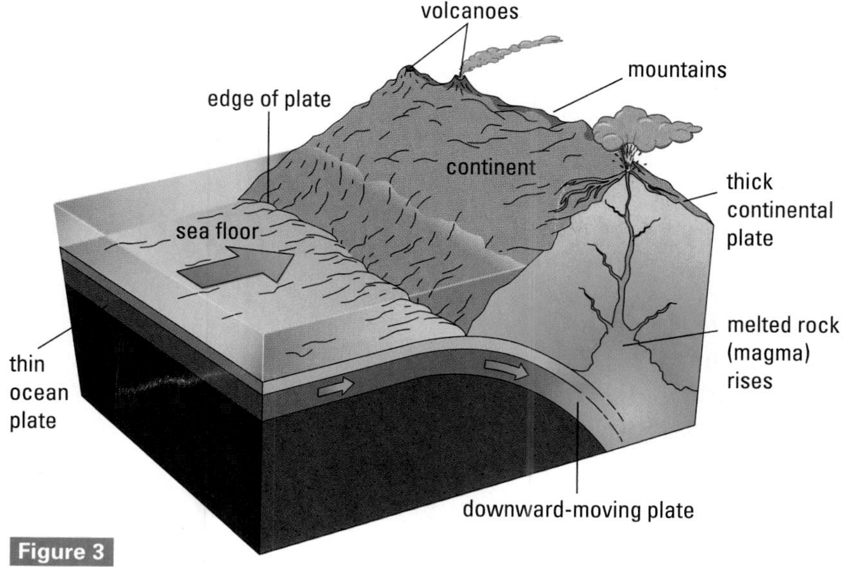

Figure 3

Because the sediment that slides under the continental plate contains water, the lava of stratovolcanos tends to be explosive.

Stratovolcanoes: Volcanoes That Explode

Stratovolcanoes are the type of volcanoes that we usually hear about in the news because they erupt so explosively, blowing ash and rock many kilometres up into the atmosphere, along with an enormous column of steam and gases.

As shown in **Figure 3**, this type of volcano forms where two plates collide, one sliding on top of the other. As the light sediments on the descending plate heat up and melt, the resulting magma rises up against the plate above and melts through it. This forms a hole so the magma can escape.

However, in contrast to the very liquid magma of shield volcanoes, the magma of stratovolcanoes is thick and sticky. Because the magma is made of melted crust and the sediment on the lower plate contains water, the lava of stratovolcanoes also contains steam under enormous pressure. It is this combination of thick magma and steam that causes stratovolcanoes to erupt so explosively. As the lava rises, the high-pressure steam escapes, carrying lava and ash with it. Mount St. Helens, shown in **Figure 4**, is a stratovolcano.

Understanding Concepts

1. Which type of volcano has very liquid magma?
2. Where are stratovolcanoes found? Why?
3. Where do eruptions occur without forming volcanoes?

Making Connections

4. Take a look at the world map of plates on page 40. On the basis of your information about plate movement, do you think that Mount Vesuvius would produce dangerous volcanic eruptions or quiet eruptions?
5. As plates move apart, the oceans between them expand. The Atlantic Ocean is expanding this way. Based on what you know, what rock would you expect makes up most of the ocean floor?

Exploring

6. (8A) Some famous volcanic eruptions had devastating consequences for the people who lived near them. Prepare a report on one of the following eruptions or on one of your own choice: Thera in about 2600 BC; Mount Pelee in AD 1902.
7. (4A) The largest volcanic eruptions in the past have given off so much dust and ash that they have formed a dust veil in the atmosphere that covered the entire planet. Research whether these dust veils made Earth's climate warmer or cooler and why.

Figure 4

Mount St. Helens is a stratovolcano in the Cascade Mountains of Washington State. In 1980, it erupted for the first time in hundreds of years.

Eruptions Where Plates Part

As you have already seen, lava also flows out onto the Earth's surface where plates are moving apart, usually on the ocean floor where the crust is thinnest. Here the lava cools quickly to form basalt in a long ridge on each side of the crack in the ocean floor. Some of these ridges may rise high enough to reach the surface, creating islands such as Iceland.

Design Challenge

SKILLS MENU
- Identify a Problem
- Planning
- Building
- Testing
- Recording
- Evaluating
- Communicating

Design and Build a Model for Using the Earth Responsibly

Human activities affect the Earth's crust. When we dig for metals and other minerals, when we dump waste on the land, or when we clear land and use it to grow crops, we make changes in the crust. Sometimes those changes cannot be reversed. When we use land, we should use it responsibly, keeping the impact on other living things to a minimum. In completing these challenges, you will explore responsible land use.

Figure 3
Farming involves intensive use of the land. It must be carefully planned.

Figure 1
Open-pit mines require extensive landscaping when they are no longer in use.

1 A Responsible Mine

Problem situation

Geologists have identified a body of rock with copper-containing ore 600 m below the surface in northwestern Ontario. The ore is under an old-growth pine forest near a provincial park.

Design brief

- Design and build a model of a mine that both removes ore efficiently and causes minimal environmental damage.

Design criteria

- In the model, rock must be safely removed from the rock face.
- The model must include a mechanism that brings rock containing copper ore from the rock face to the surface.
- The mine must be environmentally friendly. Damage to the forest and the nearby park must be kept to a minimum.
- Your model must include a plan for restoring the land once the mine is closed.
- Your model mine must be safe for miners.

2 A Safe Mine-Tailings Pond

Problem situation

After rock is brought to the surface of a mine, the desired mineral, such as chalcopyrite (which contains copper), must be separated from the rock. Usually this involves crushing the rock and mixing it with water and chemicals. Then the valuable mineral is skimmed off. The remaining wastes, called tailings, are poured into a large artificial pond. Tailings are often toxic and must not be allowed to escape into the surrounding soil and water systems.

Design brief

- Design and build a model of a tailings pond that will safely contain all the tailings from a mine until they can be treated and removed.

Design criteria

- The model tailings pond must be able to contain both toxic solids and liquids.
- Plans for testing surrounding land and water for contamination must be included.
- The model must demonstrate how the contents of the pond can be removed without affecting the environment.
- The model must include a plan for restoring the land used for the pond to its original state.

3 An Erosion-Proof Field

Problem situation

The world's human population of approximately 6 billion relies on farmers to grow food. Poor farming techniques can result in precious topsoil being washed away by rain or blown away in windstorms. Chemicals used by farmers, such as pesticides, herbicides, and fertilizers, can pollute nearby streams and rivers.

Design brief

- Design and build a model of a farmer's field in which the soil resists erosion and water runoff.

Design criteria

- The model field should have a slope of 15° with a stream at its lowest point.
- The model must show two sections: one at the preplanting stage (no plants yet) and one that is already planted.
- When the model field is sprinkled with water from a watering can, no soil should reach the stream at the bottom. You must create a test to show that soil does not enter the stream after the sprinkling.

Assessment

Your model will be assessed according to how well you:

Process

- understand the problem
- develop a safe plan
- choose and safely use appropriate materials, tools, and equipment
- test and record results
- evaluate your model, including suggestions for improvement

Communication

- prepare a presentation
- use correct terms
- write clear descriptions of the steps you took in building and testing your model
- explain clearly how your model solves the problem
- make an accurate technical drawing for your model

Product

- meet the design criteria with your model
- use your chosen materials effectively
- construct your model
- solve the identified problem

When preparing to build or test a design, have your plan approved by your teacher before you begin.

Figure 2

Tailings ponds are temporary dumping sites for waste from mining.

Unit 4 Summary

In this unit you have learned that the Earth's crust—the rocks and soil that sustain us—is constantly changing as many forces act on it, including those set in motion by human beings.

Reflecting

- Reflect on the ideas and questions presented in the Unit Overview and in the Getting Started. How can you connect what you have done and learned in this unit with those ideas and questions? (To review, check the sections indicated in this Summary.)
- Revise your answers to the Reflecting questions in ❶,❷,❸ and the questions you created in the Getting Started. How has your thinking changed?
- What new questions do you have? How will you answer them?

Understanding Concepts

- describe the Earth and its crust 4.1, 4.15
- distinguish between rocks and minerals 4.2
- classify rocks and minerals by their characteristics and by how they were formed 4.2, 4.13, 4.21
- describe how soil is formed 4.6, 4.7
- describe the origin and history of natural features of the local landscape 4.6, 4.11, 4.13, 4.20
- observe and analyze evidence of geological change 4.12, 4.14, 4.15
- identify the processes involved in rock and mineral formation 4.13, 4.21
- explain the rock cycle 4.13, 4.21

- describe mountain formation and the folding and faulting of the Earth's surface 4.15, 4.16, 4.20
- explain the causes and effects of volcanoes and earthquakes 4.15, 4.16, 4.20, 4.22

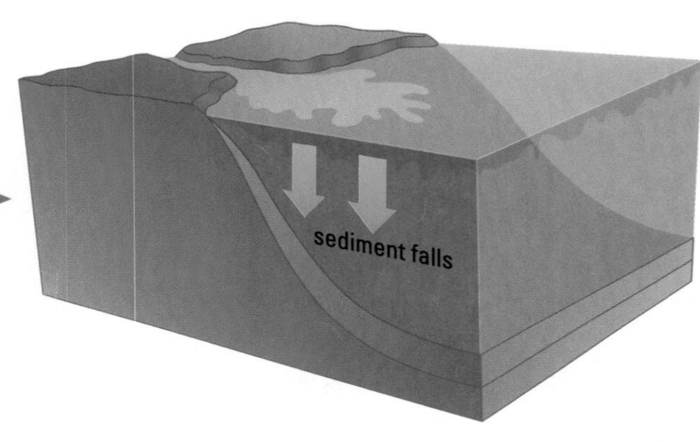

Applying Skills

- investigate the effect of weathering on rocks and minerals 4.6, 4.11, 4.12, 4.13
- classify minerals, using observations, according to their characteristics 4.2
- describe the process of mineral extraction from rock 4.3, 4.4
- observe what makes topsoils different from one another 4.8
- understand and use the following terms:

clay
cleavage
colour
continental drift
core (inner and outer)
crust
deposit
drift
drumlin
erosion
fault
flood plain
hardness
humus
igneous rock (intrusive and extrusive)
lava
litter
lustre
magma
mantle
metamorphic rock
minerals
mining (strip and underground)
mountains (block, dome, and fold)
moraine
ore
overburden
plates
plate tectonics
ridge
sand
sediment
sedimentary rock
shield volcanoes
silt
soil horizons
stratovolcanoes
subduction
subsoil
tailings
till
topsoil
weathering
zero tillage

- design and build a mountain that withstands the forces of erosion 4.12
- plot historical data of earthquake and volcanic activity in order to determine patterns and predict future events 4.17
- design, plan, and carry out the construction of an earthquake-proof building 4.19

Making Connections

- investigate ways in which humans have altered the landscape to meet their needs 4.3
- identify factors that must be considered when making informed decisions about land use 4.4, 4.5, 4.10
- investigate soil to determine its suitability for specific uses, including conservation 4.7, 4.8, 4.9, 4.10

- identify a career that uses modern technology to contribute to the study of natural geological events 4.18, 4.19

Unit 4 Review

Understanding Concepts

1. (a) Describe the structure of the Earth.
   (b) Even though the inner layers of the Earth are extremely hot, the inner core is solid. What is the reason?
2. What is the difference between a rock and a mineral?
3. Which of the following metals are not minerals: copper, bronze, gold, tin, steel, silver? Give a reason for your answer.
4. (a) What property of minerals is assessed using a scratch test?
   (b) Describe how you could use a penny in a scratch test of three minerals.
5. Why do all minerals cleave along flat surfaces when they are broken up?
6. If two samples of the same mineral have crystals of different sizes, what does this tell you about the samples?
7. (a) Explain how lichen erodes rock.
   (b) What other types of biological weathering can erode rock?
8. Ice causes erosion in two ways. What are they?
9. Is each of the following an example of mechanical or chemical weathering or both? Explain your answer.
   (a) cracks in the sidewalk
   (b) discoloured metal jewellery found in a sunken ship in the ocean
   (c) an underground cave
10. Which area would be more likely to lose its topsoil: a gently sloping area or a steep hill? Explain.
11. List the following soil particles from largest to smallest: sand, clay, silt, pebbles.
12. Why do gardeners mix sand and peat into soils that are mostly clay?
13. Surtsey, an island near Iceland, was formed recently from lava flowing out of the ridge in the middle of the Atlantic Ocean. Explain, using diagrams, how deep soil might eventually form on this island.
14. Explain how you can classify soils using your senses of touch and sight.
15. Look at **Figure 1**.
    (a) Which river is younger, a or b?
    (b) Which river is most likely to carry large stones?
    (c) Which river is most likely to be surrounded by a flood plain?

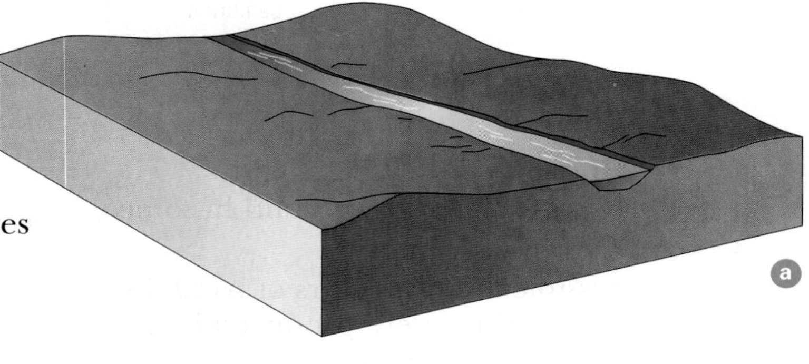

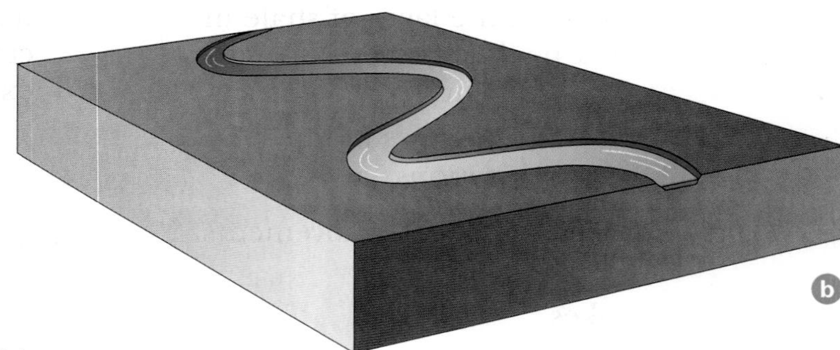

Figure 1

16. A small lake near a river has a "C" shape and a sandy bottom.
    (a) Could this lake have once been part of the river?
    (b) What other clues would you look for to support your answer?
17. In what type of rock are fossils normally found? Why?

surface
sandstone
limestone
sandstone
shale
basalt
limestone

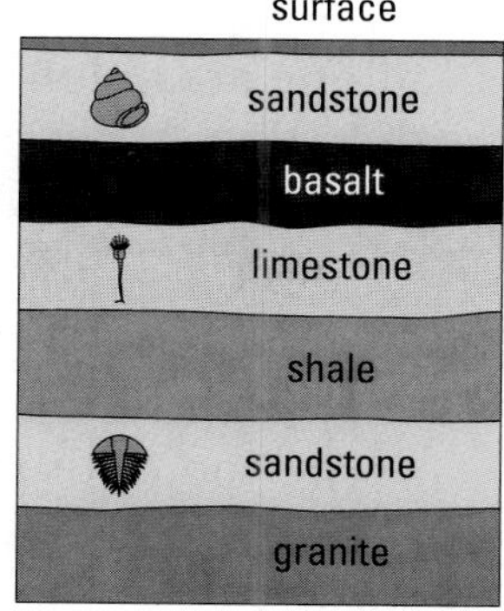

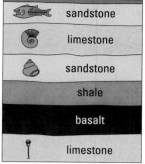

	Fossil	Epoch
	bony fish	Cenozoic
	ammonite	Jurassic
	snail	Triassic
	crinoid	Permian
	trilobite	Cambrian

Figure 2

18. **Figure 2** shows layers of rock in two locations. Fossils have been found in some of the layers.

(a) Is it possible that the layers of basalt in the two locations were produced by the same volcano? Explain.

(b) Which is older, the layer of shale in Location 1 or the layer of shale in Location 2? Explain your deduction.

(c) Explain the differences in the rocks from the two locations.

19. Explain how tectonic plate movements cause:

(a) earthquakes.

(b) volcanoes.

20. The Laurentian Mountains in Quebec are low and rounded. They were not always this shape.

(a) Describe how this mountain range may have appeared 200 million years ago. What has happened to them since then?

(b) Based on your understanding of mountains, speculate on how this mountain range formed.

21. What is the difference between intrusive and extrusive igneous rock?

22. Lava flows down the side of a shield volcano and enters ocean water.

(a) What kind of rock will be formed from the lava?

(b) Would you expect the mineral crystals in the rock to be large or small?

23. India and the island of Sri Lanka are on the Indo-Australian Plate, which, in the north, is being subducted under the much larger Eurasian Plate.

(a) Would you expect the collision of these two plates to cause earthquakes in Sri Lanka? Explain.

(b) Draw a diagram showing what is happening where the two plates meet.

(c) On the Indo-Australian plate there are areas where layers of sandstone lie on top of granite. Explain what will happen to this rock as it is subducted.

24. Imagine that you could mark a tiny crystal of mineral in a large rock sitting on the surface in central Ontario. Imagine also that you could go away for a billion years, come back, and find that crystal. List as many places as you can think of where that crystal might end up. For each place, explain how the crystal could get there.

Applying Skills

25. Match the following terms with the correct descriptions:

Description	Term
A place where two plates slide past each other	1 mantle
B molten rock on the Earth's surface	2 moraine
C partly molten layer below the Earth's crust	3 fault
D molten rock below the Earth's surface	4 lava
E deposit of gravel and loose rock left by glaciers	5 sediment
F rock particles deposited by moving water	6 magma

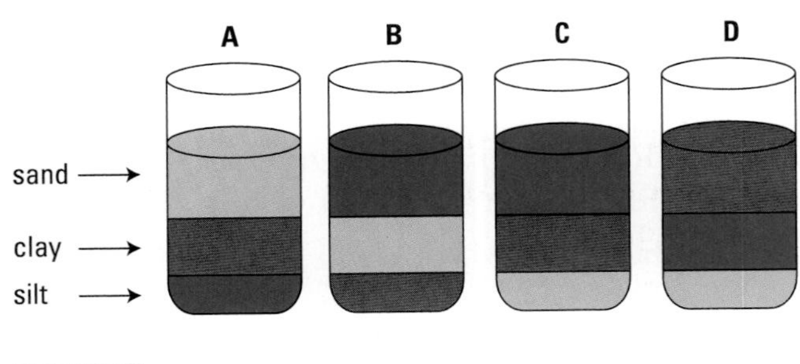

Figure 3

26. The layers produced by four soil samples are shown in **Figure 3**.
- (a) Which illustration shows an accurate representation of the layering you would expect?
- (b) Which soil sample would you recommend for planting vegetables? Explain.

27. You want to start a garden in an area where there has never been one before.
- (a) Only a few weeds seem to be growing in the soil. What does this indicate?
- (b) You notice that puddles form on the surface of the soil. What does this indicate?
- (c) What could you do to improve the soil?

28. **Figure 4** shows rocks from three different areas. In each case, identify whether the rocks are igneous, metamorphic, or sedimentary, and explain your reasoning.

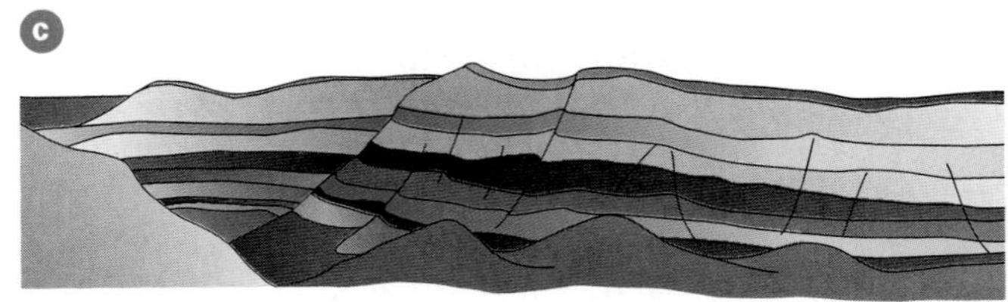

Figure 4

29. A geologist notices that small, narrow hills in one area seem to point in the same direction. When she takes samples from them, she finds that there is gravel near the surface of each one.
- (a) What type of erosion occurred here?
- (b) Did the erosion occur once over a long period of time, or at several different times? Explain.

30. "Fossils give an incomplete history of life on Earth." Is this statement true or false? Explain.

31. Why do earthquakes often occur in the same geographical regions as volcanoes?

32. A travel agent finds customers are fascinated by volcanoes. He wants to arrange a trip that will visit an active volcano. He has read predictions that volcanoes may erupt soon in Mexico, Alaska, and Iceland.
- (a) Which volcano would you advise him is safest to visit? Why?
- (b) The travel agent thinks the volcano in Alaska is safe because volcanoes in that state have caused little loss of life in the past. Is the agent's reasoning correct? Why or why not?

33. A farmer is spending a lot of money on herbicides and insecticides and is wondering what she can do to spend less. Suggest some ways she could reduce her costs. Illustrate and explain your suggestions.

34. A small earthquake occurs in southern Ontario and people are worried that it's a sign of a much bigger one to come. Is it reasonable to worry? Explain.

Making Connections

35. What factors help determine the value of a mineral?

36. If a huge diamond mine were discovered, so diamonds become common rather than rare, how might the use of diamonds change?

37. A person from Norway visits Newfoundland and notices the local hills look just like those at home. Explain the resemblance.

38. Imagine that you are planning to build a home on a steep hillside where several lots are available.

(a) What should you be concerned about when choosing a lot?

(b) What steps should you take to prevent erosion if you decide to build on a sloped lot?

(c) How might landscaping with plants help prevent erosion?

39. The land on a flood plain makes particularly good farmland.

(a) Why do you think this is the case?

(b) Is a flood plain a safe place for people to live? Explain.

40. You decide to go into the mineral mining business. After much study, you discover local deposits of five minerals. You have enough resources to mine only one. In **Table 1** these five minerals are ranked for abundance (the higher the number, the larger the deposit); ease of mining (the higher the number, the easier it will be to mine); and the value of the mineral (the higher the number, the more valuable the mineral). Which mineral would you mine? Why?

41. A woman is planning to buy a farm. When she goes to look at farms that are for sale she brings a hand lens and a shovel with her. How would she use these tools to help her decide which farm to buy?

42. Look at **Figure 5**.

(a) Using plate tectonics, explain the feature shown.

(b) East of this area there is a continent. What features would you expect to find near the coast?

(c) Many people are moving into cities along the coast. What advice would you give them? Why?

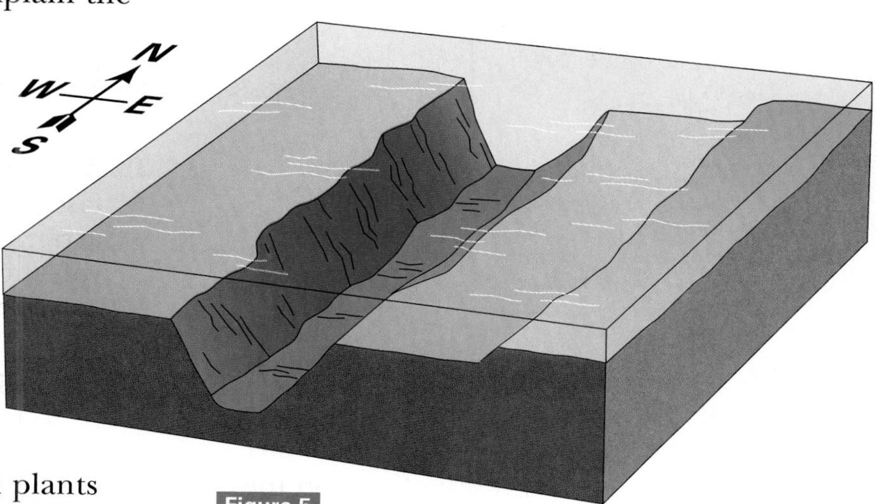

Figure 5

43. An ancient statue from a small village in Egypt, almost perfectly preserved, was moved to a large city in the United States, where it quickly eroded. What different conditions in the city might have caused this to occur? How would you reduce the erosion?

44. Using terms you've learned in this unit, design a concept map that illustrates the processes that change the Earth's crust. There is a list of terms in the Unit Summary.

Table 1

Mineral	Abundance	Ease of mining	Value
Bauxite	5	4	3
Hematite	4	5	1
Halite	3	3	2
Quartz	2	1	4
Gold	1	2	5

Unit 5

Interactions Within Ecosystems

Unit 5 Overview

No organism lives alone, closed in its own little world. On Earth, every living thing interacts with other living things. Every living thing must deal with changes in its environment, such as the amount of sunlight, the temperature, or the quality of the soil. Living things must adapt to their environment, and the environment may change because living things are there. Humans' actions have an impact on other living things. How does your presence change the world? What factors in the environment can change the way you and other living things behave? How do other living things affect you? In this unit you will explore some of these questions.

Living Things and Ecosystems

Living and non-living things interact to form ecosystems.

You will be able to:

- Identify living (biotic) and non-living (abiotic) components of an ecosystem.
- Explain the roles of producers, consumers, and decomposers within an ecosystem.
- Describe how food and energy move through food chains and food webs.
- Describe how chemicals, such as water and carbon, cycle through an ecosystem.
- Explain how communities change within ecosystems and describe how those changes can affect plant and animal populations.
- Evaluate the long-term effect of habitat loss on species extinction.
- Evaluate the economic and social benefits of environmental responsibility.

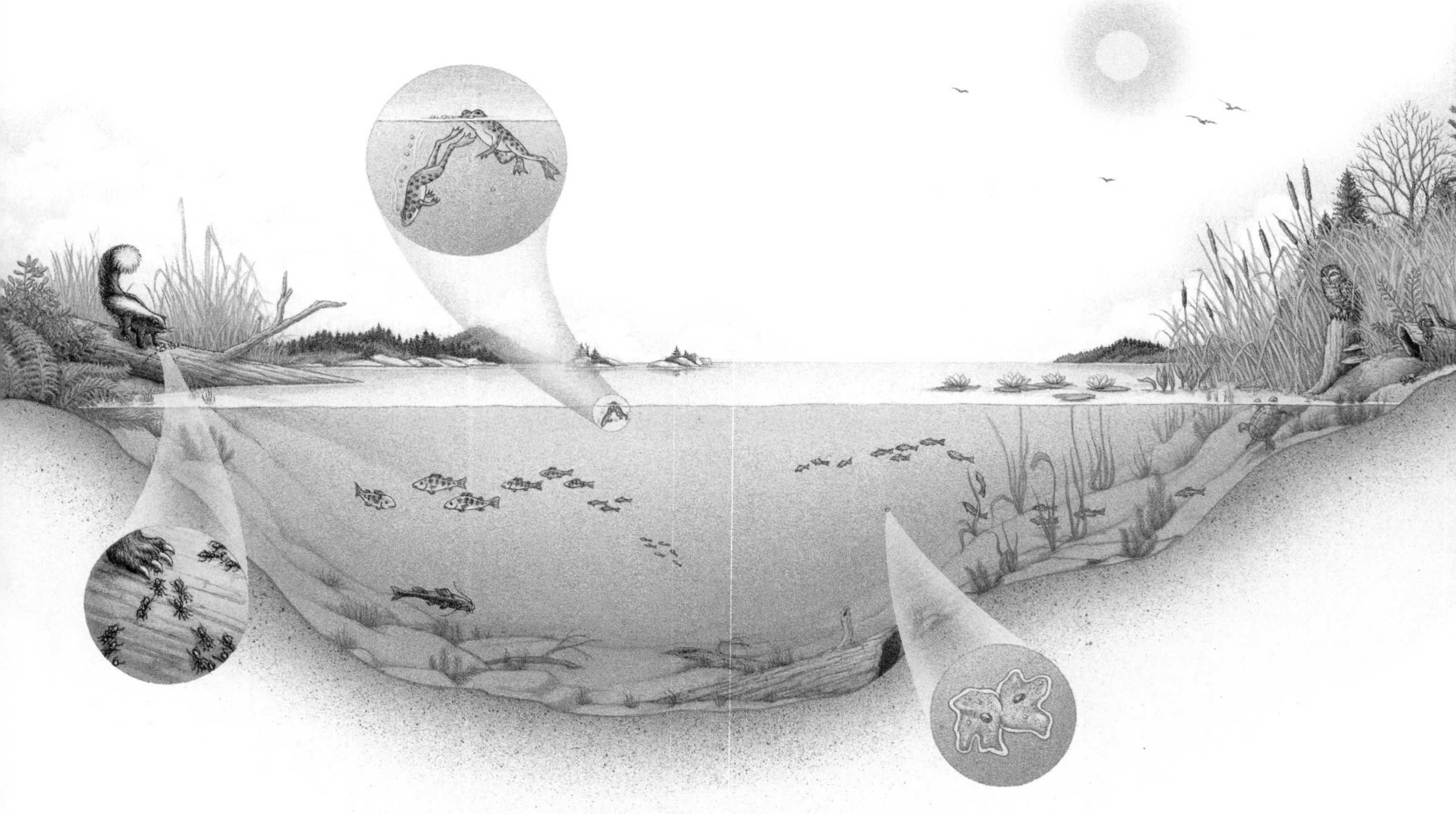

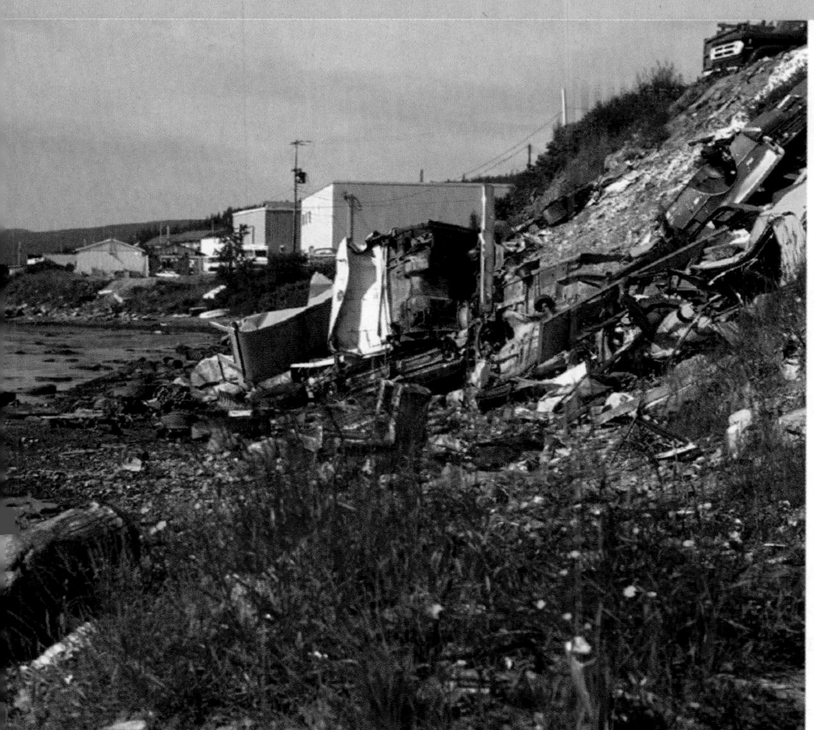

Humans, Technology, and Ecosystems

Humans and our technology have an impact on ecosystems.

You will be able to:

- Identify the benefits and risks that come with technologies and assess how they might affect various ecosystems.
- Plan experiments to investigate how ecosystems are affected by technological innovations.
- Evaluate the costs and benefits of recycling and controlling waste disposal.
- Identify economic, social, political, and environmental factors involved in sustaining ecosystems.

Design Challenge

You will be able to ...

demonstrate your learning by completing a Design Challenge.

A Solution to the Landfill Problem

Each year we generate millions of tonnes of waste. Some of that waste is recycled, but much of it goes to landfill sites. Can we reduce the amount of waste that we truck to landfill sites? And is there a way to reduce the burden that landfill sites place on the environment?

In this unit you will be able to design and build:

1 A Device or Strategy to Reduce Garbage:

Create a device or make up a strategy that will help reduce the amount of garbage being produced by your family.

2 A Biodegradable Container or Packaging Material:

Invent a container or packaging material that can be broken down quickly in a landfill site.

3 A Model Landfill Site:

Design and build a model landfill site capable of storing household garbage.

To start the Design Challenge, see page 302.

Record your thoughts and design ideas for the Challenge when you see

Design Challenge

Getting Started

Environmental Issues

1. In the middle of the 20th century, humans first saw Earth from space. Satellite images not only tell us how our planet is changing, they also give us a new way of looking at our problems. How is our planet changing? What might satellite images look like 100 years from now if we continue to treat our planet as we do?

2. Earth is often compared with a spaceship. It has been launched, and nothing more can be added to it. Because a spaceship is closed, air and water must be recycled or the astronauts will die. The same is true on Earth. Life depends on recycling. How is this recycling done? How do we depend on the recycling of matter? What is the role of living things in the recycling of matter?

Reflecting

Think about the questions in 1, 2, 3. What other questions do you have about ecosystems? As you progress through this unit, reflect on your answers and revise them based on what you have learned.

3 Humans cannot continue using resources faster than they are replaced. Can we change the way we live? What can we do to reduce the stress we put on the systems of living things on our planet? What do we do that threatens those systems?

Try This A Field Study 

There are systems of living things to explore as close as your schoolyard.

- Choose an area of the yard where there are both shady and open areas.
- Using string and popsicle sticks, mark off the area you will study.
- Measure and draw a map of your study area.
- 6D Make a table to record observations of any animals you find, including where you found them and what they were doing.
- Carefully investigate your chosen area. 6A
- Record on your map where each plant is and how tall it is. (It is easier to use symbols rather than drawing each plant.) If the area is mostly grass, record only the plants that aren't lawn grass.
- Record the locations of other living things, such as mushrooms, on your map.
- Using a garden trowel, take soil samples from three different locations within your study area. Record your observations of the temperature, water content, and content of the soil.
- Try to leave your study area exactly as it was before you began.

1. Are the shady parts of your study area different from the open areas? Use your observations to support your opinion.
2. Speculate on what each of the animals you observed eats. What evidence that you collected supports your opinion?
3. Make a list of the effects humans have on the living things you observed.

Bear Necessities

Humans are widespread on our planet. There are many of us, and we can survive in environments as widely different as hot deserts, open plains, tropical jungles, and the cold of Canada's Arctic. In all of those environments, the presence of humans has an effect on other living things and the way they interact with each other and the environment. The study of relationships between living things and between living things and their environment is called **ecology**. A Canadian example of the effects of humans can be found in the lives of the polar bears that live on and around Hudson Bay.

The Bears of the Bay

Since the glaciers of the last ice age retreated thousands of years ago, the polar bears of Hudson Bay have lived much the same way. In the winter they live on the ice of the bay. In the summer they live in more southern forests. Bears and humans have always had trouble getting along. We tend to live in the same places and eat similar things. Our niches overlap. An **ecological niche** is the way of life or role of an organism. However, until relatively recently, the only humans the polar bears would encounter were the Inuit and other Native peoples of the north who did not create landfill sites. The town of Churchill, Manitoba, has a landfill site. The town is also directly on the migration route of the polar bear, as you can see in **Figure 1**.

Figure 1
Polar bears and the residents of Churchill meet every fall.

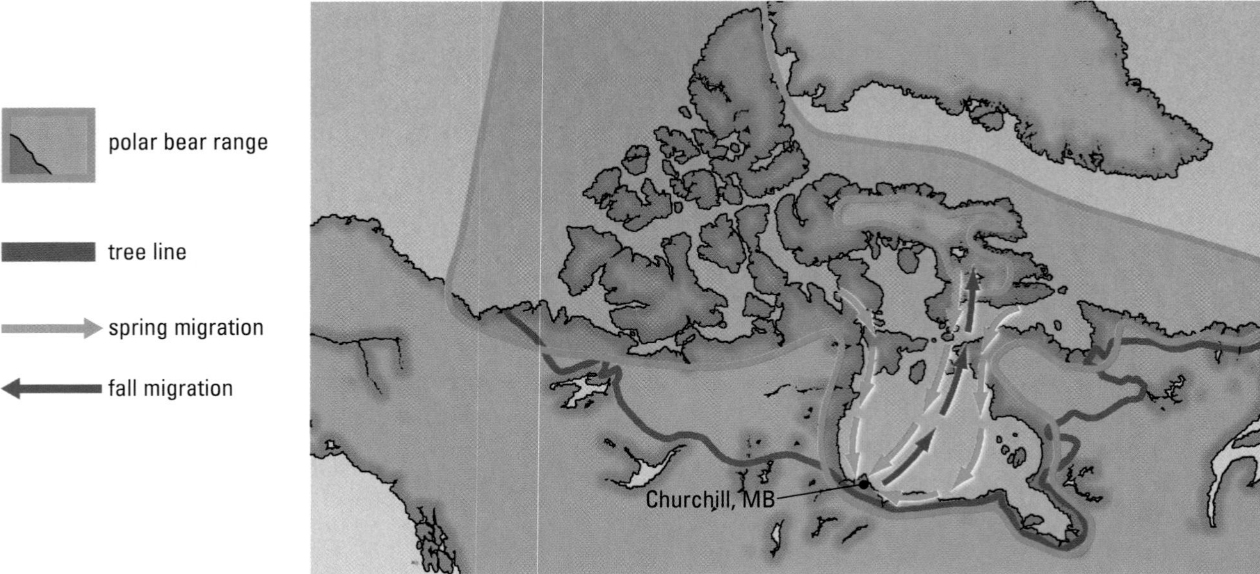

Figure 2
Polar bears look for breathing holes made by seals and wait patiently for their prey.

Polar Bears in Winter

The polar bear is not like other bears. In the winter, while other bears are sleeping, the polar bear is most active. Early in October, polar bears begin migrating north onto the ice floes forming on Hudson Bay. From freeze-up to breakup, polar bears feed mostly on ringed seals and bearded seals (**Figure 2**). The bear uses the high-energy seal meat to build a layer of fat.

Polar Bears in Summer

As the ice begins to melt in the spring, the polar bears move to the land and south to their summer retreat. During the summer, polar bears live in the forest. They spend most of the summer sleeping and lazing around, living off stored fat. By the time temperatures begin to drop in the fall, the bears have used up the energy they stored as fat the previous winter. The hungry bears begin moving north—and come to the landfill site in Churchill, the fast-food restaurant on the bear migration highway. Unfortunately, a trip to the garbage dump brings the bear into contact with humans. Hungry bears and angry humans are a bad mix—one or the other may get hurt.

Understanding Concepts

1. Ecologists insist that no organism lives alone. How do polar bears interact with other living things? How are bears affected by humans?
2. Why is the polar bear considered to be a marine mammal?
3. The polar bear lives in two different environments at different times of the year. Compare the two environments in a chart. Include factors such as temperature, wind, and amount of sunlight.

Making Connections

4. Only about 30% of a black bear's diet is made up of animals (insects, eggs, fish, and small mammals). The other 70% is vegetation. Like humans, bears are classified as omnivores. Explain how the diet of black bears could bring them into conflict with humans.

5.2

The Organization of Life

As you have seen, polar bears can tolerate a wide range of environmental conditions. They survive the bitter cold and fierce winds of an Arctic winter, and the heat of the summer. They survive on land, on ice, in fresh water, and in the cold salt water of Hudson Bay. Bears see well enough to hunt in the dark of northern winter, and the almost perpetual day of northern summer. Few animals are adapted to so many different conditions or factors.

The changes in temperature, the changes in the amount of sunlight, the strength and variation of the wind, the amount of rain or snowfall, and the presence of salt or fresh water are all abiotic factors of the polar bear's environment. **Abiotic** factors are the non-living, physical factors of an environment.

There are other factors that affect the polar bear. If seals move to a new area, the bears must also move. If there are fewer fish in the bay, there will be fewer seals, and so the bears will go hungry. Effects such as these, caused by other living things, are the **biotic** factors of the environment.

Figure 1
The organization of life

a Organism
An organism is a single living thing. Ecologists may study feeding, daily movements, or reproduction of the polar bear to help them understand the ecological niche of the organism in its ecosystem.

Organizing Relationships

No organism lives alone, not even the solitary polar bear. All organisms have relationships with other living things, as polar bears do with seals, fish, and people. They must also deal with the abiotic factors in their environment. Ecologists organize all of these relationships among organisms and their environment to help study the interactions. They do this by using terms to describe systems of living things, starting with the individual living thing (an organism) and progressing to the largest system, which includes every living thing on Earth (the biosphere), as shown in **Figure 1**.

Ecologists use the term "ecosystem" to describe a wide range of systems. Some are large and some are very small. For example, the ice-floe ecosystem of Hudson Bay is very large. The ecosystem is made up of a community that includes populations of large organisms such as polar bears and seals, and also many populations of small organisms such as algae and bacteria. However, we can also speak of a temporary spring pond as an ecosystem, with a community made up of populations of tiny organisms (see **Table 1**).

Table 1: Three Ecosystems

Ecosystem	Some populations in the community
ice-floe system of Hudson Bay	polar bears, bearded seals, ringed seals, herring, krill, algae
small pond	raccoons, wood frogs, mosquitoes, dragonflies, fairy shrimp, algae
abandoned city lot	cats, mice, ants, chickadees, crab grass, dandelions

Small ecosystems can also exist within larger ecosystems. For example, the ecosystem inside a rotting log is part of the larger ecosystem of the forest.

Biomes are usually large and contain many ecosystems. The boreal forest biome stretches from the Atlantic coast through central Canada and north of the prairies to the western mountains. This biome includes many coniferous forests, and also the ecosystems in their clearings, lakes, streams, and rivers.

Understanding Concepts

1. Explain the following terms in your own words: population, community, ecosystem, biome, and biosphere.
2. **Table 1** shows some of the populations in the community that makes up a pond ecosystem. Create a list of abiotic factors that would affect the organisms in that ecosystem.
3. In **Table 1,** the community of organisms that might be present in the ecosystem of an abandoned city lot is not complete.

(a) What other organisms might be present in the lot, either permanently or temporarily?

(b) List the biotic and abiotic factors that might affect the organisms in the abandoned lot ecosystem.

b Population
A population is the number of organisms of the same species living in an ecosystem. Ecologists might study the effects of an increasing population of polar bears on the ice-floe ecosystem.

c Community
A community is all of the populations of organisms within an ecosystem. Ecologists might study the effects on the community when one of the species becomes extinct.

d Ecosystem
An ecosystem is a system of living things that interact with each other and with the physical world. An ecologist might study how changes in snowfall affect the community that lives in the ice-floe ecosystem.

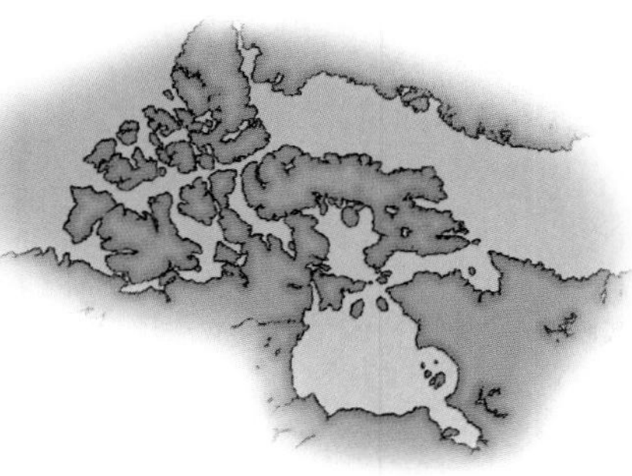

e Biome
A biome is a collection of related ecosystems. An ecologist might study how climate change affects the ecosystems of the Arctic biome.

f Biosphere
The biosphere is all of the biomes, all of the ecosystems on Earth, from the poles to the equator, from the atmosphere to kilometres into the rock of the Earth's crust. Wherever living things are found, that is the biosphere. An ecologist might study how the amount of light coming from the Sun affects the biosphere.

Design Challenge

How could you design your landfill site to discourage bears from visiting?

Adaptations for Survival

Every ecosystem has factors that make it different from other ecosystems. The ice-floe ecosystem is cold, and the water is salty; a wetlands ecosystem near a southern lake is warmer, and the water is fresh. To succeed in an ecosystem, plants and animals have special structures and behaviours, called **adaptations**. The fat that polar bears put on in winter is an adaptation. The fat helps protect the bears from the cold. In this case study, you will examine photographs of organisms and speculate on how their special adaptations help them to survive.

Changing Colour

The chameleon (**Figure 1**) is a reptile that lives in trees and feeds on insects. It is not large, so it also has to worry about being eaten by larger animals. The chameleon has an interesting adaptation that helps it survive. It can change its skin colour so it blends with its background. Animals that use colour to hide are using camouflage. The chameleon has another adaptation — a long tongue with a sticky lump at the end that it launches to catch insects.

(a) How does camouflage help the chameleon catch insects?

(b) How does camouflage help protect the chameleon from predators?

(c) What other animals can you think of that use camouflage for protection or to hide from prey?

Figure 1
The chameleon can change its skin colour to match the background.

Figure 2
The bright patterns on the wings of the monarch butterfly warn birds not to eat it.

Using Bright Colour

The monarch butterfly (**Figure 2**), which lives in southern Canada in the summer, has two related adaptations. The butterfly produces a chemical that gives its body a very bitter taste, which birds hate. Its wings also carry a bright pattern that is easy to see. After trying to eat a monarch, a bird will remember the bitter taste and the bright pattern on its wings and avoid monarchs in the future.

(d) How does the monarch butterfly benefit from its adaptations?

(e) Does this combination of adaptations make every monarch butterfly safe from birds? Explain.

(f) The combination of a poison or unpleasant chemical and bright colouring to warn possible predators is not unusual. What other animal can you think of that has similar adaptations?

SKILLS HANDBOOK: 4A Research Skills

Flying on the Wings of the Monarch

Not all animals that carry bright, distinctive colours are poisonous or taste unpleasant. The viceroy butterfly (**Figure 3**), which lives in the same areas as the monarch, looks very much like a monarch butterfly, but doesn't taste bitter. Birds who have tasted a monarch butterfly avoid the viceroy because they think it is a monarch.

(g) Compare the monarch and the viceroy butterflies. What differences do you see?

(h) Is the viceroy's adaptation as effective as the monarch's? Explain.

(i) How might the viceroy's colours affect monarch butterflies?

Other Disguises

Like the viceroy butterfly, some animals and plants fool predators or prey by pretending to be something else. Some moths scare away predatory birds by wearing spots that look like eyes (**Figure 4**).

Figure 4
The hawk moth uses its wing pattern to scare away birds that might eat it.

Many plants use strong, sweet scents or bright flowers to attract insects, but the Stapelia plant of the tropical jungle (**Figure 5**) has a special adaptation. It looks and smells just like rotting meat.

(g) Why would birds avoid animals that have large eyes in the front of their head?

(h) Why would plants attempt to attract insects?

Figure 5
A blowfly has just laid her eggs in what she believes is rotting meat. It's actually the flower of a *Stapelia* plant.

Figure 3
The pattern on the wings of the viceroy makes it look very much like a monarch.

Understanding Concepts

1. What advantages can an organism gain by:

(a) looking like another kind of organism?

(b) using camouflage?

2. The honey bee (**Figure 6**) can give a painful sting to an attacker, but the bee dies after it uses its sting. Explain how the bee's coloration is an important adaptation.

Figure 6

Making Connections

3. (4A) Every animal and plant has adaptations that help it survive in its ecosystem. Some, like most of those studied in this section, involve colour. Other adaptations may involve body shapes, or special organs, or behaviours. Choose a plant or animal to study. List its adaptations and explain how each adaptation helps the plant or animal in its ecosystem.

5.4

A Landfill Ecosystem

A casual look at a pile of garbage in a landfill might lead you to believe there is no life there. Nothing could be further from the truth. Populations of bacteria, fungi, worms, and millipedes make up a community that is working hard to **decompose** (break down) matter in the landfill, as shown in **Figure 1**.

All ecosystems contain **decomposers** to recycle matter. During decomposition large, complex chemicals are broken down into less complex chemicals. Eventually, the simpler chemicals are used by other organisms as nutrients (food). Earth has a limited amount of matter, so all life depends upon this recycling.

To understand any ecosystem, including the landfill ecosystem, you must understand the abiotic components of the ecosystem. Moisture, temperature, and oxygen levels are the important abiotic components of a landfill site. Landfills need enough oxygen and moisture to support a large number of decomposers. Without the decomposers, the garbage would stay as it was when it was thrown away, instead of being recycled. (**Figure 2**).

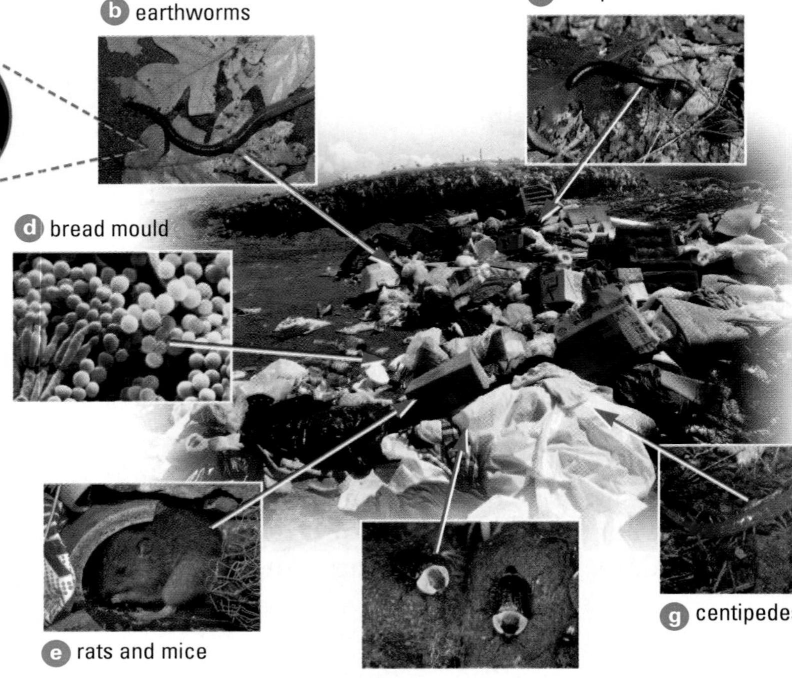

Figure 1
Biotic components of the landfill ecosystem. Bread mould, bacteria, earthworms, and millipedes are classified as decomposers. The centipede, beetle, and rat live on partially decomposed foods, but can also act as predators.

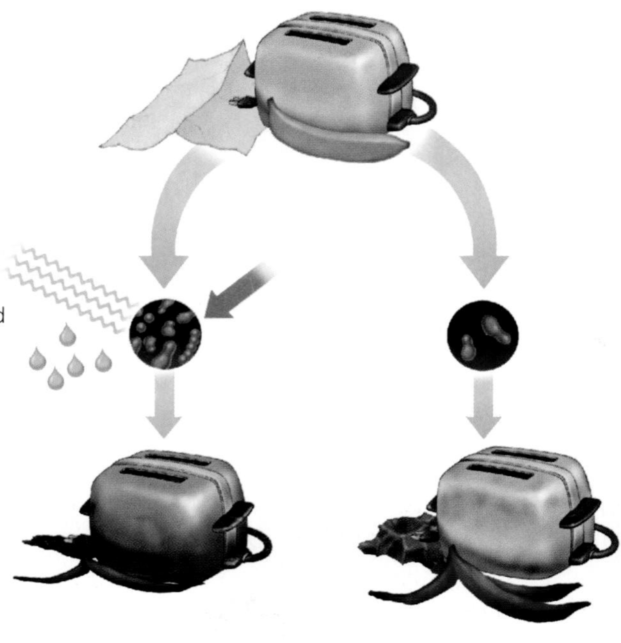

Figure 2
Abiotic components of the landfill ecosystem. Water, heat, and oxygen levels are important factors, especially for the growth of bacteria. If the landfill were sealed to prevent water and oxygen from entering, garbage would never decompose.

What Goes into a Landfill?

Our throwaway culture is leaving a legacy of garbage. Each hour North Americans throw away 2.5 million non-returnable, non-recyclable plastic bottles. Each year about 2 billion disposable pens and razors and 20 to 30 billion disposable diapers end up in a landfill site. Paper accounts for about 29% of the solid waste going to landfill sites. A typical Canadian discards 7 kg of junk mail and 55 kg of newsprint each year, as shown in **Figure 3**.

All of the garbage we produce ends up at the nearest landfill site, burying the ecosystem that used to thrive in that place. The garbage replaces the ecosystem of the field or forest with the ecosystem of the dump.

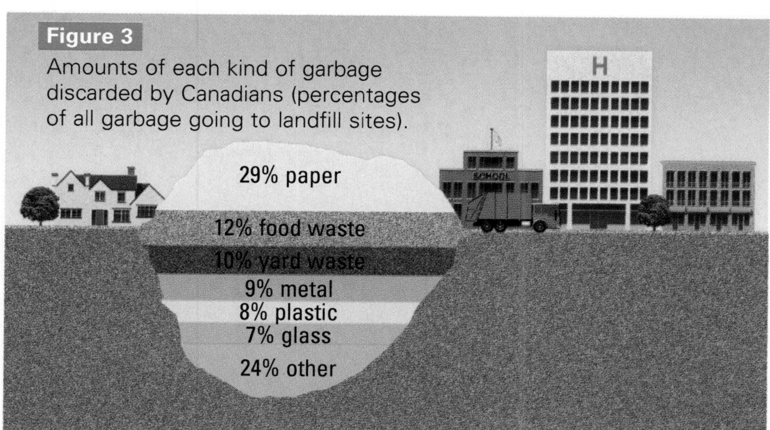

Figure 3
Amounts of each kind of garbage discarded by Canadians (percentages of all garbage going to landfill sites).

Understanding Concepts

1. Explain in your own words why decomposers are important in an ecosystem.
2. Name three abiotic and three biotic factors in:
   (a) a landfill ecosystem.
   (b) a pond ecosystem.
   (c) a grassland ecosystem.
3. Give an example of how abiotic factors affect the organisms that live in a landfill ecosystem.

Making Connections

4. Compare the top of a fallen log and underneath the fallen log. Would you expect to find the same community in both places? Explain.
5. Why would dumping garbage in the ocean not be a good solution for overcrowded landfill sites?

Design Challenge

Create a list of suggestions that would help you to reduce the amount of garbage produced by your family in one week. Check your suggestions and add to them as you go through this unit.

Try This A Trash Audit (6B)

How much trash does your family produce? You can calculate how much by estimating the volume of a full plastic garbage bag.

- Wearing gloves, shake the garbage bag until it forms a cylinder.
- Measure the radius and the height of the cylinder. Use the equations in **Figure 4** to find the volume of the cylinder.
- Multiply this volume by the number of bags that your family throws away each week.

1. Calculate how much garbage your family produces in a year.

Figure 4

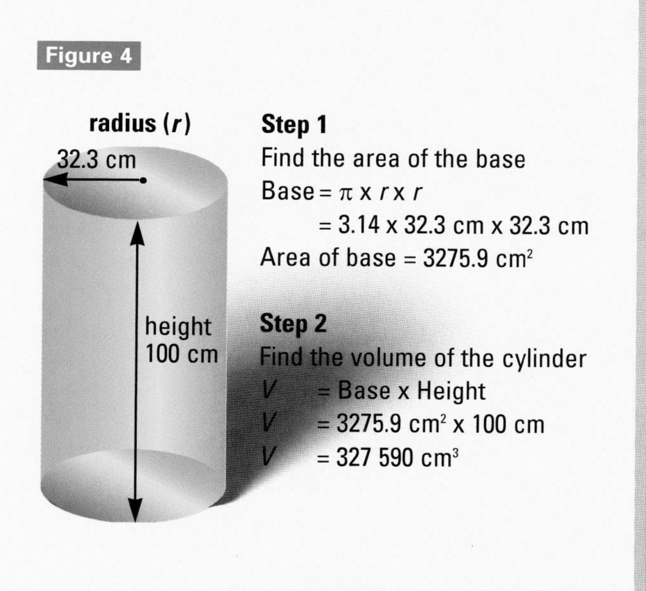

radius (r)
32.3 cm
height
100 cm
Step 1
Find the area of the base
Base = $\pi \times r \times r$
= 3.14 x 32.3 cm x 32.3 cm
Area of base = 3275.9 cm^2
Step 2
Find the volume of the cylinder
V = Base x Height
V = 3275.9 cm^2 x 100 cm
V = 327 590 cm^3

SKILLS MENU
○ Questioning ● Hypothesizing ○ Planning ● Conducting ● Recording ● Analyzing ● Communicating

What Belongs in a Landfill?

Many materials that make their way to landfill sites do not break down very readily. One of the major problems facing municipalities is finding new sites for wastes that cannot be recycled.

Question

Which solid substances are best suited for a landfill site?

Hypothesis

2C **1** Create a hypothesis for this investigation.

Experimental Design

In this investigation you will place a variety of materials in a shoe box filled with moist soil, to see which materials will break down.

Materials

- apron
- rubber gloves
- scissors
- shoebox
- masking tape
- plastic sandwich wrap
- soil
- jug of water
- spoon
- hand lens
- items for testing (newspaper, orange peel, aluminum foil, plastic bottle cap, coffee grounds, lettuce, metal tab from pop can)

Procedure

2 Line a shoebox with plastic sandwich wrap or a plastic garbage bag.

- Use masking tape to secure the plastic to the sides of the box.

3 Put about 8 cm of soil in the shoebox.

- Add enough water to make the soil moist (NOT wet).
- Arrange items for testing on the surface of the soil. (Each group will test different items.)
- Cover each item with a layer of moist soil.

(a) Why did you line the box with plastic?

4 Place the shoebox in a warm, sunny place for the next 25 days. Keep the soil moist by adding enough water daily.

(a) Make a table like **Table 1**.

Table 1: Observations

Day	Item	Observation
10	newspaper	?
10	foil	?

SKILLS HANDBOOK: 2C Predicting and Hypothesizing

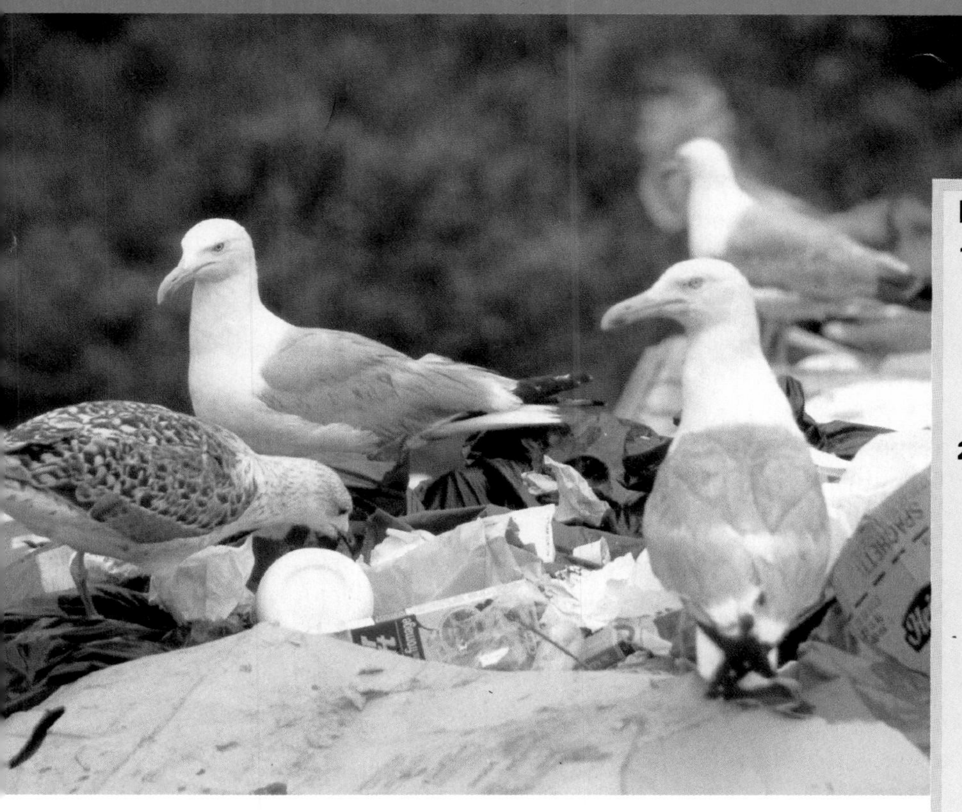

Making Connections

1. In this investigation you lined the shoebox with plastic wrap. Landfill sites don't use plastic, but they are lined with clay. Explain why landfill sites are lined with clay.
2. Disposable diapers create some problems in landfill sites. About 2 million diapers are used in Canada every day. For each of the following, comment on any environmental problem created and whether washable diapers would reduce the problem.
   (a) By mass, each diaper is 30% plastic.
   (b) Most of the rest of the disposable diaper is made of fibre from pulped wood.
   (c) Each infant produces nearly one tonne of diapers each year.
   (d) Soiled diapers (with solid wastes) are often disposed of without being cleaned.

5 On days 10, 15, 20, and 25 you should examine the covered items.
- Put on rubber gloves.
- Use a spoon to remove the top layer of soil.
- With a hand lens, examine each item.
- Make sure you cover the materials with soil after each examination.

(a) Record your observations.

(b) Why should you wear rubber gloves when examining the items?

Analysis

6 Analyze your observations by answering the following questions.

(a) Which substances decompose fastest?

(b) Do substances that decompose quickly have anything in common?

(c) Did any substances show no change?

(d) Do you think the unchanged substances would ever decompose? Explain.

Design Challenge

You have learned that some materials decompose easily and others don't. How can you use this information in your Challenge? Don't forget to examine the health, social, and economic implications in your design.

5.6

Cycling of Matter

You may not realize it, but you are made of recycled matter! Atoms of carbon, oxygen, hydrogen, and nitrogen that make up your living body may once have been in the body of a dinosaur or an ancient fern. More recently, they may have been in a fruit such as an apple or the leg of a cow. Only atoms that are here on Earth can be used to build the bodies of living organisms—no other source of matter is available. Matter must be recycled.

Through the process of decomposition, the complex matter that makes up living bodies is broken down into simple forms called **nutrients**. Living things use nutrients to build complex matter. This use and reuse of matter on Earth is called a **matter cycle**. By tracing the flow of matter through ecosystems, biologists learn how organisms depend on each other (**Figure 1**).

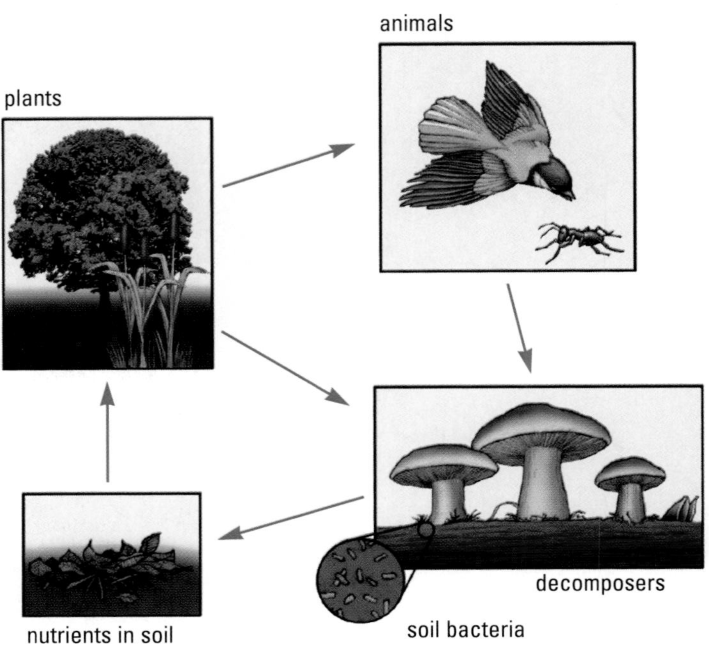

Figure 1
Decomposers break down the complex chemicals found in living things into a simpler form, which can be used again by plants. Plants assemble these simpler forms of matter to make food for themselves.

The Cycle of Matter and Energy

Most matter cycles begin with plants. Plants use energy from the sun to make a high-energy food called sugar. The process is called **photosynthesis** (*photo* means "light" and *synthesis* means "to make"). A green substance called **chlorophyll** allows plants to "capture" the energy from the sun.

Organisms that contain chlorophyll are able to make their own food and are referred to as **producers**.

Other organisms, such as animals, do not contain chlorophyll and are not able to make their own food. To get the "captured" energy, they must eat plants or other animals that eat plants. In either case, the sources of the food are plants. Organisms that rely on plants for food are called **consumers**.

Consumers that eat plants are referred to as **herbivores**, meaning "plant eaters." Consumers that eat other animals are referred to as **carnivores**, meaning "flesh eaters."

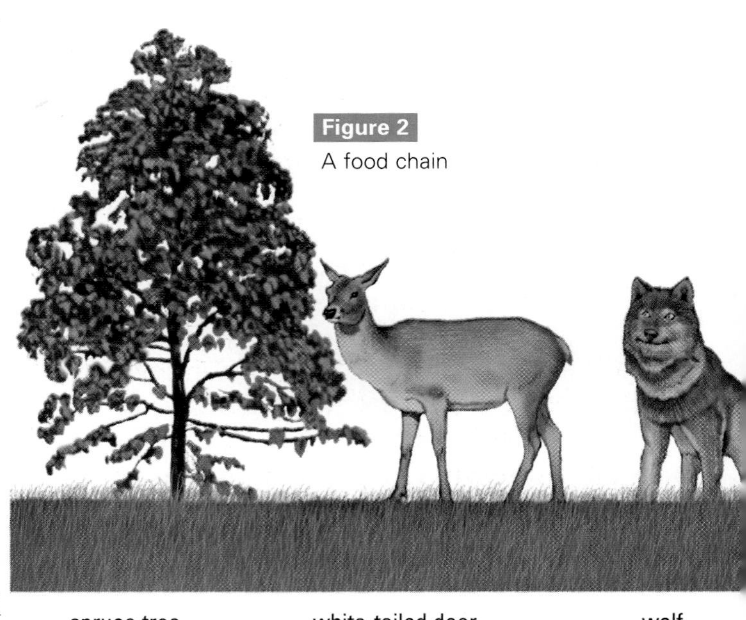

Figure 2
A food chain

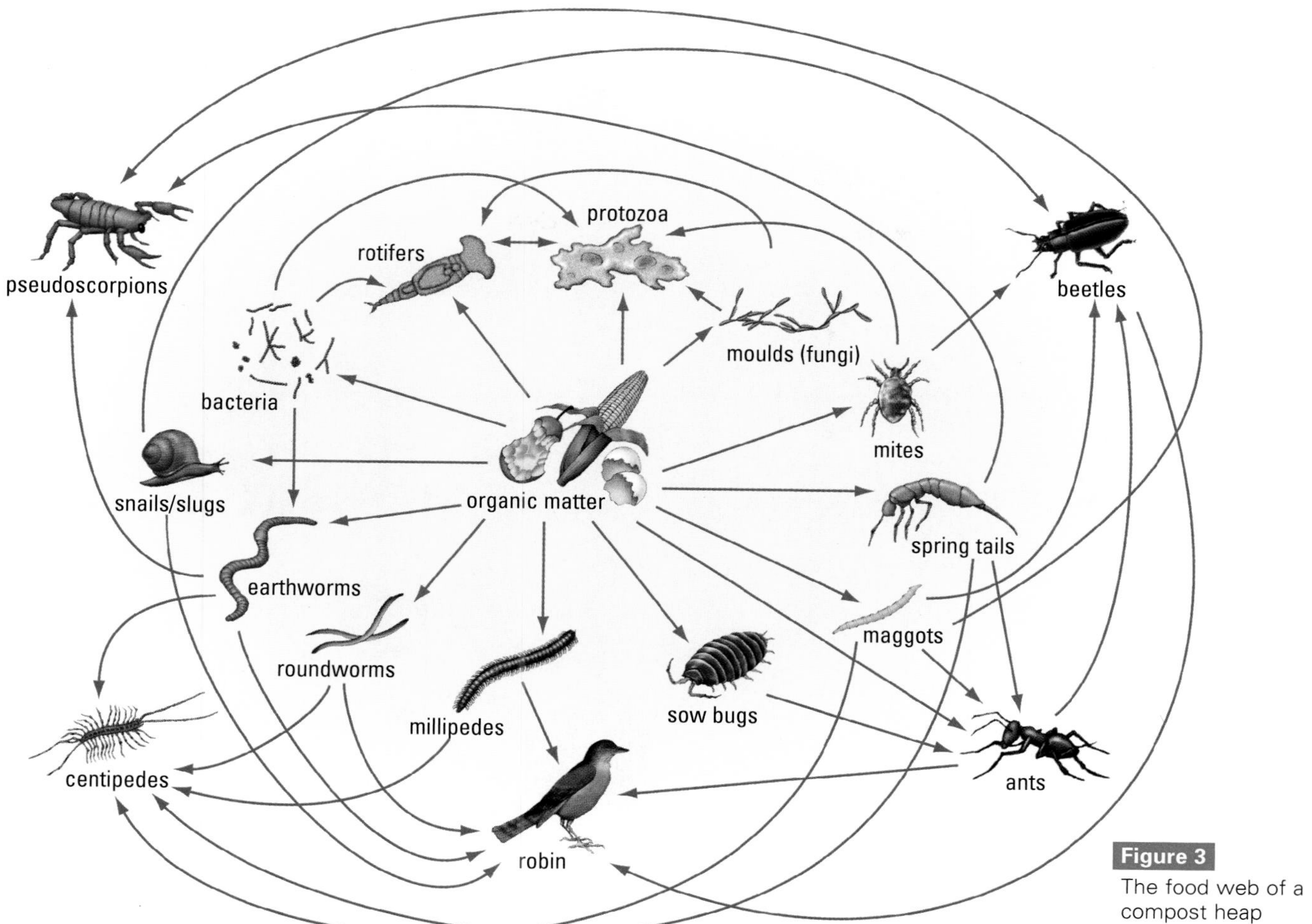

Figure 3
The food web of a compost heap

Food Chains and Webs

You can trace a simple feeding pathway, known as a **food chain** (**Figure 2**). The arrows indicate the direction in which the matter and energy are being transferred.

In most ecosystems, carnivores do not rely on only one source of food. For example, the wolf in **Figure 2** eats white-tailed deer, but it may also eat mice, ground squirrels, rabbits, ground-nesting birds and their eggs, and many other animals. The mice the wolf eats do not eat spruce buds, but they do eat the seeds, inner bark, and shoots of many different plants. It might be possible to describe these relationships with many individual food chains, but it is easier to show the relationships in a **food web**, which connects each organism with all of the organisms it eats and all of the animals that eat it. **Figure 3**, showing the food web of a compost heap, is an example of the ways in which organisms interact within an ecosystem.

Understanding Concepts

1. Why are matter cycles essential in an ecosystem?
2. Explain in your own words the following terms, and give an example of each: producer, consumer, herbivore, and carnivore.
3. **(a)** How is a food chain different from a food web?
   (b) Create an example of a food chain using the organisms in **Figure 3**.
4. **(a)** Create a food chain at least three organisms long that includes human beings.
   (b) Can you make a food web out of your chain? What other organisms could you add?

Making Connections

5. Wolves don't eat plants, but a wolf could not live in an ecosystem that didn't have plants. Explain.

Reflecting

6. Construct a food web of the organisms found in a landfill site.

Microbes in Ecosystems

Every organism in an ecosystem serves a function, even those we are afraid of. When most people think of microbes, the first image might be disease-causing viruses or bacteria (**Figure 1**). Microbes were responsible for epidemics of smallpox, the Black Death, and diphtheria that claimed millions of lives. Today the HIV virus that causes AIDS and the so-called flesh-eating bacteria evoke fear.

Figure 1

There are four kinds of microbes. Only a few of each kind are harmful to people. Some of the diseases or harm they do are listed here.

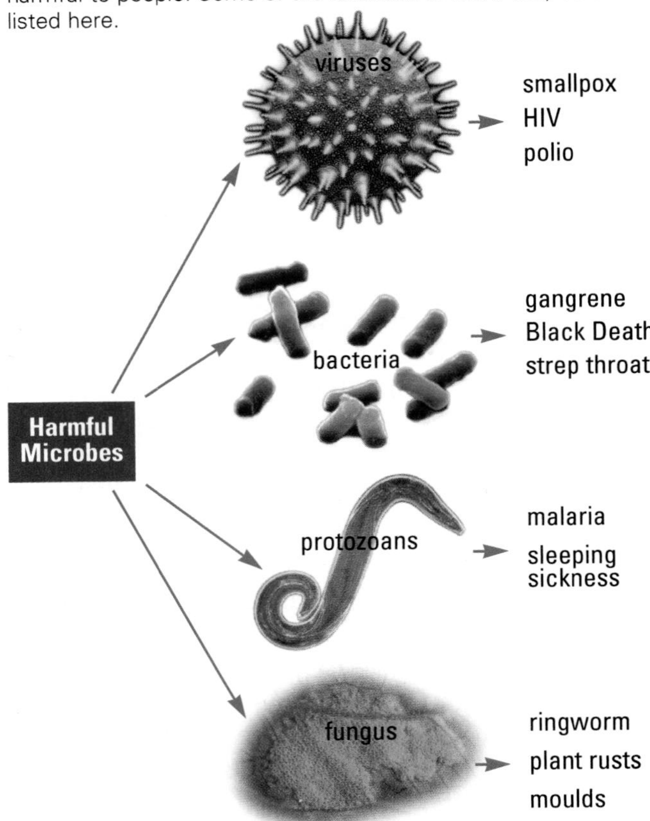

Helpful Microbes

Unfortunately, the fear of a few disease-causing microbes has given a bad name to all microbes. The vast majority of microbes do not cause disease. Some are even beneficial to humans. Bacteria are used in making cheese, buttermilk, and yogurt. Bacteria are also used in tanning leather. Yeast (a type of fungus) is used to make bread. Many different kinds of bacteria and fungi are used to produce drugs, such as penicillin (**Figure 2**).

Figure 2

Penicillin is made from this mould, a kind of fungus. Penicillin can be used to kill harmful bacteria that cause illnesses such as strep throat.

Microbes and Food

Each microbe has a role in its ecosystem. Although a specific microbe may create problems for humans, it still serves a useful function. Consider microbes that cause food to spoil (**Figure 3**). We often describe these microbes as harmful because they compete with us for our food. However, a world without these microbes would soon be in trouble. Apples would fall and pile up at the base of the tree. The leaves that drop from the trees in fall would still be there in spring, and in the following year. Recycling of matter would stop. Soon plants, starved of nutrients, would begin to die.

These microbes break down complex molecules in food and return nutrients to the ecosystem so other organisms can grow.

Microbes and Disease

Even microbes that cause disease have a function. Consider an elk infected by the bacteria that causes tuberculosis. The elk will become weaker and soon fall prey to wolves or a cougar. Vultures and small scavenging mammals might be next to feed on the remains. Later, beetles and ants would remove some of the remaining nutrients from the bones. Eventually, other decomposers, such as mushrooms and bacteria, would complete the process of recycling.

Tuberculosis is very harmful to the individual elk, but it helps the ecosystem. Elk form large herds that can eat all of the available food in an area, which endangers the plants they eat and other animals that feed on those plants. Large herds are even a danger to the elk. As food is depleted, the elk become weak and begin to starve.

Tuberculosis spreads when an elk with the disease coughs. It spreads much more easily in a large herd where the animals are weak than in a small, healthy herd. The disease keeps the ecosystem in balance by preventing elk herds from becoming too large. After some of the elk have died of the disease, food supplies will increase and the remaining elk will be healthier.

Figure 3

Moulds and bacteria spoil food, but by doing so they recycle nutrients within the ecosystem.

Understanding Concepts

1. Provide three examples of microbes that are:
   - **(a)** beneficial to humans.
   - **(b)** harmful to humans.
2. Explain why microbes that spoil food are essential to ecosystems. What would happen if all of these microbes were destroyed?
3. What purpose do disease-causing microbes serve in an ecosystem?

Making Connections

4. The flow of untreated sewage into a lake creates problems for organisms living in the ecosystem. Decomposing microbes that live in the water break down the solid wastes in the sewage and free nutrients that help aquatic plants to grow rapidly.
   - **(a)** Speculate on what might happen in a lake where plants and algae are growing and spreading rapidly.
   - **(b)** The bacteria that break down sewage use up oxygen from the lake. The more sewage there is, the more bacteria will grow to feed on it. Fish need oxygen to survive. What problem might be caused by a steady flow of sewage into a lake?
   - **(c)** In lakes polluted by sewage, trout populations decline before the populations of catfish and other bottom feeders. Why might trout suffer before less active fish like the catfish? How could you test your hypothesis?

Reflecting

5. Cattle can catch tuberculosis from elk. What kinds of dangers might this create for farmers? Knowing these dangers, should we use medicines to control tuberculosis in elk, as we do in humans?

5.8 Inquiry Investigation

SKILLS MENU
- ○ Questioning
- ● Hypothesizing
- ● Planning
- ● Conducting
- ● Recording
- ● Analyzing
- ● Communicating

Nutrient Recycling and Plant Growth

In a natural setting, as in **Figure 1**, plants grow without artificial fertilizers. The nutrients that the plants need come from decomposing matter in the soil.

Question

Would nutrients extracted from soil promote plant growth?

Hypothesis

1 Read the procedure and create a hypothesis for this investigation. (2C)

Experimental Design

In this investigation you will determine whether nutrients dissolved from the soil promote plant growth.

2 Design a chart to keep track of plant growth and your observations for both the control and experimental cartons. (6D)

Materials

- 10 presoaked pea, corn, or bean seeds
- colander
- cheesecloth
- potting soil
- large container
- 250-mL plastic beaker
- plastic storage bottle
- marking pen
- 2 milk cartons, each 2-L
- 100-mL plastic graduated cylinder
- water

Procedure

3 Line a colander with cheesecloth.
- Pour the potting soil into the colander.
- Hold the colander over a large container.
- Pour 250 mL of tap water over the soil.
- Repeat this procedure two more times, reusing the same water each time.
- Store the water in a plastic bottle.
- Using the marking pen, label the bottle "nutrient water."

4 Remove the top half of the milk cartons.
- Label one milk carton "control" and the other "experimental."
- Fill the milk cartons with soil from the colander to a height of about 20 cm.
- If you need more soil, make sure that you filter water through it as you did in step 2.

(a) Why must all of the soil used for this experiment have water filtered through it?

5 Plant 5 seeds in each milk carton.
- Using a 100-mL graduated cylinder, add 50 mL of tap water to the seeds in the carton labelled "control."
- Add 50 mL of nutrient water to the seeds in the milk carton labelled "experimental."

SKILLS HANDBOOK: (2C) Predicting and Hypothesizing (6D) Creating Data Tables

Figure 1
Plants draw the nutrients they need from the soil.

Reflecting

1. Read the comments you kept about the plants as they grew and review your data. What do you conclude about the nutrient water?

6 Each day, check that the soil is moist. If water is needed, add the same amount to each carton. Always add tap water to the seeds labelled "control" and nutrient water to the seeds labelled "experimental."

(a) Record the height of each plant every day. Also make notes on the colour, health, and appearance of each of the plants.

Analysis

7 Analyze your results by answering the following questions.

(a) Calculate the average height of the control and experimental plants each day. (If any seed in either group fails to grow, do not count it when you calculate the average.)

(b) Why is it useful to report the average height for all five plants, rather than the height of each individual plant?

(c) Plot the average growth for the control and experimental group in a line graph. Use the horizontal axis (*x*-axis) to represent time (days) and the vertical axis (*y*-axis) to represent average height of the plant. (7C)

(d) Does the data that you collected support or contradict your hypothesis? Explain why.

(7C) Constructing Graphs

Field Biologist

Figure 1
These small white cedars may be hundreds of years old.

Uta Matthes-Sears studies botany (plants) at the University of Guelph. One of the things that makes her work so appealing is that she spends a great deal of time studying plants outdoors. Equipped with the straps and harness of a rock climber, Uta scales steep cliffs in her outdoor laboratory—an abandoned quarry she has chosen because it is so much like the Niagara Escarpment.

The Escarpment is a long wall of limestone and dolomite rock that marks the edge of an ancient lake. From Niagara Falls, it passes northward near Guelph and then winds into Lake Huron, and southward into the United States.

No other trees are quite like the trees of the escarpment. White cedars, which live for only 90 years in horizontal forests, may be 850 years old in the Escarpment's vertical forest (see **Figure 1**). When the trees grow on the cliffs of the escarpment, they grow at a much slower rate.

Puzzled by these trees, Uta and a team of researchers from Guelph have done experiments to study how the cedars live in this strange environment. They have discovered that soil doesn't seem to be important to the trees.

Uta conducted a two-year experiment on 60 cedars in her quarry. She left 20 trees undisturbed (these were her control). She gave extra water to 20 trees, and fertilizer solution to another 20. Over the two years she measured how much each tree grew. She discovered that extra water had no effect on growth. She found that fertilizer allowed the plants to grow very slightly faster. Uta also found that the roots of these trees grow just as fast in bare rock as they do in soil pockets. The white cedars of the Niagara Escarpment are mysterious plants!

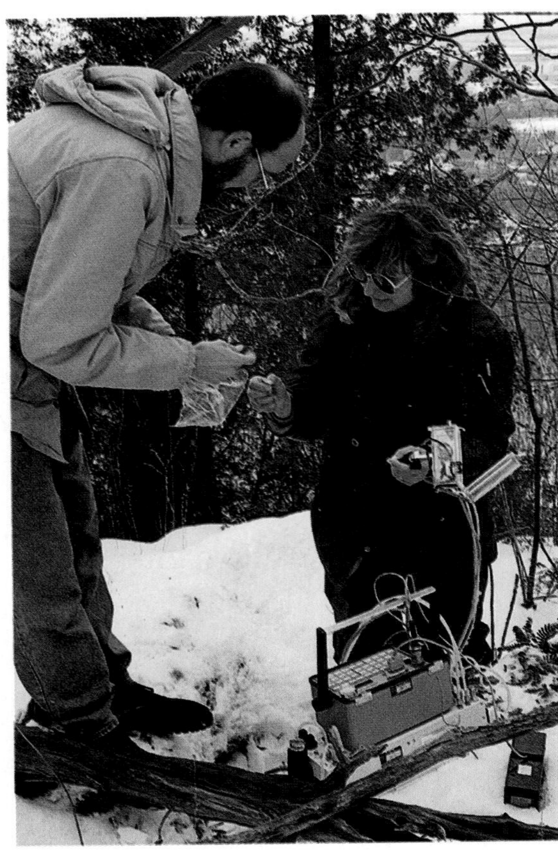

Uta is now switching her attention back to her first interest—lower plants. While she and her team were examining roots, they made an exciting discovery—many tiny organisms, including algae, are actually growing centimetres deep inside the rock of the Escarpment. "Some (scientists) have associated these algae only with Antarctica and other extreme environments," she says, "but we found them growing right here in the Escarpment."

There are easier places to study plants, but few are more interesting and exciting than the Niagara Escarpment. A field biologist in this study group needs the fitness and agility of a rock climber to scale 25-m cliffs, and the knowledge and the patience of a scientist to make careful observations and collect data.

Try This Studying Plant Distribution (6A)

Why do plants grow where they do?

- Find a north-facing and south-facing slope along a river or stream.
- Without climbing any cliffs or exposing yourself to any danger, take photographs of the plants on each slope. (Photos can be taken from a distance.)
- (6C) In your notebook make a rough map of the area that you investigated.

1. Are more large trees found along the north-facing or south-facing slope?

- On your photos, use a ruler and a felt pen to divide each slope into three horizontal areas.

2. Are more large trees found at the bottom, middle, or top section of the slope?

- Use field guides to identify as many of the plants as possible from their pictures.
- Identify different abiotic factors between the north-facing slope and the south-facing slope.

3. Are the same plants found on each slope?
4. Are the same plants found in each of the horizontal regions of the slope (top, middle, and bottom)?
5. Explain how the abiotic factors affect the types of plants found on each slope.

Ecological Pyramids

Did you ever wonder what life would be like without mosquitoes? A walk though a cool forest on a hot summer day would not be disrupted by buzzing and biting.

Dragonflies are glad there are mosquitoes. If there were no mosquitoes, there would be no dragonflies. This fearsome-looking insect scours forests and fields looking for mosquitoes (**Figure 1**). The dragonfly traps a mosquito in its front wings, then uses its forelimbs to pull the mosquito toward its mouth. All the while, its back wings keep it aloft. In a single day, the amazing dragonfly eats more than its own weight in mosquitoes, yet there never seems to be a shortage of the blood-sucking pests. Why are there always more mosquitoes than dragonflies?

Figure 1
Dragonflies catch mosquitoes on the fly.

In seeking an answer, you must follow your blood (see **Figure 2**). After a mosquito has taken its share, it stores very little of the energy available in your blood. Most of it is used just to stay alive. Flight alone requires a tremendous amount of energy.

When a dragonfly eats the mosquito, only about 10% of the energy that came from your blood is passed to the dragonfly. The rest was used up by the mosquito. The dragonfly uses energy in catching the mosquito, eating it, and breaking down the large food molecules to simple nutrients. This means that only a very small fraction of the energy from your blood is stored by the dragonfly.

Each time energy is transferred within an ecosystem, some of the energy is lost. It takes a great number of mosquitoes to keep one dragonfly alive, and a great many arm bites to keep all of those mosquitoes alive. If there were more dragonflies, there wouldn't be enough mosquitoes to feed them. That is why the dragonfly must eat many mosquitoes, why there are always more mosquitoes than dragonflies, and why walking in the forest in summer isn't always fun.

Figure 2
Energy transfer from blood to dragonfly

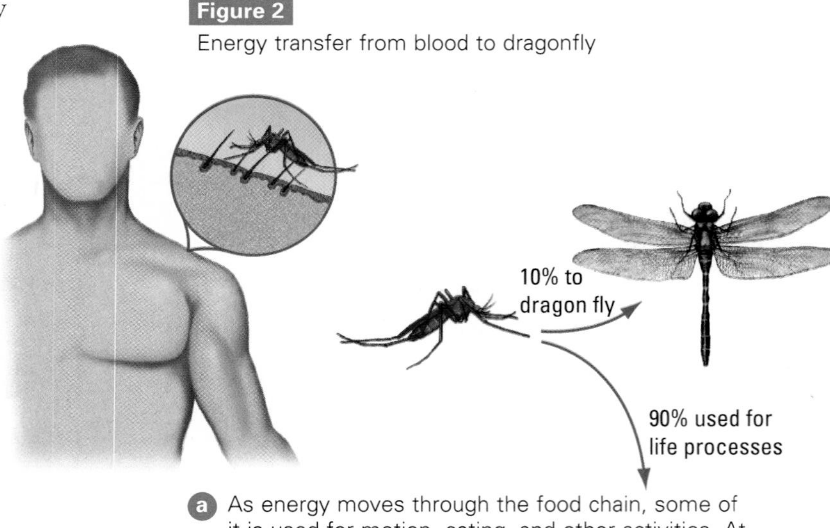

(a) As energy moves through the food chain, some of it is used for motion, eating, and other activities. At each link in the food chain there is less energy available than at the previous link.

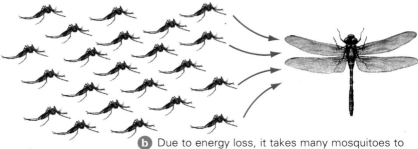

(b) Due to energy loss, it takes many mosquitoes to keep one dragonfly alive.

Food Chains in a Graph

Ecological pyramids are a graphical way to show the effects of loss of energy (**Figure 3**). Each level in a pyramid matches a level of producer or consumer in an ecosystem or food chain. At each level the amount of energy available is less. The number of organisms at each level of the pyramid usually decreases.

Figure 3

The base of the pyramid holds producers (plants). At each level above the producers, the amount of energy available is reduced. That explains why in your ecosystem you might find huge numbers of insects that eat plants, a much smaller number of shrews to eat the insects, and only a very small number of owls to eat the shrews.

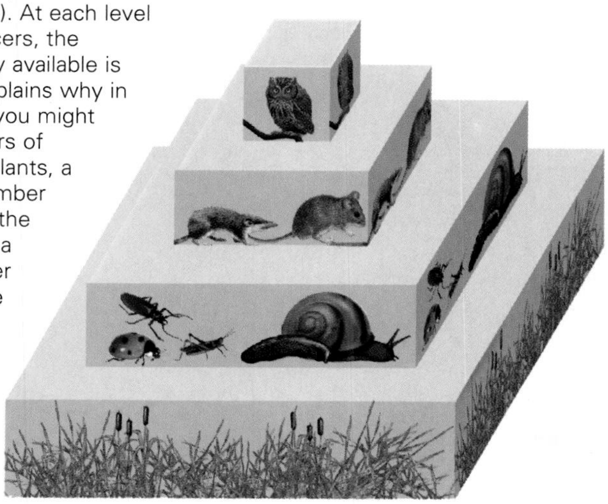

Understanding Concepts

1. Why is less than 10% of the energy the mosquito gets from its food transferred to the dragonfly?
2. Using your own words, explain why there are usually more producers in an ecosystem than consumers.

Making Connections

3. **Figure 5** shows an ecological pyramid for a forest ecosystem in the summer and winter. Why are they different?

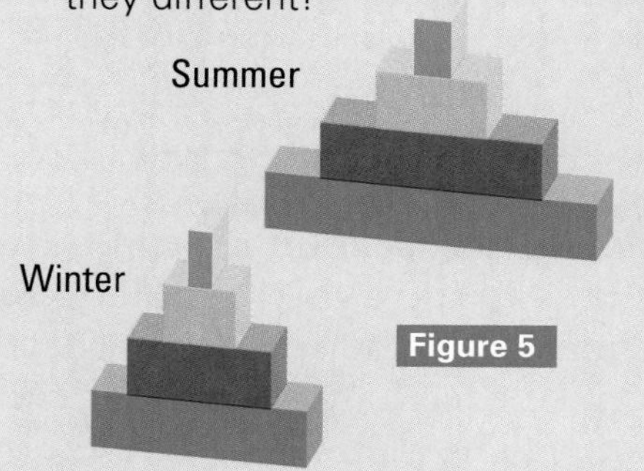

Figure 5

Reflecting

4. Using ecological pyramids, explain why animals we think of as pests, such as mosquitoes, are important to ecosystems.

Number Models

It's easy to create an ecological pyramid—at least, it's easy if you have done the very hard job of counting the organisms in a food web! Use the data in **Table 1** to make an ecological pyramid for the pond.

Table 1: A Pond Survey

Organism	Role in the ecosystem	Estimated number of organisms
algae	producers	200 000 000
aquatic insects	consumers, eat algae	100 000
small fish	consumers, eat insects	100

- Use rectangles to build your pyramid. Each rectangle represents one level of organism. The area of the rectangle represents the number of organisms at that level.
- Select a scale and build your pyramid.

Figure 4

Area = length x width
= 5 cm x 2 cm
Area = 10 cm^2

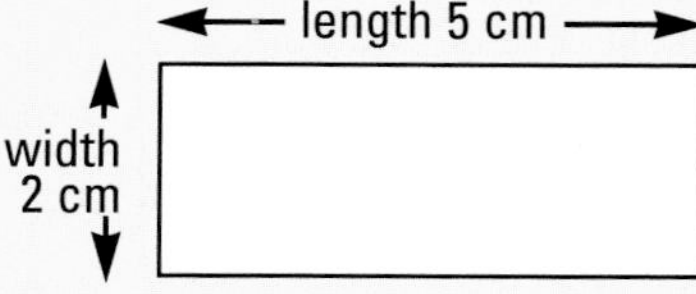

1. If you used the scale of 10 organisms for each 10 cm^2, how much paper would you need to make the rectangle for the algae? Is this a good scale to choose?

5.11 Case Study

Pesticides: Poisons in the Food Chain

As much as 30% of the annual crop in Canada is lost to pests. The pests include weeds, rusts and moulds, birds, small mammals, and insects. For each of these pests, we have created a pesticide. **Pesticides** are chemicals designed to reduce the populations of unwanted organisms, both plant and animal.

Tires and Mosquitoes

What do we do with worn-out tires? Burying tires in a landfill isn't possible. After a few years they always push through to the surface. Just storing them separately has always been a problem, because old tires can burn. As tires burn they create a thick, choking smoke.

There is another problem with tire dumps: tires make excellent troughs for collecting rainwater. The still water, warmed by the sun hitting black rubber, makes an agreeable ecosystem for hatching mosquitoes.

(a) Why is it a problem to create a favourable ecosystem for mosquitoes?

Mosquitoes and Disease

Some mosquitoes carry microbes that cause disease. Malaria is one such disease, as shown in **Figure 1**. Thousands of people in tropical areas of the world die of this disease every year.

(b) Used tires are often stored in one area and then moved to another area for disposal. What problem might this cause?

Figure 1

The malaria microbe is carried by one species of mosquito. The microbe cycles between animals such as humans and mosquitoes.

a A mosquito draws blood from an infected person and picks up the parasite.
b the parasite is transferred into the next victim's bloodstream when the mosquito bites.
c The parasite incubates in the liver and releases microbes into the bloodstream.
d Malaria microbes infect red blood cells, which rupture and send spores into the bloodstream.

Using Pesticides

Scientists developed a pesticide spray that could eliminate mosquitoes. When it was tried on an island, other effects were soon noted. Insects other than mosquitoes began to disappear, and then the number of lizards began to fall.

(c) Why did scientists want to reduce the number of mosquitoes?

(d) What do you think caused some other insects to begin to disappear?

(e) Provide at least two examples of insects that you would not want to destroy and explain why they are important.

(f) Why might the lizards begin to disappear?

The Problem Spreads

Most people on the island were not too worried about the disappearance of a few insects and some lizards. However, they took notice once the local wildcats, which had fed on dead lizards, began to get sick and die. Without the cats the rat population soon increased. Fearing an outbreak of diseases linked with rats, the local people imported domestic cats.

(g) What problems could be caused by bringing in domestic cats?

Invasion of the Caterpillars

Changes to the food web became even more obvious when caterpillar populations began to increase. Apparently, the pesticide affected wasps and other predators of the caterpillar, but it had little effect on the caterpillars. Once the predators were gone, the caterpillar population increased greatly. Eventually, caterpillars searching for food moved into fields and devastated food crops.

(h) Use pictures of a beetle, cat, caterpillar, grasshopper, lizard, mosquito, rat, and wasp to draw a food web that shows the impact of spraying with the insecticide.

Biological Amplification

Pesticides tend to stay in the bodies of animals that come in contact with them. (If pests could easily get rid of the pesticide, it would not be effective.) The result is that the concentration of harmful pesticides increases at each level in a food chain. Predators always have more toxic chemicals in their bodies than their prey, as shown in **Figure 2**.

If the body of the prey contains harmful pesticides, the pesticides will be taken in by the predator. Predators eat many prey over their lifetimes. Each time prey is eaten, the amount of pesticide in the predator increases. This process of increase at each level of a food chain is called **biological amplification**.

(i) Predict how scavengers, such as beetles, might be affected by biological amplification.

Understanding Concepts

1. Explain in your own words what pesticides are.
2. Why do pesticides create the greatest problems for carnivores?

Making Connections

3. In Atlantic Canada pesticides called pyrethoids were used to control winter moths and leaf miners in apple orchards. Unfortunately, the chemicals killed more insects than intended, including predators of red mites and apple mites. After orchards were sprayed with pyrethoids, the mite population rose quickly, damaging the trees and reducing the yield of apples. What recommendations would you make to anyone who planned to use pyrethoids?

Design Challenge

Make a list of the problems created by disposing of tires in a landfill site. What other kinds of garbage might cause similar problems? Think about some solutions.

Figure 2

The concentration of a pesticide increases as it moves up the food chain. (In this case the pesticide is DDT.) The greater the number of links in the chain, the greater the amount of biological amplification. From water to osprey the concentration of DDT increases 10 million times.

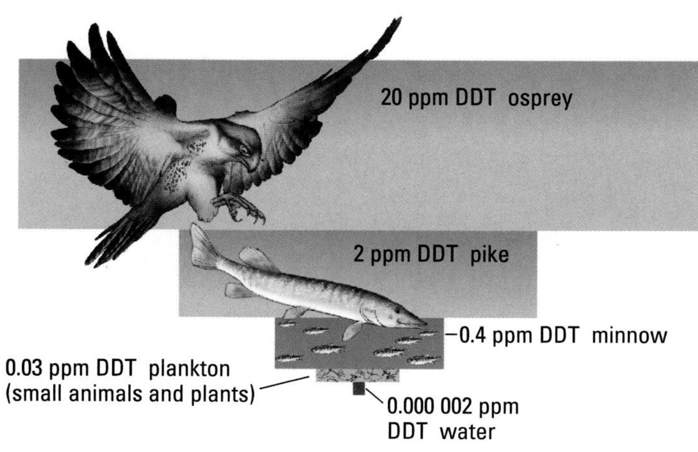

ppm = parts per million (one part per million is equivalent to one drop of the chemical in a full bathtub)

The Water Cycle

Have you ever made sand castles at the beach? When you dig a trench around the castle you may get a surprise (see **Figure 1**). The trench fills with water that comes from below the surface.

Figure 1
Water in the moat around this sand castle provides evidence that water continuously moves between the lake and the soil.

Water Beneath the Soil

There are two sources of fresh water: ground water and surface water. Precipitation that collects above the ground is called surface water. Lakes, ponds, and rivers are surface water. Surface water filters down into the layers of soil and rock. Eventually it reaches a level where the soil or rock is saturated with water. This level is called the water table. Water at and below the water table is ground water.

As water seeps downward it carries dissolved chemicals from the upper to the lower layers of the soil. This process is called **leaching**. The removal of these chemicals from the upper layers of the soil could be a serious problem for plants, which require the chemicals for growth and development. They respond by sending long, branching roots deep into soil. These help draw the chemicals back from the lower levels of the soil to the surface.

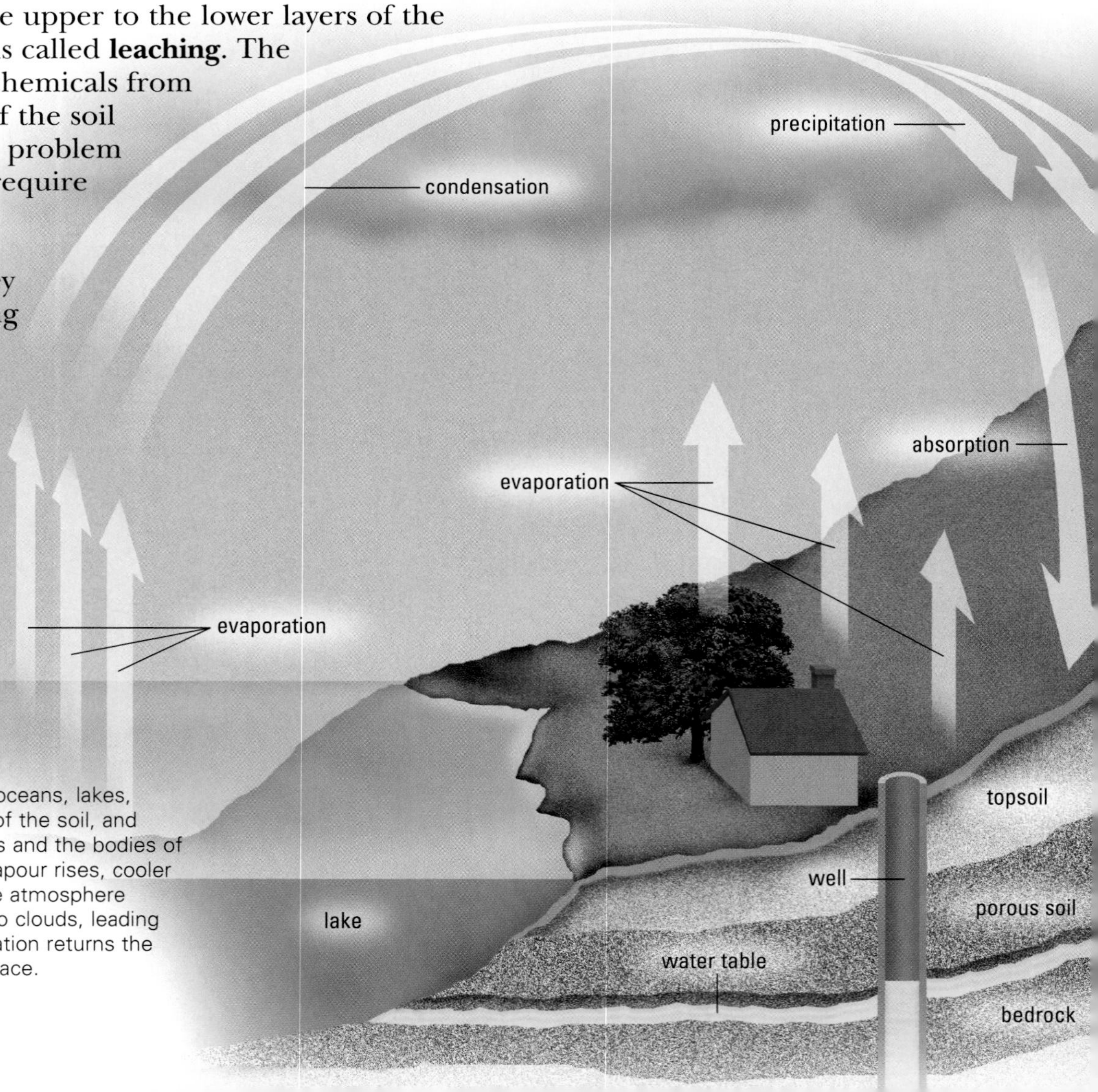

Figure 2
Water evaporates from oceans, lakes, rivers, the upper layers of the soil, and from the leaves of plants and the bodies of animals. As the water vapour rises, cooler temperatures high in the atmosphere cause it to condense into clouds, leading to precipitation. Precipitation returns the water to the Earth's surface.

The Water Cycle

Water is an important nutrient. Like other nutrients, it moves through ecosystems in a cycle. As shown in **Figure 2**, the **water cycle** collects, purifies, and distributes Earth's water. When the Sun's rays warm the Earth's surface, water evaporates and enters the atmosphere as vapour. As water enters the atmosphere, it leaves behind any chemicals that were dissolved in the water. Even the salt dissolved in ocean water remains in the ocean. Only fresh water enters the atmosphere by evaporation. Water removed from the oceans, lakes, and soil by evaporation is returned to Earth in the form of rain, snow, sleet, and hail.

Understanding Concepts

1. What is the water table?
2. Explain in your own words how the water cycle purifies water.
3. Why do minerals leach from the soil?
4. How do the roots of plants help prevent the leaching of important minerals?

Making Connections

5. List and describe two factors that would alter the amount of ground water in an area.
6. What dangers might be created by digging a hole for an outhouse at a beach cottage?

Design Challenge

How could a landfill site contaminate ground water? How might you prevent contamination?

Try This Measuring Water Cycling (6B)

How much water goes from plants to the atmosphere? You can find out.

- Put a small plastic bag around a leaf of a deciduous tree and around a small branch of a tree with needle leaves (**Figure 3**).
- Gently tie off the bag so the mouth of the bag is snug to the branch but not tight, and collect water overnight.
- Pour the water you collect into a graduated cylinder.

1. Which type of leaf cycled the greatest amount of water?
2. (2C) Create a hypothesis to explain the difference.

Figure 3

5.13 Case Study

Choosing a Waste Disposal Site

In this case study, you will evaluate problems connected with waste disposal. Landfill is one of the cheapest methods of waste disposal. A large pit is dug, replacing the existing ecosystem. Garbage is stored in the pit. Once the pit has been filled, it is covered by a cap of soil. Trees are planted and the site is left to be reclaimed by nature.

Although inexpensive, landfill sites are not ideal for disposing of all wastes. Radioactive wastes, medical wastes (such as bandages that may carry diseases), and poisonous chemicals should not be stored in an open pit. Medical wastes and some chemicals are burned instead. Other dangerous wastes can be disposed of by deep-well injection (see **Figure 1**).

(a) Explain why the well in deep-well injection must extend below the water table.

(b) Why couldn't deep-well injection be used in earthquake zones?

Figure 1

Deep-well injection of toxic waste

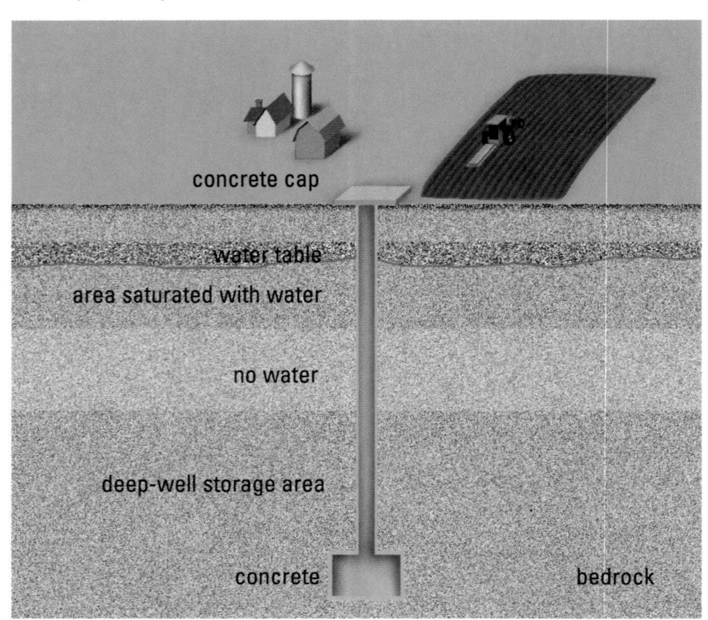

The Site

A landfill site is to be shared by the city of Cosmo and the town of Greenbelt. Possible sites are shown in **Figure 2**.

Site C is closest to the largest supply of garbage; however, the site is not considered the best by many citizens.

(c) What are some disadvantages of site C?

(d) Who do you believe opposes site C more, the people of Greenbelt or of Cosmo? Explain.

(e) Which site is farthest from a populated area?

(f) What are some disadvantages of the farthest site?

Figure 2
Possible sites for a landfill

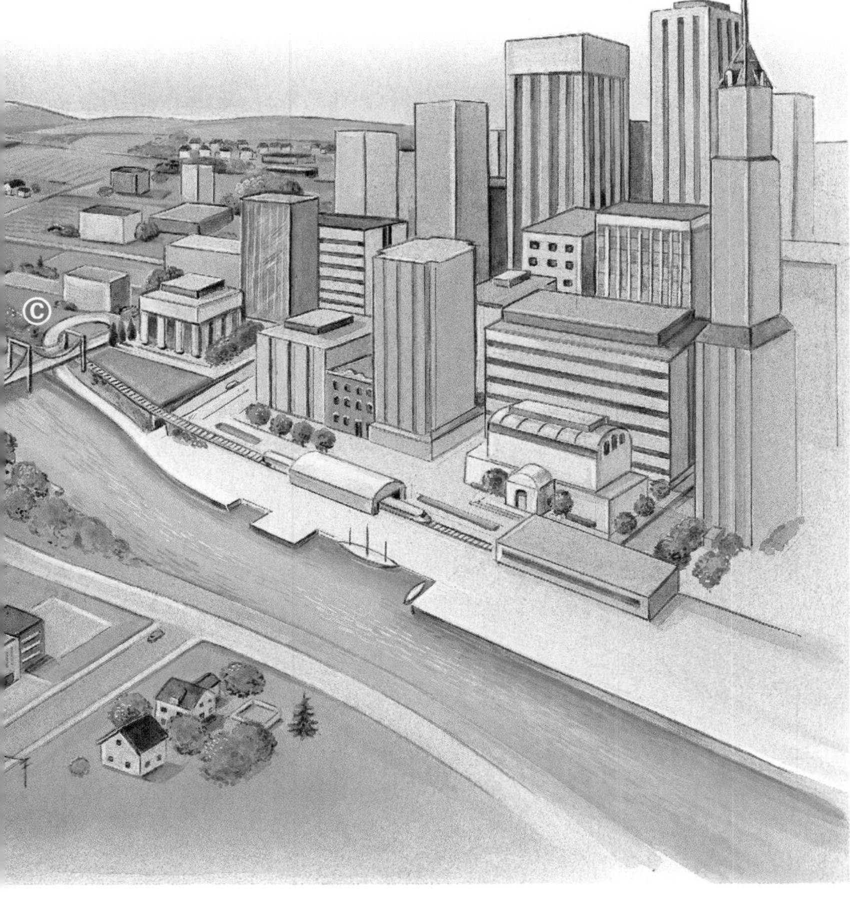

Understanding Concepts

1. Which landfill site poses the greatest ecological danger for people and organisms? Explain your answer.
2. Which landfill site would you choose? Give your reasons.

Making Connections

3. Residents of cities often prefer landfill sites that are far from their homes. What added environmental dangers are caused by choosing such a site?

Reflecting

4. A homeowner complains about not being able to throw away paints, car batteries, tires, and strong household cleaners. These must be taken to a separate site for disposal. The homeowner points out that this adds great expense to collecting the garbage. How would you respond to this viewpoint?

Getting to the Core

Core samples were collected from the soil at each potential site. Examine the results in **Figure 3** carefully before continuing.

(g) Why is it important to know where the water table is?

(h) Taking into account only the water table, which site would you choose?

(i) Why is it important to know the composition of the soil?

(j) Why might landfill site C be recommended over B?

(k) Why might landfill site D be recommended over A?

Figure 3
Core samples from sites A, B, C, and D

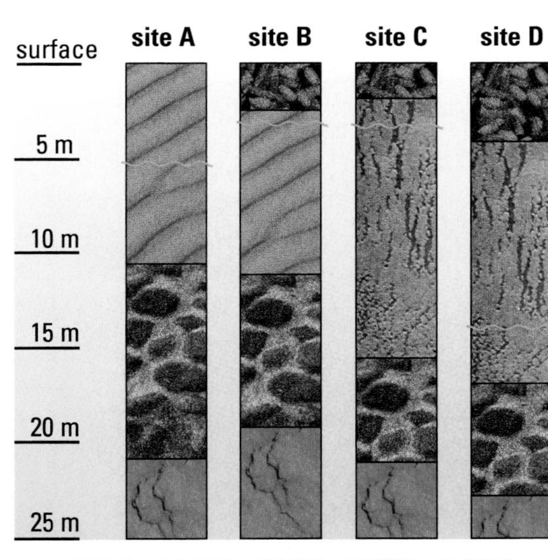

Rethinking Before Recycling

Figure 1

Of the containers in **Figure 1**, which is the best to hold juice? For many people, the first choice for an environmentally friendly juice container is a tetra box. It collapses, so it should take up less room in a landfill. The tetra box also contains paper, which you know breaks down in a landfill.

However, the tetra box (**Figure 2**) is probably the worst choice for the environment. Although it is 70% paper, it also contains an aluminum liner (6% by mass) and a plastic cover and a liner (24% by mass). The problem is that plastic and aluminum are recycled using a different process. (You probably have noticed that recycling depots have separate containers for paper, aluminum, and plastic.) There are recyclables in a tetra box that can't be recycled, so they end up in the landfill site.

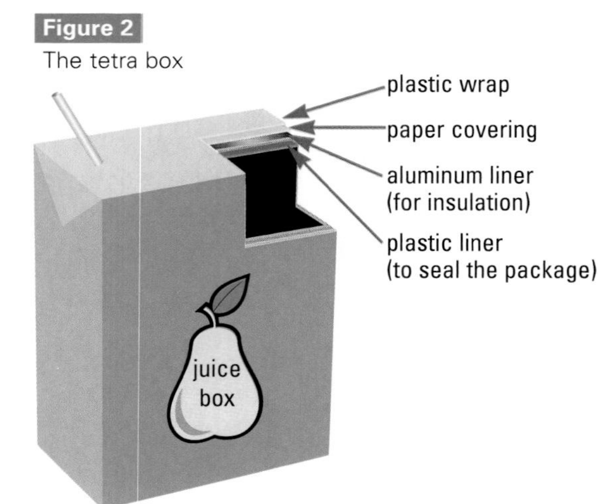

Figure 2
The tetra box

The Alternatives

What about the other containers? The aluminum can is strong. It can be used only once, but is then easily recycled, as you can see in **Figure 3**.

Plastic and glass bottles have the advantage of being reusable. After use they can be washed, disinfected, and used again. Eventually, plastic and glass can also be recycled.

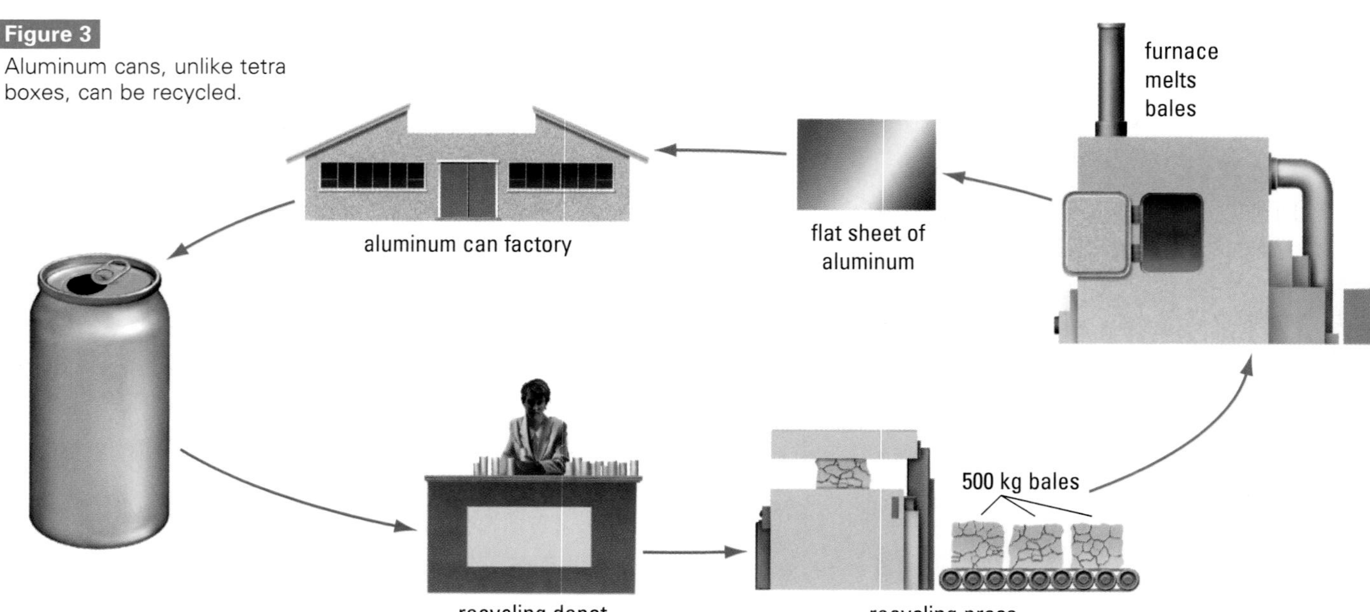

Figure 3
Aluminum cans, unlike tetra boxes, can be recycled.

Biodegradable Products

Products made from things that were once living are broken down easily by decomposers. Such products are referred to as **biodegradable**. Paper is an example of a biodegradable product. It contains cellulose, a complex substance found in plants. Bacteria and other microbes can break down cellulose into simpler substances, called sugars. The sugars can be used as a source of energy by the bacteria and other living things. Once this process has begun, it tends to move quickly. As more sugar is released for growth and reproduction, the population of the bacteria increases. More bacteria become available to break down even more paper.

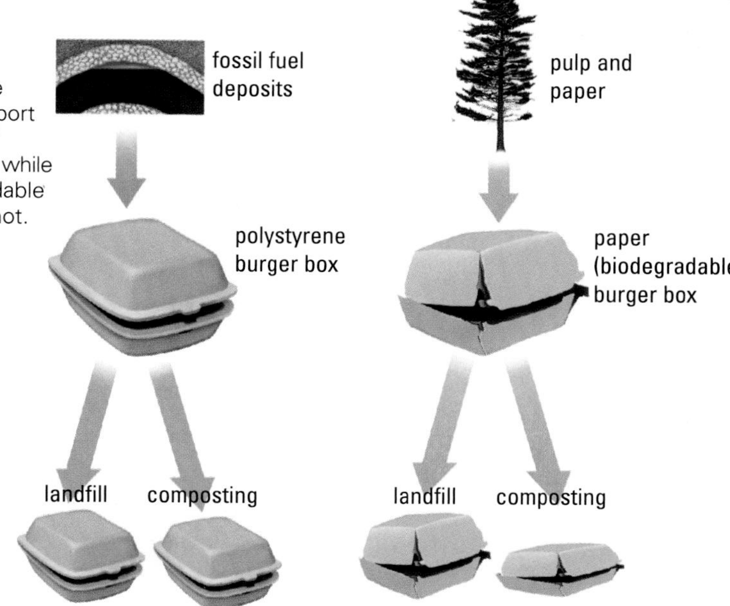

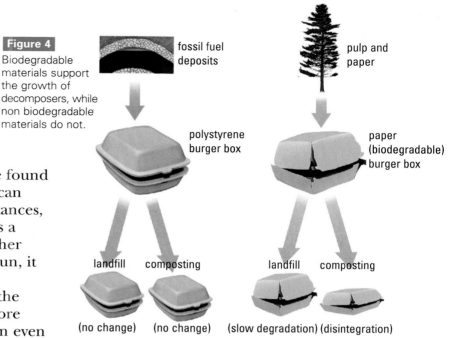

Figure 4
Biodegradable materials support the growth of decomposers, while non biodegradable materials do not.

Nonbiodegradable Products

Nonbiodegradable materials tend to be human-made chemicals. Because they do not provide food energy for the growth of decomposers, they break down very slowly (**Figure 4**). Plastics and synthetics, such as nylon, are examples of nonbiodegradable materials.

The advantage of nonbiodegradable materials is that they last a long time—you wouldn't want a pop bottle to begin breaking down in your fridge! However, this property also makes nonbiodegradable products a problem. They remain unchanged in landfill sites for many years.

Degradable Plastic

Scientists have designed special plastics that do break down. The plastic is made of tiny clumps of material that are weakly connected to other clumps. The weak connections can be broken by exposing the plastic to the sun or to oxygen, which is found in the atmosphere, in soil, and in water. The plastic will then break into small pieces.

Understanding Concepts

1. What advantage do glass and plastic containers have over aluminum cans?
2. What kind of container would you recommend to carry fruit juice? Give your reasons.
3. Explain the difference between biodegradable and nonbiodegradable products in your own words.

Making Connections

4. Why shouldn't degradable plastic be recycled with nonbiodegradable plastics?

Extension

5. (3F) Test how well different kinds of packaging protect merchandise. Put an egg in a plastic bag and then put the egg in a 2-L milk carton. Test different packaging materials by stuffing them around the egg. Drop the milk carton from varying heights. Which packaging gives the greatest protection?

Design Challenge

(9E) Make a concept map of what you have learned in this lesson. What connections can you see to your Challenge?

SKILLS HANDBOOK: (3F) Testing and Evaluating a Prototype (9E) Graphic Organizers

Garbage and the Community

Imagine a line of garbage trucks stretching from Earth halfway to the Moon (**Figure 1**). That is how long the lineup would be if all of the garbage produced in Canada since you were born were loaded into trucks. By the time you are about twenty-five years old, the lineup would reach the Moon!

It's estimated that the garbage collected from Canadian houses, hospitals, and businesses every year has a mass of about 18 million tonnes. If debris from construction and demolition is added, the amount soars to 29 million tonnes. As **Figure 2** shows, Canadians are not showing the world how to reduce garbage production.

This much garbage presents a storage problem. In Ontario alone, the garbage produced each day is more than enough to cover a football field. Many large cities that face landfill problems have looked for new sites outside their city limits. However, the surrounding communities have generally not been interested in storing their neighbours' garbage. The search for a landfill site often involves great emotion and political controversy. Who wants to live next door to a dump?

Figure 1
The garbage produced in Canada in 12 to 13 years would extend halfway to the Moon. Of course, it isn't possible to use the Moon as a landfill site.

Figure 2
Canada is not the most environment-friendly country when it comes to garbage.

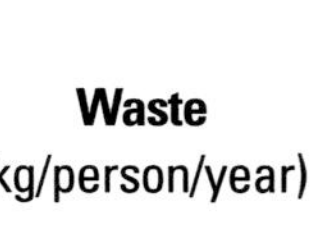

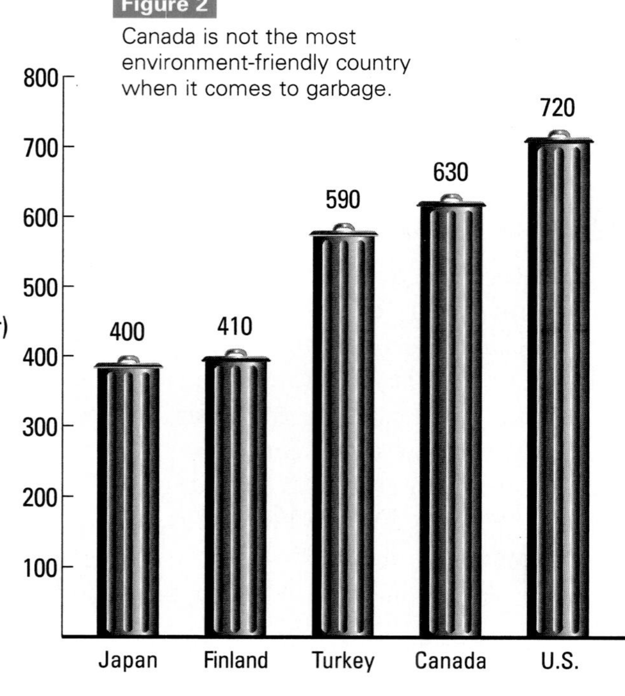

Source: Organization for Economic Co-operation and Development, Environmental Data, 1997.

Understanding Concepts

1. How much garbage would a Canadian family of four create in one year? in four years?
2. Speculate on why Canadians produce more garbage than the people of Japan.

Scenario: Cosmo's Conundrum   8D

The city of Cosmo's current landfill site will be full within two years. The city is growing, and a solution to the garbage problem must be found. One of the city councillors has put forward a proposal for a new landfill site. She says her proposal will help the site last longer, by reducing the amount of garbage that goes into it. Her proposal has not been welcomed by everyone in and around Cosmo. A public meeting will be held where everyone who wishes can make a presentation.

The Proposal

- Cosmo will create a new landfill site on farmland. (Site B in the map in Case Study 5.13.)
- Garbage will be separated by kind by the people discarding the garbage.
- City trucks will pick up regular garbage and recyclables from each home and business on a regular route. Every home and business will be given a separate container for each type of recyclable garbage:

  paper and paper products
  plastics such as pop bottles
  appliances and metals
  food waste
- Hazardous waste, such as paint, tires, batteries, and corrosive cleaners and solvents, will be picked up by a special city truck. Every resident and business in the city will be charged $50 per year for this service.

The Decision

You will take one of the roles listed. After the presentations, Cosmo's City Council must make a final decision.

The Roles

- city councillors; ask questions and vote on the final decision
- mayor; acts as chair for the meeting
- local farmers and rural residents; believe the landfill site should not be on farming land. They use wells as the source of their water.
- entrepreneurs; believe garbage collection can make money. They want to set up a company to collect garbage and dispose of it in the new site.
- representatives of a recycling company; think they can make money from recycling paper and metal but also want a subsidy so they won't lose money on food waste and appliances
- owners of large apartment buildings; are concerned that maintaining five large containers for waste will force them to construct a storage building or make other expensive modifications
- homeowners; object to paying $50 to dispose of hazardous waste, which used to be free
- environmental groups; think landfill should be at site C to encourage citizens to produce less waste

What do you think?

Comment on the decision-making process of the council. Do you agree with the decision? Explain why it is so difficult to meet everyone's needs.

5.16

Acid in the Water Cycle

Have you ever gotten a squirt of vinegar or lemon juice in the eye? If you have, you aren't likely to forget the burning sensation. Now imagine the damage that could be done by rain that is as acidic.

Measuring Acidity: The pH Scale

The pH scale is used to measure the strength of acids (**Figure 1**). Absolutely pure water (distilled water) has a pH value of seven. Solutions with a pH less than seven are considered to be acids. Normal rain is slightly acidic because the water mixes with carbon dioxide in the air to form a weak acid (carbonic acid). However, recent rain in Mexico and Brazil has been more acidic than vinegar.

The Source of Acid Rain

Coal-burning plants, metal smelters, and oil refineries provide energy and valuable materials, but at the same time produce air pollutants that contain sulfur and nitrogen. The burning of fossil fuels in cars and the processing of nitrogen fertilizers also produce these pollutants. The pollutants enter the atmosphere and combine with water droplets to form acids, as shown in **Figure 2**.

These acidic droplets act like normal water droplets in the water cycle—they eventually fall as rain or snow. The term **acid rain** is used to describe the movement of sulfur- and nitrogen-containing acids from the atmosphere to the land and water.

Figure 2
Acids created by pollutants combine with rain and snow as part of the water cycle.

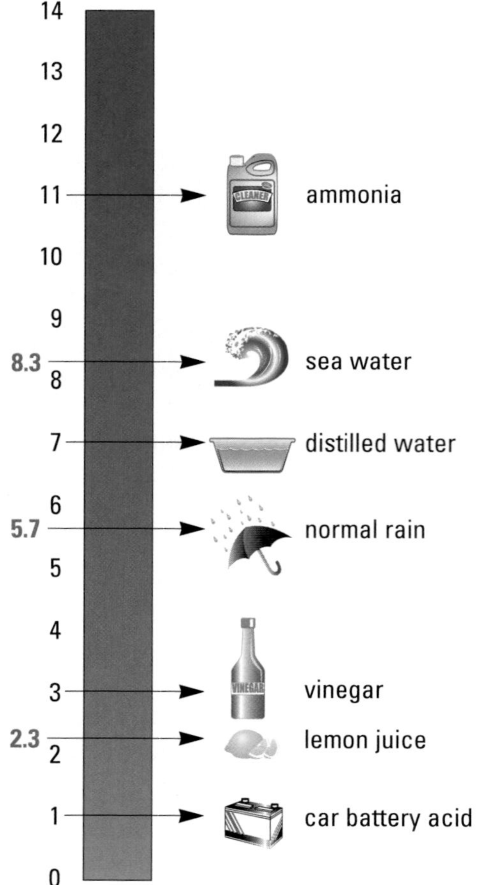

Figure 1
The pH scale ranges from 0 (very strong acids) to 14 (very strong bases). Chemicals at both ends of the scale are highly corrosive. Pure water is considered neutral.

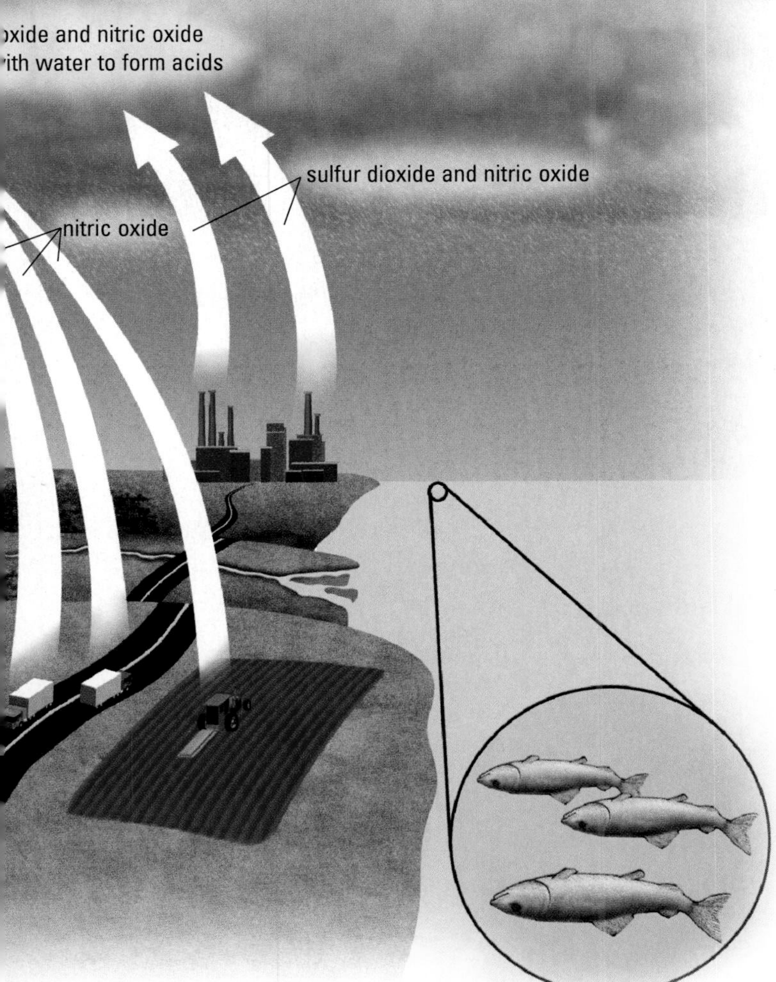

Fish die in highly acidic water

Effects of Acid Rain

Acid rain eats away marble, metal, mortar, rubber, and plastics. It kills fish, microbes in the soil, and both water and land plants (**Figure 3**). It also increases leaching of nutrients from soil.

Some areas are more sensitive than others to acid rain. Soils that have only a thin layer of rich soil on top of a solid granite base, such as those in the Muskoka and Haliburton areas of Ontario, can do little to reduce the impact of the acid before it runs off into streams and lakes. Deeper soils over limestone can reduce the acidity of the water.

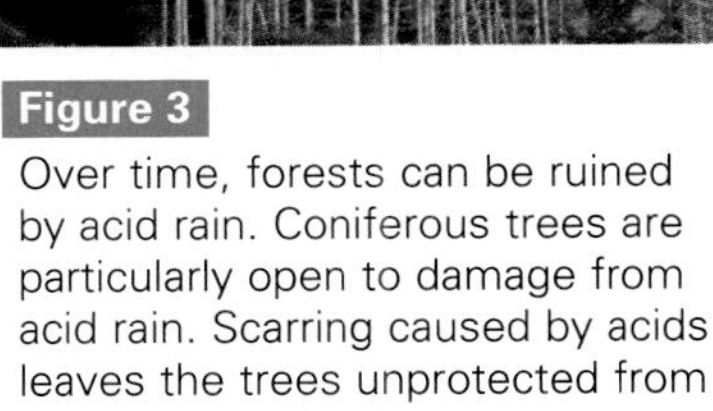

Figure 3

Over time, forests can be ruined by acid rain. Coniferous trees are particularly open to damage from acid rain. Scarring caused by acids leaves the trees unprotected from insects and infections.

Understanding Concepts

1. Why is acid rain a problem?
2. How do acids enter the water cycle?

Making Connections

3. Offer two suggestions that would reduce acid rain.
4. A lake in northern Ontario was checked in 1925 and again in 1999. Fish were collected and the following data were obtained.

Year	pH level	Number of fish		
		trout	whitefish	bottom feeders
1925	6.6	22	12	5
1999	4.6	0	0	8

(a) What has happened to the acidity of the lake?

(b) What conclusions can you draw about the effect of acid rain on fish?

(c) Other research data shows that the lake was murky in 1925 but clear in 1999. Does this indicate that the water is now better to drink? Explain.

(d) How does the acidity of a lake affect human health and the local economy?

Exploring

5. Some plants, such as moss, do (2E) well in acid soils. The acid-loving moss often grows so quickly that it steals food that could be used by other plants. Design an experiment that determines which plants do best in an acid soil. With approval from your teacher, carry out your experiment.

Design Challenge

Consider how acid rain would affect a landfill site.

5.17 Inquiry Investigation

SKILLS MENU
○ Questioning ● Conducting ● Analyzing
● Hypothesizing ● Recording ● Communicating
● Planning

Environmental Models

Environmental models allow scientists to study what could happen to the plants and animals in an ecosystem if there were changes in its abiotic components. Models help check predictions without disrupting a large area.

In this investigation you will build an ecocolumn to research an environmental problem. An ecocolumn is an ecological model that is especially designed to cycle nutrients.

Materials

- 2 or more 2-L plastic pop bottles
- pond water
- soil
- compost
- representative organisms (moss, flies, spiders, snails, etc.)
- scissors
- duct tape or binding tape (wide width)
- motor oil or vinegar
- other materials as required

Be careful when using sharp scissors.

Wear safety goggles and gloves when handling motor oil.

Always wash hands after handling soil, plants, or animals.

Question

You will investigate one of three environmental questions:

A. How would an oil spill affect an aquatic ecosystem? (You will use motor oil to test the environmental impact.)

B. How would acid rain affect an ecosystem? (You will use household vinegar.)

C. How would rapid changes in climate affect an ecosystem?

Hypothesis

1 Begin by doing research on one of the questions.
- Prepare a one-page report on the problem before beginning the investigation. (4A)
- Prepare a bibliography of the books and/or Internet sites that you used in gathering information. (8A)

2 Create a hypothesis for the question. (2C)

Experimental Design

3 Design an experiment using an ecocolumn that will test your hypothesis. Include safety precautions. (1)

4 Identify a control, if appropriate, and your independent and dependent variables.

5 Present your procedure to your teacher for approval before beginning.

Building an Ecocolumn

6 Remove all labels from a plastic bottle.
- Using scissors, remove the top and bottom of the bottle.
- Keep the top (part 1) and the middle (part 2), but discard the bottom.

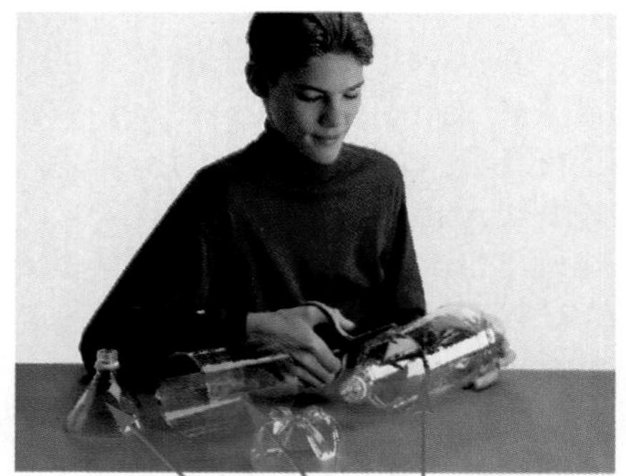

7 In a second bottle, make a cut just below where the bottle narrows.
- Discard the top, but keep the bottom (part 3).

 SKILLS HANDBOOK: (4A) Research Skills (8A) Writing a Report (2C) Predicting and Hypothesizing (1) Safety in Science & Technolo

Figure 1
A sample ecocolumn

Design Challenge

Explain the advantages of using prototype models when designing your Challenge.

8 Slide part 1 into part 2 and seal them with silicone or tape.
- Stack the combined structure on top of part 3, and seal it.

9 A sample of a more complex ecocolumn is shown in **Figure 1**. You decide on the design that is appropriate for your experiment.

Procedure

1 Carry out your experiment.

Analysis

1 Analyze your results by doing the following.

(a) Present your data in tables and graphs. (7C)

(b) Draw a conclusion from your experiment. (7E)

(7C) Constructing Graphs (7E) Reaching a Conclusion

The Carbon Cycle

Nearly 200 years ago, Joseph Priestley conducted an experiment that demonstrated that animals depend on plants. Priestley used three heavy glass jars. One of the jars was placed over a mint plant. The second was placed over a mouse. The third was placed over a mint plant and a mouse together, as shown in **Figure 1**. The mouse in jar B died. When living together, however, the mouse and plant seemed to thrive. Plants and animals need each other—but why?

Figure 1

Priestley's experiment showed that plants and animals help each other.

Photosynthesis

Plants convert light energy into chemical energy (food). However, the conversion is not a single-step process (see **Figure 2**). During the first part of the reaction, light energy is absorbed by chlorophyll in the plant's leaves. The light energy is used to split water molecules into hydrogen and oxygen. The oxygen is released into the atmosphere.

water + light energy → hydrogen + oxygen

During the second phase, carbon dioxide from the air is combined with the hydrogen that was removed from water molecules. The product is glucose, a sugar.

hydrogen + carbon dioxide → glucose

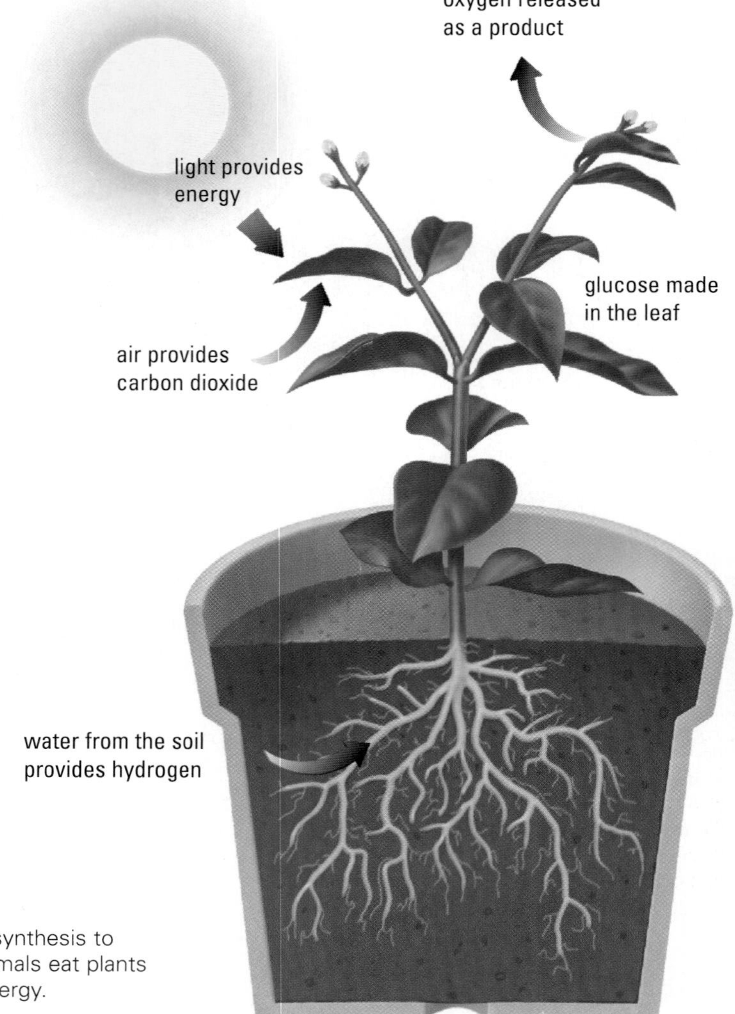

Figure 2

Plants use photosynthesis to store energy. Animals eat plants for that stored energy.

Respiration

You need energy to move. Your heart needs energy to pump blood through your body. You need energy to make new molecules for growth and to fight off disease. You need energy to breathe and to think. There is no time of the day that you don't need energy.

Your body gets its energy from food molecules, such as the sugar glucose. In your cells, oxygen is used to break down sugar molecules and release energy. This process is known as respiration. As sugar is broken down, carbon dioxide and water are released.

sugar + oxygen → carbon dioxide + water

Both plants and animals use respiration to release energy (see **Figure 3**).

Figure 3

Plants also respire. During the day, photosynthesis is working faster in plants, so they release much more oxygen than they do carbon dioxide. At night, just like animals, plants use up oxygen and release carbon dioxide as they break down sugar for energy.

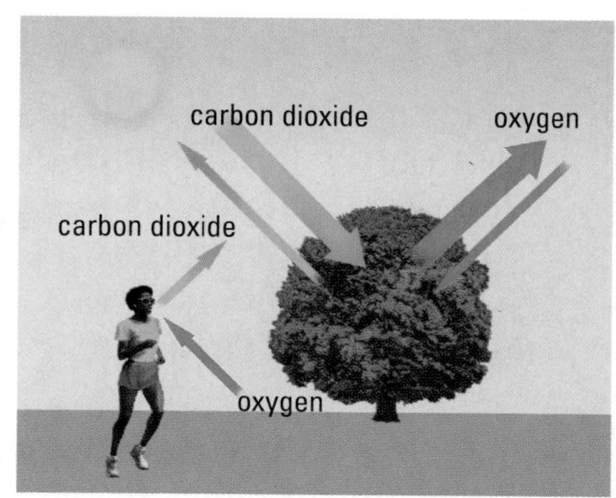

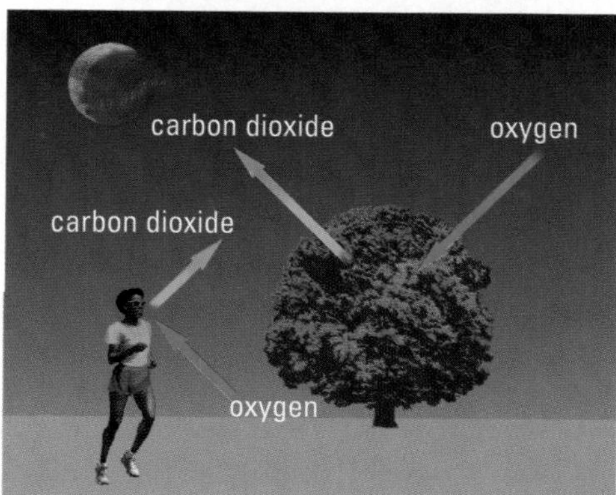

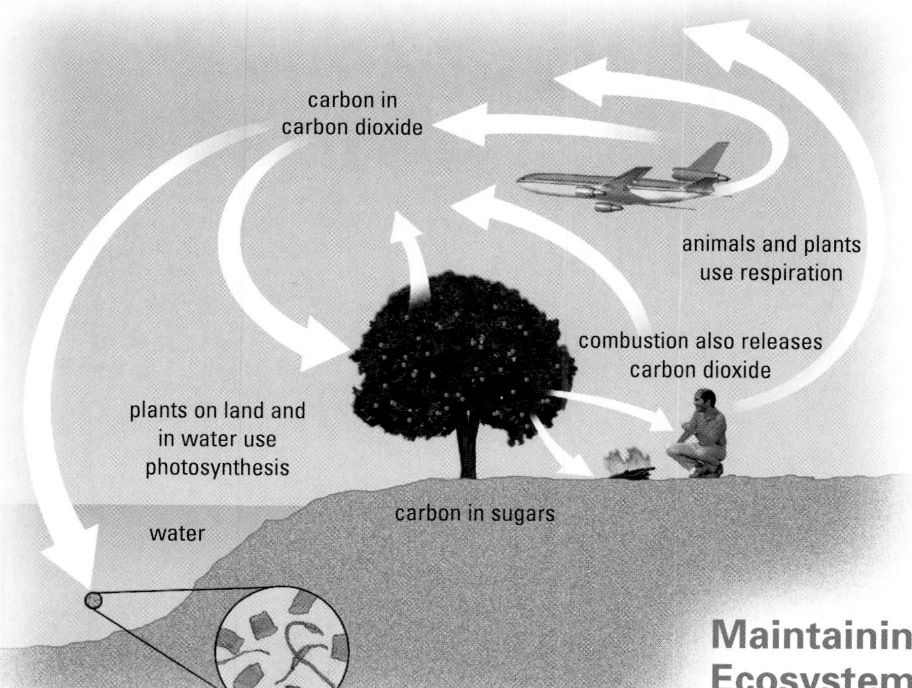

Figure 4

The carbon cycle. Carbon in carbon dioxide from the atmosphere is used to make sugars. The sugars are used by plants and animals for energy. The carbon from the broken-down sugars is then released to the atmosphere as carbon dioxide.

Maintaining a Balance in Ecosystems

In nature a balance of oxygen and carbon dioxide is maintained. The plants provide oxygen and sugars for the ecosystem, while animals provide carbon dioxide and water for the ecosystem. The processes of photosynthesis and respiration support one another. The flow of carbon through photosynthesis and respiration is called the **carbon cycle**, as shown in **Figure 4**.

The Greenhouse Effect

Have you ever noticed how warm it can be inside your car when the sun is shining, even on cool days? The heating is caused by the greenhouse effect (see **Figure 5**).

Figure 5

Greenhouses depend on a special property of glass. Glass allows radiant energy (light) from the Sun to pass through, but not the radiation emitted by warm objects.

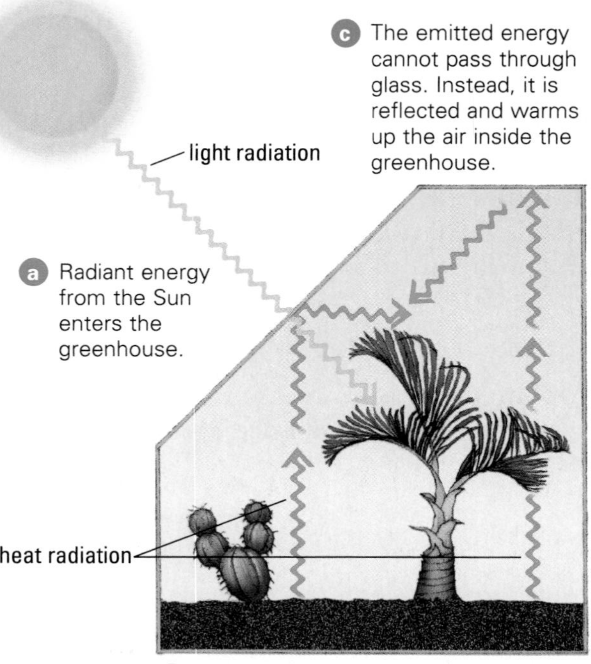

c The emitted energy cannot pass through glass. Instead, it is reflected and warms up the air inside the greenhouse.
light radiation
a Radiant energy from the Sun enters the greenhouse.
heat radiation
b The soil and plants absorb much of this energy, which warms them, and then emit radiant energy in a different form.

Global Warming

Many of the atmospheric gases that surround the Earth work like glass in a greenhouse. These greenhouse gases act like a blanket, trapping the heat from the Sun, and warming the Earth's surface. Greenhouse gases are essential for life. Without greenhouse gases the average temperature of the planet would fall from 15°C to –18°C.

In our industrialized world, vehicles, homes, and factories churn out carbon dioxide as we burn fossil fuels such as coal, oil, and natural gas (see **Figure 6**). It's estimated that the amount of carbon dioxide generated over the past 40 years has tripled because of the burning of wood and fossil fuels. Global temperatures have increased by 1°C over that same time. The rising levels of carbon dioxide, one of the main greenhouse gases, has changed the balance between photosynthesis and respiration. The increasing levels of carbon dioxide are altering the world's climate. It's getting warmer.

Try This: Greenhouse Simulation (6B) (7E)

You can simulate the greenhouse effect (see **Figure 7**).

- Put an identical ice cube in each of two plastic bags.
- Put one of the bags inside a large, inverted glass jar, with a small thermometer to measure temperature.
- Put the bag in the jar and the other bag in a sunny place.
- Use a graduated cylinder to measure the amount of melting in each bag after 10 min.
- Use thermometers to record the temperatures in each situation over the 10 min.

1. What do you conclude, based on your measurements?

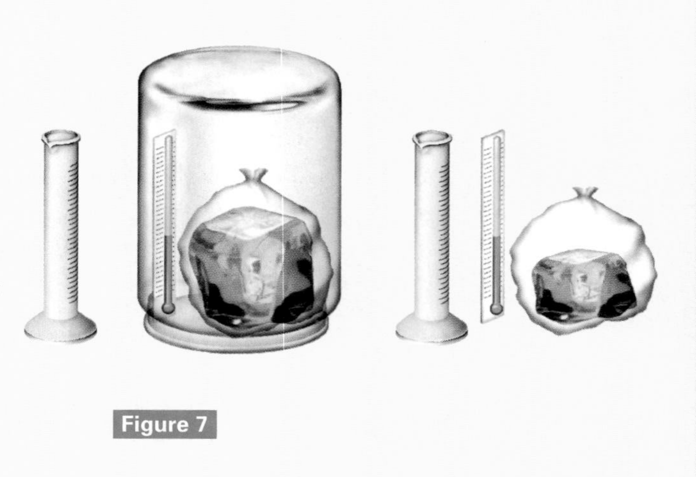

Figure 7

SKILLS HANDBOOK: (6B) Obtaining Quantitative Data (7E) Reaching a Conclusion

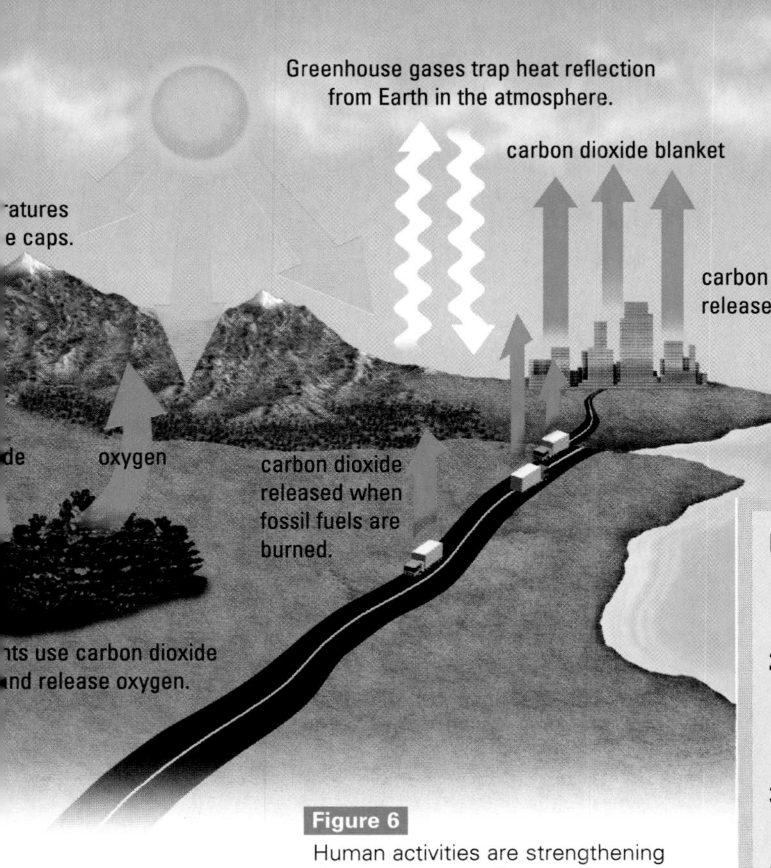

Figure 6
Human activities are strengthening the greenhouse effect.

A Warmer Climate

More warmth is appealing for most Canadians. However, higher temperatures have their drawbacks. In Canada's Arctic, ecosystems would change radically as the layer of ground that normally remains permanently frozen thawed. Snow caps and glaciers on mountains would melt and rivers would overflow, causing disruption in ecosystems and flooding in many of our southern cities.

The melting snow and ice would also raise the level of our oceans, causing drastic changes in what we now call our coasts. Port cities like Halifax and Vancouver might find much of their most expensive real estate under water.

Design Challenge

How might incineration of garbage affect the carbon cycle? In what other ways might garbage affect the carbon cycle?

Understanding Concepts

1. What is the source of energy for photosynthesis?
2. Create a chart comparing the processes of respiration and photosynthesis. Include raw materials, products, and the organisms that use the process.
3. Describe the voyage of a carbon atom as it goes through the carbon cycle.
4. In your own words, describe the greenhouse effect.
5. List two things that increase carbon dioxide levels in the atmosphere.

Making Connections

6. More than 200 years ago the Earth's atmosphere contained about 280 parts per million (ppm) of carbon dioxide. By 1993, the burning of fossil fuels had raised the level to 355 ppm. Carbon dioxide could reach 700 ppm by 2050.
   - **(a)** Draw a graph showing the increased levels of carbon dioxide in the atmosphere.
   - **(b)** Make some suggestions on how carbon dioxide levels could be lowered.

Exploring

7. Many factors affect the balance of oxygen and carbon dioxide. Research one of the (4A) factors below and create a display that (8C) explains the problem.
   - A. Deforestation means less oxygen is available.
   - B. Agricultural land is being used for housing, new factories, and landfill sites.
   - C. Increased combustion because of automobiles is increasing the amount of carbon dioxide in the atmosphere.

(4A) Research Skills (8C) Multimedia Presentations

Solutions for Global Warming

In 1997, the United Nations held a meeting on the environment in Kyoto, Japan. The hot topic was climate change due to greenhouse gases. Participating countries, including Canada, made concrete commitments to cut carbon dioxide emissions. Now opposition within Canada is mounting, saying the commitments are too difficult to achieve.

(a) What groups in Canada might not favour reducing carbon dioxide emissions?

(b) Give at least one concern each of these groups might have.

Fossil Fuels and Carbon Dioxide

Combustion (burning) is a rapid chemical reaction in which a fuel reacts with oxygen to produce heat and light. The burning of fossil fuels, such as gasoline and natural gas, releases carbon dioxide and water. As we burn more fossil fuels, the level of carbon dioxide in Earth's atmosphere has increased from 280 parts per million (ppm) 200 years ago to 355 ppm in 1993. Scientists project the level of carbon dioxide could reach 700 ppm by 2050.

(c) List at least three technologies that burn fossil fuels.

(d) How are scientists able to make projections about the levels of carbon dioxide 50 years from now?

Voices of Caution

Not every scientist accepts that higher carbon dioxide levels and global warming are unnatural. Evidence from fossils and other sources suggests that global temperatures and carbon dioxide levels have gone up and down many times in the past. For example, about 135 million years ago, long before there were any human beings, the level of carbon dioxide in the atmosphere exceeded 1000 ppm. That level is much higher than the present level.

Figure 1
Spreading sun block

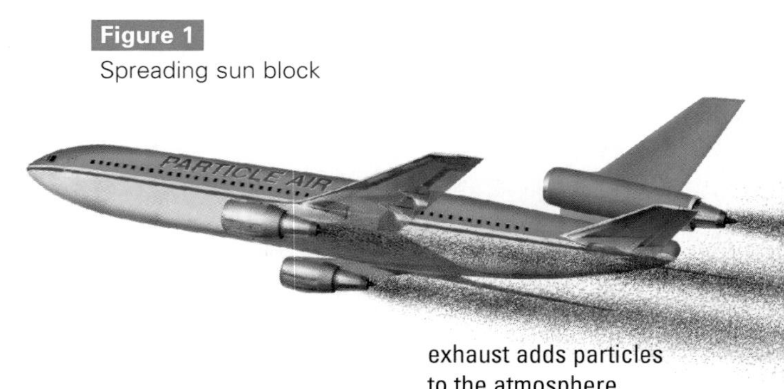

(e) Previous episodes of global warming were not caused by humans. Should we be concerned about global warming that is caused by humans? Explain your answer.

Finding a Solution

Scientists often use mini-ecosystems and computer models to test hypotheses. They are using them now to test technological solutions to global warming. Presented below are three possibilities. No plan is without its problems. You will be asked to consider the consequences of each technological fix.

Use Sun Block

The eruption of Mexico's Mount Pinatubo in 1991 shot a plume of ash and debris 20 000 m into the atmosphere. The ash spread around the Earth. Climatologists estimate that the blanket cooled the globe on average about 0.7°C, at least in tropical areas.

Could we deliberately add particles to the atmosphere? Running jet engines on richer mixtures of fuel would add particles to the atmosphere (see **Figure 1**). Burning coal adds soot to the air. Creating either kind of sunscreen would be cheap.

(f) Why would ash and particles in the atmosphere cool the Earth?

(g) What are some possible problems with this solution?

Add Iron to Sea Water

For many years naturalists have observed that some areas of the open ocean are rich in life, while other areas are barren. They discovered the iron content of the water makes the difference. In an experiment in 1995 (see **Figure 2**), a patch of ocean off the coast of South America was fertilized with half a tonne of iron. The iron caused a massive bloom of tiny marine plants, where previously only a small number had existed.

(h) How would more marine plants lower global temperatures?

(i) What negative effects might you expect from wide-scale fertilizing of the ocean? How would more marine plants affect local ecosystems?

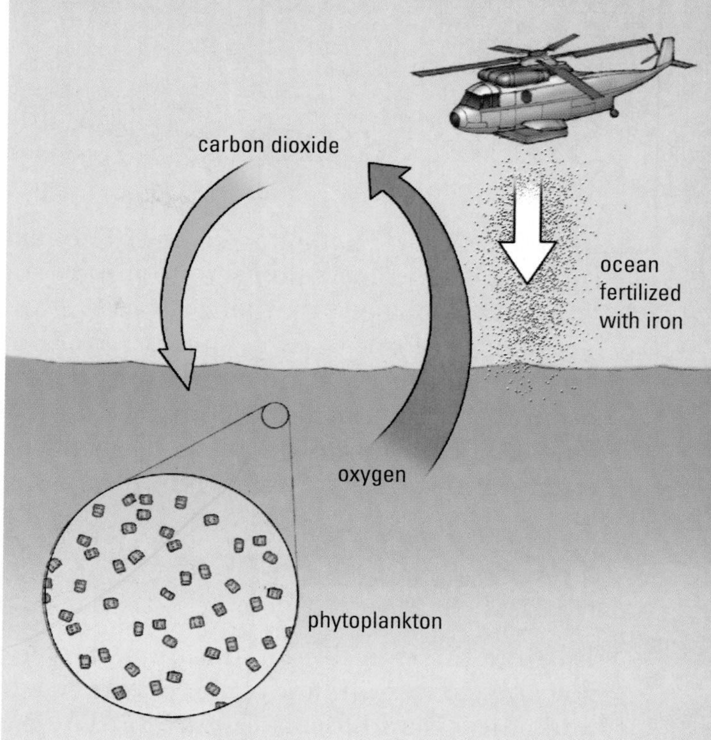

Figure 2

Fertilizing ocean water with iron might result in more photosynthesis.

Bury Carbon Dioxide

An oil company in Norway came up with a revolutionary way of getting rid of carbon dioxide. Normally, carbon dioxide created during the processing of natural gas is released into the air. In 1991 a new Norwegian tax on releasing carbon dioxide made this an expensive procedure. Norwegian oil and gas companies had to find alternatives. Pumping waste carbon dioxide into shale was one of them (see **Figure 3**).

The floor of the North Sea contains a layer of shale. It is ideal for the storage of carbon dioxide. Theoretically, it could soak up all of the excess carbon dioxide produced by countries of the European Union. One of the dangers of this process is that the carbon dioxide could combine with water to form a weak acid around the pipes.

(j) Why would it be dangerous if a weak acid formed around the pipes?

Figure 3

A Norwegian process pumps waste carbon dioxide into a layer of shale under the North Sea. Carbon dioxide moves very slowly through shale, and could stay trapped there for hundreds of years.

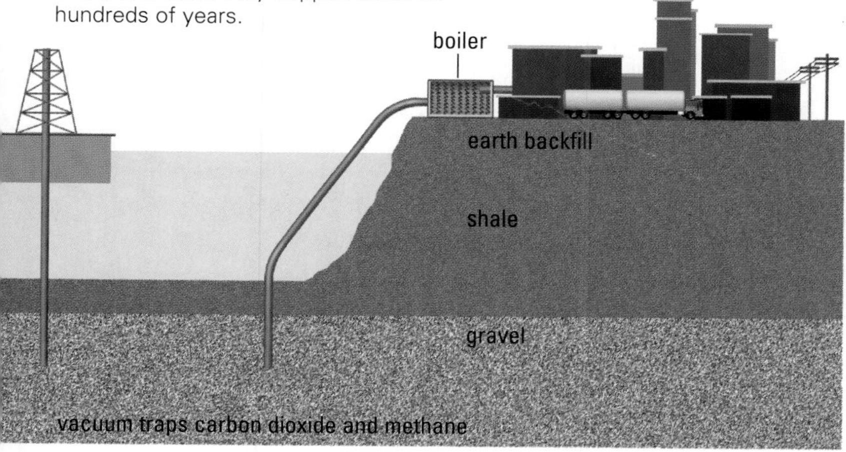

Making Connections

1. What type of things could be done around the home to reduce carbon dioxide emissions?
2. Car pools and increased use of public transportation would reduce fossil fuel usage. Make a list of benefits and problems if people were forced to car pool or use buses.

Reflecting

3. A "carbon tax" has been proposed. Anyone who bought a gas-guzzling car, van, or truck would pay the tax. Sport utility vehicles and cars with big engines would fall into this category. Make a list of advantages and disadvantages of such a tax. What solutions do you have for reducing carbon dioxide emissions from automobiles?

5.20 Case Study

Succession

Ecosystems can change over time. The process is referred to as succession. In **succession** the dominant species within an ecosystem are gradually replaced by others.

There are two types of succession. **Primary succession** occurs in an area where there was no community before. **Secondary succession** occurs after the partial or complete destruction of a community. The damaged community is replaced by another or by a series of other communities until a stable community is re-established.

Figure 1
A new volcanic island

Primary Succession: A New Island

Imagine the eruption of an underwater volcano. Lava spills above the ocean's surface and a new island forms (**Figure 1**). The new island starts off as bare rock, but a dynamic ecosystem will soon develop.

(a) Why wouldn't you expect to find animals on the new island?

The First Green

Within a short time the island begins to turn green. Lichens appear first (**Figure 2**). Because they are the first organisms to appear in such situations, lichens are called **pioneer species**.

Lichens contain two different organisms: algae and fungi. The algae have chlorophyll and are capable of photosynthesis. They make the food the lichen needs. The fungi have threadlike filaments that absorb water well. The filaments also secure the lichen to the rock.

(b) Why are lichens able to grow on barren rock?

Figure 2
Lichens are made of algae and fungi working together. The algae provide food; the fungi provide water.

Soil and Moss

Lichens begin the process of breaking down rock to make soil. Also, as they grow, die, and decompose, they create some small scraps of soil in crannies in the rock. That tiny amount of soil is enough for moss. It takes over wherever the soil is created (see **Figure 3**).

Mosses produce more food and store more water than lichens, making the ecosystem richer. As they die, the soil becomes thicker. Eventually, there is enough soil for small grasses and weeds to grow.

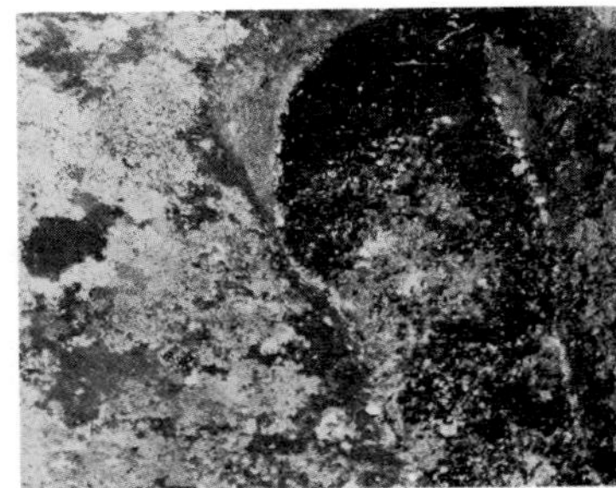

Figure 3
Mosses can absorb more water than lichens.

(c) Speculate about why moss communities would succeed lichen communities.

(d) Often marine birds stop to rest or even nest on new islands (see **Figure 4**). Because there are no predatory animals, they feel safe. How might birds stopping on the island affect succession?

Figure 4
Marine birds may have mud on their feet from previous stops. What might be in the mud?

More Plants Arrive

Most plants can grow higher than lichens and mosses. Tall plants put short plants in the shade and limit the amount of sunlight they can receive. The more soil there is, the taller plants can grow. And more soil is constantly being created as weathering breaks down rocks and as each generation of plants dies and decomposes. Eventually, the island will have enough soil to support shrubs, and then trees. This final community, called the **climax community**, remains unchanged for many years.

(e) What advantages do plants such as dandelions and crabgrass have over mosses and lichens?

Birds and Succession

As vegetation changes, the animals living in the area also change (see **Figure 5**). In addition to marine birds, the island will first host small, well-camouflaged birds, such as the grasshopper sparrow, that nest on the ground. These birds feed on grass seeds and the insects that feed on the grasses.

Each plant is eaten by different species of insects. As grass and weeds are replaced by shrubs, insects that eat grasses are replaced by insects that live on the leaves of shrubs.

The birds of the island will change as the new kinds of food become available. The original sparrows are gradually replaced by birds like the towhee that are adapted to life among shrubs and trees.

As the amount of vegetation increases, the island can support more animals, including predators such as hawks and falcons.

(f) Birds often first arrive on islands by accident, carried there by storms. What might happen to the first pair of vireos that arrived on the island 10 years after succession had begun? What might happen to a pair that arrived 40 years after?

(g) Why would a forest support more species of birds than a grassland community?

Figure 5
As the vegetation changes, the animals in the community also change.

Secondary Succession: Forest Fires

Nothing looks so devastating as the destruction of a mature forest by a fire. All that remains is a blackened landscape with a few solitary trunks pointing brokenly skyward. But in nature, nothing is final. Within a few months the ground slowly turns green. Animals move back into the area, and the forest community begins to recover.

Years later the new forest will be more vital than a neighbouring forest that escaped the fire. The pattern of rejuvenation by fire, shown in **Figure 6**, is part of the natural cycle of forest ecosystems.

(h) Speculate on why a fire might be more likely in a mature forest.

(i) Which plants act as pioneers following a forest fire?

(j) Why do grasses and weeds appear before trees and shrubs?

(k) Speculate about why grouse don't appear until conifers begin to grow.

Figure 6

Secondary succession as a result of a forest fire

(a) Stage 1: mature forest

(b) Stage 2: destruction

(c) Stage 3: pioneer species move in

(d) Stage 4: the forest returns

(e) Stage 5: a young forest

Figure 7
Secondary succession in a pond

ⓐ Stage 1

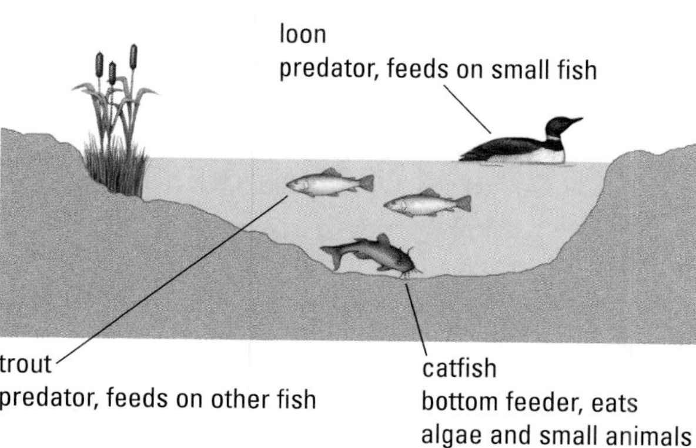

ⓑ Stage 2

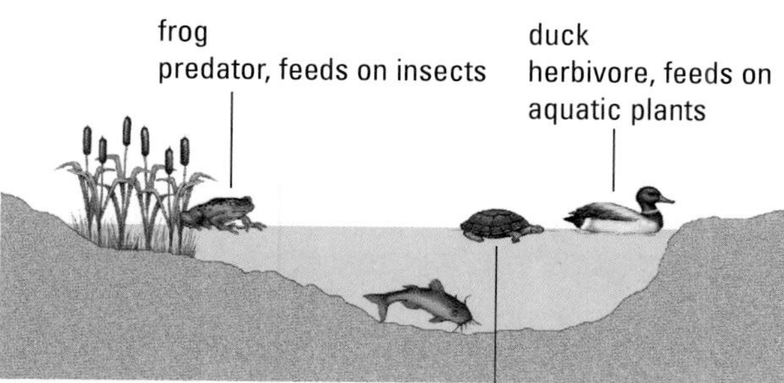

ⓒ Stage 3

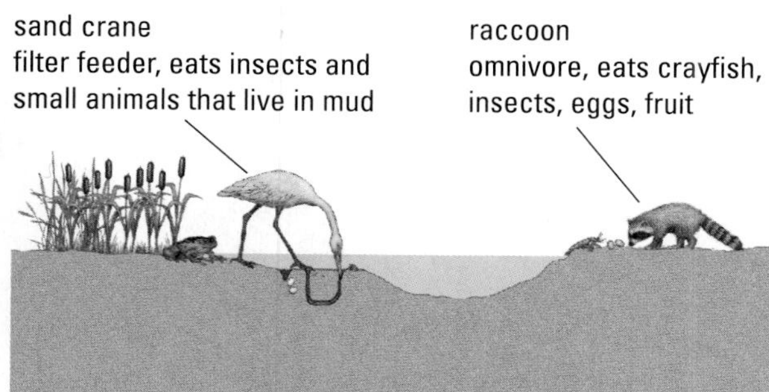

Secondary Succession: A Pond

Secondary succession is often a very slow process. **Figure 7** shows changes in a pond over many years.

(l) What happens to the depth of the pond over time? Explain how this might happen.

(m) Explain how the change in pond temperature is related to the depth of the pond.

(n) How does the change in temperature affect the type and number of plants found in the pond?

(o) Describe changes in the type and number of fish found in the pond through the three stages.

(p) Speculate as to why the trout seem to disappear after stage 1.

(q) Why might turtles be found in stage 2, but not in stage 1?

(r) Speculate about why loons are replaced by ducks.

Understanding Concepts

1. Define succession.

2. What is a pioneer species?

3. Indicate whether each item below is an example of primary or secondary succession. Give your reasons for each choice.

(a) Lichen grows on barren rock in the tundra.

(b) A farm field left untended becomes a forest.

(c) As a glacier retreats, plants grow in the areas it leaves.

(d) A dam is constructed and a forest changes into a lake.

Making Connections

4. Draw a climax community for a pond and explain why it is a climax community.

5. Hypothesize about why trout are found only in cold waters.

6. Describe succession in an abandoned lot in a city, using a series of diagrams. (6C)

Design Challenge

Speculate about the environmental impact of your Challenge. How could things be changed?

SKILLS HANDBOOK: (6C) Scientific & Technical Drawing

Logging Old Growth Forest

Forests are important resources. Forests regulate climate by recycling water and carbon dioxide. On hot days a large tree may absorb 5.5 tonnes of water from the soil and release it into the atmosphere. Between 40% and 50% of the water above a temperate rainforest comes from the trees.

In addition, forests affect the physical environment of ecosystems. The forest acts as a giant sponge, slowing runoff and holding groundwater. The root systems also hold the soil, preventing erosion and reducing the amount of sediment that washes into streams.

Forests are shelters for wildlife. The trees, both living and dead, provide nesting sites and food for many different animals.

According to one estimate, a typical tree provides $196 250 in long-term ecological value, compared with about $590 as timber.

Forests are also in decline, as **Figure 1** shows.

Figure 1

Old-growth forest in North America in 1600 and in 1998. Before the industrial revolution there were approximately 6 billion hectares of forest on Earth. Today about 4 billion hectares remain. Canada has 436 000 000 ha of forest, about 40% of the world's northern forests.

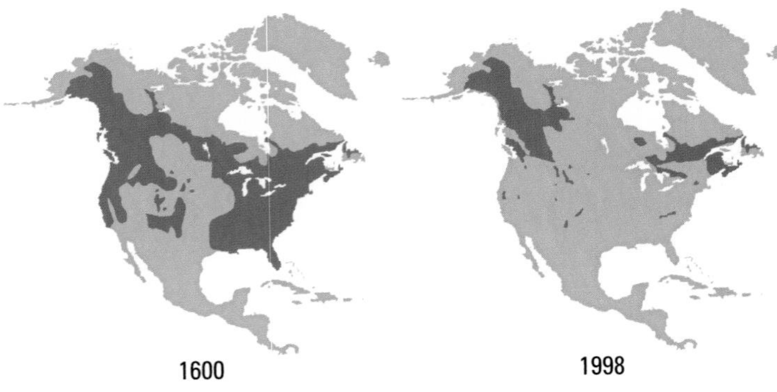

Forestry Practices

Deforestation caused by humans falls under three categories, as shown in **Figure 2**.

Figure 2

Three forms of human deforestation

a Slash-and-burn All vegetation is piled and ignited in a controlled burn to provide soil nutrients for future crops. Commonly used in tropical areas.

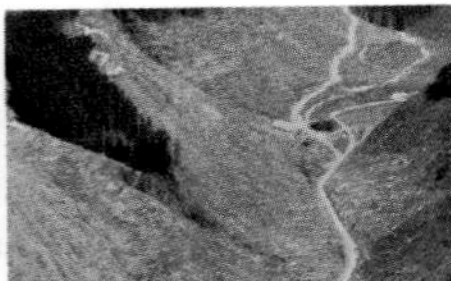

b Clear-cutting All trees are removed for use in timber or pulp. In Canada, this approach is followed by replanting the dominant species.

c Selective cuttir Only valuable trees are harvested from an area; the others are left untouched.

Table 1: Benefits and Costs of Clear-Cutting

Benefits	Costs
Reduced cost Clear-cutting is less expensive than selective cutting. The timber or pulp from a clear-cut will be cheaper for purchasers.	**More erosion** There is more soil erosion and runoff into local streams from clear-cut land.
Fewer injuries for forestry workers If a site has many pests (biting and stinging insects, crustaceans, and animals), clear-cutting reduces the hazard by eliminating places where the dangerous animals can live.	**Water loss** The removal of vegetation on the ground exposes dark soils and increases the warming of the area. In turn, this increases water loss from the soil.
Efficiency Clear-cutting permits the logging company to replant only with valuable trees that it can cut again later with less waste.	**Loss of biodiversity** Replanting with a single kind of tree decreases biodiversity within the ecosystem.
Some living things benefit As happens after a forest fire, clear-cut areas undergo some succession. Some wildlife, such as moose, benefit from clear-cuts. Low-lying vegetation, such as berries, provide them with a stable food source.	**Destruction of ecological niches** Nesting sites are destroyed, food webs are reduced. Selective logging leaves much of the forest unharmed.

Effects of a Clear Cut

It takes as much as 350 years for a forest to become an old-growth forest. Because the old trees create many ecological niches for other living things, old-growth forest ecosystems tend to have complicated food webs. They act as reserves for a tremendous diversity of wildlife. This diversity, called **biodiversity**, allows these old ecosystems to be flexible. Small amounts of damage are easily repaired. Undisturbed old-growth forests also contain an enormous number of fallen trees that slowly decompose, providing a constant source of nutrients for the soil.

By comparison, forests that have been replanted after a clear-cut have a few dominant species in what ecologists describe as a farm, not a natural ecosystem. Because there are fewer kinds of trees, there are fewer sources of food, and fewer niches for living things. The biodiversity of a farm forest is much lower. Forests that contain a single dominant species of tree are also more susceptible to disease. Because the old wood was cleared out during the logging, there are fewer nutrients available for new growth. **Table 1** summarizes the costs and benefits of clear-cutting.

After a Clear Cut

Softwoods, such as spruce and fir, are used for pulp and paper and are often considered more valuable than hardwoods, which grow much more slowly. As a result, clear-cut areas are usually planted with softwoods, as shown in **Figure 3**.

Figure 3

After a forest has been clear cut, it is planted with small trees. These trees will grow and can be harvested again decades later.

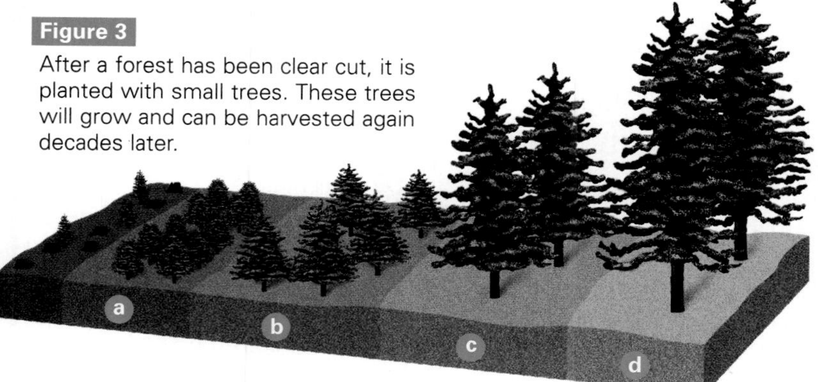

(a) 2 or 3 years: herbicides are used to prevent crowding of the more valuable softwood trees by hardwood trees.

(b) 10 years: the underbrush is removed.

(c) 35 years: the trees are checked for diseases and pests, such as the spruce budworm.

(d) 50 to 60 years: the softwood trees are large enough to harvest.

Understanding the Concepts

1. Why are forests important?
2. What are three methods used for deforestation?
3. Using your own words, explain biodiversity.
4. Identify some of the differences of forests that are replanted and have a single species of trees compared with old-growth forests that develop through the natural process of succession.

Making Connections

5. In 1929 the Pulp and Paper Act of Ontario established the principle of maintaining a sustained yield. Trees that were cut had to be replaced by replanting. Why did ecologists insist the trees be replanted? What might have happened if the trees were not replanted?
6. Compare succession in a pine forest that has been clear-cut with one that has undergone a fire.
7. (4A) The spotted owl, which lives in old-growth forest on the west coast, is one of Canada's animals threatened with extinction. Draw a map of Canada and show areas in which different plants and animals are threatened with extinction because of changing environments.
8. (4A) (6C) Forestry is big business in Canada. It accounts for billions of dollars in exports and employs thousands of people. Draw a map of Canada, showing the location of other important plants in our economy.
9. Explain how sustainable forestry practices can benefit the environment and the economy.

SKILLS HANDBOOK: (4A) Research Skills (6C) Scientific & Technical Drawing

Design Challenge

SKILLS MENU
- Identify a Problem
- Planning
- Building
- Testing
- Recording
- Evaluating
- Communicating

Design and Build a Solution to the Landfill Problem

Figure 3
Does this site encourage breakdown of materials and prevent leaks? Can you do better?

Throwing away garbage is getting more and more difficult. As we learn more about ecosystems, we discover more of the problems involved in dumping garbage. To protect ecosystems from the disruption and chemicals caused by dumped garbage, we must build our landfill sites with the future in mind. Taking care with waste costs money. Throwing away garbage used to be cheap and easy; now it is expensive and difficult. But we aren't producing less garbage, we're producing more. The need for new landfill sites is not declining. You will work on a solution to this problem.

1 A Device or a Plan to Reduce the Volume of Waste

Problem Situation

Toothpaste tubes come in a box. We take out the tube and throw away the box. An incredible 30% of the garbage that goes to landfills is packaging. And what about the other 70%—does it all have to end up in landfill sites? Does it have to take up so much space and cause so much damage to ecosystems?

Design Brief

- Create a device or a strategy that will help reduce the volume of garbage that goes from your home to landfills.

Design Criteria

- If you design a device, it must be cheap to make and maintain, reliable, easy to use, and easy to store.
- If you develop a strategy, you must include information on the difficulty of following your plan. Could it be used in both summer and winter? How much time and effort would it take to implement your plan? Will there be additional costs?

Figure 1
In Germany, tubes of toothpaste have no boxes. Each tube indicates that it meets the world's most stringent packaging laws.

2 A Biodegradable Container or Packaging Material

Problem Situation

We are filling our landfill sites with materials that do not break down, or break down very slowly. Plastic bags. Polystyrene packaging material. If they don't break down, they stay in the landfill site. Can we reduce the amounts of these materials we use?

Design Brief

- Design and create a new container or packaging material for a common product that is usually wrapped in plastic or packed in polystyrene.

Design Criteria

- The container or packaging must break down quickly in a landfill site.
- You must provide information showing that your container or packaging material is easy to use, and works well.

Figure 2
Plastic bags and polystyrene do not bre down in landfill sites.

3 A Model Landfill Site

Problem Situation

No one wants to live next to a landfill site. The smell of rotting food and the ugliness are two of the most obvious reasons. People living near landfill sites are also concerned about the possibility of dumped chemicals entering the air or their drinking water.

Design Brief

- Design and build a model landfill site capable of recycling throwaway household garbage.

Design Criteria

- You must show how your design will encourage the growth of the bacteria and fungi that decompose waste.
- You must show how your design will prevent toxic chemicals from leaving your site and entering the ground water or atmosphere.

Assessment

Your model will be assessed according to how well you:

Process

- understand the problem
- develop a safe plan
- choose and safely use appropriate materials, tools, and equipment
- test and record results
- evaluate the sustainability of your model, including the environmental, economic, and social implications, along with suggestions for improvement

Communicate

- use correct terms
- write clear descriptions of the steps you took in building and testing your model
- explain clearly how your model solves the problem
- make an accurate technical drawing for your model

Produce

- meet the design criteria with your model
- use your chosen materials effectively
- construct your model
- solve the identified problem

When preparing to build or test a design, have your plan approved by your teacher before you begin.

Unit 5 Summary

In this unit you have learned that living things and abiotic factors interact to form ecosystems, and that human technology affects those ecosystems.

Reflecting

- Reflect on the ideas and questions presented in the Unit Overview and in the Getting Started. How can you connect what you have done and learned in this unit with those ideas and questions? (To review, check the sections indicated in this Summary.)
- Revise your answers to the Reflecting questions in ❶, ❷, ❸ and the questions you created in the Getting Started. How has your thinking changed?
- What new questions do you have? How will you answer them?

Understanding Concepts

- identify populations of organisms in communities and ecosystems 5.1, 5.2
- recognize that ecosystems include living things and the abiotic factors of the environment 5.2
- identify adaptations that help organisms survive in their ecosystem 5.3

- identify producers and consumers in food chains and food webs and explain how matter cycles through chains and webs 5.6, 5.10
- explain how decomposers recycle nutrients within ecosystems 5.5
- explain the roles that living things have in their ecosystems, including the microbes that cause disease 5.7
- analyze how matter and energy are transferred from producers to consumers in ecosystems 5.10, 5.11
- evaluate the effect of pesticides on food webs 5.11
- describe how water and carbon cycle through the biosphere and ecosystems 5.12, 5.18
- identify succession as it occurs on a new island, after a forest fire, and in a pond ecosystem 5.20

Applying Skills

- investigate conditions that affect decomposition and analyze materials best suited for landfill 5.5
- record and analyze results of an investigation 5.4, 5.8, 5.17

Making Connections

- explain that plants producers are the source of energy in every food chain and food web 5.6, 5.10
- explain how decomposing matter is essential for plant growth 5.6, 5.7, 5.8
- identify and explain the benefits of recycling and analyze how products contribute to recycling 5.14
- investigate the impact of pesticide technology and analyze its effects on a food web 5.11
- investigate the effects and costs, including economic, social, health, and ecological, of landfill sites 5.1, 5.4, 5.5, 5.13, 5.15

- investigate soil nutrients and the effects of leaching 5.8
- design and conduct a controlled investigation to determine how abiotic changes affect a model ecosystem and communicate the results 5.17
- understand and use the following terms:

abiotic	ecosystem
acid rain	food chain
adaptation	food web
biodegradable	herbivore
biological	leaching
amplification	matter cycle
biome	nutrient
biosphere	organism
biotic	pesticide
carbon cycle	photosynthesis
carnivore	population
chlorophyll	primary succession
community	producer
consumer	recycle
decompose	respiration
decomposer	secondary
ecological niche	succession
ecological pyramid	succession
ecology	water cycle

- identify technologies that contribute to acid rain and explain the effects of acid rain 5.16
- explain how plants and animals depend on each other 5.18
- investigate the consequences of burning fossil fuels, and analyze some technological solutions to global warming 5.18, 5.19
- describe how forestry practices affect forest ecosystems 5.21

Unit 5 Review

Understanding Concepts

1. (a) Give examples of reducing, reusing, and recycling, and explain why each is important.
   (b) How can Canadian manufacturers change the way products are packaged?
2. Why are plants important for the survival of all living things?
3. (a) Name a greenhouse gas.
   (b) How do greenhouse gases affect the climate?
4. How do automobiles contribute to the greenhouse effect?
5. Describe changes that might occur after a landfill site is capped and returned to nature.
6. Pesticides are sprayed on a grain field to control mice. Why would a hawk have a greater concentration of pesticides in its body than a mouse?
7. (a) Identify at least two abiotic factors of the ecosystem shown in **Figure 1**.
   (b) Explain how one of those abiotic factors would affect one of the organisms.
8. Identify a producer and a consumer from the ecosystem in **Figure 1**.
9. Identify a decomposer in **Figure 1** and explain its role in the ecosystem.
10. Using organisms you can see in **Figure 1**, draw a food chain that includes at least three organisms and identify them as producers or consumers.
11. Using organisms from **Figure 1**, draw an ecological pyramid with at least three levels and include one organism at each level.

Figure 1

Figure 2

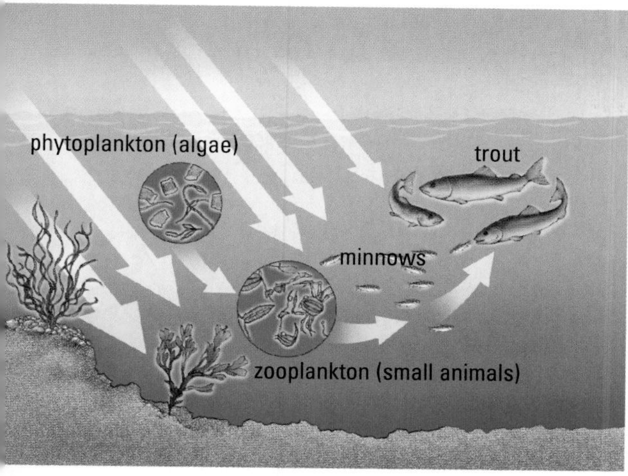

12. The primary source of energy for the ecosystem in **Figure 2** is
    (a) sunlight
    (b) zooplankton
    (c) phytoplankton
    (d) water and minerals

13. In **Figure 2** trout would be classified as
    (a) producers
    (b) consumers
    (c) decomposers
    (d) bottom feeders

14. Heavy metals accumulate in organisms, much like pesticides. If heavy metals were released into the pond in **Figure 2**, you would expect to find the highest concentration of the metals in the
    (a) trout
    (b) minnows
    (c) zooplankton
    (d) phytoplankton

15. (a) Describe succession after a forest fire in a climax forest.
    (b) Most deciduous trees are well adapted only to the warmer climate of southern Canada. What differences would you expect in succession in northern Ontario from southern Ontario?

Practising Skills

16. Based on the information in **Figure 3**, recycling which product conserves the greatest amount of energy?

17. Based on **Figure 3**, recycling which product will have the greatest effect on the carbon cycle? Give your reasons.

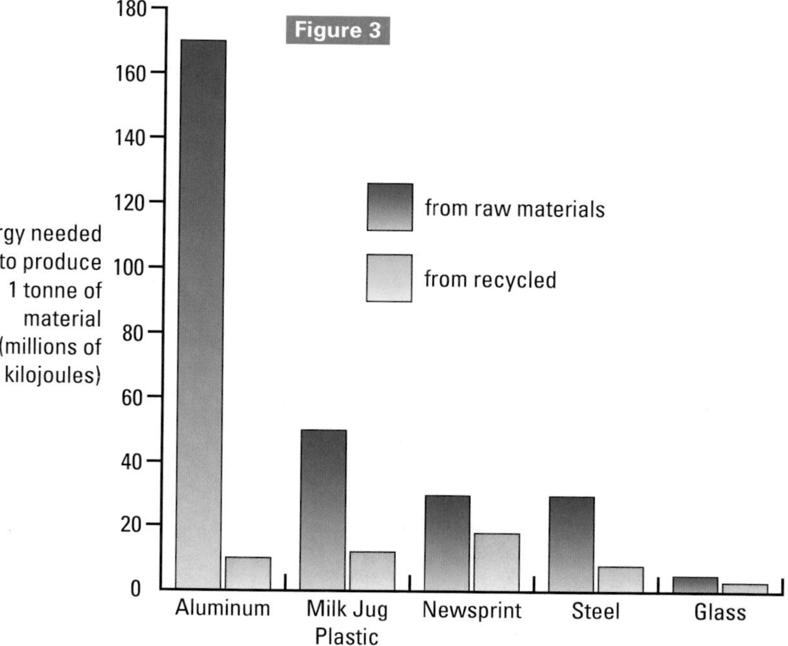

18. From information in **Figure 4**, which animal is most sensitive to acid rain?

19. Based on **Figure 4**, what is the lowest pH level at which lake trout are able to survive?

Figure 4

Organisms within a lake ecosystem are affected by acid rain. The + symbol indicates that the organism is still found in the lake when the water is that acidic.

	pH 6.5	6.0	5.5	5.0	4.5	4.0	3.5
Water boatman	+	+	+	+	+	+	+
Whirligig	+	+	+	+	+		
Yellow Perch	+	+	+	+	+		
Lake Trout	+	+	+	+	+		
Brown trout	+	+	+	+			
Salamander	+	+	+	+			
Mayfly	+	+	+				
Smallmouth bass	+	+	+				
Mussel	+	+					

Question:

How does acid rain affect the growth of germinating seeds?

Materials:

- various acidic solutions
- 4 petri dishes
- 40 seeds per group
- ruler

Design:

Germinating seeds are placed in petri dishes. Acid solutions of different pH solutions are added. The length of the seedling is measured daily.

Three groups submitted different proposals for the acid solutions:

Group 1	5 mL pH 2	10mL pH 6	15 mL pH 9	20 mL pH 12
Group 2	10 mL pH 2	10mL pH 2	10 mL pH 2	10 mL pH 2
Group 3	10 mL pH 2	10mL pH 6	10 mL pH 9	10 mL pH 12

Figure 5

A science class has designed an experiment to test the effect of pH on seed germination.

20. Write a hypothesis for the experiment in **Figure 5**.

21. Which group in **Figure 5** has provided the best procedure to test the hypothesis? Explain.

22. What are the independent and dependent variables in the experiment in **Figure 5**?

23. What question is being investigated in **Figure 6**?

24. What are the independent and dependent variables in **Figure 6**?

25. Would you expect the same results from the experiment in **Figure 6** if both plants were put in a dark cupboard? Explain.

Making Connections

26. A few billion years ago, Earth's atmosphere contained much less oxygen than it does now. Provide a hypothesis that explains why oxygen levels have increased from the early days of the planet.

27. A chemical that sterilizes soil destroys all the bacteria normally found in the soil. Predict what would happen if the sterilizing chemical were sprayed on a forest ecosystem. Explain.

Figure 6

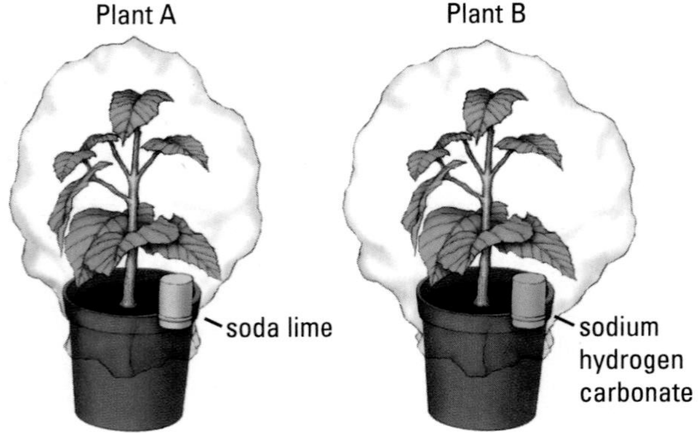

Design:

Two plants were sealed in plastic bags. Soda lime absorbs carbon dioxide. Sodium hydrogen carbonate releases carbon dioxide slowly.

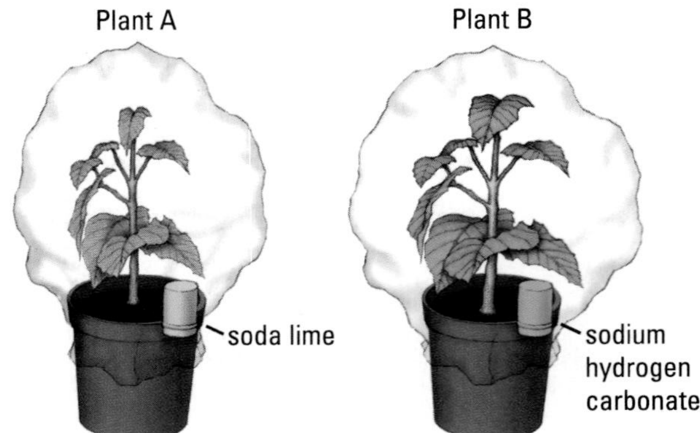

Results:

Plant B appeared green and healthy throughout the test. Plant A turned yellow and began to wilt.

28. What is the role of light in the process described in **Figure 7**?

29. Why is the waste carbon dioxide pumped back to the growth chamber in **Figure 7**?

30. How does recycling occur in **Figure 7**?

ure 7

ntists at the University of West England, in Bristol, nted a nonpolluting way of generating energy. An algae, ed *Chlorella*, is used to generate electricity.

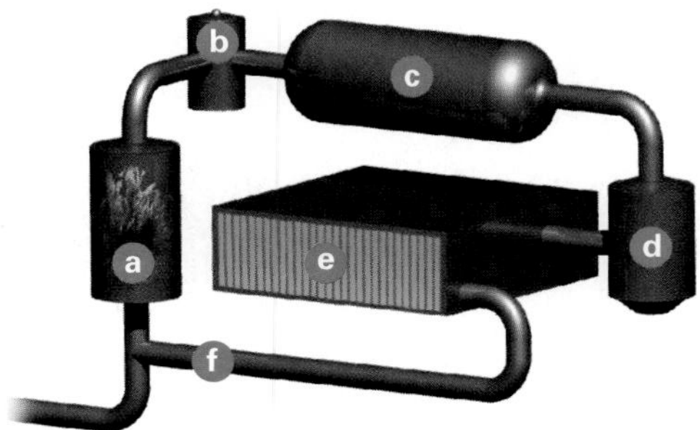

- (a) Algae are grown in a special chamber.
- (b) Water is separated from the algae by a filter.
- (c) The algae are dried using waste heat from the furnace.
- (d) The dry algae are made into a spray, which is pumped into the furnace.
- (e) The algae spray is burned to produce heat, which is converted into electricity using a boiler and turbine.
- (f) Waste carbon dioxide from the burning is directed back to the growth chamber.

31. Which matter cycle is presented in **Figure 8**?

32. What is the source of the acid in **Figure 8**?

33. In **Figure 8**, what is Process B?

34. What causes the tree in **Figure 8** to die?

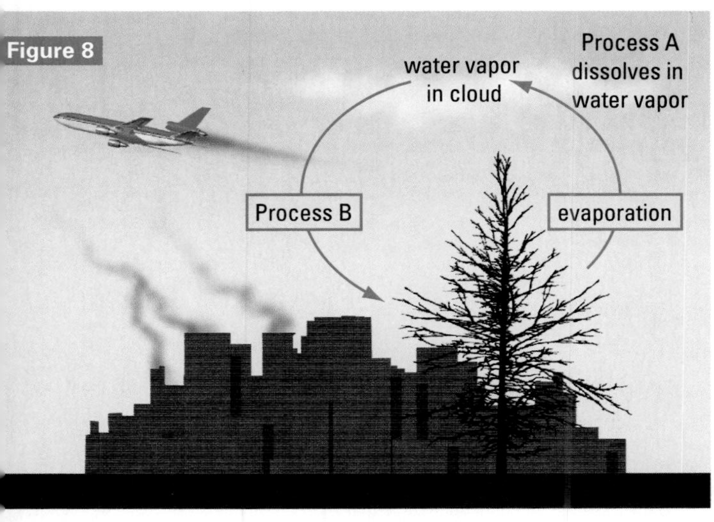

Figure 8

35. Copy **Table 1**. Using information in **Figure 9**, place a check mark (✓) in the correct box in your table.

Table 1

Description	respiration by soil microbes	respiration by rabbit	combustion by fire	photosynthesis by plant
uses oxygen	?	?	?	?
produces oxygen	?	?	?	?
requires sunlight energy	?	?	?	?
builds complex molecules	?	?	?	?

Figure 9

36. Copy **Figure 9** in your notebook and include the carbon cycle or the source of energy that drives the carbon cycle.

37. How could you increase the levels of oxygen in **Figure 9**?

38. In each of the following, which product would you consider most environmentally friendly? What are the economic and health implications? Give your reason.

(a) wrapping paper or gift bag

(b) all-in-one breakfast (individual cereal box and plastic milk container) or large cereal box with separate milk container

(c) juice in a plastic bottle or juice in a tetra box

(d) disposable batteries or rechargeable batteries

(e) paper plates or ceramic dinner plates

(f) cloth lunch bag or paper lunch bag

(g) packaging made of popcorn or packaging made of polystyrene

NARROW

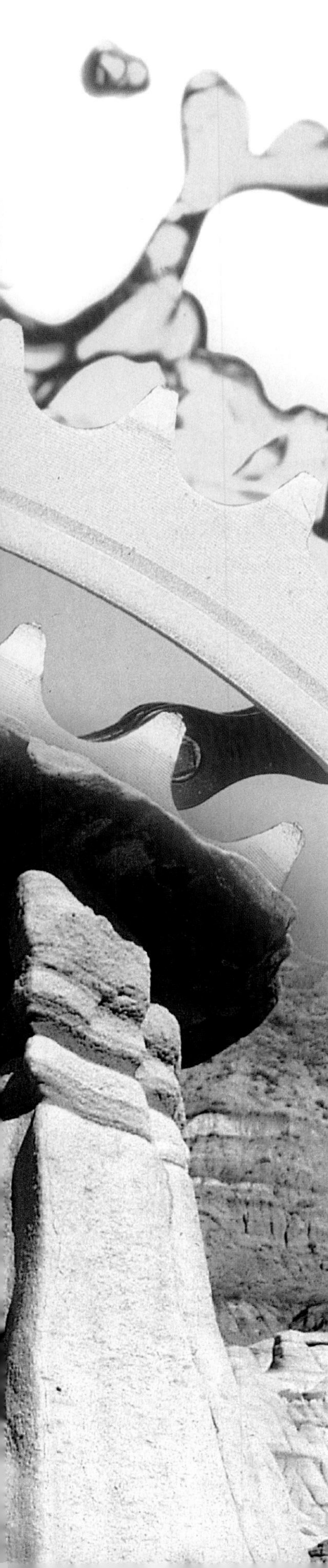

Skills Handbook

1 Safety in Science & Technology

Safety Conventions in *Nelson Science & Technology 7/8*

The investigations in *Nelson Science & Technology 7/8* are challenging, interesting, and safe. However, accidents can happen. In all of the investigations, potential hazards are identified by a caution symbol and described in red type (**Figure 1**).

Figure 1

Be careful when cutting. Always cut away from your body.

Always read the cautions carefully and make sure you understand what they mean before you proceed. If you are in doubt about anything, ask someone who knows (i.e., your teacher or a parent).

You should also look for caution symbols on the materials and products you use in your investigations. The symbols in **Figures 2 and 3** are often found on the labels of hazardous products.

Hazardous Household Product Symbols (HHPS)

You are probably familiar with the warning symbols in **Figure 2**. They appear on a number of products that are common in most households. These warning symbols indicate exactly why and to what degree a product is dangerous.

Workplace Hazardous Materials Information System (WHMIS) Symbols

The Workplace Hazardous Materials Information System (WHMIS) symbols in **Figure 3** were developed to standardize the labelling of dangerous materials used in all workplaces, including schools.

Preventing Accidents

Most accidents in the Science & Technology classroom are caused by carelessness. Following these general procedures can help you prevent them.

- Pay careful attention to instructions and take your work seriously.
- Be prepared for every investigation.

Figure 2

Hazardous Household Product Symbols (HHPS)

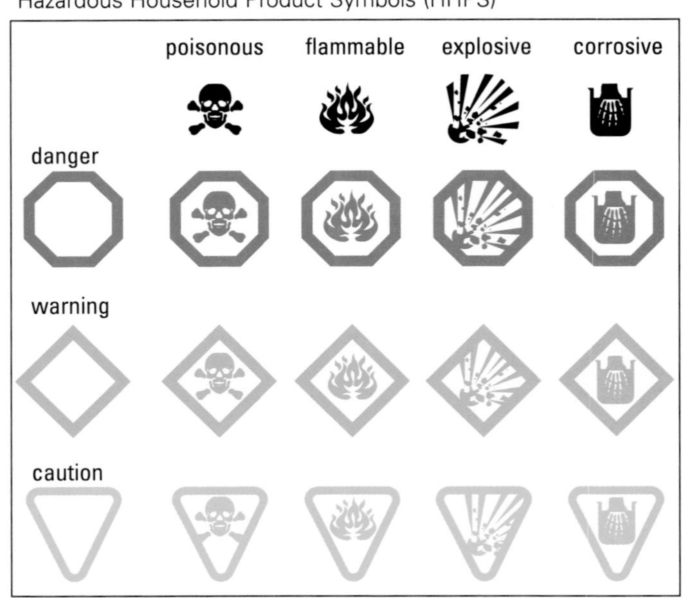

Figure 3

Workplace Hazardous Materials Information System (WHMIS) Symbols

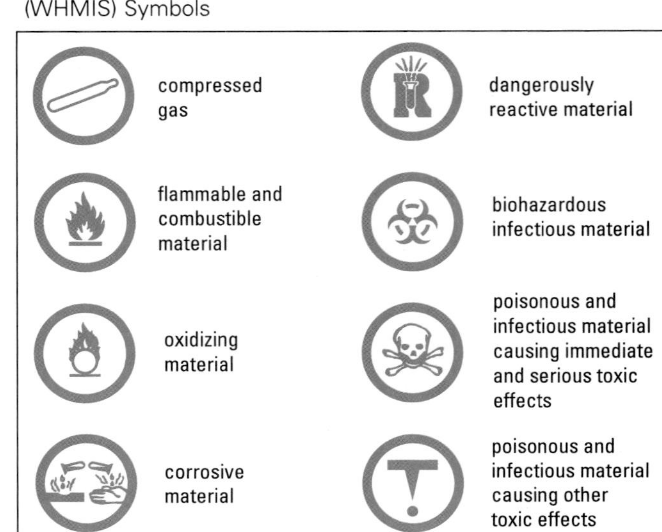

- Keep your working space clean and organized.
- Tie back long hair and don't wear loose clothing or jewellery.
- Measure and mix chemicals correctly.
- Handle hot equipment with care.
- Do not apply too much pressure to glass equipment (including microscope slides, cover slips, and thermometers).
- Use all tools, especially sharp tools, with proper care.
- Wear safety goggles.

Getting Off to a Safe Start

1. Learn the location and proper use of safety equipment, such as:
    - safety goggles
    - protective aprons
    - heat-resistant gloves
    - eye-wash station
    - broken-glass container
    - first-aid kit
    - fire extinguishers
    - fire blankets
    - water station

    Locate the nearest fire alarm.

    Know the procedures to follow in case an accident does occur.
2. Inform your teacher of any allergies or medical conditions that you may have. Do not wear contact lenses when conducting investigations—if a foreign substance became trapped beneath the lens, it would be difficult to remove it.
3. Read the procedure of any investigation carefully before you start. If there is anything you do not understand, ask your teacher to explain. Check all materials for warning labels. Make sure all tools and equipment are in good working condition and are properly secured. Clear your work area of all materials except those you will use in the investigation. If you are designing your own investigation, have your teacher check your design before you proceed.
4. Wear safety goggles and appropriate protective clothing, and tie back long hair (**Figure 4**). Remove jewellery and neckties. Wear closed shoes, not open sandals. Beware of loose clothing.
5. Return all equipment and tools to the appropriate storage facility.
6. Only use power tools if a qualified adult has trained you in their safe use.
7. Never work alone.

Figure 4

(a) Ready to conduct a safe inquiry investigation

(b) Ready to conduct a safe design investigation

Working with Chemicals

1. Do not taste, touch, or smell anything unless you are asked to do so by your teacher. Do not chew gum, eat, or drink in the Science & Technology classroom.
2. Be aware of where the Material Safety Data Sheet (MSDS) manual is kept. Know any relevant MSDS information for the chemicals you are working with.
3. Label all containers. When taking something from a bottle or other

container, double-check the label to be sure you are taking exactly what you need.

4. If any part of your body comes in contact with a chemical or specimen, wash the area immediately and thoroughly with water. If your eyes are affected, do not touch them but wash them immediately and continuously with cool water, moving from the bridge of the nose toward the outside corner of the eye, for at least 15 min. Inform your teacher.

5. Handle all chemicals carefully. When you are instructed to smell a chemical, wave the vapour toward your nose (**Figure 5**). This way, you can smell the substance without inhaling too much into your lungs. Never put your nose close to a chemical.

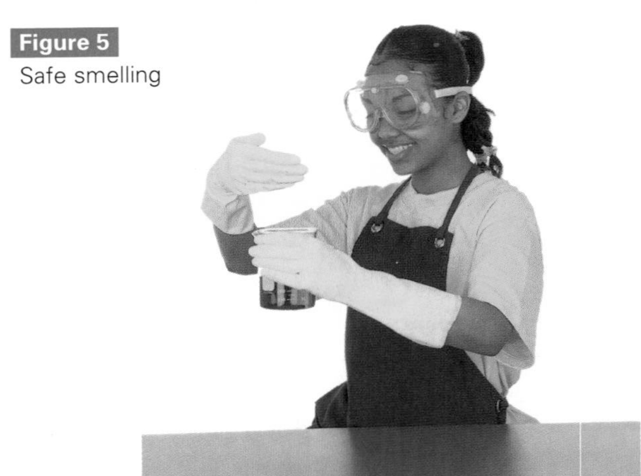

Figure 5
Safe smelling

6. Place test tubes in a rack before pouring liquids into them. If you must hold a test tube, tilt it away from you (and others) before pouring in a liquid (**Figure 6**).

Figure 6
Safe pouring

7. Clean up any spilled or dropped materials immediately, following instructions given by your teacher.

8. Do not return unused chemicals to the original containers, and do not pour them down the drain. Dispose of chemicals as instructed by your teacher.

9. Ensure the area is well ventilated when using chemicals.

10. Clean all equipment thoroughly after use.

Working with Heat

1. Whenever possible, use electric hot plates for heating materials. Use a flame only if instructed to do so. If a Bunsen burner (**Figure 7**) is used in your Science & Technology classroom, make sure you follow the procedures listed below.
    - Obtain instructions from your teacher on the proper method of lighting and adjusting the Bunsen burner.
    - Do not heat a flammable material (for example, alcohol) over a Bunsen burner. Make sure there are no flammable materials nearby.
    - Do not leave a lighted Bunsen burner unattended.
    - Always turn off the gas at the valve, not at the base of the Bunsen burner.

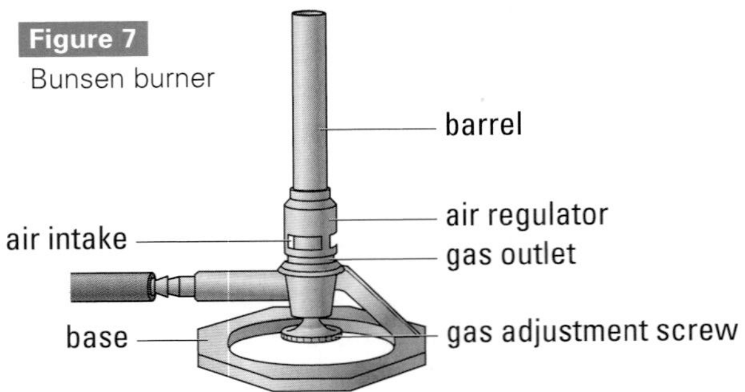

Figure 7
Bunsen burner

2. When heating liquids in glass containers, make sure you use clean Pyrex or Kimax. Do not use broken or cracked glassware. Never allow a container to boil dry.

3. When heating a test tube over a flame, use a test-tube holder. Hold the test tube at an angle, with the opening facing away from

you and others (**Figure 8**). Heat the upper half of the liquid first, then move it gently in the flame, to distribute the heat evenly.

Figure 8
Heating using a test-tube

4. Be careful when handling hot objects and objects that might be hot. Hot plates can take up to 60 min to cool completely. Test that they are cool enough to move by touching first with a damp paper towel. If you hear sizzling or see steam, wait a little longer! If you burn yourself, immediately apply cold water or ice, and inform your teacher.
5. Always have an inspected and certified fire extinguisher at hand.

Working with Light

1. Never look directly into a light source (including the Sun). Do not use magnifying lenses to observe light directly.
2. Use mirrors with care. If a mirror is broken, dispose of glass in the appropriate receptacle.
3. Since ray boxes are used in the dark, be careful when moving from place to place. Allow your eyes to become accustomed to the dark prior to beginning an activity.

Working with Sharp Tools

All tools must be used below waist level. Always wear safety goggles.

1. Saws (**Figure 9**):
    - Always use the correct type of mitre box to match the saw you are using. Be sure that the mitre box is secured to the work surface.
    - Make sure the saw blade is properly in place (the teeth of the saw should be angled away from your body).

Figure 9
The safe use of a saw

2. Drills:
    - Change drill bits carefully. To reduce breakage, always use high quality drill bits.
    - Drill on a solid, flat, secured surface. Be sure to secure the object you are drilling.
    - Always drill downwards.
3. Paper Drills:
    - Secure the cutting end.
    - Drill on a solid, flat, secured surface.
    - Use light pressure only.
4. Utility Knife:
    - Always use a metal safety ruler.
    - Cut on a solid, flat, secured surface.
    - Keep work area clear.
    - Always cut by pulling the knife toward you. Keep your other hand well out of the way. Work carefully and slowly. Use light pressure. Thicker materials may need several cuts (not more pressure).
    - Always retract the blade when finished.
5. Snips and Scissors:
    - Always carry these by the blade end.
    - Place the material being cut close to the pivot point so that it is easier to cut.
    - Snip materials so that they fall down onto the working surface.
    - When snips are not in use, secure the safety catch.

6. Hammer:
   - Hammer only the nail head. Never bang two hammers together.
   - Work on a solid, flat, secured surface.
7. Screwdriver:
   - Use a screwdriver only for its intended purpose, turning screws. Do not use as a punch, wedge, etc.

Working with Adhesives and Fasteners

1. Always read the label to ensure that what you are using is not toxic.
2. Follow directions for safe use. Be aware of first aid precautions and treatment.
3. Always use glue guns and adhesives in a well-ventilated area.
4. Glue Guns (**Figure 10**):
   - Wear safety goggles.
   - Always use a glue gun in a low traffic area of the room, near an electrical outlet. Ensure that glue gun cords are out of the work area.
   - Your work surface should be protected.
   - Always glue down to the object. Gluing should take place at the level of the work surface area.
   - To avoid burning fingers, always use a stick to position an object being glued. Never use a foreign object to force the glue through the barrel of the glue gun. Have cool water available in case of burns. Immerse burn for at least 10 min and inform your teacher.

Figure 10
Using a glue gun safely

5. Fasteners: Always use caution when putting metal fasteners in or through various materials. Whenever possible, precut the hole.

Other Hazards

1. Keep water and wet hands away from electrical cords, plugs, and sockets. Always unplug electrical cords by pulling on the plug, not the cord. Report any frayed cords or damaged outlets to your teacher. Make sure electrical cords are not placed where someone could trip over them.
2. Place broken and waste glass in the specially marked containers.
3. Follow your teacher's instructions when disposing of waste materials.
4. Report to your teacher all accidents and injuries (no matter how minor), broken equipment, damaged or defective facilities, and suspicious-looking chemicals.
5. Wash your hands thoroughly, using soap and warm water, after every inquiry or design investigation. This practice is especially important when you handle chemicals, biological specimens, and microorganisms.
6. Store chemicals and solvents in a secure, well-ventilated area.
7. Store tools and equipment in a safe place after use.

Try This: Safety Posters

In groups, create safety posters for your classroom. These may include a map of the route your class should follow when the fire alarm sounds, a map of where the safety materials (fire extinguisher, first aid kit, etc.) are located in your classroom, information about the safe use of a specific tool, or an illustrated poster outlining specific safety rules, etc.

2A Process of Scientific Inquiry

Science is knowledge of the world around us. It's also a way of learning about the world around us by observing things, asking questions, proposing answers, and testing those answers. Science is also about sharing information that encourages others to discover more. All scientists use a similar process to find answers to their questions. Let's look at an example of how this process is used before examining the specific steps.

Using the Process of Scientific Inquiry

From Curiosity to a Testable Hypothesis

After observing plants for some time, you may observe that they grow upward (**Figure 1**).

Figure 1
Why do plants grow upward?

If you're curious, you may ask yourself "Why?" You can probably think of some possible answers. For example, maybe plants grow upward because they grow toward the light. This is a hypothesis. From your hypothesis, you can make a prediction that you can test through experimentation. You could test the following prediction: "As the angle of light shining on plants steadily increases, the angle of the plants' growth should also steadily increase."

The Investigation

Once you have a prediction, you can design a test. You can think of your prediction as a statement of cause and effect. The effect you identified is the angle of plant growth. The cause you identified is the angle of light shining on the plant. Your investigation should test whether the cause will produce the effect you predict. The cause and effect can change or vary—so they are known as variables. To plan a careful, accurate investigation, you need to control the cause variable as much as possible. For example, you could investigate the growth of five identical plants, ensuring that all growing conditions—water, nutrients, temperature, kind of light, etc.—are the same (**Figure 2**). You would then change one variable, the angle of light shone on one plant, and measure the results.

Figure 2
Does changing the angle of light change the angle of growth?

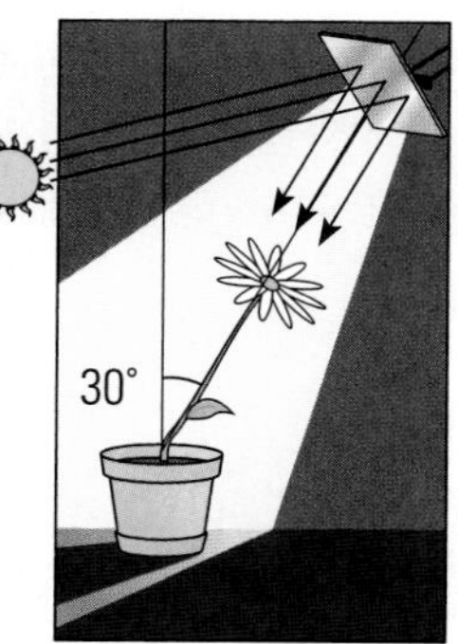

The Results

When you design your investigation, you need to think about what you are going to measure and how you are going to record your results. For instance, you might create a data table like the one in **Table 1**.

Table 1 Record of Angle of Growth

Angle of Light	Day 1	Day 3	Day 5	Day 7	Day 9	Day 11
Sample A (0º)	?	?	?	?	?	?
Sample B (30º)	?	?	?	?	?	?
Sample C (45º)	?	?	?	?	?	?
Sample D (60º)	?	?	?	?	?	?
Sample E (90º)	?	?	?	?	?	?

Once you have completed the investigation, you will have to analyze your results to see whether or not they support your hypothesis. You may create graphs based on the data you collect that will help you make sense of your results. Ultimately, your conclusions will be communicated to others in a report.

Unfortunately, you can never be sure that all possible causes of the effects have been controlled. This means that you can never be absolutely sure that your conclusions are true. However, the more closely the results match the prediction, the more confident you can be that your hypothesis was sound. If you communicate your procedure and conclusions clearly, the experiment can be repeated and the hypothesis re-evaluated. New questions may arise, and new evidence may be gathered.

The Steps in the Process of Scientific Inquiry

It is important that you follow this process and use the related skills whenever you are asked to design and conduct an experiment, if you expect to find reliable answers to the questions you pose. You can use the flow chart in **Figure 3** as a checklist. You can also refer to the more detailed sections in the *Skills Handbook* that deal with each of the specific skills necessary for each part of the process.

Try This — Detective as Scientist

Read a mystery story and describe which of the steps in the inquiry process were used by the detective to solve the crime. Use the flowchart in **Figure 3** as a checklist. The following list of questions may help you:

1. What question did the detective have to answer?
2. How did the detective reach a hypothesis? Were observation, research, or prediction used?
3. How was the hypothesis tested? Were variables controlled? Were clues observed? Were scientific instruments used?
4. How were the results of the investigation analyzed? How were observations recorded? What trends or patterns emerged? What conclusions were drawn? What new questions emerged?
5. How was the conclusion communicated?

1 Asking a Question

- Ask a question that interests you or express an idea that can be tested.

2 Making a Hypothesis

- Research information and previous discoveries that might help you answer your question.
- Develop an educated guess that answers your question. This is your hypothesis.
- Make a prediction based on your hypothesis and state it as a cause-effect relationship.

3 Designing the Experiment

- Identify all your variables.
- Decide what materials and equipment you will need to perform your experiment.
- Write a procedure that explains how you will conduct your experiment. Be sure to take safety into account.
- Draw a labelled diagram that visually explains your procedure and the material and equipment you will use in your experiment.
- Create a rough draft of tables for recording your data.

4 Conducting the Experiment

- Follow the steps in the procedure carefully and thoroughly.
- Use all equipment and materials safely, accurately, and with precision.
- Record the variable(s) you are measuring, manipulating and controlling.
- Remember to repeat your experiment at least three times. If you are collecting quantitative data, take an average. This increases the accuracy and reliability of your results.

Figure 3

The Steps in the Process of Scientific Inquiry

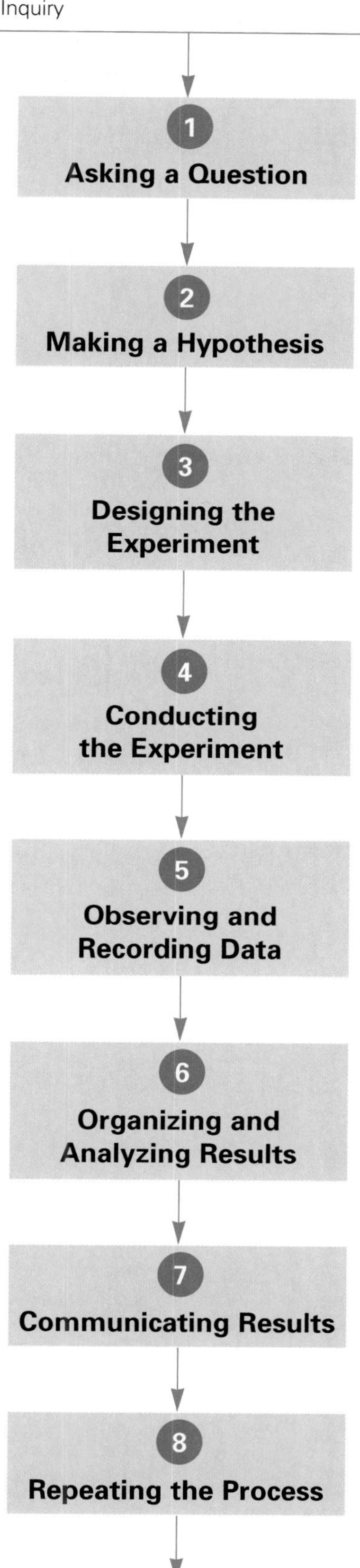

5 Observing and Recording Data

- Make careful notes of everything that you observe during the experiment.
- Record numerical data in tables.

6 Organizing and Analyzing Results

- When appropriate, create graphs to make better sense of data from your tables.
- Study all of your observations.
- Identify patterns and trends.
- Make a conclusion. Be sure that your results support, partially support, or reject your hypothesis.
- Develop an explanation for your conclusion.
- Apply your findings to your life today. Think about who will want to know about your discovery, how it will affect our lives, who it will benefit, and whether or not it could harm our world if used in a certain way.
- Reflect on your experiment. Explore any sources of experimental error in your process. Think about what changes you would make if you were to conduct this experiment in the future.

7 Communicating Results

- Write a report to summarize your investigation. In order to have their investigations repeated and validated, it is common for scientists to publish details of their research, results, and conclusions.

8 Repeating the Process

- If your experiment did not answer the question you initially asked, revise it and repeat it until the question is answered. Most scientists must complete an experiment many times before making important discoveries (e.g., a cure for cancer).

2B Asking a Question

Wondering About the World Around You

All scientific questions are asked by people who are curious about the world around them. Our curiosity is fed by observation, experience, and research. You may have noticed, for example, that balloons stick to walls if you rub them on your head (**Figure 1**). This observation might lead you to wonder about a number of things: Does a balloon stick better if you rub it more times? Does the length or texture of a person's hair affect how well a balloon sticks? Does it matter how inflated the balloon is or what colour it is?

Each of these questions is the basis for a sound scientific investigation. With a little rewording, it will become clear how these questions can be tested. Not every question that you will want an answer for *can* be tested: some are too general or too vague. Learning to ask questions that can be tested takes time and is a fundamental skill in scientific inquiry.

Questions About Cause and Effect

The first balloon-related question could be stated more usefully: "What is the effect of increasing the number of times that a balloon is rubbed on a person's head on the time that the balloon stays stuck to a wall?" You can probably already begin to plan an experiment that would answer this question. A testable question is often about cause-effect relationships. These questions often take the form: "What causes the change in variables?" and "What are the effects on a variable if we change another variable?" As you know, a variable is something that can change or vary in an investigation.

Variables and Questions You Can Test

Scientists call the cause variable the independent variable. This is the one thing in the experiment that you purposely change. For instance, increasing the number of times that a balloon is rubbed on a person's head is something you control: you are changing the independent variable.

Figure 1
What affects how well the balloon sticks to the wall?

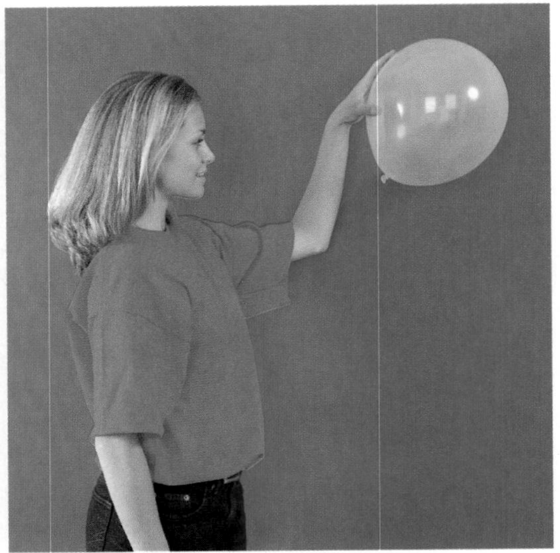

The effect variable is called the dependent variable. This is what you measure in your experiment (e.g., time, distance) and "depends" on what variable you purposely change (independent variable). The amount of time the balloon stays on the wall is the dependent variable.

A scientific question that asks what happens to a dependent variable when we change the independent variable is a question you can test. Some examples appear in **Table 1**.

Table 1 Testable Questions

Question	Independent (cause) variable	Dependent (effect) variable
How do fertilizers and phosphates affect the productivity of algae?	fertilizers and phosphates	rate of algae growth
What happens to the volume of a liquid when it is heated?	applying heat	volume of the liquid
Do all transparent materials refract light the same amount?	kind of transparent material	amount of light refracted
Does stirring affect how quickly a solute dissolves in a solvent?	stirring the solvent	rate at which the solute dissolves

Try This What's the Question?

Have you ever kicked a ball during the winter? It almost feels like kicking a brick.

1. Place a tennis ball in a refrigerator overnight.
2. Reproduce **Table 2** for recording your observations.

Table 2

Temperature of ball	Height of ball (cm)	Trial 1	Trial 2	Trial 3	Average
cold	?	?	?	?	?
room temperature	?	?	?	?	?

3. Hold a metre stick vertically with the zero end on the floor.
4. Drop the cold tennis ball from the upper end of the metre stick (**Figure 2**).

Figure 2

5. Measure the height that the tennis ball bounces back (**Figure 3**).

Figure 3

6. Do this three times (each time is called a test or a trial).
7. Repeat steps 3–6 with a ball that is at room temperature.
   - What question is being investigated in steps 1–6?
   - What question is being investigated in step 7?
   - What evidence is being gathered to answer the questions?

2C Predicting and Hypothesizing

The Hypothesis

A suggested answer or reason why one variable affects another in a certain way is called a hypothesis. Often you have some idea about this even as you ask your question. Having noticed, for instance, that a balloon sticks to the wall after you rub it in your hair, you might predict that rubbing it more will make it stick longer. You might be wrong, of course, but your prediction is probably based on past observations, on logic, and on bits of scientific theory you may remember. If you're really interested, you may even do some research based on what you already know. If you then pull everything you know together and express it, you would have a hypothesis. For instance, you might posit that the balloon sticks to the wall because it is attracted by static electricity, and that rubbing the balloon more produces a greater static electric charge on the balloon.

The Relationship Between Hypotheses and Predictions

Predictions and hypotheses go hand in hand (**Table 1**). The hypothesis is how you can explain a prediction. The prediction is what you test through your experiment. And, if the experiment confirms the prediction, you can have more confidence that your hypothesis is correct. Naturally, your experiment will not always confirm your prediction. In this case, you may need to re-evaluate your hypothesis and design a new experiment.

Try This: Answer These Questions

Support a plank with some books, so it forms an inclined plane (**Figure 1**). When you roll a jar down the plane, which will roll farther: an empty jar, or one filled with water? Write a hypothesis and a prediction to answer that question. Then carry out the experiment. How accurate was your prediction?

Now empty half of the water from the jar (**Figure 2**). How far will it roll? Write a hypothesis and prediction to answer the question, and try the experiment.

Do you need to change your hypothesis in either case?

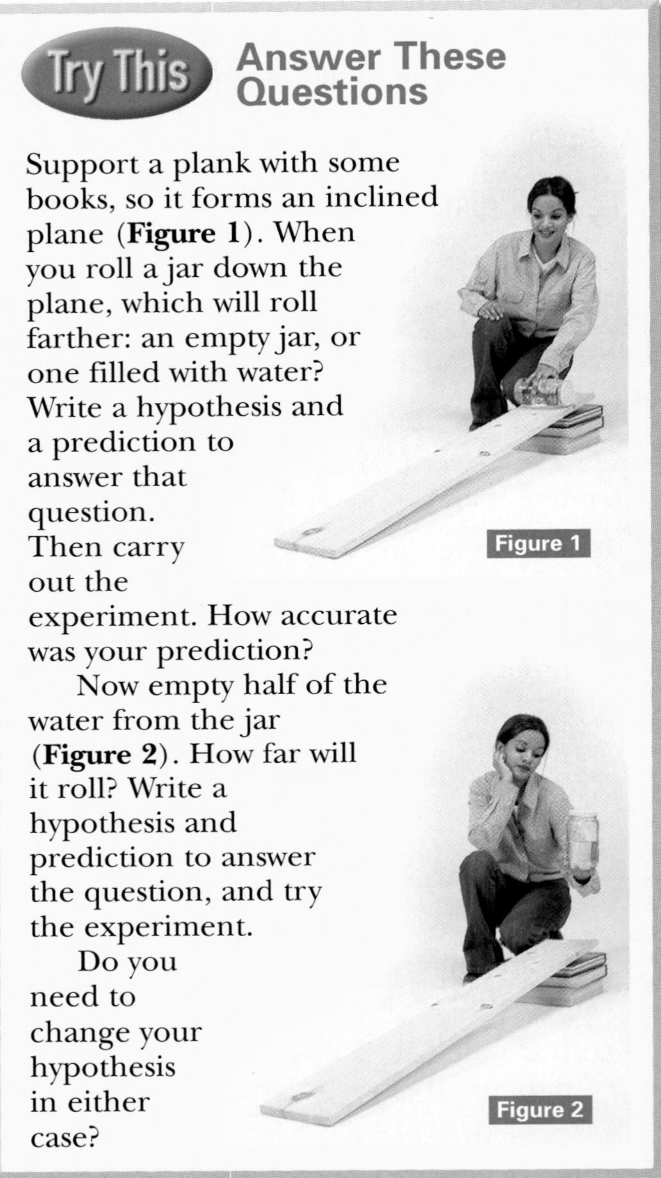

Figure 1

Figure 2

Table 1 Sample Hypotheses and Predictions

Hypothesis (possible reason for cause-effect relationship)	Prediction: Possible cause (independent variable)	Prediction: Possible effect (dependent variable)
Candy contains sugar that is used for energy by germs in the mouth, and these germs produce an acid that decays the teeth.	As the amount of candy that a person eats increases...	...the number of tooth cavities increases.
A larger sail traps more air, which then provides a greater force to a boat.	As the size of the sail increases...	...the top speed of the sailboat increases.
Salt helps oxygen in the air combine with iron in the metal of a bicycle to form rust.	As the amount of salt on a road increases...	...the amount of rusting of the metal parts of a bicycle increases.

2D Identifying Variables and Controls

You may notice that milk has a different taste if it is left out on the table for more than 3 h. What additional factors, other than the time that it has been left on the table, do you think might affect the taste of milk? You have just identified variables!

Identifying Variables

Identifying variables is extremely important to the process of scientific inquiry: it allows you to ask good scientific questions, make predictions, and design a meaningful experiment. As you know, anything that can change in an experiment is a variable. Any variable that can be changed by the experimenter is called an independent variable. For example, you might predict that if a jar has a greater mass, then it will roll farther after it leaves a ramp. The mass of the jar is the independent (or cause) variable. There are other independent variables in this experiment, shown in **Figure 1 a–c.**

The effect of changing the independent variable is called the dependent variable. The distance that the jar travels is the dependent variable.

Figure 1

a The angle of the ramp is an independent variable.

b The size of the jar is an independent variable.

c The type of liquid in the jar is an independent variable.

Identifying Controls

Scientists attempt to test only one independent variable at a time. That way the scientist knows which cause produced the effect. Controls are used to eliminate the possibility of an unknown variable.

In the jar experiment, you need to control the independent variables. To isolate the mass of the jar as the cause, you must try to change only the mass. The angle of the ramp, the size of the jar, and the type of liquid you use must always be the same—only the amount of liquid can change. If you try the experiment, you may find that the results with a half-filled jar surprise you. As a half-filled jar rolls down the ramp, water sloshes back and forth, creating friction. The friction inside the jar slows it down, and it doesn't travel as far. Friction is another independent variable that needs to be controlled. The jar in **Figure 2** with no water in it isn't affected by this variable: it is the control.

Figure 2
The empty jar on the ramp is a control.

Try This: Don't Get Burned!

Do sunscreens really prevent sunburn?

1. State a related hypothesis and prediction.
2. Identify the dependent and independent variables in your experiment.
3. What would your controls be?

Why Do Scientists Use Controls?

The following experiment shows why scientists use a control. A student notices spots of rust on the frame of her bike after riding all winter. The student hypothesizes that the rust was caused by the salt on the roads. But is salt the only variable (**Figure 3a**)? It is possible that the rusting was not caused by the salt alone. For example, the roads were also wet a lot of the winter. By comparing the amount of rusting with and without salt, you can determine just how much rusting is caused by the salt (**Figure 3b**).

Figure 3

(a) Your prediction: As metal is exposed to more salt, more rusting will occur.

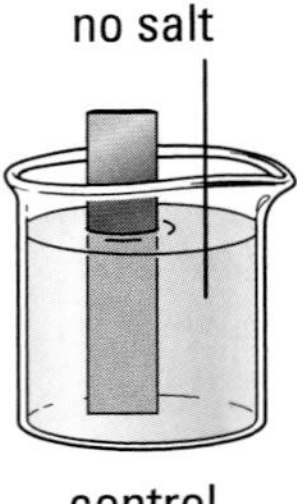

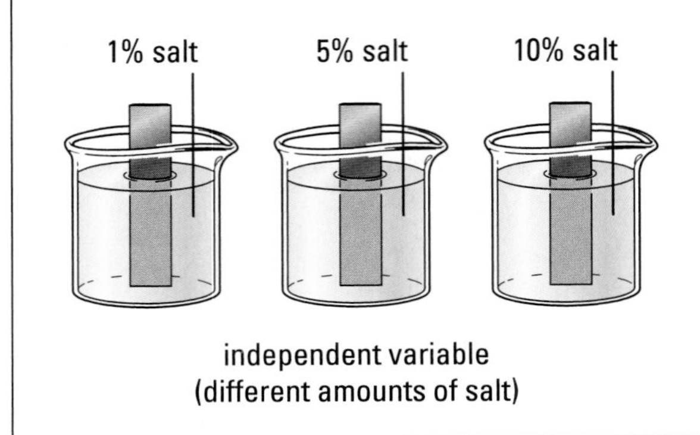

(b) The experiment: Metal placed in different solutions

2E Designing an Inquiry Investigation

Once you have asked a testable question and developed a hypothesis, you can design an investigation that will test that hypothesis. To design an inquiry investigation, you need to think of all the steps in the process of scientific inquiry outlined in section 2A. You need to visualize the investigation from beginning to end and plan for everything you'll need and every step you'll take.

Variables

Let's imagine that your question is: "Does mass affect the swing of a pendulum?" Your prediction may be: "As the mass of the pendulum increases, the number of swings per second will increase." The first step in designing your inquiry investigation is to identify your variables. Remember that an independent variable is the possible cause and a dependent variable is what the effect will be. You know you will be using different masses in your experiment (which you will have to record), and you will be measuring the number of swings per second. But you must also identify other possible independent variables so that you can control them. As you picture yourself testing the pendulum (**Figure 1**), you can probably list some of these possible causes. For instance, the length of the string, the length of the arc, the materials from which the pendulum is made—all of these may affect the swing. You must design your experiment so that these variables are kept constant.

Observations

You also need to think carefully about what you are going to measure—in this case, mass and number of swings of the pendulum. What mass are you going to start with? And how are you going to increase the mass? What unit of time are you going to use? And how long will you observe the pendulum in each case? Then you need to design a table to record your data (**Table 1**).

Table 1

The effect of mass on number of swings per second (based on 15 s of observation)	
Mass	**Number of swings per second**
1 g	?
2 g	?
3 g	?
4 g	?

Equipment and Materials

Obviously, you must also decide what materials and equipment you will use (**Figure 2**). It is useful to create a labelled diagram that illustrates the materials and equipment you will need, and the procedure you are going to use.

Figure 1
What are the independent variables?

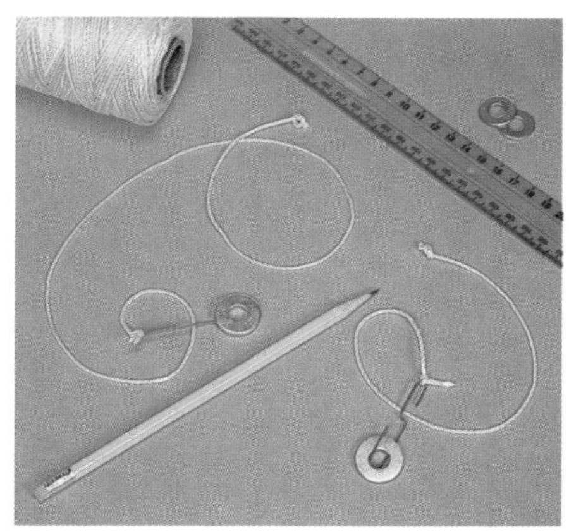

Figure 2
What materials will you need?

The Procedure

This is an essential component of an experimental design. Anyone who is interested in learning about your experiment needs to be able to understand how it was performed, so that it can be duplicated exactly (**Figure 3**). Therefore, it is important that you be able to write an experimental procedure clearly, concisely, and accurately. When writing a procedure, you should use:

- numbered steps
- passive voice (avoid using pronouns)
- past tense

Figure 3
Record every step you will take.

For example, the first two steps of a procedure could look like **Figure 4**.

Don't forget to consider all possible safety issues!

Figure 4

Procedure

1. The experiment was set up as shown in the diagram.
2. In each case, the pendulum was observed for 15 s.

Try This Write a Procedure

Think about how you would conduct the pendulum experiment. Write a procedure for this experiment, using the format explained above.

3A The Problem-Solving Cycle

The major goal of technology is to improve the world by creating products that satisfy human needs. For example, while scientists try to explain why and how the mosquito finds its prey, technologists try to create products to protect us from these annoying pests (**Figure 1**).

Figure 1

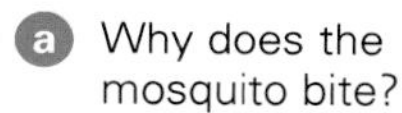

a Why does the mosquito bite?

b How can we stop the mosquito from biting?

For example, consider automobiles, computers, plastics, or the process for making decaffeinated soft drinks. Most of us are most creative when we're trying to satisfy a need. Imagine, for instance, that you and a few friends are alone at home. You're hungry, but there's not a lot of food in the refrigerator that you're really interested in. You all agree that hotdogs would be acceptable, but the power is out. Your problem is to design a method of cooking hotdogs without electricity. Luckily, your friends are with you. Working together to brainstorm possible solutions and to identify the advantages and disadvantages will help you come up with a good solution to your problem (**Figure 2**).

Figure 2

Technologists use a process of design to solve problems. Let's look at an example of how this process is used before examining the specific steps.

Using the Process of Design

What Are You Designing?

Things are usually designed in response to needs and to try to improve the quality of life.

Creating the Solution

You decide to use the energy from the Sun to cook your hotdogs. You know that aluminum foil reflects heat, so you will use it to get the most from the Sun's heat. And you want to make sure the hotdog cooks evenly. You jot down ideas and sketch out possible designs, considering all the tools and materials that you will need. You talk through how to build your hotdog cooker and realize there are a couple of things you hadn't thought of. When you think you're ready to build, you gather everything you need and go to work. Together you have built a prototype hotdog-cooker that is designed to solve your problem (**Figure 3**).

Figure 3
The Sun cooks lunch.

What Have You Learned?

The first hotdog you cook may not have turned out perfectly. Maybe the wire wasn't turning freely, and you had trouble cooking your hotdog evenly. That first hotdog was a test of your prototype, and you discovered that your design could be improved. You need to back up a few steps and modify your prototype. Once you get it working right, you may want to show some of your other friends how to make a solar hotdog cooker. Communicating the steps of the process is a very important part of the process.

The Steps in the Process of Design

The steps in the process of design are very similar to the steps used in the process of scientific inquiry. The flow chart in **Figure 5** identifies those steps. Use it as a checklist when you are required to design and test a prototype you construct in your Science & Technology class this year.

Try This Design a Mould

It's your little sister's birthday, and she loves strawberry gelatine (**Figure 4**). You've bought the powder and are trying to find something to make it in. You'd like the end result to look fun and festive. All you have are three bowls, and none of them is the right size. You've used one of the bowls in the past, and it was hard to get the gelatine out once it was set.

- Write a problem statement, choose a solution, and plan a prototype for a jelly mould that you think would solve your problem.

Figure 4

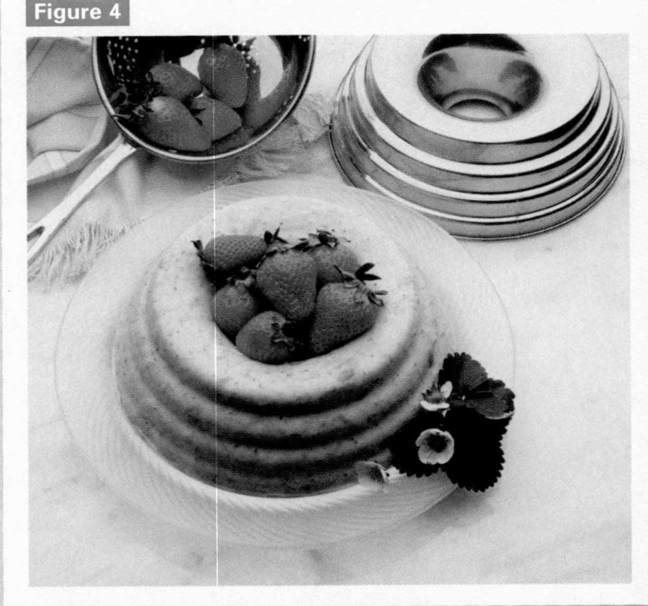

Figure 5

The Steps in the Process of Design

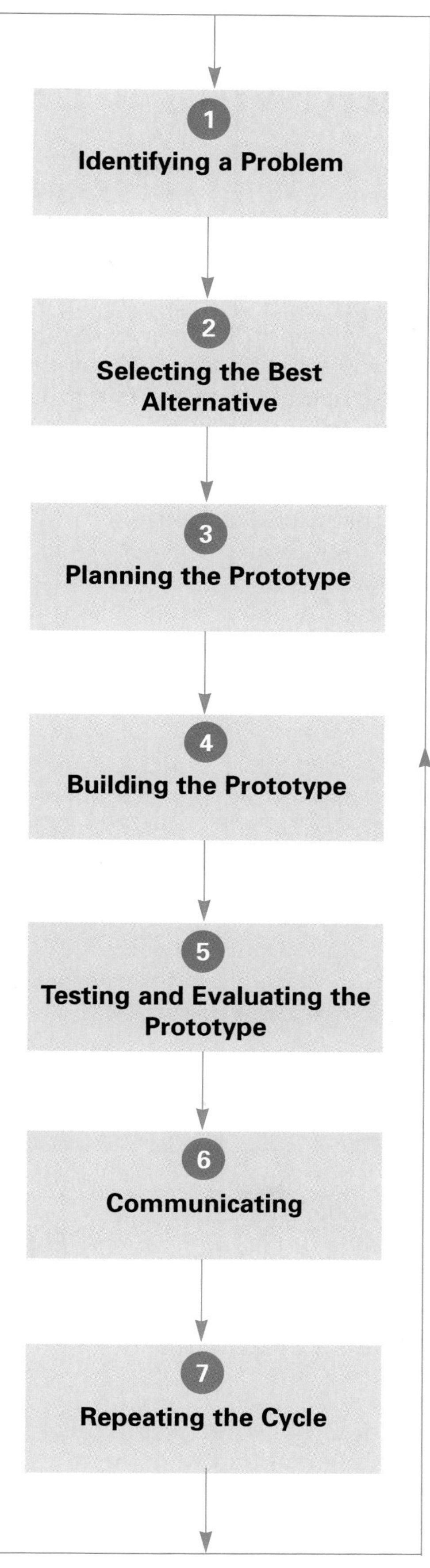

1 Identifying a Problem

- Identify and record the problem.
- Identify any limits posed by the problem.
- Research possible solutions to the problem and record new ideas.
- Restate the problem so that it clearly states what needs to be solved.

2 Selecting the Best Alternative

- Identify the constraints (e.g., human resources, time, money, environmental issues).
- Develop the design criteria (e.g., cost, reliability, safety, size, materials).
- Brainstorm all possible solutions to the problem.
- Rate the possible solutions.
- Select the alternative with the highest rating.

3 Planning the Prototype

- Draw sketches and/or schematics of your prototype.
- List materials and tools that will be needed to construct the prototype and gather them.

4 Building the Prototype

- Refer to (1) "Safety in Science & Technology" for a review of safety precautions when using tools.
- Construct a working prototype.

5 Testing and Evaluating the Prototype

- Use the design criteria to develop a test.
- Test the prototype to evaluate its ability to solve the identified problem.
- Quantify and record your test results.

6 Communicating

- Create a Design Folder that describes your process and product, and communicates your evaluation of how well the product satisfied the design criteria.

7 Repeating the Cycle

- Revise and reconstruct the prototype in order to make it more effective.
- Repeat the process until an effective solution to the problem has been developed.

3B Identifying a Problem

Identify and Record the Problem

It is important that, as you start the design process, you understand and specify the nature of the problem. Start by writing down what you believe the problem is, based on the information you have gathered. Often the problem is the need of a client. The problem may be written as a question or a statement.

Let's assume that your neighbours have a need and that they are your clients. They have ten goldfish that they dearly love. Occasionally, they go away for week-long vacations. Your neighbours are worried about how to feed the fish. They would like you to design and build a device that drops a small quantity of goldfish food into the goldfish tank twice a day (**Figure 1**).

Figure 1
Goldfish require daily feeding.

Your stated problem could be:

A device is necessary to automatically feed ten goldfish two times a day for a period of one week.

Examine and Redefine the Problem

It is important to fully understand this problem statement and to redefine the problem so that it is as clear and objective as possible. The following steps may lead you to rephrase your problem statement:

- **Be sure you fully understand the terms stated in the problem.** You may have to clarify terms or make them more precise. For example, in the given problem it is not clear how much goldfish food is to be released—the amount of food should be specified. The problem could be restated:

  A device is necessary to automatically feed ten goldfish ***0.5g*** *of food, two times a day, for a period of one week.*
- **Identify limits posed by the problem as stated.** For instance, the problem may have been expressed by someone who already has an idea about the "best" solution. In the problem statement above, it is obvious that your clients think that an automatic device is necessary to feed the goldfish. It may, however, be possible to hire a person to come in and feed the fish. Therefore, the problem may be refined to say:

  A ***method*** *or device is necessary to feed ten goldfish 0.5g of food, two times a day, for a period of one week.*
- **Research possible solutions to the problem and record new ideas.** You may find an appropriate solution that already exists. Or you may get new ideas that will help you focus your problem-solving.

Try This: Listing Needs

Generate a list of 10–15 needs that could be met through technology. Categorize the needs under the headings in **Table 1**:

Table 1

Personal needs	Class needs	School needs	Community needs
?	?	?	?
?	?	?	?
?	?	?	?

3C Selecting the Best Alternative

Identifying Constraints

For every design problem there will be factors that limit or constrain a solution. If you are designing an automatic goldfish-feeder, for instance, your clients will probably give you a limited amount of money and time to complete the project. The money and time factors are limits or constraints.

General Constraints

General constraints that should be considered for most technological designs are listed below:

- **Natural Constraints:** Will the laws of nature let me do this?
- **Time Constraints:** How long will this take? Is this a major project involving years of development and testing or a relatively short endeavour?
- **Financial Constraints:** How much money do I have to pay for the development of this?
- **Material Constraints:** What materials and tools are available to complete this project?
- **Societal Constraints:** Is there actually a need or demand for this product?
- **Ethical Constraints:** Should we be doing this? Is this harmful for society in any way?
- **Environmental Constraints:** What impact will this have on the environment?

Evaluating these constraints will influence what solutions are available and affect the specific design criteria for a project (**Figure 1**).

Developing Design Criteria

Design criteria clearly outline what your product needs to achieve if it is to successfully solve the problem for which it was designed. After answering the questions in the list of general constraints you may come up with some of the design criteria for your project. For instance, your clients may be going on vacation in three weeks. In this case, one of your design criteria would be that the automatic goldfish-feeder must be complete in three weeks.

Other design criteria will be determined by the specific nature of the problem you are trying to solve. Reliability, size, appearance, strength, durability, safety, efficiency, and maintenance are just some of the factors that may be relevant to your design.

It is useful to brainstorm a list of criteria, judging how important each is to the success of the design. For an automatic goldfish-feeder, for instance, you might consider the following design criteria:

- **Time:** The goldfish-feeder must be complete in three weeks.
- **Money:** It must cost $120 or less.
- **Reliability:** It must be completely reliable, or the fish will die.
- **Ease of use:** It is of medium importance that the device be easy to use. It has to be set up correctly, but the owner can take time to ensure that it has been correctly set up before leaving the fish unattended.
- **Appearance:** It is of low importance for the device to be attractive since it is in use only when people are away.

Figure 1

The amount of money available, for instance, will affect what materials can be used and how many people you can hire.

Brainstorming Solutions

It is now time for you to brainstorm a list of possible solutions to your problem (**Figure 2**). This may involve coming up with an idea for a new product, a modification to a device that already exists, or a new or modified process.

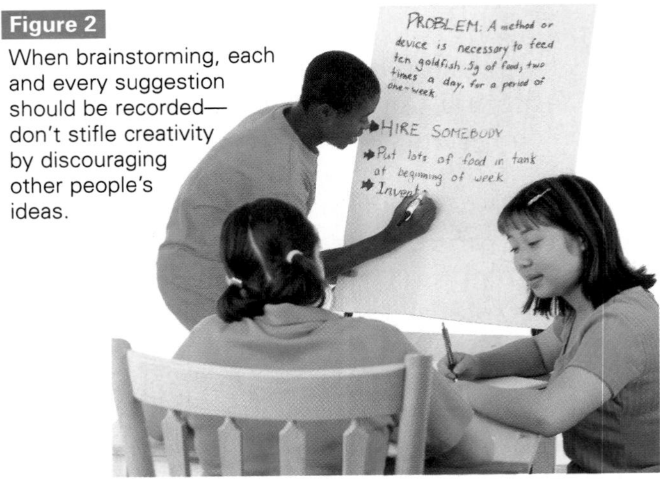

Figure 2
When brainstorming, each and every suggestion should be recorded—don't stifle creativity by discouraging other people's ideas.

After you have completed your brainstorming exercise, vote for and list the best alternatives.

Rating the Alternatives

We now need a method for choosing the very best alternative. There are different ways of rating alternatives, but it is important you measure each alternative against your design criteria.

The problem-solving matrix in **Table 1** is one way you can rate alternatives. **Table 2** provides an example of how the matrix can be used to rank alternatives to the automatic fish-feeder challenge. In this example, the lower the number, the worse the rating. Note that the criteria are measured according to different scales, depending on the relative importance of each criterion.

Table 1 **Generic Problem Solving Matrix**

	Design Criteria					
	Criterion A	Criterion B	Criterion C			
Alternatives	rating scale	rating scale	rating scale			Totals
Alternative A	?	?	?	?	?	?
Alternative B	?	?	?	?	?	?
Alternative C	?	?	?	?	?	?

Table 2 **Problem Solving Matrix – Fish-Feeder Example**

	Design criteria					
	Time	Cost	Reliability	Ease of Use	Appearance	
Alternatives	(0-10)	(0-10)	(0-10)	(0-5)	(0-3)	Totals
7-day dissolving fish feeder tablet	5	10	5	5	1	26
Put a whole lot of fish food in at the beginning of the week	10	10	1	5	0	26
Hire a person to feed the goldfish	10	10	4	2	3	29
FishFeeder Timer Device (an original device using a timer and gravity feed of premeasured food)	9	5	9	5	2	(30)

Another system uses the following rating scale:
+ = good or better than other alternatives or positive influence
0 = fair or at par with other alternatives or neutral influence
• = poor or worse than other alternatives or negative influence

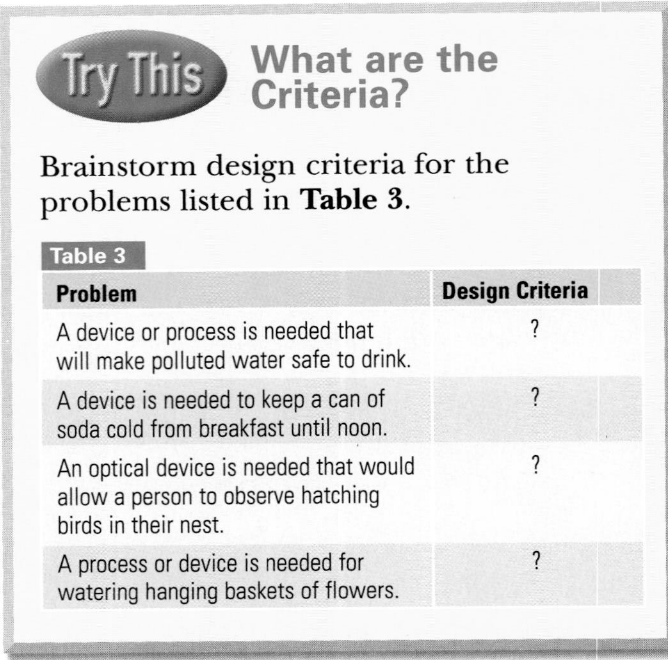

Try This **What are the Criteria?**

Brainstorm design criteria for the problems listed in **Table 3**.

Table 3

Problem	Design Criteria
A device or process is needed that will make polluted water safe to drink.	?
A device is needed to keep a can of soda cold from breakfast until noon.	?
An optical device is needed that would allow a person to observe hatching birds in their nest.	?
A process or device is needed for watering hanging baskets of flowers.	?

3D Planning a Prototype

Once you know what alternative you want to design and build, it's time to plan a prototype. A prototype is an original model that exhibits the essential features of the solution you chose. It can be a device or it can be a method that demonstrates a new or an improved process.

- **Start by making sketches and detailed drawings of your prototype.** Initially, these may be hand-drawn sketches with approximate dimensions, but you may find it worthwhile to produce a prototype drawing that shows specific measurements and working parts. (Refer to 6C "Scientific & Technical Drawing" for more details.)
  You may want to use computer-aided design programs to help you in the design process.
- **Make a list of the materials and tools you will need to build your prototype.** Examine your drawings carefully to ensure that your list is as complete as possible.
- **Write out the instructions you will follow to build the prototype.** Think this through carefully. As you set down each step in the building process, you may think of additional materials and tools to add to your list. You may also uncover potential difficulties or problems that require you to make design changes. This is not a design failure! Regular evaluation and modification of your design is an important part of the process.
- **Have others review your plan.** A fresh pair of eyes will often discover small flaws or visualize slight improvements that will enhance your design. In your Science & Technology class, you will often be asked to have your teacher approve your plan before you begin building.

Planning

Choose one of the problems in **Table 3** in section 3C and plan a prototype.

(3E) Building a Prototype

Before you begin construction, review the safety precautions for using the tools you'll need. Be sure that you have access to all the necessary materials and tools. If you are gathering these in advance, consider how you will store them for use throughout the project.

General Building Tips

- Read through your building instructions before you begin.
- If you need to, review specific tools ((5D) "Using Technology Equipment") or specific fabrication techniques ((5E) "Fabrication Techniques").
- Measure and cut materials to prepare for assembly. (Remember: Measure twice, cut once.)
- Temporarily join parts to test and evaluate their effectiveness. You may wish to use elastics, Plasticine, tape, string, and plastic tubing to assist you.
- Once you are satisfied with the components and their ability to operate, then you are ready to join the components permanently. It is important to consider methods of assembly that allow the parts to be added in such a way that they can be moved slightly, if needed.

Try This — Deconstruction

One way of learning how to build things is to take things apart (**Figure 1**). Take apart one of the things listed below and jot down anything you learn about how it is put together.

- a flashlight
- a pen
- a chocolate box
- a bicycle wheel

Figure 1

Consider the construction materials, how things are held together, the shape of the various parts, what tools would have been required, etc.

Do not take apart small appliances or electronics. You may receive an electric shock.

3F Testing and Evaluating a Prototype

What to Test

It is important to find out how well your prototype works. You need to develop a good test that will answer three basic questions:

1 Does the prototype solve the problem?
2. Does the prototype satisfy the design criteria?
3. Are there any unanticipated problems?

Does the Prototype Solve the Problem?

Let's assume you have built an automatic fish-feeder to solve the following problem:

A method or device is necessary to feed ten goldfish 0.5g of food, two times a day, for a period of one week.

To determine whether or not your prototype solved the problem, your test-period would have to be at least one-week long, you would have to record how many times a day food actually made it into the tank, and you would have to record the amount of food that was deposited at each feed.

Does the Prototype Satisfy the Design Criteria?

Let's assume that you identified and rated the importance of the design criteria in **Table 1**:

Table 1

time:	maximum importance	(rated between 0-10)
cost:	maximum importance	(rated between 0-10)
reliability:	maximum importance	(rated between 0-10)
ease of use:	medium importance	(rated between 0-5)
appearance:	low importance	(rated between 0-3)

To determine whether the prototype meets the design criteria, your test must measure against them. In some cases, the measure will be quantitative (e.g., time and cost). In other cases, your measure will be qualitative (e.g., appearance). In any case, your evaluation must be carefully recorded.

Are There Any Unanticipated Problems?

Your test may also show you weaknesses that you hadn't considered. For instance, does the position of the fish-feeder on the tank affect how much light is reaching the water? Do you need to adjust the position? Do you need to reconsider the materials you have used?

Testing Tips

The following tips will help you design and conduct your tests:

- Decide how long the test should last.
- Decide how many times the test should be done.
- Consider whether the test needs to be done in different circumstances or conditions.
- Rate each of the design criteria.
- Make and record all quantitative measurements.
- Record all qualitative observations.
- Consider potential problems that may not be related to the design criteria.
- Have other people make use of the prototype and get their feedback.
- Keep a log of your test information.

Modifying Your Design

Your test will probably give you ideas about how your design can be improved. This

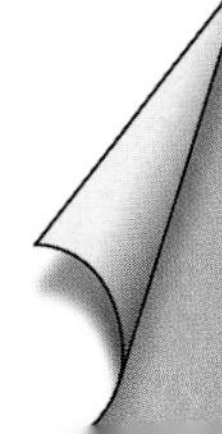

doesn't mean that you are a bad designer. The design process is a repeating cycle, not a step-by-step path to the perfect solution. You will need to go through as many repetitions of the problem-solving cycle as needed in order to come up with the best working solution. Once you have tested your prototype, it is time to re-address the problem statement, redefine your design criteria, and work on improving your device or process.

Try This: Building the Best Papercopter

A babysitter is told that his young charge can unexpectedly become very unhappy. When this happens, the only thing that will console him is watching things, like paper airplanes, fly. The babysitter can only make one kind of paper airplane, and it doesn't fly very well. The child is unimpressed. So, the babysitter's problem is to design a device that would fly long enough to amuse the child (about 10 s).

The design criteria include ease of construction, speed of construction, reliability, and accessibility of materials.

1. Follow the babysitter's plans (**Figure 1**) and build his prototype: the papercopter.
2. Now test the papercopter.
   - Make a list of things to measure and observe.
   - Conduct the test.
   - Summarize what needs to be improved.
   - List modifications to try.
   - Modify the papercopter until it solves the problem.

Figure 1

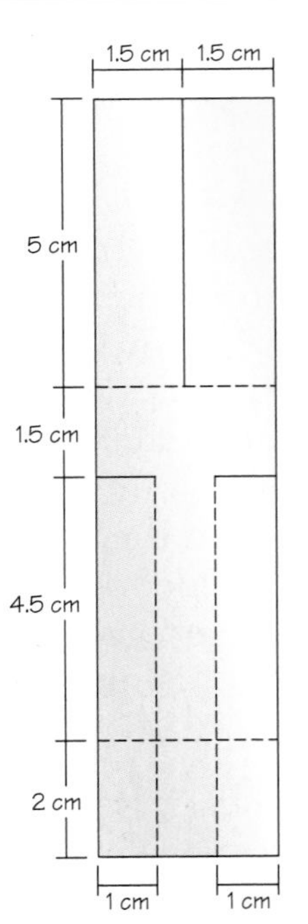

1. Cut a piece of writing paper 3 cm x 13 cm.
2. Cut along the two middle horizontal (solid) lines, and fold in.
3. Fold the bottom flap along the bottom dotted line.
4. Cut the solid vertical line at the top to create two flaps.
5. Attach a paperclip to the bottom.
6. Drop and watch the copter fly.

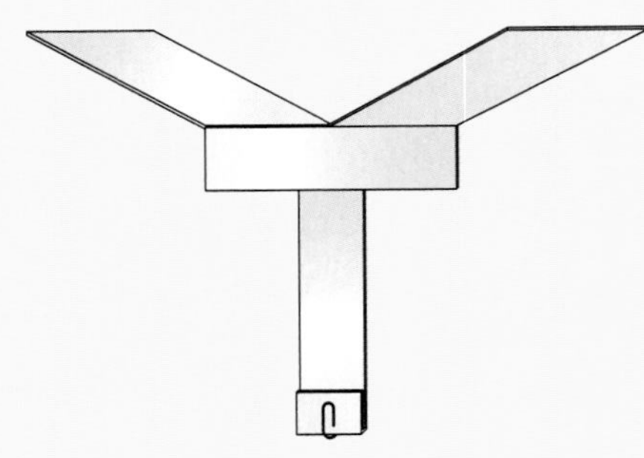

3G Patents, Trademarks, and Copyrights

What would you do if you invented an innovative product or process? Imagine you invented a "Landsurfer" and wanted to develop, sell, and market your invention. In our society, the law protects your intellectual property for a certain period of time. Anyone designing new products or processes should know the differences between and the uses of patents, trademarks, and copyrights.

Patents

A patent gives an inventor the exclusive rights to make, use, and/or sell a certain product, device, or process for a period of 17 years. The inventor must apply for the patent through the Canadian Patent Office. It is usually necessary to contact a Patent Attorney or Agent in order to search for other existing patents on your product and then to file the legal application. The inventor must prove that the invention is original, beneficial to society, and "not obvious" (i.e., something that is in common use, but has never previously been patented). The patent itself includes a number, title, and a short description. You may have noticed the words "Patent Pending" on a product or device. Because the patent process can be a lengthy one, inventors can let others know that they have applied for a patent by printing these words on the device.

Trademarks

A trademark is any name, symbol, picture, or design that an inventor or company may use to identify their products or affairs (**Figure 1**). Trademarks are often indicated by the following symbol: ™. Some well known and much used trademarks often become the actual name of a product and thus lose their legal status as trademarks. For example, aspirin and escalator were originally trademarks and have since become generic product names.

Figure 1

Copyright

A copyright protects the work of artists, composers, and authors from reproduction and/or distribution by others without permission (**Figure 2**).

Figure 2

Copyright © 2000 Nelson, a division of Thomson Learning. Thomson Learning is a trademark used herein under license.

ALL RIGHTS RESERVED. No part of this work covered by the copyright hereon may be reproduced, transcribed, or used in any form or by any means—graphic, electronic, or mechanical, including photocopying, recording, taping, Web distribution or information storage and retrieval systems—without the permission of the publisher.

Try This: Find Examples

- List 10 inventions, devices, or products that would most likely already have a patent. You may want to visit the Canadian Patent Office's web site to see some examples of current patents.
- List 10 trademarks with which you are familiar.
- List 10 things that might be copyrighted.

4A Research Skills

Sources of Information

There is an incredible amount of scientific and technological information available to you. Before you can use it, however, you have to know how to gather it efficiently. First, you need to know where to find information.

Look at the list of information resources in **Table 1**. Some resources are more useful than others in certain circumstances. Pick one or two resources that you seldom use and think of how you might use them in your Science & Technology class.

Before you start any research, brainstorm a list of the best resources for your purpose. Rank the list, starting with the most useful resource. Always use a variety of resources.

General Research Tips

Once you've decided where to look for information, you need to find the best information in the least amount of time. Using these tips will help:

- Clearly define the topic or the question you will be researching. Ask yourself: "Do I clearly understand what I'm looking for?"
- List the most important words associated with your research, and use them to search for related topics.
- Ask yourself: "Do I understand what this resource is telling me?"
- Check when the resource was published. Is it up-to-date?
- Keep organized notes while doing your research.
- Keep a complete list of the resources you used, so you can make a bibliography when writing your report. (See 8A "Writing a Report" for proper referencing formats.)
- Review your notes. After your research, you may want to alter your original problem or hypothesis.

Table 1 **Information Resources**

Information Consultants (people who can help you locate and interpret information)		
teachers	business people	
nurses	scientists	
public servants	librarians	
volunteers	politicians	
lawyers	farmers	
parents	doctors	
members of the media	senior citizens	
veterinarians		
Reference Materials (sources of packaged information)		
encyclopedias	bibliographies	
magazines/journals	newspapers	
videotapes	slides	
data bases	almanacs	
yearbooks	dictionaries	
textbooks	maps	
filmstrips	charts	
biographies	films	
pamphlets	records	
television	radio	
Places (sources beyond the walls of your school)		
public libraries	shopping malls	art galleries
parks	colleges	museums
universities	government offices	hospitals
historic sites	zoos	volunteer agencies
research laboratories		
businesses		
farms		
Electronic Sources		
world wide web (www)		
CD-ROMs		
on-line search engines		
on-line periodicals		
computer programs		

Some Specific Research Tips

Using a Library

School libraries use an organizational system, known as the Dewey Decimal Classification System, which organizes books into the major subject areas shown in **Table 2**.

Table 2 **Dewey Decimal Classification System**

Catalogue #	Subject Area	Catalogue #	Subject Area
000	Generalities	500	Natural Science & Mathematics
100	Philosophy & Psychology	600	Technology (Applied Sciences)
200	Religion	700	The Arts
300	Social Science	800	Literature
400	Language	900	Geography/History

You can usually search a library database by title, author, and/or subject area. If you have access to a computer, many library databases can be accessed online.

Always ask the librarian for help if you are having trouble finding the information you need.

Using On-line Sources

The Internet is a vast network of information that is continually growing. Many Internet navigation programs make use of several search engines. Search engines are on-line tools that find web sites (or hits) based on key words you enter into the search. When researching on-line, consider these additional research tips.

- If you have a specific web site address, go to the direct source first.
- If you need to use a search engine, find two good search engines, bookmark them, and use them. While the "Search" buttons in navigation programs are useful, they will not always give you the best search engine for your purposes.
- Learn about the features of the search engine. The better search engines make use of Boolean logic, operations that are used to combine key words when searching the Internet. In these cases, adding the word "AND" can let you narrow your search by combining two key words. Adding the word "OR" can let you expand your search by joining together two key words. Lastly, adding the word "NOT" enables you to disregard a key word. Be sure to refine your search as you continue. For example, entering the word "music" may give you 1 678 243 hits but adding "AND guitar" will reduce your search results to 18 860 hits. Including "NOT classical" will further reduce your number of hits to 2340.
- Familiarize yourself with the advanced search option within each search engine.
- Look over the first few pages of hits before you start exploring each web site. Be patient and look for the sites that seem most relevant to your topic.
- Bookmark all useful sites so you can access them readily. Put these in a specific folder if your browser allows you to do this.

Try This **Research This!**

Use the General Research Tips to research one of the following topics:

- the discovery of insulin
- eco-tourism in Costa Rica
- the invention of the telescope
- the most recent seismic activity on Earth
- the tides in the Bay of Fundy
- how pneumatics and hydraulics can be applied to everyday life
- how valves and pumps work
- the physical properties of plastics
- the manufacturing process of the product of your choice

Be prepared to communicate the information you find, bibliographic references (see 8A "Writing a Report"), how reliable your information is, and your research process.

4B Interviewing and Survey Skills

When to Use Surveys and Interviews

Surveys and interviews give you access to a very important information resource: people. If you need specialized information, interviewing experts (for example, engineers or researchers) is useful. If you want to find out if your design idea fills a common human need, a survey is an excellent tool. Surveys and interviews are both useful for learning about people's reactions to controversial scientific and technological issues.

Generally, surveys are better if you need specific information from a lot of people. Interviews are better if you need more detailed information from fewer people.

Effective Interviews

Use the following suggestions to help you decide who you are going to interview, and how to prepare and conduct the interview.

- ***Research your topic.*** Clarify what you need to learn through your interview(s).
- ***Choose your interview candidate(s).*** For instance, if you are researching water quality issues in your community, you might want to interview the municipal waterworks engineer, the health inspector, a member of a local environmental group, and a journalist who has written articles on the topic. Make contact with these people: explain your purpose clearly and arrange a convenient time and place.
- ***Prepare your interview questions in advance.*** Try to avoid simple yes/no questions—questions that require explanations will provide more information.
- ***Conduct your interview in a comfortable, quiet place.***
- ***Be prepared to ask questions that are not on your list.*** You want to make sure all of your questions are answered, but some answers will lead to other important questions. For example, if your interviewee said "The water quality is well within set specifications and much better than it was after that incident ten years ago," you may want to ask about the "incident." A good interviewer learns when to let the interview follow its own course and when to bring it back to the prepared questions.
- ***Choose an appropriate way of recording the information.*** You may want to take notes or use a tape recorder. Be sure to ask if it is okay to tape record the interview. If you take notes, be sure that this does not distract you or the person you are interviewing. If you do not understand an answer, be sure to politely ask for clarification.
- ***Be aware of your own biases as well as the biases of the person you are interviewing.*** Remember every person has opinions that have been shaped by personal experience—these are called biases. These will influence the information you get and how you respond to it.
- ***If you quote people, use their exact words and make sure you have their permission.***
- ***Be respectful of the person you are interviewing.*** End your interview on time and express your thanks in person and later with a thank-you note.

Effective Surveys

Planning the Survey

An effective survey requires careful planning. Try to think it through from beginning to end, using the following questions to help you:

- What exactly are we trying to find out?
- Who should we be surveying?
- How many people should we survey?
- Should we ask the survey questions in person and fill in the forms or send the surveys out to be filled in by the people being surveyed?
- How will we use the information? How will we want to present the data?

Answering these questions will affect how you design your survey questions.

Writing the Survey Questionnaire

Writing a good questionnaire requires skill and practice. Consider the following:

- ***Design your questionnaire so that it can be completed easily and quickly.*** The questions should be precise and concise, and the instructions should be easy to understand. Start with questions that can be answered by checking off options or giving a numbered rating, and leave the more open-ended questions to the end.
- ***Design your questionnaire so that it is easy to collate and present the results.*** It should be possible to present your results in meaningful charts and graphs. Using an appropriate software program can help you design your questionnaire and collate your results.
- ***Begin your questionnaire with questions about the respondent.*** Be sure that these questions are relevant to the topic you are studying.
- ***Write clear questions that are easy to answer.*** In order to quantify your results easily, you may want to use the Likert scale, developed by Renis Likert (1932). Start by writing positive or negative statements that relate to the issue being explored. Be sure to minimize any bias in your statements. For example, "CFCs should be banned in Canada" might be better than "Harmful CFCs should be banned in Canada."

Then, attach a five-point scale to rate public reaction to this statement. For example:

Circle the number that best describes your reaction to the following statement:

CFCs should be banned in Canada.

1 2 3 4 5

where

1 = strongly agree, 2 = agree,
3 = undecided, 4 = disagree, and
5 = strongly disagree

- ***Be courteous.*** If you are sending your survey in the mail, you may want to write a covering letter that explains your research and thanks the respondent in advance. If you are conducting the survey in person, use common courtesy.

Testing the Questionnaire

It is often a good idea to try your questionnaire on three or four people before sending it out to everyone on your list. You may need to modify the questionnaire after you have considered the following questions:

- How well did the respondents understand the questions?
- Did they give the kind of information you need?
- How long did it take to complete?

Interview or Survey?

Consider the following research questions. Would you use interviews, surveys, or both to find the answers?

- What kind of training do you need to be a water resource engineer?
- How satisfied are e-mail users with their Internet service provider?
- Should we ban the use of CFCs?
- How much of Ontario's land should be set aside as protected park land?
- Should safety ever be compromised to lower costs?
- How well is the local recycling program working?
- What technology do most people feel has the greatest impact on their daily lives?

4C Critical Thinking

Science & Technology in the News

Understanding and evaluating the results of your research is extremely important. When you do research, you can find information using the Internet, textbooks, magazines, chat lines, television, radio, and many other forms of communication. Is all of this information reliable? How do we know what to believe and what not to believe?

Every day you see and hear extraordinary claims about objects and events (**Figure 1**). Often scientific or technological evidence is used to convince us that these claims are true. This method of reporting is sometimes used to catch your attention or to make you buy something. Even serious stories on scientific research or technological innovation can be difficult to interpret, especially when they are reported in a way that makes the work sound important, official, and somewhat mysterious.

Figure 1

There are scientific and technological stories in the news every day.

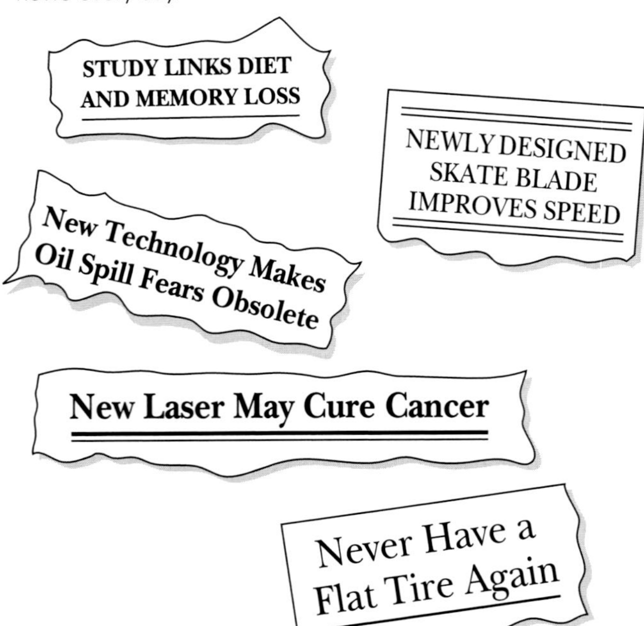

STUDY LINKS DIET AND MEMORY LOSS
NEWLY DESIGNED SKATE BLADE IMPROVES SPEED
New Technology Makes Oil Spill Fears Obsolete
New Laser May Cure Cancer
Never Have a Flat Tire Again

To analyze information, you have to use your mind effectively and critically. When you encounter a report that uses scientific or technological evidence, analyze the report carefully. You might ask yourself, for instance:

- Was the investigation conducted by a reputable laboratory or firm?
- How many times was the design or inquiry process repeated?
- What are the possible sources of error? Are they addressed?
- What do other experts say about these claims?

Try This Reading Critically

Analyze a scientific report or story from one of the following magazines by answering the questions listed above:

- *Scientific American*
- *Popular Mechanics*
- *Discover Magazine*
- *Eureka: The Canadian Invention and Innovation Newsletter*
- or a magazine of your choice

Using Critical Thinking Skills

A lot of research has been done to help people develop critical thinking skills. One very good, practical framework is known as PERCS (which comes from the word perquisite, meaning a benefit). It was founded out of Central Park East Secondary School in New York City. To prepare themselves for their world, the students at CPESS use a series of questions to help them think critically about information and arguments. These questions will help you build an educated and critical opinion about an issue.

The PERCS Checklist:

P = Perspective

- From whose viewpoint are we seeing or reading or hearing?
- From what angle or perspective?

E = Evidence

- How do we know what we know?
- What's the evidence and how reliable is it?

R = Relevance

- So what?
- What does it matter?
- What does it all mean?
- Who cares?

C = Connections

- How are things, events, or people connected to each other?
- What is the cause and what is the effect?
- How do they "fit" together?

S = Supposition

- What if…?
- Could things be otherwise?
- What are or were the alternatives?
- Suppose things were different?

Using PERCS

Try exercising your critical thinking skills. Choose any article from today's newspaper or from a popular magazine and analyze it using the PERCS checklist.

5A Using the Microscope

Because cells are small, you must make them appear larger than they really are in order to see and study them. To view cells closely, you will use a compound light microscope (**Figure 1**). It employs two lenses and a light source to make the object appear larger. The object is magnified by a lens near your eye, the ocular lens (sometimes called the eyepiece), and again by a second lens, the objective lens, which is just above the object. The comparison of the actual size of the object with the size of its image is referred to as magnification.

The parts of the microscope are described in **Table 1**.

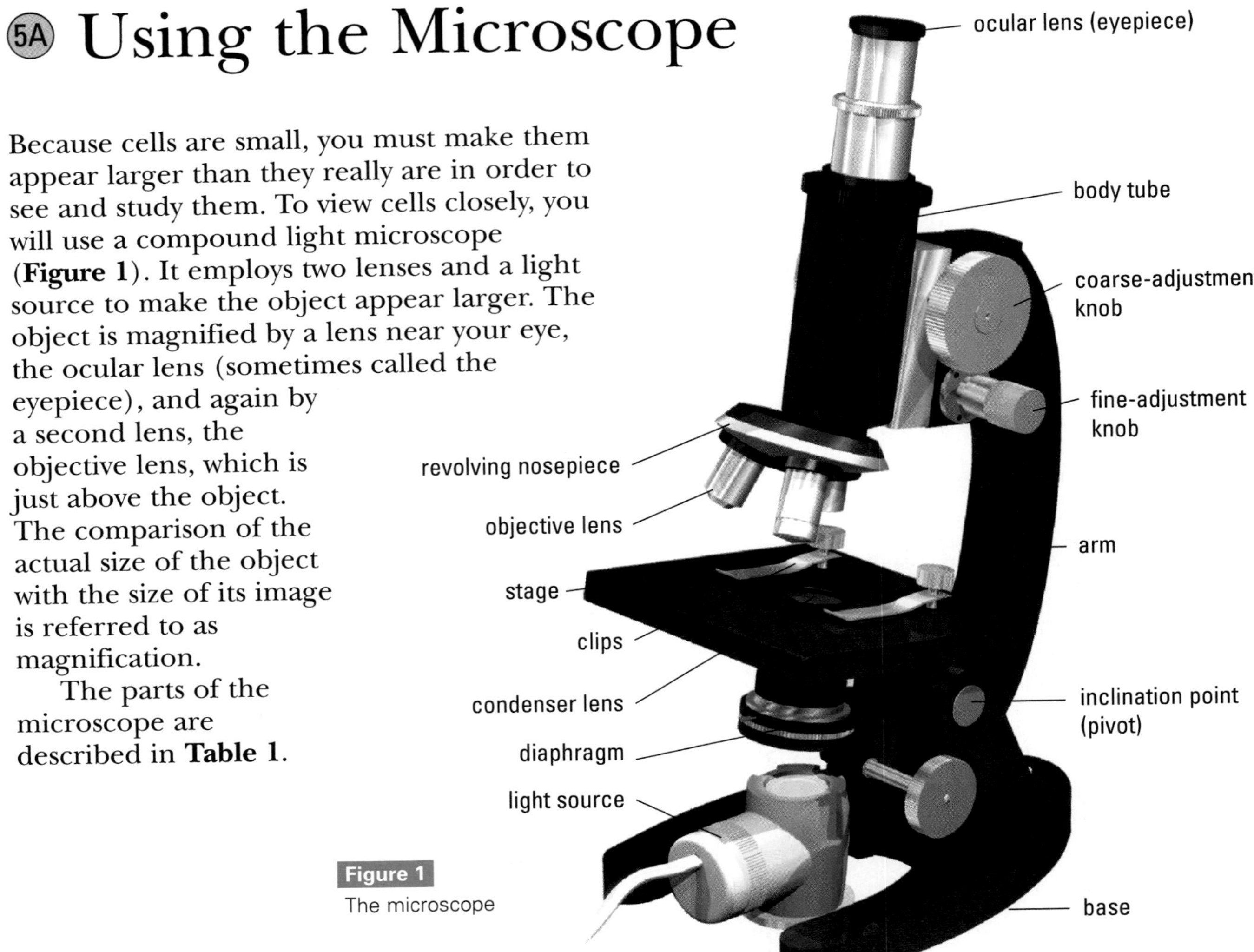

Figure 1 The microscope

Table 1 Parts of the Microscope

Structure	Function
body tube	Contains ocular lens, supports objective lenses.
clips	Found on the stage and used to hold the slide in position.
coarse-adjustment knob	Moves the body tube up or down so you can get the object or specimen into focus. It is used with the low-power objective lens only.
condenser lens	Directs light to the object or specimen.
diaphragm	Regulates the amount of light reaching the object being viewed.
fine-adjustment knob	Moves the tube to get the object or specimen into sharp focus. It is used with medium- and high-power magnification. The fine-adjustment knob is used only after the object or specimen has been located and focused under low-power magnification using the coarse adjustment.
objective lenses	Magnifies the object. Usually three complex lenses are located on the nosepiece immediately above the object or specimen. The smallest of these, the low-power objective lens, has the lowest magnification, usually four times (4X). The medium-power lens magnifies by 10X, and the long, high-power lens by 40X.
ocular lens	Magnifies the object, usually by 10X. Also known as the eyepiece, this is the part you look through to view the object.
revolving nosepiece	Rotates, allowing the objective lens to be changed. Each lens clicks into place.
stage	Supports the microscope slide. A central opening in the stage allows light to pass through the slide.

Care of the Microscope

The microscope is an important and expensive scientific instrument. It should always be used with care and patience. Here are some points to remember when using your microscope.

1. Always keep a microscope in an upright position.
2. When carrying a microscope, grasp its arm with one hand and support its base with the other (**Figure 2**).

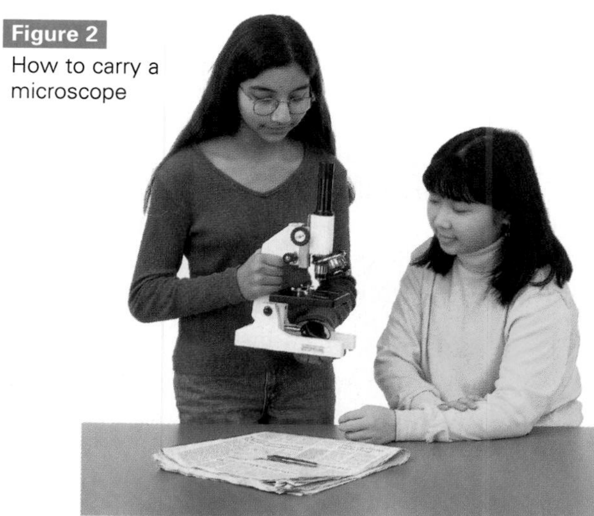

Figure 2
How to carry a microscope

3. Once you have the microscope at your workstation, turn the coarse adjustment knob to lower the objective lens to its lowest point. Focus by using the knob to move the objective lens slowly upward to bring an object into focus. You must always remember to use both knobs when adjusting your microscope or you will strip the adjustment gears.
4. Microscope lenses are made of optical glass, which is soft and scratches easily. Use special lens paper to remove any dust or dirt.
5. When you complete an investigation using the microscope, follow these steps:
   - Rotate the nosepiece to the low-power objective lens.
   - Remove the slide and cover slip (if applicable).
   - Clean the slide and cover slip and return them to their appropriate location.
   - Return the microscope to the storage area.

Basic Microscope Skills

The skills outlined below are presented as sets of instructions. This will enable you to practise these skills before you are asked to use them in the investigations in *Nelson Science & Technology 7/8.*

Materials

- newspaper that contains lower-case letter "*f*" or similar small object
- scissors
- microscope slide
- cover slip
- dropper
- water
- compound microscope
- thread
- compass or petri dish
- pencil
- transparent ruler

Preparing a Dry Mount

This method of preparing a microscope slide is called a dry mount, because no water is used. A dry mount can be used for any specimen that won't dry out while you are examining it.

1. Find a small, flat object, such as a lower-case letter "*f*" cut from a newspaper.
2. Place the object in the centre of a microscope slide.
3. Hold a cover slip between your thumb and forefinger. Place the edge of the cover slip to one side of the object. Gently lower the cover slip onto the slide so that it covers the object.

Step 3

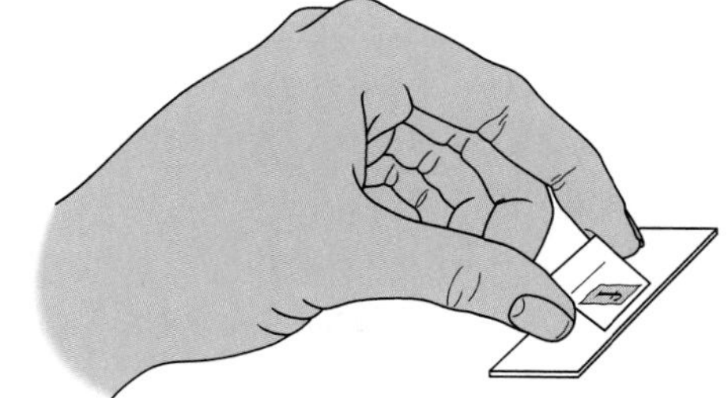

Preparing a Wet Mount

This method of preparing a microscope slide is called a wet mount, because water is used.

A wet mount is used for specimens that can dry out while you are examining them. For instance, when you use a specimen from a living thing, like an onion, the specimen must be very thin. This means that it can lose moisture rapidly: it needs to be kept moist or it will begin to shrivel and become more and more difficult to examine.

1. Find a small, thin, flat object.
2. Place the object in the centre of a microscope slide.
3. Place two drops of water on the object.

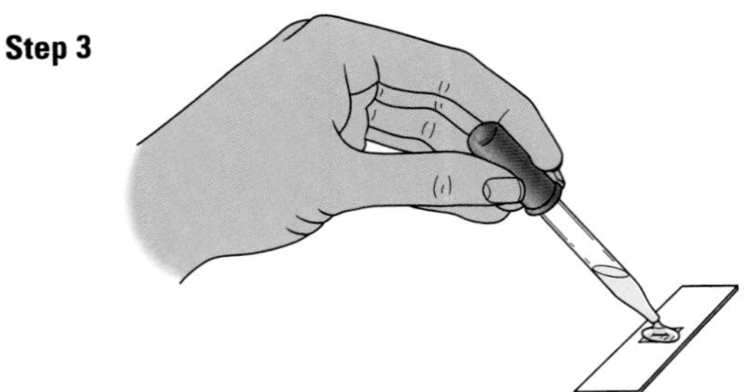

4. Holding the cover slip with your thumb and forefinger, touch the edge of the surface of the slide at a 45º angle. Gently lower the cover slip, allowing the air to escape.

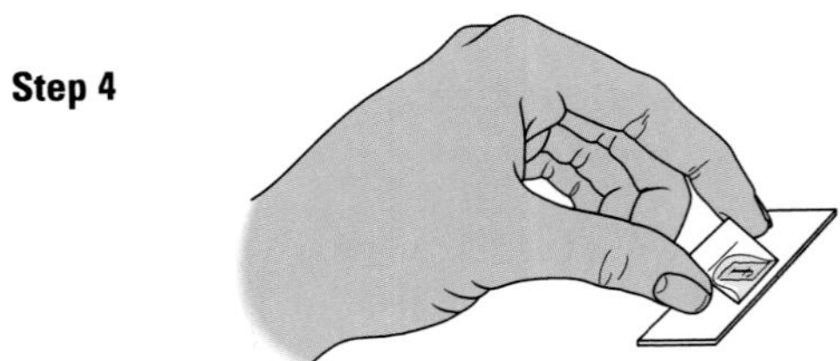

Positioning Objects Under the Microscope

1. Make sure the low-power objective lens is in place on your microscope. Then put either the dry or wet mount slide in the centre of the microscope stage. Use the stage clips to hold the slide in position. Turn on the light source.

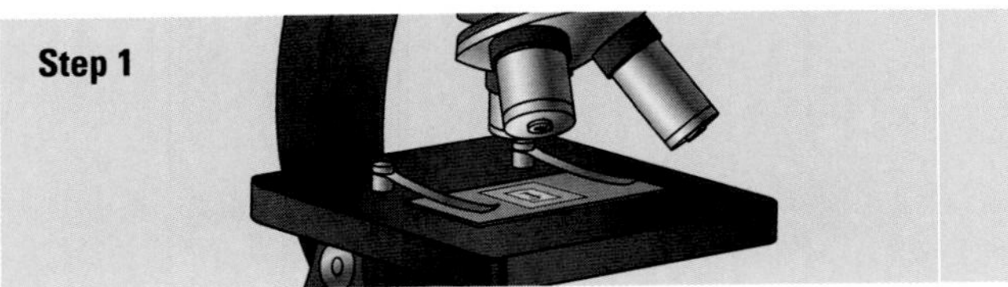

2. View the microscope stage from the side. Using the coarse-adjustment knob, bring the low-power objective lens and the object as close as possible to one another. Do not allow the lens to touch the cover slip.

3. View the object through the eyepiece. Slowly move the coarse-adjustment knob so the objective lens moves away from the slide, to bring the image into focus. Note that the object is facing the "wrong" way and is upside down.
4. Using a compass or a petri dish, draw a circle in your notebook to represent the area you are looking at through the microscope. This area is called the field of view. Look through the microscope and draw what you see. Make the object fill the same amount of area in your diagram as it does in the microscope.
5. While you are looking through the microscope, slowly move the slide away from your body. Note that the object appears to move toward you. Now move the slide to the left. Note that the object appears to move to the right.
6. Rotate the nosepiece to the medium-power objective lens. Use the fine-adjustment knob to bring the object into focus. Note that the object becomes larger.

Never use the coarse-adjustment knob with the medium or high-power objective lenses.

7. Adjust the object so that it is directly in the centre of the field of view. Rotate the nosepiece to the high-power objective lens. Use the fine-adjustment knob to focus the image. Note that you see less of the object than you did under medium-power magnification. Also note that the object seems closer to you.

Investigating Depth of Field

The depth of field is the amount of an image that is in sharp focus when it is viewed under a microscope.

1. Cut two pieces of thread of different colours.
2. Make a temporary dry mount by placing one thread over the other in the form of an X in the centre of a microscope slide. Cover the threads with a cover slip.

Step 2

3. Place the slide on the microscope stage and turn on the light.
4. Position the low-power objective lens close to, but not touching, the slide.
5. View the crossed threads through the ocular lens. Slowly rotate the coarse-adjustment knob until the threads come into focus.
6. Rotate the nosepiece to the medium-power objective lens. Focus on the upper thread by using the fine-adjustment knob. You will probably notice that you cannot focus on the lower thread at the same time. The depth of the object that is in focus at any one time represents the depth of field.
7. Repeat step 6 for the high-power objective lens. The stronger the magnification, the shallower the depth of field.

Determining the Field of View

The field of view is the circle of light seen through the microscope. It is the area of the slide that you can observe.

1. With the low-power objective lens in place, put a transparent ruler on the stage. Position the millimetre marks on the ruler immediately below the objective lens.
2. Using the coarse-adjustment knob, focus on the marks on the ruler.
3. Move the ruler so that one of the millimetre markings is just at the edge of the field of view. Note the diameter of the field of view in millimetres, under the low-power objective lens.

Step 3

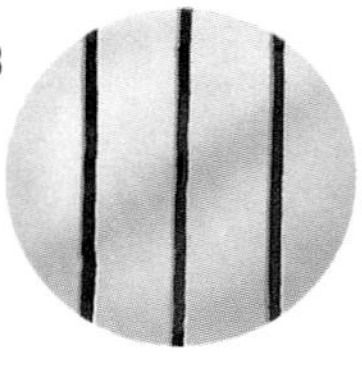

4. Using the same procedure, measure the field of view for the medium-power objective lens.
5. Most high-power lenses provide a field of view that is less than one millimetre in diameter, so it cannot be measured with a ruler. The following steps can be followed to calculate the field of view of the high-power lens.

   Calculate the ratio of the magnification of the high-power objective lens to that of the low-power objective lens.

$$\text{Ratio} = \frac{\text{magnification of high-power lens}}{\text{magnification of low-power lens}}$$

   Use the ratio to determine the field of diameter (diameter of the field of view) under high-power magnification.

$$\text{Field diameter (high power)} = \frac{\text{field diameter (low power)}}{\text{ratio}}$$

Estimating Size

1. Measure the field of view, in millimetres, as shown above.
2. Remove the ruler and replace it with the object under investigation.

Step 2

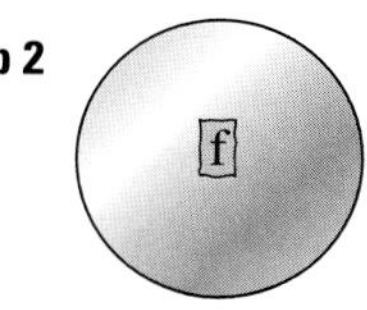

3. Estimate the number of times the object could fit across the field of view.
4. Calculate the width of the object:

$$\text{width of object} = \frac{\text{width of field of view}}{\text{number of objects across field}}$$

Remember to include units.

5B Working with Scales and Balances

Mass is an important quantitative property that is frequently measured: it is the amount of matter a substance has. A balance will give you the same measurement of mass no matter where you are, because it compares the object to another object of fixed mass acting under the same gravitational force. The electronic balance, the platform balance, and the triple beam balance are commonly used in Science & Technology classrooms.

Weight is different from mass. Weight is the measure of the force of gravity working on an object. An object will weigh different amounts in a valley, on the top of Mount Everest, and on the Moon—but it will have the same mass. Spring scales are often used to weigh things in Science & Technology classrooms.

The Electronic Balance

Electronic balances are easy to use, but they are also usually expensive and sensitive pieces of equipment (**Figure 1**). To operate an electronic balance, you simply place the sample on the platform and read the measurement on the digital display. If you want to measure the mass of a substance without including the mass of the container it is in, you can place the container on the platform and "re-zero" or "TARE" the balance. This resets the scale to zero. You can then measure the mass of the substance that you add.

Figure 1
An electronic balance

The Platform Balance

A platform balance (or equal arm balance) operates on the same principles as old scales used in commerce and, figuratively, in justice. Look at **Figure 2**. Can you see why it is called a "balance"?

Figure 2
A platform or equal arm balance

To use a platform balance, you balance your sample with known masses. Be sure that your balance is "balanced" before you use it—you may have to adjust the adjustment weights. Add masses in small amounts to come as close as possible to a balanced state. Then adjust the rider to make the final balance.

The Triple Beam Balance

The triple beam balance uses the same principle as the platform balance, but it also uses the principle of leverage (**Figure 3**). You measure

Figure 3
A triple beam balance

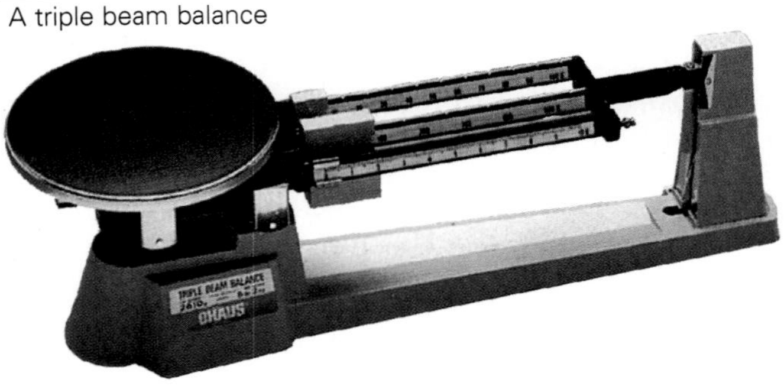

the mass of a substance by systematically adjusting the three rider beams (starting with the largest scale and ending with the smallest scale) and combining the three readings (**Figure 4**). Again, you may have to initially "zero" the scale by adjusting the adjustment weights.

Figure 4
Measuring the mass of a beaker

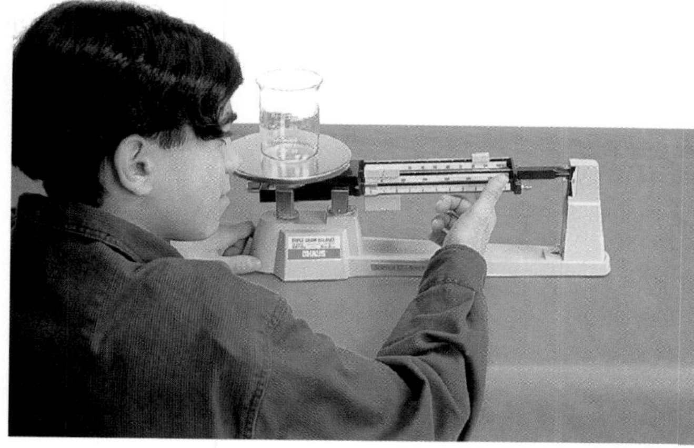

Try This **Measure Mass and Weight**

Using one of the types of balances listed above, measure the following:

- the mass of a key
- the mass of the water in a glass (you may have to think about this if you are using either a platform balance or a triple beam balance)
- the mass of a spoon of sugar

How might you measure the weight of an object in water?

The Spring Scale

The spring scale is used to measure weight (**Figure 5**). In other words, a spring scale compares the force exerted by gravity (and any other forces that are acting—such as the buoyant force) to the counterforce applied by the spring and tells you where they balance, so the measurement varies with the force of gravity. It is particularly useful for items that do not fit on platforms or are different in shape. Spring scales come in various sizes. To use the scales, place the item to be measured on the hook of the spring scale and read the weight on the scale in the clear section of the tube.

Figure 5
Spring scales

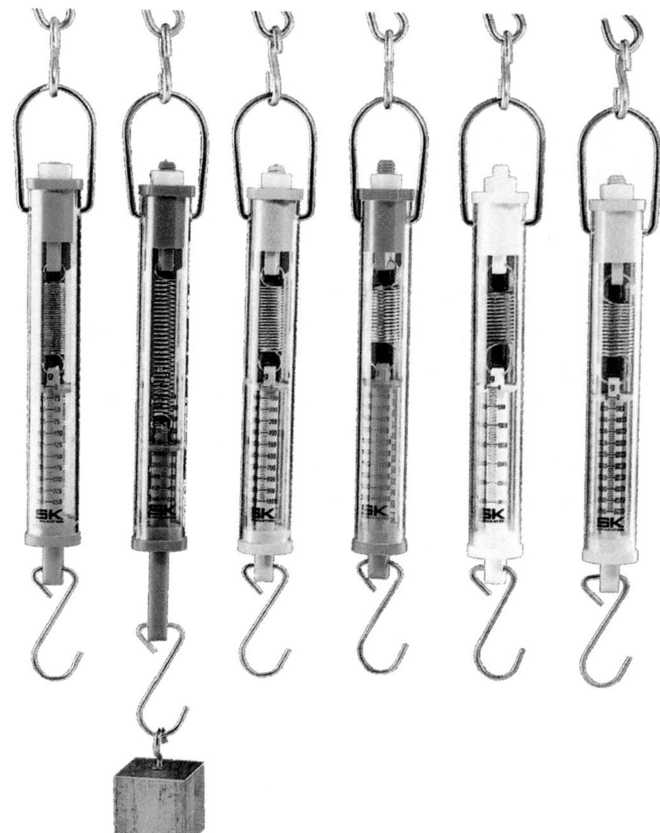

5C Using Other Scientific Equipment

You can do many investigations using everyday materials and equipment. In your Science & Technology classroom, there are other pieces of equipment. Some of these are illustrated below.

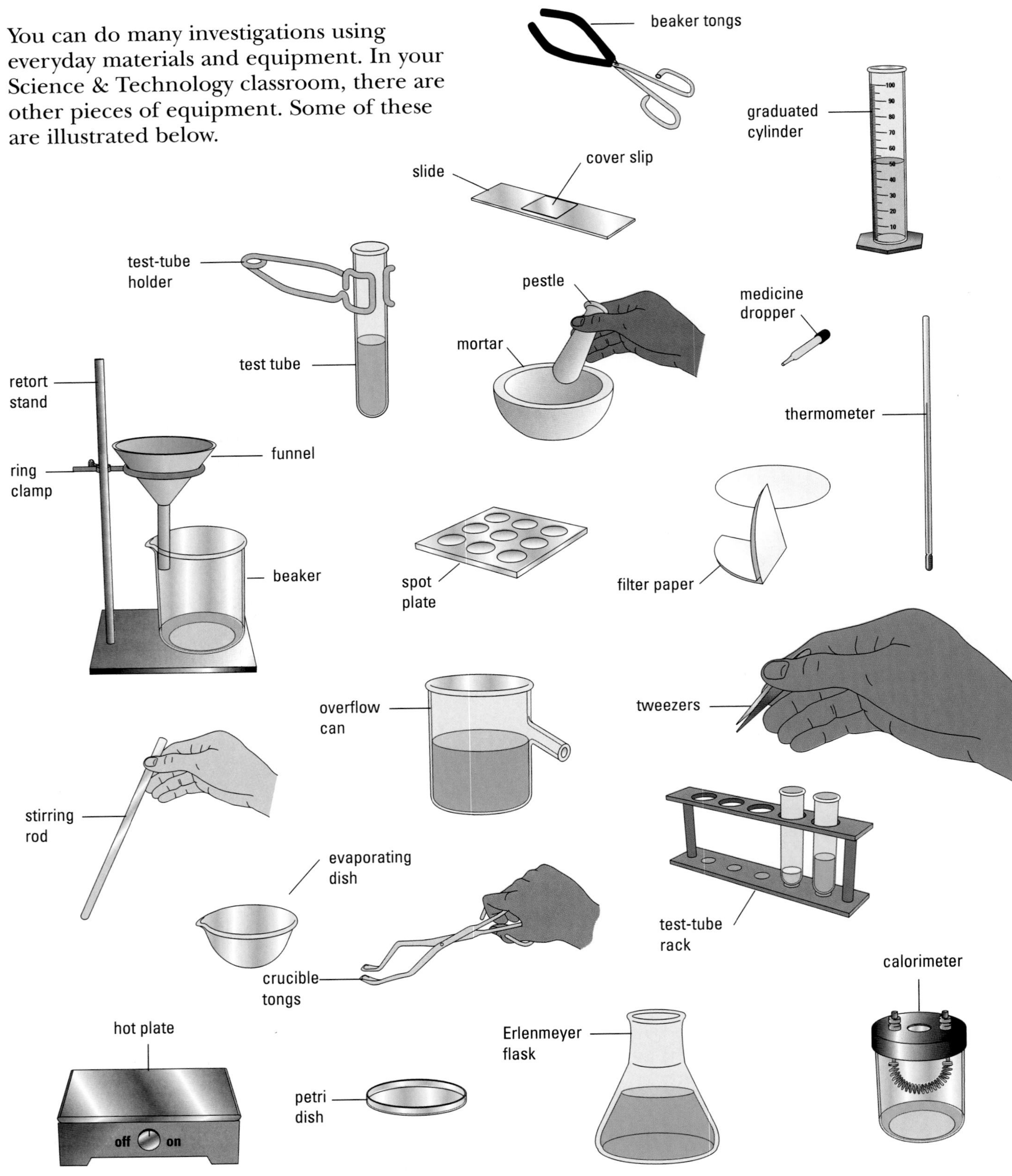

5D Using Technology Equipment

As you go through the design process, you will use various tools and materials to construct your prototypes. Some of these are illustrated below. (Refer to 1 "Safety in Science & Technology," to review the safe use of saws, drills, paper drills, utility knives, snips, hammers, and screwdrivers.)

Tools

Sawing and Cutting

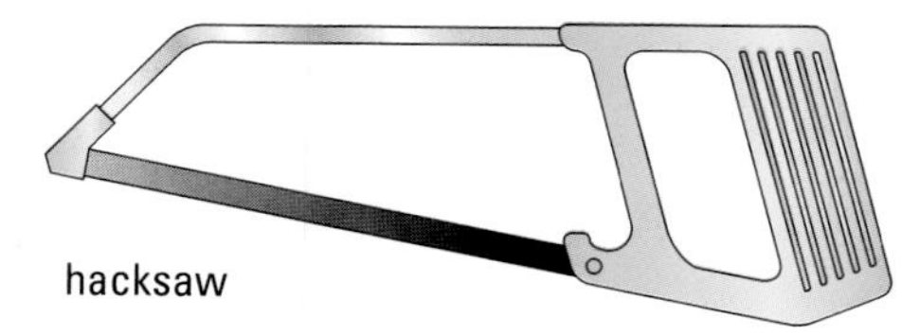
hacksaw

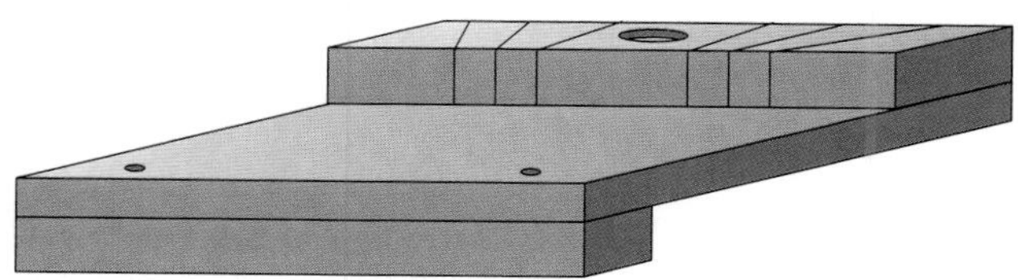
bench hook with mitre box

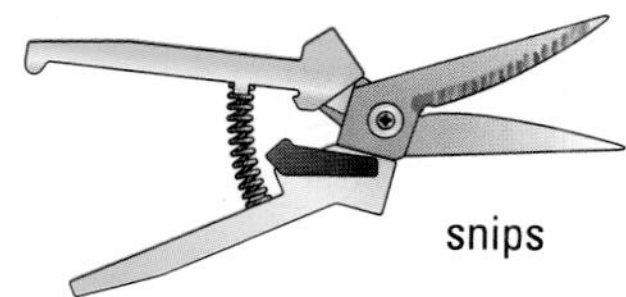
snips

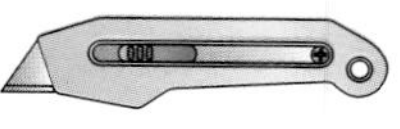
utility knife

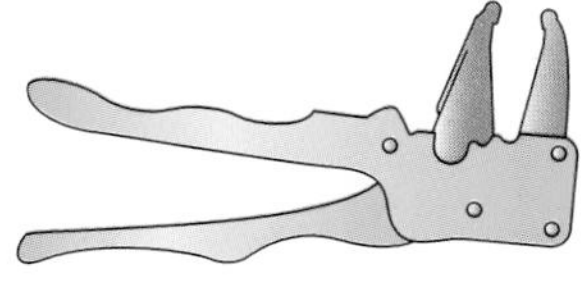
wire strippers

Joining

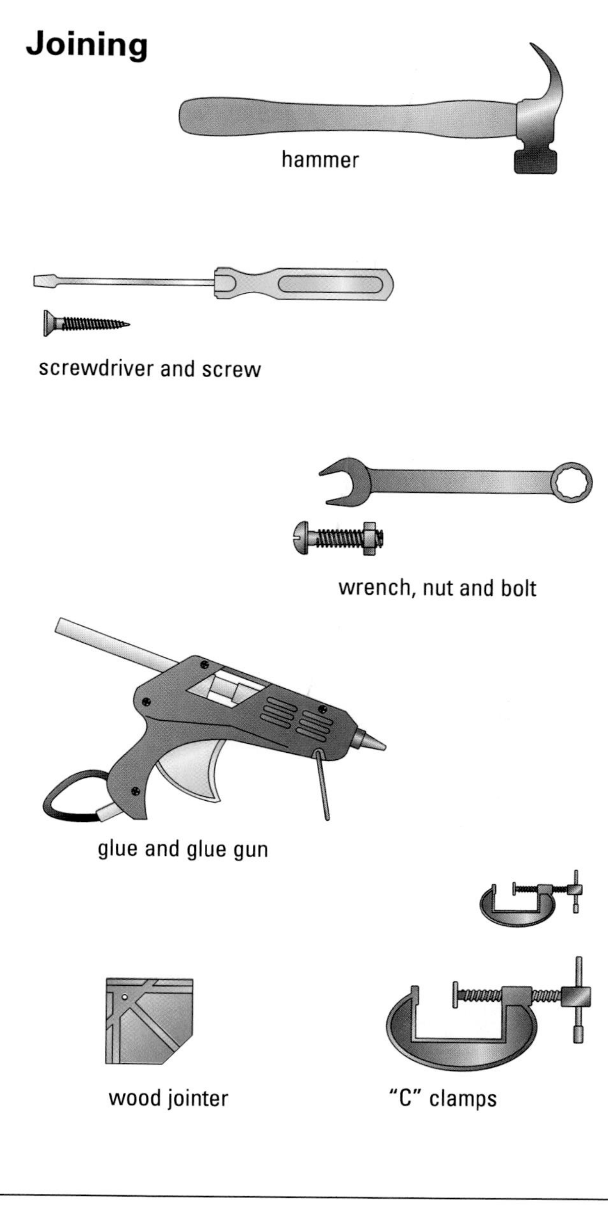

Shaping

pliers

Measuring

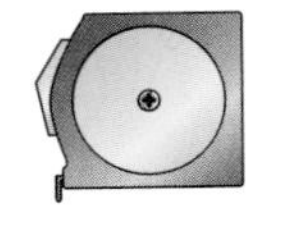

measuring tape

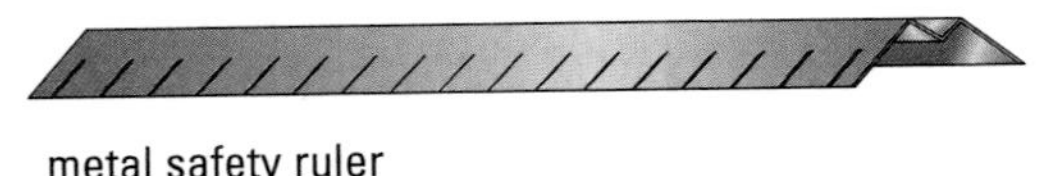

metal safety ruler

Making Holes

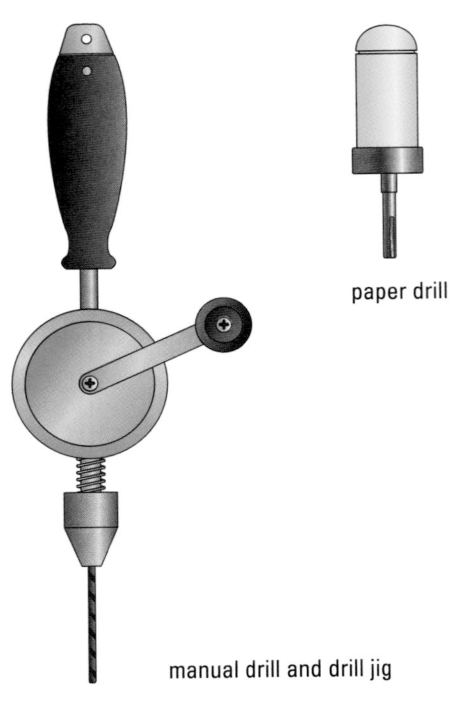

paper drill

manual drill and drill jig

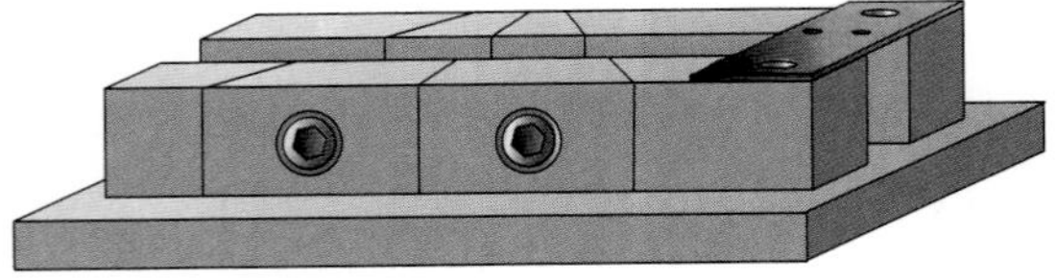

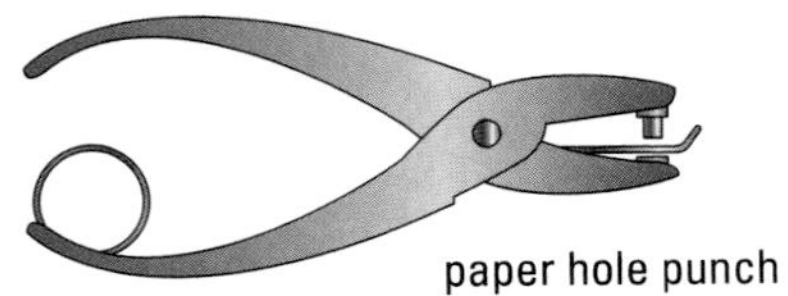

paper hole punch

Structural Parts

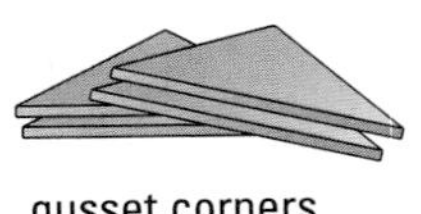

gusset corners

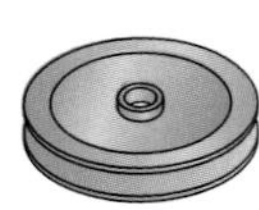

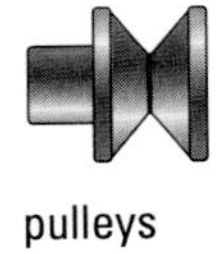

pulleys

wheels

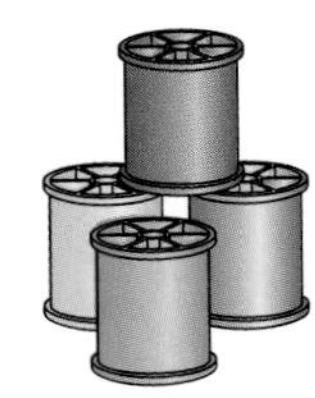

spools

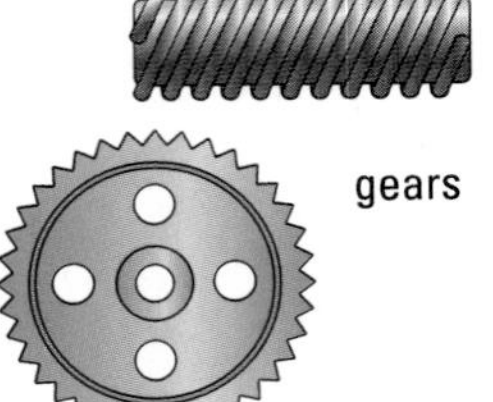

gears

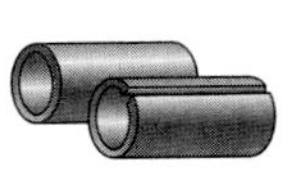

bushings

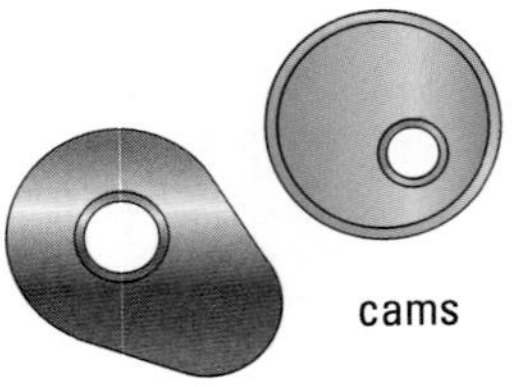

cams

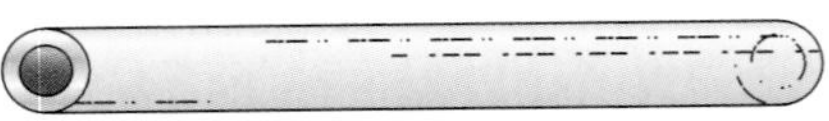

tubing

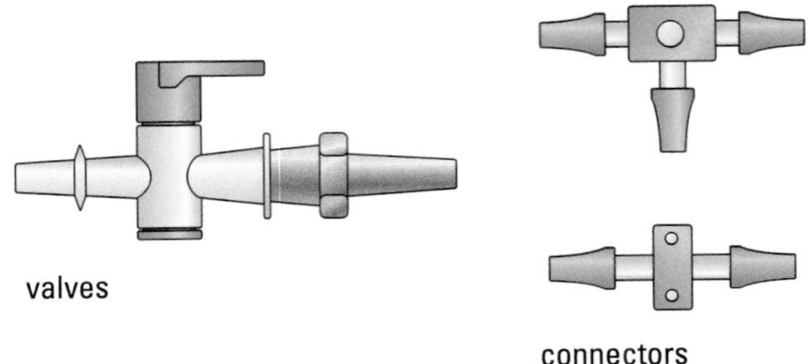

valves

connectors

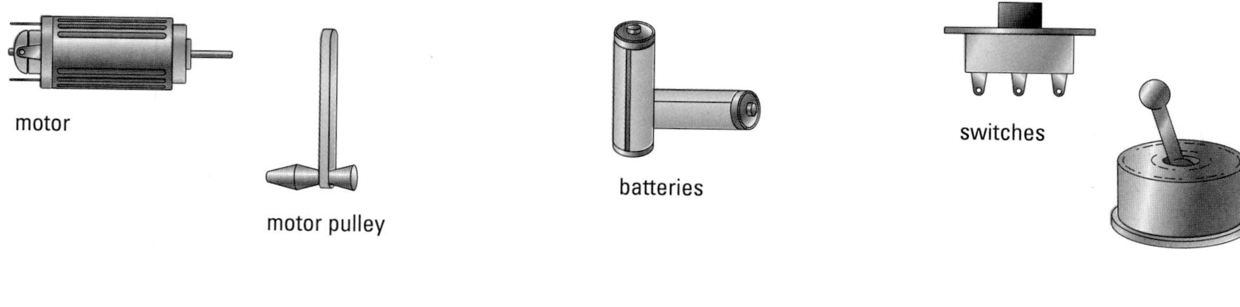

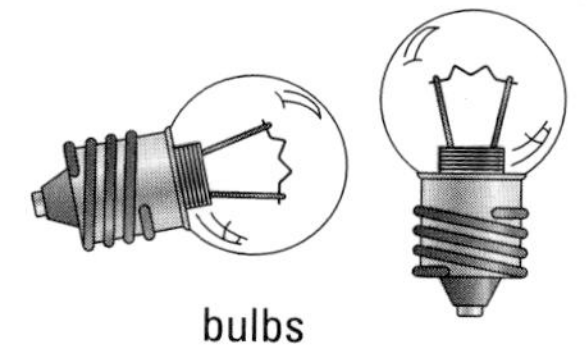

Construction Materials

There are few limits to what materials you can use in construction. The more obvious materials include:

- wood (1 cm x 1 cm basswood)
- bristol board
- metal
- corrugated plastic
- fabric

You should also consider using materials that you encounter everyday, including:

- film containers
- bread tags
- polystyrene food trays
- aluminum pie plates
- fabric
- lids
- pizza "tables"

Useful Materials

There is a wealth of construction materials available to you. Brainstorm a list of construction materials. Be as creative as possible. For each material, suggest a possible use.

5E Fabrication Techniques

There are many different fabrication techniques and skills that you can learn to help take your design from a plan to a prototype. The following section will help you learn some basic techniques. As you become more skilled, you will want to explore additional techniques. You can learn more by taking note of how things are built, by asking for expert help, and by using other information resources.

Structures

The following techniques will help you build a variety of different structures.

Joining with Adhesives

- Use the right adhesive for the materials you are using. Read labels carefully to get the best results and to work safely.
- If possible, it may be useful to roughen the surfaces being joined. A rough surface increases the gluing area and helps the glue hold.
- Make sure the surfaces being joined are in contact with each other. You may need to use a clamp or other device to apply the necessary pressure.

Figure 1 shows how to join two pieces of wood in a right angle. Spread glue on one side of a cardboard triangle, and place it on the wood so that a right angle is formed. When the glue has dried, do the same on the other side of the corner joint. This will prevent sideways twisting and keep the corner at a right angle.

Figure 1
Joining wood in a right angle

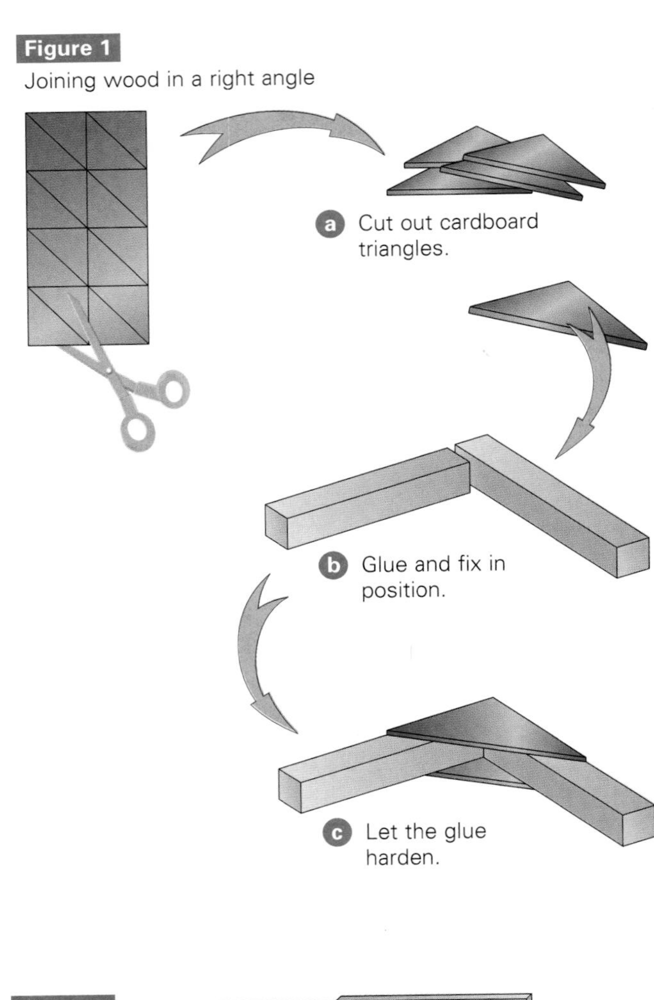
a Cut out cardboard triangles.
b Glue and fix in position.
c Let the glue harden.

Joining with Fasteners

Use the right fastener for the job. Nails, for instance, are used to join wood permanently whereas screws are better for joining things temporarily. **Figures 2–4** illustrate a few useful joining techniques.

Figure 2
Joining two strips to allow movement

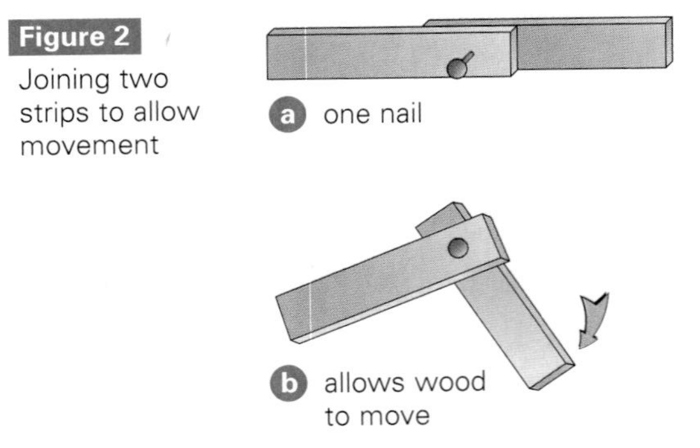
a one nail
b allows wood to move

Figure 3
Joining two strips to provide rigidity

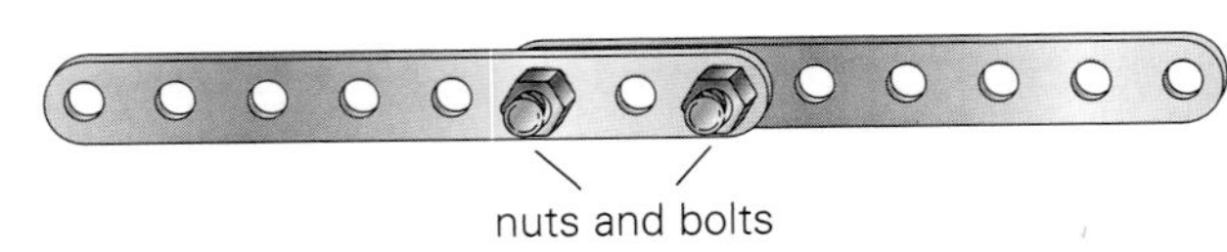
nuts and bolts

Figure 4

Making holes in materials allows you to use many different fasteners that can help you control friction better. This is useful for constructing such things as levers.

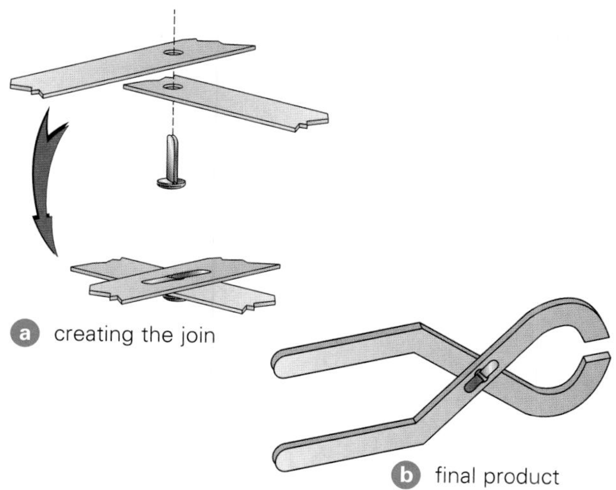

Wheels and Axles

There are two basic kinds of wheel systems: free wheels and fixed wheels. These can be understood by considering a bicycle (**Figure 5**). An axle runs through the centre of every wheel. On a bicycle, the back wheel is fixed to the axle. When the chain turns the axle, the axle turns the wheel. The front wheel is not fixed to the axle—the axle itself is fixed. When the bicycle moves forward, the front wheel turns.

Figure 5

A wheel depends upon friction to make it work. An axle runs through the centre of the wheel.

Free wheel: the bike moves forward, the tire cannot slip and so the wheel turns.

Fixed wheel: the axle turns the wheel, the tire cannot slip and so it pushes the bike forward.

- Wheels must be round. Ways of creating wheels include using ready-made wheels, using round objects as wheels, and cutting dowel into sections.
- Axles must be centred and straight. If not, the ride will be wobbly. Axles must also be loose enough or the wheels will stick.
- Wheels must have enough friction. This can be increased by roughening the surface of the wheel or covering it with a material like rubber.
- Wheels must be well attached to axles. Ways of keeping wheels on axles include plastic or rubber tubing, locking pins, and screws and washers.

Gears

A gear is a wheel with teeth. It can mesh with another gear to create different kinds of motion. Three useful types of gears are illustrated in **Figures 6–8**.

Figure 6

A worm gear drives a cog and turns the axis of rotation through 90°.

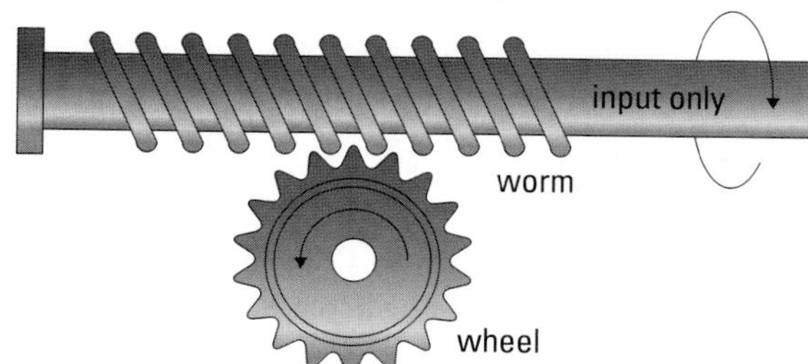

Figure 7

A rack and pinion gear converts circular movement to linear movement.

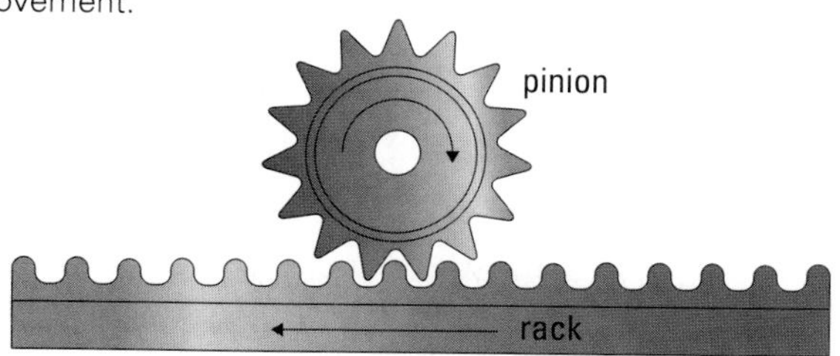

Figure 8

A bevel gear has teeth cut at a 45° angle. It changes the direction of turning through 90°.

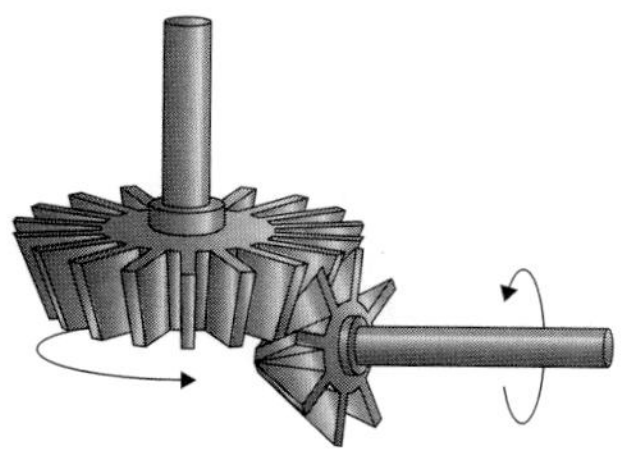

Gears are available ready-made. You can also make simple gears from corrugated cardboard and discs and dowel (**Figure 9**). For gears to work, their teeth must have a common factor. For example, a 12-tooth gear will mesh with a 4-tooth gear because they have a common factor of 3. A 12-tooth gear will not mesh with a 5-tooth gear, for example.

Figure 9
Gear construction

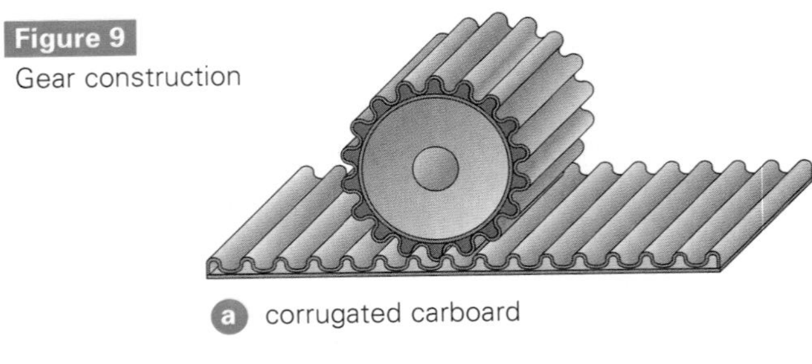

a corrugated carboard

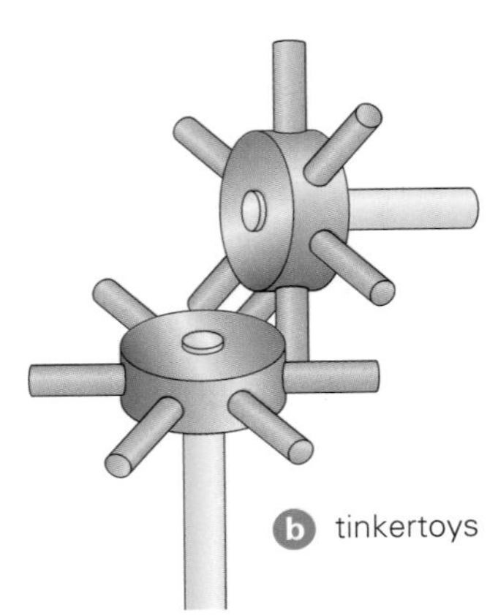

b tinkertoys

Levers

Levers can be used to change the direction and size of a movement or force. A lever is a rigid rod with a turning point (pivot). There are standard ways of linking levers together that produce specific mechanisms. Some of these are illustrated in **Figure 10**. The best way to understand how levers work is to experiment with simple materials, like cardboard strips and paper fasteners.

Figure 10
Different linkages

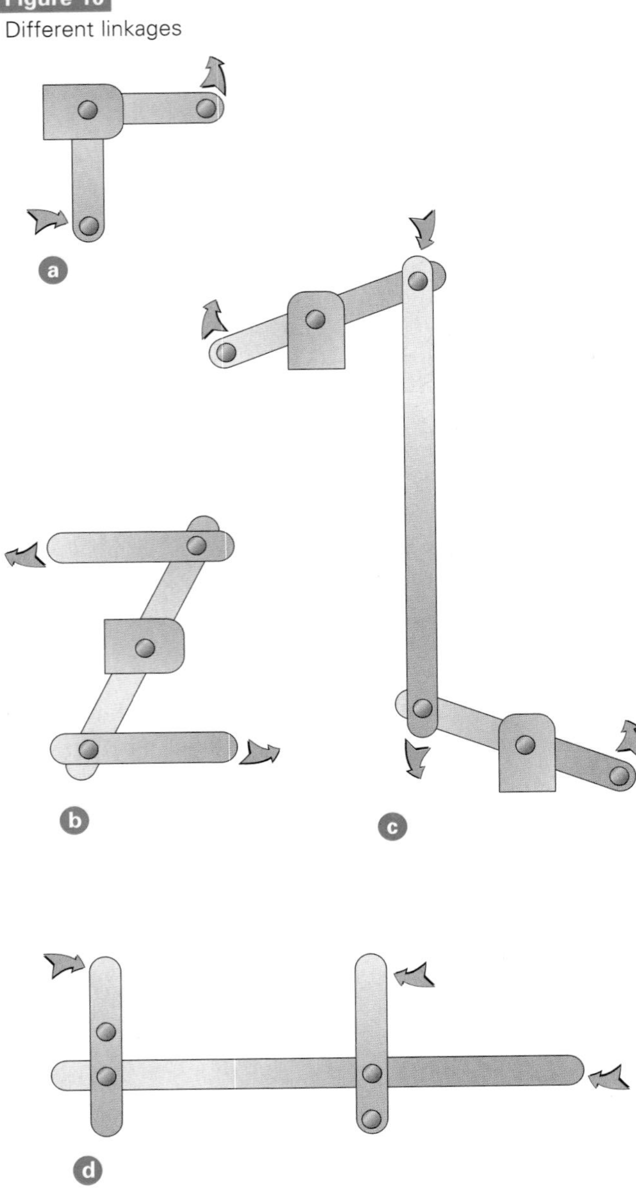

If you are having trouble with your lever, check for the following problems:

- the pivots may be too tight or too loose
- the pivots may not be in the right place
- the linkages may be connected incorrectly
- the linkages may be the wrong length
- the linkages may be out of line.

Electricity

Many of the prototypes you build will use electricity. In these cases, you will need to draw and construct circuits to control electricity. The following section outlines the basic techniques for building circuits. When in doubt about any details, ask your teacher. Think safety first.

Safety Considerations

- Only operate a circuit after it has been approved by your teacher.
- Always ensure that your hands are dry, and that you are standing on a dry surface.
- Do not use faulty dry cells or batteries, do not connect different makes of dry cells in the same battery, and avoid connecting partially discharged dry cells to fully-charged cells.
- Take care not to short-circuit dry cells or batteries.
- Do not use frayed or damaged connectors.
- Handle breakable components with care.

The Parts of an Electric Circuit

Simple electric circuits have four basic parts, shown in **Figure 11**.

Figure 11
The parts of an electric circuit

4. Connector
1. Source of electrical energy
3. Circuit control device
2. Electrical load

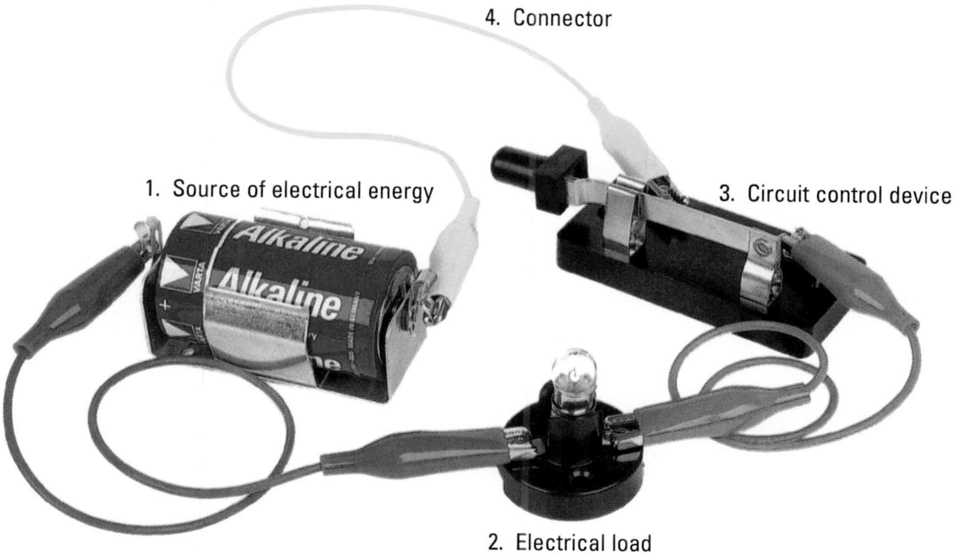

1. **A source of electrical energy:** You will typically use a combination of dry cells or a special device called a "power supply." These are direct current sources of electricity. They are much safer to use than wall outlets, which provide an alternating current source.
2. **An electrical load:** The load is the appliance that uses the electricity (e.g., lights, buzzers, motors).
3. **A circuit control device:** You will normally use one of a variety of switches (e.g., some switches turn things on and off, some switches reverse the direction of electric motors, etc.)
4. **Connectors:** These are often copper wires.

Drawing a Circuit Diagram

Before building a circuit, you should work it out on paper (**Figure 12**). There are some conventions to follow when drawing circuit diagrams: connecting wires are generally shown as straight linees or 90° angles, and

Figure 12
Schematic diagram of the closed circuit shown in Figure 11

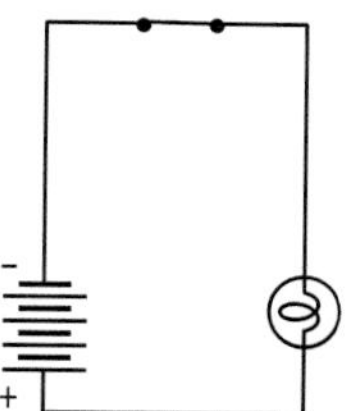

symbols (shown in **Table 1**) are used to represent all the components.

Table 1 **Symbols used in Circuit Diagrams**

	DC CIRCUITS	
Sources/Outlets		cell
		3-cell battery
Control Devices		switch
		fuse
		circuit breaker
		switch and fuse
		distribution panel
	S	switch
	S_{WP}	weatherproof switch
		push button
Electrical Loads		light bulb
		clock
		motor
		thermostat
		resistor
		variable resistor (rheostat)
		fluorescent fixture
		heating panel
Meters		ammeter
		voltmeter
Connectors		conducting wire
		wires joined
		ground connection

Constructing the Circuit

- Have your circuit diagram approved by your teacher.
- Check connections carefully when linking dry cells. Incorrect connections could cause shorted circuits or explosions. Ask your teacher for clarification if you are unsure.
- When attaching connecting wires to meters, connect a red wire to the positive terminal and a black wire to the negative terminal of the meter. This will remind you to consider the polarity of the meter when connecting it in the circuit.
- Sometimes the ends of connecting wires do not have the correct attachments to connect to the device or meter. Use extra approved attachment devices, such as alligator clips, but be careful to position the connectors so that they cannot touch one another.
- Open the switch before altering a meter connection or adding new wiring or components.
- If the circuit does not operate correctly, open the switch and check the circuit wiring and all connections to the terminals. If you still cannot find the problem, ask your teacher to inspect your circuit again.

Pneumatics and Hydraulics

Two additional systems can be used to create movement: pneumatic systems and hydraulic systems. Each of these systems is based on the fact that fluids (gas or liquid) can be "pushed" in order to make something else move. Hydraulic systems use a liquid. Water, for instance, works in low-pressure systems, whereas hydraulic oil is used in high-pressure systems. Pneumatic systems use a gas, such as air. The air must be compressed before it can be used.

These systems have three basic components:

1. Inputs: You need a reservoir of fluid and a way of moving the fluid into the system. For instance, gravity can be used to create water pressure.
2. Controls: You need a way of directing the flow of the fluid that is strong enough to withstand the pressure of the fluid. The parts of the control system include pipes to control the direction of the flow, connectors to extend the system, taps to control the amount of fluid in the system, and valves to control the direction of the flow.
3. Outputs: The moving fluid is used to activate a device.

A simple pneumatic system is illustrated in **Figure 13**. Air from the syringe is forced through the tubing and into the balloon. The balloon inflates and the hand is forced open.

Figure 13
A pneumatic hand

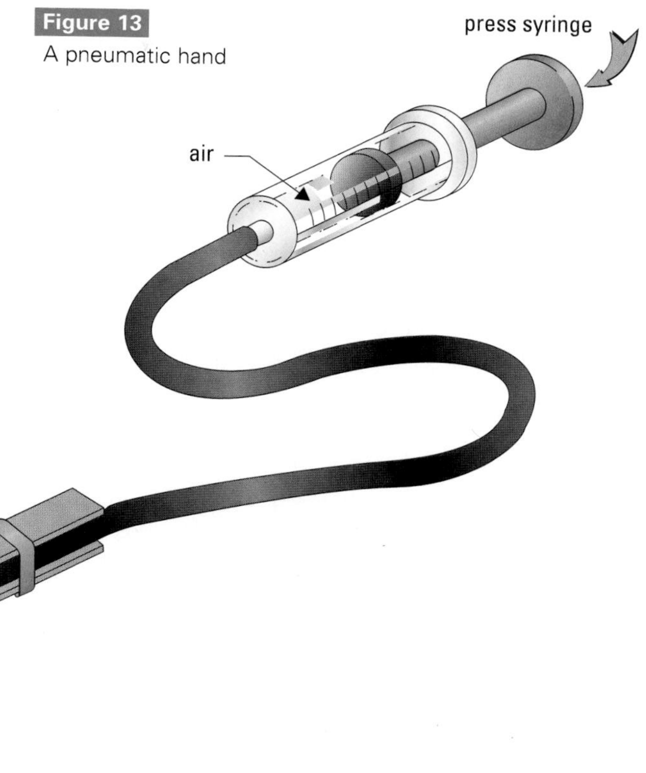

6A Obtaining Qualitative Data

Qualitative Observations

An observation is information that you get through your senses. Scientific questions and technological problems are usually based on observations. For instance, watching waves wash up onto a beach might make you wonder about the cause of tides or how to prevent soil erosion. When you describe the qualities of objects, events, or processes, the observations are qualitative (**Figure 1**).

Figure 1
The shape, the space available for sitting, and the colour of the chair are qualitative observations.

Making observations is a critical step in the process of scientific inquiry (see 2A "Process of Scientific Inquiry," Step 6). Making observations is also critical to the process of design. Evaluating a prototype according to its design criteria requires careful observation (see 3A "The Problem-Solving Cycle," Step 5). Both scientists and technologists have grouped qualitative observations into categories, based on the kind of qualities displayed and the purpose of the investigation.

Qualitative Observations in the Process of Scientific Inquiry

Common categories of qualitative observations used in the process of scientific inquiry appear below:

State of Matter: All substances can be classified as solid, liquid, or gas (**Figure 2**).

Figure 2

(a) Roller blades are solid.

(b) Water is a liquid.

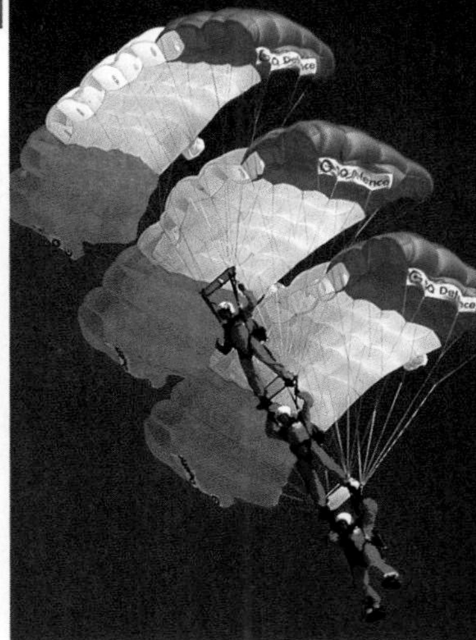

(c) Air is a gas.

Colour: Objects can be described as being any colour or any shade of colour (**Figure 3**). Materials that have no colour should be described as colourless.

Figure 3
This leaf appears green because it reflects green light back to your eyes.

Smell: Also known as odour. There are many words to describe smells, including pungent, strong (**Figure 4**), spicy, sweet, and odourless.

Figure 4
Skunks can produce a very strong odour.

Texture: The surfaces of objects can have a variety of textures, including smooth, rough, prickly, fine, and coarse (**Figure 5**).

Figure 5
These cereal flakes have a coarse texture.

Taste: Objects can taste sweet, sour, bitter, or salty (**Figure 6**). Other tastes are combinations of these basic tastes. Objects that have no taste can be described as tasteless.

Figure 6
Black olives give this pizza a salty taste.

Shininess: Also known as lustre. Objects with very smooth surfaces that reflect light easily, like mirrors, are said to be shiny or lustrous (**Figure 7**). Kitchen taps, mirrors, even well polished desktops can be described as lustrous. Objects with dull surfaces are said to be non-lustrous.

Figure 7
Most metals, such as copper and silver, appear shiny.

Clarity: Some substances let so much light through that letters can be read through them. These substances are said to be clear or transparent. Other substances that allow light through, but not in a way that allows you to see through them, are translucent. Objects that do not let light through are opaque (**Figure 8**).

Figure 8
Clarity ranges from transparent to opaque.

Other qualitative descriptions include form (the shape of a substance), hardness, brittleness (how easily the substance breaks), malleability (the ability of the object to be changed into another shape), and viscosity (a liquid's resistance to flow).

Another important characteristic that can be described qualitatively is the ability of substances to combine with each other.

Qualitative Observations in the Process of Design

The following list outlines design elements that often form the basis for qualitative observations in the process of design:

Shape: A shape is an area defined by a line. A shape can have two dimensions, like a square, or three dimensions, like a pyramid (**Figure 9**). The three dimensions are called: height, depth, and width.

Figure 9

The surface of one side of this box is a square. The box itself is a cube.

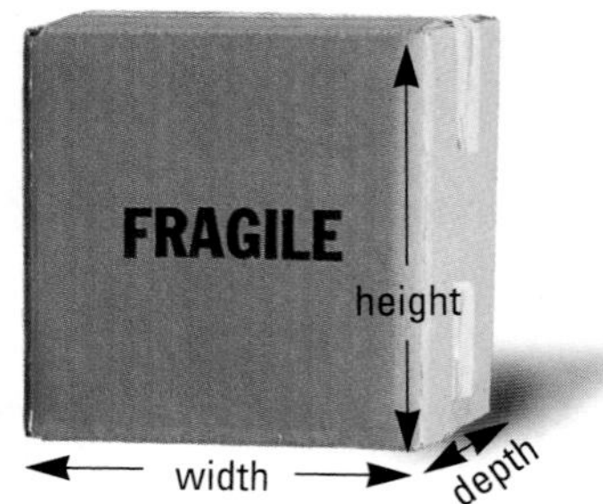

Space: Space is the area that surrounds an object or is contained within an object. All objects exist in space (**Figure 10**). We can only appreciate the form of an object by imagining or seeing the space around it.

Figure 10

The shapes of the objects in this room can only be understood because of the space around them.

Colour: Colour is important because it produces an instant response. Colour is used to enhance a design.

Texture: Texture has an effect on the appearance and function of a design.

Ergonomics: Ergonomics involves designing things so that they can be used easily and safely.

Try This — Which Qualities?

Review the categories of qualities used in the processes of scientific inquiry and design. You will notice that some appear in both lists. Are there others that you think could be useful in both processes? Provide two or three examples.

6B Obtaining Quantitative Data

Quantitative Observations

Observations that are based on measurements or counting are said to be quantitative, since they deal with quantities of things. The length of a rose's stem or a piece of wood, the number of petals on a flower, and the number of rotations of a gear are all quantitative observations.

Look at the two lines in **Figure 1**. Which looks longer? You will find that AB and CD are the same length. Our senses can be fooled. That is one of the reasons quantitative observations are important in science and technology and it is also the reason measurements must be made carefully.

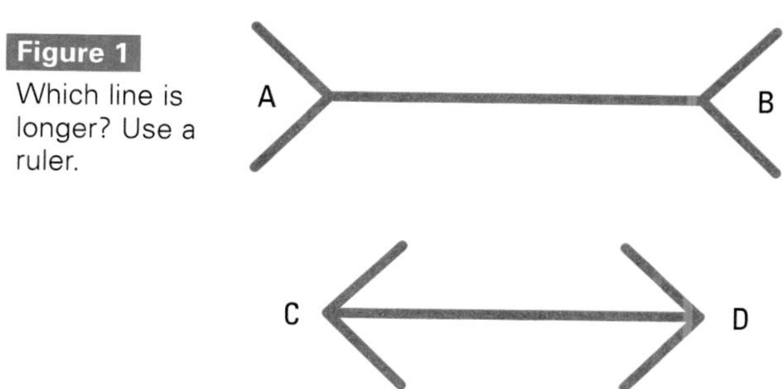

Figure 1
Which line is longer? Use a ruler.

Standards of Measurement

Units of measurement used to be based on local standards that the community had agreed to. At one time, for example, there was a unit equal to the length of a line of 16 people standing close together. Horse heights are still measured in hands, based on the width of a human hand, and measured from the ground to the horse's shoulder.

These standards may sound strange, but the unit of length that replaced most local standards, the metre, was based on an arc on the Earth that ran from the equator, through Barcelona, Paris, and Dunkirk, to the North Pole (**Figure 2**). The length of this arc, divided by 10 000 000, equaled one metre. That also sounds strange, but it established the first standard unit of length that the whole world could use.

Figure 2
The early standard for the metre was 1/10 000 000 of the distance from the equator to the North Pole.

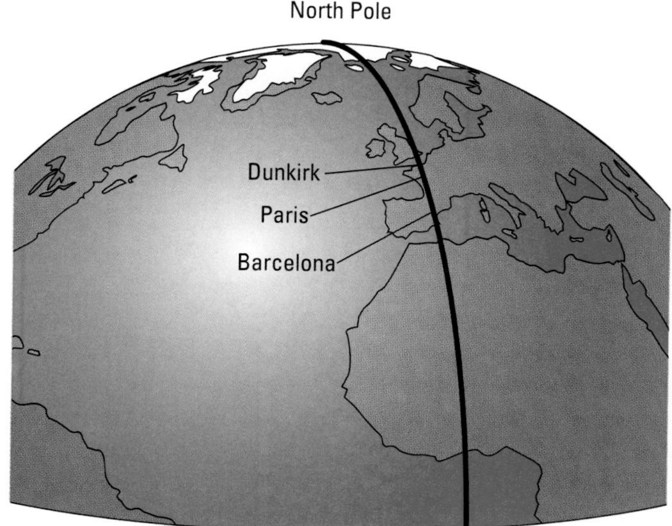

The metric system, which includes units such as the metre and the kilogram, is the one adopted by Canada. You should be familiar with, and use, the units from this international system (also called the SI system, from the French name: Système International d'Unités).

Base Units and Prefixes

There are seven SI base units, shown in **Table 1**.

Table 1 The Seven SI Base Units

Quantity	Unit	Symbol
length	metre	m
mass	kilogram	kg*
time	second	s
electric current	ampere	A
temperature	kelvin	K
amount of substance	mole	mol
light intensity	candela	cd

*The kilogram is the only base unit that contains a prefix. The gram proved to be too small for practical purposes.

Larger and smaller units are created by multiplying or dividing the value of the base units by multiples of 10. For example, the prefix deca means multiplied by 10. Therefore, one decametre (1 dam) is equal to ten metres (10 m). The prefix kilo means multiplied by 1000, so one kilometre (1 km) is equal to one thousand metres (1000 m). Similarly, each unit can be divided into smaller units. The prefix milli, for example, means divided by 1000, so one millimetre (1 mm) is equal to 1/1000 of a metre.

To convert from one unit to another, you simply multiply by a conversion factor. For example, to convert 12.4 metres to centimetres, you use the relationship 1 m = 100 cm.

$$12.4 \text{ m} = ? \text{ cm}$$

$$12.4 \text{ m} \times \frac{100 \text{ cm}}{1 \text{ m}} = 1240 \text{ cm}$$

To convert 6.3 g to kilograms, you use the relationship 1000 g = 1 kg.

$$6.3 \text{ g} = ? \text{ kg}$$

$$6.3 \text{ g} \times \frac{1 \text{ kg}}{1000 \text{ g}} = 0.0063 \text{ kg}$$

Any conversion of the same physical quantities can be done in this way. The conversion factor is chosen so that, using cancellation, it yields the desired unit.

Once you understand this method of conversion, you will find that you can simply move the decimal point. Move it to the right when the new unit is smaller and to the left when the new unit is larger. As you can see from **Table 2**, not all the units and prefixes are commonly used.

Table 2 Metric Prefixes

Prefix	Symbol	Factor by which the base unit is multiplied	Example
giga	G	10^9 = 1 000 000 000	
mega	M	10^6 = 1 000 000	10^6 m = 1 Mm
kilo	k	10^3 = 1 000	10^3 m = 1 km
hecto	h	10^2 = 100	
deca	d	10^1 = 10	
		10^0 = 1	m
deci	da	10^{-1} = 0.1	
centi	c	10^{-2} = 0.01	10^{-2} m = 1 cm
milli	m	10^{-3} = 0.001	10^{-3} m = 1 mm
micro	μ	10^{-6} = 0.000 001	10^{-6} m = 1 μm

Table 3 shows quantities that you may need to be familiar with.

Table 3 Common Quantities and Units

Quantity	Unit	Symbol
length	kilometre	km
	metre	m
	centimetre	cm
	millimetre	mm
mass	tonne (1000 kg)	t
	kilogram	kg
	gram	g
area	hectare (10 000 m^2)	ha
	square metre	m^2
	square centimetre	cm^2
volume	cubic metre	m^3
	litre	L
	cubic centimetre	cm^3
	millilitre	mL
time	minute	min
	second	s
temperature	degrees Celsius	°C
force	newton	N
energy	kilojoule	kJ
	joule	J
pressure	kilopascal	kPa
	pascal	Pa

Measuring Accurately

Many people believe that all measurements are accurate and dependable. But there are many things that can go wrong when measuring. The instrument may be faulty. Another similar instrument may give different readings. The person making the measurement may make a mistake.

Ask your teacher for two thermometers and check the room temperature. Are the readings identical? (You may want to check both thermometers over a range of temperatures—do the two thermometers always give the same readings?) Suppose you use only one thermometer, and it reads 21°C. Is the room temperature really 21°C? That depends on how reliable the thermometer is. If your thermometer is not accurate, the temperature of the room could be 19°C, 23°C, or some other value.

No matter what you are measuring, it is wise to repeat your measurement at least three times in order to be sure of an accurate result. If your measurements are close, calculate the average and use that number. To be more certain, repeat the measurements with a different instrument.

Measuring Tips

Measuring temperature: If you are measuring the temperature of a liquid, keep the bulb of the thermometer near the middle of the liquid (**Figure 3**). If the liquid is being heated and the thermometer is simply sitting in the container with its bulb at the bottom, you will be measuring the temperature of the bottom of the container, not the temperature of the liquid. (Do not use the thermometer as a stirring stick!) Similarly, if you are measuring the temperature of a solid, place the bulb of the thermometer as close to the centre of the solid as possible.

Figure 3
The thermometer is not resting on the bottom of the beaker.

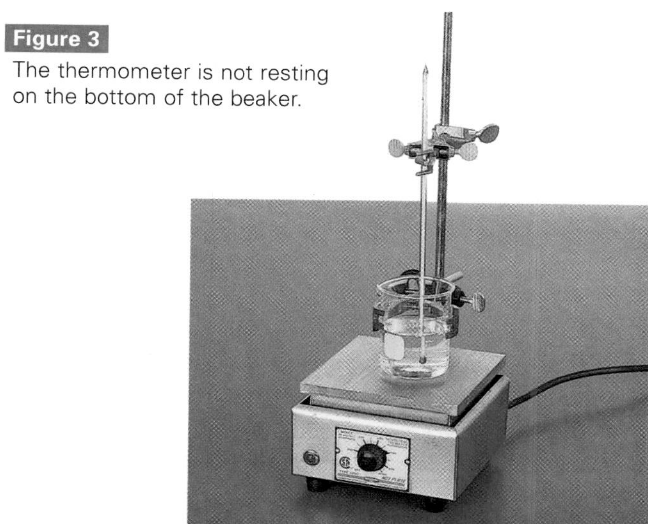

Measuring length: Choose the right measuring instrument for the task at hand. If you are measuring something quite short, for instance, you need a tool that is quite precise (i.e., that indicates small increments.) Make sure you start measuring where "0" is indicated (**Figure 4**). Many rulers or metre sticks extend past this point.

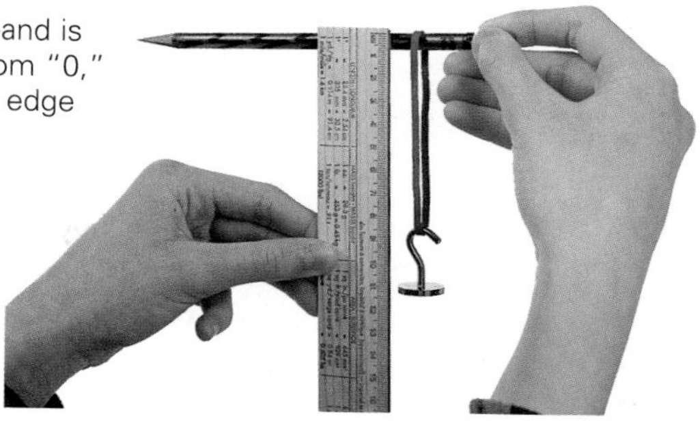

Figure 4
The rubber band is measured from "0," not from the edge of the ruler.

Measuring construction materials: Remember that when you cut some materials (e.g., wood) you will lose a bit of wood in cutting (**Figure 5**). This "bit" must remain the same to ensure square corners or exact angles. It will also affect how large the final pieces of your product are.

Figure 5
You will sometimes lose material when you cut it.

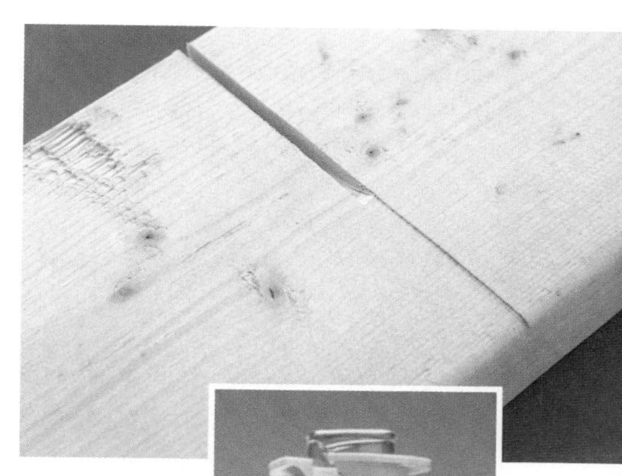

Measuring volume: As with length, it's important to choose the right measuring instrument. Make sure your measuring instrument is on a level surface. If you are measuring a solid, shake the container so that the surface is level. To measure the volume of a liquid using a graduated cylinder, measure from the bottom of the apparent curve (**Figure 6**).

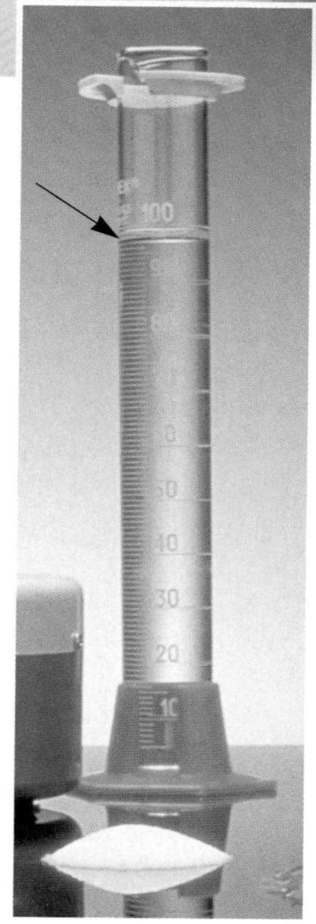

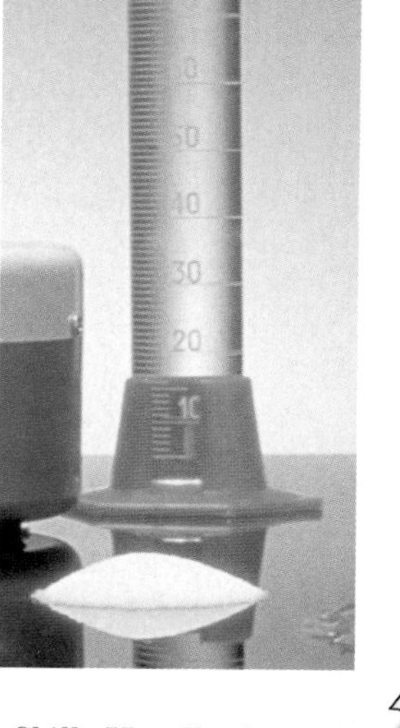

Figure 6
The arrow indicates where the measurement should be taken.

Measuring time: Measuring short intervals of time introduces a strong possibility of human error (**Figure 7**). If you are using a stopwatch to time how many times a pendulum swings in 5 s, for instance, you have to start the stopwatch at precisely the same moment as the pendulum begins its first swing. Repeating the process and averaging the results is advisable.

Figure 7
Accurate timing requires a lot of attention.

Measuring mass and weight: Refer to 5B "Working with Scales and Balances."

Measuring Quantities

Complete one of the following activities.

Activity A:

- You have been given a bag of balloons to provide motion for the balloon-powered car you have designed. Each balloon is advertised as being the same diameter. You want to verify this so that you can be certain all groups use the same volume of air to power their vehicles. Check to make sure that this is actually true.
- Decide how your group will prove or disprove this.
- Record all quantitative data in a table. What is the average balloon size?
- Compare your results with other groups.

Activity B:

- Find out what pH level means and the scale used to identify pH levels as acidic, neutral, and alkaline.
- With a partner, measure the pH levels of a variety of liquids.
- Compare your results with others in your class. Did everyone obtain the same results?

6C Scientific & Technical Drawing

Scientific drawings are done to record observations as accurately as possible. Technical drawings are used to visualize design ideas. Drawings are used to communicate, which means they must be clear, well-labelled, and easy to understand. Following are some tips that will help you produce useful scientific and technical drawings.

Before You Begin

- **Obtain some paper.** You will have to make a decision about which type of paper best meets your needs. Blank paper will be best when lines might obscure your drawing or make your labels confusing. Graph paper will be best when you are drawing something that requires exact measurements.
- **Find a sharp, hard pencil** (e.g., 2H or 4H). Avoid using pen, thick markers, or coloured pencils. Ink can't be erased—even the most accomplished artists change their drawings—and coloured pencils are soft, making lines too thick.
- **Plan your drawing.** Ensure that your drawing will be large enough that people can see details. For example, a third of a page might be appropriate for a diagram of a single cell or a gear train. If you are drawing the entire field of view of a microscope, draw a circle with a reasonable diameter (e.g., 10 cm) to represent the field of view. If you are drawing a three-dimensional object, plan for more than one view (e.g., top view, side view, etc.)
- **Leave space for labels.** In scientific drawings, the right side of the drawing is commonly used.

Scientific Drawing Tips

- **Make simple, two-dimensional drawings.**
- **Draw only what you see.** Your textbook may act as a guide, but it may show structures that you cannot see in your specimen.
- **Do not sketch.** Draw firm, clear lines, including only relevant details that you can see clearly.
- **Do not use shading or colouring.** A stipple (series of dots) shown in **Figure 1** may be used to indicate a darker area. Use double lines to indicate thick structures.

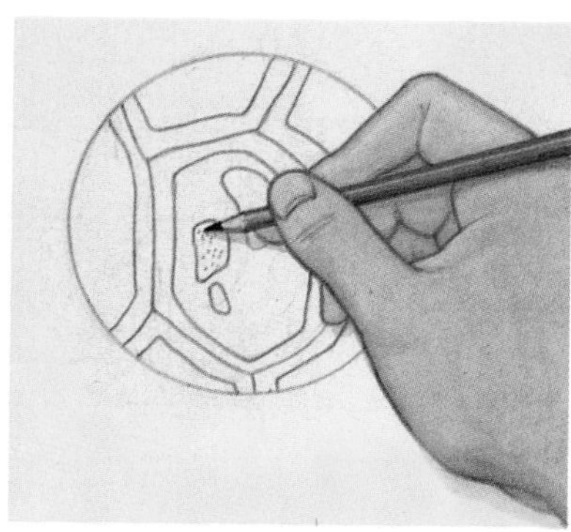

Figure 1 Using a stipple effect

Labelling

- **Label all drawings fully.** Avoid printing labels directly on the drawing.
- **Use a ruler.** Label lines must be horizontal and ruled firmly from the area being identified to the label (**Figure 2**).

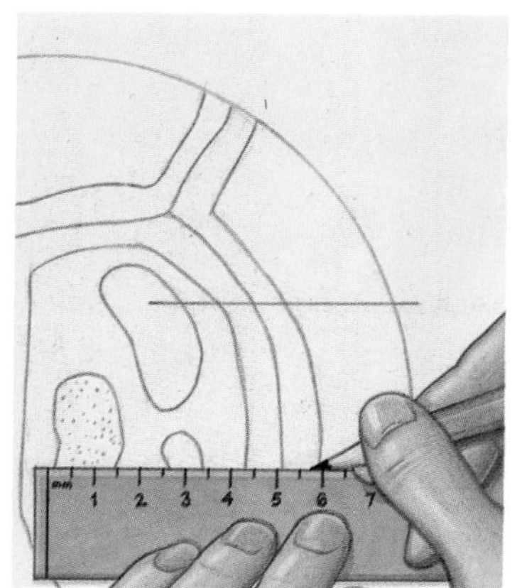

Figure 2 Neat labelling makes your drawing clear.

- **Label lines should never cross.**
- **Label drawings neatly.** In scientific drawings, it is preferable to list your labels in an even column down the right side.
- **Title the drawing.** Use the name of the specimen or prototype and any other specific information that will help identify the drawing. Underline the title.

Scale Ratio

To show the relation of the actual size to your drawing size, print the scale ratio of your drawing beside the title.

$$\text{scale ratio} = \frac{\text{size of drawing}}{\text{actual size of the specimen/prototype}}$$

For example, if you have drawn a nail that is 2 cm long (**Figure 3**) and the drawing is 8 cm long, then the scale ratio, which in this case is a magnification, is

$$\frac{8\text{ cm}}{2\text{ cm}} = 4\times$$

Figure 3
The nail as drawn is 4X larger than the actual nail.

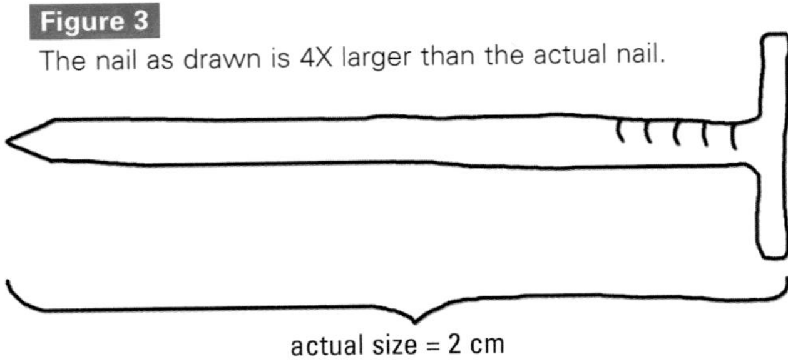

The magnification is always written with an "×" after it. In a fully labeled drawing, the total magnification of the drawing should be placed at the bottom right side of the diagram. If the ocular lens magnified a specimen 10×, the low-powered objective (4×) was used, and the diagram was drawn 3× larger that the original specimen, the total magnification of the diagram would be as follows:

$$\begin{aligned}\text{Total Magnification} &= \text{Ocular Lens} \times \text{Low-Powered Objective Lens} \times \text{Scale Ratio}\\ &= 10 \times 4 \times 3\\ &= 120\times\end{aligned}$$

The total magnification should be written on the bottom right-hand side of the diagram, as shown in **Figure 4**.

Figure 4
The magnification is 120×.

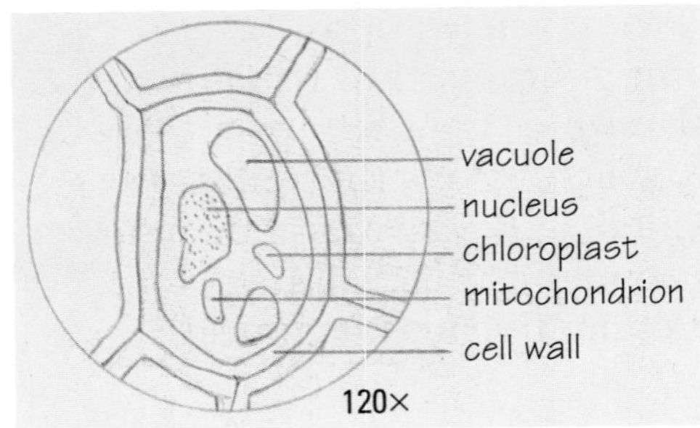

Technical Drawing Techniques

The kind of drawing you produce during the process of technological design will depend on its purpose. Some drawings are little more than doodles—rough attempts to give shape to your ideas at the beginning of the process. Some drawings will help you explain your concept to others. Some drawings are used in the plan of a prototype, along with written instructions, to help in the construction.

Sketches

When you are first brainstorming ways of solving a problem, it is often useful to sketch your ideas. The sketches help you develop and record your concept. Often a sketch will include notes to help you keep track of an evolving idea (**Figure 5**). Sketches can also help you communicate your ideas to other members of your team.

Figure 5
A sketch for a game design

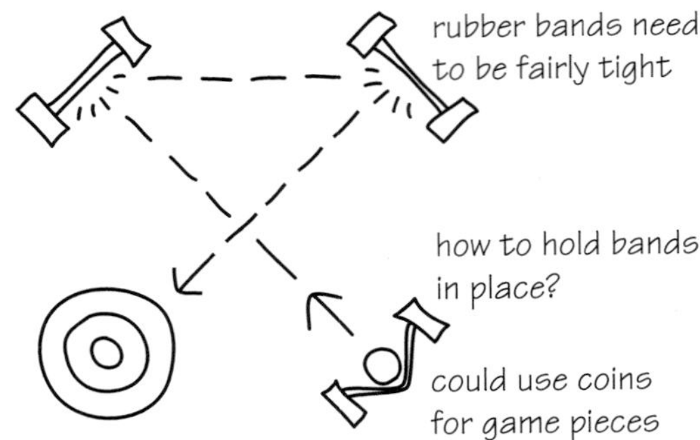

Isometric Drawings

As you refine your design, you will also refine your technical drawings. Drawings that are designed to help others understand or build your design need to be clear and accurate.

An isometric drawing represents an object in three dimensions with angles drawn at 30°. Often special isometric grid paper is used. It consists of three sets of parallel lines. Wherever the lines cross, there are three axes which represent depth, length, and height (**Figure 6**). This method of drawing allows you to use the actual measurements of the object you are drawing and provides others with a picture of the object that it easy to understand (**Figure 7**).

Figure 6

The parallel lines in an isometric grid run at 60° to one another.

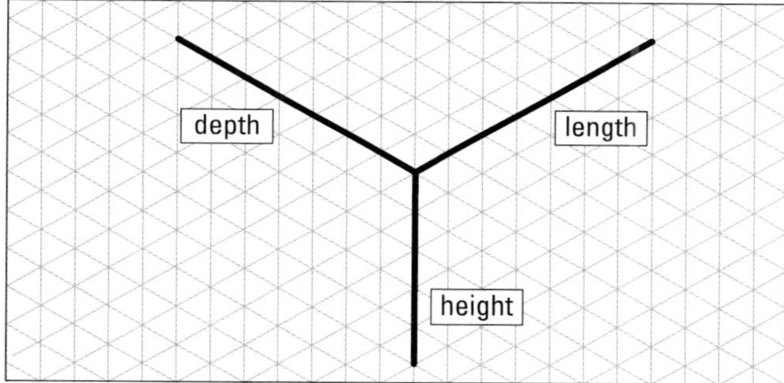

Figure 7

A model of a garage to be made from a shoebox

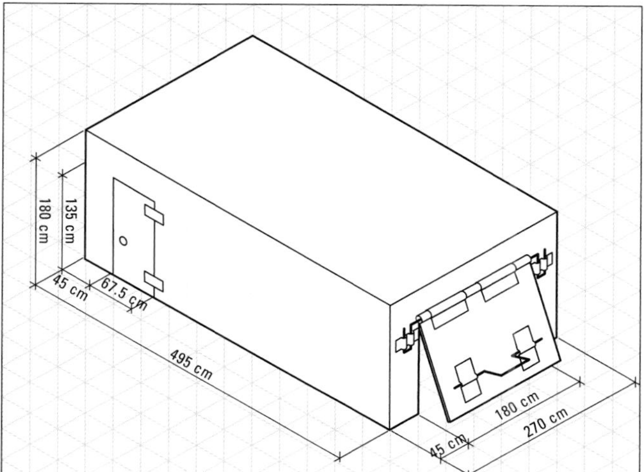

Orthographic Projection

It is often useful to create a working drawing that shows your prototype from three different views: the top, side, and front views. An orthographic projection is an accurate drawing that shows all the views and includes every detail and measurement (**Figure 8**). Each view is drawn square-on, in two dimensions. It is drawn so that the relation between the views is clear. Using graph paper makes this easier. One way of understanding the relation between each view is to imagine that the object is enclosed in a transparent box. If you drew what you saw from sides A, B and C on the box, then opened the box up, you could see how each view is related to the other two (**Figure 9**).

A complete working drawing often includes the orthographic projection, a list of parts, a list of materials used for each part, and detailed assembly instructions.

Figure 8

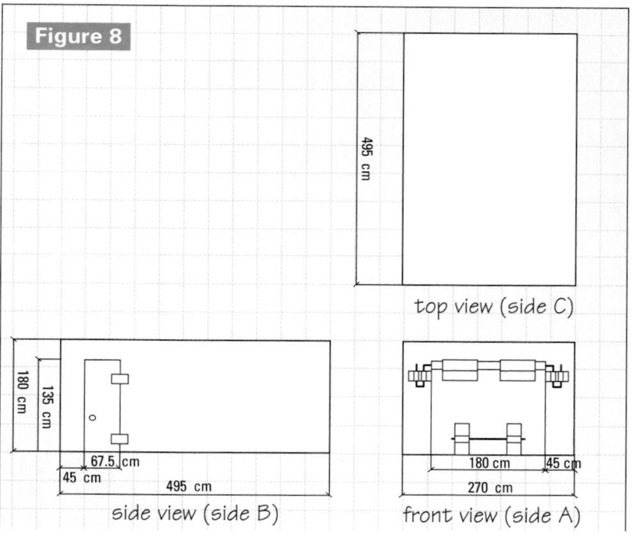

Figure 9

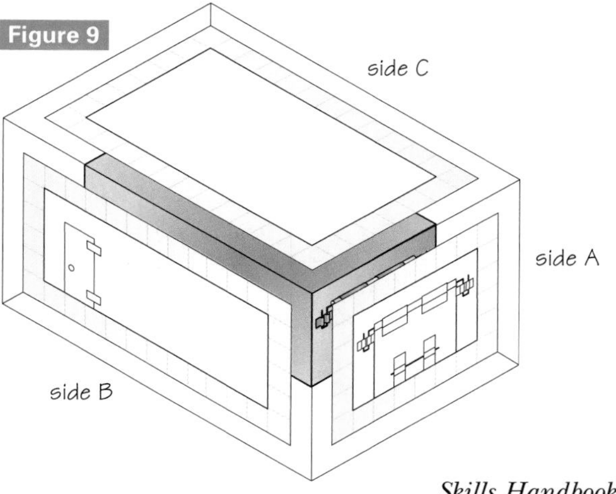

Other Views of an Object

In some cases, it may be useful to show the inside of an object. One way of doing this is to draw a cross-section (**Figure 10**).

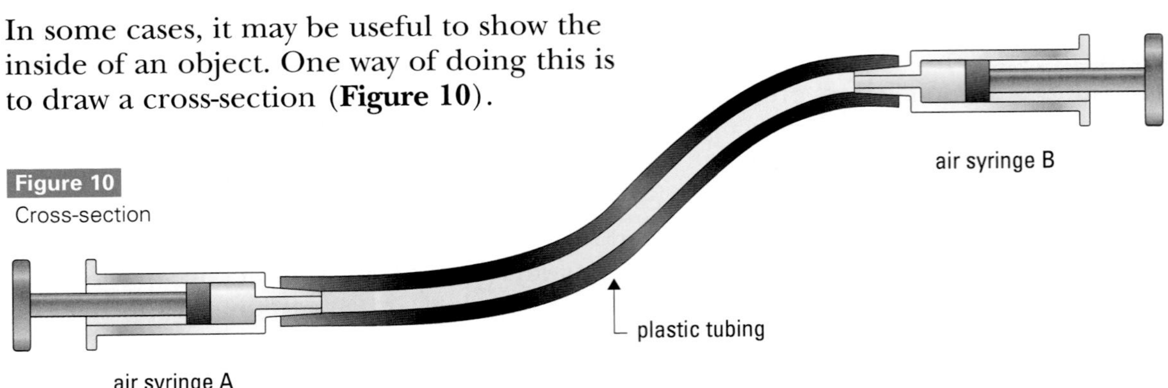

Figure 10
Cross-section

To show clearly how parts of an object fit together, an exploded view is often drawn (**Figure 11**).

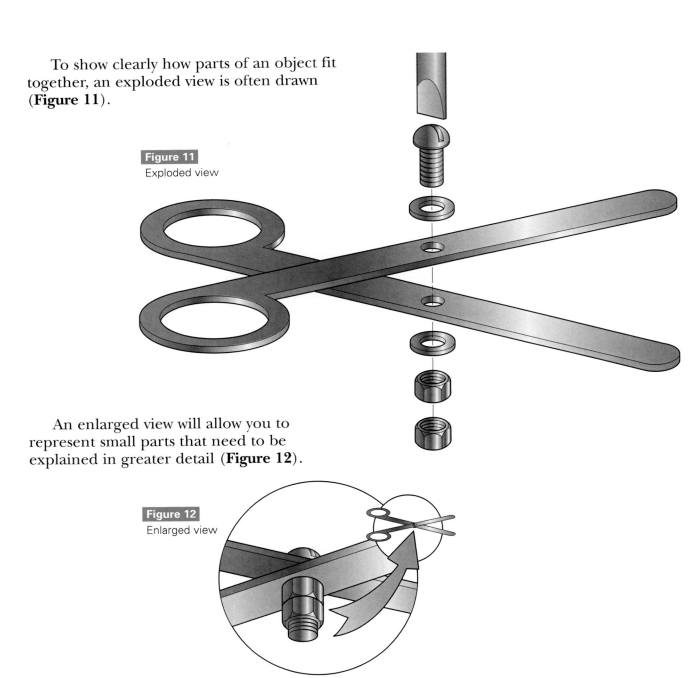

Figure 11
Exploded view

An enlarged view will allow you to represent small parts that need to be explained in greater detail (**Figure 12**).

Figure 12
Enlarged view

6D Creating Data Tables

Creating effective data tables in your investigations will help you record and analyze your data. Constructing a useful data table is one of the first steps in making sense of your experimental data. Take a look at **Tables 1, 2,** and **3** which come directly from *Nelson Science & Technology 7/8*. What similarities exist? What strategies should you employ when constructing your data tables?

Table 1 **Maturity Time and Yield of Tomato Varieties**

Variety	Time to maturity (days)	Yield for determinate varieties (kg per plant)	Yield for indeterminate varieties (kg per plant every 10 d)
A	80	n/a	6.8
B	40	n/a	2.6
C	70	n/a	5.2
D	60	10	n/a
E	70	n/a	4.2
F	65	10	n/a
G	55	15	n/a
H	50	10	n/a
I	75	n/a	5.6

Table 2 **Average Monthly Temperatures (°C) in Cities A and B**

Month	Temperature (°C) in City A	Temperature (°C) City B
J	-7	-6
F	-6	-6
M	-1	-2
A	6	4
M	12	9
J	17	15
J	21	18
A	20	18
S	15	14
O	9	9
N	3	3
D	-3	-3

Table 3 **Average Monthly Precipitation (cm) in Cities A and B**

Month	Precipitation (cm) in City A	Precipitation (cm) in City B
J	4.6	14.7
F	4.6	11.9
M	5.7	12.3
A	6.4	12.4
M	6.6	11.1
J	6.9	9.8
J	7.7	9.7
A	8.4	11.0
S	7.4	9.5
O	6.3	12.9
N	7.0	15.4
D	6.6	16.7

The following checklist will help you construct effective data tables in your investigations:

- List the dependent variable(s) (the effect) along the top of the table.
- List the independent variable (the cause) along the side of the table.
- Be sure that each data table has a descriptive, yet concise, title.
- Be sure to include the units of measurement along with each variable when appropriate.
- If you include the results of your calculations in a table, be sure to show at least one sample calculation in your data analysis.

Refer to 9C "Using Your Computer Effectively" for information about using spreadsheet programs to create useful data tables.

7 Analyzing Results

7A The Need to Graph

Making Sense of Data

Scientists and technologists often create huge amounts of data while doing experiments and studies—maybe hundreds, even thousands, of numbers for every variable. How can this mass of data be arranged so that it is easy to read and understand? That's right—in a graph. The sample tables below don't have thousands of pieces of data, but there is enough to become confusing. Can you make sense of the data in **Table 1** by simple inspection?

A graph is an easy way to see where a relationship or pattern exists. As well, it allows you to see more precisely what the relationship is, so it can be accurately described in words and by mathematics. **Figure 1** is a point-and-line graph that shows the data from **Table 1**.

The graph in **Figure 1** shows the relationship between the two variables and highlights two temperature plateaus where a change of state is taking place. In more complex relationships such as this, the need for a graph is quite clear. Data trends are much easier to visualize and understand in the organized form of a graph than as numbers in a table.

Table 1 **The Heating Curve of Water**

Time (minutes)	Temperature (°C)	Time (minutes)	Temperature (°C)
1	0	13	51
2	0	14	58
3	0	15	65
4	2	16	72
5	4	17	79
6	7	18	86
7	9	19	93
8	16	20	97
9	23	21	100
10	30	22	100
11	37	23	100
12	44	24	100

Figure 1 The Heating Curve of Water

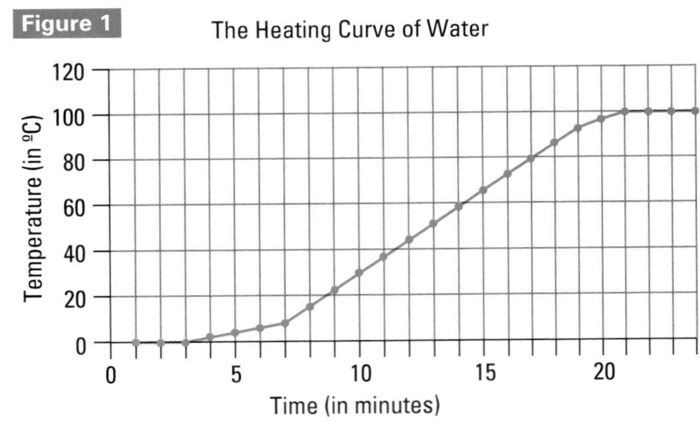

Types of Graphs

There are many types of graphs that you can use when organizing your data. You must identify which type of graph is best for your data before you start drawing it. Three of the most useful kinds are point-and-line graphs, bar graphs, and circle graphs (also called pie graphs).

Point-and-Line Graphs

When both variables are quantitative, use a point-and-line graph. The graph in **Figure 2** was created after an experiment that measured the number of worms on the surface of soil (quantitative) and the volume of rain that fell on the soil (quantitative). It is based on the data in **Table 2**.

Table 2 **Number of Worms Per Volume of Water**

Volume of water (mL)	Number of Worms
0	3
10	4
20	5
30	9
40	22

Figure 2 Number of Worms vs. Volume of Water

Number of worms

Volume of water (mL)

Bar Graphs

When at least one of the variables is qualitative, use a bar graph. For example, a study of the math marks of students (quantitative) who listened to different kinds of music (qualitative) while doing their math homework resulted in the graph in **Figure 3**. In this kind of graph, each bar stands for a different category, in this case a type of music. Notice also that the range on the vertical axis is chosen so that even the smallest bar is still visible.

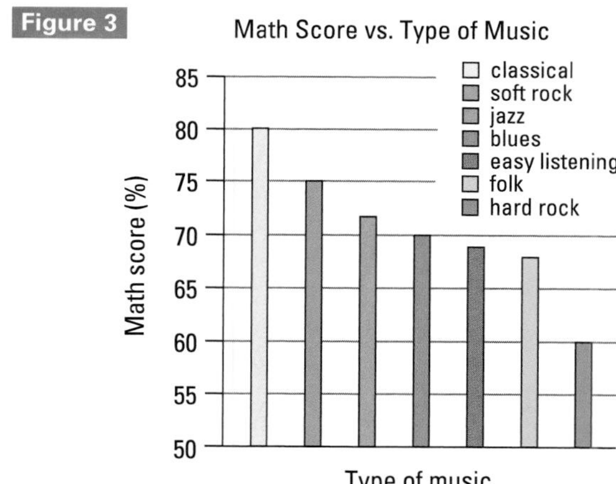

Circle (or Pie) Graphs

Circle graphs and bar graphs are used for similar types of data. If your quantitative variable can be changed to a percentage of a total quantity, then a circle graph is useful. For example, if you surveyed a class to find the students' favourite type of music, you could make a circle graph like **Figure 4**. In a circle graph, each piece stands for a different category (in this case, the kind of music preferred), and the size of the piece tells the percentage of the total that belongs in the category (in this case, the percentage of students who prefer a particular kind of music).

Figure 4 Percentage of Students vs. Type of Music

rap 17%, pop 33%, classical 10%, reggae 13%, easy listening 3%, classic rock 7%, hard rock 17%

Try This: Choose a Graph

Copy and complete **Table 3**. Determine the type of graph (point-and-line, bar, or circle) that is most suitable to illustrate the relationship between the variables in each pair.

Explain each of your choices.

Table 3

Pairs of variables	Most appropriate type of graph
1. Hardness of water Different cities/towns in Ontario	?
2. Amount of water used in a regular showerhead Amount of water used in a water-saver showerhead	?
3. List of five most abundant elements in the Earth's crust % abundance of elements	?
4. Surface area of an airplane wing Time the airplane stays aloft	?

7B Reading a Graph

When data from an investigation are plotted on an appropriate graph, patterns and relationships become much easier to see and interpret—it is easier to tell if the data supports your hypothesis or matches your design criteria. Looking at the data in a graph may lead you to a new hypothesis or to alter your design.

The graph in **Figure 1**, for example, clearly shows the relationship between the mass of an aircraft and the length of runway required for the aircraft to take off.

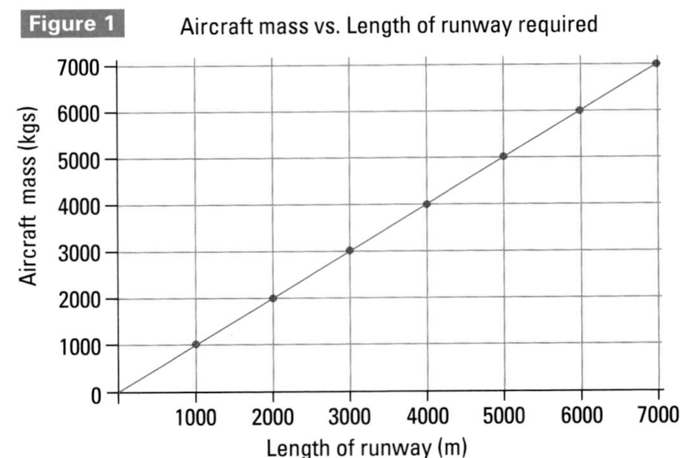

What to Look for When Reading Graphs

Here are some guiding questions as you interpret the data on a graph:

- What variables are represented?
- Is there a dependent variable? Is there an independent variable? If so, identify each.
- Are the variables quantitative or qualitative?
- If the data are quantitative, what are the units of measurement?
- Are two or more sample groups needed? If so, are they included?
- What do the highest and lowest values represent on the graph?
- What is the range (the difference between the highest and lowest values) of values for each axis?
- What patterns, trends, functions, or relationships exist between the variables?
- If there is a linear (straight-line) relationship, what might the slope (steepness) of the line tell us and what is the impact?
- Is this the best graph for the data?

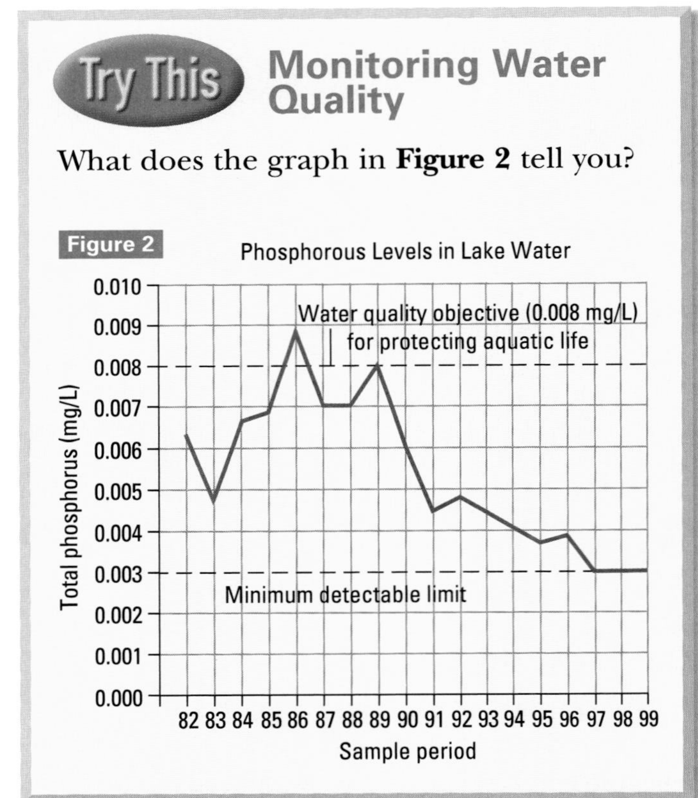

7C Constructing Graphs

Making Point-and-Line Graphs

Point-and-line graphs are common in mathematics, economics, geography, science, technology, and many other subjects. This section will help you become more skilled at drawing them, and at understanding point-and-line graphs produced by others.

As an example, the data in **Table 1** are used to produce a graph.

When making a point-and-line graph, follow these steps:

Table 1

Elevation (m)	Average height of tree (m)
1000	4
900	6
800	7
700	9
600	11
500	14
400	16
300	18
250	20
200	24
150	24
100	26
50	27
0	28

1. Construct your graph on a grid. The horizontal edge on the bottom of this grid is called the *x*-axis and the vertical edge on the left is called the *y*-axis (**Figure 1**). Don't be too thrifty with graph paper—if you draw your graphs large, they will be easier to interpret.

Figure 1

Step 1: Draw the axes.

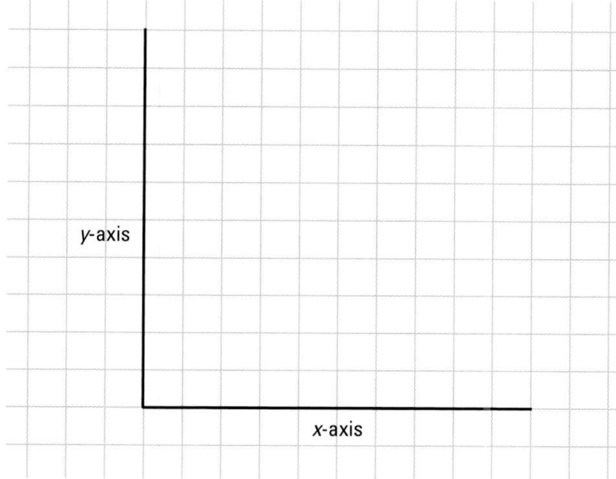

2. Decide which variable goes on which axis, and label each axis, including the units of measurement (**Figure 2**). It is common to plot the dependent variable (average height of tree in m) on the *y*-axis and the independent variable (elevation in m) on the *x*-axis.

Figure 2

Step 2: Label each axis.

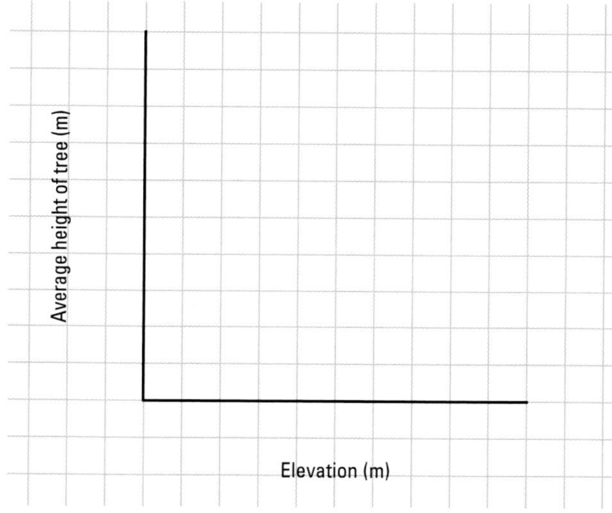

3. Determine the range of values for each variable. The range is the difference between the largest and smallest values. For the average height of tree, the maximum is 28 m, and the minimum is 4 m, so the range is: 28 m – 4 m = 24 m. For the elevation, the range is 1000 m – 0 m = 1000 m.

4. Choose a scale for each axis (**Figure 3**). This will depend on how much space you have and the range of values for each axis. Each line on the grid usually increases steadily in value by a convenient number, such as 1, 2, 5, 10, 20, 50, 100, etc. In the example, there are 10 lines for each axis. To calculate the increase in value for each line on the *x*-axis, divide the range by the number of lines:

$$\frac{28\text{ m}}{10\text{ lines}} = 2.8\text{ m/line, which is rounded up to 3.}$$

Then, round up to the nearest convenient number, which in this case is 3. The scale on the "Average height of tree" axis should increase by 3 every space. Repeat the calculation for the *y*-axis:

$$\frac{1000 \text{ m}}{10 \text{ lines}} = 100 \text{ m/line}$$

Figure 3

Step 4: Choose a scale for each axis.

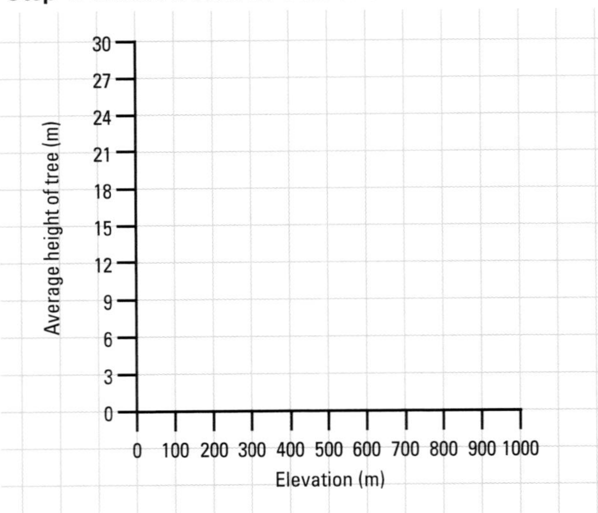

5. Plot the points (**Figure 4**). Start with the first pair of values from the data table, 1000 m elevation and 4 m trees. Place the point where an imaginary line starting at 1000 on the *x*-axis meets an imaginary line starting at 4 on the *y*-axis.

Figure 4

Step 5: Start plotting points.

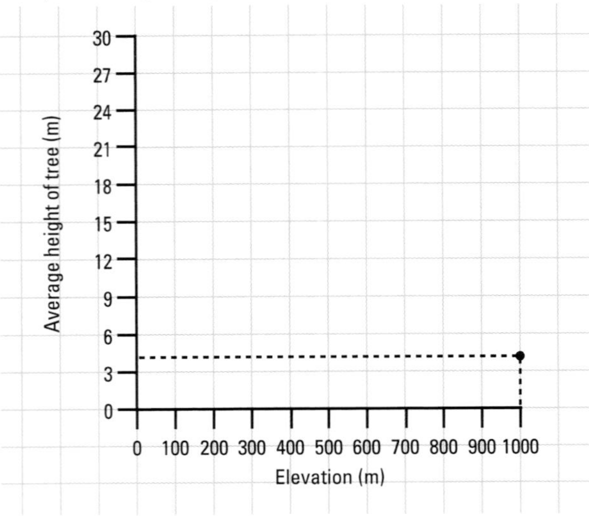

6. After all the points are plotted, and if it is possible, draw a line through the points to show the relationship between the variables (**Figure 5**). It is unusual for all the points to lie exactly on a line. Small errors in each measurement tend to move the points slightly away from the perfect line. You must draw a line that comes closest to most of the points. This is called the line of best fit—a smooth line that passes through or between the points so that there are about the same number of points on each side of the line. The line of best fit may be a straight line or a curved line.

Figure 5

Step 6: Draw a line of best fit.

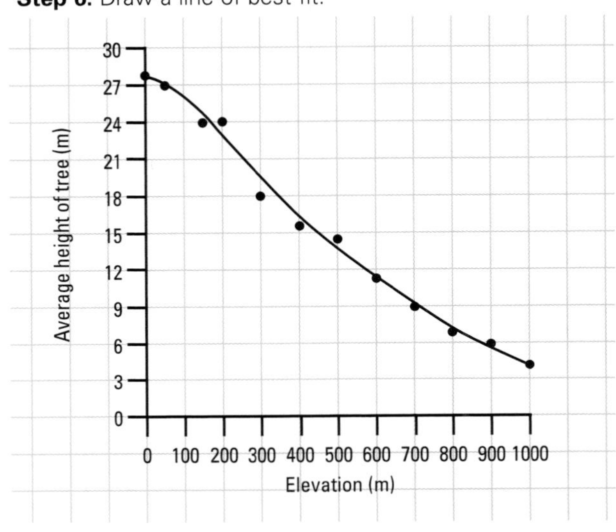

7. Title your graph.

Making Bar Graphs

Bar graphs are useful when working with qualitative data and when a variable is divided into categories. In the following example science students did a study of the kind of music students listen to while doing mathematics problems, and got the results listed in **Table 2**.

Table 2

Type of music	Math score (%)
easy listening	69
hard rock	60
jazz	72
blues	70
classical	80
folk	68
soft rock	75

Follow these steps to plot a bar graph of this data.

1. Draw and label the axes of your graph, including units (**Figure 6**). Some people prefer to have the bars based on the *x*-axis; others prefer to use the *y*-axis as the base. In the illustrations, the *x*-axis was chosen for the base.

Figure 6

Step 1: Draw the axes.

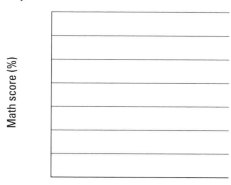

2. Develop a scale for the axis of the quantitative variable, just as you would for a point-and-line graph. In this example, the *y*-axis increases by fives, starting below the lowest value. In the illustration, 50 was chosen as the starting point, so all the bars would be visible.
3. Decide how wide the bars will be and how much space you will put between them. This decision is based on:
   - How much space you have. Measure the length of the axis on which the bars will be based, and divide that length by the number of bars. This will give you the maximum width of each bar.
   - How you want the graph to look. Decide how much less than the maximum width your bars will be, based on the visual appeal of thick and thin bars.
4. Draw in bars (**Figure 7**). Start by marking the width of each bar on the base axis. Then, draw in the top of each bar, according to your data table, and the sides. You can shade the bars equally or make each bar different from the others. It is important, however, to keep the graph simple and clear.

Figure 7

Step 4: Draw the bars.

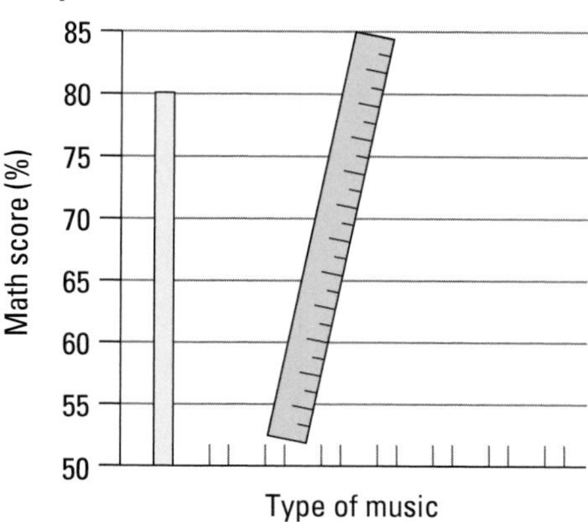

5. Identify each bar (**Figure 8**). There are several ways to do this. The best choice is the one that makes the graph easy to understand.

Figure 8

The completed bar graph

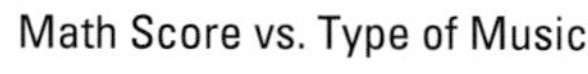

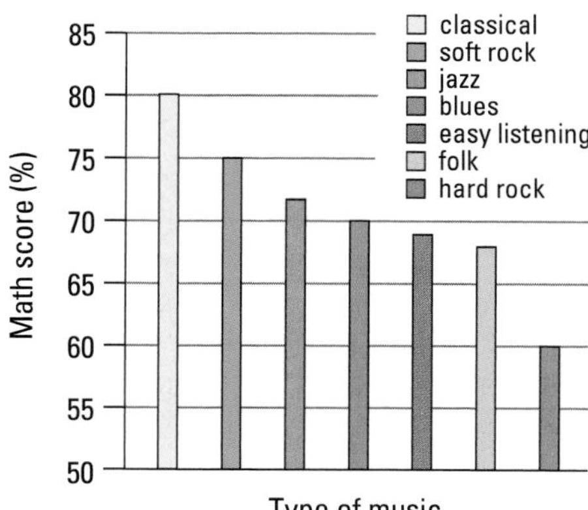

Making Circle (or Pie) Graphs

If your quantitative variable can be changed to a percentage of a total quantity, then a circle graph is useful. A sample circle graph is worked out below, using the data in **Table 3**.

Table 3

Type of music	Number of students who prefer that type	Percentage of total (% and decimal)	Angle of piece of pie (degrees)
rap	5	17% = 0.17	61.2
pop rock	10	33% = 0.33	118.8
classical	3	10% = 0.10	36.0
reggae	4	13% = 0.13	46.8
easy listening	1	3% = 0.03	10.8
classic rock	2	7% = 0.07	25.2
hard rock	5	17% = 0.17	61.2
TOTAL	30	100% = 1.00	360

Follow these steps to construct a circle graph.

1. Convert the values of your quantitative variable into percentages, and then into decimal form. In the sample, each number of students who prefer a type of music was turned into a percentage of the total number of students.

   $$\text{Percentage} = \frac{\text{number}}{\text{total}} \times 100\%$$

   $$\text{Percentage for rap} = \frac{5}{30} \times 100\% = 17\% \text{ (decimal version} = 0.17)$$

2. Multiply the decimal version of each percentage by 360 (there are 360° in a circle) to get the angle of each "piece of the pie" within the circle.

   Angle of piece of pie for rap = 0.17 x 360° = 61.2°

3. Draw a circle using a compass. To make the graph easy to read (and make), the circle should be big. The more pieces there are, the bigger the circle should be.

4. Draw in each piece of pie, using a protractor (**Figure 9**).

Figure 9
Step 4: Draw the pieces.

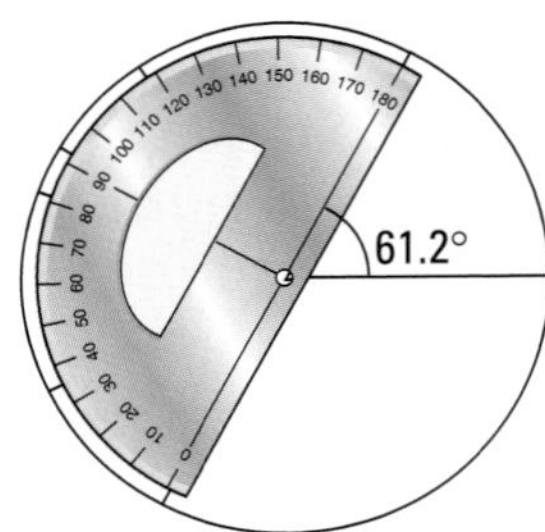

5. Shade each piece of pie using colours or patterns (**Figure 10**).

Figure 10
Step 5: Shade the pieces.

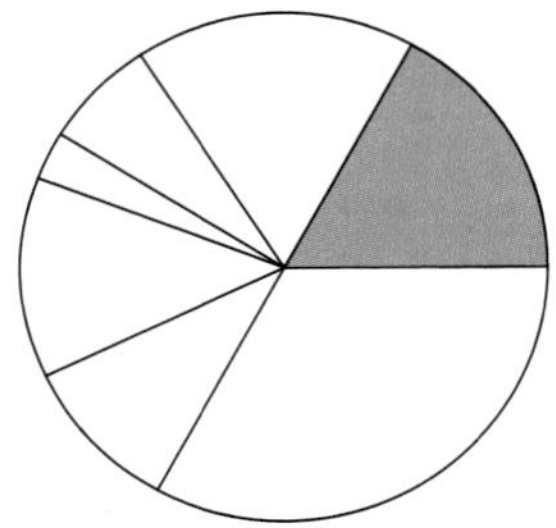

6. Label and title the graph (**Figure 11**). Put the percentage and the name of each category with its piece of pie (perhaps percentage inside and category outside the circle), or include them in a legend. Pick a title for your graph that describes the variables.

Figure 11
Step 6: The completed circle graph

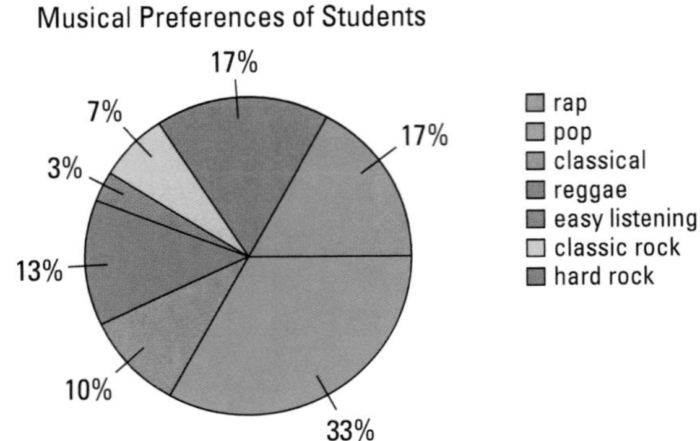

Using Computers for Graphing

You should be aware that there are many useful computer programs that can help with the graphing process. For example, Microsoft Excel is a very powerful spreadsheet/graphing program that allows for the construction of point-and-line, bar, and circle graphs as well as many other types of graphs (**Figure 12**). In addition, such programs can make use of statistical analysis to compute the best straight line or line of best fit.

Figure 12

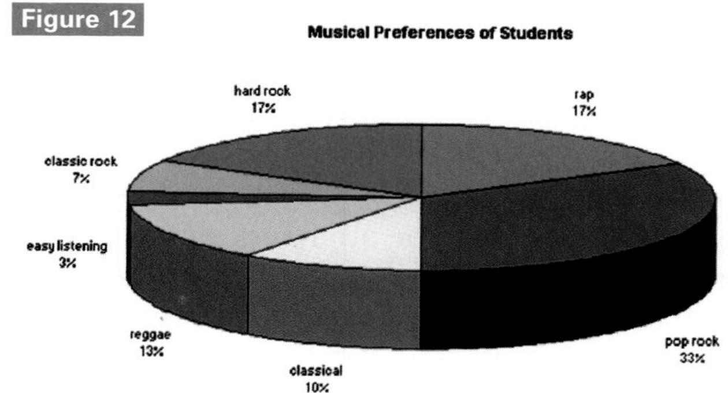

Try This Graphing

Perform the following tasks and graph the data that is given or that you collect.

1. Make labelled point-and-line graphs, with appropriate lines of best fit, for the data in **Table 4**.
2. Conduct a survey of your class or a larger group, and make bar and circle graphs from the data you collect. You could use one of the following variables or one of your own: most popular brand of sports shoe, favourite band, most interesting technological job, most well-known international structure or building.

Table 4 **Amount of force needed to close a door vs. the position on the door where the force is applied**

Distance from the fulcrum (hinges) in centimetres	Force applied in newtons
10 cm	80 N
15 cm	75 N
20 cm	70 N
25 cm	65 N
30 cm	60 N

⑦D Using Math in Science & Technology

Our world can often be analyzed, described, and predicted mathematically. For example, the mass and volume of a pure substance, when viewed in a point-and-line graph, prove to be directly proportional to one another. That is to say, as the volume of the object increases the mass of the object increases as well. If we set up a ratio of

$$\frac{\text{the mass of an object (m)}}{\text{the volume of an object (V)}} = \text{density of an object (D)}$$

we can define a new property—density—for a substance. This is just one example of how a mathematical relationship allows for the extension of our understanding.

While mathematics can sometimes appear abstract and daunting, as a scientist or technologist your ability to understand some fundamental mathematical concepts will improve your analytical ability.

Scientific Notation

In your studies, you use some very large and some very small numbers. For example, the average distance from the centre of the Earth to its crust is 6 400 000 m (**Figure 1**) and the average radius of a hydrogen atom is 0.000 000 000 05 m (**Figure 2**).

Because we don't want to spend the better part of our day writing out zeros, it is convenient to use a mathematical abbreviation known as scientific notation. The scientific notations for these two values are 6.40×10^6 m and 5.0×10^{-11} m, respectively. Can you see how this works?

Essentially,

multiply by the number 10 a total of 6 times

$$6.4 \times 10^6 = 6.4 \times 10 \times 10 \times 10 \times 10 \times 10 \times 10$$

$$5.0 \times 10^{-11} = \frac{5.0}{(10 \times 10 \times 10 \times 10 \times 10 \times 10 \times 10 \times 10 \times 10 \times 10 \times 10)}$$

divide by the number 10 a total of 11 times

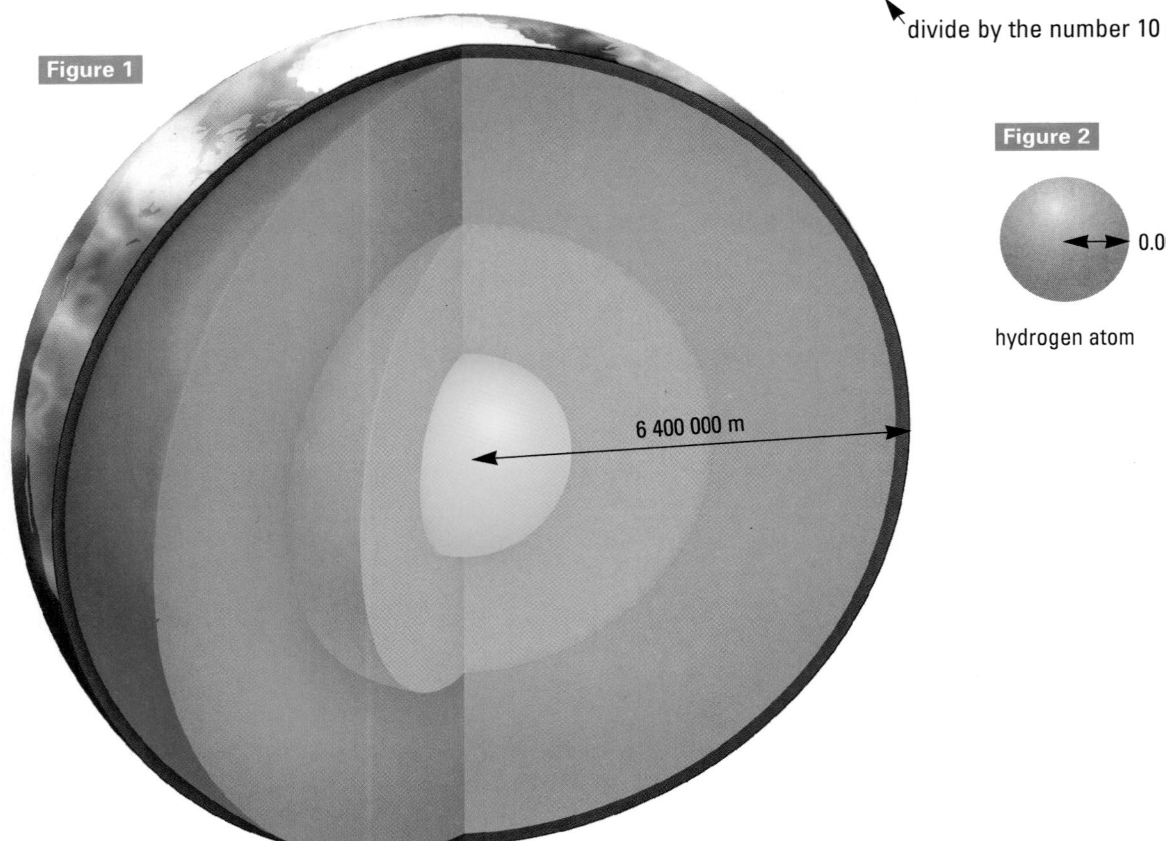

Figure 1

Figure 2

Significant Figures

Imagine you are given two pieces of string and you wish to find the total length of string that you have (**Figure 3**). You measure the length of one piece of string with an accurate scale ruler and find that it is 12.72 cm long. You measure the length of the other piece of string with an old metre stick and find that piece of string to be 14 cm long. What is the total length of string that you have? If you claim the total length to be 26.72 cm, you have assumed that the second piece of string is 14 cm—was your old metre stick able to give you this level of precision? No. You can only come to the conclusion that you have a total length of 27 cm.

Figure 3

When we take measurements and manipulate numbers in science and technology, we must look at the number of significant digits (or figures) in a number. The number of significant digits represents how carefully, and with what level of accuracy or precision, the measurement was taken.

Calculating Averages

There are many statistical methods that help us analyze the quantitative data that we collect. One of the most important of these is finding the average of a set of numbers. Calculating the average of a set of numbers allows you to reduce your findings to one representative value. For example, if we measure the heights of four students,

Suzanne = 175 cm   Jan = 185 cm
Omar = 145 cm   Molly = 180 cm

we could calculate that the average height of the group is

$$\text{average height} = \frac{175 + 185 + 145 + 180}{4} = 171 \text{ cm}$$

Predicting Using Formulas

Using various mathematical or experimental techniques, we can connect and explain phenomena by a mathematical formula. For example, you will study the following relationship:

$$\text{pressure} = \frac{\text{force}}{\text{area}}$$

If you know this formula, and you know any two of the quantities, you can predict the third. For instance, consider two people on a toboggan. If you know the area of a toboggan (1 m^2) and the force exerted on it by the two people sitting on it (1000 N), you can predict the pressure:

$$\frac{1000 \text{ N}}{1 \text{ m}^2} = 1000 \text{ N/m}^2 \quad \text{also known as 1 kilopascal (kPa)}$$

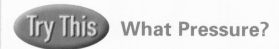

Try This: What Pressure?

A pile of scrap metal with a force of 20 000 N is dumped on a platform with an area of 25 m^2. What is the pressure on the platform?

7E Reaching a Conclusion

Scientific investigations mean very little, if anything, unless the scientist states a conclusion about the results. A conclusion is a statement that explains the results of an investigation. This statement should refer back to your original hypothesis. It should reveal whether the results support, partially support, or reject your hypothesis. Don't worry if your hypothesis is incorrect—scientists usually need to revise and repeat experiments many times in order to obtain the solutions they are seeking. Remember, science is a repetitive process. How many experiments do you think have been repeated in order to learn what we now know about cancer treatments?

In the process of design, the evaluation of the prototype is the stage at which conclusions are reached (see 3F "Testing and Evaluating a Prototype"). Your evaluation will take into consideration how effectively you solved the initial design problem. The design process is also a repetitive process: products and processes are tested and modified and, ultimately, improved.

Checking Your Hypothesis

Suppose you wanted to find out about the relationship between the amount of time spent doing homework per week and the mark you receive on your tests. Your hypothesis may be "As I increase the amount of time I spend on Science & Technology homework, my level of success on tests increases." Over a period of 10 weeks, you increase the number of hours you study by 2.5 h per week.

At the end of each week, you are given a test and record your results. At the end of 10 weeks your results have improved.

One conclusion that could be made from these results might read, "My hypothesis was correct. The results show that when I spend more time on Science & Technology homework, there is an increase in my test scores because I understand the material better." There may be other possible hypotheses and conclusions that would explain these results. When reaching a conclusion, it is important to consider all the variables, e.g., your study methods, the environment in which you studied, and the time of day (**Figure 1**).

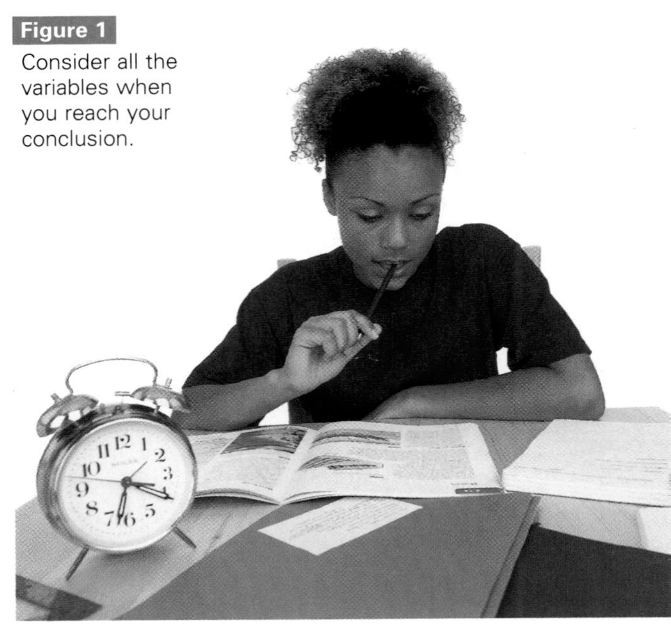

Figure 1
Consider all the variables when you reach your conclusion.

Reaching conclusions in Science & Technology investigations allows you to critically analyze results using a mix of logic, common sense, understanding, and patience.

Think Again

Consider the variables that you would have had to control in order to conduct a sound investigation to test the effect of hours of study on test results. What possible hypotheses might you want to consider before settling on your final conclusion?

7F Reflecting on Your Work

It is always important to reflect on events in order to learn from them. This is one aspect of inquiry in science and technology that is sometimes neglected, especially with beginners. Once you have been through either the process of inquiry or design, it is always advantageous to step back and think about what you did. What went well? What were the challenges? What could be improved? What would you do differently if you were to go through the process again? It is through reflection that you will improve your work and increase your learning.

When reflecting back on the process of inquiry or design, be sure to identify the types of error that may have emerged. These sources of error should be identified in the conclusion or discussion of your results and be used as the basis for improving the process the next time. For example, let's say you completed an experiment and were able to conclude that plants did grow toward sunlight. What sources of experimental error could have occurred while performing this experiment? These could include such things as variations in air temperature, inconsistent exposure to light, or differences in soil composition. Be as specific as possible when stating experimental errors. It is not good enough to simply state: "It was due to human error." Reflection is equally important when evaluating the design process. For example, once you've developed the prototype for a new type of school chair, you need to think about what modifications or improvements you should make.

In the process of scientific inquiry, experimental errors decrease the validity of an experiment. But, more importantly, they allow you to revise your procedure. That revision will increase the reliability of the results the next time you perform the same investigation. Remember, experiments are a repeating process. By repeating the process, you are improving your ideas and investigative skills.

In any investigation, it is important to recognize that what may appear to be an error in one phase may ultimately turn out to be the means to improvement or innovation.

Try This: If You Did It All Over...

Complete one of the tasks below:

- Think back to an argument you had with your parents or a friend. Now, reflect on the conflict from beginning to end. List all the things that you would do differently if you were ever in that situation again.
- Think back to a scientific experiment or technology project you have done in the past. Now, reflect on the work you did from beginning to end. List all the things that you would do differently to make it more reliable.
- Think back to a prototype you have built in the past and identify the modifications you would make in order to improve it.

8A Writing a Report

All investigators use a similar format to write reports, although the headings and order may vary slightly. Indeed, your report should reflect the process of scientific inquiry that you used in the investigation.

The Features of a Report

Cover Page: Make a cover page (**Figure 1**) that includes the following:
- the title of your investigation
- your name
- name of your partner(s) (if applicable)
- your instructor's name
- the due date

Figure 1

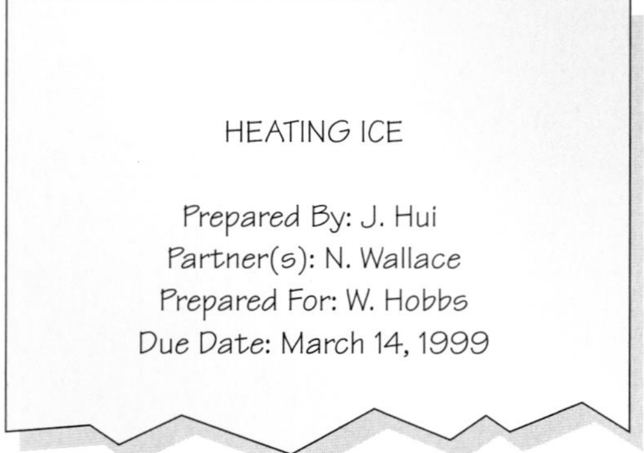

Title: At the beginning of your written report, write the title of your experiment.

Introduction: Always begin with a brief explanation of pertinent theory underlying the experiment. This includes the information you discovered by researching your topic. This section is also referred to as your "review of literature."

Purpose, Question, or Problem: Make a brief statement about your investigation. This can be written as a question.

Hypothesis: Write the hypothesis. Remember this is your "educated guess," based on your previous knowledge and the research you completed.

Materials: These include consumables (e.g., water, paper towels). Be specific about sizes and quantities. These also include non-consumables (e.g., test tube, beaker). Make a detailed list of the materials you used.

Diagram: Make a full-page diagram of the materials and equipment you used in the experiment (**Figure 2**). Remember to label and title the diagram. Your diagram can be placed at the end of your report, following the applications.

Figure 2

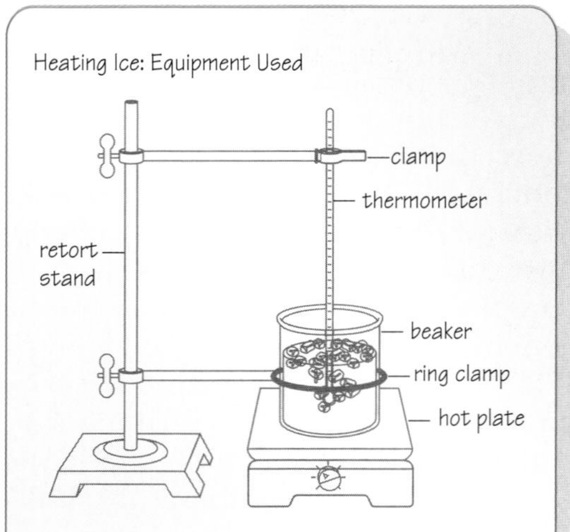

Experimental Design: List the independent, dependent and controlled variables in your experiment and summarize the procedure.

Procedure: The most important part of an investigation, when others are trying to determine if it is "good" or "bad" science, is the procedure. To be sure that your work is judged fairly, make sure you leave nothing out! Remember to write this in numbered steps, past tense, and passive voice.

Observations/Results: Present your observations and results in a form that is easily understood. The data should be in tables, graphs, or illustrations, each with a title. Include any calculations that are used. The results of the calculations can be shown in a table.

Analysis/Conclusion: Summarize the investigation as you would if you were writing a book report. Refer back to your hypothesis. Was it correct, partially correct, or incorrect? Explain how you arrived at your conclusion(s). Justify your method and describe your results. Suggest a theory to support or interpret your results. If you were assigned questions with an investigation, you would answer them here. Discuss any sources of experimental error that may have affected your findings.

Applications: Describe how the new knowledge you gained from doing the investigation relates to your life and our society. It should answer the question, "Who cares?"

References/Bibliography: Give credit for the resources you used in your research. Always cite your source(s). Failing to do so is considered plagiarism (unacknowledged copying). It is unethical and illegal.

Citing Your Information Sources

Giving Credit for Material Used Within the Report

Whenever you give credit to an author (including yourself from previous reports!) for the use of graphs, tables, diagrams, or ideas, use the following technique:

Immediately after the information is used, give the last name of the source, the date of the publication, and the page reference. For example:

The bedrock may be under soil, but it is still subject to biological weathering from plant roots (Gibb, 1999, p.22).

Writing a Bibliography

The bibliography appears at the end of your report and includes the full reference for every source you cited within your report as well as any sources you used for general reference, fact-checking, etc. It should be in alphabetical order of authors' last names. Be sure to use hanging paragraphs. The format for books, journals, web sites, newspapers, and CD-ROMs differ. To make sure you cite your sources correctly, refer to the following examples:

- **Information from a book:**

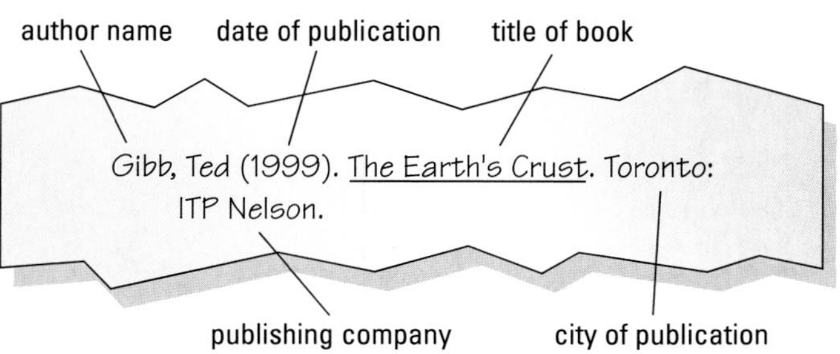

- **Information from a journal or a magazine:**

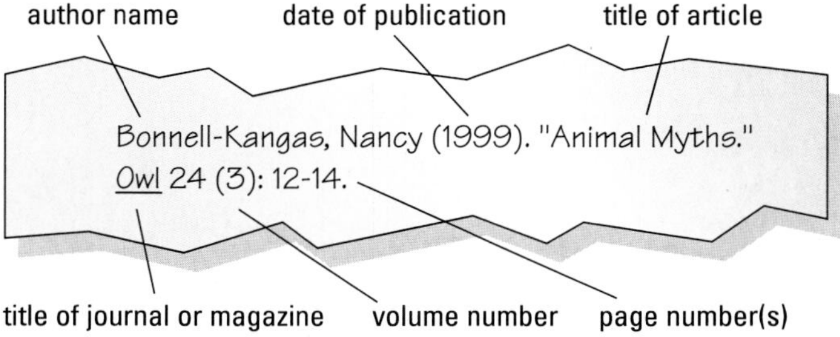

- **Information from a newspaper:**

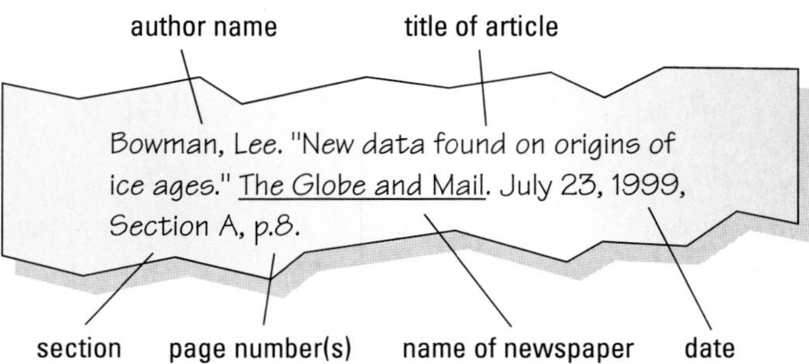

author name
title of article
Bowman, Lee. "New data found on origins of
ice ages." The Globe and Mail. July 23, 1999,
Section A, p.8.
section
page number(s)
name of newspaper
date

.nformation from a web site:

author or host name | name of home page

GCS Research Society. Great Canadian Scientists Web Site, 1996. Available HTTP: http://www.science.ca/scientists/Hubel/hubel.html

date | web site URL

- **Information from a CD-ROM:**

title of CD-ROM

Oxford English Dictionary Computer File: On Compact Disc. 2nd ed. CD-ROM. Oxofrd. Oxford UP, 1992.

year of publication | city of publication

Checklist for Writing a Report

Refer to this checklist whenever you are required to write a scientific report.

✓ Cover page
✓ Title of the investigation
✓ Introduction
✓ Purpose/Question
✓ Hypothesis
✓ Materials
✓ Diagram
✓ Experimental Design
✓ Procedure
✓ Observations/Results
✓ Analysis /Conclusion
✓ Application
✓ References/Bibliography

8B Creating a Design Folder

It is a good idea to create a folder that communicates important information about your design. The end product (or process) will rarely speak for itself. You should be able to explain why your design is useful, what steps you took in the design process, and how well the prototype meets the needs for which it is designed. In fact, you should summarize all the steps you took in the process of design as outlined in 3A "The Problem-Solving Cycle."

Features of a Design Folder

Cover Page: Create a cover page (**Figure 1**) that includes:

- name of the product or process you designed
- your name
- your partner(s) name (if applicable)
- the date the folder was completed

Figure 1

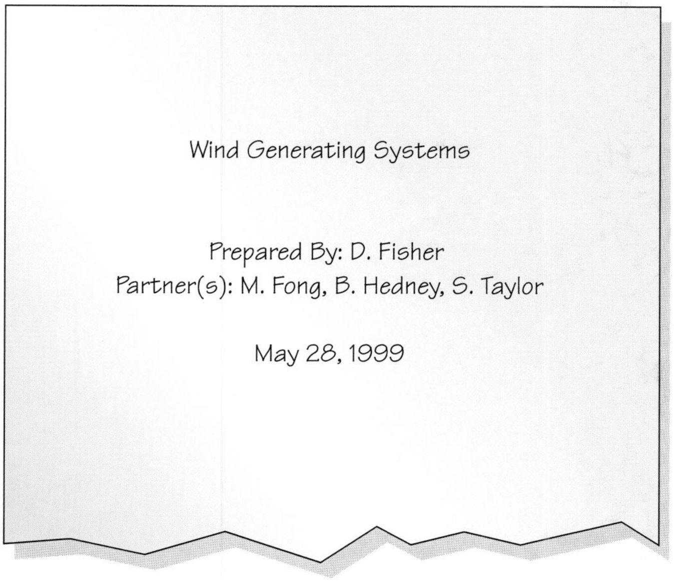

Wind Generating Systems

Prepared By: D. Fisher
Partner(s): M. Fong, B. Hedney, S. Taylor

May 28, 1999

Title: At the beginning of your folder, write the name of your product or process.

Problem: State your problem briefly and clearly and define any key terms.

Introduction: Provide background information on your problem. What was the context for your design? How did you assess the need that your design is intended to satisfy? If you conducted any interviews or surveys, summarize the results here. (Details can be placed in an appendix.) Summarize any research you did on existing products or processes that might meet your need, and explain if and how these were adapted to solve the problem you identified.

The Best Alternative: Explain how you chose the solution you did. List all the constraints, and explain and rate the design criteria. Itemize all the alternatives that you considered as possible solutions to the problem, and explain how you rated them. Include any useful charts or graphs. For instance, if you used the problem-solving matrix to choose the best alternative, include the results in this section (**Figure 2**).

Figure 2

Rating Scale: 0=Bad

Alternatives	Specifications					Total
	Safety	Cost	Durability			
	0-10	0-9	0-8			
Solar Paneled Ceilings	6	2	3			11
Water Wheel	4	0	2			6
Windmills	8	6	6			20

Design Plan: Explain how your prototype was put together and how it is supposed to function. Include well-labelled sketches and drawings to support your explanation (see 6C "Science & Technical Drawing" for samples.) Include a list of necessary materials tools. If appropriate, include operating instructions.

Tests and Evaluation: Present the results of your prototype tests. Be sure that your tests measured the prototype against the specific design criteria you used. Use tables and graphs, and/or qualitative observations to illustrate your results. Write a brief paragraph evaluating how well the prototype met your design criteria—how well did it solve your problem?

Summary: From all of your experience and data, draw conclusions as appropriate. Be certain the conclusions are based on the data obtained from the construction of your prototype, the test results, and from a thorough literature survey. Describe what worked and what didn't. Indicate what could be improved if the prototype were rebuilt. Present evidence to support your conclusions.

References/Bibliography: In addition to citing various sources (see 8A "Writing a Report" for the correct format for citing sources of information), include a list of all the people who have made substantive contributions to your project.

Checklist for Creating a Design Folder

Refer to this checklist whenever you are required to create a design folder.

✓ Cover page
✓ Name of the product or process
✓ Introduction
✓ Problem
✓ The Best Alternative
✓ Design Plan
✓ Tests and Evaluation
✓ Summary
✓ References/Bibliography

8C Multimedia Presentations

Multimedia presentations provide a lot of scope for creativity. They allow you to use a combination of colour, computer graphics (even animation), sound and video clips to communicate information in an interesting, interactive way. When you read a book, for example, you tend to get information in a linear fashion, one page after another. When you interact with a multimedia presentation (e.g., web sites, computer games, CD-ROMs, kiosks) you have much more control over what information you see and when you see it.

There are a number of different software programs that can help you create effective multimedia presentations. There are specific skills you need to use specific programs. What you can create will depend on what hardware and software you have available to you, and how well you know how to use them (or how much time you have to learn!). There are some general tips you should bear in mind, no matter what kind of multimedia presentation you are creating.

General Tips

- Be sure to have a definite and well-articulated purpose. Be sure that you know who your audience will be.
- Start by considering your introduction (where you state your main goals) and your conclusion (where you restate your main goals).
- Create a flowchart for your presentation (**Figure 1**). Consider how your audience might want to make use of the information you are presenting, and provide logical links from one place to another.
- Consider the length of your presentation. Be clear and concise!

Figure 1

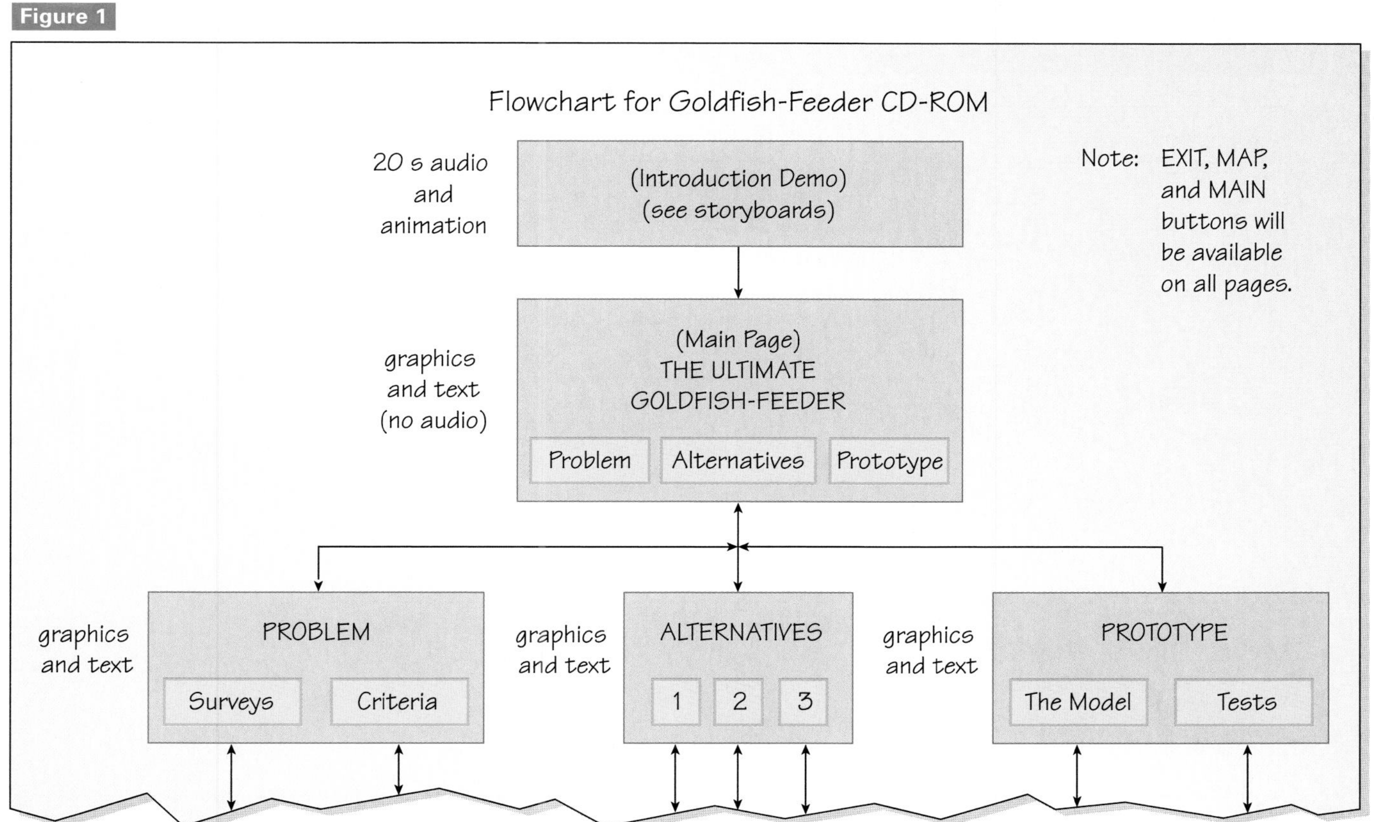

raw storyboards for your presentation (**Figure 2**). Be sure to consider all media: what are people going to see and hear at any given moment?

- Choose your audio-visual material carefully. Remember that the special effects you use should have a purpose. They should make your presentation more memorable and clarify any information you are presenting.

What Makes a Good Site?

Search the Internet for three good web sites. Choose one and analyze the way the information is presented. What are the strengths? List three ways you would improve the site. Write an e-mail to the webmaster stating what you like about the site and how it could be improved. The next time you access the site, some of your suggestions may have been implemented!

Figure 2

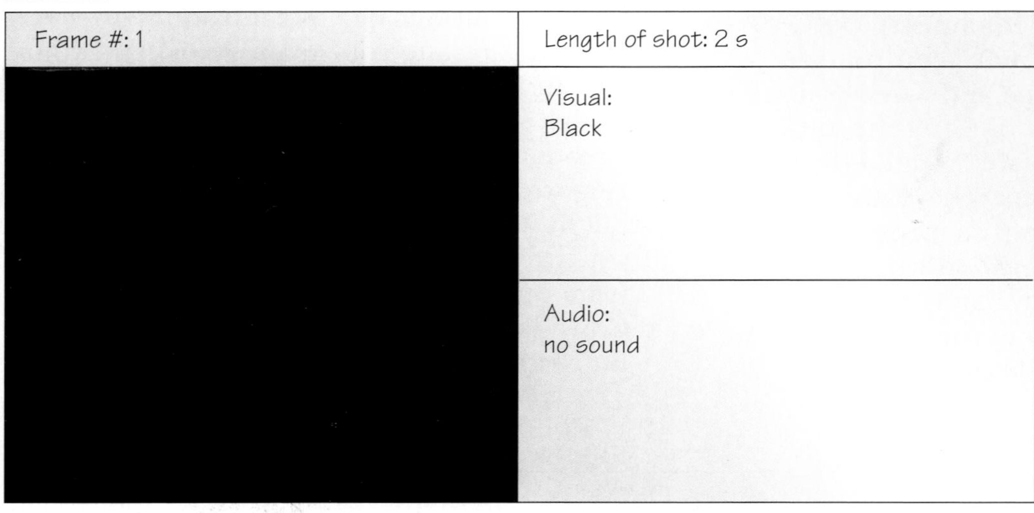

Frame #: 1	Length of shot: 2 s
	Visual: Black
	Audio: no sound

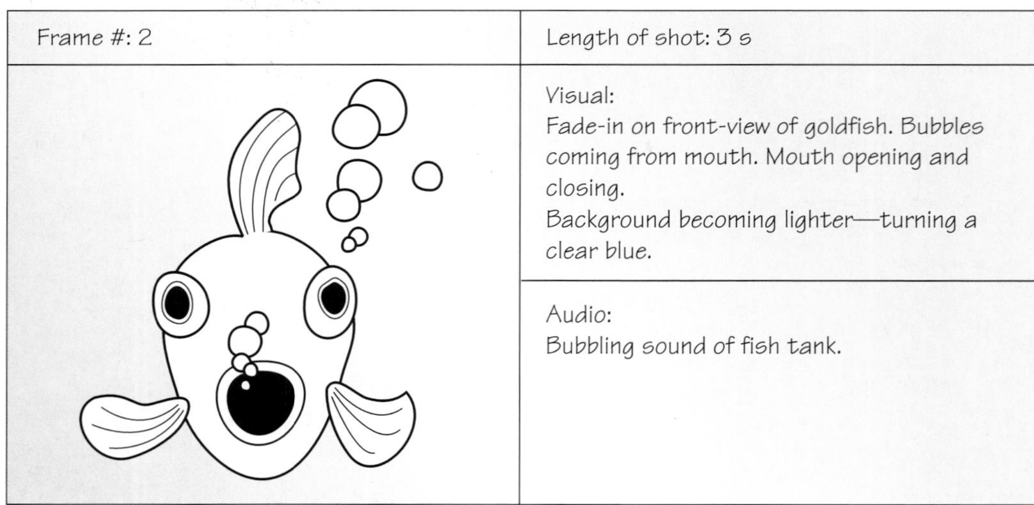

Frame #: 2	Length of shot: 3 s
	Visual: Fade-in on front-view of goldfish. Bubbles coming from mouth. Mouth opening and closing. Background becoming lighter—turning a clear blue.
	Audio: Bubbling sound of fish tank.

8D Exploring an Issue

In *Nelson Science & Technology 7/8*, you will have opportunities to explore many issues. Advances in technology and science need to be evaluated from many different perspectives—particularly since these advances are being made at an ever-increasing rate.

Figure 1 shows a helpful way of organizing the advantages and disadvantages of a given issue related to technology or science.

Figure 1
Should you use an electric toothbrush?

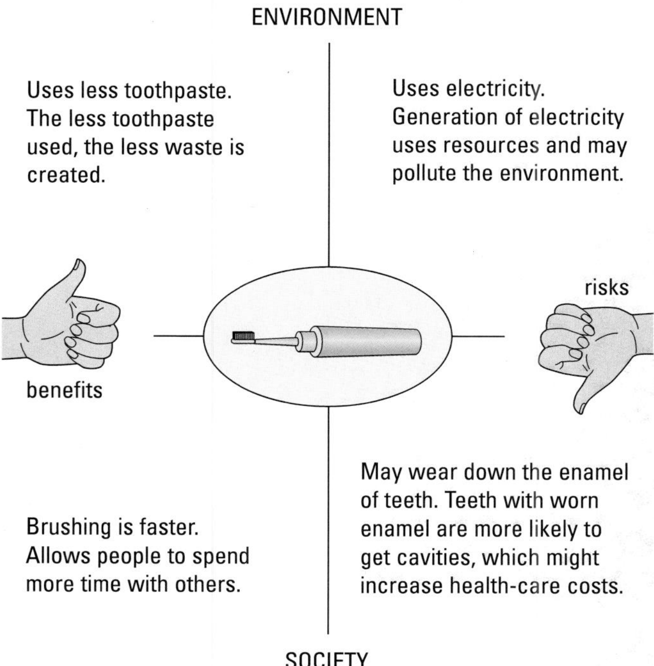

ENVIRONMENT
Uses less toothpaste. The less toothpaste used, the less waste is created.
Uses electricity. Generation of electricity uses resources and may pollute the environment.
risks
benefits
Brushing is faster. Allows people to spend more time with others.
May wear down the enamel of teeth. Teeth with worn enamel are more likely to get cavities, which might increase health-care costs.
SOCIETY

Toward an Educated Opinion

The following process will help you evaluate the advantages and disadvantages of an issue, and provide supporting evidence and arguments to the position you ultimately take on that issue.

1. Initial Research

Choose an issue that really interests you. Gather sources of information about it. Consider all the sources of information available to you (see 4A "Research Skills").

2. Formulation of a Question

Put together a question around the issue. The question should be answerable, important to our society, and debatable. You are encouraged to try this question out on your classmates, teacher, and others.

3. Further Research

Continue your research on this topic. Find at least two additional sources of information on the issue. Be sure to scrutinize the credibility of your information. Remember PERCS (see 4A "Critical Thinking")!

4. Reaching Your Position

Answer your question. Explain your position thoroughly. Be sure to consider the following:

- Have you included information from at least three articles?
- Have you stated your position clearly?
- Have you shown why this issue is relevant and important to our society?
- Have you included at least two solid arguments (with solid evidence) backing up your position?
- Have you included at least two arguments against your position and shown their respective faults?
- Have you analyzed the strong points and weak points of each perspective?

5. Communicating Your Position

There are several ways of communicating your position, each with its own format:

- Write a brief essay.
- Participate in a formal debate.
- Participate in a role-play activity, taking on the role of a specific, affected party.
- Write a letter to the editor of a newspaper.

9A Setting Goals and Monitoring Progress

Think back to the time you spent in school last year. What classes did you do really well in? Why do you think you were successful? What classes did you have some difficulty with? Why do you think you had those troubles? What could you do differently this year that would help you do better than you did last year?

What you have just done is reflect on your past behaviour in an attempt to make positive change. The things that you want to accomplish today, this week, this year—throughout your life, for that matter—are called goals. Learning to set goals and planning toward their achievement takes skill and practice.

Setting Goals

- **Honestly assess your strengths and weaknesses.** Setting goals starts with reflection. Maybe you've noticed that you do better on projects and reports than you do on tests. Your strengths may include teamwork, independent research, and analysis. Your weaknesses may include inattention in class, anxiety or stress during tests, and poor note-taking skills.
- **Brainstorm a list of realistic goals that are important to you.** Don't set yourself up to fail by setting goals that you can't achieve, or that you don't care about. State your goals in relation to your expectations of yourself—not in comparison with the performance of others. For instance, "I will increase my test results by 10% by the end of the semester" is a better goal than "I'll have the highest test results in the class by the end of the semester."
- **Make sure your goals are measurable.** You will find it easier to keep trying to reach your goals if you can tell whether or not you are getting any closer to them. Again, "I will increase my test results by 10% by the end of the semester" is a better goal than "I'm going to do a lot better on my tests."
- **Discuss your goals with someone you trust.** Other people can often help you clarify your goals. People who know your strengths and weaknesses may think of possibilities you haven't considered. Sharing your goals with someone else is also a good way of enlisting outside support.

Planning Toward Your Goals

Once you have a list of realistic goals, you need to create a plan to achieve them. There are two essential components to your plan: actions and target dates.

Taking Action

The first thing to do is to make a list of actions that might help you reach your goals (**Figure 1**). If you've made an honest assessment of your strengths and weaknesses, you know what you have to work on to achieve your goals. If note-taking is one of your weaknesses, you could strengthen that skill by arranging to meet regularly with someone who could help you develop it. If

Figure 1

Goal: To increase my test results by 10% by the end of the semester

Possible actions:
- call Mark and Akim. Ask them if they want to start a study group for tests
- meet with Mrs. Rankin to ask how I could learn to take better notes
- increase the amount of time I study each evening by 30 minutes (NOTE: this will mean giving up something else! Must decide what!)
- reorganize my desk and bookshelf
- buy a day-timer
- schedule my homework time each day
- take Fridays off if I keep my schedule from Monday to Thursday

working in groups is one of your strengths, you could build on it by starting a study group to help you prepare for tests. The key is to identify what is preventing you from achieving your goal and to plan ways of overcoming those obstacles.

When you are making your list, include incentives and rewards. If overcoming obstacles starts feeling like a punishment, you won't work at it as long or as hard.

Making a Schedule

Your goal is a target. You need to know what you want to achieve, and you need to know how long it should take to achieve it. Once you've made a list of actions, you can assign dates to them. These dates provide short term targets that, if you hit them, will make it easier to hit your overall target.

Work backwards from your ultimate target date. For instance, if you hope to achieve a 10% increase in test results by the end of the semester, how much time have you got? How many tests are scheduled between now and then? What can you achieve before the first test? What more can you achieve before the second test?

Go back to your list of actions and write in a date beside each one. Stay flexible. Your plan will evolve as you put it into action. Often, your plan relies on other people and will change depending on their schedule. A working schedule is represented in **Figure 2**.

Figure 2

Sept. 19:	Organize study space
Sept. 20:	Meet with Mrs. Rankin: 3:55 p.m. Buy day-timer
Sept. 22:	First study group (plan to meet every Wednesday)
Sept. 23:	Science & Technology Study: 4:15-5:15 (same time every Mon., Tues., Thurs.)
Sept. 24:	TEST: 11:00 a.m. Meet Sara at Mike's: 4:10 p.m. (if goals met during the week)

Once you've roughed out a schedule that looks manageable, transfer the actions from your list onto a calendar. Keep your calendar in a prominent place in your study area, and make it a habit to refer to it on a daily basis.

Monitoring Progress

When you reach your ultimate target date, you have to be able to assess whether or not you've achieved your goal. It is also important to measure your progress along the way. The more detailed and specific your plan is, the easier this will be. In fact, your plan should include regular monitoring. You might decide to review your progress at the end of every week, for instance. How many of the things that you scheduled did you actually do? For example, did you have any tests that week? If so, did your results show an increase?

The results of this monitoring may be a change in plan. For example, maybe the study group idea isn't working very well, and you're spending more time talking than studying. It's always possible to change your plan.

Don't be too hard on yourself when you review your progress. If you missed some small targets, put it behind you and keep moving forward. Adjust your goal if you have to, but don't give up.

Try This Your Goals

On a piece of paper, write three personal goals that you would like to accomplish by the end of the term or semester. Identify ways in which you will try to reach each of these goals. State how you will celebrate when you reach your goals.

Good Study Habits

Understanding anything—whether it is a life-saving technique in the swimming pool, a trumpet solo, or a Science & Technology lesson—is an active process. Studying takes on many forms. It involves learning and understanding material. Developing the following study skills can help you in your learning. You can modify these tips to help you in other school courses and in recreational activities.

Your Study Space

- **Organize your working area.** The place where you study at home and at school should be tidy and organized. Papers, books, magazines, or pictures that are strewn all over your working area will distract you from focusing on the work at hand.
- **Maintain a quiet study space.** Make sure that the place where you study is removed from distractions such as the phone, stereo system, TV, friends, and brothers and sisters. Popular study spaces include the school library, the public library, and your bedroom at home (if it has a working area). Any quiet place where you can be productive will work.
- **Make sure you feel comfortable in your study space.** You will be the most productive and study effectively if you are working in an area where you feel at ease—personalize your space.
- **Be prepared with all the materials you will need.** It is important that you have all your notebooks, textbooks, computer equipment, paper, pencil, pen, ruler, dictionary, thesaurus, and anything else you use for your work in your study space. If you have to continually get up to find a book or eraser, you won't be able to accomplish as much as you had hoped.

Study Habits

- **Prepare for class by reading material ahead of time.** It is also helpful to read or view materials from other sources, such as science magazines, newspapers, the Internet, and television programs.
- **Take notes.** To make note-taking easier, you may want to make up a shorthand method of recording ideas.
- **Review any notes you made in class the same day and add comments.** Then have a friend or relative quiz you on the material in the notes. Reinforce your understanding by answering the questions in the textbook—even if they are not assigned.
- **Use your notes and the textbook to prepare summaries.** Studying is most effective with a pen or pencil or your word processor, so you can write down the important ideas (**Figure 1**). You may want to write or type study cards to assist in making effective, point-form summaries of your notes. Look at the example in **Figure 2**. Notice there is a title at the top and all the information has been condensed into a point-form, easy-to-learn format. It's much more effective than learning material that is in paragraph form. Condense, condense, and condense!

Figure 1

- **Use graphic organizers to help you summarize a unit, or lesson.** (see 9E "Graphic Organizers"). You may want to use unit summaries in the student resources.
- **"Practice makes perfect."** This is as true for Science & Technology as it is for playing piano and shooting baskets. If you practise your study skills until they become almost automatic, you will have more time to think about how you will use them.
- **Schedule your study time.** This will help you avoid that most ineffective of all study methods, "cramming" before assignments and tests. Use a daily planner and take it with you to every class. Write all homework assignments, tests, projects, and extra-curricular commitments in it. This will assist you in organizing a daily "To Do" list that will ensure maximum use of your time.
- **Know your strengths and your weaknesses.** Take advantage of all opportunities to get help with areas in which you may have trouble. Use your strengths to help yourself and others. Form a study group and have regular meetings. You may be able to help others in some parts of the course. In turn, you may receive help from them.
- **Teach the material you have learned to someone who has not yet learned it.** Their questions will help you see what areas of the subject you need to learn more about and what areas you don't completely understand (**Figure 3**).

Figure 2
A study card

The Visible Spectrum

White Light = Roy G. Biv

- red
- orange
- yellow
- green
- blue
- indigo
- violet

- **Take study breaks.** It is important that you set study goals and take a short study break after meeting each of the goals you set. For example, you could decide that you will take a study break after crossing two items off your "To Do" list. Taking study breaks will help you rejuvenate for the next tasks on your list and will assist you in completing all your work effectively and accurately.

Study Checklist

✓ Organize your study environment. (Is it quiet? Comfortable? Organized?)
✓ Read material ahead of time.
✓ Take notes.
✓ Review.
✓ Summarize. (Make study cards, if that technique works for you.)
✓ Use graphic organizers.
✓ Practise.
✓ Schedule study time. (Use your daily planner and make a "To Do" list.)
✓ Know your strengths and weaknesses.
✓ Teach what you have learned.

Try This — Making Study Cards

Condense the information in this section of the *Skills Handbook* (9B) onto study cards. Remember to put a title at the top of each study card and make point form notes.

Figure 3

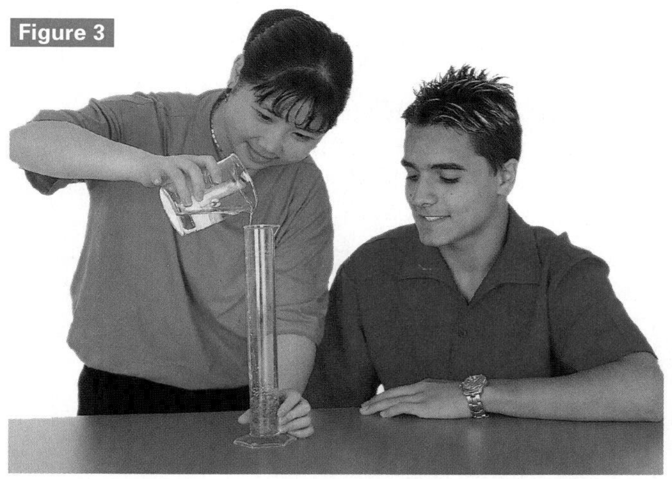

9C Using Your Computer Effectively

Computers are becoming more and more common in your learning. Most students have access to this technology at some point every week. Like your notebook, it is important to keep your computer files organized. It is also necessary to use your computer effectively—there is a time for computer work and a time for computer games and recreational surfing of the Internet. The following hints can assist you in using your computer effectively in your learning. Remember these hints can be modified to suit your needs.

General Computer Hints

- **Create a folder for all your science and technology work.** It is important that any computer work you do is kept in one folder. Otherwise, your work could be saved in lots of different locations on your computer and this means that it could become easily misplaced or even lost.
- **Organize your science and technology units in your folder.** Now that you have created a science and technology folder, organize this folder into the various units that you will study this year. Refer to **Figure 1** for a detailed glimpse of what your folders might look like.
- **Think carefully about what to name each of your documents.** Make sure that the names you give will allow you to easily identify what a particular document contains. Work that is called *Science & Technology 1*, for instance, provides no indication of what the work actually is. Be as specific as possible.
- **Back up your work.** Always make an extra copy of any work you do on the computer. Copy your work onto a disk or onto your school network. Too often students lose their work because they do not take the time to do this. It's much easier than having to complete a report or assignment all over again.
- **Maintain correct posture and form.** It is important that you don't sit too close to the screen and that you sit in an upright position with your hands formed correctly while typing. Incorrect hand positioning can eventually cause carpal tunnel syndrome. The study of how people interact effectively and safely with computers is a part of what is termed "ergonomics."

Figure 1

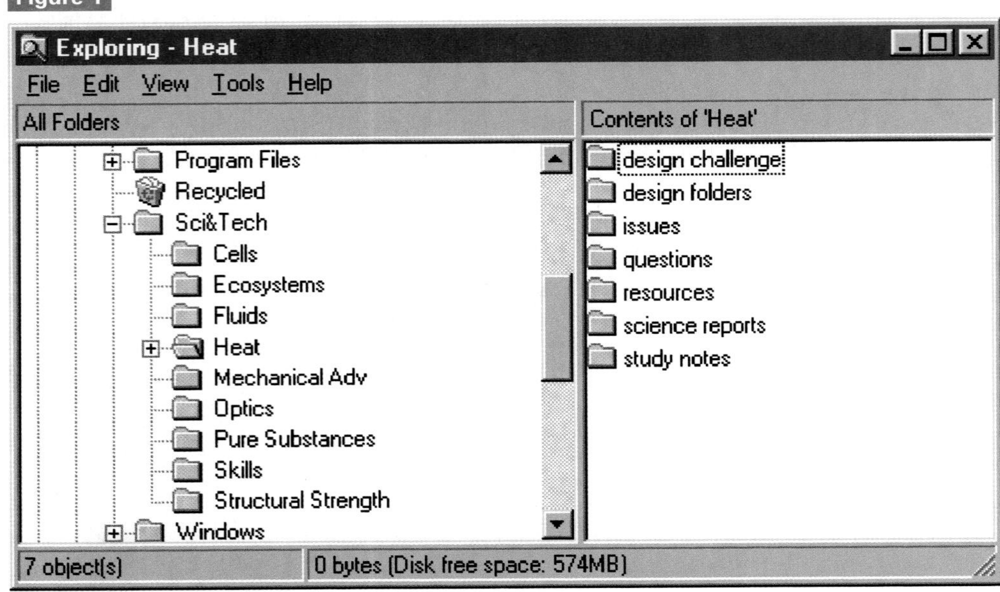

Using Spreadsheets and Databases

The computer is a powerful tool for storing, organizing, and analyzing data. Using databases and spreadsheets, you can record observations from science experiments or information acquired during the design process. You can use these software programs to sort information in different ways and to discover important relationships among variables. You can also use this software to create graphs and charts. The best way to get an overview of how spreadsheets and databases work is to explore different programs by using their built-in tutorials.

Spreadsheets

You can think of a spreadsheet as an electronic data table. To be as useful as possible, it has to be well designed. When you create any kind of data table, you should start by thinking carefully about what information you need to record, and how you will ultimately use that information.

In scientific inquiry, your spreadsheet will often be built on the variables you are using. If you are observing the viscosity of different fluids, your variables are the kind of fluid and the amount of time it takes for an object (e.g., a marble) to fall to the bottom of the receptacle containing that fluid (see **Figure 2**).

Figure 2

E7 | =SUM(B7:D7)/3

	A	B	C	D	E
1	**Viscosity of Various Liquids**				
2		**Time taken for marble to fall through the liquid**			
3	**Liquid**	**Trial #1**	**Trail #2**	**Trial #3**	**Average**
4	water	0.48	0.48	0.47	0.48
5	canola oil	0.57	0.56	0.54	0.56
6	olive oil	0.45	0.42	0.47	0.45
7	corn syrup	0.52	0.54	0.55	0.54
8					

Your spreadsheet, like any data table, should have a title. The rows and columns of your spreadsheet should be well-labelled. Specific data is entered where a given row and column intersect. This space, which you can identify by referencing the number of the row and the letter of the column, is known as a cell. Some information you will enter yourself as numbers or text. In other cells, however, you will enter a formula that tells the program to perform a mathematical function using data in other cells. For instance, in **Figure 2**, you do not type in the numerical averages—the program does this for you based on the formula you have entered. To find out what formula is required, simply use the help function of the program you are using.

As you change or add data, the results of the calculations will change. The information in your spreadsheet will also be available as graphs—and these are also automatically updated as data is changed (**Figure 3**.)

Figure 3

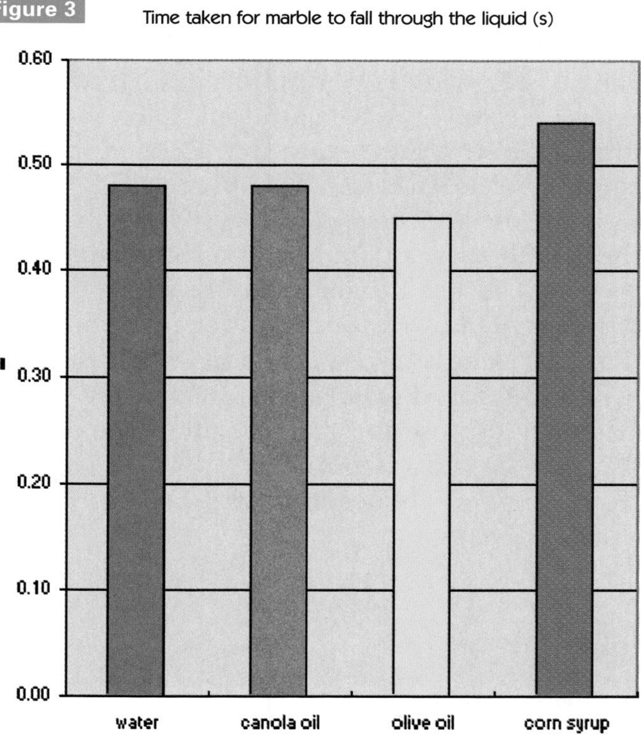

Databases

A database is another powerful tool for managing data. A good database will help you find specific information with ease, see relationships between different pieces of information, chart trends, create graphs, charts and reports, etc. Again, however, you have to spend some time designing this tool for your specific needs. A database can only give you what you need if you have designed it well.

First, you will need to become familiar with the power and uses of a database. The tutorials that are packaged with database software are good places to start. In general, a database is organized into records and fields. You can think of a record as an index card that lists all the information you need about a specific thing, person, or process. For instance, if you have conducted a survey about public reaction to the use of CFCs, each record would contain the information provided by one respondent.

Each record in a database is set up in the same way. The structure of each record is a "form" (**Figure 4**). You fill in the form with information you have gathered. Each piece of information is entered into a "field." Like spreadsheets, these fields have specific "electronic addresses." In fact, you can view information in a database as a list (**Figure 5**).

You can use the database for sophisticated analysis of your results. For instance, you can look for trends in responses to certain survey questions based on age, region, gender, etc. You can also use the data for other purposes (e.g., to create a mailing list). And, of course, you can generate accurate graphs and charts from the data.

Try This — Use a Database

Complete the tutorial for a popular database program. Now think of one project that you are working on now, or have recently completed, that would be enhanced by using a database. Design a form for that project.

Figure 4
A form designed for aircraft parts inventory

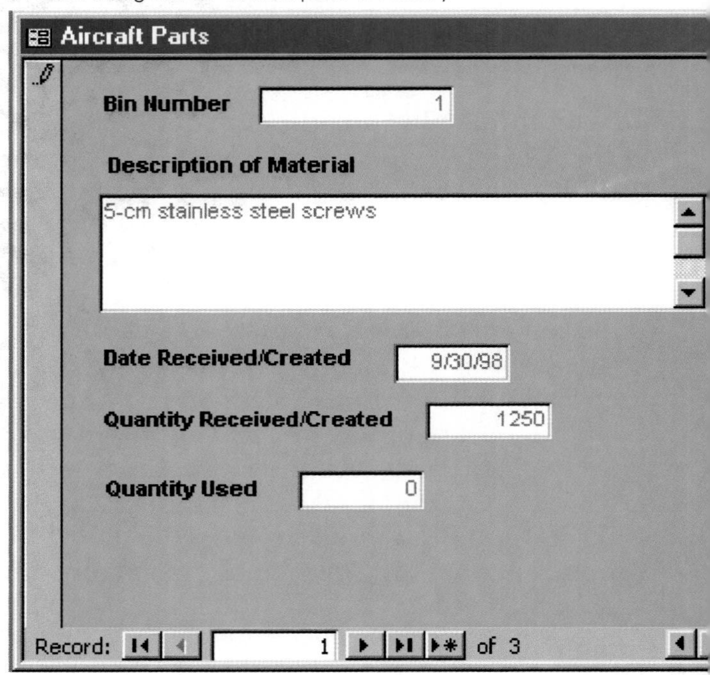

Figure 5
Inventory database in list view, showing 3 records

Aircraft Parts : Table

Bin Number	Description of Material	Date Received	Quantity Received	Quantity Used
1	5-cm stainless steel screws	9/30/98	1250	0
2	5-cm stainless steel nuts	9/30/98	1250	0
3	wheels	11/15/98	12	0

9D Working Together

Technological and scientific progress is almost always made by teams of people working together. Scientists share ideas, help each other design experiments and studies, and sharpen each other's conclusions. Technologists most frequently work in interdisciplinary teams, in which each person brings different expertise to the problem-solving process. We have all worked in a group at one time or another. In the "real world," group work is necessary and usually more productive than working alone. It is therefore important for us to be able to work in teams.

Try This: The Barge Contest

Your group will compete against other design groups to create the barge capable of carrying the greatest number of marbles.

To solve this problem, you will build a model. Models are used as small-scale tests for larger, more expensive future experiments. Cheap models also allow a trial-and-error approach that would be far too expensive for full-scale tests.

Materials

- water
- large bucket
- marbles
- 250 g of modelling clay

Procedure

1. Working with all the members of your group, create a diagram for the barge's design. Everyone in the group must agree on this design (**Figure 1**).
2. Build your barge using only the modelling clay you have been given.
3. Fill the bucket with water and place your barge on the surface of the water.
4. Add marbles to your barge, until it begins to sink (**Figure 2**).
5. Record the maximum number of marbles that could be added.
6. Evaluate your teamwork.

Figure 1

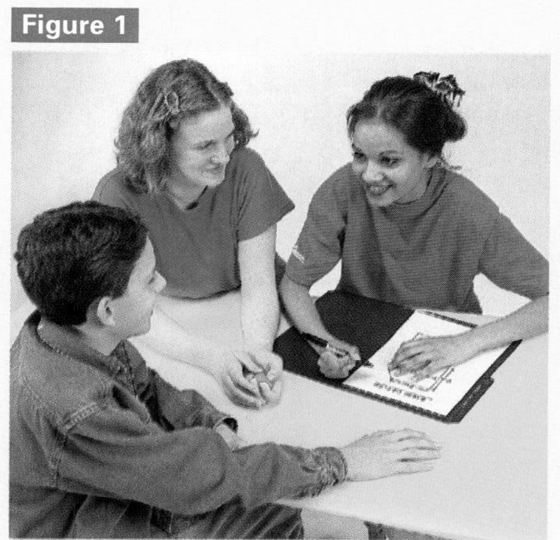

Figure 2

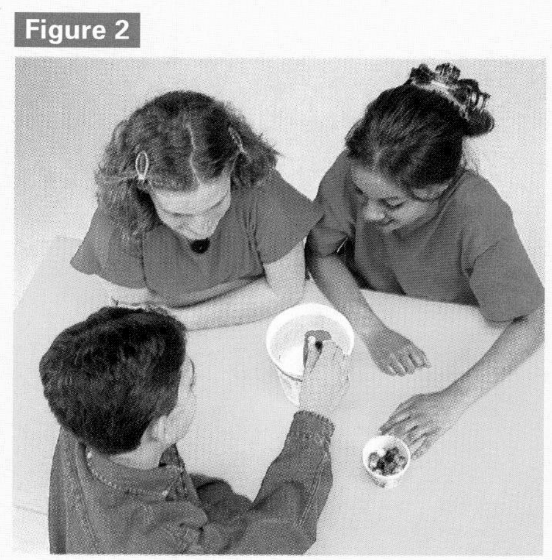

Teamwork Tips

While working with *Nelson Science & Technology 7/8*, you will spend much of your time working in teams. Whenever you do, it is useful to take the following tips into account:

- Encourage all members to contribute to the work of the group.
- Respect everyone's contributions. There are many points of view and all perspectives should be considered. Keep an open mind.
- Be prepared to compromise.
- Share the work fairly.
- Keep focused on the task at hand. Divide the various tasks between all group members.
- Support the team's final decision.
- When you are given the opportunity of picking your own team, be sure that the students you decide to work with complement your strengths and weaknesses.

Can you think of any more tips that should be considered during group work?

Evaluating Teamwork

After you've completed a task with your team, evaluate the team's effectiveness—the strengths, weaknesses, opportunities, and challenges. Answer the following questions:

1. What were the strengths of your teamwork?
2. What were the weaknesses of your teamwork?
3. What opportunities were provided by working with your team?
4. What possible challenges did you see with respect to your teamwork?

9E Graphic Organizers

When you are trying to describe objects and events, it is sometimes helpful to write your ideas down so that you can see them and compare them with those of other people. Instead of writing these ideas down in sentences, they can often be represented visually. There are a number of ways of organizing information graphically that may help you express concepts and relationships.

Concept Maps

A concept map is a collection of words (representing concepts) or pictures that you connect to each other with arrows and short descriptions. The map is a drawing of what is happening in your brain.

You may have seen concept maps similar to the one in **Figure 1**. This concept map, called a food web, shows one way of thinking about animals and what they eat. The arrowhead points to the animal that eats the animal or plant at the other end of the arrow. The arrows describe the relationship between the organisms.

Concept maps can also be drawn of other topics and in other ways. For instance, the relationships between family members can be drawn using a concept map like the one in **Figure 2**.

Figure 2
A family

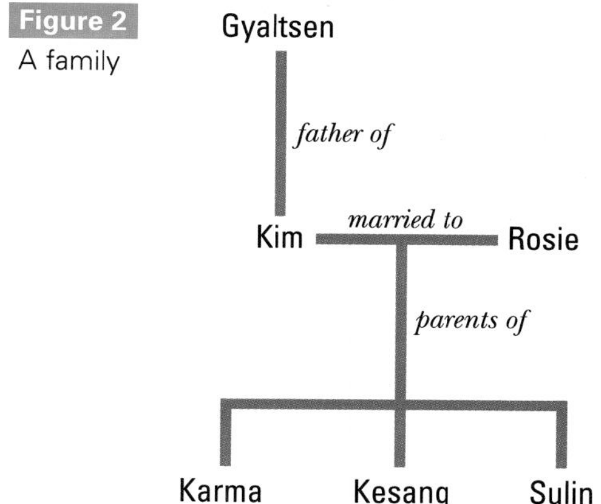

Figure 1
A food web

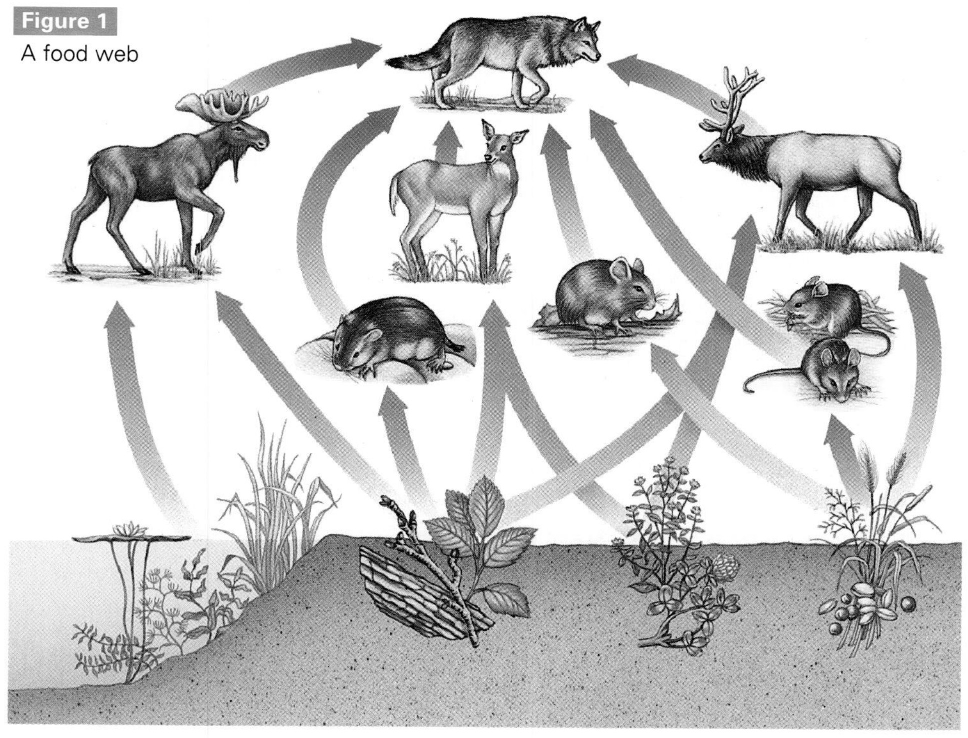

Concept maps can also be drawn to show a series of cause-and-effect relationships (**Figure 3**). You may find making this kind of map useful during the processes of scientific inquiry and design.

Sometimes concept maps can be used to show how your ideas change and become more complex as you work on a topic. You can see an example of this type of concept map in **Figure 4**.

Figure 3
Causes and effects related to plant growth

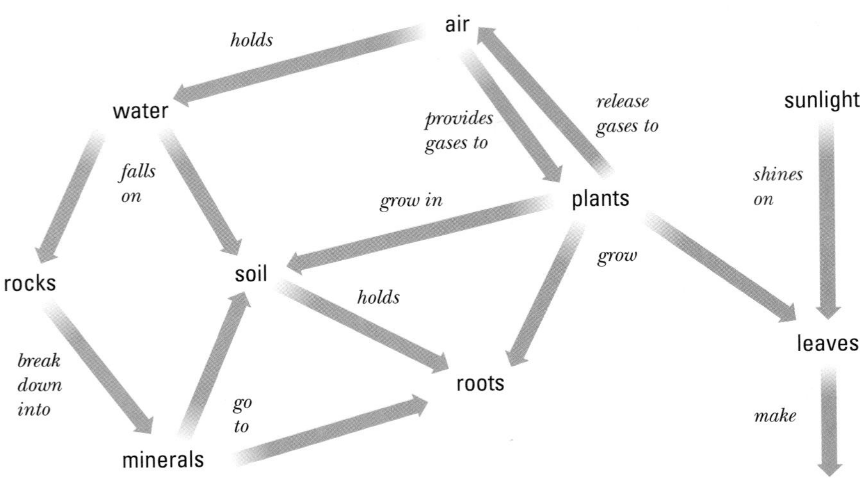

Figure 4
Concept maps evolve as your ideas evolve

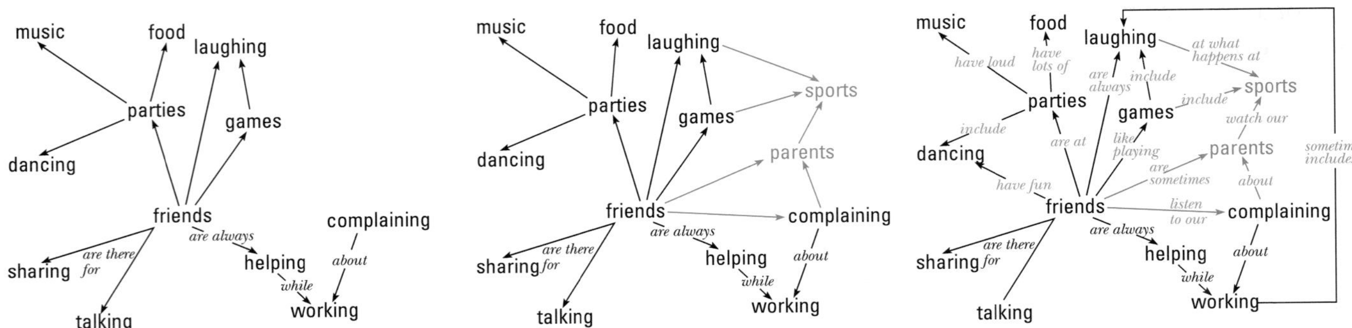

Making a Concept Map

Here are some steps you can take to help you make a concept map.

1. Choose the central idea of your concept map.
2. Write the central idea and all related ideas on small scraps of paper.
3. Move the scraps of paper around the central idea so that the ones most related to each other are close to each other. Ask yourself how they are related, and then use that information in the next steps.
4. On a big sheet of paper, write down all of your ideas in the same pattern that you have arranged the scraps. Draw arrows between the ideas that are related.
5. On each arrow, write a short description of how the terms are related to each other.

As you go, you may find other ideas or relationships. Add them to the map. When you gain new ideas—whether from research, from your investigations, or from other people—go ahead and change your concept map. You may want to add new ideas in a different colour of ink, to indicate your new ways of thinking about the ideas.

Comparison Matrix

It is often useful to use a comparison matrix to compare things according to a variety of criteria (**Table 1**). For instance, you might want to compare the properties of different materials in order to choose the best one for a particular design.

Table 1 The Heating Curve of Water

	Properties			
	Malleable	**Lustrous**	**Strong**	**Affordable**
Gold	X	X		
Silver	X	X	X	
Copper	X	X	X	X

Venn Diagram

Another simple diagram used for comparing and contrasting things is the Venn diagram (**Figure 5**). Similarities between two items are written in the area of overlap; differences are written in the separate circles.

Figure 5

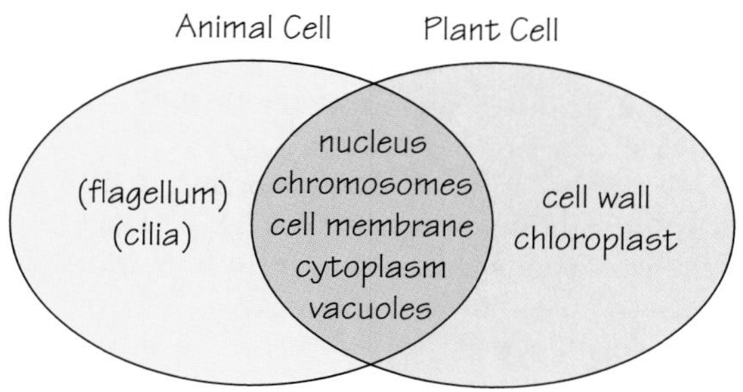

Hierarchical (Branching) Diagram

Some concepts can be broken down into subcategories. A hierarchical diagram is a useful way of representing these relationships (**Figure 6**).

Figure 6

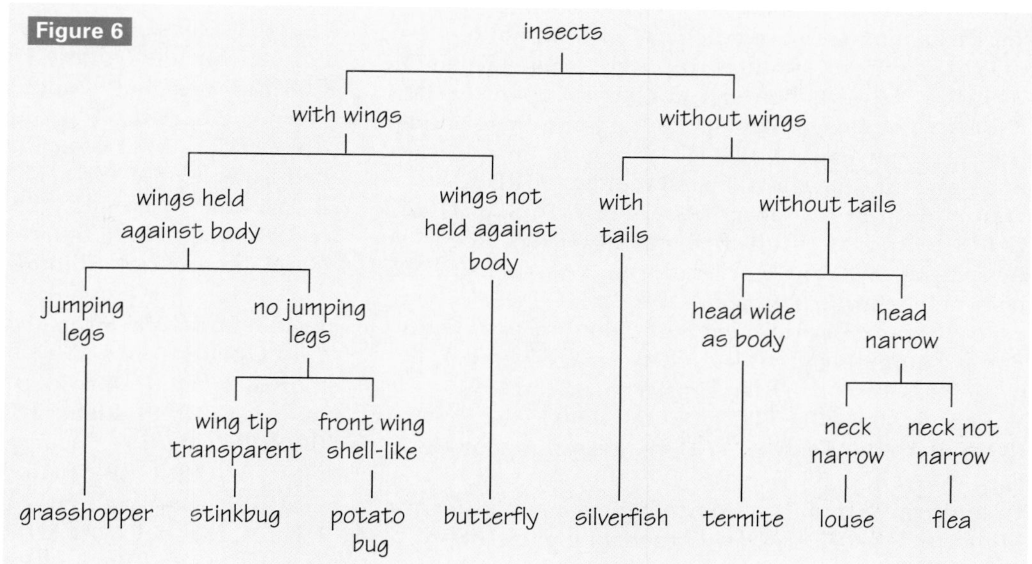

Target Diagram

A target diagram is often used to illustrate which item best applies to a given criterion. (**Figure 7**).

Figure 7

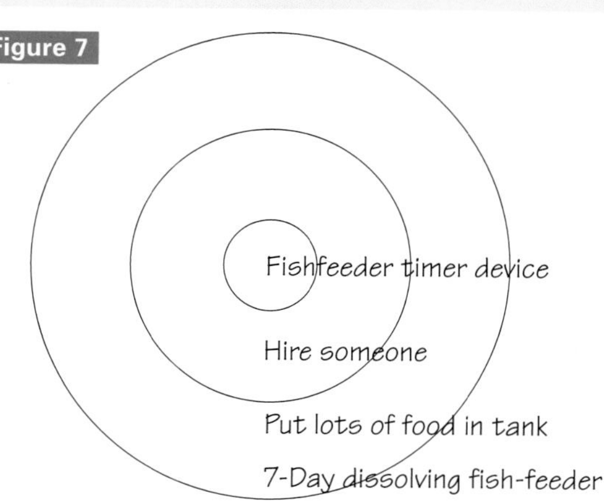

Photo Credits

Cover: I & V/Masterfile

Table of Contents: p. 4 Visuals Unlimited/Bruce Gaylord; p. 5 Visuals Unlimited/Science VU; p. 6 CORBIS/Richard Hamilton Smith; p. 8 Stephen J. Krasemann/VALAN PHOTOS.

Unit 1: Pure Substances
Unit Opener (pp. 10–11): Telegraph Colour Library/Masterfile; p. 12 Dave Starrett; p. 13 top CORBIS/Sergio Dorantes, bottom Peter Beck/First Light; p. 14 Dave Starrett; p. 15 Visuals Unlimited/John Sohlden; p. 16 Dave Starrett; p. 17 top COMSTOCK, bottom Dave Starrett; pp. 21–22 Dave Starrett; p. 23 top Visuals Unlimited/John S. Flannery, bottom Dave Starrett; p. 24 Dave Starrett; p. 25 top Visuals Unlimited/Bruce Gaylord, bottom Dave Starrett; p. 28 Dave Starrett; p. 29 Arthur Beck/First Light; p. 30 Dave Starrett; p. 31 top Dave Starrett, bottom Jeremy Jones; pp. 34–36 Dave Starrett; p. 38 top left Dick Hemingway, middle left CORBIS, bottom left CORBIS/Jeffrey L. Rotman, top right John Warden/T. W. Image Network, bottom right Henry Siplinga (HMS Photos)/The Image Bank; p. 39 top PhotoDisc, middle Jean Bruneau/VALAN PHOTOS, bottom Images BC/T. W. Image Network; p. 40 middle CORBIS, bottom Andrew Farquhar/VALAN PHOTOS; p. 41 left CORBIS/Annie Griffiths Belt, right CORBIS/Roger Ressmeyer; p. 42 top J. A. Wilkinson/VALAN PHOTOS, bottom left Arthur Strange/VALAN PHOTOS, bottom centre George Disario/First Light, bottom right Omni Photo Communications Inc./T. W. Image Network; p. 43 PhotoDisc; p. 44 Ian Crysler; p. 45 top V. Whelan/VALAN PHOTOS, bottom Ian Crysler; p. 46 CORBIS/Leng/Leng; p. 47 Dave Starrett; pp. 52–53 Dave Starrett; p. 56 Visuals Unlimited/Gurmanken/Morina; p. 58 courtesy Joanna Johns; p. 59 CORBIS/David Muench; p. 60 left Flip Chalfant/The Image Bank, right Visuals Unlimited/S. Flegler; p. 62 left CORBIS/Fernando Alda, right Visuals Unlimited/Jeff Greenberg; p. 63 Phil Norton/VALAN PHOTOS; p. 64 left CORBIS/Roger Ressmeyer, right Dave Starrett; p. 65 left Visuals Unlimited/Gurmankin/Morina, right V. Whelan/VALAN PHOTOS; p. 68 PhotoDisc; p. 69 top PhotoDisc, bottom Dave Starrett.

Unit 2: Heat
Unit Opener (pp. 70–71): J. Jamsen/First Light; p. 72 top Visuals Unlimited/Bill Banaszewski, bottom Gerhard Kahrmann/VALAN PHOTOS; p. 73 PhotoDisc; p. 74 top William Taufic/First Light, bottom CORBIS/Phil Schermeister; p. 75 courtesy Ontario Hydro; pp. 76–77 in numerical order — 1. Chip Simon/FPG, 2. Val and Alan Wilkinson/VALAN PHOTOS, 3. Visuals Unlimited/Jeff Greenberg, 4. T. W. Image Network/Joseph Borelli, 5. David Taylor/Science Source/Photo Researchers, 6. V. Wilkinson/VALAN PHOTOS, 7. T. W. Image Network/Peter Johanski, 9. Esther Schmidt/VALAN PHOTOS, 10. Diane Padys/FPG, 11. Visuals Unlimited/Cavagnero, 12. Oxford Scientific Films/Mike Tracey/Survival Anglia, 13. Visuals Unlimited/Deneve Feigh Bunde, 14. Visuals Unlimited/Bruce Glendenning; p. 78 Dave Starrett; p. 79 top Telegraph Colour Library/FPG, middle pair courtesy Boréal; pp. 80–81 Dave Starrett; p. 82 CORBIS/Lowell Georgia; p. 83 Dave Starrett, p. 84 top CORBIS/Robert Estall, bottom Dave Starrett, p. 90 Dave Starrett; p. 91 top CORBIS/Charles O'Rear, bottom Dave Starrett; p. 94 Dave Starrett, p. 96 courtesy of Susan Kern; p. 97 PhotoDisc; p. 104 Visuals Unlimited/Science VU; p. 106 Dave Starrett; p. 107 CORBIS/Mark Gibson; pp. 108–109 Dave Starrett; pp. 112–113 Dave Starrett; p. 114 top Michael Hart/FPG, bottom PhotoDisc; p. 47 top Dave Starrett, bottom courtesy Ontario Hydro; p. 54 CORBIS/Wolfgang Kahler; p. 123 CORBIS/Jeremy Horner; p. 124 top Dave Starrett, bottom Telegraph Colour Library/FPG; p. 125 left Dave Starrett, right Oxford Scientific Films/Mike Tracey/Survival Anglia; p. 126 Dave Starrett; p. 128 courtesy Alan Hirsch, p. 129 top CORBIS/Stuart Westmorland, bottom left Corel, bottom right PhotoDisc.

Unit 3: Structural Strength and Stability
Unit Opener (pp. 130–131): Corel; pp. 132–133 CORBIS/Jim McDonald; p. 134 top Dave Starrett, bottom CORBIS/Richard T. Nowitz; p. 135 CORBIS/Charles O'Rear; pp. 136–137 Dave Starrett; pp. 138–139 CORBIS/Tim Wright; p. 140 CORBIS/Tim Wright; p. 142 Dave Starrett, p. 145 top John M. Mitchell/VALAN PHOTOS, bottom Corel; p. 146 CORBIS/Richard Hamilton Smith; p. 148 top Kerri Yano, bottom courtesy Mitsu Yano; p. 151 Dave Starrett; p. 154 Dave Starrett; p. 155 Jeri Gleiter/FPG; p. 156 Dave Starrett; p. 157 top Philip Norton/VALAN PHOTOS, bottom left CORBIS/Michael T. Sedam, bottom right Associated Press AP; p. 158 Dave Starrett, p. 159 top PhotoDisc, bottom Dave Starrett; p. 161 Dave Starrett; p. 163 PhotoDisc; p. 164 Dave Starrett; p. 165 CORBIS/John Dakers/Eye Ubiquitous; p. 166 Dave Starrett; p. 168 Dave Starrett; p. 169 top left CORBIS/Morton Beebe, bottom left and top right Dave Starrett; p. 171 COMSTOCK; pp. 172–176 Dave Starrett; p. 178 top PhotoDisc, bottom Kennon Cooke/VALAN PHOTOS; p. 179 top left CORBIS/Michael S. Yamashita, bottom left Photo Fred Bruemmer/VALAN PHOTOS, top right CORBIS/Charles and Josette Lenars; p. 181 Joseph R.

Pearce/VALAN PHOTOS; p. 182 left and middle PhotoDisc, right L. O. L. Inc./FPG; p. 183 Dave Starrett; p. 184 left Dave Starrett, right Joseph R. Pearce/VALAN PHOTOS; p. 185 top left and right Dave Starrett, bottom right CORBIS/John Dakers/Eye Ubiquitous; pp. 188–189 CORBIS/Richard Hamilton Smith.

Unit 4: Earth's Crust
Unit Opener (pp. 190–191): Visuals Unlimited/Derrick Ditchburn; p. 192 top Dave Starrett, middle CORBIS/Robert Garvey, bottom (farm) CORBIS/Dave G. Houser, inset Dave Starrett; p. 193 top CORBIS/Vince Streano, bottom CORBIS/Michael S. Yamashita; p. 194 top John Cancalosi/VALAN PHOTOS, middle (inset) CORBIS/Science Pictures Ltd., bottom Corel; p. 195 top Corel, bottom G. Brad Lewis/Tony Stone Images; p. 198 (top to bottom) Visuals Unlimited/George Herben, Visuals Unlimited/Ken Lucas, Visuals Unlimited/Mark A. Schneider, Tony Joyce/VALAN PHOTOS, © Biophoto Associates/Photo Researchers, Visuals Unlimited/Ken Lucas; p. 199 left (top to bottom) Visuals Unlimited/Ken Lucas, Visuals Unlimited/Ken Lucas, Visuals Unlimited/Ken Lucas, © 1997 Custom Medical Stock Photo, Arthur Strange/VALAN PHOTOS, bottom right Visuals Unlimited/Ken Lucas; p. 201 Courtesy of Inco Limited; p. 202 Dave Starrett; p. 203 Herman H. Geithoorn/VALAN PHOTOS; p. 204 top CORBIS/Johnathan Blair, bottom CORBIS/Charles E. Rotkin; p. 206 Visuals Unlimited/George Herben; p. 207 top left Visuals Unlimited/George Herben, bottom left James R. Page/VALAN PHOTOS, top right T.W. Image Network/Images B.C., bottom right Dave Starrett; p. 208 bottom left Dave Starrett, right Janet Dwyer/First Light; p. 209 top right Tom W. Parkin/VALAN PHOTOS, bottom left Visuals Unlimited/John R. Cunningham; p. 212 middle pair Paul Till; p. 213 Pam Charbonneau/Turfgrass Institute/University of Guelph; pp. 214–215 Dave Starrett; p. 216 top Visuals Unlimited/Inga Spence, bottom Visuals Unlimited/Larsh K. Bristol; p. 217 left Visuals Unlimited/Richard Thomas, right Visuals Unlimited/Science VU; p. 218 bottom Visuals Unlimited/Steve McCutcheon; p. 220 Dave Starrett; p. 221 top Hälle Flygare/VALAN PHOTOS, bottom Harold V. Green/VALAN PHOTOS; p. 222 Geomatics Canada/Canada Centre for Remote Sensing; p. 223 top (left to right) W. Wilkinson/VALAN PHOTOS, Tom Parkin/VALAN PHOTOS, V. Wilkinson/VALAN PHOTOS, bottom left & right Kennon Cooke/VALAN PHOTOS; p. 224 bottom left Wayne Lankinen/VALAN PHOTOS, right (top to bottom) J.A. Wilkinson/VALAN PHOTOS, CORBIS/Neil Rabinowitz, John Cancalosi/VALAN PHOTOS, CORBIS/Kevin Schafer, Visuals Unlimited/Ken Lucas, John Cancalosi/VALAN PHOTOS; p. 225 CORBIS/Ken Schafer; p. 228 CORBIS/Roger Ressmeyer; p. 229 CORBIS/Bettmann/UPI; p. 231 left CORBIS/Roger Ressmeyer, right CORBIS/Michael S. Yamashita; p. 234 top CORBIS/Adam Woolfitt, middle V. Wilkinson/VALAN PHOTOS, bottom left V. Wilkinson/VALAN PHOTOS, bottom right Herman H. Geithoorn/VALAN PHOTOS; p. 235 top left CORBIS/Ric Ergenbright, top right CORBIS/Maurice Nimmo/Frank Lane Picture Agency, bottom left Tony Joyce/VALAN PHOTOS, bottom right Visuals Unlimited/A.J. Copely; p. 236 top right Pat Morrow, middle left Lisel Currie; p. 238 CORBIS/Michael T. Sedam; p. 239 Prof. Stewart Lowther/Science Photo Library; p. 240 Dave Starrett; p. 241 CORBIS/Michael S. Yamashita; p. 242 CORBIS/Jonathan Blair; p. 243 top Visuals Unlimited/Inga Spence, bottom CORBIS/Dewitt Jones.

Unit 5: Ecosystems
Unit Opener (pp. 250–251): Pete Turner/Image Bank; p. 253 Val Wilkinson/VALAN PHOTOS; p. 254 top NASA/GSFC/Science Photo Library, bottom NASA; p. 256 CORBIS/Tom Nebbia; p. 257 Stephen J. Krasemann/VALAN PHOTOS; p. 260 top Gregory Dimijian/Photo Researchers, bottom John Mitchell/Oxford Scientific Films; p. 261 top Visuals Unlimited/John Gerlach, middle left Visuals Unlimited/Kjell B. Sandved, middle right CORBIS/Chase Swift, bottom Kjell B. Sandved/Photo Researchers; p. 262 , clockwise from top right — Philip Norton/VALAN PHOTOS, CORBIS/Doug Wilson(centre image), Visuals Unlimited/Bill Beatty, John Mitchell/VALAN PHOTOS, Robin Redfern/Oxford Scientific Films, CORBIS/Ron Boardman/Frank Lane Picture Agency, A. B. Dowsett/Science Photo Library (inset), Visuals Unlimited/Doug Sokell; p. 264 Dave Starrett; p. 265 top Visuals Unlimited/John D. Cunningham, bottom Dave Starrett; p. 266 Dave Starrett; p. 268 bottom left Joyce Photographics/VALAN PHOTOS, top right, from top to bottom CORBIS/Michael Freeman, CORBIS/Lester V. Bergman, Oliver Meckes/Photo Researchers, David M. Dennis/Oxford Scientific Films; p. 269 Visuals Unlimited/Sherman Thomson; p. 270 Dave Starrett; p. 271 top Visuals Unlimited/E. Webber, bottom Dave Starrett; p. 272 courtesy of Uta Matthes-Sears; p. 273 Philip Norton/VALAN PHOTOS; p. 274 Visuals Unlimited/Bill Beatty; p. 278 Visuals Unlimited/Audrey Gibson; p. 282 Dave Starrett; p. 287 Visuals Unlimited/Arthur R. Hill; pp. 288–289 Ray Boudreau; p. 296 bottom left CORBIS/Wolfgang Kahler, top right CORBIS/Nik Wheeler, middle right Visuals Unlimited/John D. Cunningham, bottom right CORBIS/David T. Grewcock/Frank Lane Picture Agency; p. 297 left to right CORBIS/Joe McDonald, CORBIS/Joe McDonald, Robert C. Simpson/VALAN PHOTOS, CORBIS/Tim Zurowski, Rob Simpson/VALAN PHOTOS, CORBIS/Roger Tidman, Visuals Unlimited/Rob Simpson, Visuals Unlimited/Rob Simpson; p. 300 left to right CORBIS/Chris Hellier, CORBIS/Gary Braasch,

CORBIS/Owen Franken; p. 302 courtesy of Colgate-Palmolive GmbH, Germany; p. 303 top CORBIS/Marc Granger, bottom Todd Ryoji; p. 304 bottom left Visuals Unlimited/Kjell B. Sandved, top right CORBIS/David T. Grewcock/Frank Lane Picture Agency, bottom right Visuals Unlimited/Audrey Gibson; p. 305 Visuals Unlimited/Arhur R. Hill.

Skills Handbook

Unit Opener (pp. 310–311): collage of (clockwise from top left) Corel, Alan Marsh/First Light, Visuals Unlimited/Derrick Ditchburn, B. Fraunfelter/First Light; p. 313 top Ian Crysler, bottom Dave Starrett; pp. 314–316 Dave Starrett; p. 317 Paul Till; p. 320 Dave Starrett; pp. 321–324 Ian Crysler; pp. 325–327 Dave Starrett; p. 328 PhotoDisc; p. 330 Visuals Unlimited/Jeff Greenberg; p. 331 CORBIS/Richard T. Nowitz; p. 332 Dave Starrett; p. 334 Dave Starrett; p. 338 top to bottom PhotoDisc, Todd Ryoji, Dick Hemingway, Omni Photo Communications Inc./T. W. Image Network; p. 340 Dave Starrett; pp. 342–343 Dave Starrett; p. 345 Dave Starrett; p. 348 top Visuals Unlimited/Richard L. Carlton, rest Boréal; p. 349 top left Ian Crysler, bottom right Boréal; p. 357 Dave Starrett; p. 360 top left CORBIS/Rodney Hyett/Elizabeth Whiting & Associates, top right R. W. Jones/First Light, middle right (b) Bob Semple, (c) First Light, bottom right Rom Watts/First Light; p. 361 top left Visuals Unlimited/R. Lindholm, middle left Joe Lepiano/Artbase, bottom left Dave Starrett, top right Dave Starrett, bottom right Andrea Pistolesi/The Image Bank; p. 362 top left Dave Starrett, bottom left Gary Russ/The Image Bank; p. 365 left Dave Starrett, top right Joe Lepiano/Artbase, middle right Dave Starrett, bottom right Chuck Savage/First Light; p. 366 Paul Till; pp. 381–383 Dave Starrett; pp. 394–395 Dave Starrett; p. 399 Ian Crysler.

Glossary

A

abiotic: the nonliving components of an ecosystem

acid rain: rain, snow, or hail that contains acids formed from sulphur and nitrogen-containing pollutants in the atmosphere

adaptations: special structures and behaviours that help an organism to succeed in its ecosystem

alloy: a homogeneous mixture of two or more metals or metals and other substances in a solid solution

arch: a structure or part of a structure formed in a regular curve; used as a support or to create an opening in a structure

B

bedrock: the layer of rock immediately below the subsoil

bend: a structural change caused when an external force generates forces of tension and compression in a beam or member; characteristic is that the curve of the beam or member changes

biodegradable: products made from things that were once living and that can be broken down by decomposers

biological amplification: the process that results in increasing concentrations of a harmful chemical at each higher level of a food chain

biome: a collection of related ecosystems

biosphere: wherever living things are found on Earth, from the atmosphere to kilometres under the surface

boiling point: the temperature at which a substance boils

bridge, arch: a bridge that uses at least one arch, made of steel, concrete, or stone to support the bridge either from below or above

bridge, beam: a bridge made of one or more beams supported at both ends and sometimes by columns underneath

bridge, cantilever: a bridge that relies on masses at either end to support the span in the middle

bridge, suspension: a bridge that uses cables strung from towers to support the bridge from above

bridge, truss: a frame bridge that relies on a system of triangular supports (trusses) to support its load

buckle: a structural change caused by a compression force acting on a beam or member; characteristics are the wrinkling or pleating of the material

C

carbon cycle: a matter cycle for carbon as it is used and reused in respiration and photosynthesis

carnivore: a consumer that eats other animals

centre of gravity: the point in a structure at which you can picture the mass of the object being concentrated; if the centre of gravity of a structure lies outside its base of support, the structure is unstable

ceramic: a material manufactured by heating minerals and rocks; ceramics include pottery, bricks, cement, and glass

chlorophyll: a green substance found in plants; used to capture and store radiant energy from the sun

clay: soil component that consists of very small particles of rock (less than 0.002 mm)

cleavage: a property of minerals; describes the way the minerals split into smaller pieces

colour: a property of minerals; describes the appearance of the mineral; used to identify and classify minerals

cogeneration: the process of providing electricity and heat at the same time

community: all of the organisms in an ecosystem

compression: a force within a structure or part of a structure that squeezes or pushes

concentrated solution: a solution that contains a high amount of solute

conduction: the transfer of heat by the collisions of particles in a solid

cone: the shape that hardened lava takes as it spills from a volcano

consumer: an organism that cannot make its own food and must eat other organisms

continental drift: a hypothesis that continents move and that millions of years ago they were all connected into a supercontinent

contraction: a decrease in the volume of an object or substance

convection current: the motion of the fluid particles during convection

convection: the transfer of heat by the movement of particles from one part of a fluid to another

core, inner: the innermost region of the Earth and also its hottest; made mostly of solid iron and nickel

core, outer: the region of the Earth surrounding the inner core made of liquid iron and nickel

corrugation: the regular pleating or rippling of a material; used to strengthen the material, as in cardboard.

crop rotation: a process used by farmers to prevent loss of nutrients from soil, in each growing season, a different kind of plant is grown in a field

crust: the thin surface layer of rock that covers the Earth

D

database: information organized by categories; usually generated using a computer

dead load: the static load caused by gravity acting on the mass of a structure; the weight of the structure

decompose: to break down materials into smaller pieces or molecules into smaller molecules, so they can be reused in an ecosystem

decomposer: an ecological niche; an organism that breaks down materials so they can be reused in an ecosystem

deposit: an area in which the local rock contains unusually large amounts of a valuable mineral or metal

diversity: a measure of the number of different types of organisms in an area

drift: loose material that is easily scraped from the bedrock by an advancing glacier; eventually left behind when the glacier recedes

drumlins: small mounds of moraine shaped by glaciers

dynamic load: a load on a structure caused by a force other than gravity

E

ecological niche: the way of life or the role of the organism in an ecosystem

ecology: the study of the relationships among living things and between living things and their environment

ecosystem: all of the relationships among the living things in a community and their interactions with the abiotic factors in their environment

erosion: the wearing away of soil or rock by agents such as wind, water, and living things

expansion: an increase in the volume of an object or substance

F

factor of safety: a measure of how safe a structure is; to generate the factor of safety divide the maximum live load a structure can bear by the live load expected under maximum use

fastener: a device or material that holds two or more pieces of a structure together

fault: an area where rocks are broken by movement in the crust

field: an area to enter a category of information in a database

flood plain: the area on each side of a river that is covered when the river overflows its banks, mostly during the spring runoff

food chain: an organizing device that shows a feeding pathway, made up of several organisms

food web: an organizing system made up of many intersecting food chains

frame structure: a structure formed from components that are fastened together to support and strengthen each other

G

gas: a substance that fills any container it is in and takes on the shape of the container; it can flow, and it is easy to compress

glass: a ceramic product made by mixing small amounts of limestone and potash with silica at high temperatures; a solution that is a supercooled liquid

greenhouse effect: the process of trapping radiant heat inside a structure made with glass

gusset: a small piece of material used to reinforce a seam or a joint where tension forces are expected to act

H

hard water: water that contains certain dissolved substances, such as magnesium, calcium, or sulfur, which prevent soap from forming a lather

hardness: a property of minerals; describes how resistant a mineral is to being scratched

hazardous product: a substance that requires special handling and storage because it is dangerous to human health or to the environment

heat: energy that is transferred from hotter substances to colder ones

heat capacity: a measure of the amount of heat needed to raise the temperature of the substance or a measure of how much heat the substance releases as it cools

heat conductor: a substance that conducts heat well

heat pollution: wasted heat being produced by human activities

heating curve: a graph of a change of state as a substance is heated

herbivore: a consumer that eats only plants

heterogeneous mixture: an uneven mixture that contains two or more substances; samples of heterogeneous mixture may have different properties

homogeneous mixture: a mixture that is the same throughout; all samples taken from a homogeneous mixture (a solution) will have the same properties

horizons: the layers that can be found in most soil, from litter to bedrock

humus: decaying plant and animal matter that is mixed with soil

I

igneous rock, extrusive: rock formed when liquid magma cools and hardens above the surface of the Earth

igneous rock, intrusive: rock formed when liquid magma cools and hardens below the Earth's surface

igneous rock: rock formed from the hardening of liquid magma

L

lamination: a technique in which two or more layers of material are glued, fastened together, or bonded to make the material stronger

lava: magma that flows out of cracks onto the Earth's crust

leaching: a process in which water seeps downward through soil or other material, dissolving chemicals and carrying them into lower layers

liquid: a substance with a set volume that will take the same shape as the container it is in; it can flow, but it is difficult to compress

litter: material lying on the surface of soil, consisting of leaves, broken branches, fallen trees, and animals' bodies

live load: a static load; caused by gravity acting on all of the things in and on a structure that are not part of the structure

load: the effect of forces acting on a structure; static loads are caused by gravity, dynamic loads are caused by other forces

lubricant: a substance used to reduce friction

lustre: a property of minerals; describes how shiny a mineral is

M

magma: a hot, liquid solution of dissolved minerals; cools to form igneous rock

magnitude of force: a description of the strength of a force

mantle: the area between the Earth's crust and its core; it consists of magma, a thick, molten material that, when cooled, can form rock

mass structure: another name for a solid structure; a structure formed from a single unit

matter cycle: a description of how matter is used and reused by living things

matter: anything that takes up space and has mass

mechanical mixture: a heterogeneous mixture; in a mechanical mixture at least two substances are visible

melting point: the temperature at which a substance melts

metamorphic rock: rock formed when igneous or sedimentary rock is exposed to the higher temperatures and pressure deep in the Earth's crust

minerals: the building blocks of rocks; minerals are nonliving things

mining, strip: a type of mining whereby topsoil and rock are removed from the top of a deposit so that a mineral can be removed; used only for deposits that are near the surface

mining, underground: a type of mining whereby one or many tunnels are dug into rock to reach a deposit so that a mineral can be removed; often used for deposits that are buried far below the surface

mixture: any substance that contains at least two pure substances

moraines: piles of broken rock left behind by receding glaciers

mountains, block: mountains formed when movements in the crust cause blocks of crust to rise or fall

mountains, dome: mountains formed by the pressure of hot magma pushing up from below

mountains, fold: mountains formed when two of the Earth's plates collide

N

nonbiodegradable: products made from human-made chemicals; because they do not provide food energy for the growth of decomposers, they break down slowly

nutrient: a chemical that is essential for the growth of living things

O

ore: rock that contains a valuable mineral

organism: a single living thing

overburden: top layer of soil and rock that must be removed during strip mining to expose ore

P

particle theory: a theory used to explain matter and heat transfer. It suggests that all matter is made up of tiny particles too small to be seen. These particles are constantly in motion because they have energy. The more energy they have, the faster they move.

pesticides: chemicals designed to reduce the populations of unwanted organisms, both plant and animal

pH scale: a gauge, ranging from 0 (strongly acidic) to 14 (strongly alkaline), used to express the acidity or alkalinity of a solution

photosynthesis: the process plants use to make sugars out of carbon dioxide and water using radiant energy from the sun; releases oxygen

planned obsolescence: a process in which a product is intentionally designed to be replaced after a limited time

plastic: a modern material manufactured in a multistep process, beginning with oil and gas

plate tectonics: a theory that describes the Earth's crust as a set of rocky plates that are in continual motion, colliding and moving apart

plates: solid sections of the Earth's crust that float on the liquid mantle

population: the number of organisms of the same species living in a community

primary succession: succession that occurs in an area where there was no community before; ends when a climax ecosystem is established

producer: an organism that can make its own food

pure substance: any solid, liquid, or gas that contains only one kind of particle throughout.

R

radiant energy: energy transferred by radiation; examples are heat and light

radiation: the transfer of energy by means of waves

raw material: unprocessed material of any kind

respiration: the process used by living things to break down sugars for the energy stored in them; uses oxygen and releases carbon dioxide and water

ridge: a rise made of hardened lava erupting where two of the Earth's plates are moving apart; usually found on the ocean floor

S

sand: soil component that consists of largest particles of rock (0.02–2.0 mm)

saturated solution: a solution that contains the maximum amount of solute that the solvent can dissolve at the given temperature

secondary succession: succession that occurs after the partial or complete destruction of a community; the damaged community is replaced by another or by a series of other communities until a stable community is re-established

sediment: fine particles of rock and soil that are deposited by moving water; settles in layers on lake beds or sea beds

sedimentary rock: rock composed of layers of sediment

shear: two forces that act in opposite directions along the same plane inside an object; the type of structural damage caused by shear forces

shell structure: a structure that is built as solid surface around a hollow area; shell structures rely on curves (arches) to help them bear loads

shield volcanoes: volcanoes formed above a hot spot in the mantle of the Earth; eruptions tend to be frequent but not spectacular

silt: soil component that consists of medium-sized particles of rock (0.002–0.02 mm)

soft water: water that contains very small amounts of dissolved minerals; easily forms a lather when mixed with soap

solid: a substance with a set volume and a rigid shape; it cannot flow and it is very hard to compress

solid structure: a structure formed from a single unit (also called mass structure); solid structures gain their strength from the mass of the material used to make the structure —they are too massive to move or bear compression well

solubility: the maximum amount of a particular solute that can be dissolved in a particular solvent at a given temperature

solute: a substance that is dissolved in a solvent to form a solution

solution: a homogeneous mixture made of a solvent and one or more solutes; in a solution, only one substance is visible; a solution can be solid, liquid, or gas

solvent: a substance that dissolves a solute to form a solution

span: a section of bridge that lies between two supports

stable: a structure is stable if it remains on its base, undamaged, when acted on by the forces it is designed to withstand; the stability of a structure depends on the materials the structure is made from, how those materials are arranged, and how the structure's mass is distributed

static load: a load caused by the force of gravity; the dead load and the live load on a structure are both static loads

stratovolcanoes: volcanoes formed on the upper surface of a plate where another plate is plunging underneath; eruptions tend to be dramatic and destructive

structural failure: a permanent, nonreversible change in a structure, caused by internal forces (tension, compression, torsion, or shear)

strut: a member that supports a structure; the dominant force within a strut is compression

subduction: a process whereby one plate slides beneath another plate, pushes into the hot mantle, heats up, and melts

subsoil: the layer of soil below the topsoil; contains very little humus and many stones

succession: a natural process in which the dominant species in an ecosystem are gradually replaced by others

supersaturated solution: a solution that contains more of the solute than would be found in a saturated solution

symmetry, reflectional: when a line or plane can be drawn through a structure and each side is a reflection of the other side, the object has reflectional symmetry

symmetry, rotational: when the appearance of a structure is not changed if it is rotated through a specific angle, the structure has rotational symmetry

T

tailings pond: a pond built to contain toxic liquid wastes from mining

tailings: liquid waste from a mine, consisting of a mixture of small particles of rock and the chemicals used to extract the valuable mineral from ore

temperature: a measure of the average energy of motion of the particles of a substance

tension: a stretching or pulling force within a structure or part of a structure

thermocouple: a device that uses electricity to measure temperatures

thermometer: a device that uses the expansion and contraction of a liquid to measure

thermostat: a device that uses the expansion and contraction of solids to measure temperatures

tie: a member that supports a structure; the dominant force within a tie is tension

till: to break up compacted soil with a plough in order to allow water and air into the soil; prepares the soil for plant growth

topsoil: the layer of soil under the litter; contains humus and small amounts of stones

torsion: a twisting force within a structure or part of a structure; created by applying opposite rotational forces

truss: a structural element made up of a series of triangular frames; used to strengthen structures

turbidity: a measure of the amount of suspended solids in water, calculated using special meters

twist: the structural changed caused by a torsion force acting within a structure

unsaturated solution: a solution in which more solute can be dissolved at the given temperature

W

water cycle: the cycle that collects, purifies, and redistributes the Earth's water; driven by energy from the Sun

weathering, biological: erosion caused by living things

weathering, chemical: erosion caused by chemicals, such as the acid in acid rain

weathering, mechanical: erosion caused by fast-moving water, particles carried by the wind, or ice

WHMIS: (Workplace Hazardous Materials Information System) symbols found on hazardous products that identify the type of danger associated with the product and that provide information on safe handling

work plan: a plan for how a product will be built; includes the resources (materials, how materials and components will be stored, personnel assignments, and a plan for use of physical space) and a schedule that describes the sequence in which work will be done, with delivery dates

Z

zero tillage: a method of farming whereby stubble from previous crop is left in the ground, and new seed is planted into old stubble without the use of a plough; reduces loss of soil nutrients

Index